ENCYCLOPEDIA OF
THE UNITED STATES
IN THE TWENTIETH CENTURY

Editorial Board

Encyclopedia of
The United States
in the Twentieth Century

Stanley I. Kutler

Editor in Chief

Robert Dallek

David A. Hollinger

Thomas K. McCraw

Associate Editors

Judith Kirkwood

Assistant Editor

Volume III

CHARLES SCRIBNER'S SONS

Macmillan Library Reference USA

Simon & Schuster Macmillan

New York

SIMON & SCHUSTER AND PRENTICE HALL INTERNATIONAL

London   Mexico City   New Delhi   Singapore   Sydney   Toronto

Copyright © 1996 by Macmillan Library Reference USA A
Simon & Schuster Company

All rights reserved. No part of this book may be
reprinted or reproduced or utilized in any form or by any
electronic, mechanical, or other means, now known or
hereafter invented, including photocopying and recording,
or in any information storage or retrieval system, without
permission in writing from Charles Scribner's Sons.

Charles Scribner's Sons
Macmillan Publishing Company
1633 Broadway
New York, New York 10019

Library of Congress Cataloging-in-Publication Data
Encyclopedia of the United States in the twentieth century
    / Stanley I. Kutler, editor in chief; Robert Dallek,
    David A. Hollinger, Thomas K. McCraw, associate
    editors; Judith Kirkwood, assistant editor.
        p.   cm.
    Includes bibliographical references and index.
    ISBN 0-13-210535-7 (set: hc: alk. paper). —
0-13-307190-1 (vol. 1: hc: alk. paper). — 0-13-307208-8
(vol. 2: hc: alk. paper). — 0-13-307216-9 (vol. 3: hc:
alk. paper). — 0-13-307224-X (vol. 4: hc: alk. paper).
        1. United States—Encyclopedias.   I. Kutler, Stanley
I. E740.7.E53 1996
973'.003–dc20   95-22696
                                                         CIP

    5 7 9 11 13 15 17 19   20 18 16 14 12 10 8 6 4
PRINTED IN THE UNITED STATES OF AMERICA

The paper in this publication meets the requirements of
ANSI/NISO Z39.48-1992 (Permanence of Paper)

Contents

Part 5

THE ECONOMY

Contents of Other Volumes

VOLUME I

CONTENTS OF OTHER VOLUMES

CONTENTS OF OTHER VOLUMES

Alphabetical Table of Contents

ALPHABETICAL TABLE OF CONTENTS

Common Abbreviations Used in This Work

Ala.	Alabama	Me.	Maine
Ariz.	Arizona	Mich.	Michigan
Ark.	Arkansas	Minn.	Minnesota
Art.	Article	Miss.	Mississippi
b.	born	Mo.	Missouri
c.	*circa*, about, approximately	Mont.	Montana
Calif.	California	n.	note
cf.	*confer*, compare	N.C.	North Carolina
chap.	chapter (plural, chaps.)	n.d.	no date
Cong.	Congress	N.D.	North Dakota
Colo.	Colorado	Neb.	Nebraska
Conn.	Connecticut	Nev.	Nevada
d.	died	N.H.	New Hampshire
D	Democrat, Democratic	N.J.	New Jersey
D.C.	District of Columbia	N.Mex.	New Mexico
Del.	Delaware	no.	number (plural, nos.)
diss.	dissertation	n.p.	no place
ed.	editor (plural, eds); edition	n.s.	new series
e.g.	*exempli gratia*, for example	N.Y.	New York
enl.	enlarged	Okla.	Oklahoma
esp.	especially	Oreg.	Oregon
et al.	*et alii*, and others	p.	page (plural, pp.)
etc.	*et cetera*, and so forth	Pa.	Pennsylvania
exp.	expanded	P.L.	Public Law
f.	and following (plural, ff.)	pt.	part (plural, pts.)
Fla.	Florida	R	Republican
Ga.	Georgia	Rep.	Representative
ibid.	*ibidem*, in the same place (as the one immediately preceding)	rev.	revised
		R.I.	Rhode Island
Ida.	Idaho	S.C.	South Carolina
i.e.	*id est*, that is	S.D.	South Dakota
Ill.	Illinois	sec.	section (plural, secs.)
Ind.	Indiana	Sen.	Senator
Kan.	Kansas	ser.	series
Ky.	Kentucky	ses.	session
La.	Louisiana	supp.	supplement
M.A.	Master of Arts	Tenn.	Tennessee
Mass.	Massachusetts	Tex.	Texas
Md.	Maryland	UN	United Nations

COMMON ABBREVIATIONS USED IN THIS WORK

U.S.	United States		Vt.	Vermont
U.S.S.R.	Union of Soviet Socialist Republics		Wash.	Washington
v.	versus		Wis.	Wisconsin
Va.	Virginia		W. Va.	West Virginia
vol.	volume (plural, vols.)		Wyo.	Wyoming

ENCYCLOPEDIA OF
THE UNITED STATES
IN THE TWENTIETH CENTURY

Part 5

THE ECONOMY

INTRODUCTION

Thomas K. McCraw

In his presidential address of 1910 to the American Historical Association, Frederick Jackson Turner commented that "the economic historian is in danger of making his analysis and his statement of a law on the basis of present conditions and then passing to history for justificatory appendixes to his conclusions." Turner was warning both himself and his colleagues against an unseemly present-mindedness. Yet viewed in retrospect, his speech has a kind of reverse merit, not as presentist history but as prophecy. Most of the themes he discussed in 1910 remained conspicuous at the close of the twentieth century. Those themes include the globalization of American interests, the unequalled power of American industry, the energy of the workforce, the issue of national abundance, and the troubling question of economic class. This part of the Encyclopedia addresses those issues, and many more related to the American economy and its business system.

Turner did not foresee everything, of course. Writing in 1910, he could hardly have predicted the full measure of consumer materialism that would soon engulf not only the American economy but the national culture as well. Although historians have long argued about when modern consumerism first appeared, there seems little doubt that the watershed period was the 1920s. In that decade, the radio, the automobile, the refrigerator, and a lavish variety of branded packaged goods began to pour off factory assembly lines in unprecedented volume. As Susan Strasser relates in the article on consumption, a portentous economic process began in the twenties, and by the end of the century, it had turned consumption from a necessary but minimal part of one's life into an activity that rivaled work itself as a way for Americans to spend most of their time.

That change did not happen automatically, of course. In the next article, Richard S. Tedlow analyzes in close detail the ways in which modern marketing evolved. He describes the interlocking re-lationships among mass production, mass consumption, brand names, and the perhaps essential intermediary of mass advertising. Demographics and what advertisers call psychographics became the tools of sophisticated marketers who persuaded consumers that they "needed" the latest new and improved versions of whatever products the advertisers' clients happen to make. Tedlow goes on to show how different kinds of consumer goods passed through specific phases of standardization and specialization targeted to particular market segments. But, he maintains, advertising by itself could not compel anyone to buy anything. The marketplace really is a competitive arena in which the consumer decides what will "sell."

Different classes of consumers purchased different market baskets of goods and services. In "Wealth and Poverty," an article at once trenchant and poignant, James T. Patterson charts the anomalous persistence of indigence in the world's richest country. When the twentieth century began, the United States was already the number one agricultural and industrial power. Its people were more prosperous than those of any other nation—but their affluence gave only a hint of the fantastic growth that lay ahead. By the end of the twentieth century, real gross domestic product per capita in the United States had reached a level about *five times* what it had been in 1900.

Yet the distribution of the nation's wealth never appeared to be satisfactory at any time during the twentieth century, measured against the nation's democratic traditions. In the United States, as in other western democracies, there arose a "welfare" system, one of whose purposes was to alleviate poverty and spread income by means of what came to be called transfer payments. These payments grew in scale and scope, particularly after the 1950s. For a time the system seemed to be working fairly well.

As the last quarter of the twentieth century began, however, something ominous happened. For many decades up to the year 1973, real wages had grown at a annual rate of about 2 percent, year in and year out. Consequently, average pay, and by implication average living standards, had doubled about every thirty-five years. But in 1973 the trend abruptly stopped, and average real wages of production and nonsupervisory workers began a steady decline. By the middle 1990s, the hourly wage of a worker in manufacturing was only 90 percent of what it had been in 1973. (Had the prior trend of two percent annual growth continued, this 90 percent figure would have been over 150 percent.) Meanwhile, the average pay of workers in unskilled occupations had fallen even more rapidly, and commentators began to refer routinely to a permanent underclass. As Patterson shows in his essay, this was a new phenomenon in American history, one that threatened to undercut the economic egalitarianism that had formed part of the core of American culture since the nation's beginnings.

Shoshana Zuboff, in her article on work, explores the psychological as well as the economic implications of this growing bifurcation of the American labor force. She shows that during the closing decades of the century the spread of computer-mediated work created wholly new relationships, in many cases altogether blurring traditional distinctions between blue-collar and white-collar, union and nonunion, even "labor" and "management." Beginning in the 1950s and accelerating very rapidly in the 1980s, the use of integrated-circuit technology thrust the American economy into a new epoch. The spread of the computer to millions of desktops, work-stations, and home offices caused an unprecedented expansion of access to information. In the business world, this sudden availability of bountiful data to people at all levels of the organization led to a flattening of hierarchies and a broadening of management's span of control. By the end of the twentieth century, the implications of the new revolution in information were only beginning to be understood. The whole movement was not just an American phenomenon but a full-blown global trend. Zuboff's essay treats the effects of all these changes on the worker's body, the organization of business, and the psychological health of the society.

In "Industrial Production," Alfred D. Chandler, Jr., analyzes the evolving portfolio of goods produced by American business. He stresses the importance of heavy industry in the second industrial revolution (metals, machinery, automobiles, electrical goods, basic chemicals); and then of science-based products in the third industrial revolution (electronics, computers, pharmaceuticals, polymer chemicals). Chan-

dler's essay is especially informative in tracing shifts in the capital intensity of particular industries. Over the course of the twentieth century, machinery replaced labor at very different rates in different industries. Some service-oriented industries hardly changed at all, remaining labor-intensive down to the present day. In other industries, however, employees almost disappeared from the shop floor, as machine tools and computer-aided controls made their work and their very crafts obsolete. Chandler shows how and why all of this happened.

Most important of all was the sheer volume of industrial production that emerged from American factories during the twentieth century. This record of production is one of the themes of Richard H. K. Vietor's article on economic performance. In a presentation dominated by numbers and appropriately filled with graphs and tables, Vietor places the performance of the American economy in an international perspective. He shows how, during most of the twentieth century, the United States as a country outperformed all other industrial nations. But he also demonstrates that there are two other characteristics: first, the American economy went through three distinct phases, each characterized by a shift in productivity growth; and second, toward the close of the century a host of macroeconomic problems associated with the federal deficit and international competition threatened to interrupt the remarkable long-term growth performance of the economy. If that indeed happens, Vietor warns, then the time of the American Dream may be past.

All capitalist economies have their ups and downs, of course. As the economist Joseph Schumpeter once remarked, "Stabilized capitalism is a contradiction in terms." In his article on the business cycle, Michael A. Bernstein chronicles the ebb and flow of twentieth-century prosperity, and analyzes its causes and effects. Business cycles have always fascinated economists, and scholars have never come to a full understanding of the phenomenon. (If they did, and if they could then go on to prescribe practicable remedies, then economic life would become simultaneously prosperous and dull.) Bernstein's essay shows how some very sophisticated tools of countercyclical macroeconomic management emerged during the Keynesian revolution—and then retreated late in the twentieth century under the tremendous pressures of a complex mix of circumstances. Like nearly all students of business cycles, Bernstein pays particular attention to the Great Depression of the 1930s. Unlike most analysts, however, he emphasizes some of the microeconomic aspects of that baffling phenomenon as well as its monetary, fiscal, and international dimensions.

The perennial mystery of money is the subject of George David Smith and Richard Sylla's tour of capital markets. Here the authors properly insist that the twentieth century's experience with stocks and bonds, and with Wall Street in general, cannot be understood apart from the rather complex nineteenth-century background. A nation born in democratic revolution developed a uniquely decentralized banking system, and in fact went through several periods during which there was hardly a "system" at all. Because the behavior of money and interest rates has always been enigmatic to most people, the doings of financiers, even including central bankers in the service of the government, have inevitably attracted hostile attention. The common people's feelings of being bilked have multiplied in the face of well-publicized conspiracies at high levels of finance. The American press has seldom suffered from a deficiency of stories about real scandal, from the time of Jay Gould in the 1860s to that of Richard Whitney in the 1930s to that of Michael Milken in the 1980s. But Smith and Sylla eschew the sensational, and they go admirably far in demystifying the complex subject of capital markets.

As Mira Wilkins shows in her comprehensive article on foreign trade and investment, capital markets as well as product markets became more and more international as the twentieth century wore on. When the century began, a few American corporations such as Singer Sewing Machine, Standard Oil, and International Harvester had already been operating abroad for several decades. In the years after World War I, the internationalization of U.S. business expanded briskly, only to falter during the Great Depression. Then, in the period after World War II, American business interests abroad exploded in a colossal drive for markets that changed the world economy forever. Throughout the century, the composition of American trade—both imports and exports—underwent almost constant change. Who would have thought in the 1950s, for example, that by the 1970s an incoming flood of automobiles and consumer electronics from Japan would threaten powerful American producers? In her essay Wilkins also elucidates the interrelationships among trade and investment. For example, she shows why, for particular corporations that wish to penetrate foreign markets, the decision to build factories abroad was a logical and almost irresistible climax to a series of prior strategic steps.

Foreign trade and investment are regulated by all countries. In the article on economic policies, Ellis Hawley traces the winding route of government-business relations in its broadest setting. He emphasizes the antistatist tradition in America and the consequent fragmentation and relative incoherence of policy. He notes that the United States entered the twentieth century without the kind of established and mature public sector that characterized other industrial nations. From a minuscule base in 1900, government's influence on the economy grew steadily during the Progressive Era, through the First World War, then the New Deal and the Second World War, until it reached a zenith of power and prestige during the Great Society of the 1960s. But by the 1980s, government began to be seen as part of the problem, not of the solution. Economic "deregulation" was instituted for airlines, railroads, and other industries, while social and environmental regulation moved forward without much interruption. In macroeconomic policy, chronic federal budget deficits became endemic after the Reagan Revolution lowered and flattened income tax rates beginning in 1981. Meanwhile, as Hawley shows, the mixed character of American beliefs about the proper role of the state resulted in an ad hoc approach to economic policies. Overall, the government steered an uneasy course between a general commitment to the "free market" on the one hand, and essential regulatory action on the other. But the excellent overall performance of the American economy in the twentieth century suggests that this kind of inconsistent approach, rooted in no firm ideology except individualism, actually may have strengthened economic growth, or at least did not seriously interfere with it.

Jack High's article on economic thought provides a systematic background for understanding the behavior delineated in Hawley's article on economic policies. High is concerned with both advanced theory and practical application. He explains how the marginalist revolution of the late nineteenth century reoriented economic thought in the western world. He notes that some American theorists contributed to this neoclassical surge while others reacted against it. The negative reaction coalesced around a group calling themselves institutionalists, and to this day their work constitutes one of the distinctive American contributions to economic thought. High shows how and why institutionalists were overtaken by the abstract modelers who began to dominate the economics profession in the 1960s, and who have become increasingly mathematical in their approach in the years since. But the salient story in High's survey is how the United States, a backwater of economic thought prior to the twentieth century, became by the end of the century the world's leading center of both theoretical and empirical thinking.

Some of the best economic thinking has gone into the design of the American tax system, the subject of the article by W. Elliot Brownlee. This is not to say that the American system is wholly rational, that it accomplishes all of its aims, or that it is unique in the world. Like the United States, many other countries have used their tax systems for diverse purposes: to pay the expenses of government, to promote or retard certain kinds of economic activity, and to redistribute wealth and income. But few countries have taken the particular approach of the United States. As Brownlee shows in his essay, the U.S. relies overwhelmingly on personal and corporate income taxes as opposed to value-added taxes or sales taxes. Because income-tax filings are so difficult to police, the American system reposes uncommon faith in the honesty of individual and corporate taxpayers. Should this implicit covenant ever be broken on a wide scale—a possibility given the antitax ethos that surfaces periodically in American culture—then the whole American system of government might be endangered. The strain on the tax system that accompanied the enormous federal deficits of the 1980s and 1990s, however, was not an entirely new development. Two hundred years earlier, in 1795, retiring Secretary of the Treasury Alexander Hamilton had written ruefully about the problems of taxation in a republic:

> To extinguish a Debt which exists and to avoid contracting more are ideas almost always favored by public feeling and opinion; but to pay Taxes for the one or the other purpose, which are the only means of avoiding the evil, is always more or less unpopular. . . . Hence it is no uncommon spectacle to see the same men Clamouring for Occasions of expense . . . [and also] declaiming against a Public Debt, and for the reduction of it as an *abstract thesis,* yet vehement against every plan of taxation which is proposed to discharge old debts, or to avoid new [ones] by defraying the expences of exigencies as they emerge.

In the whole national history of the American people, it would be hard to find a comment more germane to the fiscal trap the country set for itself in the late twentieth century.

Tax monies have underwritten much of the infrastructure, the subject of the article by William R. Childs. The American road and highway system, the world's largest and best, has been funded by public support at every level of government: city, county, state, and federal. It has been a tremendously expensive public works program, developed continuously throughout the twentieth century. And it is only part of a complex network of transportation facilities that include railroads, airports, and waterways both inland and coastal. Without a systematic infrastructure, the far-flung regions of the country could not have been knit together to form such a tightly integrated area of free trade. And without that advantage, the phenomenal economic growth of the twentieth century likely would have been impossible. Childs' essay covers as well the parallel growth of other elements of the infrastructure, including electric power and housing, which are complex subjects in themselves.

The next two articles, "Conservation and the Environment" by Arthur F. McEvoy and "Natural Resources" by Gavin Wright, provide sophisticated analyses of the difficult tradeoffs involved in Americans' treatment of their physical environment. Starting with the transcendent point that the North American continent is richly endowed in natural resources of almost all kinds, McEvoy traces the constitutional, legal, and political approaches to the balancing of preservation and exploitation. He shows that the tensions within the conservation movement between early-twentieth-century utilitarians such as Gifford Pinchot on the one hand, and wilderness devotees such as John Muir on the other, persists down to our own time. The proclamation of Earth Day on 22 April 1970 and the establishment of the Environmental Protection Agency (EPA) in that same year marked a national commitment to a cleaner environment. The subsequent passage by Congress of legislation such as the Clean Air Act and the Clean Water Act, plus the rapid evolution of EPA into one of the most powerful of all federal agencies, underscored the official American commitment to environmental values.

In his article on natural resources, Gavin Wright argues that the remarkable record of American economic growth owed a great deal not just to the country's tremendous endowment of minerals, trees, and fertile soil, but also to the rational processing of those endowments. Americans refined and marketed all over the world the oil they pumped from the ground. They developed the world's greatest steel industry as well as mining coal and iron ore. They built paper mills to process woodpulp from their forests. And they turned American agriculture into one of the great economic wonders in the history of the world. Wright provides an economic analysis of resource-based industries and then traces the development of supporting structures to carry out the essential processes of commercialization.

No account of the course of the American economy and its business system would be complete without commentary on the engineers, lawyers, accountants, and consultants who help make it all work, and on the teachers and professors who train the labor force. In the concluding article in this part of the Encyclopedia, Kenneth J. Lipartito and Paul Miranti examine the professions and professionalization. They provide an enlightening discussion of the persistent tension between American democratic values on the one hand and the need for elite expertise on the other. How does a society that aspires to egalitarianism rationalize the separation of some of its members into self-governing professions? How does it police the malpractice of professionals? Are not many "professions" simply economic cartels designed to restrict entry and thereby raise the prices of their members' services? Where exactly is the line that separates a "professional" from the normal run of businessperson or citizen? These questions go to the heart of the American character, and one can learn a great deal about the experience of the United States in the twentieth century by examining the history of any one of the great professions.

One final word about the American economy. As the articles here and in other parts of the Encyclopedia make clear, the United States cannot be viewed as an island unto itself. At the end of the twentieth century more than at any other time in its history, the nation is part of a complex international economy that it was instrumental in creating. As the overwhelmingly dominant industrial and trading power

to emerge from World War II, the United States sponsored a series of steps aimed at developing and liberalizing national economies throughout the world. The American government relentlessly promoted transnational institutions such as the General Agreement on Tariffs and Trade, the World Bank, the International Monetary Fund, and the United Nations. Washington became the most powerful force in opening world markets and moving toward a prosperous international trading system. The American market itself was by far the most lucrative, and policymakers generously opened it to a vast array of manufactured goods from abroad. Asian exporters took particular advantage of this situation, and their products poured into the United States. The overall result, by the end of the century, was world economic growth and integration on a scale scarcely imaginable only a few years earlier.

The motives behind American policies toward economic liberalization varied across a broad spectrum: financial self-interest, Cold War efforts to build up noncommunist economies as bulwarks against Soviet expansion, and an altruistic drive to propagate "the American way of life." That way of life embodied secular materialism, perpetual economic expansion, and a uniquely high level of prosperity. It may be true, as some critics have argued, that Americans have seldom led the world in philosophy, music, literature, painting, sculpture, architecture, and other essential and precious human arts. But throughout the twentieth century, right up to the late challenges from the Europeans and Japanese, the United States did undoubtedly lead the world in the realms of business and economic performance.

CONSUMPTION

Susan Strasser

Consumption is "the sole end and purpose of all production," wrote Adam Smith in *The Wealth of Nations*. The practices and policies of American institutions have embraced and transcended Smith's definition. Over the course of the twentieth century, consumption became fundamental to corporations and government agencies attempting to affect the activities of households in the interests of both corporate enterprise and economic growth. Marketing concerns came to dominate corporate decision making about production; the Great Depression brought consumption to the fore in considerations of economic policy; and, in public discourse, individuals' status as consumers came to rival and even surpass their status as workers. Corporate and governmental efforts to influence consumption brought Americans' daily lives—their attitudes, intimate behavior, and use of both paid and unpaid time—under the influence of economic institutions, for consumption operates at the intersection of public and private life.

As a private activity, consumption is important as both pastime and work. Throughout the century, developers of stores and shopping malls elaborated on the efforts of late-nineteenth-century department-store executives to create shopping environments that would associate buying with pleasure and fantasy. Yet for many consumers, shopping was an inevitable source of frustration, since marketing strategies were designed to awaken desires that exceeded their means. Still, they had to consume: the shopping and planning that constitute the work of consumption became essential to twentieth-century household life as factory-made goods and commercially provided services supplanted household production.

Historians have differed about dating the origins of consumer culture. Some suggest that the consumer revolution arrived quite early in Britain; they describe advertising, commercialized leisure and politics, and innovative production techniques that brought many new goods into common use before 1800. Likewise, scholars of early America have pro-vided considerable evidence that neither colonial households nor their localities were entirely self-sufficient. Many of these writers have construed their own work as a challenge to students of the twentieth century, and they certainly have demonstrated that more people participated in market activity than was suggested by previous depictions of societies based on subsistence agriculture. Nonetheless, during the four decades between 1890 and the beginning of the Great Depression, American consumption patterns and consumer consciousness were transformed so substantially that a new kind of consumer society came into being. That transformation corresponded to equally profound changes in the production and distribution of goods. Although these changes were the culmination of many decades' worth of development, the historians who have offered the most comprehensive interpretations about production speak of "revolutions," and of differences in kind as well as in scale.

The innumerable new products offered by twentieth-century industry transformed both the work and the diversions of private life, saving household labor and bringing paid entertainments into American homes. The new commodities, and the new media for selling them, changed people's expectations, desires, and needs, which in turn influenced the development of the new products that followed. Those changes followed patterns evident in other aspects of the culture: stratification and variance along lines of class, gender, race, ethnicity, age, and geography. Shopping itself was gendered activity, a set of tasks that supplanted women's vegetable gardening and sewing but was more subject to derision. Advertising targeted at women informed them of new products and stimulated desire, while helping to create an image of women as hopelessly addicted to spending. Gender and other distinctions were codified in marketing strategies: market segmentation and product positioning characterized successful marketing campaigns even in the first decades of the century.

Wealthier people enjoyed remarkable new products before poorer ones; urban life changed more quickly than rural.

These uneven patterns of development were echoed in individual lives. New ways coexisted with old, and people who bought new products kept things they already had. Early-twentieth-century farmers both ordered from Sears and bartered with country storekeepers. Depression-era housewives kept chickens and lit their homes with electricity. Children of the 1950s played hopscotch and watched television. Shoppers at the end of the century used credit cards for televised home shopping and bargained with cash at garage sales.

THE NEW CONSUMER CULTURE: 1890–1929

Many of these themes are exemplified in *Middletown*, Robert Lynd and Helen Merrell Lynd's 1929 study of Muncie, Indiana, a classic sociological text that has framed ideas about American consumption in the twentieth century. Nearly every historian who has discussed the topic has used *Middletown* as a source of information or a text for exegesis. Curiously, the Lynds did not even study consumption as an activity; their index does not list "shopping," "retail," "stores," or "markets," and offers only two brief references to "consumption." Yet the transition from local and household production to consumption of goods made in distant factories pervades their analysis and constitutes their central theme.

The Lynds cautioned readers who might wish to apply their findings "to other cities or to American life in general." Muncie was not typical. The authors' desire to simplify their study by selecting a "compact and homogeneous" city overruled their intent to find a representative one; with large nonwhite and foreign-born populations, most American cities in the 1920s were anything but homogeneous. Still, their pseudonym for Muncie and their subtitle—*A Study in Contemporary American Culture*—suggest an average town with average people. Here their work corresponds to that of contemporary investigators who did wish to apply local findings broadly: market researchers, who by the time the Lynds went to Muncie had conducted a considerable number of local studies on specific questions, working for advertising agencies and publications. *Middletown* cites, for example, comparisons with a seminal market study published in 1927 by the *Literary Digest*, whose investigators had knocked on every door in Zanesville, Ohio, to inquire about household possessions. Sociologists and marketers alike constructed ideal types; the group to be studied (or satisfied) was the middle, rather than the fringes.

Even though the Lynds concerned themselves with a homogeneous group of Muncie's citizens—native-born, white Americans, living in two-parent families with children of school age—they discovered that they could not describe Muncie as a unit. Class was simply too important. They defined it by men's work activities: working-class men used and made things, while business-class men worked with people. But the division went well beyond work. "The mere fact of being born upon one or the other side of the watershed [of class]," the authors wrote, "is the most significant single cultural factor tending to influence what one does all day long throughout one's life; whom one marries; when one gets up in the morning; whether one belongs to the Holy Roller or Presbyterian church; or drives a Ford or a Buick." The two classes represented the major segments of the Muncie market for consumer products and services. All the business-class families had telephones, for example; almost half the workers' households still were without them. Business-class women bought less fabric for sewing than did working-class women. They purchased commercial canned goods, while the workers' wives put up fruits and vegetables at home.

The business class, in other words, had gone farther in a process that greatly concerned the authors of *Middletown*. By 1924 there was little connection, they pointed out, between most of the activities of paid workers and their daily human needs. "Only to a negligible extent," they wrote, "does Middletown make the food it eats and the clothing it wears. Instead, it makes hundreds of thousands of glass bottles or scores of thousands of insulators or automobile engine parts." As a result, "more and more of the activities of living are coming to be strained through the bars of the dollar sign." There was much to buy, many "new urgent occasions for spending money in every sector of living." Automobiles and movies, "inventions re-making leisure," were of particular interest as they affected the institutions of family and community that had governed all of life.

The Lynds had a sharp eye for uneven development in what the historian Daniel Horowitz calls "the transition from exotic to ordinary." They admitted that the main recreations of Muncie were still cards and dancing, that lectures, reading, music, and art were entrenched, and that the movies and the automobile "must be viewed against an underlying groundwork of folk-play and folk-talk that makes up a relatively less changing human tradition." Likewise, they stressed the less-than-universal diffusion of new household products. "A single home may be operated in the twentieth century when it comes to ownership of automobile and vacuum cleaner, while its lack of a bathtub may throw it back into another era," they wrote. "Side by side in the same block one observes families using in one case a broom, in another a carpet sweeper, and in a third a vacuum cleaner."

Middletown's use of what later came to be called oral history was among its particularly effective devices; in addition to questions about current issues, the investigators asked about Muncie life in 1890, providing a point of historical comparison with the 1920s. Thus the book described not only a particular place at a particular moment, but a profound historical transition as it affected daily life. During those years, the United States had achieved its shift from an agricultural to an industrial society, while modern organizational systems and advanced technologies for production and distribution transformed industry itself. In addition to wearing more ready-made clothes and buying more factory-made furniture, Americans of all classes began to use products that nobody had ever made at home or by hand—products like corn flakes and safety razors. New products and technologies made old ones obsolete, as, for example, electric lights replaced oil lamps. Many human activities joined the realm of commodities for the first time, as folk culture was commercialized and experiences became something to buy. The new goods provided the material basis for new habits and the physical expression of a genuine break from earlier times. Even poor urban workers, with little land for gardens or time for handcrafts, joined the expanding market for manufactured goods. People in remote rural areas shopped from the Sears and Montgomery Ward catalogs, which offered a wider range of manufactured products than any store.

In part, markets grew because of demographic change. In 1900, three-fifths of the American population still lived in rural territory, places with populations less than 2,500. The urban population surpassed the rural in the 1920 census, and by 1930, those in urban areas formed 56 percent of the population. One consequence of this urbanization was smaller households. American households in 1890 were about equally divided among those with three people or fewer (34 percent), those with four or five (32 percent), and those of six or more (35 percent). By 1930, 52 percent of households had three people or fewer, while 29 percent had four or five, and only 19 percent had six or more. These trends alone could account for substantial market growth in consumer goods: simply put, the more households, the more need for household goods, and the more urban dwellers, the less time and space for home production. The demographic changes were compounded, however, by the rising expectations and changing standards of living promoted by the growing advertising industry, and with a general rise in disposable income.

Foremost among the vast number of new commodities that revamped private life during the period were technological systems that had manifestations as consumer services. Electricity, telephones, plumbing systems, and gas lines literally connected the private household to the public world. Whereas energy production—making fires and hauling fuel and water—had once been an essential component of household work, now water, gas, and electric energy literally could be consumed. Electricity and gas reduced the grime that accumulated on every surface from lamp soot, coal dust, wood chips, and smoke. The new fuels even altered space and time. Gas and electric light merged night and day; warm winter evenings dulled the distinctions between the seasons. Space in rooms, once defined by the focus of lamp and stove, was now framed by the walls.

Electricity was not something consumers could simply decide to purchase, but a choice made available by private companies and public utilities, which generally offered electric service to industry and business first. Once there was electricity to be had, however, households plugged in. In Muncie, only 22 homes had electricity in 1899, compared to 245 commercial customers; by 1907 private homes made up more than half the two thousand customers. The electric company offered wiring services on the installment plan, and by 1929, 95 percent of the city's households had electric lights. Muncie was ahead of other towns; in the United States as a whole, 85 percent of urban and nonfarm rural dwellings had electricity in 1930. Farm homes lagged far behind; only about 10 percent had electricity in 1930.

The spread of electricity was in part due to the rapid price decrease as new power plants were built and electric companies courted domestic consumption. In 1912, when about 16 percent of American dwelling units had electric service, a kilowatt hour cost about 9 cents, while in 1920 the 35 percent who had electricity paid 7.5 cents and in 1930 the 68 percent with electricity paid 6 cents per kilowatt hour. As a result of cheaper electricity, households installed more lights, bought more appliances, and used more current. The average annual use per customer doubled between 1912 and 1930. At first, most homes used only a few electric lights; other appliances were available, but not common. By 1926, 59 percent of Zanesville houses had electric irons, 53 percent had vacuum cleaners, and 20 percent had toasters. Still, the average residential customer used only 547 kilowatt-hours in 1930; customers in 1970 used thirteen times that much.

Indoor plumbing had been available to the wealthy throughout the nineteenth century, but its widespread diffusion required the mass production of pipes and fittings, and even middle-class plumbing systems were rudimentary. The Lynds wrote that in 1890 no more than two dozen houses in Muncie had complete bathrooms, and "only about one family in six or eight had even the crudest running water—a hydrant in the yard or a faucet at the iron kitchen sink." An 1893 report published by the U.S. Commissioner of Labor stated that 53 percent of New York families, 73 percent of Chicago's, and 88 percent of Baltimore's had access only to an outside privy. As late as 1925, 7 percent of a group of mostly black and Mexican-born Chicago workers still had to go outside for a toilet. Many of the others shared facilities in the halls outside their apartments, and during the winter frozen pipes rendered useless what indoor plumbing they had. The Lynds found about a quarter of Muncie households without running water in 1924, and again commented on the unevenness of modernity. "It is not uncommon," they wrote, "to observe 1890 and 1924 habits jostling along side by side in a family with primitive back-yard water or sewage habits, yet using an automobile, electric washer, electric iron, and vacuum cleaner." Like electricity, plumbing displayed substantial urban-rural differences: in the late 1920s, 71 percent of urban families and only 33 percent of rural had bathrooms, according to the President's Conference on Home Building and Home Ownership.

Telephones were the last of the utilities to achieve universality; 59 percent of households were still without them in 1930, a figure that was to rise during the Depression as people disconnected their phones to save money. Still, during the period between 1890 and 1929 telephones moved decisively out of the category of luxuries and oddities. Virtually all businesses had them, and they were used widely for personal calls. About 20 million phones in 1930 amounted to 163 per thousand population, which may be compared with 4 phones per thousand in 1890 and 82 per thousand in 1910. All the business class families the Lynds interviewed in 1924 had phones, along with 55 percent of the workers' families.

The statistics that tell the story of public utilities so clearly are for the most part not available to describe the concurrent triumph of consumer products. It is clear nonetheless that by the turn of the century a wide variety of prepared and packaged foods were advertised and distributed to a national market. Many of the brands are still familiar. Heinz and Campbell's offered prepared sauces and soups, in essence competing with household labor and saving the time and trouble of preparation; Quaker and Pillsbury competed with oats and flour sold in bulk. These firms exploited the economies of mass production, and after 1900 their prices began to drop. By the 1920s, prepared and packaged foods could be found on many working people's tables. New technologies and the general expansion of the consumer economy similarly brought more durable goods within the reach of many. Enameled sheet-steel pots and pans, for example, became available to supplant or supplement cast iron during the 1890s. By 1919, a government list of minimal kitchen equipment for the working poor included not only enamelware, but even a few utensils made of aluminum, a luxury material twenty years earlier.

By the 1920s ready-made clothing was common among people of both sexes and all classes. Men's wear had dominated the nineteenth-century ready-made industry, while women's and children's clothes remained the product of the private home and the independent seamstress; in 1890 women's clothing constituted less than a quarter of the value of all factory-made clothing. The industry expanded because of technological change—improved sewing and cutting machines that increased workers' productivity—and organizational innovation, the sweatshops. These were small shops employing fewer than ten immigrant workers. They were supervised by contractors who rented lofts or used their own tenement apartments, bought sewing machines on the installment plan, and got raw materials on credit from manufacturers. By 1914, the value of factory-made women's clothing surpassed that of men's wear. Within a decade, making clothing—once a task that occupied most women's every spare moment and, for some, a source of craft satisfaction—became a choice. Two-thirds of the working-class women the Lynds interviewed in 1924 spent less than six hours a week sewing and mending; half the business-class women spent less than two hours. According to the head of the fabric department of Muncie's largest department store, demand for yard goods was "only a fraction of that in 1890."

The transition from home to factory production

was a central concern of the theorists and teachers of the home economics movement, comprising a variety of people and organizations who came together in the American Home Economics Association in 1908. In the courses they designed for degree students at the land-grant colleges and for young women in public schools, home economists defined shopping and planning for consumption as women's work, increasingly essential to family life as household production became less so. During the 1920s, home-economics graduates began to work in industry. They created recipes for utility companies to use in promoting gas and electric stoves and for food manufacturers to print in their advertising; they designed curriculum materials for home economics classes that explained and promoted manufacturers' products; and they represented "the woman's point of view" in company policy discussions.

While home economists concerned themselves primarily with household work, a full consideration of consumption during the period must also note changes in leisure-related consumption. Here, too, mass production, urbanization, and new fuels made possible new products and services for people of all classes during the forty years before the Great Depression. Kodak, for example, sponsored a revolution in photography, an extremely expensive and highly technical hobby at the beginning of the period; the company manufactured cameras that were easy to operate and offered products priced for the middle class. Photography also came within the reach of working-class people, who patronized photo studios for formal portraits and had their pictures taken by roving photographers on outings to the amusement park or the beach.

Amusement parks themselves represent another kind of leisure consumption: the buying of experience. Brooklyn's Coney Island was the mecca—not one establishment but several, beginning with Sea Lion Park, which opened in 1895. Steeplechase Park opened two years later, and twenty-two-acre Luna Park in 1903, the latter a fantasy land of minarets, turrets, and 250,000 electric lights. The amusement park, the historian David Nye writes, "inverted central values of American society—thrift, sobriety, restraint, order, and work—and exploited technology for pleasure. . . . It transformed the public into a crowd to be manipulated into spending money for momentary pleasures and gaudy visions of self-transformation." By 1919, there were at least 1,500 amusement parks in American cities.

Amusement parks served as one of the initial venues for motion pictures, also presented as part of vaudeville shows. Nickelodeons—storefront theaters featuring shows composed of one-reel films—first opened around 1905. Within two years, there were about two thousand such theaters in the United States, including over two hundred in Manhattan alone. By 1910, about 26 million Americans attended weekly shows at ten thousand nickelodeons. Because movies cost less than live theater, and because silent films could be understood by everybody, they were especially popular with immigrant workers. Around 1914, larger theaters, equipped with carpets, ushers, and other marks of refinement, were built to bring the new, longer feature films to the middle classes. After World War I, theater entrepreneurs began to operate large movie palaces—ornate buildings designed with grand staircases and decorated in exotic styles, attracting large middle-class audiences who came by streetcar for the movies and stage shows. During the 1920s, chains of such theaters, each seating two to three thousand patrons, were built in every large city, coexisting with the rowdier local movie theaters in working-class neighborhoods. The Lynds found nine motion picture theaters in Muncie, each showing two or three movies a week.

As *Middletown* suggested, the single most important product in the new culture of consumption was the automobile. With the exception of a house, it was the largest item in a family budget; it spawned and supported ancillary industries and businesses ranging from tires to highway construction to parking lots; it engendered such new approaches to activities as drive-in movies, supermarkets, and motels; it stimulated financial markets with the development of insurance and consumer credit; it opened up new communities and changed both the physical and the economic landscape. The automobile, in short, established a vast number of opportunities for investment far beyond its own industry and caused equivalent repercussions in lifestyle.

Henry Ford, already a manufacturer of medium-priced automobiles, introduced his Model T in 1908. Its immediate popularity enabled his company to grow rapidly and paid for continual development in manufacturing processes both before and after the inauguration of the assembly line in 1913. The price of a Model T—$950 in 1909—dropped to $290 by 1924. Even so, Ford began to lose market share in the twenties: the company sold 55 percent of new American cars in 1921, and 30 percent in 1926. General Motors had by then introduced yearly model changes, and established manufacturing facilities and an organization capable of adapting to and fostering those changes. As a marketing device, the yearly model change symbolizes the advent of the consumer culture, in contrast to the Model T, a symbol of production efficiency.

By the end of the 1920s, automobiles were a central feature of American consumer culture. In 1930, 23 million passenger cars were registered, almost one for each of the 30 million households. The development of a substantial resale market for second-hand cars both kept the new car market afloat and broadened the influence of the automobile; used-car sales surpassed new-car sales for the first time in 1927.

Some of those who wanted new cars but could not pay the price purchased them on time credit. For many decades, the installment plan had enabled seamstresses and farmers to buy sewing machines and harvesters—capital goods for small businesses. Now it became part of the selling strategy for expensive consumer products. Three major companies financed the postwar auto boom by offering loans to consumers, including the General Motors Acceptance Corporation, established in 1919. But the habit went beyond car-buying. "The rise and spread of the dollar-down-and-so-much-per plan," the Lynds wrote in *Middletown*, "extends credit for virtually everything—homes, $200 over-stuffed living-room suites, electric washing machines, automobiles, fur coats, diamond rings—to persons of whom frequently little is known as to their intention or ability to pay."

Credit on a more modest scale had long been the norm at country general stores, small-town Main Street shops, and stores in urban neighborhoods. The face-to-face personal relationships that went along with the retail credit, home delivery, and other services that small retailers provided were challenged during the first decades of the twentieth century by new kinds of retailing. Chain stores had begun in the grocery trade well before 1890, but they remained small until after 1912, when A&P introduced "economy stores," small cash-and-carry operations run by two people. By the end of 1913, A&P had 585 stores; it opened 1,600 more during 1914–1915, an additional 2,600 before the end of 1919, and reached 15,700 at its peak in 1930. For the most part, however, industrial workers who lived from paycheck to paycheck continued to patronize local stores that offered credit.

Chains depended on the central tenet of mass retailing: turnover. Merchandise that sat on a shelf took up space that could be used repeatedly by more profitable stock; capital could reap continual profits if it were invested and reinvested in things that sold. This principle—moving goods into and out of the store as quickly as possible—was first developed by nineteenth-century department stores and brought to its apotheosis by the big Chicago mail order houses, Montgomery Ward and Sears, Roebuck. Ward's was already selling about 24,000 separate items when Sears began to expand during the early 1890s. By 1900, Sears had surpassed its rival, and in 1906, the company moved to a forty-acre tract, where two thousand people opened and processed more than nine hundred sacks of mail every day.

While some mass retailers manufactured goods to sell under their own labels—especially Sears, which in 1906 owned or held a major interest in sixteen manufacturing plants—others attracted customers by offering low prices on branded, nationally advertised products. Cut-rate prices on these products challenged the central marketing strategy used by successful mass producers, who hoped to establish brand loyalties strong enough to overcome price sensitivity: belief in the qualities of Kellogg's or Ivory that would convince customers to pay whatever they cost. The branding strategy altered the balance of power in the chain of distribution. Before the 1880s, wholesalers wishing to distribute white soap took bids from manufacturers and then promoted what they bought to retailers, who sold it to their customers. But when people began to ask for Ivory, a product that could be obtained only from Procter and Gamble, the wholesalers had to buy from that company. To the extent that manufacturers could convince people to rely on advertising rather than on their grocers' opinions, branding offered manufacturers a more predictable and controllable market, with protection against competition and industry price fluctuations. Mass producers making such branded products as packaged crackers or toothpaste or chewing gum, which sold for only a nickel or a dime, had difficulty lowering the price by a penny or two to increase demand. To sell more, they had to advertise.

Advertising agencies introduced new services to promote branded products. Moving beyond their decades-long role of brokering advertising space in periodicals, agencies at the turn of the century began to hire copywriters and artists. The most advanced agencies and the biggest companies conducted campaigns—coordinated efforts based on market research that brought advertising together with other kinds of promotion such as free samples and store demonstrations. By 1911, Heinz had a large enough sales force to change 25,000 store displays in coordination with magazine advertising. The next year, Procter and Gamble introduced its new shortening, Crisco, with the most elaborate and expensive marketing campaign ever seen. The J. Walter Thompson agency tested different sales promotion plans and conducted a general analysis of the shortening market; the product was launched with full-sized free samples sent to every grocer in the United States, along with advertisements in several national magazines.

Such campaigns demonstrate that modern marketing concepts were well in place before World War I. Market segmentation may be seen in any number of examples. Many companies produced what later came to be called flanker brands, different versions of a product under different brands, each advertised to a particular segment. The 1910 Edison phonograph line ranged from the $200 Amberola, with a sapphire needle and an oak or mahogany cabinet, to a bare-bones model selling for $12.50. The Arbuckle Brothers coffee company packaged Yuban for wealthy urban people and Ariosa for rural markets and poor urban ones. Procter and Gamble both promoted Ivory for use on clothes and sold Star, a laundry soap targeted at consumers who could not afford to use Ivory that way.

The new campaigns took advantage of and contributed to major developments in the advertising media. New mass publications had national circulations and depended for their revenues on advertising, not subscriptions; these magazines and newspapers were designed to highlight the ads, which were larger and embraced new design principles such as the use of white space. Newspapers and magazines had published commercial messages for centuries, but usually in separate sections full of closely packed small ads; now the periodicals literally functioned as advertising media. Likewise, although billboards are the oldest of media, new national and regional firms developed systems during the decades after 1890 that would offer advertisers the ability to get signs posted simultaneously in distant places. Advances in lithography made it possible to reproduce huge color images; electricity made night as important as day for commercial purposes.

Advertising—when it was successful—functioned to create demand. People who had never used toothpaste or oatmeal that came in a box had to learn that they might want to buy them. In the process of learning about those products, and about branded packaged products in general, their expectations about their daily lives changed, as did their needs and desires. At the same time, many products failed, and spectacular campaigns like the one for Crisco were exceptional. Early-twentieth-century ads attempted to build consumer trust in manufacturers, but trust in local merchants still motivated many purchases. Manufacturers exploited those motivations, but also had to adapt to them and court the retailer along with the consumer. People buy some goods and do not buy others; they use what they buy in their own ways, giving products their own meanings as well as taking meanings from the advertising.

The historian Daniel Boorstin has described late-nineteenth- and early-twentieth-century America as a land of "consumption communities," Lucky Strike smokers or Chevrolet drivers "with a feeling of shared well-being, shared risks, common interests, and common concerns." Distinguishing them from earlier communities of Pilgrims or pioneers, Boorstin comments that consumption communities were less exclusive, "held together by much thinner, more temporary ties." The metaphor is compelling; advertising did encourage individuals to consider products as central to their well-being and to identify fellow users of a brand as special people. But consumption communities were not merely invisible; they existed only in the realm of advertising. In fact, real communities continued to exist and to influence taste, and manufacturers courted them consciously, advertising in ethnic newspapers and targeting particular products at particular areas of the country; ethnic communities sometimes incorporated elements of mass culture more than they were assimilated by it.

Rather than finding themselves in some new kind of community, twentieth-century Americans were increasingly alone in the marketplace, cut loose from the relationships that had once brought people the things they used. Formerly *customers,* purchasing the objects of daily life from craftspeople or storekeepers whom they knew, Americans became *consumers* during the first decades of the century, buying mass-produced goods as participants in a complex network of distribution, a national market that promoted individuals' relationships with big, centrally organized, national companies. They got their information about products not from the people who made or sold them, but from advertisements created by specialists in persuasion. These changes, though by no means universal or complete on the eve of the Great Depression, were accelerating processes that had taken firm hold on American daily life.

THE PEOPLE AS CONSUMERS: 1929–1945

Those processes were so relentless that the march of consumption as a way of life and an element of culture was not halted either by the shortage of purchasing power during the Great Depression or by the shortage of goods to purchase during World War II. Sales of some consumer goods even increased during the period. Two innovations in selling—national radio and the supermarket—gained broad popularity. Moreover, the modern concept of the consumer came into its own during this time.

Hindsight implies a significant break following the stock market crash of 1929, and some writers' attempts to make sense of history by means of periodization place the birth of twentieth-century consumption patterns and attitudes during the 1920s and suggest that they were stalled by the Depression. In fact, however, mass media, mass retailing, and the fundamental elements of mass marketing were in place even before World War I and, for most Americans, the twenties never roared. While GNP and per capita income rose, people did not share equally in prosperity. Wages, especially for the unskilled and semiskilled workers who predominated in industrial employment, rose modestly or not at all. Unemployment was high in whole industries, especially agriculture, coal, and textiles. Even for skilled workers, industrial work was often seasonal; the "fully employed" got laid off frequently. The Lynds found that 74 percent of Muncie families earned less than the Bureau of Labor's standard for a minimum cost of living. Coming to the city during its 1924 recession, they stressed the intermittent and unstable nature of employment. When in 1937 they published *Middletown in Transition,* which studied the effects of the Depression, they emphasized that hard times had not begun overnight, nor all at once. One quarter of the city's factory workers had lost their jobs by 1930, while most business-class jobs continued through 1931.

Nationwide, retail sales dropped by 48 percent from 1929 to 1932. They then rose slowly during the rest of the decade without achieving the 1929 level. People bought less, did without, and practiced countless small economies in their daily lives. Some kinds of consumption changed more than others, however. The physical volume of sales remained constant in food stores and almost constant in general-merchandise stores from 1929 to 1935. Residential use of electricity and consumption of gasoline continued to go up despite the Depression. In Muncie, jewelry stores were the hardest hit, with a decrease of 85 percent in dollar sales between 1929 and 1933, followed by lumber yards, car dealerships, and candy stores. Restaurants suffered a drop of 63 percent in sales. Stores selling men's clothing lost more than those featuring women's wear. As in the nation at large, gasoline still sold; purchases of new cars went down, but not overall car registrations. "While, therefore, people were riding in progressively older cars as the depression wore on," wrote the Lynds, "they manifestly continued to ride."

One major consumer durable, the electric refrigerator, even achieved widespread diffusion during the Depression. Less than one-half of 1 percent of Zanesville families owned them in 1926. Five years later, market researchers for Time, Inc., estimated that 90 percent of American families were still without them. During the thirties, however, 10 million refrigerators were sold, thanks at least in part to an aggressive advertising campaign. In 1935, almost eight times the number of refrigerators were sold annually as in 1929, and by 1940, 56 percent of American households owned them. Consumers Union pointed out in 1938 that because higher-income people already had refrigerators, poorer people represented the largest potential market. But manufacturers continued to develop expensive models and to try to convince the wealthy that their refrigerators were obsolete. "Although the cream has been skimmed," the CU report complained, "the industry would like to skim it again."

Radios, too, sold steadily during the Depression. Radio was still a hobby when broadcasting started in 1920: headsets had to be assembled and properly tuned, while noncommercial radio stations broadcast local, amateur talent. By 1924, radios with loudspeakers were designed to look like furniture, making it possible for whole families to listen to increasingly professional broadcasts. In 1927, 84 percent of the households in Zanesville and 63 percent of those in thirty-six other cities studied by the R. O. Eastman company had no radio, statistics the New York researchers noted with some surprise. From 1930 to 1936, the total number of radios nearly doubled, from 12 million to nearly 23 million, a figure that did not include approximately 3 million car radios, nearly nonexistent in 1930. By 1940, about 80 percent of American households owned radios.

Commercial sponsorship by companies producing nationally advertised products dominated the airwaves during the Depression. In the early days of radio, there had been some concern among advertising professionals and government regulators that people accustomed to entertainment without commercial interruption would resent it. Initially, programs incorporated commercials by featuring "branded performers" like Paul Oliver and Olive Palmer, who performed for the Palmolive Company; Goldy and Dusty, the Gold Dust Twins; the Ipana Troubadours; and the A&P Gypsies. By 1928, national networks had been established on an explicitly commercial basis, selling expensive radio time. New forms of sponsored programming emerged, most notably with *Amos 'n' Andy,* sponsored by Pepsodent beginning in 1929, and Eddie Cantor's *Chase and Sanborn Hour,* which went on the air in 1931. The variety show format took off the next season, with new programs featuring Jack Benny, George Burns and Gracie Allen, George Jessel, and Fred Allen—and words from their sponsors.

During the daytime, women learned homemaking skills and product use from a variety of radio homemakers. Most of these shows were local. Individual radio stations—many of them owned by utilities and appliance manufacturers—hired women to offer household hints, recipes, and product advice on the air. There were, however, some important national homemaking programs during the 1930s. CBS hired a college-trained home economist, Ida Bailey Allen, for its "National Homemaker's Club." The U.S. Department of Agriculture sponsored "Housekeeper's Chat" featuring "Aunt Sammy," played by fifty women in fifty radio stations reading identical scripts prepared by USDA home economists. General Mills had at first supported multiple Betty Crockers, but, after network radio, she was played by one woman broadcasting from Minneapolis, backed by a test kitchen, promoting scientific cooking and praising the company's products. The other important selling innovation of the 1930s, the supermarket, was a direct result of the Depression, its success due to low prices. Self-service had been introduced in 1916 in the Piggly-Wiggly chain, but the modern supermarket depended on a population equipped with automobiles and accustomed to branded goods. This combination had been achieved by 1930, when Michael Cullen, who called himself "the world's greatest price wrecker," opened his first King Kullen store in Queens, New York. Cullen and later supermarket entrepreneurs either built new stores on cheap land or modified empty factory buildings outside major urban areas, opening huge stores with expansive parking lots. They offered neither credit nor delivery. Customers picked out their own goods rather than asking clerks to retrieve their purchases (and, potentially, making product choices based on the clerks' opinions). Whereas Piggly-Wiggly had offered wire baskets for customers to use in the store, the new supermarkets of the 1930s offered shopping carts that could hold large quantities. People with cars were not constrained in their purchasing by how much they could carry home. Here was the full expression of the turnover principle. It threatened not only the individual grocer, but the nonsupermarket chain store as well. Even huge chains like A&P were composed of many small stores.

To convince the supermarket shopper to pick one brand over another, Depression-era copywriters devised a number of strategies. They intensified their appeals to economy, of course, and increased their use of what the historian of advertising Roland Marchand calls the "Parable of the Democracy of Goods." A 1931 *Ladies' Home Journal* advertisement for Pond's beauty products, for example, displayed photographs of women from the Vanderbilt, Morgan, Astor, Belmont, Drexel, and du Pont families, who were said to use Pond's products "despite their democratic simplicity and modest price." Above all, the advertising industry aimed to keep people wanting things and spending whatever money they did have. The manufacturers the ad people served continued to offer revised products. In the hard-hit home-building industry, model homes and architectural competitions glamorized the latest fashions; the 1939 World's Fair in New York featured twenty-one single-family houses in a "Town of Tomorrow." "Style," commented the author of a 1937 report on consumption during the Depression, "continued as an active force throughout the depression. 'Streamlined' became an almost universal slogan. . . . While no statistical evidence is at hand, casual perusal of fashion magazines suggests that women's dresses and hats went through style transformations between 1930 and 1936, much as in more prosperous times."

Although it did not appear in advertisements, a new set of concepts about consumption and consumers entered public discourse during the Depression. Predepression marketing had brought individuals' attitudes and the use of their unpaid time increasingly under the influence of large corporations and other economic institutions, but consumption was fundamentally understood as private activity. Now it came to be seen as having public repercussions—serious consequences for economic enterprise and growth—and the consumer gained a new place in public discourse.

At first, common sense (and President Herbert Hoover) suggested that things would get better if people would just spend their money. "This whole depression business is largely mental," the Muncie afternoon paper wrote in a June 1930 editorial. "If tomorrow morning everybody should wake up with a resolve to unwind the red yarn that is wound about his old leather purse, and then would carry his resolve into effect, by August first, at the latest, the whole country could join in singing, 'Happy Days Are Here

Again.' " "This 'underconsumption' note," the Lynds commented, "alternately wheedling and belaboring the individual citizen overboard in midocean for not throwing away his life belt—went on year after year through the depression, linked with the argument that depressions are 'merely psychological.' "

The life belt, of course, was savings. There had been a steady upward trend in personal saving for the period from 1915 to 1929. The Liberty Loan campaigns of World War I reinforced the savings habit among working people, and the economic uncertainty of the early 1920s strengthened it. Among kinds of personal savings, there was substantial growth in savings-and-loan deposits, an approach suited to small savers. John Maynard Keynes called attention to the broader social relationship between savings and consumption in his *General Theory of Employment, Interest and Money* (1936). Keynes attempted to specify the consumption function, the direction and magnitude of the variables that affect how a society will divide its income between consumption and savings. According to him, "the propensity to consume" followed a "psychological law"—that, in the economist James Tobin's words, "the community will divide an increase in income in some regular proportion between an increase in consumption and an increase in saving."

While there is doubt among historians as to the actual influence of Keynesian theory on Franklin D. Roosevelt's economic policy, certain New Deal programs contributed to consumption and to the development of consumer culture. "The dole" represented "the hitherto abhorrent notion that the consumer must be furnished with purchasing power whether he works or not," wrote Stuart Chase, an accountant who turned to popular writing, in the *Nation* in 1933. The Public Works Administration and other work relief projects extended recreation opportunities and expectations by building facilities in national parks, and tennis courts and swimming pools in cities. A number of agencies helped to transform rural life and contributed to the ever-increasing consumption of electricity: the Tennessee Valley Authority, established in 1933, and its experimental subsidiary, the Electric Home and Farm Authority; the Rural Electrification Administration, created in 1935; and, once they began to sell power, the Grand Coulee and Bonneville Dams of the Columbia Basin Project, begun in 1933. By 1941, 35 percent of farm dwelling units had electric service, and total residential use of electric energy had almost tripled since 1929.

Other New Deal programs suggest a growing consumer consciousness. The chief of the short-lived and controversial National Recovery Administration, Gen. Hugh S. Johnson, exhorted consumers to rally behind the NRA by purchasing products branded with its symbol, the Blue Eagle. At the same time, he excoriated the concept of consumer representation through the NRA's Consumer Advisory Board, which had little power. "Who is a consumer?" he demanded. "Show me a consumer." Similarly, although a Consumers' Council was established within the Department of Agriculture, it was weakened by the perplexing question of whether a separate consumer interest existed and who might represent it. Late in the Depression, in 1938, revisions of Progressive Era legislation exhibited the concept of consumer interest by extending the powers of the Food and Drug Administration and the Federal Trade Commission. The FDA's jurisdiction would now include cosmetics and therapeutic devices. Drug manufacturers were required to demonstrate the safety of new products before putting them on the market. The FTC was granted the power to regulate deceptive practices as well as unfair ones, giving the agency jurisdiction over deceptive advertising, among other business practices.

The demands for these legislative revisions and for consumer representation in the federal government came from a growing consumer movement. Consumer activism was not entirely new. Concerns about unsafe food and drugs had resulted in two important pieces of legislation in 1906, the Pure Food and Drug Act and the Meat Inspection Act. Part of the broader Progressive movement to regulate large firms, the coalition of muckrakers, business interests, and women's groups that lobbied for those laws had not formulated clear concepts of the consumer or of consumer interest. In fact, the only Progressive Era activists to call themselves consumers— the National Consumers' League—were actually interested in questions of production. The League used the boycott as an instrument of moral power to press for better conditions for workers.

When the consumer movement emerged during the thirties, however, it was not without a longstanding intellectual tradition. Beginning with *The Theory of the Leisure Class* (1899), the most important thinker to address himself to the question of consumption had been Thorstein Veblen. While his indictment of leisure-class consumption was hardly an expression of the consumer's interest, Veblen formulated ideas that were to become fundamental to the consumer movement. He offered an institutional analysis, a challenge to the idea that more was better, and an antipathy toward waste, expressed in striking phrases like "conspicuous consumption" and "captains of industry." In fiction, the key critic of consumption was Sinclair Lewis, who presented his analysis in three novels published during the twenties, *Main Street, Babbitt,* and *Dodsworth.* The intellectual historian Neil Harris calls *Babbitt* "perhaps the most detailed portrait of American consumption in our fiction" and describes the novel as "an endless set of inventories. . . . Lewis is at pains," he writes, "to outline the symbolic system which surrounds the objects."

Stuart Chase provided the intellectual link between Veblen and the consumer movement. In two popular books, *The Challenge of Waste* (1922) and *The Tragedy of Waste* (1925), Chase declared that many new products had nothing to do with human needs and were in fact detrimental, inefficient, or just worthless. *Your Money's Worth: A Study in the Waste of the Consumer's Dollar,* written with F. J. Schlink and published in 1927, made recommendations. "Our whole thesis," Chase and Schlink wrote in the final chapter, "may be expressed in a hypothetical case. Two men are discussing the merits of a famous brand of oil. Says one, 'I know it must be good; it sells a million dollars worth a year. You see their advertisements everywhere.' But the other says, 'I do not care how much it sells. I left a drop of it on a piece of copper for 24 hours, and the drop turned green. It is corrosive and I do not dare to use it.'" The book described an "experiment station" that Schlink had established as part of a consumer's club in White Plains, New York. It recommended more sophisticated testing labs staffed by technical experts and funded by universities and government agencies.

Schlink responded to the interest and financial support generated by *Your Money's Worth* by forming Consumers' Research, Inc., and transforming his "Consumer's Club Commodity List" into *Consumers' Research Bulletin,* devoted increasingly to rating products and offering guidance for consumption decisions. Within five years, the magazine had a circulation of 42,000 subscribers, and the organization was publishing a variety of books and pamphlets as well. In 1933, Schlink and Arthur Kallet, a Consumers' Research board member, published *100,000,000 Guinea Pigs: Dangers in Everyday Foods, Drugs, and Cosmetics,* a blood-curdling indictment that became one of the best-selling books of the decade. The authors advocated, among other things, mandatory lists of ingredients on food packages. By 1935, Consumers' Research employed more than fifty people full time and had considerable credibility, including

a list of sponsors such as well-known journalists from major liberal magazines. Dissatisfaction among the CR staff led to union organizing efforts in 1935, and ultimately to the formation in 1936 of a new organization, Consumers Union, whose bulletin, *Consumers Union Reports* (later *Consumer Reports*), surpassed *Consumers' Research Bulletin* in circulation in 1938. Like the previous organization, Consumers Union had influence well beyond its subscription list. It was frequently quoted in other periodicals, and advertisements reported the results of its tests, not always honestly.

With the beginning of emergency preparations for World War II, Consumers Union began to track civilian supply. After American participation in the war began, the organization started a newsletter that traced issues like price controls, quality deterioration, and other wartime domestic economic issues. Over the years between Pearl Harbor and V-J (Victory over Japan) Day, per capita consumer purchases in fact went up. Shortages, rationing, and curtailed production of consumer durables, however, gave a working population with money to spend a sense that they were sacrificing to the war effort *as consumers.*

The government began to restrict consumer-durables production in 1941, and the next year it ended the production of motor vehicles and electrical appliances (including radios) for civilian use. Other civilian purchases increased: per capita consumption of food went up, as did that of clothing, household soft goods, cosmetics, toys, jewelry, paper products, alcohol and tobacco, and electricity. In general the figures jumped with the beginning of the war and continued to rise slowly for its duration.

Rationing, however, began in 1942. Ration boards were established in every county in the United States, with volunteers recruited to handle the paperwork. President Roosevelt announced a ban on the use of gasoline for pleasure driving, and cars bore stickers announcing how much fuel they were entitled to. Rationing was managed for food and other goods through the use of books that held stamps for items on the ration list such as sugar, coffee, or shoes. Clothing other than shoes was not rationed, but its production was regulated so as to conserve fabric. The government outlawed doubled-breasted and three-piece suits, full skirts, knife pleats, and cuffs on men's trousers. The War Production Board stated that it wished to "assure the women and girls of America that there will be no extremes in dress styles during this war . . . and that their present wardrobes will not be made obsolete by radical fashion changes."

Wartime propaganda assigned an important place

to the consumer. "Give your whole support to rationing and thereby conserve our vital goods," the Office of Price Administration wrote on the ration book distributed in 1943. "Be guided by the rule: *If you don't need it,* DON'T BUY IT." Consumer consciousness of waste was promoted in scrap drives that probably served the war effort more as propaganda than to gather critical materials like rubber and metal. People were encouraged to use only one razor blade per week, to turn in old toothpaste tubes when they bought new ones, and to bring waste fat back to the butcher for use in nitroglycerin manufacture. "Use it up, wear it out, make it do, or do without," went the slogan.

Advertising, meanwhile, made promises about the future. Automatic washing machines, for example, had been introduced immediately before the war. Because of the machine's advantages over the older wringer washers, the Bendix automatic had gained 55 percent of the market before the war stopped production. Other companies developed automatic washers and promoted them before they could sell them. "Some day soon . . . you'll be free from the drudgery of Washday!" read one such pamphlet issued by a major manufacturer in 1944. "Come 'V Day' . . . the hard work of clothes washing will be done for you." The Minnesota Mining and Manufacturing Company used a similar pitch for Scotch tape, which, they wrote in an ad, had been "drafted for service on battle lines and in war plants. When these war jobs are done, the tape will all be back again." Such advertising, combined with government propaganda, rationing, and shortages of consumer durables and building supplies, created pent-up demand at the end of the war.

LEVITTOWN AND THE MALL: 1945–1970

Throughout the Depression and the war, economic necessity and shortages had preserved an everyday awareness of thrift. The United States was still populated by a large proportion of migrants from agricultural societies on both sides of the Atlantic. Most adults had grown up learning how to get along with little; they knew how to use simple tools—whether needles or hammers—to make and fix things. The skills and habits of the past, reinforced during the fifteen years before 1945, shaped individual attitudes and fueled intergenerational debates about spending and consumption habits for many decades thereafter. Those born during and after the war knew only a prosperous economy and a well-developed consumer culture.

Per capita GNP fell in the initial postwar period, but it grew by 15 percent in constant dollars during the fifties, and by 32 percent during the sixties. Meanwhile, the population increased, by nearly half between 1945 and 1970. Despite some immigration, the foreign-born population was smaller in 1970 than before the war; the cause of the increase was the well-known "baby boom." The birth rate, 86 per 1,000 women of childbearing age in 1945, shot up to 102 the next year, and to 113 in 1947. It peaked at 123 in 1956, returning to World War II levels ten years later.

As factories returned to civilian production and wartime material shortages ended, personal consumption expenditures increased yearly during the period immediately following the war. Pent-up demand got satisfied by automobiles, radios, and washing machines. New products were introduced: consumer durables like clothes dryers, first introduced in 1946; household products like Procter and Gamble's new detergent, Tide, launched in 1947; and new materials and components like transistors, invented in 1947 and first marketed in hearing aids in 1952, or polyester, introduced in 1953.

Between 1946 and 1958, short-term consumer credit increased fivefold, to almost $45 billion. By far the largest component of this was automobile financing. Gasoline companies and department stores offered instant credit to account holders who presented cards to make their purchases. Third-party credit cards represented a small but embryonic element of consumer credit. Diners Club was formed in 1949, the first card that allowed purchasers to buy goods and services at a variety of establishments across the country. It gained favor primarily among salesmen, who used it to entertain clients or to cut down on the amount of cash they carried on the road. The Diners Club concept introduced a middleman between the customer and the retailer, who no longer had to extend credit as a matter of personal service. Now it was purely a financial product. In 1958, the company met its first formidable competition: American Express, Carte Blanche (a Hilton Hotels subsidiary), and the two largest banks in the country, Bank of America and Chase Manhattan, all entered the field. At the end of the 1960s the groundwork was laid for the great expansion that followed. In 1966 Bank of America licensed its BankAmericard and several other large banks joined together to create the Interbank Card Association, which in 1969 purchased the name "Master Charge" from a smaller bank consortium.

Mortgages were the largest element in personal

debt, and real estate was the most striking single development of postwar recovery. The wartime shortage of houses was notorious. By 1945, residential construction had been dormant for sixteen years. Six million Americans were doubling up with relatives or friends by 1947, and half a million were living in temporary housing. The Veterans Administration created its mortgage-guarantee program in 1944, offering mortgages with no down payment. Congress followed after the war with legislation that favored residential construction and financing: abandoning wage and price controls, extending income-tax benefits for owner-occupants, providing tax benefits to savings and loan associations, and funding research on new building technologies. Single-family housing starts rose steadily from 114,000 in 1944 to 1,692,000 in 1950. In current dollars, total residential nonfarm mortgage debt more than doubled between 1945 and 1950, and more than doubled again by 1956.

The government programs of the late 1940s and 1950s changed the role of the real estate developer. In the housing boom of the 1920s, developers had purchased land, platted lots, laid out streets, and installed sewers; they had sold lots or parcels to individuals or to small builders who built a few houses or a few blocks. In the 1950s, it became profitable for developers to build the houses, a practice that resulted in large suburban subdivisions full of almost identical "homes." The best known development was Levittown on Long Island. Between 1947 and 1951, Levitt and Sons, already a major developer because of government contracts to build barracks and war workers' housing, turned 4,000 acres of potato farms into dozens of curved streets and 17,450 homes accommodating about 82,000 people. In this development and others, the company was notable for its production techniques, which relied on economies of scale, prefabrication, and nonunion labor doing routinized piecework. By 1950 the company produced a four-room house every sixteen minutes. The houses incorporated new designs emphasizing picture windows, open living spaces, private sleeping areas, and built-in features—a refrigerator and washing machine in 1949, a television in 1950.

Like the Levitt projects, housing developments all over the country situated relatively inexpensive, architecturally similar houses in low-density areas outside of cities. Their populations were decidedly homogeneous, racially and economically. The size and homogeneity of the developments contributed to the creation of the suburban lifestyle: child- and family-centered and consumption-oriented. Middle-class expectations for both family size and mate-

rial well-being demanded more expenditures on household goods than ever before.

Despite abundant indoctrination about their proper place in the home, women entered the paid labor force. The statistical point may be made in several ways. Women were 29 percent of the labor force in 1950, 37 percent in 1970. A third of women worked for pay in 1950, only half of them full-time, while by 1975 nearly half of women worked, more than 70 percent of them full-time. Among married women, 14 percent were in the labor force in 1940, 22 percent in 1950, 31 percent in 1960, and 41 percent in 1970. The bulk of the increase was among women over forty-five, although by 1970 one-third of women with children under six years old were employed outside the home. Most women held stereotypical women's jobs and were paid substantially less than men. Low status in the workplace was reinforced by assumptions that women's paid jobs were secondary to their roles as consumers, housewives, and mothers, though they might be necessary to embellish the family lifestyle.

Some of the propaganda came from television, a growing force in the culture and an increasingly important selling machine. In 1947, with ten stations on the air, 7,000 televisions were sold in the United States. Three years later, 7.3 million TVs were in American homes and ninety-eight stations served fifty-eight markets. By 1955, 66 percent of households had a television; in 1970, the medium was essentially universal, in 96 percent of households. At first, almost all American television stations were affiliated with networks, which sent programs to the affiliate by means of transcontinental cable and on 16mm film.

In the 1950s, the networks offered sponsors (for varying amounts of money) a basic network of stations in the largest cities, an additional second tier of stations in smaller but desirable markets, and a third tier of small communities that gave essentially national coverage. At first, advertisers followed the model set by radio, sponsoring complete shows—often with corporate names in the title, like the Texaco Star Theater or the Gillette Cavalcade of Sports. Advertising agencies produced many of these shows; the networks simply sold the time to sponsors and televised the product. By the mid-1950s, production costs mounted and companies began to share programs, sometimes continuing to underwrite a complete show but alternating weeks with other sponsors. In the wake of the 1958 quiz-show scandals—and because of rising costs of production—the networks and the leading advertising agencies reformed the sponsoring relationship. They adopted a strategy similar to that of magazines: networks would sell commercial time to several companies for a show or series and not identify an individual show with a sponsor. This magazine advertising format was actually already in existence, especially on ABC, then the least wealthy and least popular of the networks. As early as 1953, ABC made arrangements with Warner Brothers and Walt Disney studios to produce television shows, and sold the advertising to multiple sponsors.

For Disney's part, the deal was one piece of the financing for Disneyland—like television, an example of the new consumption of experience. Walt Disney had commissioned the Stanford Research Institute in 1952 to analyze possible locations for this pet project. They chose a site near Anaheim and the projected Santa Ana Freeway. Besides the agreement with ABC to produce the weekly hour-long "Disneyland" program, the Disney group received initial funds from five-year leasing agreements with corporations including American Motors, Kodak, Pepsi, and Trans World Airlines. These firms agreed to develop exhibitions similar to the ones that companies had sponsored at world's fairs since the mid-nineteenth century. After a difficult start in July 1955, Disneyland was a huge success. Over a million people visited within six months; by the end of the first year, Disney had paid off $9 million in loans; and after 1956 the park paid for itself, including expansion and upkeep.

Developers of other theme parks attempted to replicate Disneyland's success. During the 1960s, they produced some major failures (notably Freedomland, USA in the Bronx) and a few successes (especially Six Flags over Texas and Six Flags over Georgia) but the heyday of theme parks was still in the future. Like Walt Disney himself, these developers were attempting to capitalize on—and advance—the commercialization of leisure and experience.

Nearly every commentator on the theme park remarks on the perfect control that it exercises through design of space over the behavior of visitors and staff. Some have compared it to the other important enclosed environment that developed during the 1950s, the shopping center. "Little at the shopping centers is left to chance," writes Neil Harris. "Along with Disneyland they were early experimenters in the separation of pedestrian and vehicular movement, and the isolation of service activities from customers." Deliveries were made, but not so they would intrude on the shopping experience.

Suburban shopping had come with the automo-bile. Sears and Montgomery Ward located their initial retail stores in the outskirts of cities during the 1920s. Like the supermarkets of the next decade, they used cheaper land than downtown department stores and offered free parking. Throughout the country, but especially in California, developers experimented with planned clusters of stores during the 1920s. The Depression and war slowed construction and development, but the concept of the shopping center was already well known. Postwar developers had grander plans, grouping small stores with large ones that would serve as magnets, bringing shoppers from far away. The first regional complex, Northgate Shopping Center near Seattle, opened in 1947 with two department stores anchoring a pedestrian walkway lined with forty smaller retailers. Thanks to increased highway construction, many other shopping centers followed suit.

The next development was the fully enclosed, climate-controlled mall, beginning with Southdale Center in Minnesota, which opened in 1956. Heated and air conditioned, Southdale had stores on two levels and a garden court with sculpture, trees, and benches—a protected, self-contained environment. In surroundings such as this, as in the spectacular department stores of the late nineteenth century, consumption was confounded with leisure. Despite the potential frustrations of shoppers responsible for buying what they came for within limited time and limited budgets, shopping at the mall was an experience sold by the real estate developer as a pleasurable activity.

Southdale's developer, Victor Gruen, later made the extravagant claim that shopping centers "can provide the need, place and opportunity for participation in modern community life that the ancient Greek Agora, the Medieval Market Place and our own Town Squares provided in the past." In fact, shopping centers very often destroyed both their surrounding landscapes and the quality of downtown life. Moreover, the rights of freedom of speech and assembly in these privately owned public spaces became very troublesome matters of prolonged legal dispute. Picketing, speechmaking, and distributing pamphlets—part of the business of the agora and the town square—are anathema at the mall.

In the world of consumption that took shape after World War II, buying became something of a surrogate for liberty, and freedom of choice a matter of purchasing. This was Vice President Richard Nixon's point on one of the cooler battlegrounds of the Cold War, his kitchen debate with Soviet Premier Nikita Khrushchev in 1959 at the opening of the

American National Exhibition in Moscow. Standing at a model home display, the two sparred over the merits of American and Soviet appliances. "To us, diversity, the right to choose . . . is the most important thing," Nixon contended. "We have many different manufacturers and many different kinds of washing machines so that the housewives have a choice."

The nature of the choices, however, was itself a topic of debate. Vance Packard's 1957 book *The Hidden Persuaders* attacked the psychological techniques used in advertising, asserting that consumers were being manipulated. The next year, John Kenneth Galbraith published *The Affluent Society,* which suggested that the quest for fulfillment through private consumption was inundating public life, shortchanging expenditures on public goods like schools, museums, and hospitals. Ralph Nader published *Unsafe at Any Speed* in 1965. The book exposed the defects of the Chevrolet Corvair, accused the automobile industry of ignoring consumers' desires for safe cars, and launched Nader's career as the leader of the modern consumer movement. It became a bestseller the next year, after Nader testified at Senate hearings.

Nader's position on automobile safety was not entirely new, and there were significant calls for consumer protection before he established his organization, the Center for the Study of Responsive Law. *Consumer Reports* had published studies of automobile safety since 1946, and had released a technical publication, *Passenger Car Design and Highway Safety,* in 1962. John F. Kennedy had made consumer protection a campaign promise, and in 1962 delivered a message to Congress that articulated a consumer bill of rights. In 1962, the Kefauver-Harris amendments to the Federal Food, Drug, and Cosmetics Act required that new drugs be tested for efficacy and safety. In 1964, President Johnson appointed the first presidential assistant for consumer affairs, Esther Peterson, an activist in the women's and labor movements. She was fired two years later for her outspoken style.

Six months after the Nader testimony of 1966, the National Traffic and Motor Vehicle Safety Act was signed into law, the first of a number of consumer protection laws of the 1960s. These included acts regulating the safety of meats, poultry, toys, flammable fabrics, and radioactive materials, and the 1968 Consumer Credit Protection Act establishing truth-in-lending. Nader's organization, staffed by idealistic young people who scrutinized the regulatory agencies, was central to the creation of a broad-based consumer movement, and to the passage of these acts and those that followed.

The young people who became Nader's Raiders shared with many of their siblings and classmates in the creation of the counterculture of the late 1960s and early 1970s. Counterculturalists eschewed material success and voluntarily minimized their purchasing at a time of unprecedented increase in the range of products available and in general income levels. They shopped at food co-ops and secondhand stores, and ordered books and tools by mail after discovering them in *The Whole Earth Catalog.* This series of books, the consumer bible of the movement, promoted an ethic of local self-sufficiency, with attention to both traditional methods and high-tech products. Within a decade, corporations and individual entrepreneurs had adopted and transformed the countercultural identity into a market segment that, while not dominant, could support such product lines as Celestial Seasonings herb teas. Blue jeans, the emblematic countercultural clothing for both genders, were restyled and sold for high prices, emblazoned with fashion designers' names.

SILICON CHIPS AND WORKING MOMS: SINCE 1970

While rapid and significant technological change characterized the history of consumption throughout the twentieth century, it dominated the century's closing decades. Consumer goods and the act of consumption were transformed by the many new technologies that revolutionized the creation, transfer, use, and sale of information. By 1971, the development of the silicon chip had shrunk the mainframe computer and popularized the pocket calculator, and by the mid-seventies, hobbyists were building personal computers. The related new inventions were legion—lasers, fiber optic technologies, and devices that could digitize sights and sounds so they could be processed and transferred as information.

From these new technologies came new products, both goods and services. Personal computers remained the province of hobbyists and hackers until 1979, when Apple released the first electronic spreadsheet. By 1984, 19 million PCs were in use, a figure that almost doubled within three years. Half of them were located in people's homes. Digital technology and lasers were combined in compact discs and their players, introduced in 1983; sales of the discs surpassed those of long-playing record albums in value in 1987, and in numbers the next year.

The same technologies transformed shopping, by

enabling large retailers to build sophisticated merchandise tracking systems and to gather information on their customers' buying habits. For consumers, the new systems first manifested themselves in the bars and numbers of the Universal Product Code, which started to appear on packaged products during the early 1970s. Despite this manufacturer cooperation, the systems were slow to catch on because of the cost of installing new check-out counters. As late as 1978, only 1 percent of the nation's supermarkets had the scanners and computerized cash registers needed to read the codes and calculate sales. The systems became commonplace during the next decade. By the early 1990s, the giant Wal-Mart discount chain operated the largest privately owned satellite system in the country, connecting all its scanners to a central computer. The scanners usually did away with price tags on the goods, discouraging consumers from keeping track of their total expenditures as they shopped.

The new technologies also contributed to separating consumers' purchasing from their budgeting processes by facilitating the extension of credit cards. By the late 1960s, there were two major bank card organizations, BankAmericard and Master Charge. The systems had stabilized, their initial kinks had been ironed out, and they were ready for expansion, which they achieved through mass mailings of unsolicited cards. The Federal Trade Commission banned this practice in 1970, but credit cards took off anyway, thanks to vigorous promotion, the installation of major new computer systems during the early 1970s, and the 1977 entrance of credit unions and savings and loan associations into the field, offering lower rates. The number of bank credit cards in circulation doubled during the 1970s, while the volume of charges increased by fourteen times. By the end of the decade, nearly half of American consumers had cards. Credit card debt continued to grow during the 1980s, representing 14 percent of annual disposable personal income in 1982, 18 percent in 1986. The cards also represented an increasing proportion of total installment payments, replacing retailer financing. Over the whole period from 1970 to 1986, the average outstanding balance for those who did not pay their bills in full (a group that remained steady at 50 percent of cardholders) rose from $649 to $1,742, in real terms. Meanwhile, innovation continued in products offered to both consumers and retailers. Carte Blanche brought the segmentation concept to credit cards by introducing its gold card in 1972, followed by American Express in 1975 and VISA in 1982. Computer connections at the cash register, which checked authorizations and reported charges without using the merchant's bank to process credit slips, were commonplace by the early 1990s.

Two other technologies created new products and changed the nature of marketing by overthrowing network television's hold on home entertainment. Cable television, connecting homes to a central antenna, had been introduced in 1949 as a way to bring TV transmission to rural and mountainous areas. It remained small, however, until the mid-1970s, when new networks offered programming to cable operators by satellite. Home Box Office began satellite transmission in 1975, with a heavyweight boxing championship match; it was followed by Turner Broadcasting in 1976. By 1989, there were twenty-three national cable networks. Consumers subscribed in response to more programming: while 15 percent of American television households had cable in 1976, more than half did by 1987. Cable offered advertisers a way to segment markets into more pieces and target audiences more precisely, with whole channels devoted to country-music fans or lovers of the outdoors or Spanish speakers. Cable was particularly vulnerable to economic vicissitudes, however: like the telephone in the Depression of the 1930s, the cable subscription could be disconnected when times got hard. And eventually, cable channels had to contend with the next form of video marketing; by 1989, 20 percent of cable households subscribed to pay-per-view services that offered programming without advertising.

Network television suffered not only in competition with cable service, but also with a new consumer durable product, the videocassette recorder. Sony introduced its Betamax in 1975, and JVC its Video Home System (VHS) not long afterwards. At first there was considerable confusion surrounding the two incompatible formats—in 1977, Consumer Reports cautioned against a hasty choice—and only 4 percent of television households had bought VCRs by 1982. Growth over the next few years was extraordinary, and by 1987, 52 percent of television households had decided, increasingly for VHS. Even when they were used to record commercial television programs, the recorders threatened the advertising function of the medium. Time-shifting (recording a show and playing it back at the consumer's convenience) made it more difficult for advertisers to predict demographics. The remote control devices that came with VCRs gave viewers the opportunity to fast-forward through recorded commercials, a practice soon called zapping; this term, along with channel surfing, was also applied to the use of remote controls to change channels, again often to avoid advertising. Moreover, VCRs were increasingly used as playback decks for rented films whose only commercials were trailers for other movies offered by the distributor. By 1989, there were forty thousand home video stores renting films, including major chains whose practices resembled those of other mass retailers, resting on high volume and offering low prices.

Cable TV and video were part of a general expansion in industries selling products for recreation and leisure. Personal-consumption expenditures for recreation, $43 billion in 1970, grew to $115 billion in 1980 and $247 billion in 1988, in current dollars. Some, like video games, had a basis in the new technologies. From Pong, the electronic tennis game of the 1970s, to PacMan, the arcade wonder of the early 1980s, to Super Mario Brothers, Nintendo's most successful home game at the end of that decade, electronic games increased in conceptual and technical sophistication. Other recreation industries depended more on new marketing concepts. Club Med, for example, sold packaged foreign vacations on the Disneyland model, offering contained environments where visitors could play, without having to handle money or speak foreign languages.

An expansion in leisure industries, however, did not signify an expansion in leisure time. In fact, it took an increasing number of wage earners per capita and per household to pay for all the VCRs and vacations charged on the VISA cards. Women continued to enter the labor force in record numbers, as they had during the previous period. Women constituted 38 percent of paid workers in 1970, 40 percent in 1975, 43 percent in 1980, and 45 percent in 1988; put another way, women's labor force participation rate rose from 43 percent in 1970 to 57 percent in 1988. Among married women, 32 percent had worked for pay in 1960, 57 percent by 1988. Whereas 19 percent of married women with husbands present and children under six had worked in 1960, 57 percent of those women were working by 1988. And a record 73 percent of women with children aged six to seventeen were in the labor force, a participation rate higher than that of single women. In order to attain middle-class lifestyles, many of the children worked, too, staffing McDonalds and Kentucky Fried Chicken rather than babysitting or raking leaves. During the decade of the 1970s, the labor force participation rates of sixteen- and seventeen-year-old men went from 47 percent to 50 percent, and of women that age, from 35 percent to 44 percent.

While more household members worked, household size shrank, averaging 3.3 in 1960, 3.1 in 1970, 2.8 in 1980, and 2.6 in 1989. The decrease was largely due to more one-person households, which increased by 69 percent between 1970 and 1980. More people stayed single longer. The median age at first marriage rose more than two-and-a-half years for both women and men between 1970 and 1988, and the proportion of never-married people more than doubled for men aged twenty-five to forty and for a slightly younger cohort of women. Divorces had climbed steadily for decades; the rate doubled between 1965 and 1988, when it reached half the marriage rate. Many divorced and single people lived alone, each with a full complement of household goods. The housing and recreation industries promoted the singles lifestyle; solitary living was to be an occasion for greater consumption, not deprivation.

Single people and employed married women (most of whom retained primary responsibility for their households) constituted a market for fast foods and other consumer products that promoted the ideal of convenience. While the number of other restaurants declined 9 percent during the sixties, fast-food outlets nearly tripled. By the end of the seventies, a third of the nation's food dollars were spent on restaurant meals; by 1985, 73 million people ate out on any given day, about a third of the population; and by 1988 restaurants accounted for 41 cents of every food dollar. Fast food revamped American eating habits; the use of cooking oils and frozen potatoes skyrocketed. For those who stayed home, packaged convenience foods offered savings of time at a price, especially products designed to be heated in microwave ovens. The first home microwave, the Amana Radarange, was introduced in 1967; by 1980, the appliance could be found in 19 percent of American households, and eight years later, in 70 percent. Part of the increase was due to the introduction during the mid-1980s of new microwaveable foods, whose dollar value in 1987 increased 64 percent over that in 1986.

Child-care products and services likewise eased the double burdens of women in the labor force. Child-care services, once exclusively a cottage industry, became a province of nationally franchised businesses. The largest one, KinderCare, was launched in 1969 and by 1988 had 1,100 centers in forty states, serving 115,000 children. Disposable diapers, which eased a disagreeable task, were a great success despite their initial high price and a continuing controversy over their environmental effects. First test-marketed by Procter and Gamble in 1961, they accounted for 25 percent of diaper changes in 1970, 65 percent in

1980, and 90 percent by 1990, according to the company.

Disposable diapers—like disposable razors and the wrappings of a Big Mac—were consumed in a literal sense, used up with one-time use, a concept that had become familiar at the turn of the century with the throwaway Gillette razor blade and the Quaker Oats box. Indeed, many of the marketing methods and consumption patterns of the late twentieth century were extensions of earlier practices and tendencies. Trends towards standardized consumption, for example, may be easily observed throughout the century. But however much Disneyland's Main Street, USA may offer the impression that the business districts of old-fashioned small towns were as alike as contemporary malls, they in fact reflected regional differences, ethnic heritages, and distinctive personalities that may not be seen at the Gap or the other chain retailers that fill the malls. The Mall of America, the consumption theme park that opened in Minnesota in 1992, provided a representation of qualitative change, well beyond standardized consumption: the mall *as* America, America as mall. Its seventy-eight acres included a thousand hotel rooms and, in the middle of the mall, a seven-acre amusement park developed by the creators of Knott's Berry Farm, a famous California theme park.

By the end of the century, commercial culture no longer maintained a sharp distinction between products and the media that sold products. Music videos served as commercials for compact discs and tapes, and, at the same time, as programming for the television networks that presented them. Movie theaters showed commercials. Film producers arranged deals with consumer product manufacturers to display products in films, in return for help with financing. Even literature described objects by brand name, although Bobbie Ann Mason and other young writers of the 1980s were not paid by the brands they named. By incorporating product images constructed by manufacturers, the writers found shorthand ways to convey impressions of their characters, endangering their own chances for classic status by using referents that generally have shorter shelf lives than generic nouns.

Such writers were particularly effective because, by the end of the twentieth century, consumption was held to be a source of identification and satisfaction that surpassed work for most people, and rivaled it for everybody. Shopping had become so identified with leisure that shopping centers were touted as destinations for vacations. Clothes were labeled on the outside, and consumers wore T shirts advertising the products they used and the vacations they took. Brands no longer were even arguably representative of consumption communities, but became individual statements about desires and about status with respect to other individuals, whether ghetto youth displaying their sneakers or Wall Street traders flaunting their watches. By purchasing and amassing standardized products, individual consumers created lifestyles that came as close to fulfilling their physical and psychic needs and to representing their tastes as their budgets and their time and tolerance for shopping would allow.

SEE ALSO Mass Media and Popular Culture; Leisure and Recreation; Sports; Music; Literature; Visual Arts; Clothing and Appearance (all in volume IV).

BIBLIOGRAPHY

As suggested above, virtually all writers on twentieth-century American consumption consult Robert S. Lynd and Helen Merrell Lynd, *Middletown: A Study in Modern American Culture* (1929) and *Middletown in Transition: A Study in Cultural Conflicts* (1937); see also Robert Lynd's "The People as Consumers," in vol. 2 of *Recent Social Trends in the United States* (1933). Daniel Boorstin opened many of the topics of this essay to modern historical inquiry in *The Americans: The Democratic Experience* (1973). Stuart Ewen contributed a provocative seminal analysis in *Captains of Consciousness: Advertising and the Social Roots of the Consumer Culture* (1976).

Since that time, a number of works have made significant conceptual contributions that go beyond the specifics of their topics and time periods. Susan Porter Benson, in *Counter Cultures: Saleswomen, Managers, and Customers in American Department Stores, 1890–1940* (1986), analyzes shopping in the context of the work process, demonstrating the importance of the relationships of selling. Roland Marchand's *Advertising the American Dream: Making Way for Modernity, 1920–1940* (1985) is a thorough portrait of advertising and the advertising industry. Daniel Horowitz provides an intellectual history of attitudes about consumption in *The Morality of Spending: Atti-*

tudes toward the Consumer Society in America, 1875–1940 (1985). Two books opened the field of the history of leisure: Roy Rosenzweig, *Eight Hours for What We Will: Workers and Leisure in an Industrial City, 1870–1920* (1983); and Kathy Peiss, *Cheap Amusements: Working Women and Leisure in Turn-of-the-Century New York* (1986). David E. Nye's *Electrifying America: Social Meanings of a New Technology* (1991) stands out among a number of excellent books on electricity for its blend of business history, technological history, social history, and cultural history. Richard Wightman Fox and T. J. Jackson Lears, *The Culture of Consumption: Critical Essays in American History 1880–1980* (1983), is an important collection of essays; see especially Fox's "Epitaph for Middletown: Robert S. Lynd and the Analysis of Consumer Culture."

Michael Schudson, *Advertising, the Uneasy Persuasion: Its Dubious Impact on American Society* (1984), provides the best sociological treatment of advertising. Norman Isaac Silber, *Test and Protest: The Influence of Consumers Union* (1983), provides information on that organization from archival sources. Richard Tedlow, in *New and Improved: The Story of Mass Marketing in America* (1990), describes modern marketing using case studies of major consumer products and retailers.

Neil McKendrick, John Brewer, and J. H. Plumb, in *The Birth of a Consumer Society: The Commercialization of Eighteenth-Century England* (1982), offer the strongest argument that a consumer society developed before the end of the eighteenth century. Andrew R. Heinze's *Adapting to Abundance: Jewish Immigrants, Mass Consumption, and the Search for American Identity* (1990) provides a detailed case study on the question of consumption and immigrant assimilation.

Lizabeth Cohen, *Making a New Deal: Industrial Workers in Chicago, 1919–1939* (1990), offers rich detail on consumption patterns between the two world wars. For detailed estimates of consumption during World War II, see Combined Committee on Nonfood Consumption Levels, Combined Production and Resources Board, *The Impact of the War on Civilian Consumption, in the United Kingdom, the United States, and Canada* (n.d. [1949]). Roland S.

Vaile, *Research Memorandum on Social Aspects of Consumption in the Depression* (1937), provides statistics and commentary.

Kenneth T. Jackson, *Crabgrass Frontier: The Suburbanization of the United States* (1985), offers detail on housing within the context of suburban development. Lewis Mandell, *The Credit Card Industry: A History* (1990), provides information about that late-twentieth-century form of consumer credit. Neil Harris, *Cultural Excursions: Marketing Appetites and Cultural Tastes in Modern America* (1990), collects the author's imaginative and wide-ranging essays on these topics.

Larry May, *Screening Out the Past: The Birth of Mass Culture and the Motion Picture Industry* (1980), is the best introduction to movie-industry history. J. Fred MacDonald, *One Nation Under Television: The Rise and Decline of Network TV* (1990), describes the history of the television industry through VCRs and cable. Judith A. Adams, *The American Amusement Park Industry* (1991), offers information about amusement parks and theme parks.

Among works by economists, James Tobin's article, "The Consumption Function" for the *International Encyclopedia of the Social Sciences* offers a concise account of Keynes's consumption theory and of the modifications proposed by later economists. Raymond W. Goldsmith, *A Study of Savings in the United States,* 3 vols. (1955), is the best source of statistics on this topic.

Susan Strasser, *Never Done: A History of American Housework* (1982), and *Satisfaction Guaranteed: The Making of the American Mass Market* (1989), offer more fully realized versions of my point of view, and details on the diffusion of household products, the transition from household production to consumption, and the nature of turn-of-the-century mass marketing.

Much of the research on these topics was, at the time this article was written, in the form of unpublished dissertations and conference papers. Future readers will want to consult published works by the authors of those papers, especially Susan Porter Benson, Kathleen Donohue, Carolyn Goldstein, Dana Frank, Charles McGovern, and Susan Smulyan.

MARKETING

Richard S. Tedlow

Prior to the twentieth century, the term *marketing* was rarely if ever used in any business in the United States or anywhere else. Businesses had sales or distribution functions through which the output of their factories was delivered to their customers.

Sales implies at least an element of persuasion. The salesperson's job usually includes convincing a prospective customer to purchase a particular item that the salesperson has in stock. *Distribution* suggests an emphasis on logistics. The word almost seems to imply that the sale has been made, and the firm now must concern itself with physically transporting the merchandise to the customer. These meanings are still clearly evident in, for example, the full name of the marketing department at Michigan State University: Department of Marketing and Logistics.

The transformation from *sales* or *distribution* to *marketing* has an import transcending semantics. The marketing function in the modern American business comprehends a variety of tasks, many of which would have left an executive of a century ago by turns skeptical, astonished, bewildered. The basic responsibilities—persuasion and logistics—remain, but they have been fundamentally transformed. And new responsibilities have been added.

Textbooks have come to define the purview of the marketer as encompassing the four P's: 1. product policy, 2. price, 3. place, and 4. promotion. (Something of a stretch was required to achieve the alliteration. Place—which is also sometimes called push—means distribution, and promotion refers to advertising and other forms of communication.) Even these four P's do not include all the responsibilities of the modern marketer, as we shall see presently, but a brief discussion of them will shed light on the changing nature of the critically important relationship between manufacturing and marketing (or production and distribution) in American business.

The term *product policy* refers to the array of products a firm chooses to make available to the consumer. For example, the product policy of the Coca-Cola Company until 1955 was to sell one product (the branded, carbonated soft drink Coca-Cola) in two forms: the six-and-a-half-ounce hobble-skirted bottle, the other a glass prepared at a soda fountain or in a restaurant. In 1955, Coca-Cola's product policy changed. That year it brought out a king-size twelve-ounce bottle. This change in packaging represents a change in product policy, and although it seems like a small matter to the outside observer, it can have considerable repercussions for the company and its distribution network. As table 1 illustrates, Coca-Cola's product line is very broad by comparison to what it was in 1954.

The meaning of price, the second of the four P's, is obvious. Yet pricing is as subtle and as technically complicated a task as any that confronts the marketer. Bearing on the decision are a host of variables including production economics, competitors' prices, value of the product to the customer, the nature of the relationship with the customer, and the ability to add value to the product in ways that do not demand cash expenditure by producer or customer.

Place means distribution; it is sometimes used interchangeably with push, a term close to slang. The phrase *push money,* for example, was often used in the 1940s in the cosmetics trade to refer to money paid, often under the table, to cosmetics salespeople in major outlets such as department stores. These incentives were aimed at motivating the salesperson to reply "Revlon" (to choose a random example) when approached by a customer asking, "What nail polish do you recommend?"

Distribution systems can become extraordinarily complex. They encompass the movement of tangibles such as the product itself in one direction and money in the other, and also of intangibles such as information, reputation, and loyalty. This is true even for a product whose core characteristics are uncomplicated, as figure 1, a diagram of the Coca-Cola distribution system in about 1950, illustrates.

Throughout the twentieth century, an issue in

Table 1.   THE PRODUCT LINE OF
COCA-COLA IN 1993

Classic	Caffeine Free Coke Classic
diet Coke	Coca-Cola
Sprite	Cherry Coke
Caffeine Free diet Coke	mr. PiBB
diet Sprite	diet Cherry Coke
Minute Maid	Tab
diet Minute Maid	Fresca
Fanta	Caffeine Free Tab
Mello Yellow	Others

SOURCE: *Beverage Industry,* March 1993, p. 6.

marketing for certain classes of products has been
the extent to which a manufacturer should own its
distribution system. Among major automobile manufacturers, this issue was settled relatively early. Henry
Ford decreed in November 1916 that the Ford Motor
Company would make no sales directly to the end
user. Rather, the Ford Motor Company set up a
network of company-owned wholesalers that managed the final assembly of the vehicles and sold them
to thousands of small retail dealers all over the country. These retailers sold the car to the consumer.
Alfred P. Sloan, Jr., of General Motors, Henry Ford's
great rival, agreed with this strategic decision. In his
view, car selling at the retail level was basically a
trading business, one best managed by a small entrepreneur with an intimate, firsthand knowledge of the
trading area.

Although this structure was adopted by what
came to be the Big Three American automobile
manufacturers, it was not universally accepted. Mer-
cedes-Benz, for example, forward integrated into retailing. When a firm vertically integrates, it combines
under one ownership successive stages of production
and distribution; thus, to "forward integrate" or to
"integrate forward" into retailing means that a manufacturer (or wholesaler) is purchasing its own retailers.
In 1990, about 40 percent of the output of the giant
Mercedes works near Stuttgart was purchased by the

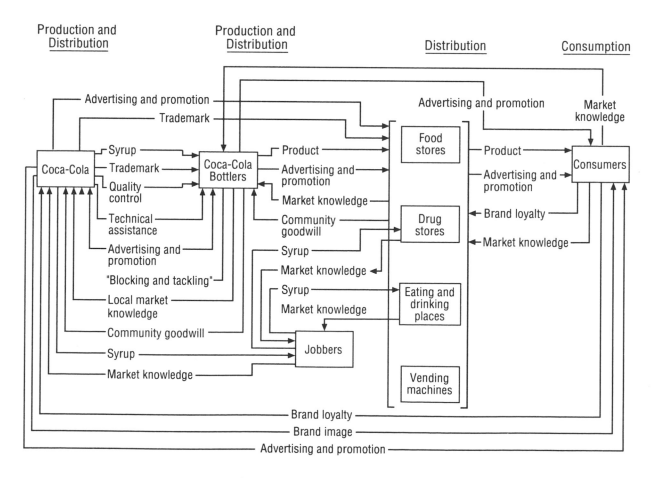

Figure 1.   The Coca-Cola distribution system around 1950.

consumer right at the factory with no intermediary. Attempts at structures such as this in the United States were only made occasionally by marginal producers. In industries other than automobiles, this kind of dominant design rarely emerged. Distribution systems have tended to grow piecemeal. New arrangements were made to suit the needs of the day, but old arrangements, crafted for a time when the product in question held a different position in the market, were very hard to terminate. As a result, numerous companies have found themselves competing against their own distribution system. Not surprisingly, distribution has often been fraught with interpersonal tension, and legal action has not been uncommon.

As an example, think of the Coca-Cola system in 1954. If you were working for Coca-Cola, you wanted to make money by selling your product at a profit. If you were an independent Coca-Cola bottler, you wanted to see lots of Coke sold *in bottles*. If you owned a chain of soda fountains, you wanted to see lots of Coke sold *in drinking glasses* and you wanted the jobber who sold you the syrup to get it for you at the lowest possible price. If you were a franchisee of a large national chain, you wanted your franchiser, which might be large enough to do business directly with Coca-Cola headquarters in Atlanta, to obtain syrup at a competitive price and perhaps to promote the beverage jointly with your chain. The potential for the appearance, if not the reality, of unfairness in such an arrangement is obvious.

Distribution systems, enmeshed in history and explicit contractual agreements, are probably the most difficult element of marketing to change. Features can often be added to a product and prices change constantly, as do advertising campaigns. Not so with distribution.

Promotion, the fourth of the four P's, refers to marketing communication. This can include paid advertising, the most obvious element in the marketing program; unpaid advertising in the form, for example, of favorable word-of-mouth; and public relations, a catch-all term that includes matters ranging from managing the general reputation of the corporation to the placement of "news" about a company or product in the editorial columns of the press, to the funding of publicity events.

Promotion is the most technology-sensitive aspect of marketing. Some consumer package goods, such as Pepsodent toothpaste, reaped great rewards from early recognition of the impact of radio as an advertising medium. With television came the opportunity both to show and tell potential consumers about a product. Revlon is one of a number of firms that became major factors in their industries because they recognized early the efficiency of telecasting to a mass market. In the 1990s the cable revolution is making possible more precise market targeting.

Thus, the four P's. This brief tour hardly does justice to the elements of marketing strategy, but it does begin to suggest categories that will help us chart the changes in marketing over time.

Embedded even in this sketch of marketing strategy is a profound conflict that surfaced soon after the industrial revolution and has periodically faded and intensified down to the present day: the conflict between marketing and manufacturing.

In times of shortages this conflict tends to dissipate. After World War II in the United States, for example, the floodgates of pent-up demand burst. In dozens of consumer and industrial product categories, companies were producing at capacity to meet demand. The rising tide of a rapidly growing market benefited many business firms.

In more recent times, however, as the auto-industrial age has reached maturity and as the American macroeconomy has grown consistently more slowly than its competitors, growth in business has often meant not holding on to share of an expanding market but taking share from a competitor who is trying to take it from you. At times like these, the inability of marketing and manufacturing to coexist has led to serious disruptions in businesses. These problems of coexistence can be seen most clearly in the first two of the four P's, product policy and price.

Every marketer wants his or her company to manufacture what the customer wants to buy. The reason is obvious. It is far easier to sell a customer something he or she wants than to convince the customer to purchase something he or she is not enthusiastic about. This is doubly true when a competitor is right at the customer's doorstep, willing and anxious to sell a product that satisfies.

The problem is that designing the perfect product for every customer is impossible, even though flexible manufacturing is at century's end making affordable variety more a possibility than ever before. Not only does variety add expense in manufacturing, it also increases the defect rate. In 1982, Ford offered almost seventy thousand option combinations on the Thunderbird. The smaller, less expensive Japanese automobiles that were penetrating the American market offered as few as thirty-five. It was easier to keep the defect rate low with the Japanese car than with the Thunderbird.

Product variety causes problems all through the

distribution channel. Think, once again, of Coca-Cola introducing its king-size bottle in 1955. It sounds simple; but hundreds of Coca-Cola bottlers that year had to purchase millions of twelve-ounce bottles, since their previous stock had been only six-and-a-half ounce bottles. And they now had to run two bottling lines where before they ran one. And the problems did not end there. Coca-Cola did not want to give up shelf space formerly devoted to the six-and-a-half-ounce bottle in order to stock the king-size bottle in supermarkets. To the contrary, it wanted more shelf space for the new product. But no well-run supermarket had empty shelf space waiting for Coca-Cola's new product, so some other product would have had to be removed. The next question was: Removed from where? The supermarket had traditionally stocked Coca-Cola on a shelf the height of which matched the six-and-a-half-ounce bottle. Either the shelf height had to be changed, or the king-size bottle had to be put somewhere else.

I have begged the reader's indulgence to walk through this chain of events in some (but by no means complete) detail to suggest the difficulties involved in a matter as seemingly simple as increasing the number of bottle sizes available. From the firm's point of view, all these difficulties were worth undertaking because the customer wanted a bigger bottle. If Coca-Cola did not provide it, some other company would. In fact, some other company already had. Pepsi-Cola had been marketing a twelve-ounce bottle since 1934. Coca-Cola resisted meeting this particular "Pepsi Challenge" for over two decades in part because of the difficulties just described. But Pepsi's king size played a key role in transforming what was a virtual Coca-Cola monopoly in the nationally branded soft-drink market into the duopoly that exists in the 1990s.

What this means is that if one company, however dominant, does not serve shifting consumer needs, another company will. And yet does the consumer really want all this variety, or would he or she prefer to do without limitless and often trivial choice—especially when that choice raises prices and lowers quality? This trade-off is one that must be faced industry by industry, product by product on an ongoing basis. Seventy thousand varieties of Thunderbirds were more than Ford could handle in 1982. One bottle size was not enough for the soft drink consumer in 1955.

We can thus see that both product policy and price, which textbooks place within the realm of marketing, have a clear impact on manufacturing. When the marketer demands variety in product of-fering in order to compete effectively in the marketplace, complexity and costs on the factory floor increase. When the marketer demands a lower price to meet or beat the competition, he or she may be bumping up against cost constraints in the plant and increased costs in the distribution system itself.

Often, however, the marketer's view of price setting is very different from the manufacturer's. The manufacturer must think first of cost: price below it and you go out of business. The marketer must think first of customer value (i.e., either the value the customer places on the product or the value the customer perceives in the product): price above it and you go out of business just as quickly. Behind this trade-off lie conflicting views of what a business is and how it works. The manufacturer wants the marketer to sell what the plant makes. The marketer wants the manufacturer to make what the customer wants to buy. The result of ineffective coordination between these two is dead stock (work-in-process and finished goods inventory that no one wants) or stockouts (product in demand that the company is unable to supply).

THE INTEGRATION OF MASS PRODUCTION AND MASS DISTRIBUTION

The problems described above seem to result to some extent from the effort to coordinate manufacturing and marketing within a single enterprise, the necessary coordination to be undertaken by a general as opposed to a functional manager. Could these problems be avoided if there were no such coordination?

This is another way of asking what the boundaries of the firm should be, a question of great practical and theoretical significance. There certainly is no easy answer. The boundaries of firms differ according to the industries in which they compete, particular market conditions, and the underlying economics of the business. Generally speaking, during the past century, there has been a trend toward the integration of mass production and at least some elements of mass marketing.

Vertical integration came at different times in different industries. When cotton manufacture on the spinning jenny was inaugurated in the United States in 1791, the manufacturing and marketing functions were carried on by separate firms. Yarn output from Samuel Slater's mill in Pawtucket, Rhode Island, was marketed by the independent partnership of Almy & Brown. The same was true of the early mills built by the Boston Associates in Waltham and Lowell, Massachusetts.

The result of this arrangement was not a happy one. As Nathan Appleton, one of the original Boston Associates, recollected of the output of the mill that Francis Cabot Lowell had just put up in Waltham, "Mr. Lowell said to me one day that there was one difficulty which he had not apprehended, the goods would not sell." Appleton's solution was to consign the mill's output to the shop of one Mrs. Bowers, who would see to its sale.

The textile industry, one of the drivers of the first great industrial revolution in Britain in the late eighteenth century, has historically been vertically fragmented (with a few important exceptions). Technical breakthroughs took place in an unplanned fashion in various areas of production, and the whole "value chain" (i.e., those activities that add value to a product at each step of the process of production and distribution) would be reoriented as a result.

We can use woolen manufacture as an illustration. Wool travels a road with many stops from the back of a sheep to a customer's coat. First, the sheep have to be raised and cared for. Next, they have to be sheared. Third, the fleece must be cleaned. Fourth, it must be combed to transform it from a collection of knotted balls into skeins of relatively parallel strands of fiber. Fifth, this fiber must be twisted into yarn. Sixth, the yarn must be woven into cloth. Seventh, the cloth has to be dyed. Finally, the dyed cloth has to be cut for blankets, coats, or whatever its final use might be. And last, the item in question has to be sold. Figure 2 charts the way this process worked at the dawn of the first industrial revolution, two centuries ago.

From the eighteenth century onward, each of these steps was automated at different times and in different places. When automation occurred, there would be shortages for inputs and bottlenecks at the output stage, thus summoning forth new innovation.

Consider, for example, step four above: combing. For all history until the late eighteenth century, wool had been combed by hand. An individual would brush it with a device similar to a wire dog brush. This was highly labor- and time-intensive. With the development of the carding engine, a machine could now comb more wool in a day than could formerly be combed by hand in weeks. Rather than stay at home brushing wool, the shepherd could take it to a carding engine and have it combed quickly and easily.

The development of the carding engine had an impact on the adjacent elements of the value chain.

1. Raise sheep for fleece.
    ↓
2. Shear the sheep.
    ↓
3. Clean the fleece.
    ↓
4. Comb the fleece into parallel fibers.
    ↓
5. Twist the fiber into yarn.
    ↓
6. Weave the yarn into cloth.
    ↓
7. Dye the cloth.
    ↓
8. Cut the cloth into apparel, blankets, etc.
    ↓
9. Sell the finished product.

Figure 2.   Steps in the manufacture of wool in the late eighteenth century.

There was a capacity for more wool, which meant there was a need to develop more efficient shearing methods. Shearing devices were indeed developed. On the other end, there was a glut of combed wool waiting to be spun into yarn. The response was successful experimentation with and eventual adoption of more efficient spinning engines. In the whole, complex, multilevel value chain just described, no single actor coordinated the process. Things just seemed to happen. The owner of the carding engine did not advertise wool carded by his engine as the best in the country. Nor did he invest in spinning machinery to make sure there was a market for the wool combed by his engine. Nor did he integrate backward into sheep ranching to assure supply so that his engine would run full and steady. Rather, every activity was coordinated by the "invisible hand" of the market. No one in this value chain thought in terms of four P's. There was no effort made at marketing strategy. Indeed, in the demand-driven commodity era of the late eighteenth century, there was no marketing as we know it today.

We must emphasize that this process was far more complicated and confused than the bare outline just presented suggests. Fibers in the first industrial revolution ran the gamut from jute to silk. Their different properties, especially with regard to coarseness and strength, had a great deal to do with the historical evolution of machinery to process them. Figure 2 is thus a stylized representation of the "great booming buzzing confusion" of the industrialization of the textile industry. But the basing dynamic—that machinery new to the world caused bottlenecks at various stages of production that in turn demanded the invention of new machinery—is vital to understand.

To a remarkable degree, the textile industry was still vertically (and horizontally) uncoordinated well into the twentieth century, especially in Britain. There, individual firms manufactured and marketed independently of one another. Thus, there was no need for professional management to coordinate these functions, even at that late date when leading businesses in so many other industries were functionally integrated. In the late eighteenth century, the British textile industry was showing the way to the future. A century and a half later, it was desperately holding on to the past.

Why is it that managerial coordination of manufacturing and marketing came to so many industries in the United States from the 1880s onward, despite the problems that such coordination posed? Why did the British textile industry and, indeed, so much of British industry in general, decline to adopt this coordinated structure? And what implications did the new coordination have for the development of marketing in twentieth-century American business?

We know the answer to the first of these three questions because of the research of Alfred D. Chandler, Jr. His conclusion is nowhere more succinctly stated than in his Pulitzer Prize–winning book, *The Visible Hand:*

> By integrating mass production with mass distribution, a single enterprise carried out the many transactions and processes involved in making and selling a line of products. The visible hand of managerial direction had replaced the invisible hand of market forces in coordinating the flow of goods from the suppliers of raw and semi-finished materials to the retailer and ultimate consumer. The internalizing of these activities and the transactions between them reduced transaction and information costs. Most important, a firm was able to coordinate supply more closely with demand, to use its working force and capital equipment more intensively, and thus to lower its unit costs. Finally, the resulting high volume throughput and high stock-turn generated a cash flow that reduced the costs of both working and fixed capital.

Chandler provides in rich detail the historics of those companies that, by integrating mass production and mass distribution, came to define the essential attribute of "the modern industrial corporation." He groups them under three general categories: (1) users of continuous-process technology; (2) processors of perishable products; and, (3) machinery makers whose products demanded aftersale service.

Let us examine two of Chandler's many narratives in order to understand better why marketing and manufacturing were integrated within individual firms. We can then begin to grasp the nature of modern marketing. The two stories concern the American Tobacco Company and the Singer Sewing Machine Company.

The cigarette and the sewing machine bracket the extremes of consumer product marketing. A cigarette is a low-ticket (i.e., inexpensive), non-ego-intensive, impulse purchase. There is no negotiating or trading at the point of sale. Quite the opposite is true of a sewing machine. It is a planned purchase and ego intensive: at one point in its history, it served not only as machinery but as a large piece of furniture. It was so expensive that, like the automobile in modern times, (the most expensive branded consumer good most people ever buy), the sewing machine often required financing. The manufacturer had to lend the consumer part of the purchase price in order to make the sale. Also like the automobile and, obviously, unlike the cigarette, the sewing machine required aftersale service. It really was an investment, a durable good supposed to last many years.

Why, then, did the American Tobacco Company and the Singer Sewing Machine Company integrate manufacturing and marketing?

Prior to the 1880s, tobacco was consumed in a number of forms. It was smoked in pipes or cigars, chewed, or sniffed as snuff. Cigarettes, as Chandler puts it, were "a new and exotic product," and they were not easy to mass produce. "The most efficient hand worker could only produce 3,000 a day." In 1881, the cigarette industry was dominated by a few firms, which marketed the product in geographically circumscribed areas.

James Buchanan Duke was looking for a way to break into the tobacco industry. He found it with a machine patented by the inventor James Bonsack. While still in its experimental stages, this machine could roll more than twenty times as many cigarettes a day as the most efficient manual laborer. Soon it could produce 120,000 cigarettes a day. Fifteen Bonsack machines could satisfy world demand in the early 1880s. Obviously the company that controlled this production breakthrough possessed a competitive weapon of great potential power. This power was only potential, however, because the Bonsack machine was of little use without tobacco to feed into it and customers to purchase its output. Duke's greatness lay in his lightning recognition of this fact and his rapid moves to see the cigarette industry as a system rather than merely the lengthened shadow of a remarkable machine. On the input side, tobacco presented all the problems typical of agriculture. The vicissitudes of the weather were compounded by the unreliability of curing facilities and led to wild fluctuations in availability and price. Duke solved much of this problem by building his own curing facilities and keeping enough tobacco in inventory to assure the utilization of his works.

As "output soared," Chandler observes, "selling became the challenge." To meet this challenge, Duke built a marketing structure with a budget to match. He established a global presence with notable speed by concluding marketing arrangements with wholesalers and dealers around the world. American Tobacco locked up the home market through the establishment of a nationwide web of sales offices.

> These offices, headed by salaried managers, became responsible for both the marketing and distribution of the product. The office kept an eye on local advertising. Its salesmen regularly visited tobacco, grocery, drug, and other jobbers, and a few large retailers to obtain orders.

American Tobacco's advertising budget reached $800,000 in 1889. This is an astonishingly high figure for the time. One hundred years ago, such funds could be expended on what by today's standards would be a narrow choice of media. Plentiful space must have been bought in newspapers and magazines. Much of this money must also have gone into signs. One imagines the nation plastered with pictures of American Tobacco's brands.

Here, in sum, we have a marketing program—the four P's—designed to implement a marketing strategy:

1. Product policy: the cigarette. This was, in the early 1880s, a relatively new product and thus an effective tool for opening up the tobacco market against competitors already well entrenched in pipe tobacco, cigars, and other products.

2. Price: low. As Chandler observes, because "packages of cigarettes were priced in 5-cent increments—5 cents for the standard package and 10 cents to 25 cents for the better brands—there was little room for price cutting, particularly in the all-important cheaper brands." To be sure, there was always room to cut price to those distributors who ran independent businesses and who bought in bulk from American Tobacco. But the basic point here is that cigarettes were conceived of as a mass-marketed product. That meant that the purchase price for the consumers had to be as low as possible.

3. Place (or push, i.e., distribution): intensive, but not direct. "Intensive" means that American Tobacco wanted its brands to be available in as many places as possible. Such availability served two purposes. Since cigarettes were thought of as impulse purchases, American Tobacco wanted to make it as easy as possible for the consumer to satisfy that impulse when it occurred. If a potential customer wanted a smoke at a particular time and there was no place to purchase the product, American Tobacco lost a sale. Second, intensive distribution lessened the chances that an American Tobacco customer might try another brand that might have been available rather than do without a cigarette altogether. Having sampled this other brand, the customer might, to his or her surprise, have found it preferable. The result was that American Tobacco lost a customer.

Thus, the distribution strategy was intensive but indirect. "Indirect" means that although the company found it both useful and necessary to establish a network of offices to guide the flow of product from factory to sales outlet, full forward integration into retailing was apparently never successfully effected. Why not?

At a certain stage in the value chain, it became uneconomical for American Tobacco to own its distribution system. Cigarette jobbers typically handled a variety of products, not just cigarettes. For them, profit was made through economies of scope, to use Chandler's terminology once again. The need for very low-cost, high-volume, intensive distribution made cigarettes an attractive product for them. It was "plus business" for a system already in place.

For American Tobacco, to own its own retailers would have required massive capital investment as well as knowledge of real estate all over the country. The company did, in fact, invest in the large United Cigar Store chain, but this investment failed to generate dominance of the cigar industry. Retailing cigarettes to consumers was a fundamentally different operation from the core of American Tobacco's competence. Moreover, such forward integrating was not necessary. American could manage a distribution system owned by others to everyone's satisfaction because there was a way for all to make money.

4. Promotion. The key lay in mass consumption, and the key to opening up the wondrous profit possibilities of a mass market for cigarettes lay in the fourth "P"—promotion; specifically, advertising. Advertising was the engine that drove the marketing machine for American Tobacco as surely as the Bonsack inno-

vation drove production. The $800,000 expended on advertising amounted to almost 18 percent of sales in 1889 and was twice the amount of the company's profits. American Tobacco relied not only on the push of intensive distribution, but also on the pull of what may have been the largest advertising budget in the history of the world to that time. The goal was a complete program. Advertising would stimulate people's interest both in this relatively new product category (primary demand) and specifically in American's brands (selective demand). When the interest of consumers was thus piqued, the intensive distribution placed the product near at hand so that interest could be satisfied through a purchase.

Let us now take a look at the other extreme on the spectrum of consumer products in the late nineteenth century, the sewing machine. The sewing machine has been described as "the first consumer appliance" and "the first product to be sold under a consumer installment plan." It was expensive and complex. A successful sale often demanded demonstration in a showroom. Purchasers required aftersale service. In order to handle the marketing end of the business, all three leading sewing-machine firms (Wheeler & Wilson, Grover & Baker, and I. M. Singer) developed a network of independent agents. This strategy had the signal virtue of requiring little capital outlay on the part of the manufacturer. However, it soon proved to be less effective than was hoped. Chandler explains why:

> [Independent agents] had little technical knowledge of the machines and were unable to demonstrate them properly or service and repair them. Nor were the agents able to provide credit, an important consideration if customers were to pay for these relatively expensive goods.

In sum, these independent franchisees were unwilling or unable to provide all the marketing services that were vital to compete successfully in this product category in post–Civil War America. In 1885, Singer opened a plant in Scotland capable of producing ten thousand sewing machines a week. When one contemplates all the parts involved in a sewing machine, one realizes the scheduling challenge such volume production posed. In addition to concerning itself with the flow of product through its own complex and growing factories, Singer also found itself having to worry about the flow of product through distributors who seemed not to have their heart in the business or to understand the big picture. The agents committed the cardinal sin in a high-fixed-cost business such as Singer's. As Chandler reports, they failed to maintain inventories properly. They waited until their stocks were low and then telegraphed large orders, requesting immediate delivery. They seemed to be always either understocked or overstocked. Moreover, [they] were frustratingly slow in returning payments on the machines to the central office.

Singer had turned to independent agents in the hope of finding help in opening markets for this new product while conserving its own capital for investment in production. Instead, the company found itself being starved of capital, which its own distribution system was withholding from it. The second price of this inefficient distribution system was an intensification of scheduling problems at the plant due to the peak-and-valley inventory habits of the distributors. The distributors seemed to be taking an "old-fashioned" view of the business; evincing little faith in its long-term profit potential, they wanted to squeeze as many dollars out of it as quickly as possible.

The Singer owners, especially Edward Clark, whom Chandler describes as "Singer's partner and the business brains of the partnership," were, by contrast, thinking big and thinking long term. By 1860, Clark had begun slowly and with meticulous care to replace independent agents with salaried managers directly responsible to the firm. He was "constantly on the outlook" for such people, knowing that this new, vertically integrated structure would never be any better than those who staffed it. Once completed, the company-owned branch-office network "made possible aggressive marketing, reliable service and repair, and careful supervision of credits and collections; it also assured a steady cash flow from the field to the headquarters."

Singer's two major competitors did not give the distribution function the attention it demanded, and they suffered the consequences. Grover & Baker went bankrupt in the depression of the 1870s. Wheeler & Wilson watched Singer succeed with vertical integration but understood its importance too late. It tried to create its own internal distribution system quickly, "failing," as Chandler observes, "to give careful attention to the selection of personnel, the development of procedures, and other organizational matters."

This failing is apparent not only in hindsight but to shrewd contemporaries as well. As Clark observed to one of his British executives, "I am certain the W & W will lose by these operations this year more than £50,000. This business cannot be made in this slap-bang style." A century before academicians were writing about the difficulties and delicacies of distribution, leading practitioners understood them quite well. Soon after the turn of the century, Singer acquired Wheeler & Wilson. Thus the real key to Singer's success lay not in its production facilities, not in its patents, and not even in its marketing system. It lay in all those things combined, which amounted to its total organizational capability.

Throughout the twentieth century, academics have published articles and books with titles such as "Can the Cost of Distributing Food Products Be Reduced?" or *Does Distribution Cost Too Much?* The explanation for this line of inquiry is that marketing, until the post–World War II era, has not been given sufficient recognition for adding value to the product sold. Not only scholars but also average citizens have thought it somehow not right that an item that might cost a given amount were it bought at the factory gate should cost far more after passing through the marketing system. This attitude has been shared by some business people. The remark has been attributed to various entrepreneurs that "I know half my advertising budget is wasted. I just don't know which half." Henry Ford hated marketing. He fired his best marketers, who went to work for General Motors; and he considered retailers to be merely speculators. His factory, Ford always felt, was where the magic really took place.

The truth is, as the American Tobacco and Singer stories illustrate, that manufacturing and marketing need each other in order to make a business profitable in the modern world. Making the right product at the right price and having that product where the customer wants it when the customer wants to buy are no less important than any other business function.

Yet we noted earlier that the owner of the carding engine, a century before the creation of American Tobacco, was able to produce combed wool at a profit without vertically integrating. Why? The reason is that early manufacturing arose out of an agricultural matrix. Early textile machinery could be found on farms. This machinery did not represent a large capital investment. Some of these early machines could be made by hand. In fact, many early factories were little more than sheds in which handicraft production took place. The Latin roots for the word *manufacture* mean to make by hand. If there were no wool to comb or combed wool to sell, the owner could simply return to his farm tasks.

Firms like Singer and American Tobacco did not enjoy similar freedom. Their factories were the largest in history, and the equipment in them represented a huge investment of capital in fixed, dedicated form. Those factories cost a fortune whether they were running or not. Therefore, it was absolutely vital that they be kept running. In business after business, that meant integrating mass marketing with mass production. Vertical integration became the defining trait of the second industrial revolution, which took place toward the close of the nineteenth century and marked the true birth of modern marketing.

Perhaps the most important lesson to be learned about marketing in the twentieth-century business economy is that it is important. Mass production in giant works representing high fixed costs with special-purpose assets is impossible without mass marketing to guide the product from the factory gate to the customer.

Through much of the twentieth century, the builders of giant enterprises have recognized that their mass-marketing system could stand on an equal footing with their mass-production facilities as a barrier to the entry of new competition. Properly managed, mass production working together with mass distribution can generate super-competitive profits, high market share, and great wealth. In some product categories, the case can be made that marketing is a more important arena for capturing competitive advantage than is manufacturing. This is true for Coca-Cola. It is a trivial assignment to produce a soft drink indistinguishable from Coca-Cola in taste. Getting a bottle of that new soft drink onto a supermarket shelf is another matter. Soap presents a similar picture. As an executive of Pears remarked long ago, "Any fool can make soap. It takes a clever man to sell it."

Some theorists have come to believe that marketing is, in fact, the most important business function. And, to pile irony upon irony, while sounding a deafening drumbeat of complaint against the costs of marketing, legislators in this century have often passed measures making it difficult to decrease those costs, such as the so-called fair-trade laws. For its part, the executive branch of the federal government has also erected roadblocks to reducing marketing costs, especially in its interpretation and enforcement of the antitrust statutes. We are left with a picture of a critical business practice—believed by some to be the most critical—being attacked for inefficiency while having inefficiency imposed upon it by some of the very people lodging such complaints.

Let us turn our attention at this point, however, not to public policy, but specifically to marketing itself. How did marketing change from 1900 to 1950, from 1950 to 1980, from 1980 to the present day? What are the possible futures of marketing given its evolution? A full answer to these questions demands an understanding of the differences between consumer marketing and business-to-business or industrial marketing. It also requires an appreciation of the new challenges posed by the marketing of services. In this essay, the focus will be on the marketing of consumer products because it is in that realm that innovation has usually taken place.

A METHODOLOGICAL PLAN OF ACTION

To illuminate the subject, the historian of marketing has numerous methodologies from which to select. Perhaps the ideal would be to start with the organizational structures of the nation's largest companies and see when they first began devoting special, formal effort specifically to sales or distribution. We could see how these departments evolved from selling to marketing and how their funding increased. Work such as this has indeed been undertaken for some aspects of marketing and for brief time periods. However, a full-scale investigation along these lines would be prohibitively time consuming and expensive even if the relevant corporate records were available, which they are not.

Another approach would adopt industries rather than companies as the unit of analysis, charting the routes taken by the products of various industries from factory gate to end user. When such an examination had been completed, the researcher would be left with two questions to answer. First, why are, say, independent agents used more often than a company-managed sales force in some industries than in others? Second, why does the use of agents versus a company force change over time?

Analysis of industries can be done more readily than analysis of companies because almost all the necessary data are available from published censuses. An example is provided in figure 3. This remarkable chart is explained in great detail in tabular form in the volume from which it is drawn.

There are, unfortunately, problems with this approach. For one, it cannot take into account changes within its categories. For example, "Intermediary Trade" in the food industry is bound to mean something very different in 1929 and in the 1990s. More important, this approach leaves the company and with it the individual manager behind. It therefore can show us change but cannot explain how that change came about. It is all structure, no strategy.

A third methodological option for exploring marketing history is to select some specific aspect of the function and examine it extensively. The history of what people said they have done—the intellectual history of marketing—has appeared in numerous sources. These sources are readily available because they are published. But they often prove to be a weak reed on which to lean. People may not address the questions that interest us the most. They rarely use quantitative data when writing about their ideas. And the relationship of what people actually did, what they wanted to do, and what they say they did often proves impossible to sort out.

Another possibility is to select a specific market segment and see how marketers have addressed it. This has also been done, most recently and most successfully in a monograph by Stanley C. Hollander and Richard Germain describing changes over time in marketing products to the youth segment.

Yet another option is to select a set of cases that seem particularly revealing of the history of marketing practice. This has been the decision that I have made for my own work. As with all these approaches, the use of case studies has drawbacks. By definition, one leaves out a great deal. The breadth of coverage is sharply limited. The resulting history cannot claim to be truly comprehensive. Furthermore, the representative character of the cases can be discussed and suggested; but it cannot be proven. Nevertheless, cases offer noteworthy advantages. What one sacrifices in breadth, one gains in depth. Not every marketing advance by every company can be covered, nor can a paragraph be devoted to every smart marketer. The great counterbalancing advantage is the chance to search with greater depth for how marketing history is really made.

What case studies reveal is that there are two basic causes for change in marketing strategy. One is the need to develop new ways to market new products. The other is to come up with innovative methods to mount an attack on the company that has mastered these new methods. Ideas for change in marketing do not arise out of thin air. They come from concerted attention to a business challenge. Marketers do not take risks to make history; they take risks to make money.

The use of case studies does not preclude other ways of looking at marketing. To the contrary, it demands at least a cursory examination of the tools at the disposal of the marketer. These tools were often developed by innovators who had no intention of affecting marketing practice, but the marketers who seized upon them and applied them to their businesses often reaped great rewards.

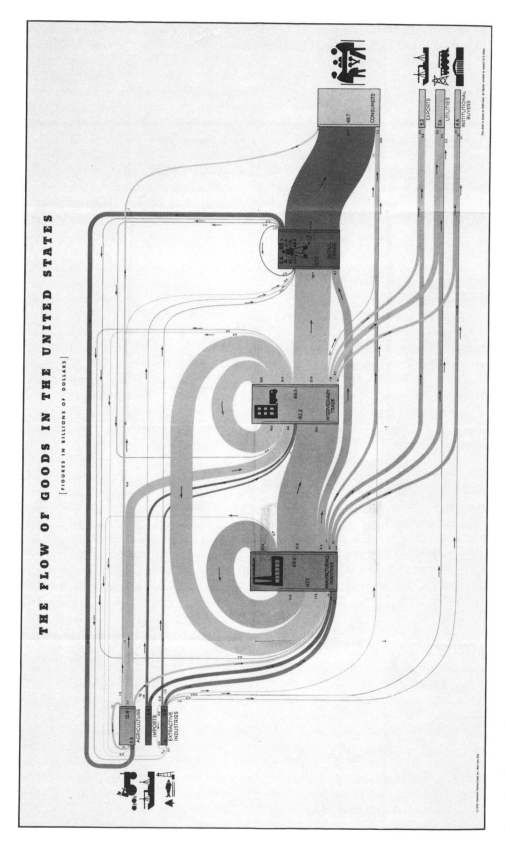

Figure 3. The flow of goods in the United States. This flowchart was prepared by the Twentieth Century Fund in 1938. It is based on 1929 data, with all figures rounded to the nearest $1.0 billion.

PHASE I OF MARKETING: THE FRAGMENTED MARKET, PRIOR TO THE 1880s

The previous assertion is vividly illustrated by the development of the railroad and the telegraph in the nineteenth century and by the invention of radio and television in the twentieth. None of the leading marketing firms had anything to do with these innovations. Procter & Gamble, considered by many to be America's most effective consumer marketer, did not invent the railroad or the telegraph. Neither did American Tobacco, Singer, or Duke. But without them, these great marketers never would have become great. And because these firms exploited the new transportation and communication technology as quickly as they did, they gained first-mover advantages that served them for decades to come.

Prior to the railroad and the telegraph, the United States was divided into relatively isolated geographic fragments. The Constitution may have formed a customs union among the states, but the realities of geography spoke louder. Transportation was so arduous and expensive, information so tardy and inaccurate, that there was no national market in the modern sense.

"A coal mine," reported a committee of the Senate in 1816, "may exist in the United States not more than ten miles from valuable ores of iron and other materials, and both of them be useless until a canal is established between them, as the price of land carriage is too great to be borne by either." At that time, it took about two and a half months to send a wagonload of freight pulled by a team of four horses from Massachusetts to South Carolina. And this was in the relatively developed eastern region of the 850,000 square miles that made up the nation after the Revolution.

In his first inaugural address in 1801, Thomas Jefferson said of this vast expanse that it provided its citizens "with room enough for our descendants to the thousandth and thousandth generation." Two years later Jefferson doubled the nation's size by the purchase of the Louisiana Territory from Napoleon. He dispatched Captain Meriwether Lewis and Lieutenant William Clark to explore this acquisition soon after its purchase.

Lewis and Clark departed St. Louis in May 1804. They wintered far up the Missouri River among the Mandan tribe in present-day North Dakota. They departed as the ice broke up on the river in early April 1805. From there, they trekked across plains and mountains, reaching "Cape Disappointment at the entrance of the Columbia River into the Great South Sea, or Pacific Ocean" in November, seven months later. Along the way, in addition to encountering native Americans from numerous tribes and "feasting [their] eyes" on some of the most beautiful scenery in the world, expedition members found a rich abundance of game: "We can scarcely cast our eyes in any direction without perceiving deer, elk, buffalo, or antelopes." Perhaps most impressive to Lewis was the pelt of the sea otter, which he described as "the richest and most delicious fur in the world that least I cannot form an idea of any more so. It is deep silkey in the extreme and strong."

Pelts and furs were the original impetus to opening up the proverbial "trackless wilderness." The first American businessperson to "think continentally" (to borrow a phrase from Alexander Hamilton) was John Jacob Astor, who quickly moved to engross as much of the nation's fur trade as he could through his American Fur Company, which he incorporated in 1808. The American Fur Company had some modern characteristics. First, unlike most businesses of the day, it was a legally constituted corporation. Second, it had a continental reach. Astor's firm was divided into geographic areas, within which trading posts were established to acquire the furs trapped by woodsmen and ship them east. Fur was the ideal product to form the basis for Astor's business, since it was in great demand and was neither bulky nor heavy. Low bulk and weight meant that transportation costs could be kept within reason. High demand meant that consumers were willing to absorb those costs and pay a price that allowed a healthy profit.

The third aspect of Astor's business that was modern in nature was its global context. Astor negotiated with Russia's consul general in the United States about provisioning Russian outposts. Eventually, he succeeded in turning his nationwide fur business into the pivot for a worldwide trading empire.

Nevertheless, Astor's achievements are more properly viewed as the climax of the old way of doing business rather than as the inauguration of the new. His company was not a tight-knit, carefully managed organization. It is probably better thought of as a magnet for independent entrepreneurs—fur trappers in Oregon, spice merchants in the East Indies, or sea captains sailing their own ships. Astor's major function was as an arbitrageur. His capital investment, though large at the time, was tiny by later standards.

Because the fixed, special-purpose capital investment in his business was small, Astor could sustain a complete cessation of commerce such as occurred during the War of 1812 and survive financially. He was also able to exit the business with relative ease, which he did in 1834. Unlike so many of the firms founded in the 1880s, the American Fur Company did not prove to be long-lived. It was in bankruptcy less than a decade after Astor's departure. Another aspect of Astor's business that marks it more as the ending of the old rather than the beginning of the new is that he made no effort to brand his merchandise so that the final consumer would know it had passed through his hands. This stands in stark contrast to the world of Duke and Singer.

In the 1980s and 1990s, much was written about the pressure being put on national and international manufacturers' brands by store-promoted, private-label merchandise. Commentators have speculated that over the long term brands will decay toward commodity status on the grounds that, with the exception of legal protection like that afforded by patents, all attempts to differentiate a brand can and will be copied, with the eventual result being a price war.

This may or may not be the case as the twentieth century gives way to the twenty-first, but it definitely was not the case as the nineteenth century gave way to the twentieth. The nineteenth century was, for most consumers, a world of unbranded commodities—of tea from chests, biscuits from barrels, and flour out of sacks from the local grist mill. This was equally true for apparel as well as for food products and also for industrially marketed goods.

It has been said that the United States was a nation that was born in the country and moved to the city—and now, it could be added, to the suburb. Certainly during most of the nineteenth century, the nation was predominantly rural, with its farmland dotted by thousands of "island communities."

Slowly but inexorably, the balance between rural and urban population changed during the course of the nineteenth century. In 1800, the nation's population was 5.3 million with only 322,000 (or 6 percent) living in urban territory, which the census defined as settlements with a population of 2,500 or greater. By 1900, there were 76 million people living in the nation, with 30 million (or 40 percent) living in urban areas. Only with the census of 1920 did a majority (51.2 percent) of the U.S. population live in cities, and even at that late date the census defined a city as having a population of only 8,000 or more.

These demographic realities had important implications for nineteenth-century marketing. On the farm, many of life's necessities could be obtained without recourse to a formal market. The household unit could produce furniture and clothing. A family could grow a variety of foodstuffs for its own consumption, and it could barter the remainder for other goods or services within the local area or sell to a local dealer for shipment to a distant market.

The general store at the rural crossroads of a small village carried a bewildering variety of merchandise in very cramped quarters, often as small as four hundred square feet. Tea, flour, sugar, liquor, shoes, axes, kegs of nails, spices, and saddles were crammed into the available floor space; harnesses and a host of other goods hung from the rafters. A store in Arrow Rock, Missouri, in the 1820s was located in a clearing shared with deer, snakes, and other denizens of nearby woodland. The simple two-room structure was built of logs held together by clay and lime. One room, windowless, was used to store goods; the other was used as a salesroom, with bolts on the door and windows for protection against robbers. As Gerald Carson observes in *The Old Country Store* (1954), there was little organization in such stores:

> A great deal of time was wasted in looking for articles that were not in place or had no place. . . . Flies swarmed around the molasses barrel and there was never a mosquito bar to keep them off. There was tea in chests, packed in lead foil and straw matting with strange markings; rice and coffee spilling out on the floor where a bag showed a rent; rum and brandy; harness and whale oil. The air was thick with an all-embracing odor, an aroma composed of dry herbs and wet dogs, or strong tobacco, green hides and raw humanity.

One authority has estimated that $5,000 to $6,000 was sufficient for the pre–Civil War frontier merchant "to purchase a good stock, and much of this could be obtained on credit." Merchants often traveled to large cities such as New York and Philadelphia in the East and Chicago and St. Louis in the West to obtain their wares. Difficulties caused by the primitive state of transportation lent an element of risk to the acquisition of inventory.

The pace of business in the country store was slow through most of the 1800s. A day might not see much more than a dozen customers. Because of the absence of an adequate currency, trade was often carried on by a system of money-barter, whereby customer and merchant would exchange goods with money equivalents used as a standard of value. Price was a matter for negotiation, and if sharp dealing was not the rule, neither was it the exception. The flamboyant poseur and impresario Phineas T. Barnum remarked of his experience as a youth keeping store in Connecticut in the 1820s: "The customers cheated us in their fabrics, [and] we cheated the customers with our goods. Each party expected to be cheated if it was possible."

The merchant's relationship with the manufacturer was a distant one. There was little, if any, direct buying. Purchases were made from wholesalers or jobbers, and the daunting logistical problems were solved through recourse to a thick and intricate web of middlemen. National brands were rare but not completely unknown; Walter Baker's Chocolate was apparently stocked by the store Abraham Lincoln tended in New Salem, Illinois, in 1833, and branded patent medicines were ubiquitous. But only with the growth of the big consumer packaged-goods firms in the last two decades of the nineteenth century did manufacturers begin their concerted effort, through national advertising and preemption of shelf space, to develop a marketing program combining both pull and push.

Until that time, merchants dealt primarily in undifferentiated commodities, and their advertising was largely restricted to announcing the availability of products. Advertising, in a setting characterized by a poor communications infrastructure and commodity products, offered scant assistance. Writing in 1939, historian Lewis E. Atherton observed that the "primary aim" of advertising before the Civil War was "to give the location, business, and services of a store, or to acquaint the public with any unusual changes occurring in the life of the firm. Little effort was spent in trying to increase sales through creating new desires for goods." Advertising had yet to become an active tool for selling.

Morris Adelman observed that the "nearest thing we ever have had to monopoly in grocery retailing was the old village grocery store," but this observation is accurate only for certain settings. If only one store was accessible to a wide trading area, consumers were indeed confronted with the choice of buying goods there, making the goods themselves, or going without them. On the other hand, this "vast network of minuscule monopolists" could be disrupted by the presence of more than one store in a village. For farmers who traveled twenty miles over country roads for their provisions, it made sense to shop as many stores as they could easily reach. Competition would then take place on the basis of price, because such modern nonprice allures (enticing shop-window displays and attractive furnishing and fixtures within the store itself) as are today grouped under the term *shopping experience* did not play a significant role. Distinctions between planned and impulse purchases, so central to retail strategy today, were largely irrelevant to the rural dweller of the nineteenth century. Every trip to the store took planning and effort. Rural

merchants appreciated the importance of access to the consumer, access insulated from competition, as was evidenced by their attempts to open additional stores when problems of capital, communication, and control could be overcome. Traveling salespeople, with their wares in their wagons, combed the countryside. They brought products directly to the consumer's door and added an increased element of competition.

The picture that emerges of the nineteenth-century country store, then, is of an institution without most of the tools at the command of today's retailer. Storekeepers' access to merchandise was sporadic and inconsistent. Their stores were general indeed, more likely to carry whatever goods were available from suppliers than those that the customer wanted. The pace of business was so slow that merchants had to rely on margin (the difference between the cost of acquiring a product and the selling price) rather than turnover (the speed with which a given stock of goods is sold and then restocked) as the key to their financial success. Merchants located in proximity to competition lost control over their prices. The necessity of extending credit to customers whose ability and willingness to pay their bills was questionable put the merchants' solvency at risk. They received minimal help in selling from the wholesalers from whom they bought or from the manufacturers from whom the wholesalers bought.

The above discussion contains the defining characteristics of what I call Phase I of the history of marketing. One of these characteristics was market fragmentation. Note that I draw a sharp distinction between the market fragmentation of Phase I and the market segmentation that helps define Phase III. (Phases II and III will be discussed in the pages that follow.) The fragmentation of Phase I was geographic, not demographic (related to age, income, and education), or psychographic (related to the consumer's lifestyle). It was not the product of a strategy. Rather it resulted inexorably from the brute facts of logistics in a topographically varied nation of 3 million square miles.

In this slow-moving world, products passed through many hands between acquisition of the raw material and final sale, as in the example of the woolen coat. Each of those hands charged for expenses and took as much profit as it could capture. Everyone in the system made money on high prices, high margins, and low unit sales.

This world was transformed by the revolution in transportation and communication represented by the railroad and the telegraph. The railroad-building binge, which followed the invention of the telegraph and which would not have been possible without it, got underway in the late 1840s. There were 3,332 miles of railroad tracks in operation in 1840 and more than twice that a decade later. By 1860, that number had increased to 30,000 miles.

What did this mean for national marketing? Travel time from New York to Chicago provides an answer to that question. In 1800, it took a month and a half to journey between the two cities. In fact, in that year, only New York was a city; Chicago was hardly even a settlement, located at the outer reaches of the known world. By 1860, the railroad had cut the time for the trip from New York to Chicago (which was by then very much a city) to a day and a half.

The Civil War and the depression of 1873 slowed the trend toward the nationalization of the American market. Nevertheless, the rail network grew to more than 90,000 miles by 1880. Then, with the Civil War and the depression over, the nation experienced a railroad building boom the like of which was never seen anywhere else before or since. Over 70,000 miles of track were laid, bringing the total in 1890 to 166,703 miles. By the system's peak in 1916, there were about a quarter of a million miles of railroad track in operation.

In the course of one lifetime, Chicago, *the* nineteenth-century city, exploded from a settlement of mud huts to a metropolis of a million-and-a-half people. Because it became the nation's railhead, Chicago was the perfect location for the two great marketing firms of the first half of the twentieth century, Sears, Roebuck and Montgomery Ward. Headquartered there, Sears and Ward were able to supply first their mail-order customers and later their stores by gathering goods from all over the nation to their main warehouses and then shipping them nationwide.

The railroad and the telegraph were two exogenous technological developments, that is, they emerged independently of the corporations whose history they were to transform. But the firms that seized upon the availability of the railroad-and-telegraph infrastructure changed the way of doing business in the United States and created companies that would dominate their markets and produce profits for generations. In the process, these businesses drove the practice of marketing from Phase I to Phase II.

PHASE II: THE UNIFIED MARKET, 1880s–1950s

We can use the carbonated soft drink industry to exemplify this transition from Phase I to Phase II of

marketing. Throughout the nineteenth century, there were virtually no barriers to entry into this industry at the local level. The very absence of such barriers made the creation of a national brand highly problematic. Any drugstore proprietor, of whom there were thousands in nineteenth-century America, could serve a patron a glass of water mixed with sugar plus extracts of whatever happened to be handy. The sugar and other additives were meant to make the beverage more interesting, and their addition justified an extra charge.

Although there were no barriers on the production side to getting into this business, there were massive barriers on the distribution side. The product had to be sold to soda-fountain operators and their suppliers as well as to other vendors. This meant, for example, that Coca-Cola had to have a trained sales force that was highly mobile. In addition to a sales force to deal with the trade, Coca-Cola needed to publicize its product and make it as attractive as possible to consumers. Thus the company had to establish push through the trade and pull from the soft drink-consuming public. The ultimate goal was to turn two common English words—*coca* and *kola*—into an inviolable proprietary trademark.

So Coca-Cola salespeople took the train to their assigned towns like well-prepared shock troops. They were heavily armed with large quantities of advertising material such as signs and circulars, carried with them in a large trunk. Their goal was to sell Coca-Cola syrup, to show fountain operators how best to serve it, to reacquaint them with the company's selling plan, and to negotiate with the local bill-poster to see to it that advertising signs were placed wherever possible. These activities had to be executed quickly, since the typical salesperson seldom remained in a town for more than twenty-four hours. Then it was back on the train to the next stop.

Without a railroad network Coca-Cola would never have been able to build and manage a national sales force on an economical basis. Nor would it have been able to ship the syrup to those druggists who ordered it in those far-flung towns. Without newspapers and magazines, which increased their circulation at the turn of the century because of the growth of a literate public with the spare change and the curiosity to read them, Coca-Cola would not have been able to create the pull to complement its push through the channels of distribution.

All these things—railroad, telegraph, newspapers, magazines, high literacy rates—were essential for Coca-Cola to transform its beverage into one of the great national and, by World War II, international brands in the history of marketing. But none of these things did Coca-Cola create. It owned neither railroads nor telegraph lines. Rather, it creatively put these tools together to market its quite pedestrian product. In so doing, it built monumental barriers to the entry of new competition by being the first mover in constructing what was a unique marketing system and, just as important, by continually improving that system. Coca-Cola, along with Procter & Gamble, Johnson & Johnson, American Tobacco, Heinz, and a few others, led the world of marketing into an era so new that it constituted a fundamental discontinuity with the past.

This new era I call Phase II of marketing. The most important characteristic differentiating Phase II from Phase I was speed. Thanks to the telegraph, market information and orders for product could move with the speed of electricity. Salespeople and the product itself could move with the speed of steam-driven engines on rails. Taking advantage of these new realities, firms such as those named above began to understand that they could make more money by doing a lot of business with a lot of customers quickly than by doing a little business with a few customers slowly.

A key ingredient to this new approach to the market was price. Low prices meant low profit margins, but these low margins were more than acceptable given the immense increase in volume made possible by the new market reach, due to the railroad. Penetration pricing (setting prices low in order to gain market share and make money on sales volume) was the rule of the day for consumer-product manufacturers in the 1880s. For Coca-Cola, penetration pricing was essential because the product could be cheaply and easily copied. For American Tobacco, it helped eliminate the resistance to its new product, the cigarette, and ensure that its expensive investment in manufacturing with the Bonsack machine paid off. For other firms, low prices led to greatly expanded use and expanded use led to recognition all over the nation. This kind of recognition led to demand pull, meaning that the manufacturer was no longer at the mercy of the many-layered distribution system. It was now possible for a company like Johnson & Johnson, founded in 1886, the same year as Coca-Cola, to introduce its baby powder and gain such name recognition that if a customer could not find this particular brand of baby powder in one store, he or she might choose to shop for it in another.

The development of continuous-process machinery, another set of technological innovations in addition to those in transportation and communication, was critical in bringing about this new world.

To understand this development, we must return to the factory. By the 1880s, a series of incremental advances in machinery and manufacturing technology had made it possible to produce a standardized product in large volume and, just as important, to package it in small units. Continuous-process machinery, as Chandler notes, was "invented almost simultaneously for making cigarettes, matches, flour, breakfast cereal, soups and other canned products, and photographic film."

Thus, by the end of the last century the manufacturer had at his disposal a whole new collection of tools that had been unavailable to his predecessors. When he could put his own name on his product thanks to this new machinery, when he could announce it everywhere thanks to advertising, and when he could ship it anywhere thanks to the railroad, he could endow his product's name with an unprecedented meaning and power. The manufacturer could create a supername—a brand.

The brand was the object of marketing strategy in the Phase II era and distinguishes it from Phase I. What, then, is a brand? The American Marketing Association provides a straightforward definition: "a brand is a name, term, sign, symbol or design, or a combination of them that identifies the goods or services of a seller and differentiates them from those of a competitor."

This is as good a definition as any, but it neglects the magical component of truly successful brands. In his effort to uncover the "essence" of a brand, pioneer motivational researcher Ernest Dichter talked in the 1940s and 1950s about its "soul." Advertising executive Shirley Young has said simply that a "brand is a friend." James E. Burke, CEO of Johnson & Johnson from 1976 through 1989 and the man most responsible for saving Tylenol from the tampering incidents of the 1980s, has said that a brand is the "capitalized value of the trust between the customer and the company."

What Burke was alluding to is that a branded product is reliable and consistent. It ought to be available when and where needed. It is a "friend" in that it puts your mind at ease. You do not have to search for information when you make your purchase. You know exactly what you are getting. The fact that the brand's owner is willing to advertise it conveys the message, explicit or implicit, that the owner believes in the brand's efficacy enough to stand behind it. After all, the leverage that a branded product provides can operate in reverse if the product does not perform properly. There is no place for the manufacturer to hide. That is the reason for the

Table 2. LEADING BRANDS, 1925 AND 1985

Product	Leading Brand in 1925	Position in 1985
Bacon	Swift	Leader
Batteries	Eveready	Leader
Biscuits	Nabisco	Leader
Breakfast cereal	Kellogg	Leader
Cameras	Kodak	Leader
Canned fruit	Del Monte	Leader
Chewing gum	Wrigley	Leader
Chocolates	Hershey	No. 2
Flour	Gold Medal	Leader
Minted candies	Life Savers	Leader
Paint	Sherwin-Williams	Leader
Pipe tobacco	Prince Albert	Leader
Razors	Gillette	Leader
Sewing machines	Singer	Leader
Shirts	Manhattan	No. 5
Shortening	Crisco	Leader
Soap	Ivory	Leader
Soft drinks	Coca-Cola	Leader
Soup	Campbell	Leader
Tea	Lipton	Leader
Tires	Goodyear	Leader
Toothpaste	Colgate	No. 2

SOURCE: Thomas S. Wurster, "The Leading Brands: 1925–1985," *Perspectives* (1987) as reprinted in David A. Aacker, *Managing Brand Equity: Capitalizing on the Value of a Brand Name* (1991), p. 71.

saying, well known in the advertising industry, that nothing kills a poor product more quickly than good advertising.

The true value of a brand is difficult to measure directly. Various proxy (i.e., indirect) measures have been developed, none completely satisfactory. The heart of the problem is that much of a brand's value lies in such imponderables as trust and friendship. We do know that for generations, Americans have been willing to pay more for branded merchandise in certain product categories. Table 2 is a comparison of leading brands in 1925 and in 1985 in twenty-two product categories.

Here, then, we have the final defining characteristic of Phase II marketing: the creation of a brand designed to unify, define, and dominate a market. Table 3 provides in capsule form what I view as the characteristics of Phases I and II in the history of marketing.

Phase II marketing aimed to sell product to everyone, everywhere. It was truly the era of mass marketing. This is quite apparent in Phase II advertising. Here is the text of an advertisement for Coca-Cola which was placed in a nationally circulated magazine in 1905:

Coca-Cola is a delightful, palatable, healthful beverage. It relieves fatigue and is indispensable for business and professional men[,] students, wheelmen [bicycling enthusiasts] and athletes, relieves mental and physical exhaustion and, is the favorite drink for ladies when thirsty, weary, despondent.

This advertisement covers a lot of ground. The transcripts of Coca-Cola sales and advertising-planning sessions clarify the point of view that produced advertisements like this one. At one such meeting, an executive began by declaring that "to formulate a proper selling plan, one must analyze the class of people whom he is desirous of reaching." This statement suggests some kind of scheme of segmentation, designed to classify people according to certain characteristics in order to target them effectively. However, this same executive then explained: "In other words, our advertising must be an appeal to each class of people." That is another way of saying that all Coca-Cola was really looking for were thirsty throats. If you had one, the company aimed to satisfy that demand. This was true whether you were rich or poor, young or old, free-spirited or conservative in your style of living. It was true no matter what section of the country you called home, no matter what racial or ethnic group you belonged to, or what your religious beliefs were. In other words, Coca-Cola's marketing strategy at the turn of the century was pursued without regard for the whole host of considerations which became of vital importance in the later Phase III world of marketing segmentation.

Coca-Cola achieved its goal of market dominance. By the 1920s, investment analysts came to understand that this *market* dominance derived directly from *marketing* dominance (not from patents or investment in bricks and mortar) and furthermore that marketing dominance could be as valuable as any other barrier to entry.

Evidence of Coca-Cola's market power was everywhere. It out-advertised its nearest competitor by four to one by the late 1920s and achieved brand recognition to match. This created pull, which kept the distribution system functioning smoothly. "Evidently," according to *Barron's* in 1932, "of every 100 persons entering a drugstore, 61 patronize the soda fountain, and of these, at least 22 buy Coca-Cola. These startling figures . . . impress [the retailer] with the public preference for Coca-Cola, and discourage his active pushing of any competitive drink."

This quotation from *Barron's* makes it clear that by the Great Depression, Coca-Cola had won two battles. By building its brand and creating pull, it raised a barrier to entry by competitors. At the same

Table 3.   PHASE I AND PHASE II IN THE HISTORY OF MARKETING

Phase	Characteristics	Approximate Dates
I Fragmentation	High margin per unit Low volume of unit sales Limited geographic market Expensive and slow transportation and information Commodity products	To the 1880s
II Unification	Low margin per unit High volume of unit sales National mass market Less expensive and far faster transportation and information Branded products	1880s–1950s

time, it kept the distribution system in line; druggists were unable to engage in active pushing of another brand, even if the druggist could make more money from another brand. As far as bottlers were concerned, during this period, "either you bottled Coca-Cola or you were poor."

Coca-Cola's market power made it, by the end of the 1920s, one of the nation's most profitable companies. With very conservative accounting, it earned in profits in 1929 almost two-and-a-half times its investment in property, plant, and equipment. Such lavish profitability with such a small capital investment and easily copied product should have invited entry by competing firms. There were none of the barriers beloved of economic analysis: no big plant up on the hill that cost a fortune to build, no patents, no special Bonsack-type machine that alone could fill a substantial percentage of world demand.

What Coca-Cola did have, however, proved every bit as effective. A web of contracts tied up the national bottling system with exclusive agreements. Brand loyalty was so strong that customers would "accept no substitutes." Coca-Cola and many other branded manufacturers of this era had won the age-old battle of "the brand versus the power of the store." Intangible though it may have been, this brand loyalty was bankable. Coca-Cola proved that a "power brand" could command a price comfortably above its costs.

How could a competing firm attack an entrenched brand that appeals to all segments of society and that dominates all the key elements of the system that makes up its business? This was a challenging assignment, attempted by many because of the lure of the enormous profits that seemed so easily within reach, but achieved by only one.

The standard method of attempting to establish a cola competitive with Coke was to do what Coke did but to do it better. Companies tried time and again to beat Coca-Cola at its own game. This was the same competitive strategy adopted by Wheeler & Wilson in its losing battle against Singer at the turn of the century. The problem was that every such attempt was met by the cumulative impact of Coca-Cola's first-mover advantages.

Manufacture was no problem. Virtually anyone with minimal capital could produce a nice-tasting, sugared, carbonated water that would be indistinguishable from Coca-Cola in a blind taste test.

Then, however, the difficulties started. Production may have been easy, but one next faced the challenge posed by figure 1: how was the product to be bottled? Coca-Cola, by 1930, had tied up nearly every existing effective bottler with exclusive contracts. A potential competitor could solve this problem by integrating forward, that is, by building, owning, and operating its own bottling plants. But this meant entering a new business with all the troubles that entails and, most important, all the capital that requires. Heightened demand for capital increases the denominator in the return-on-investment fraction, making it more difficult to achieve high rates of return. Simply put, higher capital investment would demand higher profits to make the investment attractive. Those higher profits could be generated either by charging more, thus increasing margins but decreasing sales, or by selling more at a competitive price, a difficult goal to achieve.

It would take more than capital to create a bottling network. It would require executive talent and a sales force at each bottling plant to sell the product to retail outlets. Furthermore, since there was no particular reason to believe the market would grow quickly as the 1920s drew to a close, all this investment and human effort would have to be aimed at taking share away from existing players.

Instead of trying to have the beverage bottled, an entrepreneur could have approached jobbers with the hope of getting the beverage sold by the glass through restaurants and soda fountains. But why would jobbers want to do business with a new entrant? The most efficient jobbers were already distributing Coca-Cola. Even if they did not have exclusive contracts, they might be risking their relationship with Coca-Cola if they put a big effort behind a new product. More important, jobbers would find it very difficult to sell a new entrant to their own customers, which were soda fountains, drug stores, and restaurants. That was so because the patrons of those establishments, influenced by so much advertising for so many years, wanted Coca-Cola.

Thus, in order to sell to jobbers, the new entrant would need a highly persuasive sales force. But where was such a cadre of paragons to be found? The best salespeople in the industry already worked for Coca-Cola. The new entrant would either have to hire people from Coca-Cola or find salespeople from outside the industry. The first option could be achieved only by offering far higher salaries than Coca-Cola was willing to pay. But Coca-Cola could quickly match any salary that a plausible competitor could offer. And every penny more paid to the sales force was a penny less in profit, and profit was why entry into the business was attempted in the first place.

Without superb jobbers and bottler support, it would be very difficult to penetrate the food stores, drug stores, or eating and drinking places, or to establish a network of vending machines that could be easily stocked. A potential competitor could enter the distribution network by offering higher margins to these businesses, but that posed two problems. First, every penny one gave to them was a penny less in profit. Second, in any bidding war, Coca-Cola had a very full war chest. It could force up the price of anything required to succeed in this business—the salary of a salesperson or the annual advertising budget, to select two examples—so that any market share won would prove a Pyrrhic victory.

Finally, a potential new entrant into the cola business could attack the consumer. Once again, however, we are stuck with the simple question: how? Back in 1912, the Advertising Club of America had voted Coca-Cola the best advertised product in the United States. The following year, Coca-Cola's advertising budget increased slightly to $1.186 million. Table 4 provides information on what that sum of money could purchase that year. Indeed, from 1892 through 1929 inclusive, Coca-Cola spent an estimated cumulative total of $45 million on advertising. Think of that figure and take another look at table 4, which shows what $1.186 million could buy in one year.

Competing with Coca-Cola by doing what it was already doing but doing it better was highly problematic. Thus, potential competitors were left with the second option for market entry: a fundamental reconfiguration of the delivery of value to the consumer and to all the participants in the value chain. This is not easy. Timing, determination, and vision are vital. But because this was the route that Pepsi-Cola took in the 1930s, it succeeded in not being buried in the "copycat's graveyard" along with the more than seven thousand other beverage companies that had tried to compete against Coca-Cola on a national basis. Instead, it has emerged over the years as a giant consumer food company capable of matching Coca-Cola step for step and occasionally getting a step ahead.

The key to Pepsi's entry was its control over a chain of about two hundred luncheonettes in the mid-Atlantic states. This chain (actually an amalgam of three chains—Loft, Happiness, and Mirror) fell into the hands of Charles G. Guth in 1931. Guth quickly recognized that his stores moved a great deal of Coca-Cola. He demanded a sharper discount than he was receiving from Atlanta.

Coca-Cola refused. One of the principal reasons that it had become so strong in every aspect of marketing was to be in the position to reject just such demands. Furthermore, the system depicted in figure 1 could, in one sense at least, be thought of as having the defects of its virtues. If Guth received a sharp discount, others would demand the same. The wonderful fabric of profit woven over a half century might begin to fray at the edges.

And there was the added fact that Guth had no place else to go. Coca-Cola felt it could gamble on not giving him the price he wanted because the company figured that he could not do without its product, and, what is more, Coke assumed that Guth knew this quite well. Coca-Cola was right. Guth could not do without its beverage, and he did know it. What Coca-Cola did not comprehend, however, was the particular personality of this individual, Charles G. Guth. He was the kind of man who refused to be treated as Coca-Cola was treating him. He decided to stop carrying Coca-Cola, even though doing so might mean he would hurt his own company.

Soon after his battle with Coca-Cola, Guth was approached with an offer to buy Pepsi-Cola. In 1931, Pepsi-Cola, which had been founded in North Carolina in the early 1890s, was bankrupt for the second

Table 4.   ADVERTISING MATERIAL DISTRIBUTED BY THE COCA-COLA COMPANY IN 1913

Units	Material
200,000	4-head cutouts for window display
5,000,000	Lithograph metal signs from 6″ × 10″ to 5′ × 8′
10,000	Enamel metal signs 12″ × 36″, 18″ × 45″
60,000	Fountain festoons
250,000	Special signs for bottlers 12″ × 36″
50,000	Cardboard cutouts for window display
60,000	4-head festoons for soda fountains
10,000	Lithograph metal display signs
20,000	Lithograph metal display containing reproduction of bottles
50,000	Metal signs for tacking under windows
200,000	Fiber signs for tacking on walls of refreshment stands
2,000,000	Trays for soda fountains
50,000	Window trims
250,000	5-head window displays and mirror decorations
1,000,000	Japanese fans
50,000	Christmas wreaths and bell decorations for fountains
50,000	The Coca-Cola Company song
1,000,000	Calendars
50,000	Thermometers
10,000,000	Match books
50,000,000	Doilies (paper)
	24-sheet posters for billboards 10′ × 20′
	Oil-cloth signs for storefronts
10,000	Large calendars for business offices
144,000	Pencils
	Transparent signs for windows and transoms
20,000	Blotters
10,000	Framed metal signs for well displays
5,000	Transparent globes, mosaic art glasswork
	Art glass signs
25,000	Baseball score cards
	Celluloid display cards
$300,000	Newspaper advertising
	Magazine, farm paper, trade paper, religious paper ads
	Other forms of advertising

SOURCE: Richard S. Tedlow, *New and Improved: The Story of Mass Marketing in America* (1990), p. 53.

time. A judge was later to describe it as "a corporation which in point of actual fact was the mere shell of a corporation with practically nothing in the way of assets except a formula, a trademark, and the franchise of a corporation to engage in the work of erecting a business thereon." No assets. No organization. No sales. Merely a trade name known by no one and a formula of such questionable appeal that when Guth himself tasted it, he pronounced it "unsatisfactory." Guth bought the company for $12,000. It did not seem like much of a competitor at the time, so the price probably seemed right to all concerned. In 1993, PepsiCo had a market value of over $25 billion.

Guth began selling Pepsi-Cola rather than Coca-Cola through his chain of stores in 1931. Sales of soft drinks at the chain dropped, as did total sales. Some of this slump was doubtless due to the Great Depression, but the switch from Coke to Pepsi was probably a contributory factor. The loss of sales for Loft and its associated chains was, obviously, bad for Guth as president. However, the chain's soft-drink business did not collapse completely. Even if it sold one glass of Pepsi-Cola in 1931, that was one more glass than Pepsi had sold in 1930. And—this is a key point—Guth personally owned Pepsi-Cola; Loft, the company of which he was president and without which Pepsi was as worthless in 1931 as it was in 1930, did not. Although it was bad for Guth in his role as president of Loft to see business dwindle there, it was fantastic for him as owner of Pepsi-Cola to see any product at all sold. This was a trade-off he happily made.

Thus, Pepsi-Cola came out of its second bankruptcy essentially as a retailer's brand that, in this legally and ethically questionable case, the retailer happened not to own. Pepsi-Cola after Guth bought it became what today is called a private label. By capturing the point of sale for Pepsi, Guth circumvented many of the difficulties just discussed in competing with Coke. He did not have to worry about bottlers because he was not selling Pepsi in bottles. Thus, instead of trying to beat Coca-Cola at its own game, he turned the industry on its head. He felt that a retailer could be the channel commander (the firm in the value chain of companies from raw material to finished product that exercises the most power and is therefore the most profitable) as effectively as a manufacturer.

Once Guth bought Pepsi and got to know the business, he realized how much money there was to be made. He especially wanted to get into bottling, with its fat margins. This he tried to do from the time of his purchase of the company in 1931 through late 1933, encountering all the problems just enumerated and achieving very little success. Finally, in late 1933 and early 1934, Guth and some associates came up with the twelve-ounce bottle. They decided to sell twelve-ounce bottles of Pepsi-Cola for the same nickel price for which Coca-Cola sold its six-and-a-half-ounce bottles.

The twelve-ounce strategy was possible because of one specific circumstance, and it became successful because of another set of circumstances. The specific circumstance was Coca-Cola's reaping such high profits from its six-and-a-half-ounce bottle. Coca-Cola was living in that best of all worlds: low prices, high volume, and surprisingly high margins. Guth realized that the actual liquid being sold made up such a small portion of Coca-Cola's costs that even if volume were doubled and the nickel price preserved, profits remain extremely generous.

Profit margins were a necessary but not a sufficient reason for the success of Pepsi's strategy. Let us look at what other circumstances made it work. First, there was the national context: 1934 was a depression year. Pennies mattered in a way that they had not in the previous decade. As one industry executive later recalled, "Twelve full ounces of a recognized cola for only five cents meant a hell of a lot." Second,

just as was the case when it turned the industry upside-down by attacking Coca-Cola from its retail base, Pepsi-Cola's adoption of the twelve-ounce bottle was not an attempt to beat Coca-Cola at its own game, but rather to change the rules of the game. The last thing Coca-Cola would want to do was to endorse a movement in the industry toward selling twelve-ounce bottles for 5 cents. The disruption this would cause was mentioned earlier. Beyond the operational problems, such a switch would cost Coca-Cola money.

Pepsi-Cola, on the other hand, had nothing to lose in 1933 and 1934. The company had no business through bottles. Any profit was better than no profit. Obviously, giving more for the same price had a very powerful consumer appeal. Thus Pepsi was able, not to fight Coke's strength, but to look at Coke's strength as rigidity. If there were first-mover advantages, Pepsi was showing that there could be late-mover advantages as well.

With its move to twelve ounces for a nickel, Pepsi provided a vivid lesson that many companies even in the 1990s seem incapable of learning: in the long run, the consumer rules. If you do not want to serve the consumer because it is not as profitable to do so as you would like, someone else will steal your business. A trade magazine reported in 1940 that "The very active research department of the Coca-Cola Company has . . . determined by tests that the average person who buys a drink is completely satisfied with the 6-ounce bottle and in fact does not want more than that at a clip."

This statement was nonsense on a number of grounds. First, there is no evidence that Coca-Cola had a very active research department in 1940. Second, even a moderately active research department should have had access to the *Biennial Census of Manufacturers* of the U.S. Census Bureau. These published reports showed that twelve-ounce bottles accounted for 6.8 percent of sales of bottled carbonated soft drinks in 1935, 15.4 percent in 1937, and 26.4 percent in 1939. Third, it should not have taken any research at all to figure out that people would prefer to receive more product for the same price if they had a choice.

This story deserves emphasis because it has been relived so many times in business history. In the 1920s, for example, Henry Ford wanted to keep marketing the Model T Ford. This was the product that had made his name a household word not only in the United States but around the world. It had made him a billionaire. It dominated the domestic market, accounting for a unit share of over 55 percent in 1921.

But the market for automobiles in the United States was changing in the 1920s. In 1908, when the Model T was introduced, the automobile was a new, dangerous, and unreliable product. The mass market wanted most of all a car that would work at an affordable price. Consumers wanted an appliance that would take them from place to place, without breaking down in the middle of nowhere, in the middle of the night, in the rain. That is precisely what the Model T was.

By the 1920s, however, the nation and the market had changed. The infrastructure of the auto-industrial age had been put in place to a far greater degree than at the turn of the century. Roads were better, repairs were more easily available, and cars were equipped with self-starters and headlights. Consumers had become more familiar with automobiles. The second- and third-time buyer of the 1920s was far more knowledgeable than the first-time buyer of the 1910s.

Moreover, the nation had changed dramatically during the 1910s. By the 1920s, there was more leisure time. Motion pictures and radio were satisfying and at the same time further stimulating the desire for entertainment. The economy was booming, so more people had the money to afford what had once been luxuries.

In this new environment, people wanted more from an automobile. They wanted their car to work, of course. It still had to serve as an appliance to take them from place to place. But, by the 1920s, most cars on the market, not only the Model T, were far more reliable than any cars had been at the turn of the century. The something extra that people now wanted was style, fashion, excitement. This was a change that Henry Ford refused to acknowledge for two reasons. The first was ideological; with his artisan mentality, Ford believed that as a matter of principle, people ought to want a simple vehicle that delivered what it promised. But the second reason was quite practical; Ford's gigantic works were geared up to be better and better at what they did the previous year. This was a great advantage in a period of certainty, but more a burden than a benefit in the face of discontinuous change. Yet that is what the 1920s were for the automobile industry.

To choose one example, Henry Ford has often been quoted to the effect that the "public can have any color car it wants as long as it is black." Ford probably never actually made this statement, but it did express his sentiments. These sentiments, however, have been misinterpreted. Ford has been thought of as being the victim of hubris to such an extent that he felt he had the power to dictate to the market concerning matters such as the color of cars. He is thought of as believing that the public should want only what he wanted and what he wanted them to want.

This is the truth, but only half the truth. The other half is that colors were an operational dilemma of the first magnitude for Ford. Production of the Model T demanded speed of throughput for economical manufacture. It took very little time to apply baked-on black enamel, whereas the only nonblack paint available for application to automobiles in the early 1920s took hours to dry. Minutes were precious in Ford's system. The warehousing of thousands of slowly drying cars would have upset his economies of speed.

What Ford saw as a problem Alfred Sloan at General Motors saw as an opportunity. Sloan's approach was not to dictate to the market but to satisfy it. DuPont, which owned a controlling interest in General Motors and worked closely with it, developed Duco, a quick-drying paint. The result was the "true blue" Oakland, later renamed Pontiac, in 1924.

Time and again, when Ford was rigid, Sloan was flexible. Under Sloan's leadership, General Motors developed and organized its five-name-plate product offering: Chevrolet, as *Fortune* wrote, "for *hoi polloi*, . . . Pontiac for the poor but proud, Oldsmobile for the comfortable but discreet, Buick for the striving, Cadillac for the rich." Moreover, these cars changed every year to convey a sense of style and fashion, and, not incidentally, to make obsolete the inventory of customers who had purchased last year's model. Unlike Ford with its Model T, General Motors did not have to compete directly against its own used cars, since models were different each year, or at least seemed to be.

The strategy of General Motors in the 1920s was to change the game being played. Sloan was explicit about this:

> With Ford in almost complete possession of the low price field, it would have been suicidal to compete with him head on. No conceivable amount of capital short of the United States Treasury could have sustained the losses required to take volume away from him *at his own game*. [Italics added.]

There are similarities between the stories of Ford and General Motors in the 1920s and Coca-Cola and Pepsi in the 1930s. The Model T can be seen as similar to Coca-Cola from the point of view of market position and the role they played in the history of their industries. Both products were leaders. Indeed, both not only responded to demand, but in part created the markets they served. For Coca-Cola, there was nothing inevitable about the creation of a brand in an industry with such low manufacturing hurdles as those that characterized carbonated soft drinks. By the same token, there was nothing inevitable about the mass marketing of automobiles. At the turn of the century, when automobiles in the United States and Europe were being produced essentially on a custom-made basis and were priced far beyond the reach of the mass market, many people thought that there never would be a low-priced automobile that was both durable and inexpensive. Looking back from 1925, one journalist remarked: "That a time should come when horses would be a rare sight on city streets seemed, in 1900, one of the least credible of prophecies."

Coca-Cola and the Model T became the dominant design for products in their respective industries. It was against them that others were compared. These products were not only dominant from the point of view of their core, physical characteristics; the organizational systems their companies pioneered shaped the way people conceived of marketing in their respective industries. In both cases, first-mover advantages made attacking these businesses by playing their own game difficult if not impossible. Some fundamentally new insight was required for how to deliver value to the consumer. And the times had to be right for that new insight to become an effective business reality.

Perhaps most important, neither General Motors nor Pepsi-Cola were offering me-too products. To the contrary, both were providing powerful reasons to switch. General Motors offered change and variety. Pepsi offered more product for the same price.

PHASE III OF MARKETING: THE SEGMENTED MARKET, 1950s–1990s

In Phase II of the history of marketing, we saw how entrepreneurial firms exploited a new business infrastructure to mass-market branded merchandise on a national and eventually global basis. *Massification* and *unification* are terms appropriate to Phase II. The key term that defines Phase III is *segmentation*.

As is true of the transition from the Phase I world of localized fragmentation to the Phase II world of national unification, the transition from Phase II to the Phase III world of demographic (which refers to age, income, and education) and psychographic (which refers to lifestyle) market segmentation was greatly facilitated by developments that had very little

to do with marketing practice itself. The two most important of these developments were "ether" advertising as it was originally called (that is, advertising through the air first on radio and then on television) and, second, broad changes in American culture, which exercised a profound influence on the nature of consumer demand.

Advertising by radio and especially by television brought the selling message about consumer products directly into the home with a drama and immediacy unprecedented in the history of marketing. Not even the barrier of literacy stood between the company and the consumer, as it did with much print advertising and packaging. Radio and television gave birth to the commercial jingle, which was easy for consumers to keep in mind long after the commercial was over. Television was made to order for purposes of demonstration. It also enabled the advertiser to communicate a selling message through pictures and through the creation of an ambience that might be quite unconnected to the product claims of the advertising copy itself or even to the actual characteristics of the product. The Pepsi Generation advertising campaign of the 1960s (described below) is a good example.

The use of television for commercial advertising became permissible in North America long before it did in Europe or Japan. There were 6 commercial television stations in the United States in 1945 and 411 a decade later. Some of the most famous programs regularly attracted very large audiences and it soon became apparent that certain types of programs attracted certain classes of viewers. All this meant that the opportunities for segmenting markets—that is, for concentrating the selling appeal on one particular group of potential customers who might be defined by their age, income, and education (demographics) or by their lifestyle (psychographics)—were greatly enhanced.

In addition to this new technology that had been placed in the hands of marketers, the American consumer market after World War II was ripe for segmenting. Never before in American history had the generation gap been so broad and so deep. Take the example of an American born in 1947, as I was. My parents grew up during the Great Depression, which made a life-long impression on them; I grew up during the 1950s and 1960s. They grew up in poverty, while I had money in my pocket as an adolescent, not because I had earned it, but because times were good in the United States and my parents could give it to me. My parents lived through World War II; for me World War II was something to experience through John Wayne movies. My parents grew up before the atomic bomb; I after it. My parents grew up before television; like most Americans of my era, I watched about a thousand hours a year for the first two decades of my life.

When we put all this together, the generation gap becomes more understandable. My parents' generation and my own had very different experiences of life and very different expectations from it. My generation—known as baby boomers in the United States because of the population explosion in the late 1940s—looked for badges of belonging that could serve both to link us to others in our age group and to differentiate us from our elders. These badges could be of different types. In music, it was Elvis Presley reaching the nation with records and live performances through radio, television, and motion pictures. Not long after him, the Beatles achieved the same level of attention.

In this hothouse environment, entertainment could have effects on products that were quite unpredictable. A good example is the story of the Levi's 501s, the basic blue jean that had for years been produced by Levi Strauss & Co. Levi Strauss posted sales of $8 million in 1945. In fiscal 1990, its sales were $4.25 billion, making it the world's largest branded-apparel manufacturer. What accounted for this remarkable growth?

In the mid-1950s, three motion pictures were made that featured rebellious but sympathetic teenage males who were alienated from their families, looking for fellowship from their young male comrades, and clumsily searching for love from the opposite sex. *The Wild One* starred Marlon Brando and *East of Eden* and *Rebel without a Cause* starred the ill-fated James Dean. By chance, the antihero protagonists in all three of these films wore Levi's 501s. These garments, which previously had been identified primarily as work clothing or western wear, now became known as the uniform of rebellion. All this happened without Levi Strauss having to spend any advertising funds. There is a lot more to the story of Levi's growth from an $8 million to a $4.25 billion firm than these three films. But the films did not hurt.

If there could be music for this new generation of privileged/alienated youth and clothing for them, too, could there not also be a soft drink targeted specifically at them? Marketers at Pepsi-Cola answered in the affirmative, and the Pepsi generation was born "comin' at ya, goin' strong." One of the most successful marketing-communication campaigns in history, the Pepsi Generation succeeded in

segmenting the carbonated-soft-drink market along both demographic and psychographic lines.

During the 1930s and 1940s, Pepsi had appealed for business strictly on price. Its slogan, a classic radio jingle, was:

Pepsi-Cola hits the spot.
Twelve full ounces, that's a lot.
Twice as much for a nickel, too.
Pepsi-Cola is the drink for you.

As this jingle suggests, Pepsi asked for business on the grounds that it gave you more product for the same price as the competition. Its commercials were laced with an announcer repeating "Nickel, nickel, nickel."

In the late 1940s, rising sugar prices forced Pepsi either to raise its prices or to lower the number of ounces it sold for a nickel. The business almost went bankrupt until a new CEO was able to reposition the product by associating it with a stylish, upper-middle-class lifestyle. After Donald Kendall became CEO in the early 1960s, the company targeted this new generation that seemed to be separated by such a gulf from its elders. This was the creation of the so-called Pepsi Generation.

Pepsi's basic idea was quite simple. Coca-Cola had always sold itself as the standard-bearer of changeless, ageless Americana. "We're tradition," Coca-Cola said of its product. "No, you're not," Pepsi, in essence, replied, "You're old." The Pepsi generation commercials were loud, brash, and aggressive. Needless to say, they never mentioned price. In fact, these commercials were not about the product at all. They were about the people whom the company wanted to portray as using it. For one spectacular television commercial, "Surf Football," Pepsi's advertising agency shipped a camera crew to the California beaches and shot thousands of feet of tape of young, beautiful, alluring, healthy-looking adolescent women and men playing a pick-up game of touch football at the water's edge. There was a jingle in the background and words were spoken, but the real message was in the picture of beautiful, insouciant youth. And the real message was "Buy a Pepsi and you, too, can be like us." A written description does not do justice to this advertisement nor to the series of those like it produced by Pepsi. The essence of the message was the image presented to the public. The Pepsi generation would have been impossible without television.

If this demographic and psychographic segmentation had taken place only in one industry, it would constitute merely a footnote to the history of marketing. However, in the post–World War II era, the great American mass market began to split into innumerable segments in product categories ranging from low-ticket, impulse-purchase items such as carbonated soft drinks all the way to expensive, ego-intensive consumer durables like automobiles. The mass market was also segmented at the retail level, with the decline of stores such as Sears and the A&P and the rise of specialty stores.

In the automobile industry, as we have seen, there was a time when the American market was dominated not merely by one company but by a specific product—the Model T Ford. The Model T was, as we have noted, the automotive equivalent of the six-and-a-half-ounce bottle of Coca-Cola in the soft-drink industry. It was the standard, the one car with which everyone could feel comfortable and confident.

The automobile industry differs from the soft drink industry in that its segmentation began decades earlier. By the late 1920s, General Motors had successfully attacked the Model T's dominance by bringing out its product array, characterized as the "car for every purse and purpose." When combined with the annual model change, this segmentation scheme gave General Motors a grip on the American market that has only recently loosened.

A look at how automobile marketing changed from 1925 to 1965, however, shows that General Motors' early segmentation was not yet fully articulated by the late 1920s. It was based primarily on age and income: Chevrolet for the young and relatively less financially well-off, Cadillac for the old and rich. By the 1960s, automobile marketing had become far more segmented and segmented along far more dimensions than was the case with GM's quintet of cars in the 1920s.

In the 1960s, the marketing of over-engineered and over-powered cars was aimed precisely at the children of the generation gap who were wearing their Levi's and listening to the Beatles sing "I Wanna Hold Your Hand" as they sipped their Pepsi. The 1960s were the era of "pony" and "muscle" cars like the Pontiac GTO, the Ford Mustang, and the Plymouth Fury. Psychographic segmentation was combined with demographics in the 1960s as it had not been in the 1920s.

Please note once again that I draw a careful distinction between the market fragmentation of Phase I and the market segmentation of Phase III. Consumer markets were fragmented a century-and-a-quarter ago not out of managerial choice, but because of the geographical barriers and logistical realities I described in the section on Phase I. But since the 1960s, aggressive executives searching to transform latent opportunities into profits have deliberately segmented markets. The Pepsi Generation is the perfect example. This market segment did not naturally arise and march to Pepsi's corporate headquarters demanding a cola all its own. Rather, Pepsi's marketers sensed an opportunity presented by changing times and through great television advertising turned this potential into something kinetic. Unlike geographic market fragments of old, modern market segments are virtually created by clever marketers who produce marketing programs that reconfigure and exploit latent consumer interests.

Table 5 provides a checklist for the three phases in the history of marketing.

TOWARD THE FUTURE: TRENDS IN MASS MARKETING

In the mid 1990s, the business press is full of articles about how new information technology is bringing about a profound change in marketing. What the railroads were to marketing in the last quarter of the nineteenth century and television was in the second half of the twentieth century, computer-collected and analyzed information will become in the future. Inventory, it has been said, is the price paid for the lack of information; and the information revolution is lowering that price in the factory, in the distribution system, and at the point of sale.

Information technology permits just-in-time systems, which in turn facilitate the manufacture of a wide variety of products in short runs in situations where scale economies can still be captured. All through the distribution system, information allows this greater variety to be managed without overstocks or stock-outs, and the end result is that the consumer has a greater variety of products from which to choose. The customer is thus more satisfied when he or she walks out of the store.

The automobile industry well illustrates these trends. Nissan has been experimenting with a new flexible manufacturing system the ultimate goal of which, according to the general manager of the engineering team that developed the system, will be "to produce any vehicle, at any time, at any production location, by anybody and in any volume required." We are told that some day soon a customer will be able to order from the dealer precisely the automobile he or she wants and have it delivered to specification in a matter of days rather than months. In other

Table 5.   THE THREE PHASES IN THE HISTORY OF MARKETING

Phase	Characteristics	Approximate Dates
I Fragmentation	High margin per unit Low volume of unit sales Limited geographic market Expensive and slow transportation and information Commodity products	To the 1880s
II Unification	Low margin per unit High volume of unit sales National mass market Less expensive and far faster transportation and information Brand products	1880s–1950s
III Segmentation	Value pricing—to capture as much margin as brand loyalty allows Volume of unit sales high enough to achieve scale economies in manufacturing and marketing Global market with numerous demographic and psychographic segments Enhanced research capabilities leading to more precise segmentation Brand proliferation with brands targeted at specific segments	1950s–Present

words, the industry has changed completely from the days of the Model T, which was marketed according to a strictly cost/price strategy based on rigid standardization.

Micromarketing is becoming one of the most oft-repeated terms in the marketing lexicon. It means hypersegmentation, segmentation to the nth degree. Some marketers seem actually to have a vision of every customer constituting a segment of one. One hears terms such as *particle marketing,* which suggest this kind of minute segmentation. Forces pushing the world toward micromarketing are not solely on the supply side. It is, in other words, not solely caused by the development of the new information technology which has made it economically possible.

There is also a demand for micromarketing on the part of the buying public. To state the obvious, people want what they want, not something made for a putative mass market. Consumers are becoming more demanding, and, in their efforts to satisfy this trend, marketers are intensifying it. In other words, the more customized people want their products, the more marketers seek to customize them. The more that marketers make this effort, the greater is the perception on the customers' part that they can get exactly what they want. If that means caffeine-free diet Coke in a twelve-ounce can, then that is what it shall be. The older six-and-a-half-ounce standard package of Coca-Cola no longer satisfies.

With the demand there and the technology to satisfy it, the advent of micromarketing as a fourth phase in marketing's development should come as no surprise. This development fits a number of the themes discussed in this essay. It is another example of a major change in marketing that results from technical developments that arise outside the control of the product marketers in question. It means greater choice for the consumer. It means that the marketer will take one step closer to every marketer's dream: to sell the potential customer precisely what the customer wants. This is so much easier than trying to convince the customer to buy what the factory has made. And once again, as with the railroad and television, the firms that can adapt their product policy and their distribution systems to the new reality have the chance to capture first-mover advantages that may last for generations.

There is, however, another side to the micromarketing story that deserves our attention. When so many experts are looking in one direction (toward micromarketing), perhaps it would be interesting to look in the opposite direction. When we do, we see at least two major forces that might inhibit micromarketing: customer confusion and saturation of the distribution channels.

With regard to consumer confusion, consider the following passage from a 1985 article in the *New York Times:*

> There are in the United States today, 23 kinds of Nine Lives cat food. Revlon makes 157 shades of lipstick (41 of them pink) and Tower Video offers 5,000 video cassettes for sale or rent. The Love drugstore chain carries 41 varieties of hair mousse.

This article's basic point—whether there is "such a thing as too much choice"—is, if anything, more valid in the 1990s than it was in 1985. The article also speaks of the "new bewilderment" as confused customers are confronted in the marketplace with scores of distinctions without differences.

The response of companies to such observations are reasonable and predictable. Speaking of its 157 shades of lipstick, a Revlon spokeswoman said: "There is someone who wants each of them or they wouldn't be there. We don't make products to sit on the shelf."

Let us give some thought to the final phrase, "on the shelf"; it draws our attention to the second major force, saturation of the distribution channels. Manufacturers may want to satisfy every consumer desire as precisely as possible, but they must reach consumers through a distribution system that must operate within its own constraints. There is a finite amount of shelf space in the retail outlets of the United States and of the world. If we conceive of every woman in the United States wanting her own shade of lipstick even if the lipstick industry could produce that great a variety, there is still the problem of that shelf.

The distribution system has become the neck in the hourglass through which manufacturer must reach consumer. At some point—perhaps when Revlon produces its 158th lipstick shade—the retailer will be forced to say "enough."

Indeed this is already happening. The balance of power in American marketing in a number of product categories is shifting to the retailers, because they control the scarce resource, shelf space. This is a resource they are selling in shelf-allotment programs. It is because of the scarcity of shelf space that manufacturers have to devote a greater percentage of their brand management budget to trade promotion rather than to consumer promotion or to mass-media advertising. And this is one reason why advertising agencies are suffering.

In light of these observations, it might be instructive to take a brief look at a development in the U.S. shampoo market in the mid 1980s. Prior to Procter & Gamble's introduction of Pert Plus in 1985, the $1 billion U.S. shampoo market was highly segmented, with over eleven hundred products competing, none of them holding a commanding share. According to a 1990 *Wall Street Journal* article, when the Pert Plus combination shampoo and hair conditioner moved from Procter & Gamble's research laboratories to test market, "top management responded with a yawn." The product "didn't even rate a new brand name. . . . Instead it was pumped into moribund Pert shampoo, then barely clinging to 2 percent of the U.S. shampoo

market. 'Nobody paid a lot of attention to it,' [according to CEO] Edwin L. Artzt."

The shampoo market was notorious for its fickle consumers. They flitted from one brand to another, and this apparently congenital absence of repeat-purchase behavior made investment spending to build a brand pointless. Pert itself was, according to the *Wall Street Journal,* "perilously close to extinction in late 1985 when reformulated Pert Plus was halfheartedly test-marketed." Artzt said that, "We weren't in the mood to put a lot of money into a 2% share brand."

The halfheartedness of the test marketing of Pert Plus is illustrated by the fact that Procter & Gamble invested little in advertising and promotion. Nevertheless, consumers took to the product almost instantaneously, doubling sales in half a year. "We just damn near missed it," said Artzt. As of mid 1994, estimates of Pert Plus market share ranged from 12 percent to 14.3 percent.

What Procter & Gamble did with Pert Plus was take a step back from the Phase III world of market segmentation to the Phase II world of mass marketing rather than a step forward into the predicted Phase IV world of micromarketing. Instead of splitting one product into two—for example, bringing out Diet Coke in addition to Coca-Cola—Procter & Gamble created one product where there were formerly two—that is, it made a combination shampoo-conditioner where there had previously been separate shampoos and conditioners. The reason that the company did not at first believe the numbers Pert Plus was generating and recognize its own success— remember that CEO Artzt said, "We just damn near missed it"—is that Pert Plus bucked a trend. The trend, as all the articles proclaim, is toward more variety. Pert Plus succeeded by doing the opposite of what everyone said: it diminished variety.

Without access to P&G's research, we cannot say with confidence why Pert Plus succeeded. But some plausible guesses can be advanced. Shampoo is a low-ticket, non-ego-intensive, impulse purchase item for many consumers. That is why there is so much brand switching. With Pert Plus, Procter & Gamble took some of the pain out of hair care. The customer now had to make only one decision rather than two. He or she had to buy only one package, thus saving time, weight, and space. This matters in an age in which people travel a lot.

This is not the first time that a product has succeeded by doing the opposite of what everyone else was doing. In the 1950s and the 1960s, when American automobile manufacturers were producing "muscle" and "pony" cars in ever-greater variety,

Volkswagen achieved global success with its Beetle. The Beetle strategy was a precise replica of the Model T Ford strategy—a simple, inexpensive, reliable appliance that performed the commodity function of transporting the owner from place to place. In a world of Mustangs and GTOs, the Beetle was an anomaly, certainly in the American market. This anomalous positioning was brilliantly transformed from a problem to an opportunity by the advertising of William Bernbach. The Volkswagen Beetle is as clear an example as one will find of a Phase II success in a Phase III world. It was the only model in the history of the automobile industry to outsell the Model T Ford.

On the other hand, as the stories of Sears and the A&P illustrate, bucking a trend can be disastrous. A firm must have a clear strategic vision and execute it skillfully, as did Volkswagen, rather than merely drift, as did these two big retailers.

Sears, for example, was forced to close down its century-old catalog at a time when many catalog operators flourished. Why did Sears fail while others succeeded? There are many reasons, but basically the problem was that for years, Sears made small changes where fundamental reconceptualizations were in order. In the great days of the Sears catalog in the 1920s, catalog merchants were located in major cities and serviced primarily rural customers. Thus, Sears and Montgomery Ward both based their catalog warehouse operations in Chicago to serve a rural market.

By the 1980s and 1990s, the context of the American market had changed fundamentally. Many major catalog firms, such as L. L. Bean and Land's End, were located in rural areas and served urban markets. Their markets were carefully segmented, the service they provided was rapid, and their products were of high quality. Sears, meanwhile, was tinkering at the margins. The company tried to change the look of its catalog without really changing the heart of its approach to the American consumer. Slowly, and by imperceptible steps, Sears left its market behind. It worried about the shadow, while its new competitors focused on the substance.

The story of the A&P is similar. For years, America's largest food retailer built its consumer franchise on its private-label merchandise rather than on manufacturers' brands. In the 1990s, supermarket chains such as Canada's Loblaw mounted a major challenge to manufacturers' brands through their own private-label programs. The difference is that private label at the A&P came to mean not only low price but low quality. That is not true at Loblaw. Loblaw

achieved some success bucking the trend toward dominance of manufacturers' brands because it had a clearly thought-out strategy. A&P, by contrast, simply tried to do each year what it had done the year before.

In marketing, as in every business function, strategy and implementation go hand in hand. Excelling at one while failing at the other inevitably leads to disaster.

A NOTE ON INDUSTRIAL MARKETING: THE PROSPECTS FOR CONVERGENCE

This essay has dealt almost exclusively with the mass marketing of consumer products. Yet, a look at figure 3 shows that a great deal of marketing is industrial rather than consumer. Some estimate that industrial-product marketing accounts for more than half of the marketing in the United States.

Industrial marketing itself is not easily defined. Clearly, a sale by General Electric of a jet engine to Boeing would be an example of industrial marketing. One company is selling a product to another. The sale is highly technical, involving well-paid engineers and contacts at the highest levels of both companies. A well-trained sales force and purchasing system are vital. Advertising plays a relatively minor role.

The advertising that is employed is designed not to make a sale (as it might be with a product such as Coca-Cola), but to establish in the minds of the purchasers that a particular company is supplying their market. A good illustration of the role that advertising is expected to play in industrial marketing is the well-known "purchasing-agent" advertisement run by McGraw-Hill, owner of numerous trade publications. A gimlet-eyed purchasing agent stares skeptically from the page. He says:

> I don't know who you are.
> I don't know your company.
> I don't know your company's product.
> I don't know what your company stands for.
> I don't know your company's customers.
> I don't know your company's record.
> I don't know your company's reputation.
> Now—what was it you wanted to sell us?

The goal here is to suggest that advertising can serve as a door opener in industrial marketing. No one would purchase a jet engine on the basis of an advertisement. The hope is that the establishment of at least minimal name recognition would allow the selling process to begin.

Industrial marketing refers not only to the jet engine transaction, but also encompasses the purchase of inexpensive items in small lots, such as Scotch tape by a law firm. It also includes the sale of goods by one company to another that are eventually targeted at the consumer market. For example, when Cone Mills sells denim to Levi Strauss and when Levi Strauss sells blue jeans to J. C. Penney, both transactions are considered industrial marketing, even though the final product, the blue jeans, is purchased by an individual consumer. This is a different chain from that of the jet engine. In order to be more inclusive, the term *business-to-business marketing* has begun to replace *industrial marketing*. The former label will probably be more common in the future.

Historically, industrial marketing has been under-recognized in business schools and, indeed, in industrial-marketing firms themselves. The pioneer industrial marketing scholar at the Harvard Business School, E. Raymond Corey, wrote in 1962:

> Surveying the great volume of marketing literature, one is struck by the fact that a relatively small amount of it is devoted to the problems and techniques of marketing industrial goods. Instead, particular interest has been shown in consumer goods selling. . . .
>
> Modern techniques of merchandising (product planning), advertising, and market research, for example, were widely applied in consumer goods marketing before being used to any great extent in the industrial goods area. In the latter area, too, the marketing function tended in many cases to be shared by, and possibly overshadowed by, managers in other functions. In the late 1930s, for example, the president of one large industrial company cryptically described his firm's marketing approach in the phrase, "400 Engineers and 8 Salesmen," and sought to implement this concept in his organization.

Finally, industrial products are very often highly technical products, and perhaps those who would study and write about the problems involved in marketing industrial products have been deterred to some extent because of their technical character.

This description would appear to be quite accurate with regard both to the 1930s and the 1960s. But there are indications that in the 1990s, business-to-business marketing may be adopting some of the techniques that have long characterized marketing to consumers.

There are increased efforts to establish awareness of firms in the industrial sector. Such efforts include both mass-media advertising and the sponsorship of high-profile events in, for example, the sporting world.

Yet more intriguing is the effort being made to appropriate the hallmark of consumer product marketing: the brand. In the computer industry, for example, many millions of dollars were spent in the 1990s to establish and solidify brand loyalty (e.g., "Intel Inside"). The purpose is to command higher prices by creating demand pull on the part of the end user. The result is that although consumer product marketers will continue to spend far more on advertising as a percentage of sales than their industrial counterparts, and industrial marketers will continue to have more technically trained sales forces, consumer and industrial marketers are beginning to segment markets using similar tools. And they are beginning to look more like one another than ever before.

SEE ALSO Industrial Production; Economic Performance; Infrastructure; Natural Resources (all in this volume).

BIBLIOGRAPHY

The foundation for modern business history, for most of my work in general, and for most of this particular essay is Alfred D. Chandler, Jr.'s seminal work, *The Visible Hand* (1977). The architecture of this essay is drawn from my *New and Improved: The Story of Mass Marketing in America* (1990). See also the new introduction written for the Japanese edition of this book (published by Yushodo Press in 1992) and my contributions to Richard S. Tedlow and Geoffrey Jones, eds., *The Rise and Fall of Mass Marketing* (1993). There are two very good books on advertising: Roland Marchand, *Advertising the American*

Dream: Making Way for Modernity (1985) and Daniel Pope, *The Making of Modern Advertising* (1983). For a different view of many of the subjects covered in this essay, see Susan Strasser, *Satisfaction Guaranteed: The Making of the American Mass Market* (1989).

The following sources are arranged in alphabetical order by author. Morris A. Adelman, *A&P: A Study in Price-Cost Behavior and Public Policy* (1959) is an illuminating study of this firm, based on voluminous antitrust records. There are numerous company histories that make a contribution to our understanding of marketing. One such is by the editors of *Adver-*

tising Age magazine, *Procter & Gamble: The House that Ivory Built* (1988); Louis E. Asher and Edith Heal, *Send No Money* (1942) is a very interesting memoir of Sears, Roebuck by an executive. An understanding of the history of the mass media is essential to understanding the development of marketing. The best secondary sources are four books by Erik Barnouw: *The Golden Web: A History of Broadcasting in the United States, 1933–1953* (1968); *The Image Empire: A History of Broadcasting in the United States from 1953* (1970); *The Sponsor: Notes on a Modern Potentate* (1978); and *A Tower in Babel: A History of Broadcasting in the United States to 1933* (1966). Anna P. Benson, *Textile Machines* (1983) provides a brief and useful guide to machinery early in the Industrial Revolution. For a brilliant overall view of American culture in the twentieth century and the role of the media and consumption therein, see Daniel J. Boorstin, *The Americans: The Democratic Experience* (1973). Gerald Carson, *The Old Country Store* (1954) provides useful material on its subject. Boris Emmet and John E. Jeuck, *Catalogues and Counters: A History of Sears, Roebuck and Company* (1950) is a superb history of a company that was of great importance in the development of marketing. James J. Flink, *The Automobile Age* (1988) is a valuable single-volume history of this vital industry. Stanley C. Hollander, a pioneer historian of marketing, has made many important contributions to the field. Particularly useful are his "George Huntington Hartford, George Ludlum Hartford, and John Augustine Hartford," in *Dictionary of American Biography* edited by John A. Garraty (1977); "The Marketing Concept: A Deja-Vu" in *Marketing Management: Technology as Social Process* edited by George Fisk (1986); "The Wheel of Retailing," *Journal of Marketing* 24 (July 1960); and co-authored with Richard Germain, *Was There a Pepsi Generation before Pepsi Discovered It? Youth-Based Segmentation in Marketing* (1992). E. J. Kahn, Jr., *The Big Drink: The Story of Coca-Cola* (1960) contains many interesting anecdotes about the company. David L. Lewis, *The Public Image of Henry Ford: An American Folk Hero and His Company* (1976) is the standard work on the public relations of Henry Ford, the man and his company. Malcolm P. McNair and Eleanor G. May, *The Evolution of Retail Institutes in the United States* (1976) contains valuable insights and statistical data. Milward W. Martin, *Twelve Full Ounces* (1962) is a fascinating memoir of Pepsi-Cola by an executive. For an outstanding presentation of the First Industrial Revolution in Britain, see Peter Mathias, *The First Industrial Nation: An Economic History of Britain, 1700–1914* (1993). Martin Mayer, *Madison Avenue, U.S.A.* (1958) is an enlightening journalistic account of the advertising business in the 1950s. There are numerous autobiographies of advertising executives. Among the best known is David Ogilvy, *Confessions of an Advertising Man* (1963). Joseph C. Palamountain, *The Politics of Distribution* (1955) is an excellent, scholarly discussion of its subject. Richard W. Pollay has provided the standard bibliography on the history of advertising in *Information Sources in Advertising History* (1979). Glenn Porter and Harold C. Livesay, *Merchants and Manufacturers: Studies in the Changing Structure of Nineteenth-Century Marketing* (1971) is outstanding and has become the definitive work on its subject. The best work treating modern marketing and advertising in the perspective of overall business management today is Michael E. Porter, *Competitive Advantage: Creating and Sustaining Superior Performance* (1985). David M. Potter's *People of Plenty: Economic Abundance and the American Character* (1954) provides an excellent explanation of the place of advertising in the United States following World War II. Michael Schudson, *Advertising: The Uneasy Persuasion* (1984) is an interesting analysis of advertising by a sociologist. John Sculley with John A. Byrne, *Odyssey: Pepsi to Apple, A Journey of Adventures, Ideas, and the Future* (1987) contains some interesting observations about PepsiCo by an executive. Alfred P. Sloan, Jr., *My Years with General Motors* (1963) may be the most important autobiography ever written by an American business executive. For a history of public relations, see my *Keeping the Corporate Image: Public Relations and Business, 1900–1950* (1979).

WEALTH AND POVERTY

James T. Patterson

When Alexis de Tocqueville visited the United States during the 1830s, he was impressed by the absence of social distinctions among ordinary Americans. "Nothing," he concluded in his *Democracy in America* (1835), "struck me more forcibly than the general equality of condition among the people." Like many other observers of the American scene, Tocqueville perceived not only a general equality but also great opportunity and very prosperous conditions. He was correct: the United States was remarkably free of the twin banes of European life—huge disparities of wealth and widespread destitution. To a degree never before seen on earth, Americans were a people of plenty.

Standards of living at that time should not be romanticized, for they were modest indeed compared to middle-class norms in the twentieth century. Life on the farm and in the small towns throughout the eighteenth and nineteenth centuries involved much hard labor and produced little disposable cash income. Prior to 1863 the vast majority of African Americans were slaves. American Indians, uprooted from their land, suffered greatly from poverty and disease. Small farmers and landless rural workers struggled to make ends meet; many, especially in the postbellum South, fell into sharecropping or tenancy. Periodic busts in the ever-spreading commercial market ruined farmers and townspeople alike. And cities housed a class of visibly impoverished people that shocked contemporaries. As early as 1815 conditions in New York City were so depressed that municipal authorities felt obliged to give public aid to nineteen thousand people, one-fifth of the city's population. The novelist Charles Dickens, visiting the notorious Five Points District of New York City in 1842, wrote in his *American Notes* (1842) that it was "as if the judgment hour were at hand and every obscene grave were giving up its dead."

But to most Americans in the early nineteenth century abundance seemed vast, and poverty not only anomalous but virtually un-American. Egalitarian ideas stemming from the American Revolution—buttressed by widespread participation in the rapidly expanding commercial market—promoted a deeply held popular faith in the existence of equality of opportunity and in the potential to advance in life. This faith persists, despite extraordinary socioeconomic changes, to the present day, and is central to any understanding of America's distinctive approach to the subsequent rise of the problems of poverty and inequality. Most people, Americans have stubbornly believed, could—and should—"make it" by working, and without relying on charity or publicly financed assistance.

Americans have of course made exceptions to this tough-minded approach. Certain small categories of people—widows, orphans, the disabled, the elderly without family—have been considered "deserving" of help. But even for the "deserving," most Americans have agreed, the amount and duration of assistance should depend on what cost-conscious local officials decide to do. Public aid, following Elizabethan poor-law practices brought to colonial America, therefore tended from the beginning of the American experience to be grudging and stingy. Poor people who had not established lengthy local residence—ordinarily several years—who were thought to behave immorally, or who were able to work, rarely received help. They were the "undeserving" poor, and had to shift for themselves.

The plight of the undeserving, increasing numbers of whom were recent immigrants as of the 1840s, evoked cold reactions even from officials concerned with the problem. Robert Hartley, founder at that time of the New York Association for Improving the Condition of the Poor, wasted little sympathy on such people. "They are content to live in filth and disorder with a bare subsistence," he wrote in his annual report of 1851, "provided they can drink, and smoke, and gossip, and enjoy their balls, and wakes, and frolics, without molestation."

The majority of Americans have repeatedly

echoed Hartley's response to the supposedly undeserving poor, even in the otherwise much changed socioeconomic conditions of the United States since that time. More than people in other industrialized nations, Americans have continued to believe strongly in the existence of equality of opportunity and to oppose potentially expensive governmental policies to aid the "undeserving" poor. When they have acted to help the "deserving," it has been with the hope and expectation that these people, too, will soon learn to help themselves. These ideological parameters, rooted in the material abundance of the United States, go far to explain America's subsequent reluctance to mount a national attack on poverty and inequality.

POVERTY AND INEQUALITY AT THE TURN OF THE CENTURY

By the 1870s many sensitive observers were lamenting what they perceived as an increase in poverty and inequality in the United States. This stemmed from rapid industrialization, which opened a widening gap between the earnings of a relatively small number of skilled people who were amply rewarded in the new economy and the lower wages of growing masses of the unskilled. It derived also from sharp increases in immigration, first in the 1840s and 1850s and again after 1880. Historians now doubt that this inequality was increasing much (if at all) prior to the 1860s, but agree that it was becoming both significant and obvious by the 1870s and 1880s. By this time workers and poor farmers were expressing rising class resentments, which erupted in independent political action, a great many strikes, and widespread social unrest. Such writers as Henry George and Edward Bellamy bitterly exposed the disturbing inequality of American life.

Urban and industrial expansion at that time drew millions of people from overseas and from impoverished areas of the countryside into urban factories and the often alien new world of wage labor. In the long run this mass movement to the city drained a good deal of poverty from destitute rural areas, both in the United States and abroad. Industrialization, moreover, gradually generated better health and living conditions, as well as rising per capita income and wealth. Before 1900, however, the greatly expanding supply of urban workers frequently exceeded the demand, creating what Marx called a reserve army of poorly paid laborers. Many worked sixty- to seventy-two-hour weeks in unhealthy and dangerous conditions.

Workers especially dreaded depressions such as the disastrous crisis of the mid-1890s, which caused widespread unemployment. But millions of Americans were insecure even in "good" times. Between 20 and 40 percent of manufacturing laborers were out of work at some point in any year between 1885 and 1900. More than half of these workers were unemployed for four months or more in the year. Unemployment, historians think, was higher in the late nineteenth century than it was (save during the Depression of the 1930s) at most times after 1900.

The result of these changes was a "discovery" of poverty in the late nineteenth century. It was a discovery that concentrated almost single-mindedly on the economic plight and social disorder of *urban* workers, especially the masses of immigrants who poured into the United States between the 1880s and 1914. Jacob Riis, a Danish-born photographer and journalist, was one of many who exposed the dangers that this urban poverty, if left unchecked, held for the stability of American society. His *How the Other Half Lives* (1890), which featured piteous photographs of the poor, estimated that between 20 and 30 percent of New York City residents lived in poverty.

Many others joined Riis in sounding the alarm. Such settlement house workers as Jane Addams, cofounder of Chicago's Hull House (1889), and reformers as Florence Kelley, a leader in the fight for factory inspection and child labor regulation, enlisted young, idealistic, socially conscious reformers in the fight against urban poverty. Most of these activists eschewed moralistic views of the poor, arguing instead that poverty was rooted in structural forces within the economy. As E. B. Andrews, president of Brown University, put it in a magazine article in 1892, "a great many men are poor without the slightest economic demerit. They are people who do the best they can, and always have done so. . . . Yet they are poor, often very poor, never free from fear of want."

Robert Hunter, a former Hull House worker, did more than any other activist to summarize what was known about turn-of-century poverty in his passionately argued book, *Poverty,* published in 1904. Hunter readily conceded that many poor Americans were undeserving. These were "paupers," a "class of people who have lost all self-respect and ambition, who rarely, if ever, work, who are aimless and drifting, who like drink, who have no thought for their children, and who live more or less contentedly on rubbish and alms."

But *poverty,* Hunter insisted, was a "much broader

term than pauperism. Many, many thousand families, who are in no sense paupers, are in poverty. Those who are in poverty may be able to get a bare sustenance, but," he emphasized, "they are not able to obtain *those necessaries which will permit them to maintain a state of physical efficiency*." He added, "a sanitary dwelling, a sufficient supply of food and clothing, all having to do with physical well-being, is the very minimum which the laboring classes can demand." Using this empirical definition of poverty (and setting a minimum standard of $460 a year for a family of five in the North and $300 in the rural South), Hunter estimated that "in fairly prosperous years" there were around 10 million Americans, or nearly one-eighth of the population, in poverty. Most of the poor, he said, were in northern industrial regions, where 6.6 million people, or 20 percent of the population in these areas, were poor.

Having defined, described, and quantified poverty, Hunter went on to warn of its long-range consequences: the rise of a socially dangerous group of long-term poor people—or what later writers were to term an underclass. Poverty, he wrote, "is a culture bed for criminals, paupers, vagrants, and for such diseases as inebriety, insanity, and imbecility." The poor resist their decline, but many will "go to pieces and become drunken, vagrant, criminal, diseased, and suppliant." By then "the degeneracy of the adults infects the children, and the foulest of our social miseries is thus perpetuated from generation to generation." Hunter's metaphors of disease, his worry about a "culture" of poverty, and his fears of intergenerational contagion mirrored concerns that alarmed not only his contemporaries but also many subsequent observers of poverty in the United States.

As even friendly readers pointed out at the time, Hunter's findings were open to dispute. Like many contemporary reformers concerned about urban-immigrant poverty, he underestimated the extent and depth of destitution in rural areas, especially the South, which then as later had the highest incidence of poverty in the United States. Few blacks, 90 percent of whom still lived in the South, had any cash income at all. His minimum standard (later called a poverty line) of $460 for a northern family of five was, many thought, too low. Father John Ryan's *A Living Wage* (1906) was one of many careful studies of the cost of living (then rising steadily) that set the minimum at $600 or higher. Using this definition, Ryan and others estimated that at least 30 million, and maybe as many as 50 million Americans—or 40 to 60 percent of America's population—were "poor" at any given time in those years.

Whatever one's definition of a minimum standard of living at the turn of the century, it was bare indeed by later, more comfortable standards. A family of five earning $600 a year ordinarily lived, whether in the country or the city, in a small, crowded, ramshackle dwelling without central heat, indoor toilet, or running water. It subsisted on nutritionally unsatisfying diets heavy in bread and potatoes. Poor rural people suffered greatly from diseases of poverty such as pellagra and hookworm. City dwellers faced serious threats from contagious diseases, notably tuberculosis. Most urban slums of those years were considerably more crowded and unhealthy than those of recent times. The average height of native-born white Americans, indeed, actually declined between the 1830s and the 1880s—a sign, historians think, of declining nutrition among the poor and working classes.

The use of quantified minimum standards of living marked a notable shift away from most older definitions of poverty, which had blamed it on personal failings rather than on environmental forces. All informed observers of poverty since that time have followed in this tradition of estimating the cost of living for various-sized households, figuring the income and assets of these households, and then determining the number defined as poor. Still, the turn-of-the-century debates over the number of people who were poor reveal a continuing problem involved in looking at poverty over time: definitions of what it means to live below a minimum standard tend to be highly subjective and therefore to reach widely differing estimates of the extent of poverty.

Absolute poverty lines such as those employed by Hunter and Ryan have two other limitations. First, absolute lines are snapshots of the number of people below a line at any given time. They provide a useful numerical measure of incidence at the moment of the snapshot, but they say nothing about the economic status of individuals over longer periods of time. They cannot tell us whether the people who were poor in 1904 were the same people who were poor in 1900 or in 1910. The same limitation applies also to snapshots of income distribution; these, too, may fail to describe the extent of individual social mobility.

Lacking reliable data for that era, we cannot offer precise answers to such questions. But studies since that time have found that while many Americans endure long-term destitution, most people who fall into poverty suffer from such shorter-term problems as illness, layoffs, or the presence of large numbers of young children in the household. Historical studies have also revealed evidence of slow but mostly upward intergenerational occupational mobility of individuals in modern America—30 to 40 percent of the sons of geographically stable blue-collar workers managed to move into middle-class occupations between 1880 and 1930. Many other workers, while remaining in low-status blue-collar occupations, concentrated successfully on acquiring property and sinking roots into reasonably stable, secure communities. Many of these people rose from rags to respectability. For the turn of the century, therefore, it may be inferred that the long-term or intergenerational poor, like later generations of the welfare poor or of the underclasses, were numerically considerable but nonetheless a minority of the poverty population.

While this conclusion provides some grounds for satisfaction, the flip side is that snapshots of absolute poverty (like snapshots of unemployment) considerably undercount the likelihood of an individual ever being poor. This commonsense but often overlooked reality is confirmed in later surveys that underline a central fact about poverty in modern industrial societies: it stems from a very wide variety of sources, including illness, disability, old age, family breakup, death of a breadwinner, technological displacement, and from structural forces in the economy, especially rural stagnation, unemployment, underemployment, and low wages. Together these forces expose a substantial proportion of people to intermittent poverty even during relatively prosperous periods. The proportion so exposed in Hunter's time—when the longer-run economic benefits of industrialization were only beginning to appear—was surely a good deal larger than in most later eras or than snapshots by Hunter and his contemporaries managed to reveal.

Absolute poverty lines also say nothing about the larger distribution of wealth and income, or about what later writers were to call relative poverty. Data concerning such distribution are simply unreliable before 1940, but scholars tend to agree that the sharper inequities that became obvious to contemporaries by the 1870s persisted, sometimes (as in the 1920s) becoming more pronounced, except for temporary changes in a more egalitarian direction during World War II. For every person who has been counted as trying to manage on an income below contemporary definitions of minimum standards of living, there have been at least as many more who have existed on incomes at or barely above the minimum. Many of these people became poor in later snapshots. In 1900, the percentage of Americans who

were relatively poor, or near-poor, or in-and-out-poor, was high indeed.

All this information about living standards, together with the increasingly visible deprivation of the cities, was fundamental to the discovery of poverty and inequality at the turn of the century: both were more obvious then than they had been in the preindustrial era or even in the memories of adults at the time. Indeed, while the distribution of income was probably no worse in 1900 than in 1930, poverty was more widespread around 1900 than at most subsequent periods of American history. According to definitions of minimum standards of living used by contemporaries—definitions that have become considerably less stringent over time to reflect more expansive notions of decent life—scholars have estimated that perhaps 50 percent of Americans were poor at any given time in the depression years of the 1890s, 40 percent or more around 1900, 35 percent or so in 1915, 35 to 45 percent during the Great Depression of the 1930s, 30 percent in the late 1940s, 25 percent in the mid-1950s, and (depending on highly contentious recent definitions) between 6 percent and 15 percent in the late 1960s and early 1970s, and between 10 and 15 percent in the 1980s and early 1990s. If one applies the minimum definitions used in the harsher years of the early 1900s to later periods, the decline in the percentage numbered as poor is more dramatic still. However these data are interpreted, one fact is clear: the turn-of-the-century years were indeed the "bad old days" of the recent past.

WEALTH AND POVERTY, 1900–1929

The majority of American social scientists in the three decades before 1929 were convinced of two things: the average standard of living was improving rapidly, and purposeful human action, combined with the happy potential of the market, could ultimately prevent all but a few vestiges of poverty and economic injustice. The two beliefs, indeed, were related. The economic progress of these years stimulated confidence that equality of economic opportunity still defined American life and that knowledgeable reformers could smooth the ragged edges of social injustice.

With the advantages of hindsight we can see that some of this optimism was misplaced. This was an era, like the late nineteenth century, of pronounced regional disparities in wealth and income, with millions continuing to flee to cities from hard-pressed rural areas. Persistent structural problems plagued workers in certain occupations, notably agriculture, textiles, and mining. Blacks and millions of recent immigrants continued to suffer long-term destitution. Sudden, sharp jolts to prosperity, especially during recessions in 1913–1914 and 1921–1922, shattered the lives of huge numbers of people. More than 3.6 million workers, nearly 10 percent of the work force, lost their jobs during the crash following World War I.

Inequality also persisted. Willford King, using scattered data to estimate the distribution of wealth in 1915, concluded that the richest 2 percent of the population controlled 60 percent of the wealth, the middle classes (33 percent of the population) commanded 35 percent, and the poorest 65 percent of the population had only 5 percent of the wealth. Inequality of income, while considerably less skewed than that of wealth, continued to anger activists on behalf of the underprivileged. Moreover, income inequality probably grew a little after the war: later estimates concluded that the top 5 percent of income recipients between 1921 and 1930 had 30 percent of the national income, and the top 1 percent had 14 percent. At the other end of the scale, the percentages in absolute poverty ranged, according to contemporary definitions of minimum subsistence, between 30 and 35 percent at any given time even during the supposedly prosperous and roaring 1920s.

Hindsight makes it clear that the optimists also exaggerated the extent of change resulting from purposeful human action. Private philanthropy rarely—then or later—focused much effort on the problem of poverty, and corporate benefit plans affected very few workers until after World War II. Recognizing the need for governmental involvement, Progressives demanded public action. Most states by 1920 provided for workmen's compensation and regulation of working conditions affecting women and children in selected trades. A few states set aside modest sums to assist deserving poor mothers (mostly widows) with children. Progressives especially welcomed the advent of federal income taxes, which increased considerably (for the very wealthy) under the need for increased revenue during World War I. In 1917, the richest 1 percent of taxpayers paid 70 percent of the money raised from the tax.

But American social legislation in the predepression years still lagged behind that of many industrializing nations at the time. Germany had established social insurance covering sickness, old age, and widowhood as early as the 1880s, and England introduced unemployment insurance for selected industries before World War I. By contrast, no American state established unemployment insurance before 1932, and only a few provided public money for old-age pensions. Conservatives rewrote the tax laws in the 1920s, ending the progressivity that had existed in 1917. Old values remained strong: poverty, most Americans continued to believe, was something to be combated primarily by individual effort or by private charity. What little public aid there was continued to come mostly from cost-conscious municipalities, not from the central government, and to go to small numbers of the deserving poor.

Many forces combined to inhibit the growth of public welfare in predepression America—and the expansion of it to northern European levels since. One was racial, ethnic, and regional division. The vast size and bewildering cultural pluralism of United States society have always made it hard for Americans to develop much sense of social solidarity or to reach consensus on passage of generous social policies. The United States differs dramatically in this very important respect from smaller, more homogeneous nations such as Sweden and Germany.

Another inhibiting force, especially in those years, was the divided and truncated nature of central government in the United States. The federal system, shunting a range of responsibilities to the state and local levels, reflected popular faith in states' rights and discouraged significant legislative initiatives from Washington. The United States, moreover, lacked a strong, well-trained civil service such as existed in Germany and England. On the contrary, many state and local governments in the United States seemed either woefully inefficient or flagrantly corrupt before 1929: they were hardly the places to entrust the management of public money for the poor or the unemployed. Doubts about state capacity, indeed, continued to be so widespread that many advocates of better social welfare turned to corporations rather than the state in their quest for the generation of benefits.

A third obstacle to social welfare policies was the self-interest of economic elites, notably large farm owners and employers, who benefited from an abundance of cheap labor and who feared that social benefits would discourage the all-important work ethic. These interests dominated local governments, which controlled the allotment of public aid, such as it was. Organized labor, which in Europe posed a sometimes countervailing force, not only remained far too weak in the United States to combat these elites, but tended until the 1930s to resist the spread of federal social policies. Samuel Gompers, head of the American Federation of Labor, considered Congress to be a creature of capital. What the state created it could dominate. Workers, he argued, ought to depend mainly on their unions, especially on strikes and collective bargaining, not on social legislation.

Two other forces were especially important in blocking social legislation in those and later years. One was the power of traditional ideas, including faith in individual effort as the key to progress, and in the market as a mechanism superior to intervention by the state. The second was continuing popular confidence in the availability of economic opportunity. It followed that the government need not do much to help the needy. The years after 1922 seemed especially to be a "New Era" of apparently unending prosperity and economic opportunity. As Herbert Hoover said in accepting the Republican presidential nomination in 1928, "We shall soon, with the help of God, be in sight of the day when poverty will be banished in the nation."

Hoover's view of the predepression years captured the heady spirit of the era. Guarded opinions, though more accurate in hindsight, made little sense to most Americans at the time. Instead, contemporaries celebrated the indisputable evidence of economic growth, which expanded greatly under the stimulus of military spending during World War I and then, in the mid- and late 1920s, under a boom in production of consumer goods such as the automobile. This economic improvement was irregular and unbalanced: substantial gains in productivity were not translated into comparably high increases in real wages. Still, economic progress was considerable over time. Per capita purchasing power rose by more than 20 percent between 1909 and 1929.

This improvement meant that not only the growing middle classes but also regularly employed blue-collar workers could live more comfortable lives. Diets became more varied and nutritious, featuring higher amounts of fruits, vegetables, and dairy products, and the average height of native-born whites rose sharply, passing 1830 levels by the late 1920s. Deaths per capita from epidemic diseases of poverty like tuberculosis decreased dramatically, falling behind diseases of affluence like heart ailments and cancer as leading causes of mortality. The homes of many urban workers acquired central heating, indoor plumbing, and hot water. Electricity, available only to a favored few in 1900, reached perhaps 80 percent of all nonfarm dwellings by 1929. By that time there was one telephone for every 2.5 nonfarm residences in the United States. And an automobile revolution had swept the land. In 1910 there had been 1 car for every 265 people in the country; by 1928 the

figure was 1 for every 6. Millions of working-class families owned automobiles by the eve of the Great Depression.

By any comparative standard this progress was little short of astonishing. In 1928 the distinguished British biochemist J. B. S. Haldane estimated that roughly half the human race was struggling in a state of "partial starvation." Dismal conditions of this sort persisted in parts of the United States at that time, notably among the poorest people, mainly blacks in the rural South, among some recent immigrants, and among American Indians confined to reservations. But many of these people lived in out-of-the-way places, visible to only the most determined of reformers. Many contemporaries agreed with the French observer André Siegfried, whose optimism echoed Tocqueville's a century earlier. America, he wrote in *America Comes of Age* (1927), "has again become a new world. . . . The American people are now creating on a vast scale an entirely new social structure which bears only a superficial resemblance to the European. It may even be a new age."

DEPRESSION AND THE WELFARE STATE: A BREAK WITH THE PAST

The Great Depression of the 1930s hit the United States harder and lasted longer than was the case anyplace else in the world. In the process it prompted lasting changes in attitudes toward the role of government. The welfare state that emerged by the late 1930s was small, involving public programs for social security, work relief, unemployment insurance, and public aid for certain categories of people. But it proved expandable in the years to come. Indeed, events of the 1930s forced a sharp break with the past. As the social worker Josephine Brown put it in 1940, "during the ten years between 1929 and 1939, more progress was made in public welfare and relief than in the three hundred years after this country was first settled."

The dimensions of suffering during the Depression were staggering. To begin with, there were persisting structural problems in the economy. Millions of people and their families continued to depend on the low-wage, insecure jobs they had held before the Depression. An aging population meant growing numbers of people over sixty-five—rising from 6.7 million (5.4 percent of the population) in 1930 to 9 million (6.8 percent) by 1940—who were often the last to be hired and the first to be fired. And there were millions of farmers and farm workers (still about 22 percent of the work force in 1930), miners, migrants, disabled people, poor women, blacks, and other neglected minorities who had been in depression all along. For some of these always varied "old poor," the Depression meant more of the same; for others, such as farmers and farm workers, the 1930s were catastrophic.

The plight of this already needy population, however, received relatively little attention during the 1930s. Contemporaries focused less on poverty than on unemployment, the great tragedy of the era. It is probable that around 13 million people were out of work at the depth of the Depression in 1933. This was approximately 25 percent of the labor force. Other estimates set the figure at 15 million and the number of family members with no breadwinner at three or four times that—or 45 to 60 million people in a population of 125 million. There were 750,000 or so young people entering the job market every year who swelled the numbers of people who wanted work but could not get it. The huge increase in joblessness—and in the numbers who had to accept lower real wages during the era—meant a sharp drop in per capita income, which fell by 28 percent (in constant dollars) between 1929 and 1933.

Although conditions improved slightly in the mid-1930s, a sharp recession descended in 1937–1938, and real per capita income in 1939 was still a little below what it had been in 1929. The number of unemployed at most snapshots in time during 1939 was around 9.5 million, or 17 percent of the work force. They joined the predepression poor to sustain the poverty population at very high levels. Franklin D. Roosevelt's statement in 1937 that "one-third of [the] nation" was "ill-housed, ill-clad, ill-nourished" was by many contemporary definitions conservative. The percentage was probably closer to 40 or 45 percent.

It is true that even high estimates of poverty in the 1930s do not appear exceptionally frightening when placed in comparative or historical perspective. Similarly high percentages of Americans, after all, had been counted as poor in Hunter's time—when to be so categorized meant living on less than many poor people did in the 1930s. And while America's depression was especially deep-seated, the nation still had resources that seemed fantastic to people in other parts of the world. When Russians saw the film *The Grapes of Wrath,* they marveled that the "Okies"—forced off the Plains by drought—had cars. The humorist Will Rogers quipped that the United States was the only nation in the history of the world that went to the poorhouse in an automobile.

But the Depression dragged millions of white working people into destitution, pushing economic deprivation and insecurity into the very center of contemporary thought and politics. It was no longer possible, as it had been for most Americans prior to 1929, to imagine that poverty mainly afflicted blacks, urban immigrants, or other small classes of the supposedly undeserving. Moreover, Americans in the 1930s did not know very much about how the Russians or other poor people lived. Like most people throughout human history, they measured their situation by their own standards and expectations. Although these expectations were modest in the 1930s by comparison to those of the postwar era, they were higher than they had been in Hunter's time, and they had been formed in an age, the 1920s, that had promised perpetual progress. For the millions of newly unemployed and their families, the surprise and shock of the 1930s had an almost elemental force that stunned them at the time and scarred them for the rest of their lives.

The suddenness of the downturn overwhelmed public officials as well. By 1931 private charities had exhausted most of their resources, and advocates of the unemployed were imploring town and state officials for funds. But these authorities, too, lacked the resources—and often the will—to do much for the needy. By 1932 popular demands turned to Washington and the administration of President Hoover. Like most political figures at the time, he did not consider relief and welfare to be federal responsibilities; after all, they never had been. Although he grudgingly approved a congressional appropriation loaning money to states for relief, he adamantly opposed federal grants to individuals in need.

Franklin D. Roosevelt, who took control in March 1933, did not have well-considered answers to the economic crisis. But he was far more flexible than Hoover, and the desperation of the citizenry in early 1933 virtually forced the government to do something. The result was the New Deal, a hodge-podge of relief and reform policies that sought mainly to relieve the insecurity of the new, unemployed poor, rather than to tackle the deep-seated structural sources of poverty. Still, FDR's efforts dramatically expanded the federal responsibility for dealing with economic conditions in the country.

The Roosevelt administration concentrated on relief in 1933 and 1934. Creation of the Federal Emergency Relief Administration (FERA), the Civilian Conservation Corps (CCC), and the Civil Works Administration offered public aid, either in the form of a dole or in work relief, to nearly 30 million people during these years. Total government spending (federal, state, and local) for such purposes reached the sum of $3 billion in 1935, fifteen times the amount spent three years earlier.

Although unprecedentedly liberal, these expenditures still fell far short of meeting the needs of the poor and unemployed. FERA gave families around $25 a month in aid, compared to the $100 deemed by many social workers to be a minimum subsistence at the time. Moreover, Roosevelt and Harry Hopkins, his top relief administrator, soon worried mainly about the long-term psychological consequences of a dole, which FDR in 1934 publicly called a "narcotic." The federal government, he said, "must and shall quit this business of relief." The result was abolition of the dole under FERA and passage in 1935 of the Social Security Act and of legislation setting up a Work Projects Administration (WPA) that committed the New Deal to work relief thereafter. For the next few years the WPA (later named the Works Progress Administration) provided public employment to between 2 and 3 million unemployed Americans (mostly male heads of families) per month. Average wages per recipient were around $55 a month, or $660 per year.

The WPA, the nation's largest experiment in civilian public employment, did much to improve the infrastructure of the United States. Workers on its rolls built or repaired 651,000 miles of roads, 39,000 schools, and more than 400 airfields. Special projects assisted writers, artists, and actors. Recipients of WPA money were deeply grateful to FDR and the government for such aid in time of need. Liberals hailed the effort, demanding mainly that the funding be vastly increased and the coverage extended. A majority of the able-bodied unemployed, they noted, did not manage to get on the rolls.

But the agency aroused increasingly hostile reactions, especially among conservatives. The WPA, they said, was a crass and expensive form of political patronage; it was wasteful and inefficient—a boondoggle for lazy hangers-on; the work, usually manual labor, developed no useful skills and produced little lasting public gain. Worst of all, they said, prolonged existence on public relief was promoting a dangerous ethic of dependency, rewarding the undeserving poor and destroying the entrepreneurial work ethic that had made America great.

A few of relief administrator Hopkins's field agents in the late 1930s came to share this pessimistic view of the effect of long-term relief on people. "Clients," one wrote in a confidential report to Hopkins, "are assuming that the government has a responsibility to provide. The stigma of relief has almost disappeared except among white-collar groups." But only a small minority of relief recipients in the 1930s—those to whom there appeared to be no local alternative to public aid—appeared to develop such expectations from government. Most Americans yearned instead for "real" work in the private sector, often resisting as long as possible the stigma of going on public relief. "I'd rather be dead and buried," one told a relief administrator. Another added, "I would hide my face in the ground and pound the earth." Although millions of needy people had to swallow their pride and accept public benefits of one sort or another in the 1930s—an extraordinary 35 percent of the population lived in households receiving governmental social benefits at one time or another during the decade—most of them jumped at the chance for private employment when good times began to return at last in the 1940s.

Even before then, however, the conservative view of welfare, as public assistance was coming to be called, was powerful politically. As early as 1939 antiwelfare members of Congress, many of them Republicans, succeeded in trimming WPA appropriations. Although the WPA was more useful than they maintained, they prevailed by proclaiming traditional American attitudes: faith in the work ethic, trust in the marketplace, resistance against potentially expensive government social policies. Public employment programs never again commanded much popular support, even in the context of the war on poverty in the 1960s.

Fortunately for later generations of needy Americans, the New Deal managed to establish programs that were more durable than the WPA. One was categorical assistance, included in the landmark Social Security Act of 1935. This was assistance to special categories of poor Americans—indigent people over sixty-five, the blind, and dependent children in needy households headed by women. The legislation provided for federal matching grants to states that appropriated money for such purposes. The programs affirmed the traditional belief that these categories of people were the deserving poor who might properly qualify for modest public support.

The categorical-aid programs fell far short of pleasing liberal advocates of public assistance. To begin with, the categories were exclusive: millions of other poor Americans, including masses of unemployed, underemployed, and low-wage poor, did not qualify. Their only hope was to find a place on the WPA, to get private charity, or to secure so-called general assistance, ill-funded and elusive programs available in some localities. The virtual exclusion of these poor, working-class people, then and later, from public aid has remained a striking feature of the American welfare state.

Most states proved fairly generous in appropriating money for old-age assistance (OAA). But funds for dependent children were scanty, in part because states had small resources to spare and in part because Congress set low-level maximum federal contributions. In 1940 the average grant per family in the Aid to Dependent Children program (ADC) was $32.10 per month, which was approximately one-fourth of the amount then deemed by experts to be a subsistence income for a family of four. Moreover, the size of federal grants depended on the generosity of the participating states. Some of the wealthier states responded quickly, but poorer ones, especially in the South, did not. Grants to recipients varied widely—in 1939 from a low of $8.10 per month per family on ADC in Arkansas to $61.07 in Massachusetts. These variations, too, remained distinctive characteristics of welfare, American style.

Liberals especially lamented the localism enshrined in the categorical-assistance programs. Thanks mainly to conservative amendments imposed by Congress, state and local authorities enjoyed considerable discretion in administering public aid. The result, particularly in management of the ADC program over time, was often hard on applicants. Many states required that recipients live in "suitable homes," a euphemism for white households without illegitimate children. This and similar rules had the intended effect of discriminating against black or immigrant families. Mothers who managed to find paying jobs had the amount of their wages subtracted from grants—or were removed from the relief rolls entirely. This feature, which remained central to the program until 1967 (and again after 1981), raised disincentives to work.

Many states enforced absent-father rules. These denied ADC to families where the father (or any other employable male) was suspected of living in or visiting the mother's home from time to time. Although critics complained that these rules encouraged marital breakup—fathers would leave home so that their children could get aid—conservatives retorted that the regulations were necessary to save money, cut down on fraud, and prevent immoral behavior. The rules necessarily promoted prying by administrators into the personal lives of clients.

In all these ways the categorical-assistance programs reflected historically durable American beliefs and practices: state and local authorities should control relief; costs should be minimal; only the deserving (mostly white) need apply; the able-bodied should work. Many people hoped that the federal role could be cut back or even abolished when and if prosperity returned. Welfare, they imagined, would wither away over time.

To a considerable degree, that happened to the OAA program, which covered the elderly poor who did not qualify for federal old-age insurance: as social security expanded its coverage over time, it significantly reduced the need for OAA. But ADC did not wither away. On the contrary, it provides a classic illustration of the way in which government policies can have unanticipated long-range consequences. Advocates of ADC in the 1930s expected it to supplement already existing but underfunded state programs that aided small numbers of especially deserving single mothers, usually widows. They did not imagine that it would be extended to large numbers of other mothers, notably divorcées or never-married women. But that is what later happened, especially in the hands of liberal administrators in the 1950s and 1960s. By then the program—renamed Aid to Families with Dependent Children (AFDC) because it added a caretaker grant to the parent as well as to the children—began to offer aid to millions of families headed by unmarried or separated women. Such was the unanticipated legacy of categorical assistance in the 1930s.

By far the most important legacy of the New Deal era, however, was not categorical assistance, but rather two other key provisions of the Social Security Act: unemployment compensation and old-age insurance. These programs, like ADC, disappointed many liberals. The unemployment plan was not funded from general revenues, but mainly from taxes on employers. It helped only certain groups of people who had jobs in 1935 or later and were then laid off; it did nothing for most of the unemployed in 1935. The program permitted states considerable leeway in setting standards and initially exempted from coverage some of the neediest groups in American life, such as domestic and agricultural workers. The benefits, which tended to approximate half-pay for up to twenty-six weeks, were smaller relative to wages than those in most other industrialized nations. They varied from state to state, thereby offering firms an incentive to move to low-benefit states. Later, Congress provided federally financed extended benefits in periods of recession, but in the early years of the plan workers who used up their benefits ordinarily had no place to turn for help.

The old-age insurance program, which Americans called social security, also evoked criticisms from liberals at the time. Unlike such plans in other countries, it did not receive funding from national income taxes. Instead, it was financed by regressive payroll taxes (1 percent at first) on both employers and workers. Benefit levels varied, depending mainly on the size of a worker's contributions over time, but remained small until the early 1970s. The old-age insurance plan did not cover people who were sixty-five or older in 1935, and it at first exempted many of the nation's poorest people. Until amended in 1939 it offered only small, lump-sum death benefits to widows or other survivors.

For all its limitations, however, social security gradually developed into far-and-away the biggest of American social programs. Amendments over time not only covered widows and survivors but also raised the benefits and vastly expanded the coverage to almost all elderly Americans with significant work experience by the 1970s. Disability insurance for people over fifty was tacked onto it in 1956 and Medicare, or health insurance for the elderly, in 1965. In 1972 these benefits were "indexed," so as to keep pace with inflation. Thanks to social security, the problem of poverty among the aged, a widespread source of fear and suffering throughout American history, has been much alleviated.

Many circumstances account for the immense growth of social security over the years. One of these was the availability, especially after 1950, of surpluses in the central reserve fund. Another has been the increasingly powerful political voice of the aged, who have high rates of voter participation and manage to mobilize in ways that poor single mothers, for instance, do not. Members of Congress have not dared to cut back the program in any significant ways. Equally important, advocates of social security, including FDR, have shrewdly described it from the start as social insurance, not as welfare. Unlike welfare, it costs the government very little (mostly in administrative expenses). And workers, having contributed payroll taxes, believe they have a right to benefits, just as they may have a right to payments from private insurance. While the insurance analogy is inexact, the point is that Americans believe in it. Moreover, social security is near-universalistic, providing benefits to most people who have worked for a certain amount of time, and inevitably, therefore, offering more to the nonpoor than to the poor. For all these reasons, social security has maintained much broader popular support over the years than have welfare programs such as AFDC or other means-tested schemes that target highly identifiable and easily stigmatized groups of the supposedly undeserving poor.

In evaluating the early welfare state, liberal critics highlight many liabilities. The United States, unlike many other nations, did not establish governmentally supported national health insurance, and it spent relatively little money on public housing. It made no serious effort to promote a more egalitarian distribution of family income (which nonetheless developed slightly during the 1930s, thanks to smaller families and to much reduced immigration). New Deal agricultural policies mainly assisted large prosperous farmers and had the effect of driving ever larger numbers of poor rural residents into the cities. Millions of the nation's neediest people—migrant and low-wage workers, poor women and children, and masses of unemployed who could not get relief—suffered greatly during the 1930s.

The gaps in these programs stemmed from significant forces, among them the perception in that budget-conscious era of real fiscal constraints, fear by policymakers of hostile rulings from a conservative Supreme Court, and the opposition to social welfare from well-entrenched lobbies. After the late 1930s the American Medical Association did much to prevent passage of health insurance, and real-estate interests fought public housing. Historically durable popular attitudes continued to be important: few Americans, Roosevelt included, were eager to support public programs that would cost a lot of money, damage the individual work ethic, elevate blacks or other minorities, or give the undeserving more than short-term emergency aid. Insurance, yes; welfare or public employment, no.

But the positive effects of New Deal programs over time have been important. Once established, social security and unemployment insurance developed increasing political support, and grew steadily. Even categorical assistance proved expandable—another category, Aid to the Permanently and Totally Disabled, was created in 1950. These programs, moreover, helped to shape popular expectations of the state. By the 1960s poor people, like Americans generally, were much more demanding than citizens in the 1930s had ever thought of being.

WEALTH AND POVERTY, 1940–1963

Real per capita GNP grew at an average rate of nearly 3 percent per year in the United States between the early 1940s and mid-1960s, thereby promoting a level of prosperity that staggered the contemporary imagination. The result was not only rising per capita income, which increased (in constant dollars) by nearly 80 percent between 1940 and 1965, but also steadily diminishing percentages of people in absolute poverty, even by the rising definitions of what it meant not to be poor. This was a fantastic era in which rapidly escalating popular expectations—of the meaning of the Good Life, of the future, and of the duties of government—transformed American life.

A number of forces coalesced to produce the growth of these years. The first was the enormous stimulation of governmental defense spending during World War II. Federal expenditures increased more than tenfold between 1939 and 1945, at which time deficit spending as well as government expenditures climbed to record-high percentages (before or since) of gross domestic product. Although low wages continued to afflict many workers, including dramatically increasing numbers of women who were entering the labor force, the wartime years were wonderful economically for millions of people. Unemployment plummeted, overtime pay proliferated, and real income generally increased. Thanks in part to these advances, in part to tax increases (which rose considerably for the wealthy and for the first time affected the middle classes), in part to prolabor policies of the War Labor Relations Board, and in part to unprecedentedly large-scale movement of poor people out of ill-rewarded farm labor into the better-paying (and more unionized) urban-industrial economy, World War II witnessed a substantial move toward greater equality of wages: the bottom gained on the middle, and the middle gained on the top.

No further trend toward a more egalitarian distribution of income characterized the postwar years— for the next three decades the poorest fifth of American families continued to receive between 4 and 5 percent of aggregate national income, while the richest fifth got between 45 and 46 percent. Federal spending, moreover, declined rapidly—by more than two-thirds between 1945 and 1948. But prosperity persisted until the early 1970s. Pent-up wartime savings boosted enormous growth in consumer goods industries, which faced little real competition from the devastated economies of Japan and Western Europe. Cheap oil, which replaced coal as the major source of energy, greatly facilitated profitable enterprise. Generous government benefits to veterans and their families—the GI bill—promoted huge growth in higher education, homebuying, and suburbanization. And the considerable increase in the supply of better-educated people tended to moderate the rise in pay for skilled workers, while other forces, including pressure from labor unions, sustained the price of less skilled labor. The result was the retention into the early 1970s of the more egalitarian wartime wage patterns.

These developments, in turn, stimulated all kinds of economic activity, including residential and commercial construction, car manufacture, trucking, and road and highway building. Increased defense spending during the Korean War provided additional stimulus to growth. A baby boom in the 1940s and 1950s further boosted consumer goods industries. By the mid-1950s the United States, which had 6 percent of the planet's population, made about half of the world's manufactured products. It had 75 percent of the world's automobiles, 60 percent of the telephones, and 30 percent of televisions and radios. By 1960, there were more automobiles in Los Angeles County than in all of South America or Asia. Although unemployment continued to be worrisome, reaching a high of 7.5 percent in the recession of 1958–1959, it ordinarily hovered at around 5 percent, far below the levels of the 1930s.

Standards of living improved markedly amid this prosperity. In 1940 one-third of homes still lacked running water, two-fifths flush toilets, three-fifths central heating, and one-half electric refrigerators. Conditions for rural people, more than one-fourth of the population, were especially uncomfortable. By the 1960s, however, electrification and indoor plumbing were the norm. Diets were much more nutritious, leading to continuing increases in the average stature of native-born Americans. Home ownership reached unprecedented highs: more than 60 percent of heads of households owned homes in the early 1960s. Few societies in world history had ever enjoyed such distribution of property.

The estimated percentage of people in absolute poverty, too, declined during these years, from around 27 percent (41 million people) in 1950 to 22 percent (39 million people) in 1960. Many of the people defined as poor, moreover, lived far better than anyone could have imagined in the 1930s: in Harlan County, Kentucky, one of the nation's poorest areas, 42 percent of homes by 1960 had phones, 67 percent had television, and 59 percent had cars. In a book on American society in the 1950s the economist Harold Vatter concluded, "the remarkable capacity of the United States economy represents the crossing of a great divide in the history of humanity."

Economic growth made possible most of these improvements, but social benefits also expanded in these years. Many of these advances came from contracts negotiated between large employers and strong labor unions, some of whom still placed more faith in contractual benefits than in publicly administered programs. The result by the 1960s was a corporate welfare state featuring a range of private old-age pension plans as well as health-insurance contracts that Americans purchased through such greatly expanding organizations as Blue Cross–Blue Shield. These corporate programs were more important in the United States than in most other Western countries. Moreover, belonging to such plans often prompted divided loyalties: why, workers asked, should they pay higher taxes for public welfare—much of which, it seemed, was going to the undeserving—when they were already contributing hard-earned money for privately negotiated benefits? To advocates of better public services, the rise of corporate welfare was a mixed blessing indeed.

Still, millions of Americans during the postwar years also participated willingly in expanding government-sponsored social services. Only 1.3 million Americans received old-age or survivors insurance in 1940; 14.8 million people did in 1960. Coverage under unemployment insurance was extended to many occupations that had been excluded in the 1930s. ADC supported 700,000 children in 1940; a broadened AFDC aided 3 million mothers and children in 1960. Expansion of these programs by no means led to creation of a generous social safety net in the United States, which continued to lag behind most other Western nations in this respect. But the growth of the welfare state, public as well as corporate, was nonetheless steady over time.

The apparently limitless expansion of the American economy in the postwar years understandably generated not only optimism but complacency. Contemporaries imagined that class distinctions were disappearing, even that public welfare would soon be unnecessary. Convinced of the blessings of affluence, few Americans paid much attention to poverty, and many who did were rhapsodic about what lay ahead. *Fortune* magazine predicted in 1960 that "real poverty" would largely be abolished in the United States by 1969.

Beginning in the late 1950s, however, a few writers began to rediscover poverty. Especially significant was publication in 1962 of *The Other America,* an impassioned exposé of poverty in the United States by the radical social activist Michael Harrington. The hard-core poor, he said, numbered between 40 and 50 million people, most of them "invisible" to unseeing contemporaries. This was 25 percent or more of the population, and numerically as high as in the mid-1930s. Harrington's exposé, and others in the press, helped to touch a popular nerve at the time. Shortly before his death in November 1963, Presi-

dent John F. Kennedy told his advisers to develop programs to help the needy. His successor, Lyndon Johnson, then launched a "war" on poverty in 1964.

Rising interest in poverty spurred contemporary efforts to be more precise about it, resulting—for the first time in American history—in adoption of a generally accepted governmental definition of what it meant to be poor. This was the idea of a poverty line, which was derived from Department of Agriculture estimates of the cost of food for various-sized families. On the assumption that families spent about one-third of their income on food, economists multiplied food costs by three to get figures of minimum costs of living. The poverty line for an urban family of four in 1959, it was concluded, was around $3,000 per year. The line has risen since then, adjusted to take into account the increasing cost of living.

This is how government officials, journalists, and others have ordinarily defined poverty in the United States since that time. In doing so, they have rekindled old debates about the very meaning of the word. On one side of these debates are a number of writers, including many conservatives, who reject any line that measures income alone. The average American in the postwar years, they point out, has personal assets, such as cars, that must be considered in determining the true meaning of wealth or poverty. Economic progress in the United States, they say, has succeeded in minimizing real deprivation, or poverty in any commonsense definition of what that word means in terms of absolute living standards.

Liberals on the other side of the debate agree that absolute definitions of poverty are both crude and arbitrary. Reformers in many other countries, they add, properly scoff at the utility of such lines, arguing instead that measures of income distribution best describe progress (or lack thereof) in a nation's economy. American liberals also think the official line is too low, partly because it fails to come to grips with rising expectations in the culture. By the early 1960s, they point out, even low-income families considered as almost essential all sorts of things—cars, televisions, household conveniences—that they had not owned in the past. They also yearned to have enough money, unavailable at the level of the poverty line, for such basic items as toys and books for children, records, a family pet, or even haircuts, and for such larger needs as funds for emergencies, retirement, college educations, or help for an ill or elderly parent. Many Americans, moreover, had to set aside rising amounts of money for housing, the costs of which exploded after the 1960s. Most people, accordingly, spend a good deal more than two-thirds of their income on basic items other than food. Multiplying food expenditures by three therefore results in poverty lines that are low both from the standpoint of necessary expenditures and from cultural expectations.

Disputes over the nature of the line are of more than academic interest. A low line limits poverty to the poorest of Americans, especially blacks, Indians, Hispanics, and welfare recipients, and promotes the perception that only they are poor. Higher lines would include larger numbers of people who labor full time at low-wage jobs but who, under the lower official definition, may make enough to hover above the line. If the public perceived these kinds of "deserving" people, too, as poor, it would have a better sense of the varied and structural bases of poverty. In that case, some reformers dream, pressure for more liberal policies might ensue.

Americans nonetheless continue to use the official poverty line. This is not because it has much of an effect on public policies: on the contrary, social-welfare programs by themselves bring very few poor Americans up to a poverty-line standard of living. Rather, it is because the official measure, as adjusted to consider changes in the cost of living, provides easily understood snapshots of absolute poverty as it has risen and fallen over time. Widespread use of the lines by the early 1960s was in this sense a significant manifestation of the contemporary rediscovery of poverty and of the ever more quantified efforts to define it.

The rediscovery of poverty, like the discovery in Hunter's time, drew its strength from three somewhat different beliefs that, while hardly new, grew in power during these years. The first was the sense that poverty was rooted in economic forces. Harrington, like Hunter and many others before him, deluged his readers with statistics showing the tenacity of poverty. Although most reviewers of his book thought he exaggerated his case, they agreed that certain groups—blacks, the sick and disabled, the aged, female-headed families, small farmers—were especially susceptible to poverty. Contemporary studies showed that more than 40 percent of blacks, for instance, were poor at the time, compared to around 12 percent of whites. Approximately 43 percent of farm families struggled on incomes below the poverty line, compared to 17 percent of the rest.

Contemporary studies also tended to confirm Harrington's attention to historically important structural causes of poverty, such as low wages: roughly one-third of all poor people at the time lived in households headed by an able-bodied, non-elderly worker who was employed full time during the year. A majority of all poor Americans were sick, disabled, older than sixty-five or younger than eighteen. Disadvantaged in the labor market, many of them needed public support.

The second belief was that there was a rapidly spreading, long-term poverty, as Harrington put it, which threatened to destroy American values. Harrington considered this a new poverty, but others before him, including Hunter, had made the same point. The new poverty, Harrington said, demoralized people, draining them of drive and producing an intergenerational culture of poverty. "To be poor," Harrington wrote, "is not simply to be deprived of the material things of the world. It is to enter a fatal, futile universe, an America within an America, a twisted spirit." Once this sort of destitution takes hold, "it tends to perpetuate itself from generation to generation because of its effect on the children. . . . There is a very real possibility that many, even most, of the children of the poor will become the fathers and mothers of the poor. If that were to take place, then America, for the first time in history, would have a hereditary underclass."

Concern about a culture of poverty affected not only reformers like Harrington, who highlighted the problem in order to promote political action, but also many conservatives, who blamed the culture of poor people, notably of blacks (and white Appalachians), for their lowly standing in society. In doing so all these observers exposed a worrisome fact: some Americans in the 1960s, as in the past, were mired in long-term poverty that they passed on—often with dysfunctional behavioral problems—to succeeding generations. But the vast majority of poor people in the 1960s continued to suffer mainly from structural-economic forces. These, not inherited, puncture-proof cultural disabilities, persisted as the major sources of poverty in the nation.

The third belief supporting the contemporary concern with poverty may have been the strongest: the sense that conditions such as these should not—more important, need not—persist in a society as abundant as the United States. The power of this belief expanded with the growing affluence of the age. It greatly enhanced the confidence of contemporary social scientists, who imagined that society had the cash and the competence to ameliorate, or even abolish, destitution in the United States. In this sense the rediscovery of poverty in the 1960s resembled the discovery of it at the turn of the century: in both eras reformers damned poverty as anomalous and imagined that the nation possessed both the resources and the expertise to do away with it.

President Kennedy, only dimly aware of poverty at the start of his tenure, came to share this concern, and this confidence. Contrary to the arguments of radical scholars like Frances Fox Piven and Richard Cloward, he did not decide in 1963 to attack poverty because he feared a rising tide of social unrest. Although the civil rights movement was escalating at that time, provoking considerable violence among segregationists, it was still predominantly southern, nonviolent, and interracial, and Kennedy was not much worried about the rise of mass unrest in the United States in 1963. On the contrary, he and other policymakers perceived 1963 as a hopeful time of accelerating economic growth for most Americans. Government efforts against poverty in the early 1960s, unlike those against insecurity in the 1930s, were rooted in confident good times, not in the ruck of depression or unrest.

Nor did Kennedy, as Piven and Cloward also maintained, act in order to solidify his political support among the poor, especially blacks. On the contrary, poor people were as divided and as powerless in the early 1960s as ever. Many blacks were disfranchised. Very few observers considered the poor to be a political force. Rather, Kennedy decided to act because he heeded the counsel of people like Walter Heller, who headed his Council of Economic Advisers. Heller was gladdened by economic growth, which had already cut down poverty among people who worked. But he recognized that growth was only very slowly reducing poverty among the poorest of the poor: the elderly, female-headed families, and minorities. A rising economic tide, Heller thought, would not float all boats. Government might. Kennedy, an activist by temperament, finally agreed in late 1963.

WARS ON POVERTY, 1963–1973

Lyndon Johnson was also an activist. During the mid-1930s he had served as Texas administrator of the National Youth Administration, a New Deal welfare program. He believed that government should act to relieve human suffering. Moreover, he was anxious to carry forward Kennedy's programs. When Heller told him about plans to fight poverty, Johnson was enthusiastic. "Push ahead full-tilt on this project," he commanded. Following frenetic planning sessions, he asked Congress for funds to mount a war on poverty.

Rapid congressional approval of Johnson's request, on partisan votes in 1964, resulted in far-and-away the most highly publicized federal effort against poverty since the 1930s. The multipurpose legislation authorized creation of residential Job Corps centers to promote work training, work-study programs for youths in needy families, and Volunteers in Service to America (VISTA), a kind of domestic peace corps. Other, lesser clauses in the legislation authorized loans for farmers and small businessmen. The law also provided federal funding for community action plans, which were supposed to ensure "maximum feasible participation" of the poor in designing local strategies against poverty. To administer many of these programs Johnson created the Office of Economic Opportunity (OEO) and named Sargent Shriver, a Kennedy brother-in-law, to run the agency.

Shriver was enthusiastic and politically adept, but almost from the start he faced serious difficulties. One was funding. Even during its peak between 1964 and 1966 the war-on-poverty programs commanded only around $1 billion a year in federal money, much of which was transferred from other areas of the budget. Liberals complained justifiably that such a sum (which was much less in real dollars than appropriations for WPA in the mid-1930s), could scarcely do much to help a poverty population of 35 million or more at the time.

Reformers complained equally loudly that almost none of the money went directly to the poor. Instead, funds primarily paid educators, bureaucrats, and entrepreneurs who ran the training and community action programs. In this respect the OEO effort differed greatly from the New Deal. Roosevelt and Hopkins, confronted by mass unemployment, had established relief and works programs that funneled government checks into needy households. Johnson and Shriver, by contrast, took a longer-range, more paternalistic view. Poor people, they thought, had to be helped to help themselves. They should get "opportunity," a time-tested Jeffersonian idea, not welfare. One later critic angrily concluded, "the War on Poverty produced a classic instance of the American habit of substituting good intentions for cold, hard cash."

Johnson was open and unapologetic in taking this approach. Despite his involvement in work-relief programs during the 1930s, he resisted the idea of public employment in the 1960s. He considered it both expensive and demoralizing in the long run, and he thought it would create few permanent, meaningful jobs. Like Roosevelt, like most Americans, Johnson had a special horror of large-scale, long-term public-welfare programs. "We are not content," Johnson said, "to accept the endless growth of relief rolls or welfare rolls. We want to offer the forgotten fifth of our people opportunity, not doles." Shriver concurred. "I'm not at all interested in running a hand-out program or a 'something for nothing' program." Shriver repeatedly emphasized that the war on poverty was a "hand up," not a "hand out." It would open up doors to opportunity, not lay down floors for subsistence.

If the OEO had restricted itself to such modest goals, it might have attracted relatively little attention. But it also provoked heated political opposition over its community action programs, which soon sprang up in a thousand American cities. Most of these agencies emphasized the widening of opportunity, often through noncontroversial Head Start and Upward Bound efforts benefiting children. But many of them also financed legal-services programs that defended poor people against local bureaucrats and social workers. And a few supported militant community activists, including civil rights workers, in challenges to city hall.

Some of Shriver's top aides sympathized with such militants. Community action, they thought, was supposed to circumvent the "tired, old bureaucracy" and the "corrupt urban machines." It was intended to involve the maximum feasible participation of the poor. But the majority of warriors against poverty had hoped mainly to stimulate local involvement. They doubted that poverty, which was rooted in national, structural problems, was very susceptible to local solutions. And they neither anticipated nor desired disruptive activity in the cities. Daniel Patrick Moynihan, a designer of the war, later described what was happening as "maximum feasible misunderstanding." Community action proved to have all sorts of unintended consequences.

Established urban leaders reacted with outrage to these consequences. As early as 1965 the mayors of Los Angeles and San Francisco accused OEO of "fostering class struggle." Mayor Richard Daley of Chicago, a power in Democratic national politics, exclaimed that leadership by the poor "would be like telling the fellow who cleans up to be the city editor of a newspaper." In July 1965 the U.S. Conference of Mayors passed a resolution demanding that OEO recognize city hall or existing relief agencies as proper channels for antipoverty money.

By this time Johnson himself was tiring of such disputes, which threatened to undermine his political base in the cities. Where, he asked Shriver, did OEO find so many "kooks and sociologists"? Increasingly absorbed in the agony of Vietnam, he paid less and less attention to OEO. He also came to believe that OEO activists and beneficiaries were among the people inciting riots that broke out in urban ghettos after 1965. Congress, meanwhile, responded to the outrage from the mayors. Beginning in 1965 it gradually stripped OEO of discretionary powers, set up rival bureaucracies (such as the Model Cities program of 1966), and transferred OEO's functions to other existing agencies. OEO was a weak and dying effort well before Johnson left office in 1969.

In retrospect the war on poverty was a mixed blessing. On the one hand, some of its programs, notably Head Start, maintained long-range popular support, even in the Republican administrations of the 1980s and 1990s. This popularity testified to the emphasis that Americans throughout the twentieth century have placed on promoting opportunity among the young. Legal services, while controversial, encouraged a number of successful challenges to restrictive welfare practices, such as state-residency requirements that deprived poor people of assistance. Job-training programs were also controversial: many trainees dropped out; others learned skills that were irrelevant; some who did well would probably have risen in life without the training; a few displaced other workers, thereby enraging the displaced. Many analysts, however, continue to think that carefully coordinated job training, which is widely employed in Germany and some other nations, is modestly cost-effective. Surely, they add, it is often better than welfare alone, which does little to help people help themselves.

Despite some such positive results, the war on poverty—hastily conceived, ill-funded, often ill-administered—was at most a skirmish. Millions of poor people, especially in neglected rural areas, had no contact whatever with a community-action agency. Very few poor people received any money. Worst of all, perhaps, the warriors against poverty aroused large expectations. Give me the tools, Shriver said, and OEO could wipe out destitution in ten years. This was wildly unrealistic. As many critics pointed out, government should avoid whetting popular expectations that cannot be met. For this and other reasons the long-run legacy of the war on poverty—as exemplified by OEO—was to prompt widespread doubts about the competence of liberal policymakers, and about Big Government in general. No social agency of the Johnson years did more to arouse the conservative political revival that flourished in the country after 1966.

This conservative reaction, while understandable, was at the same time one-sided. What it overlooked was that the OEO was but a small part of a much wider campaign against poverty in the 1960s and early 1970s. Johnson, indeed, called for a Great Society to attack destitution at a number of levels. In so doing he placed poverty on the national agenda as had no president before him.

Thanks to commanding congressional majorities, especially in 1965, Johnson achieved passage of an array of social legislation that liberals had been seeking in one form or another for years. This included large-scale federal funding for elementary and secondary education, with most of the aid supposed to go to poor school districts. It also included Medicare, that provided (via payroll taxes) health insurance to the elderly, and Medicaid, a federal-state (and sometimes local) matching-grant program that greatly increased the availability of medical services to the welfare poor. The Johnson administration expanded funding for food stamps and rent supplements, both of which went primarily to the poor. All these programs caused government employment to mushroom. Later estimates concluded that 2 million people, including 850,000 African Americans, got public-sector jobs helping to operate the Great Society. Most of these people were not poor.

The 1960s and early 1970s (including the Nixon years) also witnessed unprecedented growth in existing social programs that dated from the New Deal era. Congress increased social security benefits seven times between 1965 and 1975, and added the automatic cost-of-living feature in 1972. The result by the early 1980s was that the percentage of elderly Americans who were poor was slightly smaller than was the percentage of the population as a whole. Given the historic susceptibility of the elderly to poverty, this was an achievement of extraordinary significance. In 1972 Congress also established Supplemental Security Income, or SSI. This legislation nationalized, indexed, and greatly liberalized the previously federal-state categorical-assistance programs for the needy aged, blind, and disabled. Reformers hailed SSI as a major step toward centralized financing of the American welfare state.

Most remarkable of all was the astonishing growth in these years of AFDC. Johnson did not welcome this development. Neither did the majority of Americans, who denounced AFDC for throwing money at "welfare mothers." Congress refused to nationalize or index AFDC when it created SSI for the aged, blind, and disabled in 1972. AFDC, instead, remained a poorly funded federal-state program, with some of the same old problems, notably wide state-by-state variations, that liberals had always decried.

Nonetheless, AFDC was transformed in the 1960s and early 1970s. The number of people on its rolls leaped from 3.1 million in 1960 to 6.1 million in 1969 to 10.4 million in 1974, at which point the program grew only slightly for the next fifteen years before mushrooming again as a result of the recession of the early 1990s.

This explosion in the 1960s did not stem from any huge change in the numbers of female-headed families which were poor: on the contrary, the number of such families rose only slowly during this prosperous era. Rather, it reflected a liberalization of eligibility and a rise in the percentage of these newly eligible people who were certified for coverage. Most of these families were headed by divorced, separated, or never-married women. For the first time in American history, large numbers of supposedly undeserving poor people were receiving aid from the national government.

Piven, Cloward, and others were to argue that public unrest, notably the urban riots of the mid- and late 1960s, accounted for the willingness of relief officials, scared and anxious to please, to liberalize eligibility and to certify applicants for help. Given the coincidence of all these developments in time, there is a certain surface plausibility to this view. But the rolls began to grow significantly before the riots, which also created angry public backlash against blacks, including welfare recipients, that worked the other way. It is more convincing to see the welfare explosion as the result of two other powerful forces operating in the culture.

The first was a welfare rights movement of the 1960s. The poor of the 1960s, their expectations whetted, were far more demanding than the poor of the 1930s had been. The second was the greater readiness of liberals, including not only legal-services advocates in the communities but also federal AFDC officials themselves, to support such demands by easing eligibility requirements and certifying people as deserving of aid. In 1961 AFDC officials took steps to stop states from rigid application of the suitable-home rules that had helped deny benefits to people. In the same year Congress temporarily approved AFDC-UP (Unemployed Parents), which authorized states to provide matchable money for two-parent families with children, providing neither parent had a job. In 1962 the program became permanent. Although only half the states initially availed themselves of this option, they included many of the bigger ones. The goal of AFDC-UP was to undermine absent-father regulations and to encourage needy two-parent families to stay together.

Both these forces, in turn, owed a good deal to the long-term revolution in expectations that accompanied the extraordinary affluence of postwar America. Well before the 1960s these expectations had broadened cultural definitions of the Good Life, and of minimum subsistence. The prosperity of the 1960s, a period of substantial and uninterrupted economic growth, greatly enhanced these expectations. Prosperity contributed also to the perceived capacity of government to create effective public policies. In a society so affluent it was a relatively simple matter to legislate in order to give poor people a slice of the bigger pie.

The great moral force of the civil rights movement further abetted such expectations. Rights consciousness pervaded significant parts of society, energizing the aged, women, and minority groups to an unprecedented degree. Mass communications, notably television, further intensified such feelings—much more than in the past, deprived people could see for themselves how badly off they were compared to others. Many among the elderly (Gray Panthers) mobilized effective campaigns for better social security benefits. Even poor people began to organize by joining the National Welfare Rights Organization, which lobbied militantly (though briefly and counterproductively) for more generous and humane administration of relief. They also insisted on their right to food stamps, Medicaid, and the other federal programs that proliferated in the mid-1960s.

This transformation of attitudes marked a significant break with previous periods of American history. Reformers of earlier generations, from Hunter to Hopkins, had called for better benefits. But relatively few poor people had had the driving sense of entitlement—and empowerment—to mobilize on their own behalf. Much of this old world passed in the 1960s, when rising numbers of rights-conscious people—poor as well as nonpoor—replaced the older language of "benefits" and "programs" with one of "rights" and "entitlements."

This new language affected social scientists, too, many of whom had come to criticize the hodgepodge of existing public programs aimed at particular segments of the poverty population. In the mid- and late 1960s they began exploring ideas for "income maintenance" to provide a guaranteed minimum standard of living. Some called for passage of a negative income tax, through which poor people would have the right to automatic cash payments through the Internal Revenue Service. The Nixon administration, following advice from Moynihan, advocated in 1969 a Family Assistance Plan that would have guaranteed all families with children a minimum in federal money. Confronted by opposition, Nixon ultimately did not work hard for the plan, and Congress finally rejected it in 1972. But the very fact of its recommendation—by a supposedly conservative Republican administration—testified to the rights consciousness that peaked at the time.

The government social agencies of these years did not always accomplish what they were supposed to do. Not only the OEO but also other Great Society programs encountered criticism, much of it from the Left. Medicare covered only the elderly and, like social security, offered more to the nonpoor than to the poor; it fell well short of providing universal health coverage. Both Medicare and Medicaid lacked controls on costs, which swelled enormously. Only a small amount of federal aid to education reached poor school districts, and that which did failed to promote much improvement: many (not all) urban schools seemed as bad as ever by the 1990s. Well-organized groups, such as the elderly, benefited more than children from the Great Society.

Students of Great Society programs have noted also that equality of opportunity, not greater equality of condition, was the driving ideology behind liberal social policies of the era. Neither Kennedy nor Johnson tried to make the tax structure more progressive—the 1964 tax law lowered top income tax rates from 90 percent to 70 percent—or to alter the distribution of wealth or of income, which did not change during the 1960s and early 1970s. The best-off fifth of households in 1971 received around 44 percent of all household income after taxes; the bottom fifth got around 4 percent. Wealth distribution, as always, was much more skewed.

The persistence of such inequities, which became increasingly obvious in the mass-media age, was galling to many people, especially in the midst of such high expectations. Relative poverty, usually defined as the condition of people whose incomes were 50 percent or more below the national median, remained steady even when absolute poverty declined.

Even so, the 1960s and early 1970s, like the 1940s and 1950s, were for most people a time of significant upward movement in real incomes. The result was the unprecedented amelioration of absolute poverty in the United States. A total of 39 million people, or around 22 percent of the population, was poor by government definition in 1960. By the early 1970s the number had dropped, thanks mainly to improvements in the lives of the poor who worked, to around 25 to 26 million, or between 11 and 12 percent of the population. These percentages were all-time twentieth-century lows. Some optimistic observers, noting that rapidly increasing in-kind (noncash) benefits such as food stamps and Medicaid were not counted officially as personal income, and that many people failed to report some of their income, set the estimates of actual poverty as low as 6 percent of the population by the mid-1970s. "The day of income poverty as a major public issue," one observer commented in 1977, "appears to be past." Other optimists added that even those defined as poor lived fairly well. "If poverty is defined as a lack of basic needs," one said, "it's almost been eliminated."

The main reason for this considerable improvement—as for the longer range improvement of the twentieth century—was overall economic growth, some of it stimulated by defense spending for the Vietnam War. But social programs helped. These grew more dramatically in real terms during these years than during any other comparable period of time. Federal, state, and local government social-welfare expenditures (including social security, unemployment insurance, various forms of public assistance, and medical programs, but not including education) had risen slowly but steadily in the 1950s, from 7.6 percent of GNP in 1952 to 10.6 percent in 1960. They then increased to 12.9 percent in 1967 and to 19 percent in 1973, where they remained, with minor fluctuations, for the next twenty years. The real value of such benefits increased by two-thirds between 1967 and 1978, most of this from social security, Medicare, and Medicaid. By the late 1970s they combined with earnings and other sources of income (alimony, child support, inheritance, savings, gifts) to lift 40 percent of otherwise poor people over the poverty line. When conservatives said of government that "nothing works," they exaggerated, to say the least.

STAGNATION AND THE UNDERCLASS, 1973–1993

A few analysts have insisted that the American economy coped reasonably well from the early 1970s to the early 1990s in the face of varied and sometimes unprecedented stresses. They emphasize the impressive growth in the number of jobs, which increased from 85,846,000 in 1975 to 112,440,000 in 1987, a jump of 31 percent, faster than population growth. These writers correctly have reminded us that no nation was likely to have the especially favorable competitive international conditions that benefited the economy of the United States after 1945, and no postindustrial economy should expect to sustain

the remarkable growth rates that the United States enjoyed during the succeeding twenty-five years.

But relatively few students of the American economy in these years found much cause for self-congratulation. On the contrary, virtually everyone writes a gloomy story. It goes like this. By the late 1960s the reluctance of Johnson and Congress to increase taxes to support the Vietnam War produced inflationary pressures. By the same time other nations, notably Germany and Japan, had shaken off the trauma of World War II and had become strong competitors of the United States in the world economy. Oil-producing countries sharply hiked the price of oil, thereby increasing all prices and the cost of doing business. Baby boomers and women entered the work force in rapidly rising numbers, which drove down wages and threatened to increase unemployment. Immigration swelled considerably—the United States was home to nearly 20 million foreign-born people by 1990, the highest number in American history. Although many of these new arrivals brought needed assets to the American economy, they crowded job markets in some areas, and they added considerably to the number who were poor.

Structural changes in the economy were especially problematic. Employment grew primarily in the service sector, where productivity growth was low and where jobs, many of them filled by women and relatively ill-educated young people, tended to be low-wage. Unemployment rates rose in the 1970s, to 10 percent and more during the recession of 1979–1982. The unexpected combination of inflation and stagnation—stagflation, journalists called it—mystified many economists. All they could do was lament a paramount fact: the American economy, which had grown in real terms by nearly 3 percent per year between 1948 and 1966, increased by only 2 percent per year between 1966 and 1973, and stumbled along at rates averaging 1 percent thereafter. A few years witnessed negative percentages.

This silent depression, as many named it, badly eroded the confidence that had sustained support for social services in the 1960s and early 1970s. These still lagged behind other industrialized nations, all of which raised more taxes and spent more on social policies per capita than did the United States. Advocates of national health insurance—unavailable in only South Africa and the United States among major industrialized countries—labored in vain during these years. More than 35 million Americans, 14 percent of the population, had no health insurance in 1991. Reformers of Medicaid were equally frustrated. It assisted most of the poor on welfare, but was unavailable to most of the much larger population of working poor people in American society. The lack of such provision, and the fact that many service-oriented jobs did not provide health insurance, strengthened disincentives for the welfare poor to work.

Advocates of more centralized AFDC or Medicaid also despaired: both programs continued to depend on varied state regulations and appropriations. The administration of President Ronald Reagan cut back on federal funding for AFDC and food stamps, and replaced the Comprehensive Employment and Training Administration (CETA), a controversial public employment program that had developed in the 1970s, with efforts to stimulate private employment. Federal aid to cities fell by 60 percent during the 1980s. Hard times led states, too, to cut back funding: real AFDC benefits per recipient declined by 30 percent between 1973 and 1992.

Amid such developments it was hardly surprising that the years after 1973 witnessed considerable increases in officially computed absolute poverty. This rose from a low of around 11 to 12 percent of the population in the early 1970s to between 13 and 15 percent in the period since that time. A total of 35.7 million Americans (14.2 percent of the population) were officially defined as poor in snapshots in 1991. (The official line for a family of four at that time was $13,924; median household income for the nation as a whole was $30,126.) Mainly because of considerable increases in housing costs, the percentage of household heads owning their own homes declined in the 1980s, and the numbers of homeless people grew rapidly, to between 1 and 3 million (according to hotly debated estimates) in the early 1990s. Compared to the often terrible poverty that existed elsewhere in the world—estimated to affect 1 billion people in the early 1990s—destitution in the United States was trivial. But absolute poverty afflicted higher percentages of people in the United States than almost anywhere else in the industrialized world, and it was obviously rising. There were nearly 10 million more poor Americans in 1991 than there had been twenty years earlier.

The 1980s, most observers agree, also witnessed a rise in inequality of income, with the top 20 percent of earners receiving 46.5 percent of all household income in 1991 and the bottom 20 percent receiving 3.8 percent (compared to 44.4 percent and 4.1 percent respectively in 1981). These changes wiped out the egalitarian thrust of the 1940s, returning the distribution of income to the status of 1940. Contrary to the claims of some reformers, this development

was not the result of changes in federal income tax laws during the Reagan years: the share of the total federal income tax burden borne by the rich rose between 1981 and 1988, at which point the wealthiest 5 percent of income earners paid nearly 50 percent of all such taxes. But regressive sales and social security levies (the latter up to 7.65 percent for employers and employees alike by 1990) continued to tighten the budgets of many working people. Especially important as sources of greater income inequality were two structural forces: first, crowding of the work force by masses of women and baby boomers; and second, rising disparities of pay between relatively small numbers of well-educated, skilled people on the one hand and much larger numbers of less well-situated workers on the other. These disparities appear to stem primarily from technological changes and stiffer international competition, both of which place high premium on education and skill.

Median real household income rose slightly in the 1980s, but this improvement ceased in 1991, when the median dropped from $31,203 to $30,126 in 1991 dollars. Moreover, the modest gains of the late 1980s masked considerable changes among subgroups: female-headed families, in particular, continued to fall behind. Household incomes depended increasingly on two or more family members working for pay, often at low-skill jobs that paid less in real terms than they had twenty years earlier. Low wages, indeed, remained major sources of poverty and inequality: in 1990 a total of 14.4 million workers, or 18 percent of the full-time labor force, earned wages at or below the poverty level.

Inequality of wealth (as opposed to income) in the United States greatly alarmed reformers, who bewailed the conspicuous consumption of the very rich in the late 1980s. An IRS–Federal Reserve Bank study in 1992 found that wealth distribution had changed hardly at all between 1962 and 1983, at which point a monied few began to gain considerably. By 1989 the richest 1 percent of Americans possessed 37 percent of the nation's wealth, up from 31 percent in 1983. Their net assets totalled $5.7 trillion, more than the $4.8 trillion held by the bottom 90 percent of people. The distribution of wealth, economists believed, was more highly skewed in the United States than in most other industrial nations.

Careful analysts reply correctly that gloomy snapshots such as these tend to understate the continuing potential for the socioeconomic mobility of individuals in the United States. Almost 50 percent of individuals (aged twenty-five to fifty-four) living in families in the bottom 20 percent of income earners in both 1967 and in 1977, they point out, had moved to a higher quintile ten years later. Approximately half of the people in the top quintile in each of these years had fallen into a lower one a decade later. More than two-thirds of those who began in the middle 20 percent had moved either up or down in ten years. Total income of relatively poor individuals (those in the bottom 20 percent in 1967 or 1977) grew considerably during each decade—by 72 percent (in 1991 dollars) between 1967 and 1976 and by 77 percent between 1977 and 1986. The income of the richest 20 percent of individuals at the start of each decade, by contrast, increased by only 5 percent and 6 percent respectively during these same ten-year periods.

Other analysts, however, draw less happy inferences from these data. Some of the very rich, they concede, lost place over time—where else could they go?—but few fell far, and roughly 50 percent held their standing, just as 50 percent of the poor held theirs. The poor who gained were mostly young people who had nowhere to move but up (ordinarily only a little way) as they grew older, achieved seniority in work, and received better pay. Moreover, there is no evidence to suggest that the mobility of individuals was better in the 1970s and 1980s than in the past. Given the rising inequality of earnings between skilled and unskilled people, this suggests that the lifetime incomes of Americans entering the labor market in the 1980s and 1990s were likely to become more unequal in the future.

Growing inequality of income, other critics insist, is but the tip of a larger iceberg of social injustice. Relatively poor Americans have had to confront glaring inequities affecting their very standing as citizens—in the management of the draft during the Vietnam War, in the allocation of health care, in the quality of schools. People in many working-class neighborhoods have especially resented the rise of crime and violence in public space near their homes. Scattered evidence suggests that the social classes were moving apart in the 1980s: some studies of geographical mobility in the North in those years indicated rising levels of residential segregation by social class as well as by race.

Reformers in the 1980s and early 1990s were especially discouraged by evidence that supported the concern of Harrington and Heller in the 1960s about poverty afflicting particularly deprived groups, especially minorities. A total of 32.7 percent of African Americans were poor by official definition in 1991, compared to 28.7 percent of Hispanics, 13.8 percent of Asian Americans, and 11.3 percent of whites. Poverty rates among American Indians on reservations was as high as 60 percent. Median family income for black families was around 58 percent of that for white families. The median household wealth for blacks in 1988, at $4,170, was less than one-tenth of that for white households. Male unemployment rates were twice as high for African Americans as they were for whites.

Social scientists correctly ticked off an array of statistics to qualify these pessimistic insights into late-twentieth-century race relations: poverty rates for blacks (as for whites) have been much higher in the past—90 percent in the 1930s, approaching 50 percent as recently as the early 1950s; blacks made unprecedented educational and economic progress after 1945, with their median incomes rising relative to those of whites; the earnings of employed black women by 1990, when controlled for education, approximated those of white women. These writers emphasized also the continuity of stubborn structural forces affecting nonblack, nonurban Americans as of the early 1990s: a majority of poor Americans were non-Hispanic whites; approximately 50 percent of poor Americans still lived in rural, small town, or suburban areas; the states of the old Confederacy continued to have the highest incidence (16 percent in 1991) of poverty. Statistics such as these highlight the persistence of the many and varied structural sources of poverty, notably low wages and underemployment, that blighted the economic progress of the twentieth century.

Still, there was much disturbing evidence that small, angry clusters of central city African Americans remained mired during the 1980s and 1990s in an underclass. Moynihan had warned about this possibility as early as 1965, when he issued *The Negro Family: The Case for National Action,* a report that directed attention to rapidly rising rates of black unemployment and especially of family breakup. In 1965, he noted, 25 percent of black babies being born were illegitimate, and 25 percent of black families were headed by women. Perceiving a "tangle of pathology," he lamented the existence of a "startling increase in welfare dependency."

Moynihan's report provoked cries of outrage from defenders of black traditions and values, who railed at his unflattering depiction of black family life, and neither he nor other writers dared say much about the subject for the next fifteen years. Evidence of trends in the 1980s, however, forced the subject into the open again. And the evidence was striking indeed. As unemployment among young black males exploded, to 40 percent or more in many urban areas, increasing numbers of them were being arrested for crime and drug addiction. By 1990 it was estimated that almost one-fourth of all African American men in their twenties were either in jail, on probation, or on parole. This contrasted to one-sixteenth of young whites. More black males were in jail than in colleges and universities.

Statistics concerning family life among African Americans were even more graphic. The percentage of black families headed by women rose from 17 percent in 1950 to around 50 percent in the early 1990s. Similar percentage increases affected white families—family breakup was a rapidly rising national (and west European) phenomenon. But the percentage of female-headed white families was far lower—growing from 5 percent in 1950 to 16 percent. In this same period the percentage of black births that were out of wedlock increased from 17 to 64 percent, as contrasted to figures for whites, which rose from 2 to 18 percent. One predictable result of such trends was poverty: 68 percent of black children in families headed by women were poor in 1988, as opposed to 17 percent of black children in two-parent families.

These developments underline the important role that demographic changes—as opposed to economic trends alone—can have on poverty and income distribution. If the family structures of 1970 had persisted over the next two decades, the percentage of African American children in poverty would have declined from 40 to 28 percent. Instead, the sharp rise in the percentage of black families headed by women caused the overall poverty rate of black children to rise during those twenty years to roughly 46 percent (as opposed to 16 percent for all white children).

Family changes of this magnitude were historically discontinuous. They appeared to confirm the age-old fears of Hunter, Harrington, and others of an intergenerational culture of poverty. Welfare statistics suggested such a trend. Although the majority of AFDC mothers in the 1980s stayed on the rolls for three consecutive years or less, there was considerable reenrollment, and some 30 percent of new recipients remained for parts of eight consecutive years or more. The statistics regarding African Americans were eye-opening. Roughly 72 percent of all black babies born between 1967 and 1969 had spent some time—usually many years—on AFDC, and the percentages for later cohorts were rising. These numbers reflected the growth of a deeper, longer-lasting dependency than had been the case in the past. The Congressional Budget Office warned in 1985, "the average black child can expect to spend more than 5 years of his life in poverty; the average white child, ten months."

Dramatic as these data are, they, too, have to be seen in a broader historical and comparative perspective. Sociologists such as W. E. B. Du Bois at the turn of the century, E. Franklin Frazier at mid-century, and many others had long lamented the existence of very high levels of unemployment, hard-core poverty, and illegitimacy among African Americans. Thanks in part to population growth, the numbers of African Americans in the urban underclasses of the early 1990s were probably higher than they were in the 1960s. But it is unclear whether the percentages were. Only around 20 percent of the African American poor then lived in such ghettos. Although definitions of the underclasses vary—the term, indeed, is both nebulous and stereotyping—many scholars think that the total number in 1990 was at most 2 million people. This was less than 1 percent of the total population, and less than 6 percent of the total poverty population.

What was worrisome, however, was that the numbers of such people were apparently growing as of the early 1990s. Their anger (along with that of many nonpoor people) was spectacularly revealed in the Los Angeles riots of 1992, which were bloodier than any in the 1960s. The condition of these embittered ghetto residents presents a formidable challenge to American life in the years to come.

All of these problems—stagflation, low productivity growth, gaps in the safety net, growing inequality of wealth and income, increasing poverty, family disorganization, racial division, an angry underclass—provoked often loud and angry debates among advocates of various public policies in the 1980s and early 1990s. Liberals fell to the defensive in many of these debates. In the prosperous, confident 1960s they brought forth ambitious proposals for income maintenance and welfare reform. In the gloomier 1980s and 1990s they fought rear-guard battles against writers (and political leaders) who reminded them that many such programs cost huge amounts of money that was nowhere to be found in the deficit-ridden federal budgets of the era. Meanwhile, other writers deplored the rise of "behavioral deviancy" and welfare dependency. Charles Murray, an articulate conservative, attracted widespread interest in 1985 by arguing in his aptly titled book, *Losing Ground: American Social Policy, 1950–1980,* that welfare encouraged such deviancy and dependency. He advocated abolition of virtually all social programs in the United States.

In fact, writers like Murray exaggerated the supposedly negative effects of welfare by itself. Other studies showed that historically persistent structural problems, especially the prevalence of low-wage labor and of irregular employment, continued to be the major sources of poverty and dependency. These problems, indeed, grew at the same time—in the late 1970s and 1980s—that welfare was being cut back. Still, popular hostility to widespread welfare maintained its deep roots in American thinking. In 1991–1992, a recessionary period, several states sharply reduced allotments for welfare or mandated standards of personal behavior (no more illegitimacy, no truancy) for all who expected to stay on the rolls.

The debates went on, with little consensus in sight. More and more people deplored the costs of welfare, especially AFDC and food stamps, and the dependency that these programs sometimes seemed to foster. Many Americans, extolling the value of work, wanted to limit the amount of time—say, to three years—that parents without preschool children might stay on AFDC, at which point the mother (or father) should be expected to accept training, education, or work. Views such as these lay behind the passage in 1988 of the Family Support Act, which increased federal funding to states for such purposes and called for at least one-fifth of eligible welfare parents to accept such a change by 1995. The act also intensified federal efforts to force fathers to make good on court-mandated child support payments. The law reflected the concern of Moynihan and many others that poverty among children, which rose to 21.8 percent among children under eighteen in 1990, was one of the most frightening realities of modern American domestic life.

Other advocates continued to press for a wide variety of changes in public policies. Many conservatives (and others) sought to diminish the power of governmental bureaucrats through support of regulations conferring enhanced tenant ownership of public housing units and of vouchers that would enhance parental choice of schools and child care. Conservatives also backed legislation offering tax breaks to businesses that agreed to locate in low-income enterprise zones. These ideas, which called for decentralization of the decision-making process, and emphasized greater educational and entrepreneurial opportunity, appealed to time-tested American values. As of the early 1990s they managed to receive a more respectful hearing than had been possible in earlier eras.

Liberals countered with a list of long-held objectives: nationalization and liberalization of AFDC and Medicaid; more financial aid to central-city schools; governmentally supported national health insurance; better federal funding of job training, Head Start, Upward Bound, child care, public housing, food stamps, and work-study; tax-supported grants and loans to the needy for higher education. They campaigned especially for more attention to structural problems that had worsened, especially the plight of the low-wage working poor, who remained largely outside of the categories of federal aid. As of the early 1990s these working Americans qualified for federal earned-income tax credits, and for food stamps, but rarely for Medicaid or other forms of means-tested public aid. Millions earning the minimum wage made less than welfare recipients.

A few liberals, undaunted by substantial public opposition, called for establishment of large-scale public employment programs, like the CCC or the WPA, to provide work experience and restore the national infrastructure, and for more progressive taxes. Other liberals recommended family allowances or larger tax exemptions for poor families with children. And many—liberals and conservatives alike—urged macroeconomic policies to improve the nation's competitive ability and promote economic growth. Everyone yearned for programs that could add to the number of well-paying jobs.

The variety of such proposals underlines two central facts about America's historical experience with poverty and inequality. First, in the 1990s these problems continued to have a wide range of structural sources: no simple legislation promised to abolish poverty or significantly to redistribute wealth. Second, since the 1960s most Americans agreed that government must play some role in combating economic and social problems. The moralism of nineteenth-century American attitudes toward the poor, and the often facile optimism that prevailed in the days of Herbert Hoover, no longer prevailed.

As of the early 1990s, however, the historian is struck less by changes in American thinking about poverty and welfare than by major continuities throughout the twentieth century. Chief among these was the persistence of popular faith, especially strong among politically influential middle-class whites, in the value of hard work, and in the long-run economic opportunities available to those who would make the effort. Government, many Americans continued to think, could help, but it surely did not have all the answers. Social insurance was all right, welfare was not. Poverty, people recognized, had structural roots over which some people—the deserving—had no control. But most of the poor,

Americans still thought, were undeserving. Given the persistence of such views, which survived immense social and ideological changes since the Victorian era, the chances for significant expansion and redirection of federal social policies seemed uncertain at best in the early 1990s.

SEE ALSO Class; Race (both in volume I); Depressions and Recessions: The Business Cycle (in this volume).

BIBLIOGRAPHY

Several books provide broad interpretive surveys of major topics treated in this essay. They include Jeffrey Williamson and Peter Lindert, *American Inequality: A Macroeconomic History* (1980), an authoritative historical account; Jacqueline Jones, *The Dispossessed: America's Underclasses from the Civil War to the Present* (1992), a panoramic and critical survey; Michael Katz, *Poverty and Policy in American History* (1983), which studies the evolution of ideas and policies over two centuries; James Patterson, *America's Struggle against Poverty, 1900–1985* (1986), which deals with attitudes and governmental problems; Frances Fox Piven and Richard Cloward, *Regulating the Poor: The Functions of Public Welfare* (1971), a spirited and controversial left-wing critique of welfare policies; John Witte, *The Politics and Development of the Federal Income Tax* (1985), a solid account of twentieth-century tax policies; and Stephan Thernstrom, *The Other Bostonians: Poverty and Progress in an American Metropolis, 1880–1970* (1973), a valuable treatment of social mobility in modern America.

Comparative approaches include Peter Flora and Arnold Heidenheimer, eds., *The Development of Welfare States in Europe and America* (1981), on social legislation; Mary Furner and Barry Supple, eds., *The State and Economic Knowledge: The American and British Experiences* (1990), which contains thoughtful essays about economic ideas and public action; and Gaston Rimlinger, *Welfare Policy and Industrialization in Europe, America, and Russia* (1971), which highlights policy differences.

Studies that offer thorough coverage of poverty and unemployment in the late nineteenth and early twentieth centuries are Robert Bremner, *From the Depths: The Discovery of Poverty in the United States* (1956), which explores attitudes toward the poor between the early nineteenth century and the 1920s; and Alexander Keyssar, *Out of Work: The First Century of Unemployment in Massachusetts* (1986), a detailed historical reconstruction of the subject during the same years. Key primary sources from these years include Jacob Riis, *How the Other Half Lives* (1890), a classic exposé with photographs that helped open America's eyes to poverty; Robert Hunter, *Poverty* (1904), a well-written study that stressed the structural roots of low income in the industrial system; and John Ryan, *A Living Wage* (1906), an influential study of the cost of living.

Important books that deal with social problems and policies in the early twentieth century include Clarke Chamber, *Seedtime of Reform: American Social Service and Social Action, 1918–1933* (1963), which focuses on reform activity during that period; and William Brock, *Welfare, Democracy, and the New Deal* (1988), which evaluates the Roosevelt administration. Edward Berkowitz, *America's Welfare State from Roosevelt to Reagan* (1991), offers a well-informed survey. Some primary sources provide insight into contemporary thinking in those years. Among the most revealing are Willford King, *The Wealth and Income of the People of the United States* (1915); Abraham Epstein, *Insecurity: A Challenge to America* (1933), a classic account of poverty and policy by a leading reformer; Paul Douglas, *Real Wages in the United States, 1890–1926* (1930), a well-researched and informative study; and *Recent Economic Changes* (1929), the fact-filled report of President Herbert Hoover's Committee on Recent Economic Changes.

Especially helpful in describing and explaining post–World War II trends in the distribution of wealth and income are Frank Levy, *Dollars and Dreams: The Changing American Income Distribution* (1987), a well-written study by an economist; Richard Polenberg, *One Nation Divisible: Class, Race, and Ethnicity in the United States since 1938* (1980), a historian's graceful survey; and Kevin Phillips, *The Politics of Rich and Poor: Wealth and the American Electorate in the Reagan Aftermath* (1990), which bewails rising inequality in the 1980s. Gregory Duncan, *Years of Poverty, Years of Plenty: The Changing Economic Fortunes of American Workers and Families* (1984), reports important data from the University of Michigan Panel

Study of Income Dynamics, a key longitudinal exploration of trends. Two much-acclaimed contemporary books are John Galbraith, *The Affluent Society* (1958), which complained of the dearth of public services; and Michael Harrington, *The Other America* (1962), a passionate exposé of poverty.

There is a long shelf of books on welfare and economic policy after 1960. Among the best are Daniel Moynihan, ed., *On Understanding Poverty: Perspectives from the Social Sciences* (1968), a collection of excellent articles; Henry Aaron, *Politics and the Professors: The Great Society in Perspective* (1978), a shrewd assessment of policies of the 1960s and 1970s; and Sheldon Danziger and Daniel Weinberg, eds., *Fighting Poverty: What Works and What Doesn't* (1986), which focuses on policy questions as of the mid-1980s. Cathie Martin, *Shifting the Burden: The Struggle over Growth and Corporate Taxation* (1991), analyzes major tax legislation between 1964 and 1986. Charles Murray, *Losing Ground: American Social Policy 1950–1980* (1985), is an influential conservative critique of liberal social programs. David Ellwood, *Poor Support:*

Poverty and the American Family (1988), is a clear, brief account of the subject. Mickey Kaus, *The End of Equality* (1992), offers an earnestly argued brief for reforms to promote greater equality.

The literature concerning recent American race relations and the underclasses is extensive. A balanced and comprehensive source of information is Reynolds Farley and Walter Allen, *The Color Line and the Quality of Life in America* (1987). Ken Auletta, *The Underclass* (1982), aroused public attention to ghetto problems. William Julius Wilson, *The Truly Disadvantaged: The Inner City, the Underclass, and Public Policy* (1987), offers careful description and analysis of urban black poverty. Nicholas Lemann, *The Promised Land: The Great Black Migration and How It Changed America* (1991), tells the story of post–World War II migration of African Americans to Chicago. Christopher Jencks, *Rethinking Social Policy: Race, Poverty, and the Underclass* (1992), is a collection of original and well-informed essays. Michael Katz, ed., *The "Underclass" Debate: Views from History* (1993), contains many scholarly essays.

WORK

Shoshana Zuboff

In twentieth-century America, forms of work entirely new to human experience have been created, struggled over, diffused, and then replaced by even newer forms. This process of invention, decline, and regeneration is as tumultuous at the century's end as it was at its beginning. It has been a drama that pits ancient dilemmas against profound technological development and discontinuity; a century that triumphed over so much toil, even as it continued to lurch and weave in a perennial engagement with "the labor problem." It is an American century that broke faith with five-thousand-year-old agrarian rhythms in order to invent a new world limited only by the human imagination.

The story of work in twentieth-century America has also been the story of the worker's body, engaged in the rigors and disciplines of the new factory, and too often broken on the rack of machine power and speed. But as the century progressed, a tendency toward the abstraction of work increasingly saved the worker's body from the suffering and depletion to which it had always been subjected. This came about in part through higher levels of automation that marginalized the worker from the physical aspects of work. It also reflects a more general shift in employment that absorbed more of the laboring population in white-collar, knowledge-oriented activities, whose demands on the body (with some important exceptions associated with clerical work) have tended to be of a very different nature. Indeed, the twentieth century is the first in human history in which the majority of a working population is exempt from the excesses of physical exertion and sacrifice that had always been work's implacable companion.

In considering a century's experience of work, we must sacrifice a certain amount of nuance and complexity in favor of broad strokes and generalizations. This essay focuses on the principal technological and organizational developments that have shaped the nature of work for three broadly defined groups—blue-collar workers, clerical and office workers, and the upper echelons of the white-collar work force, particularly managers and executives.

THE INVENTION OF MODERN WORK, 1900–1929

Even those of us who see ourselves as the martyrs of future shock must strain to imagine the tumult, dislocation, and sheer volume of change that overwhelmed the first decades of this century. The year 1900 belonged to the classic period of American rural life, but that condition was not to last much longer. In the forty years from 1880 to 1920, the urban growth rate was double that of the previous eighty years. In 1800, only 6 percent of the population lived in urban communities of more than 2,500 people. By 1880 that figure was 28 percent, by 1900 40 percent, and by 1920 more than 50 percent.

The move from country to city implied immense changes in the nature and circumstances of work. For many it signaled a shift from self-employment to wage-earning status in one of the many new manufacturing establishments of that time. Between 1880 and 1920 the number of wage-earning employees in manufacturing grew from 2.7 to 8.5 million.

During the period from 1880 to 1900 alone, the average plant size doubled in eleven of the sixteen largest industries, and the volume of industrial production more than doubled, as did the number of industrial workers and manufacturing plants. The aggregate annual value of all manufactured goods almost tripled. In the steel industry, production increased from 1.4 to 11 million tons annually, surpassing that of the United Kingdom and establishing the United States as the world's largest supplier of iron and steel. Between 1860 and 1920, the U.S. population a little more than tripled, but the volume of manufactured goods increased about thirteenfold. Indeed, the United States was first in the world in industrial production by 1890, with double the output of Germany, its closest rival, by 1910. All this in a country where the industrial economy had only begun to emerge a mere fifty years earlier. Consider the inventions introduced to the human landscape in the decades around the turn of the century—the electric light, telephone, automobile, airplane, typewriter, linotype, phonograph, cash register, air brake, and refrigerated car—to name only some of the most prominent.

But this magnificence was shot through with misery. Here was the amazing wealth of the Gilded Age barons whose homes and feasts were legendary. Here was the comfortable prosperity of a newly emerging urban middle class. But over there was the poverty of millions of new immigrant workers, crowded into the tenements of America's new urban centers: men, women, and children seeking work daily in the sweatshops, slaughterhouses, and factories, glad to earn a dollar a day and frequently much less, often living in filth, short on food and medical care, without insurance or any form of security.

Modern work was invented in the manufacturing enterprises and offices of the new industrial colossus during these first years of the twentieth century. Most of the characteristics that we associate with modern organizations—scale, systems of administration, labor discipline, job specialization, standardization, simplification of tasks, the wage system, the division of white- and blue-collar work, centralization of control, professional management hierarchies, the value of efficiency, and mass production—were the innovations of this period.

The Rise of Mass Production and Scientific Management. The definitive standard for the twentieth-century workplace was set by the modern factory, with its exotic conditions and peculiar human demands. What was this new work of making things? What did it mean for the worker's body? How did labor-management clashes over interests and control set the stage for new relationships in the decades to come?

Despite the change of the nineteenth century, most scholars agree that the workshop of 1800 and the small factory of 1880 differed more in degree than in kind. In the pre-1880 factory, the operation of the plant was still in the hands of foremen and skilled workers and, with the exception of the mill towns known for their size and mechanization, the factory remained a collection of small craft shops. Home and community, farm and workshop still dominated the nineteenth-century economy. Most people used goods that they themselves or one of their neighbors had made. They ate food they had grown or that had been produced by local farmers.

Work remained rooted in producing the daily necessities of life, as it had been throughout human history. By the late nineteenth century, however, nationwide transportation and communication systems were creating a mass market, stimulating consumption and economic growth. The historian Alfred Chandler has documented the ways in which new machinery, production processes, and organizational innovations were required to dramatically increase manufacturing throughput and therefore permit a small work force to produce an immense output.

The first casualty of the new methods of mass production was the integrity and scope of craftwork. Craft know-how represented long years of apprenticeship and experiential learning involving activities that were often physically punishing. Workers endured exhaustion and risk, because only by using their bodies in that way could they achieve the precious skills that would be the ultimate source of their authority, power, and autonomy. Suffering and skill were inextricably linked, thus framing a recurring ambivalence toward "labor-saving" technology.

For example, ironmaking was an industry that depended upon combinations of skill and strength. New technology utilizing steam power to pound and roll metal together, and new puddling furnaces based on chemical reactions rather than mechanical action, had made the production process cheaper and had increased output. These innovations were not entirely labor-saving, however. In many cases they required new skills, even as they increased the physical demands of work. As the historian Raphael Samuel observed,

> The puddler, who had the key role in the new process, was given a task that was simultaneously highly skilled and exhausting, turning a viscous mass of liquid into metal. He worked in conditions of tremendous heat, violently agitating the metal as it boiled, rabbling it from side to side in the furnace, and then gathering it at the end of a rod while the molten liquid thickened. . . . The men had to relieve each other every few minutes, so great was the exertion and so intense was the heat, but even so it was said that every ounce of excess fat was drained from them. . . . Few puddlers, it was said, lived beyond the age of 50.

In 1911 an observer of the American steel industry tried to convey the notion that skilled work did not imply diminished physical exertion: "New skills, like the puddler's, the catcher's, or the machinist's included very heavy manual work. As one worker speaking about working in a steel mill declared: 'Hard! I guess it's hard. I lost forty pounds the first three months I came into the business. It sweats the life out of man!' "

The work of skilled craftspeople relied upon a special sort of knowledge, one that had always defined the activity of making things. It was knowledge that accrues to the sentient body in the course of its activity; knowledge inscribed in the laboring body—in hands, fingertips, wrists, feet, nose, eyes, ears, skin, muscles, shoulders, arms, and legs—as surely as it was inscribed in the brain. It was knowledge filled with intimate detail of materials and ambience—the color and consistency of metal as it was thrust into a blazing fire, the smooth finish of the clay as it gave up its moisture, the supple feel of the leather as it was beaten and stretched, the strength and delicacy of glass as it was filled with human breath. These details were known, though in the practical action of production work they were rarely made explicit. Few of those who had such knowledge would have been able to explain, rationalize, or articulate it. Skills were learned through observation, imitation, and action more than they were taught, reflected upon, or verbalized. As James J. Davis, later to become Warren Harding's secretary of labor, told John Fitch, author of a 1911 study of steelworkers, he had learned the skill of puddling iron by working as his father's helper in a Pennsylvania foundry: "None of us ever went to school and learned the chemistry of it from a book. . . . We learned the trick by doing it, standing with our faces in the scorching heat while our hand puddled the metal in its glaring bath."

Effort may have signaled sacrifice and self-protection, but it was also the occasion and context for the development of this intimate, robust, detailed, and implicit knowledge. Such knowledge formed the basis of the worker's bargaining power as well as what the historian David Montgomery has called the "functional autonomy" of the craftsperson. Their autonomy was derived through decades of sustained physical involvement during which the knowledge of each craft was systematized, not in explicit rules, but in the course of practical action. It is appropriate that such knowledge be referred to as "know-how," for it was derived from and displayed in action, and meant knowing how to do, to make, to act on.

The craftworker's know-how was also an important source of social integration. The foreman was typically a worker who had turned his experience into superior competence. He achieved his position by virtue of technical skill, and such opportunities were a source of real mobility for an ambitious worker. The fact that workers were required to "use up" their bodies kept them distinct from those who employed them, but the skills mastered in physical activity provided an opportunity for independence, mobility, and ambition.

In the new factories, the number of jobs requiring skilled workers was sharply reduced, though not entirely eliminated, as engineers and efficiency experts designed machinery and specified more minute divisions of labor. Shoemakers became factory machine operators in forty subdivided tasks—beaters, binders, bottomers, crimpers, dressers, and so on. Many other skilled crafts fell to new machinery and the increasing subdivision of labor. The historian Daniel Rodgers quotes a New York City machinist complaining of the breakdown of skill in his trade: "[Ten years earlier,] the machinist had considered himself a little above the average working man. . . . but today he recognizes the fact that he is simply the same as any other ordinary laborer." Although the range of craft jobs was narrowed, a new class of semi-skilled jobs was created, opening up employment opportunities to the vast ranks of unskilled immigrants, farm workers, and laborers.

The man who emerged as the chief symbol of this rationalization of the labor process was Frederick Winslow Taylor, with his philosophy and methods of "scientific management." His agenda was to increase productivity by streamlining and rationalizing factory operations. Reflecting and refining the broad movement toward "systematic" management that had begun in the late nineteenth century, Taylor advocated sweeping reforms that would substitute precise methods, information, and procedures for the frequently chaotic and tradition-bound rules of thumb that had guided factory management. His emphasis was on time-study, rationalization of task execution, and the differential piece rate, and these were the innovations most often adopted by the large manufacturers. But his system also entailed more extensive reforms, including new standardized methods of cost-accounting, production planning, and a system of "functional" foremanship.

To achieve efficiency, Taylor believed, it would be necessary to penetrate the labor process and force it to yield up its secrets. In order that effort be rationalized, the worker's skills had to be made explicit. In many cases, workers' perceptions of their own interests prevented them from articulating their know-how, but there was yet another involuntary barrier. These skills did not easily yield themselves to explication; they were embedded in the ways of the body, in the knacks and know-how of the craftworker.

Proponents of scientific management claimed

that observing and explicating workers' activity was nothing less than scientific research. Their goal was to slice to the core of an action, preserving what was necessary and discarding the rest as the sedimentation of tradition or, worse, artifice spawned by laziness. Taylor's disciples were driven by a vision of truth that would place managerial control on a footing of absolute objectivity, impervious to the commotion of class conflict or the stench of sweating bodies. The principal method of acquiring such knowledge was the time-study and, later, with the influence of Frank Gilbreth, the time-and-motion study. Here, "expert" observations of worker performance made it possible to translate actions into units of time and reconstruct them more efficiently.

The data from the time-study sheets became the possession of management and helped to fuel an explosion in the ranks of those who would measure, analyze, plan, report, issue orders, and monitor the various aspects of the production process. Armed with such data, planners, time-study experts, and production specialists (frequently organized as a staff group for the plant manager) became responsible for analyzing and organizing work tasks, controlling and monitoring their execution, coordinating functions, managing the flow of materials, and keeping records.

Taylor despised wasted effort at work, whether it resulted from deliberate self-protection or from ignorance. His single-minded devotion to the purification of effort gave rise to a set of practices that, whether adopted in whole or in part, transformed the nineteenth-century factory into the modern mass production facility. The essential logic of his approach followed three steps. First, the implicit knowledge of the worker was gathered and analyzed through observation and measurement. Second, these data, combined with other systematic information regarding tools and materials, laid the foundation for a new division of labor within the factory. It became possible to separate planning from task execution, to increase the fragmentation and thus the simplicity of production jobs, and so to minimize the amount of skill and training time associated with efficient operations. Third, the new system required a variety of specific control mechanisms to ensure the regularity and intensity of effort while continuing to supply managers and planners with the data necessary for adjustment and improvement. These mechanisms included the development of incentive payment schemes, monitoring systems, and standard operating procedures.

Taylorism meant that the body as the source of skill was to be the object of inquiry in order that the body as the source of effort could become the object of more exacting control. Once explicated, the worker's know-how was expropriated to the ranks of management, whose prerogative it became to reorganize that knowledge according to its own needs and motives. The growth of the management hierarchy depended in part upon this transfer of knowledge from the private sentience of the worker's active body to the systematic lists, flowcharts, and measurements of the planner's office. In 1912 a prominent naval engineer writing in the *Journal of the American Society of Naval Engineers* listed the seven laws of scientific management. His first law, from which all others followed, stated that "it is necessary in any activity to have complete knowledge of what is to be done and to prepare instructions as to what is to be done before the work is started. . . . [T]he laborer has only to follow direction. He need not stop to think what his past experience in similar cases has been."

Firms varied widely in the degree to which they adopted scientific management. Daniel Nelson's careful study has shown that significant aspects of Taylor's program were most frequently implemented by large firms in which parts of the operation were characterized by mass production techniques. These firms, while numbering perhaps only in the hundreds, employed hundreds of thousands of people and created the template for what would become the standard operating procedures of the large corporate enterprise.

In these operations, systematic analyses of production tasks and related administrative functions were developed. This information in turn underlies a dramatic expansion in the numbers of middle managers (many of whom had been trained as production specialists) as well as in the scope of their functions. Managing this new explicit knowledge base became an important part of the new middle manager's role. Scientific management argued that rigorous understanding, the stuff of formal education and specialized training, had to be applied to the know-how of the worker if production were to become maximally efficient and, therefore, maximally profitable.

Men like Taylor and Gilbreth, who were firmly committed to raising the total level of worker output by easing the arduousness of physical tasks, looked both to new equipment and to new principles of work organization in order to accomplish their goal. For example, after a meticulous study of bricklaying, Gilbreth introduced an adjustable scaffold for piling up bricks. His invention eliminated the worker's bending over and lifting the weight of his body "a thousand times a day," and increased a worker's output from 1,000 to 2,700 bricks daily. Gilbreth claimed that workers typically responded to his innovations with gratitude, as their jobs were made easier. The complexity of workers' responses to scientific management had much to do with the dilemmas created by the body's dual role in production. As rationalization depleted the worker's skill base, or eliminated opportunities to further develop skills, there were reactions of loss and threat. Yet where rationalization offered less strenuous ways to accomplish physical tasks while improving tools, working conditions, and wages, there is evidence to suggest that many workers who were at first suspicious accepted and even welcomed the innovations of Gilbreth, if not Taylor.

Taylor believed that the transcendent logic of science, together with easier work and better, more fairly determined wages, could integrate the worker into the organization and inspire a zest for production. He also believed it was necessary to share the fruits of such productivity increases and saw the differential piece-rate system, a central tenet of scientific management, as a method of uniting workers and managers in a bond of common interest. But incentive wages are devilishly hard to administer, and all too often managers attracted to differential wage schemes succumbed to shortcuts that promised fast gains. Managers would frequently reduce piece-rate wages as workers learned to meet the standards. This led to the complaints of overwork with which unions relentlessly dogged proponents of Taylorism.

Effort was thus purified—stripped of waste—but not always eased; and resistance to scientific management harkened back to the age-old issue of the intensity and degree of physical exertion to which the body should be subject. As long as effort was organized by the traditional practices of a craft, it could be experienced as within one's own control. Stripped of this context, demands for greater effort only intensified the desire for self-protection, and tended to amplify the divergence of interests between management and workers. Scientific management diminished the mutual dependence of the traditional employer-employee relationship, promoting the maximum interchangeability of personnel together with the minimum reliance on their availability, ability, or motivation.

The erosion of craft by the new machines and methods of mass production was accompanied by a dramatic increase in the size of the manufacturing enterprise. For example, in the 1850s the Baldwin locomotive works, with its 600 employees, had been a giant among factories. By 1880, there were 3,000 hands at Baldwin, and 8,000 by 1900. The McCor-

mick Reaper Plant in Chicago grew from 150 employees in 1850 to 4,000 in 1900, and 15,000 in 1916. Whereas in 1870 only a handful of factories employed more than 500 workers, by 1900 there were 1,063 factories with 500–1,000 employees, 443 with more than 1,000 wage earners, and 70 with more than 2,000. By this time iron and steel plants had overtaken textile mills as the largest employers, with the three largest steel works boasting nearly 10,000 employees each. A decade later their size was rivaled by the growing auto industry. According to Daniel Nelson, the Packard auto plant employed 4,640 workers in 1910 and the Buick factory employed about 4,000. Ford's Highland Park plant grew from 13,000 employees in 1914 to 33,000 in 1916 and 42,000 in 1924, when Ford's River Rouge plant boasted 68,000 workers.

These numbers are suggestive of the marked and rapid expansion of the manufacturing sector during the period. In 1880 there were approximately 2.7 million wage earners in manufacturing, in 1900 there were 4.5 million and by 1920 about 8.4 million. While smaller workshops persisted, they employed an increasingly lower proportion of the workforce, such that by 1919 in the northern states, three-fourths of all wage earners in manufacturing worked in factories of more than 100, and 30 percent in giant enterprises of more than 1,000.

Thus in the first decades of the twentieth century the work of making things had been redefined for most manufacturing employees. For the craftworker whose bodily effort had always signified an investment in precious skills, this link was often severed. The new work required a constant but more circumscribed exertion without the opportunity to develop the special know-how that had served as a source of unique power and autonomy. Factories tended to be dark and dirty, with few provisions for washing or taking meals. In most northern states the typical work day was ten to twelve hours, six days a week, and in many southern states it was even worse. As tasks were speeded up and made interdependent with ever more powerful machinery, accident rates appear to have soared. The economist John R. Commons and his associates concluded that accident rates reached an all time high between 1903 and 1907. Other studies pointed to power machinery as the most frequent cause of accidents. The most hazardous of all industries were iron and steel. In 1909–1910 nearly one-quarter of the full-time workers in 155 plants suffered some type of injury, and according to the historian Herbert Gutman, nearly 25 percent of the recent immigrants employed at the Carnegie South Works were killed or injured each year between 1907 and 1910—3,723 in all.

Workers' Responses to New Production Conditions   The task of factory supervision was now to extract the maximum effort from the work force without, in most instances, being able to offer the rewards that had been associated with the accumulation of skill. Moreover, employers were now faced with successive waves of immigrant labor, primarily southern and eastern Europeans, as well as rural migrants including Appalachian whites and southern blacks. At the turn of the century foreign-born workers represented over half of the manufacturing labor force. The majority of these were without advanced skills and willing to do any job to make their "stake" and improve their family's lot. Many planned to return home when they had made enough money to buy some land or pay off debts. Yet despite this eagerness for wages, their preindustrial work habits were an ever present challenge to manufacturers, foremen, and engineers.

Until the 1880s the management of production was left to skilled workers and their foremen. Many craftworkers were organized into trade unions that had united to form the American Federation of Labor (AFL) in 1886. As most foremen had risen from the ranks of skilled labor, they shared common knowledge of the technical aspects of production as well as the implicit social contract that defined the employment relationships. For example, the International Typographical Union exercised almost complete control over much of shop life, including hiring and firing, discipline, apprenticeships, distribution of overtime, the filling of temporary vacancies, and the exclusion of nonunionists from the composing room during work hours. Sometimes craftworkers acted as independent contractors inside a plant, agreeing to deliver to the firm a certain quantity for a certain price but otherwise exercising effective control over production within the factory or shop. Prior to the Homestead strike in 1892, which broke their union, craftworkers in the Carnegie steel mills worked in accordance with rules openly limiting production to a set quota and calling for the expulsion of rate busters. One company official complained, "The method of apportioning the work, or regulating the turns, or altering machinery, in short every detail of the great plant was subject to the interference of some busybody representing the Amalgamated Association."

Breaking craft control of production and gaining the freedom to make technological innovations and substitute semi-skilled for craft labor were among the major goals of firms in the last decade of the nineteenth century and first decades of the twentieth. By 1901, the newly created U.S. Steel achieved that goal by forcing a confrontation with the remaining lodges of the Amalgamated Association of Iron, Steel, and Tin Workers, breaking the union, and introducing open shops into all its plants, which employed 168,000 workers. Management wrested control of production from skilled workers and was thus able to accelerate capital investment and the rationalization of work practices.

When mass production and the simplification of tasks opened the doors to unskilled workers and curbed the craft unions' power, many of the foremen's production-related responsibilities were taken over by the newly trained engineers and production specialists. Indeed, one of Taylor's primary objectives was to break the foreman's lack of knowledge about the production process, tasks, and skill requirements. But foremen continued to hold more or less complete responsibility for all other aspects of the employment relationship from hiring to job assignments, wages, and supervision. They were charged with keeping labor costs down, and one way of doing this, particularly when the going wage rate had risen, was the ruthless application of all their supervisory prerogatives to the single goal of extracting the maximum effort from each worker.

The foreman was the "undisputed ruler of his department, gang, crew, or shop." To most workers he was a despot, holding their fates in his hands with little accountability to superiors or procedures for due process. When, in 1912, a congressional committee investigated U.S. Steel, the members attempted to understand just how the foreman operated. They learned that foremen throughout American industry practiced something known as the "driving method," an approach to supervision that combined authoritarian combativeness with physical intimidation in order to extract maximum effort from the worker. The driving method was well suited to work that depended upon the exertion of the human body. The foreman's profanity, threats, and punishments were meant to goad the worker into fear and submission. There were constant exhortations to work harder, work faster, give more. Fear of unemployment was the ultimate factor in enforcing obedience, and foremen fired their workers with alarming frequency, mindful of the need to stimulate submissiveness among those who remained.

The foreman's control extended over every aspect of employment. He hired new hands from the crowds of men, women, and children that gathered at the factory gate. His selections were arbitrary, sometimes based on ethnic stereotypes, the size and apparent strength of a candidate, or were guided by his own network of kin and acquaintances. Eager workers often resorted to bribing the foreman with gifts or money. Foremen assigned workers to their jobs with similar favoritism or bias. The ample supply of workers meant that those that did not work out could simply be replaced. The foreman also had power to set wages—both day and piece rates—often meting out different wages for the same work based on whom he chose to reward and punish.

Workers had many reasons to resist the driving method of supervision and the time-study experts' reorganization of work tasks, but all of them shared the same intent—to set forth an alternative standard for the effort and discipline to which the worker's body should be subject. Where craft unions were strong, they continued to restrict the foreman's authority by setting production standards, maintaining their own shop rules, regulating manning levels and working hours, insisting on seniority as the basis for allocating jobs and promotions, and challenging wage rates. They sought to establish closed shops and regulate the foremen's right to dismiss members. A 1915 government report on the pottery industry summarized relationships between employers, craft union members, and the rest of the unskilled work force: "The union workmen have steadily refused to accede to the manufacturer's demand that a record of their actual hours worked be kept, and the time and earnings of their employees, as they feared that such records would be used to their detriment at the wage scale conference every two years."

While many foremen escaped these formal constraints as the numbers of organized workers in manufacturing was still small (about 6 percent of the total in 1900 and 12 percent in 1912, almost all concentrated in the skilled trades), skilled and unskilled workers nevertheless participated in more informal methods of withholding effort. When employers cut the piece rate, workers responded by only turning out enough to make a living wage. Most important was workers' collaboration to set production rates and pressure those who ignored them. As Daniel Nelson has noted, "There were numerous stories of new employees who were approached by older, presumably wiser, workmen. 'See here, young fellow, you're working too fast. You'll spoil our job for us if you don't go slower.' If a friendly admonition did not have the desired effect and the man was judged a 'rooter' or 'rusher,' social pressure, threats, and even violence might follow."

Traditional sensibilities toward work, suffused with the rhythms of a chatty, sensual, and fun-loving humanity, continued to be articulated well into the century. In 1914, a machinist gained prominence when he debated Taylor and remarked, "We don't want to work as fast as we are able to. We want to work as fast as we think it's comfortable for us to work. We haven't come into existence for the purpose of seeing how great a task we can perform through a lifetime. We are trying to regulate our work so as to make it auxiliary to our lives."

More than a decade later things had not changed much. Stanley Mathewson's report, *Restriction of Output among Unorganized Workers,* written in the late 1920s but not published until 1931, revealed the extent of workers' ability and determination to undermine and resist the inroads of scientific management, particularly wage incentive systems and the time-study. Sometimes they found allies in foremen anxious to demonstrate high efficiency ratings within their departments. He observed

> foremen working at cross purposes with time-study men and showing workers how to make time studies inaccurate; workmen killing time by the hour because the day's "limit" had been reached; men afraid to let the management learn of improved methods which they had discovered for themselves; older workers teaching youngsters to keep secret from the management the amount they could comfortably produce in a day; managements trying first one "wage incentive" plan, then another, in an effort to induce men to do what we believe they really wanted to do in the first place.

Methods of withholding labor varied somewhat from industry to industry and might be modified according to economic conditions, but the underlying spirit was everywhere the same—to protect the body by tempering exertion. Work banking, goldbricking, soldiering—these are the terms that convey the legacy of this clash between two wildly different conceptions of the standard of exertion and discipline to which a body should conform.

Unskilled workers, sometimes in combination with their unionized coworkers, often found no outlet for their voice other than militant activity. There were sporadic but violent strikes in the years before World War I, with militia and police squared off against an immigrant work force. These strikes, while dramatic, were seldom successful. Sometimes they were tragic. More frequently, unskilled workers found that the only truly effective means to express their resistance to factory practices was to quit. Turnover rates during the first decades of the century were astonishingly high, even during periods of significant unemployment. For example, textile mills, meat-packing plants, automobile plants, steel mills, and machine works often showed annual turnover rates of 100 percent. One survey showed that between 1905 and 1917, the majority of industrial workers changed jobs at least once every three years. Between 1907 and 1910, turnover in the woolen industry was between 113 percent and 163 percent. It reached 232 percent in New York City garment shops in 1912 and 252 percent in a sample of Detroit factories in 1916.

With this behavior a new generation of workers joined the many who had gone before them whose agrarian sensibilities bridled at the seemingly unnatural demands of industrial effort. Their quit rates reflected workers' rejection of the new conditions of labor, as well as the increasingly severe pressures by employers and foremen. Many scholars have argued that the introduction of steam power and, later, other forms of costly equipment, did much to consolidate the new behavioral norms. This was because employers, in an effort to fully utilize their capital investment, became more ruthless in their willingness to dismiss workers who did not comply with the regularity of effort required to efficiently exploit the new machinery.

Ultimately the foremen's role over the immediate conditions of work was curbed by employer initiatives in the name of scientific management. Production specialists and middle managers interceded to establish cost controls, rationalize the flow of work, and improve record keeping. In parallel, more firms turned toward a set of progressive management techniques generally referred to as "welfare work" in which personnel specialists took responsibility for managing important aspects of the employment relationship, including hiring and firing, work assignments, and wage rates.

The Ford Motor Company: A Standard for the Century. The single example that best typifies the achievements of mass production, in combination with a new attention to what engineers of the day referred to as "the human element of production," is the Ford Motor Company. Ford eventually became the standard not only for automobile manufacture, but for all large-scale production. Incorporated in 1903 with $28,000 raised from ordinary citizens, it was not until 1913, with the introduction of continuous assembly line production in the new Highland Park factory in Michigan, that the company really began to make history. Auto production was at first representative of most skilled manufacturing. Crafts-

men worked at benches, fitting and assembling parts and components to the motor block. A full day was needed for the assembly of one engine. Assemblers, molders, machinists, and many other skilled craftsmen were assisted by less skilled workers who moved materials, provided tools, and so on.

Henry Ford's single-minded goal was to produce a standard automobile according to uniform procedures that would permit a dramatic decline in unit costs, thus making his Model T accessible to the masses. To this end, he began to mechanize the manufacture and assembly process in earnest. While Ford claimed that he did not employ Taylor's program, the general principles of scientific management guided the work of Ford's managers and engineers. The constant improvement of machines and their substitution for hand work was at the core of Ford's innovations. By 1911 there was a machine for painting wheels that handled six rows at a time, painting, drying, and varnishing 2,000 wheels a day. Another new machine drilled forty-five holes in the cylinder block from four different angles in ninety seconds. Spot welding made it possible for one man with a machine to do the work of eight hand riveters.

The second line of attack involved the minute subdivision of labor and the rigorous separation of planning and execution. In 1912, H. L. Arnold, an industrial journalist, described Ford's cost-cutting methods in terms of three principles: "a broad survey of the field of effort with a wholly free and unfettered mind, the careful examination of existing conditions, and the elimination of every needless muscular movement and expenditure of energy." He concluded that "the minute division of labor, is effective in labor-cost reducing in two ways: first, by making the workman extremely skilled, so that he does his part with no needless motions, and secondly, by training him to perform his operation with the least expenditure of will-power and hence with the least brain fatigue." Ford's engineers subdivided even the simplest of tasks and in doing so achieved dramatic economies. For example, one three-minute operation involved joining pistons and rods, oiling and replacing a pin, inserting and tightening a screw, and installing a cotter pin. The engineers divided the job into four components and doubled the output. Most jobs were reduced to a repetitive motion that could be timed in seconds.

Even before the introduction of the moving assembly line, machines were grouped closely together in proximity to the article being worked on. The chassis moved from station to station, and it was worked on progressively, but the speed of the line was still more or less under the workmen's control. The final and crowning innovation in Ford's manufacturing process was the development of overhead conveyors combined with the operation of a moving assembly line. Even the crude moving lines tested between 1913 and 1914 reduced chassis assembly times by more than 50 percent. When the lines were further refined, chassis assembly time had dropped from twelve and one half hours to one hour and thirty-three minutes. By the end of 1914, the Highland Park plant could produce 1,200 automobiles a day, compared to 100 a day in 1908. By 1923, Ford estimated that 79 percent of all his manufacturing jobs required no more than one week to learn. In 1924, skilled workers were estimated as no more than 5–10 percent of the auto work force, an elite group of toolmakers, draftsmen, and experimental room hands.

Henry Ford wrote the *Encyclopaedia Britannica's* first entry on the subject of mass production, and in it he recognized many of the great themes that have to come to define work in twentieth-century America. First he described the ascendancy of management and the engineering world-view as it gained authority over the design, planning, and administration of production. He explained the elimination of the worst excesses of bodily effort, and the migration of the substantive content of work to the managerial domain: "A cardinal principle of mass production is that hard work in the old physical sense of laborious burden-bearing, is wasteful. The physical load is lifted off men and placed on machines. The recurrent mental load is shifted from men in production to men in designing. . . . Mass production lightens work, but increases its repetitive quality." He pondered debate over the degradation of the skilled craftsman, acknowledging that the scope of traditional craft skills had been narrowed dramatically, but noting that many who would have been consigned to unskilled labor now had the opportunity for jobs of at least a semi-skilled nature. Most important, the significant increase in engineers, managers, clerks, and other white-collar specialists represented a wholly new development in the labor market—a mass demand for knowledge workers. "The craftsmanship of management absorbs the energies of many thousands of men who, without mass production methods, would have no creative opportunity." The phenomenon he thus described was not only a unique historical development, but the foreshadowing of a spectacular century-long trend—the rise of knowledge work on a mass scale, a radical departure from most of what had been work's human history.

In Henry Ford's world, and in the many organizations that would imitate his practices in the decades ahead, complexity and substantive work content shifted from the factory floor to the manager's desk. The jobs that were left behind required neither skill nor excessive strength, but rather a certain attentiveness, alertness, and stamina. Workers complained about the pace of the line, and about their inability to exert any control over it. Ford managers reported that men often broke down mentally and physically from the tension and speed of assembly work.

Ford's workers expressed themselves in a variety of ways, but the most dramatic was the rate at which they simply walked out of the factory never to return. Lateness and absenteeism were endemic. While turnover was a problem throughout the auto industry, at Ford the rates were staggering. At the Packard Motor Company in 1913, the turnover rate was 200 percent, while in the same year at Ford turnover reached 370 percent. In that year, 52,000 workers were hired in order to maintain a workforce of 13,600. A survey conducted during March 1913 showed that of 7,300 who had left that month, 1,276 had been discharged, 870 had formally quit, and the rest, 5,156, had simply walked out.

In October 1913 Ford management launched an extensive program aimed at rationalizing and stabilizing the employment relationship. The program borrowed some innovations from the employment reform movement known as welfare capitalism. For example, it established an employment department that took over the foreman's remaining responsibilities for work force management—hiring, firing, job assignments, wage rates. But its more famous initiative was utterly unique: Ford raised most workers' wages to $5.00 a day, up from $2.50, and decreased daily working time from nine to eight hours. The Ford program was effective in the short run, but by the end of World War I it was clear that labor-management acrimony had been temporarily suppressed but not transformed. The Ford Motor Company and the mass production industries it exemplified would spend another thirty years in a bitter struggle over the conditions of work that were to define industry for the rest of the century.

The Genesis of White-Collar Work and the Executive. At the turn of the century, only 17.6 percent of the economically active U.S. population was engaged in white-collar occupations—management and administration, professional and technical careers, clerical or sales jobs. But since then, these occupations have grown faster than any other categories. Forms of work that were just being invented at the turn of the century now provide gainful employment for a majority of the work force. This story of social invention is also the framework for yet another workplace drama—the migration of women from home to office in unprecedented numbers.

The label "white collar" (adopted by census administrators and sociologists alike) is worthy of reflection. It strikes at something essential about the genesis and meaning of these occupations—namely, the way in which they were seen as counterpoint and contrast to the physical burden of other forms of labor. At the heart of white-collar work was the promise that the body would be protected from the kind of animal effort that turns collars grimy with sweat and soil.

The genesis and evolution of white-collar work is in many ways the precise opposite of the historical path that led from craft to mass production. There we saw complex activities that involved acting-on materials and equipment. In contrast, the crucible of white collar work was the role of the owner-managers and the complex of skills involved in running an enterprise. Their know-how—part intuition, part experience—also depended upon their bodies as the medium for their art. But rather than acting-on materials, these executives used their bodies in the service of acting-with—that is, for communication and interpersonal influence. As the size and complexity of their organizations increased, the owner-managers found themselves hiring people to take on more of their supervisory responsibilities, thus contributing to the growth of middle management. In addition, other aspects of their activities (such as production planning, product development, coordination of sales and distribution, marketing, finance) were carved out and systematized, thus becoming the occasion for the proliferation of staff functions. This process of occupational differentiation was repeated at the plant or regional level, where the general manager's work became the source of additional line and staff roles. Ultimately, it accounted for the origin of modern clerical work, as the most easily rationalized features of jobs at lower managerial levels were carved out, pushed downward, and used to create a wholly new class of simpler tasks.

An important feature of this process at each organizational tier was that the higher-level positions out of which new jobs were carved did not disappear. They were not eliminated or "de-skilled," as in the case of the manufacturing crafts. On the contrary, each of these higher-level positions came more than ever to be viewed as uniquely skilled and valuable. Middle managers, functional specialists, and the earliest clerks were thus directly descended from the executive process. Their jobs incorporated important components of executive work. It was not until the intensive introduction of office machinery and principles of work organization drawn from scientific management that this line of descent was broken. It was then that a new kind of clerical work was invented, work that more closely resembled the laboring body acting on paper and equipment, requiring the regularity of physical effort and perpetual concentration associated with the factory.

The first generation of industrial capitalists were owner-employers whose comprehensive, action-oriented, and undocumented know-how absorbed a wide range of management functions. These owner-managers were engaged in activities ranging from invention to finance to direct supervision of their shops and small factories. Their know-how was wrung from trial-and-error experience during a time when few resources existed for practical training. They steeped themselves in operational detail, personally reviewing reports and production data. Without staff to collect information or formulate advice, planning consisted of little more than a response to perceived needs and opportunities. In fact, the term "management" had little meaning until well into the nineteenth century.

Owner-managers depended on oral communication in a world where written documentation and correspondence were stored in boxes, pigeonholes, and difficult-to-read press books (bound volumes of tissue paper sheets onto which copies of letters had been impressed). Most business enterprises were small enough that orders, instructions, and reports could be given orally. The treasurer of one company in 1887 defended the lack of written documentation in his organization: "We do not think printed rules amount to anything unless there is somebody around constantly to enforce them and if such a person is around printed forms can be dispensed with." Most calculations associated with commercial accounting were done mentally and communicated orally. Many successful merchants and entrepreneurs were well known for the speed of their mental calculations, and many "how-to" books included tricks and shortcuts to aid in rapid mental arithmetic. Owner-managers frequently surrounded themselves with sons, nephews, and cousins—a move that facilitated oral communication through shared meaning and context and eased the pressure for written documentation. The executive process was and still is defined by this core of implicit know-how that depends on the executive's presence, influence, and communication.

But it was the process of carving out those aspects of executive activity most subject to rationalization that underlay the structural articulation of the modern organization.

The management scholar Peter Drucker has railed against owner-managers like Henry Ford and Werner von Siemens precisely because they refused to recognize the necessity of middle management functions, insisting instead on surrounding themselves with "helpers" who were dependent upon the boss's implicit knowledge, directives, and whims. During the 1920s and 1930s, there were earnest interpreters of business practice who, flushed with the success and rational appeal of scientific management, argued strenuously that executive activity should be subjected to the analytic rigors of Taylor's principles. One of these was the social worker turned management consultant Mary Parker Follett. In 1925 she told a conference of personnel administrators in New York City that "the next step business management should take is to organize the body of knowledge on which it should rest. . . . We need executive conferences with carefully worked out methods for comparing experience which has been scientifically recorded, analyzed, and organized." She deplored the idea that executive leadership involved an "intangible capacity" or that executives relied on "hunches" in making decisions. She praised the still-youthful trend toward functional management based upon expert knowledge.

Nevertheless, as late as 1938, Chester Barnard, an executive turned scholar, wrote a lengthy treatise, *The Functions of the Executive,* that eloquently discussed the implicit, experience-based, action quality of executive skills. In a summary description, he wrote: "The process is the sensing of the organization as a whole and the total situation relevant to it. It transcends the capacity of merely intellectual methods, and the techniques of discriminating the factors of the situation. The terms pertinent to it are 'feeling,' 'judgment,' 'sense,' 'proportion,' 'balance,' 'appropriateness.' It is a matter of art rather than science, and is aesthetic rather than logical." Barnard believed that communication was the dominant function of management and, as he put it, "the immediate origin of executive organization."

Thus, the attacks on the executive process launched by disciples of scientific management did not succeed at eliminating its core of art. That does not mean, however, that executive work was not rationalized—it was, but in a manner that was in sharp contrast to the rationalization of the worker's craft. To put it bluntly, workers lost what was best in their jobs, the body as skill in the service of acting-on, while executives lost what was least attractive in their jobs, retaining full enjoyment of the skilled body as an instrument of acting-with.

In this way, during the first two decades of the twentieth century, the combined pressures of mass production, vertical integration, and expanding markets blasted the owner-manager's role into a hundred fragments, each of which materialized in a new tier of management or a new set of specialized staff functions. Now, on the shop floor, there were armies of workers without the skills, information, or authority to manage their own work. In factory and firm offices, meanwhile, there appeared an empire of paper reflecting both the new complexities of the production process and those of the firm's external transactions with ever more complicated supply chains and a geographically dispersed network for sales and distribution.

The growth of the managerial occupation was significant from the very first years of the new century. Between 1900 and 1910 there was a 45 percent increase in this occupational group, as compared to a 37 percent increase in manual workers and a 6 percent increase in farm workers. From 1910 to 1920 those numbers were 14 percent, 19 percent, and −1 percent, and from 1920 to 1930 they were 29 percent, 14 percent, and −9 percent respectively. The new middle managers became the backbone of a new salaried class, distinct from the merchants, tradesmen, and entrepreneurs of the prior century.

By mid-century, managerial hierarchies in U.S. businesses tended to be quite similar as they all participated in an almost universal set of design principles involving span of control, divisionalization, functional specialization, and formal rules and procedures. But historians have recently shown the quite diverse ways in which these managerial bureaucracies developed. For example, Alfred Chandler, Olivier Zunz, and others have looked to the railroads in the late nineteenth century as the prototype for much of the development of middle management in both structure and practice. Zunz's detailed examination of how middle management practice evolved at the Chicago, Burlington and Quincy railroad is generally instructive, as the railroad forged a model of middle management practice, not only for other rail companies but for emerging industrial and retail organizations as well. Mid-level executives sent out to supervise the railroads' regional expansion were left on their own to invent what they required. They hired clerks and workers and developed systematic procedures for handling the work of their departments. They determined pay, handled employee discipline, and made recommendations for promotion and career development of their subordinates. They represented the company, frequently in opposition to labor, and were also canny businessmen, responsible for the profitability of their part of the business and frequently in control of large financial resources.

This new world of middle management was charged with the invention of corporate bureaucracy. It included a strong analytical component, as managers and staff specialists collected reams of data from their own production processes that they now had responsibility for deciphering and acting upon. Because these roles drew strongly on their origins in the executive process, it was also a world rich in the demands of acting-with—that is the direct involvement of bodily presence for communication and influence with peers, subordinates, and superiors. As early as 1902, a "how-to" book written for young aspirants to business success warned, "Be manly, and look it. Appear the gentleman, and be a gentleman. What's the good of unknown good? Negotiable intrinsic value must have the appearance of intrinsic worth."

There were few objective criteria for judging the future potential of managers. Advancement tended to depend less upon formal criteria than upon such factors as the impressions of a superior private connection, or kinship. One study, exploring the emergence of business schools at the turn of the century, explained that "while the earlier versions of the success theme had set forth ownership of large enterprises as the ultimate goal, now the focus was on rising into the managerial elite. Schooling took on new value, and the more one could obtain the better. Less emphasis was put on improving "character" and more on improving "personality"; to get ahead, one had to get along with others, conquer self-created fear, and develop personal efficiency."

The classic text among the success literature of the period was written by Dale Carnegie. Originally published in 1926 as *Public Speaking and Influencing Men in Business,* the now familiar title, *How to Win Friends and Influence People,* appeared on a new edition brought out ten years later. The book was used as the official text for training aspiring management recruits in such major organizations the New York Telephone Company and the American Institute of Banking. Carnegie told his readers that their success or failure depended upon the impression they made in the four kinds of contacts that people have: "We are evaluated and classified by four things: by what we do, by how we look, by what we say, and how

we say it." By 1938 Chester Barnard was telling his readers that "learning the organization ropes" was a matter of learning the "who's who, what's what, why's why, of its informal society."

The diffusion of the executive process tended to be a source of social cohesion among the various levels of management securing their middle-class status, and of identification with those who controlled their firms. It provided a basis upon which these various groups could generate a rationale for a coincidence of interests between them, even where there was considerable disparity in wages between the upper and lower levels of the managerial hierarchy. At every level, managers were united in their assumption of accountability for the organization's performance. Emerging as a new class within the enterprise and the society at large, managers thus continued to draw their authority from their identification with the interests of ownership. But that was not always sufficient to justify their rights in the eyes of those they would command. Throughout these first decades of the century, the new managerial class cast about for the rationales, the symbols, and the ideologies that would support its claims to the unique and exotic authority of the manager's role—claims that were all the more fragile for the democratic political culture in which they were put forth.

At the turn of the century one important new source of legitimacy was found in Darwin's concept of natural selection and its translation into sociological terms by the English philosopher Herbert Spencer. The characterological virtues that had been widely accepted as crucial for success were imbued with the weight of inescapable biological truth. Social Darwinism fueled a new emphasis on the material basis of character and formed part of an intellectual movement that sought to identify individuals for purposes of placing them in the appropriate occupation and hierarchical position.

Journalists and academics of the period defended these doctrines as providing the scientific rationale for the facts of economic life. They did not simply extol the traditional virtues of the successful businessmen but saw characteristics such as aggressiveness, materialism, and even selfishness as necessary requirements in the struggle for existence. One academic, writing in the *American Journal of Sociology* in 1896, reasoned: "It would be strange if the 'captain of the industry' did not sometimes manifest a militant spirit, for he has risen from the ranks largely because he was a better fighter than most of us." Well-known Gilded Age journalist E. L. Godkin, founder of the *Nation* and the editor-in-chief of the *New York Post,* frequently called upon Darwinism to justify the importance of the businessman to society. They were "explorers of the race" who undertook huge risks. "The great capitalist," he wrote, "is generally a man who has been appointed by natural selection."

Scientific management provided another important rationale for managerial authority. Taylor boasted that his approach substituted "joint obedience to fact and laws for obedience to personal authority." Fundamental to this theme was the notion that only a special class of men—formally educated, specially trained, able to reason scientifically—was fit to control this knowledge and administer the organization on the basis of the insight it made possible. As Taylor put it, "I can say without the slightest hesitation that the science of handling pig-iron is so great that the man who is fit to handle pig-iron and is sufficiently phlegmatic and stupid to choose this for his occupation is rarely able to comprehend the science of handling pig-iron."

In the emerging rationale, "college-bred men" and scientific experts would impose technical standards on production for the good of all organizational members. The emphasis on the professional and scientific orientation of the manager lent force to the growing conviction, informed by Social Darwinism, that managers and workers were intrinsically different—each with their own psychology and social orientation. One historian of scientific management, Samuel Haber, observes that in the early years of the movement, Taylor attributed middle-class values to the workers whose effort he sought to rationalize. By the 1920s, however, the concept of the worker had changed dramatically. "The worker has a psychology all his own," insisted one of Taylor's followers. "We are absolutely wrong in judging the psychology of the worker from ours." Haber summarized this new perception: the worker was no longer to be thought of as an individualist; he was most comfortable, and could be managed most efficiently, in a group; he had little desire to rise or to increase his income substantially; he wanted the security and enough pay to satisfy comparatively limited desires. The emphasis on authority as derived from formal preparation and the ability to master systematic knowledge served the growing class of managers, who were increasingly differentiated from the firm's owners, as well as from first-level supervision.

Of the prominent businessmen born in the United States between 1831 and 1875, about two-thirds attained only a high school education, while the remaining third had some formal higher education. For those born between 1875 and 1920, the picture changed dramatically. Two-thirds of these managers had attended college, which distinguished them from the owner-entrepreneurs, whose educational preparation remained minimal. Access to the ranks of those who command had narrowed and was coming to depend, at least in part, upon the credential of a formal education. The professionalization of the managerial class was well under way by the turn of the century (as evidenced by the establishment of professional societies, journals, and graduate schools of business administration), and scientific management lent a new vibrancy and purpose to these efforts. Colleges and professional schools were to be the new crucibles from which the talent to manage the complex industrial enterprise would emerge. By the 1920s Taylor's system occupied a prominent place in the curricula of the new schools of business administration at Harvard, Dartmouth, and the University of Pennsylvania.

Not surprisingly, the strongest opposition to this systemization, professionalization, and growth of middle management frequently came from the foremen whose role was considerably narrowed. And, as the historian Sanford Jacoby has noted, there were also traditionalist employers and top executives who resented Taylor's system as an "impetuous abstraction of their prerogatives," because it "transferred the initiative away from them and questioned their natural superiority." But this train was not to be stopped. Middle management had become the repository for the explicated knowledge of the shop floor as well as of the executive suite. If middle managers' claims to the authority of ownership were a bit strained, they could nevertheless claim unique authority derived from their domination of information, as they controlled its interpretation and communication. That authority was accepted in large measure because enough people believed that those who had made it to the managerial ranks were smarter, a "superior class of people," for whom it was most natural to deal in the coin of knowledge. The increasing exoticism of modern industrial work—its pace, scale, discipline, regularity, and complexity—seemed to require specialists to direct, control, and coordinate it. More than ever, the worker was confined to the exertions of the laboring body, and managers were increasingly defined in terms of their distance from, and administration of, physical effort.

The Etiology of Clerical Work. The same process that produced middle managers and staff specialists accounts for the origins of modern clerical work. Those aspects of the middle manager's job that were most subject to rationalization, such as filing, record keeping, and correspondence, were carved out and used as the platform for a new class of lower level jobs.

The clerks of the nineteenth century were men who used their positions as points of entry to a business career. The premodern office was small. Relationships were personal rather than bureaucratic. Typically, business managers wrote out their own correspondence in longhand, although a very large office might employ a stenographer, usually male, who took dictation and copied from his notes. Copybooks, pressbooks, and pigeonholed desks were the tools used to order and disseminate documents. The distinction between clerical and managerial functions was not rigidly drawn and bookkeepers frequently were required to assume wide-ranging responsibilities for their office, department, or firm. An 1841 merchant's magazine recounted, "The majority of clerks are young men who have hopes and prospects of business before them. . . . A good clerk feels that he has an interest in the credit and success of his employer beyond the amount of his salary." In 1871 an observer described clerical work as requiring "knowledge of languages, skill in accounts, familiarity with even minute details of business, energy, promptitude, tact, and delicacy of perception."

Even in the federal bureaucracy, clerks enjoyed wide-ranging responsibility. During the Civil War, women were hired into clerical positions, and retained employment opportunities there that surpassed anything available to them in the private sector. The testimony of one woman who worked as a clerk in the 1870s examining the accounts of Indian agents reveals the range of her accountability: "For years I worked faithfully . . . the work being brain work of a character that requires knowledge not only of the rulings of this Department, but also those of the Treasury, Second Auditor, Second Comptroller, and Revised Statutes; demanding the closest and most critical attention, together with a great deal of legal and business knowledge." The experiences of another late-nineteenth-century clerk, Jane Seavey, have survived in her correspondence. As a clerk in the Internal Revenue Bureau, she was put in charge of the recording room, where she was credited with introducing "a new system of organizing work in her section, a method of filing adopted throughout the Treasury Department and used as a model for other agencies as well."

As the size of enterprises grew, it became increasingly difficult to operate by word of mouth. Written communication was required in order to ensure clarity in both lateral and subordinate relationships. There was a growing need for internal documentation, record keeping, and external correspondence. People and systems were needed to produce, maintain, and access the burgeoning load of written information.

By the turn of the century large firms showed an unabating appetite for office workers. Whereas in 1870 only about 1 percent of the U.S. work force was in clerical occupations, by 1900 this group had grown to 3 percent and by 1940 to 10 percent. In the first decade of the century alone, clerical occupations experienced a 127 percent growth rate. Between 1910 and 1920 one-quarter of all new nonfarm employment was clerical. More than any other single factor, the introduction of office machinery made it possible to relieve the pressure on the traditional office organization by carving out those functions subject to routinization from the more integrated activities of the early clerk. The most significant mechanical intervention was the typewriter, which was first introduced in the American market in the mid-1870s and was selling at a rate of 60,000 per year by 1893.

The typewriter introduced a decisive separation between the composition and production of correspondence. The historian JoAnne Yates offers statistics that show how rapidly and universally this new division of labor took hold. In 1890 there were already 33,000 people employed as stenographers and typists; by 1900, 134,000; by 1910, 387,000; and by 1920, 786,000. A new trained work force of typists and secretaries reduced the amount of time that higher paid executives spent on correspondence. The neat typewriter text also reduced the amount of time necessary to locate and read documents. These new clerks helped to create the new conventions and standardized formats of business communication.

It was mostly women who were called upon to fill this new class of jobs. The rapidity with which well-educated native-born white women filled the ranks of the clerical work force is one of the most dramatic workplace stories of the century. Women were virtually absent from the private sector clerical work force in 1870. The years from 1880 to 1890, when the typewriter was introduced to most American offices, saw the greatest increase of female clerical workers of any decade—a more than tenfold increase from 7,000 to 76,000. During the same year the enrollment of women in commercial schools jumped from 2,770 to 23,040, an increase of 732 percent, compared with an increase of only 140 percent for male students during that decade. In 1890, 64 percent of all stenographers and typists were women; by 1920, the figure had risen to 92 percent. By 1900 women accounted for 25 percent of all clerical jobs and for 62 percent by 1950. In the decade from 1910 to 1920, 69 percent of the change in female nonagricultural employment was due to the increase in the number of female clerks. From 1870 to 1930, almost one-quarter of women's increased nonagricultural labor force participation is accounted for by clerical work.

The introduction of typewriters, the bookkeeping machine, and other forms of office equipment made it possible to extract from the clerk's job some of the laborious manual tasks associated with copying, preparing and checking data, printing, preparing mail and internal correspondence, billing, timekeeping, and routine arithmetical calculations. At the same time, the new machines could be operated by individuals with far less training than had been necessary for the clerk of the mid-nineteenth century.

As portions of the early clerical function were carved out and routinized with a combination of lower-paid labor and mechanical support, the traditional clerks who had functioned with quasi-managerial responsibilities typically were not displaced. Just as executives were freed to exercise their art when middle managers absorbed a portion of their activities, so these traditional clerks were pushed further toward the managerial arena, often assimilating even more of the executive process as they now supervised the new, lower-status clerical workers. During the forty years from 1890 to 1930, typists and stenographers had grown to constitute 22 percent of the clerical labor force, but there was also an impressive growth in the number of bookkeepers, cashiers, and accountants—all high-status, and male, clerical positions. These employees typically inherited supervisory responsibility over entire offices of clerks who performed some fragment of the earlier, more comprehensive clerical task, such as bookkeeping. A 1914 study of Boston clerical workers reported that the bookkeeping function was now staffed by "many clerks who each do a small part of the bookkeeping. . . . The results of the work of these many clerks are collected and combined by one bookkeeper, usually a man."

In 1925, the same year that Mary Parker Follett made her speech exhorting managers to become more scientific, William Henry Leffingwell published his well-known text, *Office Management Principles and Practice,* which he dedicated to the Taylor Society in appreciation of its "inspirational and educational influence." Leffingwell was obsessed with the notion of bringing rational discipline to the office in much the same way that Taylor and his men were attempting to transform the shop floor. He summed

up the message of his book with one sentence: "In a word, the aim of this new conception of office management is simplification." Leffingwell wrote in detail about his work in the Curtis Publishing Company, which included a large mail-order operation. He had reorganized the flow of work so that 500 pieces of mail could be handled each hour by one clerk, as compared to an earlier standard of 100. No aspect of the office was too trivial for Leffingwell's attention. He not only addressed major functions like correspondence, record keeping, and communication but also applied his logic to the subjects of light, heat, ventilation, desks, chairs, tables, filing cabinets, forms, office supplies, mail, and office machinery of every variety. He considered work flow, measurement, standards, planning, and control for every aspect of the clerical day, hour, and minute.

The transcendent purpose of Leffingwell's approach to simplification was to fill the clerical workday with activities that were linked to a concrete task and to eliminate time spent on coordination and communication. This concern runs through almost every chapter of his 850-page text; it is revealed most prominently in his minutely detailed discussions of the physical arrangement of the office and in his views on the organization, flow, planning, measurement, and control of office work. Leffingwell advocated what he called "the straight-line flow of work" as the chief method by which to eliminate any requirement for communication or coordination. The ideal condition, he said, was that desks should be so arranged that work could be passed from one to the other "without the necessity of the clerk even rising from his seat [for when a] clerk is not at his desk he may be working, but he is not doing clerical work effectively."

Recognizing that the growth in the size of the office was a major force that would increase the coordinative demands on the office worker, Leffingwell saw his own principles of organization, together with the appropriate use of mechanical devices, as the chief bulwark against the threat of inefficiency and chaos: "A larger volume of business requires a large force of clerks to handle it; . . . this . . . makes the necessary communication between them more difficult, and there will be much walking back and forth between them for this purpose, unless some means is adopted to prevent it and save the time thereby expended. . . . Routine . . . tends to reduce communication." Layout, standardization of methods, a well-organized messenger service, desk correspondence distributors, reliance on written instructions, delivery bags, pneumatic tubes, elevators, automatic conveyors, belt conveyors, cables, telautographs, telephones, phonographs, buzzers, bells, and horns—these were some of the means Leffingwell advocated in order to insulate the clerk from extensive communicative demands.

Scientific management reoriented the office on a new axis, so that clerical workers would no longer be able to absorb even vestigial elements of the executive process, with its requirements for mutual presence and interpersonal skill. Before this reorganization, the functions of supervisors and their clerks had been ambiguously defined. Procedures were determined loosely enough that coordinative responsibility had to be shared, if only informally. The application of scientific management to the office sought to redefine clerical work and to set clear boundaries on the downward diffusion of coordinative responsibility. The new concept of clerical work tried to eliminate the remaining elements of skill related to acting-with, in favor of tasks that were wholly devoted to acting-on.

This severance of clerical work from its executive origins also helps to explain the dramatic change in sex composition of office work. The premodern clerk was an integral part of the firm and the skills he commanded were grounded in the particular language and procedures of that business. As clerical work was mechanized and routinized, the skills it required were now of a more general nature—typing, filing, dictation. As women were expected to work only until marriage, this new class of jobs appeared well suited to them in several ways. Firms were no longer reluctant to hire women for the short term, as the training investment for the new clerical work was minimal. Indeed, as the jobs were physically taxing, repetitive, and short of any promise of career mobility, it was women anticipating a short stint in the labor market that found them most acceptable. Despite the limitations of the new clerical work, it offered respectability and sense of gentility to young women in need of a living wage who had few attractive alternatives in the economy of the early twentieth century.

THE DIFFUSION AND CONSOLIDATION OF MODERN WORK: 1930–1970

The forty years that constitute the middle of the twentieth century saw the consolidation, diffusion, and institutionalization of the forms of modern work spawned during the century's spectacularly innovative first decades. From 1930 to 1970 the industrial work force, its unions, and employers struggled over legislation and shop floor practices to define the rights and obligations of managers and workers. The relative shift from a goods-producing to a service-dominated economy and the continued growth of the industrial bureaucracy entailed startling increases in the numbers of white-collar workers—managers, professionals, and clerks. This development contributed to an important century-long trend toward the abstraction of work; a trend reflected in the shift from making things to producing services, from working directly on materials to developing and applying knowledge or administering people and processes.

Between 1950 and 1976, the U.S. working population increased by 47 percent, while civilian employment expanded by 48 percent. The gender story here is also of significance. Women accounted for 60 percent of the total increase in the size of the labor force between 1950 and 1976. The ratio of men to women in the workplace stood at 2.5 to one in 1950, but at only 1.5 to one by 1976.

The manufacturing sector dominated the labor market for only a few decades. Indeed, manufacturing employment as a percentage of the working population had been declining since 1920, even as the absolute numbers of people employed in that sector continued to grow. In 1929 it employed 45 percent of the working population; by 1975 that number was 32 percent. In 1940 as many people were employed producing services as in producing goods and by 1950 the balance had shifted toward the service sector. The year 1960 saw six of every ten people employed in the service sector, and by 1975, almost seven of ten.

Too much emphasis on the growth of the service sector, however, can be misleading. It includes a wide range of commercial activities that encompass both highly skilled occupations, such as lawyers and bankers, as well as unskilled occupations such as waiters and janitors. Industries counted within this sector include distributive services such as wholesale and retail trade, communications, transportation, and public utilities; producer services such as accounting, legal counsel, marketing, banking, architecture, engineering, and management consulting; and consumer services such as restaurants, hotels, resorts, and entertainment. The largest source of growth in service sector jobs during this period was in government employment, particularly at the level of state and local government: about 6 percent of the labor force in 1930 and 16 percent by 1970. Much of this growth was accounted for by the expansion of educational institutions and the services that support them, as well as by government agencies related to the administration of health, justice and national defense.

The changing occupational profile of the U.S. economy is even more revealing than are these sectoral shifts. It was during the 1930 to 1970 period that America became a truly white-collar society. White-collar employment increased from 29 percent in 1930 to 48 percent in 1970, a gain of more than 65 percent. In contrast, blue-collar occupations accounted for almost 40 percent of the work force in 1930 and fell slightly to nearly 37 percent in 1970.

The most striking change in overall employment during this period involved the agricultural sector. While on the decline since the turn of the century as a proportion of the employed population, the absolute number of people working in agriculture continued to grow until 1930. Significant advances in productivity precipitated a steep decline in employment, which accounted for only 3.1 percent of the work force by 1970, down from 21.2 percent in 1930.

Throughout this period the largest single occupational group was that of semi-skilled workers, representing the core of the mass production enterprise. As late as 1968, fully 60 percent of all these workers continued to be employed in manufacturing as factory operatives. Others worked as inspectors, maintenance personnel, operators of material-moving equipment, and so on. Of those in the nonmanufacturing sector, the largest group was composed of drivers of trucks, buses, and taxicabs. While the growth of mass production limited the expansion of craft work, it had a much more dramatic effect on unskilled labor. That group dwindled from 11 percent of the workforce in 1930 to 4.7 percent in 1970, while craft-based occupations remained more or less steady at 12.8 percent in 1930 and 13.9 percent in 1970.

The fastest growing occupations were those employing professional and technical workers. These include the learned professions of law, medicine, and the clergy; professors, writers, artists, and entertainers; teachers, librarians, counselors, health professionals, social workers; and technicians in engineering, science, and other fields. These occupations increased from 6.8 percent of the labor force in 1930 to 14.6 percent in 1970. The second fastest growing occupational group was that of clerical workers, increasing from 8.9 percent in 1930 to 17.8 percent in 1970. A third occupational category that saw significant growth was that of nondomestic service workers. This group is somewhat difficult to categorize as it includes both jobs with significant skill levels, such as nurses and police, as well as unskilled employment, including waiters, attendants, janitors and ushers. Such low-level service jobs remained the last refuge for unskilled labor in an increasingly knowledge-based economy.

The number of managers grew from 7.4 percent of the work force in 1930 to 10.5 percent in 1970, but these numbers conceal an internal revolution in the nature of managerial employment. Between 1940 and 1970 the percentage of salaried managers increased by almost 70 percent, from 44.5 percent to 74 percent of all managers. This reflects the increasing professionalization of management, as entrepreneurs and small businesspeople gave way to salaried employees in large private and public enterprises.

Indeed, by the end of this period most Americans were wage or salary employees in some sort of medium-to-large scale organization. By 1970, nearly 20 percent of the nonagricultural labor force worked in government agencies, and an additional 30 percent were employed by businesses with more than 500 people. This half of the labor force does not include the many other workers employed by large organizations such as hospitals and universities. Over 12 million Americans, nearly 15 percent of the 1970 work force, were employed in firms of over 10,000 people. In manufacturing, the dominance of large firms was even more notable, reflecting as it did the burgeoning of managerial hierarchies within that sector. For example, in 1970, 60 percent of all persons employed in manufacturing worked in firms of 1,000, 42 percent in firms of 10,000, and about 15 percent were in firms employing over 100,000 people.

The trend toward the abstraction of work also rode the wave of an educational revolution in U.S. society. In 1940, only one out of every twenty-two people employed had a college degree. Most of those were trained in the classic professions of law, medicine, and the clergy. But during the 1950s, stimulated by the GI bill, which provided educational stipends to veterans of World War II, the U.S. higher education system entered a period of exceptional expansion. By the mid-1970s college graduates accounted for nearly one-fourth of the total labor force of approximately 90 million.

Labor and Management. The spirit of scientific management and bureaucratic organization spread across the economy, as three new groups came to dominate organizational life. First, there were the members of the new managerial hierarchies—top management, middle management, supervisory personnel, and staff specialists; second, production workers, most of whom were semi-skilled; and, finally, the clerks, primarily women. The country moved from the boom years of the 1920s through the depression decade of the 1930s and the war years of the 1940s, as debate and confrontation intensified over the identity, rights, and obligations of each group. The outcomes of these struggles differed dramatically for reasons that are directly linked to the genesis of each form of work.

During the 1920s, it had seemed that business could do no wrong as production and consumption enjoyed uninterrupted expansion after the recession of 1921–1922. Business leaders hoped that the combination of welfare capitalism and specialized personnel administration would be sufficient to stabilize the new industrial work force and win its acceptance of a new effort bargain. But in the early 1930s, as recession turned to depression and unemployment settled over the country, the public began to lose patience with big business. Americans turned to Roosevelt and the Democratic party, and public opinion on such matters as workers' rights to organize and bargain collectively began to soften. In 1932, the same year that Roosevelt was elected, the Norris-LaGuardia Act was passed. Although it provided little direct support for the union movement, it did remove the legal basis for court injunctions in labor disputes, making it more difficult for employers to use union scare tactics. Within the business community, factions clashed as progressive companies tried to make the case that only improved labor relations—company unions, improved communication, and labor-management problem solving—could head off labor conflict and ultimately unionization. Union organizers received a huge boost from Section 7a of the National Industrial Recovery Act passed in 1933.

By 1935, that act had been overturned by the Supreme Court, but labor and its congressional allies succeeded in the passage of much stronger legislation in the form of the Wagner Act, with its newly institutionalized National Labor Relations Board (NLRB) meant to oversee disputes arising from the legislation. The Wagner Act guaranteed the rights of workers to join unions and required management to engage in collective bargaining if the majority of workers so desired. The NLRB took on broad powers to decide cases of representation, prohibit managers from continuing unfair labor practices, and reinstate workers unfairly dismissed for union activity. It also worked to bring labor and management together in conferences and for more informal dispute resolution. The effect over the long term was to diminish the degree of virulent antiunionism, and in some cases, to increase the subtlety of firms' union avoidance tactics.

The same year the Wagner Act was passed the Committee for Industrial Organization (CIO) was formed under the auspices of eight AFL unions. Its purpose was to promote the organization of workers in the strategic core of mass production industries. Until that time, the AFL's disinclination to organize rank and file workers had left millions of semi-skilled wage earners without a formal political voice. The AFL rejected this initiative and expelled all but one of the unions in 1938. Later that year the committee, including the United Mine Workers, the Amalgamated Clothing Workers, and the International Ladies Garment Workers, held its first conventions, electing John L. Lewis of the United Mine Workers as its leader. After a series of very dramatic strikes in the late 1930s, rapid progress was made in organizing workers in steel, textiles, meatpacking, autos, rubber, and the electrical equipment industries.

The CIO constituted a new more militant power base in American trade unionism, evidenced by the increase in violent labor-management confrontation in the late 1930s. The year 1937 saw nearly 500 sit-down strikes, including the famous Flint sit-down strike, in which the United Auto Workers successfully won the representation of the General Motors work force; and the Battle of the Overpass, which marked the fight to organize Ford Motor Company; U.S. Steel surrendered to the United Steel Workers, and steel workers fought to organize the mid-sized steel companies in the Memorial Day Massacre. In total, 4.7 million workers struck in 1937, as compared to 2.1 million in 1936. The AFL added 886,000 new members to its locals, but the explosive growth was in the CIO, whose membership jumped from 88,000 in early 1937 to 400,000 by the fall. By the end of that year, business faced a more formidable, well organized union opposition, fortified by government support and frequently benefiting from widespread public sympathy. The CIO also sponsored periodic efforts to organize the burgeoning ranks of office clerks, whose work was increasingly proletarianized. In 1937 the CIO grant charters to three white-collar unions: the United Office and Professional Workers of America (UOPWA), the United Federal Workers (UFW), and the State, County, and Municipal Workers of America (SCMWA). During the late 1930s and throughout the 1940s UOPWA enjoyed some success in organizing white-collar employees, but a combination of jurisdictional barriers, sex discrimination (most office workers were female), and an inherent lack of affinity within the CIO toward these occupations drove such efforts to the margins of the CIO's political objectives.

As the historian Howell John Harris has documented, there was a spectrum of business response to these new circumstances. Most managers continued to regard unionism as a threat to the basic values of property rights and an inversion of the ideology of Social Darwinism, both of which were critical components of the rationale for managerial authority. Some major firms, like Ford and the "Little Steel" companies, mounted a virulent opposition, willing to use any and all tactics to beat back unionization. Some, like Goodyear and International Harvester, shared the objective of resisting unionism but tended to use more subtle tactics to delay and limit its incursions. Others were more realistic. General Motors reluctantly accepted the need to negotiate with a union, and set the tone for other centrist firms by adopting a hard-nosed, legalistic bargaining strategy in order to limit the union's gains and drive back any encroachment of managerial prerogatives. Still other firms, like General Electric and United States Rubber, saw their task as "constructive accommodation" rather than full-blown resistance. Their labor relations strategies favored fair-minded problem solving and collaboration; in their formula, recognition and respect would be the quid pro quo for labor peace and stability.

By 1938, after another recession and several years of well publicized labor turbulence, the political pendulum began to swing once again in a more conservative direction. The unions sought to gain control of their more militant factions, viewing "responsible unionism" as the only way to survive in a more hostile environment. Even within the CIO, rank and file organizations that had drawn their life from grass roots activism were now becoming bureaucratized and business-like. In kind, the business community began to shift its emphasis from resistance and union busting to a strategy of stabilization and containment based on a narrow approach to collective bargaining that endeavored to protect managerial prerogatives.

Wartime brought more change to the labor relations environment. The federal government made many concessions to business in order to win its cooperation in meeting the demands of a wartime economy, but labor's cooperation was needed too. The unions were important enough to inhibit any efforts to erode the power of the Wagner Act or the validity of collective bargaining. Government support in return for labor's wartime "no strike" pledge helped to fuel union expansion. Labor entered the war with the strength of having already organized most of the basic and mass production industries. By 1946, almost 70 percent of all manufacturing workers were covered by collective bargaining agreements.

Total union membership had risen to 15 million, more than one-third of the nonagricultural labor force. Government policy, wartime full employment, and the threat of industrial conflict all created pressures for harmonious relations during this period, thus helping to consolidate and institutionalize labor's legitimacy. Both the Great Depression, and the quasi-command economy of the war years had weakened the public's belief in management's exclusive right to control. The labor movement emerged from the war years with a greater sense of its institutional role in politics, the economy, and industrial relations, while business emerged poised for expansion and ready to use every possible means to prevent labor's influence from spreading any further. The fundamental belief in property rights may no longer have been entirely persuasive to workers, but it continued to unify the business community and animate its sense of sacred purpose as the representatives of shareholders with a responsibility to maximize profitable production in their interest. These beliefs were typically cloaked in a technical rationale. Industrial organizations had become so complex, the reasoning went, that efficient operations required exclusive managerial control. As historian Harris has put it, "Technical necessity denied the possibility of any nonhierarchical power structure in industry. There had to be single source of authority, a single line of command, with no confusion."

By the war's end, the difficulties of reconversion to a civilian economy, a dramatic increase in strike activity, and the postwar "Red Scare" helped to swing public opinion back toward business and the conservatives. In a labor-management conference sponsored by the Truman administration, management representatives under the leadership of the National Association of Manufactures (NAM) insisted on giving broad definition to managerial prerogatives, and formally protecting these from negotiation under collective bargaining agreements. Their definition went well beyond corporate strategy, and included such matters as the definition of job content, work assignments, the evaluation of workmanship, the scheduling of operations and shifts, and the maintenance of discipline and control. Labor argued that such definitions restricted the natural evolution of collective bargaining and imposed a priori limits on individual agreements. Nevertheless, the union representatives formally acknowledged management's rights to run the enterprise and endorsed a role for the unions based on reacting to contractual infringements with formal grievance procedures. In this way both sides declared their interest in creating dependable mechanisms for the orderly administration of conflict.

In the years immediately following the end of World War II, NAM continued to work to curb the power of the Wagner Act and the NLRB, seeking legislation that would balance labor's power with legislation that supported management's rights. It was in this context that in 1947 congressional conservatives won, over presidential veto, passage of the Labor-Management Relations Act (also known as Taft-Hartley). This legislation included measures making it easier for firms to resist the expansion of bargaining rights, excluding supervisory personnel from unionization, enabling states to pass "right to work" laws, and barring communist-led unions from the protection of the NLRB.

The lines that separated and defined labor and management were pretty clearly drawn by the time the postwar consumer boom engulfed the American economy. Unions had become responsible, centralized, bureaucratic organizations, imposing order on their militant factions and oriented to the newly legalistic and business-like administration of collective bargaining agreements in the service of an institutionalized adversarialism. In general, they restricted themselves to improving the financial security of their members through higher wages and benefits. Firms were content to buy labor's acquiescence to this apolitical role, passing these cost increases on to consumers in an expanding economy. While there were important strikes during this period, they were typically orderly efforts to establish wage patterns in core industries. Management and labor had achieved what the labor economist John Dunlop called a "shared ideology"—a mutually held belief in the legitimacy of managerial control over the business enterprise and the rightful separation of their spheres of influence. During the boom decades of the 1950s and 1960s, management tended to follow this "realistic" approach to unionism, while simultaneously using a variety of methods to limit its own vulnerability to the labor movement.

In 1955 the AFL and CIO merged under the combined leadership of Walter Reuther, President of the United Automobile Workers, and George Meany, an AFL official. The new AFL-CIO represented 15 million workers, though it still did not include the United Mine Workers, Railroad Workers, and some others from communist-influenced unions that had been expelled from the AFL in the early fifties. In contrast to Meany, Reuther believed in a broad social vision for the labor movement, and the conflict between the two leaders eventually led to the UAW's withdrawal from the Federation. The UAW and the Teamsters Union, together with two smaller unions, then formed the Alliance for Labor Action, intending to operate on a wider canvas of social issues. When Walter Reuther was killed in a plane crash in 1970, that movement lost its visionary leader.

Thus it took almost three decades, including a depression and a world war, to fully define managerial authority and establish its hegemony in the workplace. The unions fought to pull their members into the middle class, accepting higher wages and the promise of increased consumption as the price for loss of control over the conditions of work. There seemed to be little on the horizon to offer any serious threat to managers' rightful control over the nature of work, its content, organization, and evaluation. Managers were to manage, workers were to grieve but prosper, and both groups tacitly accepted the sense of the differences between them. This sense of "difference" between the two groups, and the moral vision from which it originated, was firmly inscribed in U.S. labor law during these decades.

The New Managerial Hierarchy. As forces set into motion earlier in the century continued to develop and mature, the boundaries separating workers, managers, and clerks grew ever more rigid, creating three groups whose identities, histories, and future possibilities were utterly separate. It was in this period (1930–1970) that professional management came into its own, successively incorporating activities that enabled a finer degree of control over every aspect of individual businesses.

From 1900 to 1940, the population of the United States increased by 73 percent, the labor force by 81 percent, the ranks of direct labor by 87 percent, and the numbers of administrative personnel in business enterprises—those engaged in managerial decision making, coordination, supervision, planning, record-keeping, buying, and selling—by 244 percent. From 1897 to 1947 the ratio of administrative personnel to direct labor changed from 9.9 percent to 22.2 percent. In a landmark study of this phenomenon published in 1951, the economist Seymour Melman concluded that this trend in the growth of administrative overhead appeared to be consistent across businesses and industries. Moreover, it was not a function of size, mechanization, technical complexity, or of any one of a host of other variables that many had assumed were responsible. Instead, he hypothesized, it was due to the perpetual addition of new functions and activities, a process propelled by managers' attempts to control more of the factors that bore upon the performance of the firm. This meant both more staff engaged in recordkeeping and data analysis, and more executive management to address an increasing proliferation of activities related to marketing, strategic planning, finance, and the like.

During the ensuing decades, Melman's analysis appeared to be correct. Between 1960 and 1980, the ratio of managers (including line and staff) to establishments increased by 280 percent, while the average number of production employees decreased by about 50 percent, with increases in administrative positions occurring in virtually every sector of the economy. Knowledge-specialists, middle managers, and executives all presided over the new empire of paper and the information it contained. They were groomed to be the guardians of information—to know what it meant and what to do about it. Education continued to be a principal determinant of eligibility for these new and expanding roles. Managers and specialists relied on the techniques and forms of analysis acquired in their colleges and professional schools. The actual differences in formal educational attainment between managers and workers helped to fortify the felt differences between these groups. By the late 1930s human relations experts like Elton Mayo at the Harvard Business School exhorted managers to engender unity and consensus in the organization by understanding the workers' social system and the needs, motivations and desires that animated them.

As managers attempted to adapt and apply the lessons of Mayo and his followers, the theme most frequently sounded was that of "communication." If management did a better job of listening to workers' perspectives and, in turn, provided them with more facts about the enterprise, then the possibilities of unified command would be enhanced. Academics pleaded the case that a policy of improving communication and sharing information was the cornerstone of industrial harmony. As the managerial hierarchy grew in size and complexity, so did the demands on another salient dimension of managerial skill—the manager as an interpersonal operator in the political vortex of an intricate bureaucracy.

Meetings, socializing, and paperwork dominated the lives of executives and managers. During the 1950s, as the society endeavored to understand this new social class, William H. Whyte and Melville Dalton each published what would become classic studies of the executive manager at mid-century. Both emphasized the manager's presence and demeanor as the medium for skilled acting-with. "You're always selling," an executive observed to Whyte in *The Organization Man,* "everything I do is subject to review by all sorts of people, so I have to spend as much time getting allies as I do on the project. You have to keep pace with people on all levels. Sometimes I get worn to a frazzle over this." "You've got to endure a tremendous amount of non-contributory labor—this talking back and forth, and meeting, and so on," lamented another, "the emptiness and the frustration of it can be appalling. But you've got to put up with it." Whyte concluded that this intense involvement with others according to a prescribed set of norms and values was at the heart of the manager's work—getting things done through other people. The further up the pyramid one climbed, the more demanding the role. Success put a premium on the theatrics of conformity, managing the impressions of subordinates, peers, and superiors at the expense of one's own tastes and opinions. Executives worked long hours and submerged themselves in the business of the corporation to the exclusion of family or leisure pursuits. While on the job, they displayed an intricate interpersonal know-how worthy of a seventeenth-century French courtier.

Dalton's study, *Men Who Manage,* also explored this complex interpersonal world of conformity and loyalty, conflict and conflict suppression, cliques and group rivalry. Skills in communication and interpersonal influence were critical to the success of line and staff alike. He likened these theatrics of conformity to the protective camouflage that other species use to evade predators: "In today's vast systems of rationality, the individual conforms as he evades their schemes of detection. Some members find room for personal choice and ingenuity as they strain and thrill in meeting appearances. Others conform to avoid conflict and to maintain the demanded tranquility and uniformity." These interpersonal capacities were seen to be at the core of the managerial experience in every study from C. Wright Mills's 1951 classic, *White Collar,* to Rosabeth Kanter's mid-1970s book, *Men and Women of the Corporation.*

Kanter's descriptive study of corporate life underscored the salience of shared presence and communication as the core of the manager's work. Visible participation in the meanings and values of one's immediate group helped to build a joint experience base. Managers could thus assume that they shared a common language and understanding, providing many shortcuts for communication in a pressured, rapid-fire world. Most of the managers she studied spent about half of their time in face-to-face communication. Kanter concluded that the manager's ability to "win acceptance" and to communicate was often more important than substantive knowledge of the business. These talents required self-control—the cautious management of the private self that freed up the body as a public vehicle for the sculpted show of expression and persuasion. Such skills, rooted in bodily presence and implicit know-how, were vital in order to move others toward the fulfillment of a manager's objectives. This was Machievelli for the new elite and its aspirants, charged with the administration of complexity in the glory days of America's public and private enterprises.

The Progress of Mechanization and Its Consequences.   By the late 1920s, new machine tool technology, especially the semi-special machine, had done much to increase the speed, flexibility, and continuity of manufacture in many mass production industries, further reducing the firm's need for skilled workers. For example, the A. O. Smith Corporation in Milwaukee, producers of automobile frames, automated its production process with the latest mechanical, hydraulic, and electrical devices. It was considered capable of making all the automobile frames needed in the United States with only two hundred men. But the pace of ambitious innovation slammed to a halt with the onset of the Great Depression. During the thirties, labor was cheap, and most manufacturers were disinclined to invest in expensive new machines and production processes.

The next major changes in the manufacturing arena came in the early 1940s, as the pace of production quickened with the war effort. By that time, most mass production workers were unionized and labor was again becoming more expensive. During this period, the ideal of continuously automated production firmly took hold. A noteworthy pioneer effort was organized by the United States Army Ordnance Department in its Rockford, Illinois, arsenal in 1941. There the army constructed a plant that would produce artillery shells. Responding to the high wages and frequent militancy of newly unionized mass production workers, and determined to avoid wartime labor shortages, the army conceived of a production system more or less entirely operated by women. To accommodate this goal, a process was designed that integrated conveyors, simple robots, and sophisticated machining equipment. One observer described the production process as "monitored by girls who preside over large consoles of signal lights and switches." The logic was to increase continuity of production, reduce the need for human intervention and skill, and substitute a smaller, cheaper cadre of women workers for a larger, more expensive male work force.

The success of the Rockford arsenal provided a model for American industry's aspirations during the coming decades. The assumption was that more automatic equipment could be combined with cheaper labor to enable greater control of production as well as significant productivity increases. By 1947 the Ford Motor Company had established an automation department, and between that year and the mid-1950s Ford reported investments of $2 billion dollars in new plant and equipment, approximately one-quarter of which was specifically targeted toward automation programs.

Most studies of work and workers between the 1940s and the early 1960s focused on the progress of mechanization and its consequences. The sociologists Lloyd Warner and J. O. Low studied a New England shoe factory in the mid-1930s, and again in the mid-1940s. They were surprised to discover that extensive mechanization had virtually eliminated skilled work; and they observed such rigid boundaries between workers and their managers that the notion of upward mobility had all but vanished. Charles Walker and Robert Guest, who studied assembly-line work in 1949–1950, characterized it as machine paced, repetitive, and minutely subdivided, requiring minimal skills and surface mental attention. Walker and Guest discovered that despite what then appeared to be significant levels of mechanization in auto assembly, many of the jobs were still quite physically taxing, especially those that required lifting heavy parts and tools. While workers complained about the lack of skills, variety, and mental challenge on the job, those complaints ranked below their dislike of the physical demands of the job. When they considered the possibility of transfers or promotions, remote though they were, their motives had little to do with status or financial achievement. Instead, they wanted to escape physically punishing work. And so the conundrum repeated itself, right through the middle of the century. The progress of industrial technology meant reductions in physical effort, but tended to limit the opportunity for skill development and social advancement.

This paradox of the body's dual role in production is nowhere better illustrated that in James Bright's 1958 study of automation in American industry and the subsequent reinterpretation of his findings by Harry Braverman in 1974. Bright studied thirteen manufacturing facilities, including automobile engine plants, a refinery, a bakery, an electrical-part manufacturer, plating plants, and others. He observed varieties of automation in production and materials handling, and concluded that workers were receptive and, in many cases, enthusiastic toward the new automated equipment. Why? "Automation takes the heavy labor out of a job. . . . The gain to management is productivity; the gain to labor is a much easier job. . . . In one engine plant a grizzled veteran manning a push button signal light control panel governing some hundred feet of machinery was interviewed. . . . He said, 'Sure I like it better. It's a lot easier. I can tell you one thing—I'll last a lot longer on this job.'" Self-preservation would induce the worker to accept automation.

Bright also clearly stated automation's effect on skills: "As the controls become more sensitive and responsive to the requirements of the operation, environment, and the task, the machine assumes responsibility, just as it has already assumed skill, knowledge, and judgment requirements." He noted that this was one of labor's biggest "headaches" with automation, but he believed that new wage determination systems, coupled with sensitive implementation processes, could overcome any resistance engendered by skill dilution.

In Braverman's influential critique of what he called the "degradation of work" in this century, he used Bright's study to make a very different point. Where Bright saw the glass half full because the physical demands of work were curtailed, Braverman saw the glass being drained as workers' skills were absorbed by technology. For Braverman, the transfer of skill into machinery represented a triumph of "dead labor over living labor," a necessity of capitalist logic. Braverman believed that employers, by substituting capital (in the form of machinery) for labor, merely seized the opportunity to exert greater control over the labor process. As the work force encountered fewer opportunities for skill development, it would become progressively less capable of exerting any serious opposition to management.

Most analyses of industrial organization during the middle decades of the twentieth century have taken up one of these viewpoints, and worker ambivalence toward automation has been a persistent theme in these accounts. Since skilled work is less automated, it also tends to involve more exertion, bodily alteration, dirt, and discomfort. Studies of workers in industries such as autos, machine tools, and textiles each observed the same dilemma—workers avoiding promotions to skilled positions whose work was too heavy, too dirty, and too noisy.

By the early 1960s, scholars had begun to ask whether these dual effects of lightening the physical burden of labor while reducing skill demands would continue to be magnified with successive levels of automation. As the range and depth of automation increased, further limiting the contribution of physical effort to the production process, would it further reduce skill requirements and thus continue to widen the gulf between workers and management? Based on his comparative studies of plants in the chemical, textiles and other industries, the sociologist Robert Blauner formulated in 1964 the now-classic U-curve hypothesis. Comparing levels of social integration across industries at distinct stages of automation, he found the highest levels within those industries that had the least (printing) and the most (chemical) automation. He found that workers in these craft-based and continuous-process industries were considerably less socially alienated and more socially integrated than their counterparts in the mass production industries of textiles and automobiles. He further argued that rather than exacerbating industrial tensions according to some presumed linear function, higher levels of automation actually begin to reverse some of the most prominent negative tendencies associated with the rationalization of manufacturing work. Continuous-process operators experienced a greater degree of identification with their managers and more loyalty toward their companies, resulting in a heightened sense of mutuality and collaboration. If the technology necessitated that an operator assume responsibility for monitoring and controlling broad sections of the plant, how could management regard its workers as adversaries? Hence, "the alienation curve begins to decline from its previous height as employees in automated industries gain a new dignity from responsibility and a sense of individual function."

Eligibility for these positions of responsibility depended on skill and seniority, for the know-how and judgment required could only be developed through many years of working at a variety of jobs in the plant and of observing a wide range of equipment operating under diverse conditions. The fact that this competence was experience-based helped orient the operator toward the stratified occupational structure within the work force. Because skill was cumulative, know-how gathered at the lower status levels would be relevant to performance at higher levels, and the prospect of advancement served as an important integrating mechanism. Responsibility was both a measure of the skill level of the operator and of the dependency relationship between management and its workers. Like that of the early craftworker, the exclusive knowledge of the continuous-process operators lashed them to their managers with bonds of reciprocity.

In the terms of this discussion, we can see that even in these settings, the worker's body, through the sensual information it accumulated based on its physical involvement in the production process, remained a crucial source of skill. This defined the extent to which the worker was likely to be a fully integrated member of the organization. The operator's knowledge continued to depend upon sentience, and it was the personal, specific, bodily character of this knowledge that continued to differentiate the operator from the manager. As long as their knowledge was concrete and specific rather than conceptual and technical, workers would be confined to a lower status set of roles. Without a conceptual understanding of the process in which they worked, or, indeed, of their own actions, workers would find it difficult to make a contribution to that domain of more comprehensive functions typically labeled "managerial." Despite the high level of social integration in many continuous-process organizations, a fundamental aspect of Tayloristic logic was preserved. The collaborative atmosphere of continuous-process industries derived from the minimal emphasis placed upon the worker's physical sacrifice. However, the body as the operator's source of skill remained a strong link to the industrial past and continued to demarcate the boundary between those who gave of their bodies in the service of production and others who did not.

Thus the progress of mechanization, and later automation, has been the result of the transformation and migration of knowledge about work. First, knowledge that was sentient and experience-based was made explicit, and in this way subjected to rational analysis and perpetual reformulation. This facilitated the migration of knowledge from labor to management with its pointed implications for the distribution of authority and the division of labor in the industrial organization. In the case of Blauner's chemical plant, operators' sentient knowledge could not be explicated. Their skills were left intact, but in a way that continued to circumscribe their role in the organization. Once again the differences between the managers and the managed were fortified. Workers were meant to give of their bodies, and this knowledge rarely transcended the sentience of implicit know-how. That other, more "educated," knowledge—conceptual, explicit, scientific, objective—was meant to be the exclusive domain of their managers.

During the 1960s, the term "automation" began to eclipse "mechanization." Computer-based technologies developed primarily through massive defense-related R&D programs were making themselves felt in the back offices of many businesses as the preferred method for recording and storing vast transaction histories—bookkeeping, payrolls, accounts receivables. These new technologies were just beginning to make their way into the manufacturing process, principally in the more advanced continuous process operations such as chemical and petroleum refineries. But there were fiery debates among academics, businesspeople, trade unionists, and policy experts as to their impact on work, workers, and the society at large. Most of those engaged in the debate viewed computer-based automation as a big leap forward in the progress of mechanization. Until this time, no amount of flexible machinery and mechanical conveying devices could really be counted on to eliminate the worker from work. But with computers, and the concept of the feedback loop that was at the heart of the cybernetic vision, the ideal of workerless production seemed finally attainable. As the labor expert Charles Killingsworth told a Senate panel in 1960, "Automation is the mechanization of thought, sensory, and control processes. . . . Automation means the substitution of mechanical brains for human brains." The basic formula remained the same as that pioneered in the Rockford arsenal—technology would substitute for people, making it possible to employ dramatically fewer, less skilled, and therefore cheaper, workers.

With computerization on the horizon, the incremental changes of previous decades began to appear insignificant in comparison to this promised revolution in productivity. Many scholars debated the likely effects of automation on overall skill levels in the society, but for some expert observers the entire focus of concern shifted from the nature of work and its consequences for the worker to whether there would be any work at all. Once workers and managers became candidates for obsolescence in the newly envisioned cybernetic society, many people wondered how society would endure if work could no longer be counted on as the foundation for individual identity and social meaning.

The Office. Scientific management and mechanization continued to gather force in the office. By the late 1940s, an exposition of office equipment featured more than 3,000 devices for the mechanization of clerical work, from translating typewriters to automatic envelope openers, from programmable calculators to prototype televisions for remote supervision. Office architecture followed, with clerks arranged in long lines of desks in large open areas in order to create a straight line production flow. In some offices, conveyor belts were employed to carry paper from one clerk to the next in true assembly line fashion. Factory methods migrated to the office, bringing simplified, rationalized work tasks as well as a new increment of physical misery and strain.

Complaints about clerical work became complaints about bodies in pain. In 1960, the International Labour Organization conducted a lengthy study of mechanization and automation in the office. It concluded that "in contrast to the mechanization of production processes, which often relieved workers of physically tiring jobs, mechanization introduced work of this nature into offices where it had not existed before." The study identified the chief sources of physical complaints as follows: fatigue induced by the increased speed of output, heavy lifting, standing, bending, the intensity of work measurement made possible by mechanization, the noise level of machines, and eyestrain. It found that the nervous tension generated by the new forms of office work were an even greater threat than the physical exertion. Clerks complained of being "treated like trained animals" because of the "uniformity and excessive simplification of the work of many machine operators." It also noted that these clerical jobs were peculiar in requiring a high degree of monotonous and repetitive activity coupled with the demand for continual attentiveness to the work at hand: "Tabulating machine operators, for instance, even when the controls are set for them and an automatic device stops the machine when something goes wrong, cannot let their attention flag." Irritability, nervousness, hypersensitivity, insomnia, headaches, digestive and heart troubles, states of depression were but some of the disturbances that office employees reported.

That same year, 1960, the Berkeley professor Ida Hoos was readying for publication her remarkable study, *Automation in the Office.* Her interest was in the effect of the computer on office work, and she pioneered an understanding of the various occupations associated with data processing. Hoos recognized that the mechanization of clerical work had almost completely stripped it of any remaining vestiges of the executive process. She found that the clerks now associated with data processing—primarily key punch operators—had been pushed even further into the zone of acting-on, and the women who occupied these jobs experienced a sharper and more bitter sense of disconnection from their white-collar colleagues. Hoos and the managers she interviewed believed that with clerical jobs becoming so factory-like, they could become a springboard for a resurgence of white-collar union organizing activity. Further, the staffing policies in the offices

she investigated were clear—to keep "the girls" working at key-punch machinery as long and as hard as possible, and when they wanted something different or something better, to let them go. Turnover was preferable to managing a career ladder that would somehow have to bridge the discontinuity between the work of these clerks and their managerial brethren.

As widespread as these new forms of clerical work had become, the reach of scientific management and mechanization was still far from complete. Throughout the late 1960s and the 1970s, management periodicals continued to devote considerable attention to the urgent need for an engineering approach to office work. Productivity, they cautioned, would never increase in the service sector unless the techniques of industrial engineering were applied to the tasks of the clerk. One such periodical, *The Office,* featured an article in 1969 by the director of a New Jersey industrial engineering firm who said: "We know from our company's studies that manpower utilization in most offices—even those that are subject to work measurement controls—rarely exceeds 60 percent. In some operations the percentage of utilization may fall below 40 percent. At least 17 percent of the time, employees are literally doing nothing except walking around or talking." In 1970, *Business Week* reported that companies were reducing their payroll costs by millions, using factory techniques to measure "how office workers work." One industrial engineer indicated that 75 percent of his firm's work measurement jobs were of offices, as compared to 25 percent just five years earlier: "Clerical jobs are measured just like factory jobs. The analysts add together scientifically predetermined time standards from human motions to find the time standard for a specific job—the standard by which a worker's efficiency then is measured." The progress of these efforts, however, continued to be confounded by the persistence of elements in the diverse repertoire of clerical work that could not be rationalized. Measurement efforts overwhelmed the lowest paid and most routinized clerical jobs, while tending to bypass higher-paid jobs entirely—jobs that continued to absorb, however weakly, many aspects of the executive process.

The problem was that jobs could only be measured successfully once they were converted to the dimension of acting-on and insulated from activities related either to acting-with or to more complex intellectual effort. Kanter's description of the secretarial function also illustrates the difference between clerical jobs as acting-on and clerical jobs as acting-with. She found two broad groupings of secretaries—

those who worked in a "pool" and those who were assigned to a particular boss. Secretaries disliked working in the pool arrangement, where jobs could be measured by the amount of typed output. Managers tended to avoid interaction with these typists, treating them instead with a purely "utilitarian" attitude, like input-output devices. In contrast, secretaries who worked for a single boss were required to absorb many subtle responsibilities associated with coordination and communication. They "could stop worrying about their own skills and work on their relationship with the boss. They participated in the behind-the-scenes transformation of chaos into order, or rough ideas into polished, business-like letters and documents. . . . They set the stage for an atmosphere that was designed to awe or impress visitors. They served as a buffer between the boss and the rest of the world, controlling access and protecting him from callers. And on occasion, they were asked to collude in lies on behalf of this front." For secretaries, much like their bosses, the salience of these acting-with skills clearly put a premium on their bodies as an expressive instrument of interpersonal politics. Personal secretaries were supposed to look and behave in a certain manner; dress, posture, and physical attractiveness were each important.

Thus, clerical work in the last decades of the century was still marked by considerable diversity and internal contradiction. Some clerical jobs continued to represent the furthest reach of the executive process. Despite efforts at simplification, they continued to absorb elements of responsibility for coordination and communication that precipitated from the managerial function and could be traced to the executive role. However, the continued combination of scientific management and mechanization did succeed in enlarging that second sphere of clerical work marked by a discontinuity with its historical origins. In that sphere, office workers were decisively driven into the demands of acting-on engulfed in the rhythms of the laboring body, isolated from their superiors, treated like extensions of the equipment that ruled them, only to be used up and, often, discarded.

THE STRUCTURE OF THE U.S. ECONOMY AT CENTURY'S END, 1970–2000

The invention of modern work resulted in some of the most successful commercial enterprises on earth. But each powerful legacy harbors the secret of its own demise, and the mighty force that was the American workplace is no exception. The new division of labor that characterized modern work was a source of almost miraculous efficiency, but as conditions changed, it took on a rigidity that contradicted the very spirit of inventiveness from which it had drawn life.

The essential premise behind the division of labor was that complexity would be removed from the lower levels of the organization, converted to information, and passed on to those in management with the special skills and training to decipher it, consider its meaning, make decisions, and issue orders. Mechanization, and later automation, were important tools used to accomplish and maintain this arrangement. Managers were the guardians of the organization's knowledge base, a practical fact that drew upon, and was supported by, the evolution of labor law. All of this meant simplicity and rationalization below, specialization and differentiation above. Elaborate chains of command and systems of control were required for communication, supervision, and coordination within the managerial hierarchy as well as between managers and those in the factories and offices who would execute their commands.

The experience of work in the industrial bureaucracy reinforced the sense of difference among the groups that inhabited it. Some have characterized these differences as the division of mental and manual work, but this was not exactly the case. Managerial work certainly had an important intellectual component related to information analysis and decision making. More than any other members of the organization, management had access to the grounds of knowledge that underlay the varied functions of the enterprise. This knowledge, conceptual and explicit, was necessary in order to be able to analyze, question, and improve productive and administrative processes. But managerial work was also body work in the service of acting-with—the elaborate interpersonal theater of inclusion, communication, and influence. Indeed, the more that was learned about managers' so-called rational and scientific processes of decision making, the clearer it became that even these tended to be highly contextual, based on a feeling for issues and people.

In contrast, the factory worker's role rested squarely in the domain of the laboring body. This did not necessarily mean an absence of intelligent activity. For those who continued to exercise craft skills, their knowledge was prodigious but of a special nature—implicit, felt, known through the effort of acting-on materials and equipment. For the semiskilled or unskilled laborer, work was more narrowly

1116

defined as the exertion of their bodies with regularity, discipline, and attention. The white-collar office worker ran the gamut between these two extremes. Some absorbed enough of the executive process to involve them in the work of coordination and communication, while others worked at tasks so simplified as to convert them to laboring bodies, a mere extension of their typewriters and keypunch machines.

This was the legacy of modern work as it entered the last third of the century. During these final decades, as the specter of a new millennium slowly gathered force, each earlier solution would come to be regarded as a new problem, each hard-won innovation as a new obstacle. Everything would be questioned as once-brilliant formulas failed, and ultimately it would become clear that the American workplace was once again under construction, ready to be reinvented for a new century.

During the last three decades of the century, the U.S. economy began a painful and tumultuous shift from an industrial to a service-oriented information economy. Between 1972 and 1986, the U.S. employment base added over 27 million jobs, a growth rate of 32 percent. Moderate projections calculated by the Bureau of Labor Statistics foresee slower growth between 1986 and the year 2000—21 million jobs or a 19 percent increase. The structural changes in the economy already evident at mid-century became dramatically more pronounced toward the century's end. Whereas in 1972, goods production, including manufacturing, mining, and construction, represented about 28 percent of U.S. employment, by 1986 it had declined to about 22.1 percent, and is expected to decrease even further to 18.6 percent by 2000. In absolute terms this translates into only 1 million new jobs in this sector between 1972 and 2000. Manufacturing is responsible for nearly all of the sector's decline both historically and over the period projected to the year 2000. In contrast, the service sector, broadly defined, continued to expand. Its share of employment increased from 59 percent in 1972 to 66.6 percent in 1986, and is projected to account for 71 percent of all employment by 2000. Between 1979 and 1987, 98 percent of all new jobs were created in the service sector, as compared to 79 percent between 1973 and 1979.

As the character of the work force changed, so did the appeal of labor unions. Union strength was concentrated in the traditional industrial sector, where employment levels were stagnant or diminishing. While significant gains in union participation rates were made among public sector employees, the labor movement failed to mount a successful strategy for attracting the growing numbers of white-collar workers in the private sector. Unions' share of all nonagricultural employees fell from a peak of 33 percent in 1953 to 25 percent in 1980, and then to 16 percent in 1990 (including 12 percent of the private sector work force compared to 36.5 percent in the public sector). Scholars have become increasingly concerned about current employment trends and their implications for the U.S. work force. These concerns center on the fact that service sector employment encompasses a wide variety of industries offering jobs of vastly different qualities when it comes to skill demands and wage profiles. Some industries within the service sector are capital intensive, making extensive use of information technologies and offering jobs marked by high skill demands, high wages, and stable career structures. Another group of service industries is marked by low productivity, relying on low-cost labor in jobs with little opportunity for skill development or earnings enhancement. For example, the economists Eileen Appelbaum and Peter Albin reclassified the sectoral division of industries according to their degree of knowledge and information intensity. They described a two-tier economy, with knowledge-based work rapidly expanding parallel with an even more rapidly growing number of low-paying service jobs. Specifically, they found that within the service sector, information and knowledge-oriented services created over 9 million jobs between 1973 and 1987, absorbing more than 5.7 million college-educated workers at wages better than or comparable to those offered in the traditional manufacturing industries. During the same period, another group of service industries marked by low information and knowledge intensity added 11 million jobs, 7.7 million of which were characterized by median earnings one-third or more below the median in the industrial sectors, and in which the proportion of part-time jobs reached as high as 40 percent. In addition, these low-paying "dead end" jobs have been filled largely by women.

Other scholars have argued that these structural trends should not be extrapolated into the future. For example, the economist Lester Thurow has maintained that as service sector productivity increases, its expansionary tendencies will decline. Manufacturing employment will grow again, he argues, as the United States endeavors to right its balance of payments through increased exports or substitution of domestic for overseas goods. Sectoral competition for workers will lead to rising wages in the service sector, further increasing incentives to improve productivity with new technology.

Whatever the future holds for the structure of the economy, it is clear that earlier trends in the occupational profile of the U.S. labor market have continued to intensify. The absolute levels of blue-collar employment are expected to be nearly the same in the year 2000 as they were in 1972. In contrast, executives, managers, professionals, and technicians increased their share of employment from 20 percent in 1972 to 25 percent in 1986, and another increase to 27 percent is projected by 2000, a gain that translates into 19 million new jobs for this group despite significant managerial "downsizing" from the late 1980s through the mid-1990s. These increases included a 61 percent rise in the numbers of professionals and technicians and a 41 percent increase in the ranks of managers and administrators. During the fifteen years between 1975 and 1990, the number of managers in the manufacturing sector alone more than doubled, from approximately 1.2 to over 2.5 million, in spite of well-publicized attempts to eliminate excessive layers of the managerial hierarchy in these industries. During that same period, clerical work continued to expand, increasing by 103 percent between 1972 and 1986, though some predictions foresee a leveling off or even diminishing of these rates of growth to the end of the century. Sales and service workers will have increased their share of employment by 5.5 percent between 1972 and 2000, which represents 18.5 million jobs. Some 40 percent of the workers in the information and knowledge intensive services have a college degree, compared to 17.1 percent in the other services. Workers with at least one year of college account for 63 percent of those employed in the information knowledge intensive services and only 40 percent in the other services. There is a similar disparity in the distribution of professionals, managers, and technicians—34 percent in the information intensive industries, compared to 14.6 percent in the others. Thus the century-long trend toward the abstraction of work continues to be marked by the growth of professional and quasi-professional employment together with the shift toward services and away from goods production.

The introduction of new information technologies was another important new factor contributing to, and frequently accelerating, this historical process. As information technology was applied across every sector of the economy, it tended to increase the abstractness of work, creating computer-mediated jobs at every level of the organization, many of which required information management and analysis. This meant that information intensive work was no longer the precinct of the traditionally knowledge-based occupations as it began to cut across industries and job classifications.

Work Reform in the 1970s.   By the early 1970s, the quid pro quo struck by labor and management had begun to wear thin. The formula that ceded control over the conditions of work to management in return for improved wages and benefits had operated well with a generation of depression-scarred workers for whom the equation of success with economic stability and consumerism made sense. The vitality of the postwar economic expansion allowed these expectations to be met with steady increases in earnings, the increased availability of reasonably priced high-quality consumer goods, and a stable social system based on widely shared middle-class values. Indeed, between 1950 and 1973 the median disposable income of Americans doubled, from $5,600 to $12,000 (in 1970 dollars), putting the good life well within the reach of millions.

But by the early 1970s, pollsters, academicians, journalists, and policy experts were calling attention to what they believed was a significant shift in the values and expectations characteristic of what they dubbed a new breed of younger, better educated Americans. Fueled by postwar existential philosophy and its various iterations in the popular psychologies of the 1960s and 1970s, by the sexual revolution, by the civil rights movements among African Americans and women, and by the domestic conflict over the Vietnam War, the new values taught that individual moral calculations provided a basis upon which to accept or reject the demands of organized social life. Self-fulfillment became a psychological, rather than an economic, challenge as the children of professional and working-class families alike demanded greater responsiveness from political and educational institutions—demands that gradually spread to private enterprise as well.

Work in America, a report published by the secretary of health, education, and welfare in 1973, was meant to respond to what it called "blue-collar blues," "white-collar woes," and "managerial malaise." It declared that significant numbers of Americans in every occupational category were alienated from their work and concluded that workers wanted to be the masters of their immediate environments and to feel that they and their work are important. Another study, conducted by Roxanne Bucholz, surveyed blue-collar workers, clerks, and managers and found a shared belief in "the importance of having a chance to learn new things on the job and grow in the knowledge of oneself." The mismatch between employee expectations and the realities of the workplace was viewed as responsible for the high levels of absenteeism, turnover, and walkouts, as well as the low levels of productivity, that characterized this period.

It was in this context that work reform efforts gathered force in the early 1970s. They represented a further evolution of the work of the human relations movement in management education ignited by Elton Mayo's Hawthorne studies and elaborated on by his colleagues and disciples over a twenty-year period. They also built upon the conceptual work of theorists such as Abraham Maslow, Frederick Hertzberg, and Eric Trist. The new work reform activities ranged from job enrichment to quality circles to the redesign of the social and technical dimensions of the factory. What they had in common was a frontal assault on the assumptions that had guided the evolution of work organization since scientific management redefined the American workplace in the first decades of the century.

Social scientists and management consultants were invited to advise, design, and evaluate work arrangements that might provide psychologically enhancing work experiences. Their logic called for holistic task cycles to replace the simplification and fragmentation of jobs, varied and interesting task content, feedback on one's work, autonomy in task execution, and the ability to experience the results of one's efforts. Some went further, calling for participatory management and the plantwide redesign of work and social systems. One leader in the work reform movement, Richard Walton of the Harvard Business School, stated the case in broad terms in an article entitled "How to Counter Alienation in the Plant," which described his collaboration with General Foods managers to design a new approach to factory work at the Gaines Pet Food Plant in Topeka, Kansas. He argued that employees wanted challenge, mutual influence, interesting work, and less emphasis on competition. Fulfilling these objectives would lead to productivity growth and improved social outcomes. "We must coordinate the redesign of the way tasks are packaged into jobs, the way workers are required to relate to each other, the way performance is measured, and rewards are made available, the way positions of authority and status symbols are structured, and the way career paths are conceived." In Topeka and other similar efforts, a key design element was the autonomous work group that provided self-management opportunities related to task execution, coordination, training, and problem solving. Such

teams often integrated support functions such as maintenance, quality control, and even some engineering and personnel responsibilities. Tasks were designed to include administrative functions requiring planning, problem diagnosis, and coordination. Pay systems were established to reward workers for increasing their range of skills and team leaders replaced the traditional foreman.

As had been the case earlier in the decade, corporations varied widely in their willingness and ability to engage these developments. There was a progressive minority represented by firms such as Procter and Gamble, General Foods, TRW, Exxon, General Motors, Cummins Engine, and many other less prominent companies that invested resources into experimenting with and institutionalizing many of these new forms of work organization. Others adopted a more cautious approach, embracing discrete elements such as job enrichment or quality circles, while the rest seemed to cling to the status quo with renewed fervor.

Even where companies made strong commitments to implementing innovative work arrangements, there were serious limitations. The principles upon which alternative plants were founded rarely migrated beyond the factory walls. The rest of the firm continued to operate as before, with managerial functions cleaving and multiplying at a prodigious rate. Moreover, only a minority of firms thoroughly institutionalized the new forms of work organization. In these companies, personnel were trained in the skills necessary to contribute to the new environment, recruitment and reward systems were aligned with the new skill and role requirements, and change management skills were nurtured. Typically, these firms had carefully measured the comparative performance of innovative and traditional plants and had convinced themselves of the superior economic as well as human outcomes associated with the new approaches.

In contrast, the majority of firms that ventured into the new arrangements were unable to sustain them. Turnover in top or plant level management, poorly informed designs, lack of follow-through or middle management commitment, acrimonious labor relations, knee-jerk responses to perceived changes in market conditions, and plain unwillingness to relinquish managerial prerogatives all undermined many well-intentioned efforts. Despite such setbacks, new ground had been broken, providing a valuable road map for the thousands of companies that would experiment with, and eventually institutionalize, some degree of change. The work reform movement also created a cadre of managers, consultants, and workers with a deep understanding of the social technology required to invent and sustain new plant designs. They became a source of social know-how that would be drawn upon in the still stormier decades ahead.

Intelligent Technologies Reinvent Work for a New Century.   The final years of the 1970s and the early years of the 1980s are now considered by many to define a watershed in American economic history. The oil crises of the 1970s left a legacy of volatile energy costs, which in turn soured old markets and created new market opportunities. At the same time, learning curve pricing led to impressive price-performance ratios for new microprocessor-based technologies, resulting in significant new communications and information-processing capabilities. In this context, global trade accelerated as market information could be more rapidly and accurately coordinated through real-time information systems. Once secure domestic markets, such as existed in the American automobile industry, became the targets of more efficient foreign, and particularly Japanese, competition.

During those same years, microprocessor-based technologies also began to transform the interior of the workplace. Robotics, numerically controlled machine tools, computer integrated manufacturing systems, integrated information and control systems, on-line real-time transaction systems, and an endless variety of management information and data base management systems began to reorganize and reorient work tasks at every level of the enterprise. By the mid-1980s it was clear that there had been a revolution in the technological infrastructure of the firm. That change was not limited to the machine worlds of the factory and back office; it pervaded every aspect of the corporate enterprise and every occupational level within it. Between 1984 and 1989 the percentage of employees who reported using a computer at work increased by over 50 percent, from 24.6 percent to 37.4 percent. Women, Caucasians, and highly educated workers were more likely to use computers than men, African Americans, and the less educated workers. Except in firms of fewer than twenty people, about 40 percent of all white-collar workers used personal computers extensively. Moreover, many service industries, such as banking, insurance, real estate, communication, and public administration, reported that 60 percent of all employees used computers. Some scholars regard these developments as evidence of a shift to a postindustrial society, in which service-oriented knowledge-based occupations dominate the economy. Others prefer the notion of an "information economy." Still other scholars observe that despite these important structural developments, the new economy still required diverse stakeholder groups to clash, struggle, and negotiate over the classic issues of power and control, ownership and opportunity. They note that the "information economy" has further limited the options of the educationally disadvantaged, creating two tiers of employment with wholly different kinds of jobs, workers, and opportunities in each.

Amid these controversies, two major points are clear. First, the global integration of markets changed the nature of competition for American firms, much as the railroad and telegraph did by the end of the nineteenth century. Whereas the mass production approach excelled at volume and standardization, and considered variations in quality to be a necessary cost of these benefits, the new competitive conditions put a premium on very different outcomes. American firms found that their customers now demanded greater degrees of customization and consistently high quality. The new environment rewarded ever-diminishing product and service delivery cycle times along with perpetual innovation. Second, information technology fundamentally altered the nature of work across industries and occupations, thus constituting a true discontinuity in industrial history, one that called into question virtually every aspect of the modern functional hierarchy.

As the presence of information technologies exploded in the workplace during the 1980s, many managers believed it would at last provide a solution to "the labor question." The common assumption was that the new computer-based technologies provided a straightforward means of labor substitution, consistent with the automation paradigm laid down in the Rockford Arsenal decades before. The ideal was to create self-acting and self-regulating machine systems, independent of human intervention. Advanced computer-based technologies seemed finally to be able to fulfill this promise.

Yet, this vision was never realized. My own research on information technologies in the workplace, along with the work of other scholars, has helped to demonstrate the unique characteristics of these new technologies and their effect on the nature of work. These insights help to explain why managers have so frequently been thwarted in their efforts to accomplish the ultimate in automation. As information technologies are used to reproduce, extend, and improve upon the process of substituting machines for human agency, they simultaneously accomplish something quite different. The same microprocessor-based devices that automate equipment also register data about those automated activities, thus generating new streams of information. Computer-based, numerically controlled machine tools or microprocessor-based sensing devices not only apply programmed instructions to equipment but also convert the current state of the equipment, product, or process into data. For example, scanner devices in supermarkets automate the checkout process and simultaneously generate data that can be used for inventory control, warehousing, scheduling of deliveries, and market analysis. The same systems that make it possible to automate office transactions also create a vast overview of an organization's operations, with many levels of data coordinated and accessible for a variety of analytical efforts.

Thus information technology, even when it is applied to automatically reproduce a finite activity, is not mute. It not only imposes information (in the form of programmed instructions) but also produces information. It both accomplishes tasks and translates them into information. The action of a machine is entirely invested in its object, the product. Information technology, on the other hand, introduces an additional dimension of reflexivity: it makes its contribution to the product, but it also reflects back on its activities and on the system of activities to which it is related. Information technology not only produces action but a voice that symbolically renders events, objects, and processes visible, knowable, and sharable in a new way.

Information technologies are characterized by a fundamental duality. On the one hand, these technologies can be applied to automate operations according to a logic that hardly differs from that of the nineteenth-century machine system—replacing the human body with a technology that enables the same process to be performed with more continuity and control. However, these new technologies simultaneously generate information about the underlying productive and administrative processes through which an organization accomplishes its work. They provide a deeper level of transparency to activities that had been either partially or completely opaque. In this way information technologies supersede the traditional logic of automation. The word I have coined to describe this unique capacity is *informate.* Activities, events, and objects are translated into and made visible by information when a technology informates as well as automates.

The informating power of intelligent technology can be seen in the manufacturing environment when microprocessor-based devices such as robots, programmable logic controllers, or sensors are used to translate the three-dimensional production process into digitized data. These data are then made available within a two-dimensional space, typically on the screen of a video display terminal or on a computer printout, in the form of electronic symbols, numbers, letters, and graphics. Such data make possible a quality of information that did not exist before. The new technology not only tells the machine what to do—imposing information that guides operating equipment—but also tells what the machine has done—translating the production process and making it visible.

In the office environment, the combination of on-line transaction systems, information systems, and communications systems creates a vast information presence that now includes data formerly stored in people's heads, in face-to-face conversations, in metal file drawers, and on widely dispersed pieces of paper. The same technology that processes documents more rapidly, and with less intervention, than a mechanical typewriter or pen and ink can be used to display those documents in a communications network. As more of the underlying transactional and communicative processes of an organization become automated, they too become available as information in a growing organizational data base.

In its capacity as an automating technology, information technology has a vast potential to displace the human presence. Its implications as an informating technology, on the other hand, are only beginning to emerge. The distinction between automate and informate provides one way to understand how these new technologies represent both continuities and discontinuities with the traditions of industrial history. As long as these technologies are treated narrowly in terms of their automating functions, they perpetuate the logic of the industrial machine that over the course of this century has made it possible to rationalize work while decreasing the dependence on human skills. However, when a technology also informates the processes to which it is applied, it increases the explicit information content of tasks and sets into motion a series of dynamics that transform the nature of work and profoundly challenge the legacy of modern work.

As the informating process unfolds, the organization is increasingly imbued with an electronic text that explicitly represents many forms of data that were once implicit, private, or minimally codified. Thus, the work environment becomes increasingly "textualized," that is, more information about the organization's work is codified, integrated, and presented through the medium of an electronic text. Under these conditions, the nature of work becomes more abstract, since it depends upon an understanding of, responsiveness to, and ability to manage and create value from information. In an informated environment, skills are redefined. The application of an informating technology does not simply imply the destruction of older forms of knowledge. Instead, it requires the construction of a new kind of knowledge, one that is more analytical and conceptual.

The informating process represents a radical discontinuity in the history of work and the evolution of industrial technology. Earlier generations of machines decreased the complexity and substantive content of work tasks, making it possible to employ people with ever-lower levels of skills. In contrast, an informating technology increases the explicit information content of tasks. As a result, it tends to increase the intellectual character of work. The force of this discontinuity can be appreciated in light of the history reviewed in this essay. Managers have been the guardians of the organization's explicit knowledge base, and much of their authority has derived from their special accreditation for those responsibilities. The iron curtain drawn between management and labor has been more or less defined by tasks that were stripped of information content on the one side, and the new managerial tasks toward which that information migrated, on the other. In the context of an informating technology, that iron curtain is no longer feasible as tasks at every level are frequently reinvested with substantive information content.

These new conditions open up possibilities for firms struggling with the hypercompetitive conditions of the global marketplace. In an earlier era of domestically defined mass markets, firms concentrated on increasing the volume of production while lowering unit costs, and industrial work organization reflected those objectives. In the new economy of the late twentieth century, consumers are empowered with information and choice. Firms are shifting their strategic objectives toward quality, speed, flexibility, customization, and customer responsiveness, all of which are easier to achieve when complexity can be dealt with at the point it enters the organization. But this new logic requires that employees at the point of production, at the customer interface, or in the process of service delivery, have the cognitive skills to engage competently with the new electronic text in order to create value from information. It also means providing those employees with the freedom and authority to express and act on what they can learn, for the more blurred the distinction between what people know, the more fragile and pointless become the relations of domination and subordination between them.

Thus it appears that the competitive conditions at the heart of the new information economy no longer favor the principles of work organization and management refined during the many decades of this century. The purpose and function of the managerial hierarchy are severely attenuated. New principles of work organization are required that redistribute knowledge and authority, where learning (and the creation of added value derived from that learning) supplant the control orientation of the industrial bureaucracy. The implications of these developments extend well beyond the shop floor to the work of every occupational group within the enterprise. In other words, the final decades of the century mark the beginning of a new period of profound historical adaptation for the American workplace. The economic potential of the new information infrastructure will be thwarted until new principles of organization and management are devised that are appropriate to the work of this new age: the rapid transformation of information into value.

Many scholars have now documented the contours of this new challenge and the arduousness of the change it entails. It is clear that informating technologies alone will not carry the burden of these changes, though by transforming the nature of work at the task level they are creating pressure for more systemic organizational reinvention, new qualities of skill, new roles, new organizational structures. It is also clear that firms are quite varied in their responses to these pressures for adaptation. Some have joined the challenge, citing competitive objectives such as quality improvements. Others have endeavored to exploit new technological capabilities in the redesign of operations, or to reduce costs through simplifying the managerial hierarchy, without substantive efforts to develop new work force skills or a new division of labor. Still others continue to reproduce the status quo. The challenges of adaptation earlier in this century led to the formation of, and concentration of power within, the managerial hierarchy. The challenge to the firm at the century's end points to the need for a devolution of that very power structure. It is likely to be a slow and painful process that will move forward only as the status quo is repeatedly battered by the pragmatic claims of competitive conditions that favor new forms.

These developments are quite dramatic in light of the history of manufacturing work in this century. No longer is physical strength and a willingness to suffer bodily exertion the hallmark of the worker's role. For the first time, the worker is drawn into the abstract precincts of explicit information that have been the manager's exclusive world as technology returns to workers what it once took away—but with a crucial difference. The worker's knowledge had been implicit in action. The informating process makes that knowledge explicit: it holds up a mirror to the worker, reflecting what was known but now in a precise and detailed form. In order to reappropriate that reflection, the worker must be able to grapple with a kind of knowledge that now stands outside the self, externalized and public. New intellectual skills become the means to interact competently with this objectified text, to reappropriate it as one's own, and to engage in the kind of learning process that can transform data into meaningful information and, finally, into insight.

In the clerical sector, scholars have followed the evolution of office automation and its effect upon the continued evolution of the executive process. During the late 1970s and early 1980s, office automation followed the pattern observed by Ida Hoos in the early 1960s. Computer-based technologies were used to further fragment and simplify tasks. Clerks found themselves riveted to video terminals with high-volume quotas for data entry or simple transaction functions, their productivity perpetually measured and tracked by the very systems through which they accomplished their tasks. The generally underspecified nature of much clerical work had required clerks to retain at least some slender hold on the executive process—identifying and locating documents or holding informal discussions with supervisors or peers over the best way to handle a nonroutine event, etc. Now, the computer system became a unitary resource; everything required of a clerk could be accomplished without leaving the terminal. Socially isolated behind their video screens, these clerical functions were denuded of any last traces of substantive responsibility for coordination and communication—in other words they were finally and decisively severed from the executive process. All that remained was to automate these jobs out of existence.

Like the keypunch operators before them, most clerks confronting the first waves of the "information economy" found themselves the losers. Confined to the simplest forms of acting-on, office employees became increasingly engulfed in sensations of physical discomfort. In my own work I interviewed hundreds of clerks working under these new conditions and frequently asked them to draw pictures that expressed their sense of the job before and after computerization. The most striking feature of their many pictures was the similarity among them. Over and over clerical workers depicted themselves in their computer-mediated tasks as suffering from hair loss, impaired eyesight, contorted facial muscles, a decrease in bodily dimension, rigidity of the torso, arms, and face, inability to speak or hear, immobility, head-

aches, and enforced isolation. The clerks portrayed themselves as chained to desks, surrounded by bottles of aspirin, outfitted with blinders, closely observed by their supervisors, surrounded by walls, enclosed without sunlight or food, bleary-eyed with fatigue, solitary, frowning, and faceless.

Toward the close of the twentieth century, the emphasis in the back office moved away from the highly automated and de-skilled job. These rote tasks were often either completely automated or reintegrated into new multiactivity jobs that, with the aid of a powerful computer work station, combined tasks once allocated among data entry clerks, supervisory-level clerks, and professionals. The newly skilled clerks that filled these jobs could exercise considerable levels of responsibility and judgment. In these cases, eighty years of routinization of the executive process began to reverse itself. Activities that were once carved out of more complex tasks and became the occasion for the elaboration of a new set of lower level roles began to be reintegrated upward. In many cases, the new clerical work once again requires specific knowledge of the business and the product.

Changes in the nature of managerial skill combine processes evident in manufacturing with those emerging in the back office. Managers and executives have found more of their work depending upon intelligent interaction with the new electronic text as the internal and external dynamics of the business are made transparent and accessible. Managers can monitor and administer larger sectors of activities based on objective data, rather than relying on observation and verbal report. As the emphasis shifts toward adding value through analysis and prediction based on explicit quantitative information, managers and executives find themselves having to develop the kinds of cognitive skills that emphasize abstract thinking, a theoretical understanding of the business, analytical problem solving, and procedural reasoning. As more sectors of data are integrated, it becomes possible to compare business segments, shops, or product lines on a global basis, while examining data on any business unit in almost infinite detail. Managers can experiment with business models and hypothesis testing to develop deeper insights into commercial dynamics. It also becomes possible to intervene swiftly when troubling patterns are surfaced or exceptions to standard operations are flagged. This can put a greater premium on strategic skills involving diagnosis and planning, and also can create a vulnerability to micromanaging across levels of responsibility.

Although it has not supplanted the earlier core of skills related to acting with—the demands of interpersonal influence, coordination, and communication—

the informated environment has expanded the domain of skills associated with the creation of value from abstract information. The skills of acting-with continue to be important, but may be applied in new ways. Where subordinates are becoming responsible for managing information related to substantive business activities, the manager is no longer required merely to supervise and control. Instead, managers must oversee and encourage work force skill development and help create the kind of social environment in which more members participate in and contribute to the business process. New forms of personal influence are associated with the ability to learn and to engender learning in others. Further, as the information infrastructure makes the organization more transparent, the degree of horizontal integration is also increased. It becomes possible to track business processes across functions, and increases the need for interfunctional coordination and problem-oriented team work. Hence, the manager's acting-with skills are also directed toward a new level of integration and interdependency with peers across the enterprise. Vertical and horizontal integration create relations that are more intricate, fluid, and unpredictable, less determined by status, position, or role. Dynamic relations among individuals with informed opinions come to replace hierarchical relations between classes of employees.

The new technological environment has also affected the manager's job in another way that bears directly on the historical evolution of the executive process. Many managers, linked to their personal computers, laptops, or executive workstation in the course of fulfilling their daily responsibilities, now find themselves writing their own reports, maintaining files, updating their calendars, or doing any one of a dozen other routine clerical functions in the course of accomplishing their complex tasks. In other words, the manager's role has begun to reabsorb many of those activities that were carved out, routinized, and precipitated into lower level clerical work. Computer power and ease of use has made it possible for the manager to operate without the legions of clerical support considered necessary in an earlier technological era.

Thus, the changes in the nature of work related to new information technologies coupled with the competitive demands of the global economy appear to favor a general upgrading in the skill requirements of work in many occupations. In the language of natural selection, the firms moving in this direction are most likely to be selected for growth. These outcomes depend, however, upon managerial choice as it sets about interpreting labor market conditions, customer demands, product characteristics, competitor moves, and so on. These choices require a fundamental rethinking of managerial prerogatives and how they bear upon the distribution of knowledge and authority in the workplace. As such, they are anything but a fait accompli—emotional grief, political struggle, negotiation, and the occasional celebration will line the path of historical adaptation. In some cases, this adaptation will be led by insightful managers committed to a new economic and moral vision. In the vast majority of cases, however, adaptation will occur over a longer time frame, and only as a result of the relentless pressures of a marketplace in search of new forms of value.

Thus, the story of work in the twentieth-century United States has been rewritten not once but twice. First, work was severed from its roots in land and craft. For the first time in history, the majority of a working population migrated from the natural world to the machine world. The new mechanized work demanded little from the brain, but still much from the body. A new class of knowledge workers was invented to direct, control, and advise the growing industrial leviathan. Everything we know about modern work organization was invented or perfected in the effort to maximize the efficiency and productivity of this new machine world.

But by the century's end, the breakdown of mass markets and a new technological infrastructure based on information technology were calling into question these very tenets of modern work. The new information economy drove change in two directions. On one side, knowledge work proliferated across occupations and organizational levels, exploding the old division of labor and challenging the sources of authority from which it derived. On the other, relatively low-skilled service jobs offered little in the way of challenge, advancement, or finanical security. And across this spectrum, simple physical work drifted to the margins of economic activity. The challenge for the next century became not one of work's demise, but rather, its utter reinvention. How do we adapt to these new modalities of work while ensuring that the whole society has access to them?

SEE ALSO Class; Race; Ethnicity and Immigration; Gender Issues (all in volume I);
The Professions (in this volume).

BIBLIOGRAPHY

Several excellent treatments of the invention and institutionalization of the new precepts of modern work in the early part of the century are available in Reinhard Bendix, *Work and Authority in Industry* (1956); Daniel Nelson, *Managers and Workers: Origins of the New Factory System in the United States, 1880–1920* (1975); Daniel Rodgers, *The Work Ethic in Industrial America, 1850–1920* (1976); and Sanford Jacoby, *Employing Bureaucracy: Managers, Unions, and the Transformation of Work in American Industry, 1900–1945* (1985). In-depth explorations of workers' responses to the new industrial conditions can be found in Herbert Gutman's now classic essays, *Work, Culture, and Society in Industrializing America: Essays in American Working Class and Social History* (1977), as well as in David Montgomery, *Workers' Control in America: Studies in the History of Work, Technology, and Labor Struggles* (1979), and David Brody, *Workers in Industrial America: Essays on the Twentieth Century Struggle* (1993). Perspectives on the new conditions of work shared by turn-of-the-century intellectuals are explored in James Gilbert, *Work without Salvation: America's Intellectuals and Industrial Alienation, 1880–1910* (1977). For a penetrating social history of the early years at Ford, see Stephen Meyer, *The Five Dollar Day: Labor Management and Social Control in the Ford Motor Company, 1908–1921* (1981).

For specific discussions of Taylor, his views, and his contributions, see Frederick Taylor, *The Principles of Scientific Management* (1911) as well as a collection of then contemporary essays in Clarence Bertrand Thompson, *Scientific Management* (1922). A superb critique of Taylor's movement is available in Samuel Haber, *Efficiency and Uplift: Scientific Management in the Progressive Era, 1890–1920* (1964). For a fascinating psychohistory of Taylor, see Sudhir Kakar, *Frederick Taylor: A Study in Personality and Innovation* (1970). See also Gilbreth's own writings in Frank B. Gilbreth, *Motion Study* (1911). An important history of workers' responses to Taylorism is available in Hugh Aitken's *Taylorism at the Watertown Arsenal: Scientific Management in Action, 1908–1915* (1960). A close analysis of changes in the material processes of production is David Hounshell's *From the American System to Mass Production, 1800–1932* (1984). See also Siegfried Giedion's unique history of the diffusion of the mechanized world view in *Mechanization Takes Command* (1969).

Olivier Zunz provides an important account of the invention of managerial work in *Making America Corporate, 1870–1920* (1990). There is a fascinating description of the evolution in means of corporate record-keeping and communication in Joanne Yates, *Control through Communication: The Rise of System in American Management* (1989). For a comprehensive look at the rise of female clerical employment, see Elyce J. Rotella, *From Home to Office: U.S. Women at Work, 1870–1930* (1981).

A thorough overview of changes in the structure of the economy and occupational distribution during the postwar years is available in John Dunlop and Walter Galenson (eds.) *Labor in the 20th Century* (1978). Elton Mayo, *The Social Problems of an Industrial Civilization* (1945), introduced a social-psychological perspective on industrial work, thus paving the way for the influential human relations school in organization theory. Other excellent studies that followed in the social-psychological tradition are Lloyd Warner and J. O. Low, *The Social System of the Modern Factory: The Strike, A Social Analysis* (1947); Robert Guest and Charles Walker, *The Man on the Assembly Line* (1952); Ely Chinoy, *Automobile Workers and the American Dream* (1955); and Floyd Mann and Richard Hoffman, *Automation and the Worker: A Study of Social Change in Power Plants* (1960).

The ardent debate over technology's role in degrading or enriching work is defined by the opposing views of James Bright, *Automation and Management* (1958) and Harry Braverman, *Labor and Monopoly Capital* (1974). That debate is further exemplified in the empirical work of Robert Blauner, *Alienation and Freedom: The Factory Worker and His Industry* (1964), as regards blue-collar work and Ida Hoos, *Automation in the Office* (1961), for the white-collar ranks of back-office employees.

Early and influential studies of the unique work of managers, executives, and other white-collar types can be found in Melville Dalton, *Men Who Manage: Fusions of Feelings and Theory in Administration* (1959); Chester Barnard, *The Functions of the Executive* (1938); William Whyte, *The Organization Man* (1956); and C. Wright Mills, *White Collar; The American Middle Classes* (1951). For a detailed overview of managerial activity see Peter Drucker, *Management* (1973). Henry Mintzberg, *The Nature of Managerial Work* (1973), broke new ground in a close-up empirical study of what top managers actually do. One of the best accounts of the many facets of corporate life is in

Rosabeth Kanter's *Men and Women of the Corporation* (1977). Michel Crozier's *The World of the Office Worker* (1971) is also a very useful study. In Robert Schrank, *Ten Thousand Working Days* (1978), there is an unusual first-person account of the contrasting nature of work in the factory and office. James Green, *The World of the Worker: Labor in Twentieth-Century America* (1980), provides a good overview of developments in organized labor. John Howell Harris, *The Right to Manage: Industrial Relations Policies of American Business in the 1940's* (1982), is a penetrating analysis of industrial relations and managerial legitimation.

Many of the unique structural and occupational shifts of the late twentieth century were first discussed in Daniel Bell, *The Coming of Post-Industrial Society: A Venture in Social Forecasting* (1976). Michael Piore and Charles Sabel argure for an end to the Fordist paradigm in *The Second Industrial Divide: Possibilities for Prosperity* (1984). Highly competent analyses of late-century developments in the structure and content of occupations are available in two edited collections: Eileen Appelbaum and Peter Albin (eds.), *Labor Market Adjustments to Structural Change and Technological Progress* (1990), and Paul Adler (ed.), *Technology and The Future of Work* (1992). The debate over new computer-based technologies and their impact on the nature of work continues with Feldberg and Glenn's "Proletarianizing Clerical Work: Technology and Organizational Control in the Offices," in Andrew Zimbalist (ed.) *Case Studies in the Labor Process* (1978); Joan Greenbaum, *In the Name of Efficiency: Management Theory and Shopfloor Practice in Data-Processing Work* (1979); Harley Shaiken, *Work Transformed: Automation and Labor in the Computer Age* (1985); David Noble, "Social Choice in Machine Design: The Case of Automatically Controlled Machine Tools," in *Politics and Society* 8 (1978); and Shoshana Zuboff, *In the Age of the Smart Machine: The Future of Work and Power* (1988). A critical analysis of workplace relations is Richard Edwards, *Contested Terrain: The Transformation of the Workplace in the Twentieth Century* (1979). Two very useful analyses of changing skill requirements in the late-century economy are Russell Rumberger, "The Changing Skill Requirements of Jobs in the U.S. Economy," in *Industry and Labor Relations Review* 34:4 (1981), and Kenneth Spenner, "Technological Changes, Skill Requirements, and Education: The Case for Uncertainty," in Richard Ayers and David Mowerys (eds.), *The Impact of Technology: Change in Employment and Economic Growth* (1988). Two thoughtful analyses of developments in labor relations during the late century are Charles Heckscher, *The New Unionism: Employee Involvement in the Changing Corporation* (1988), and Robert McKersie and Thomas Kochan, *The Transformation of American Industrial Relations* (1987).

INDUSTRIAL PRODUCTION

Alfred D. Chandler, Jr.

The changing processes of production in the United States during the twentieth century were both a response to and a cause of the transformation of an economy that was rural, agrarian, and commercial into an economy that was urban and industrial. Fundamental to this transformation was the development of new products and new processes. Technologies of production—those that involved more than hand production—were either mechanical processes (i.e., used machinery) or chemical processes. Throughout the twentieth century these processes of production have become more science based; physics and metallurgy have been applied to mechanical systems and chemistry and biology to chemical systems.

Throughout the century, technological innovation brought the substitution of machinery and chemical equipment for human labor in the processes of production. This shift can be best defined by the changing ratio of labor employed to investment in capital equipment, a ratio that has increased throughout the twentieth century.

The substitution of capital equipment for human labor differed from industry to industry, however, and these differences reflected the different basic processes of production in each industry. In industries where the processes were primarily chemical, the ratio of capital to labor rose more rapidly than in industries where the processes were mechanical (i.e., where raw materials were processed by machines). Among the mechanical industries the ratio of investment in capital equipment to the number of production workers rose most rapidly in industries that fabricated basic metal products and turned them into machinery, vehicles, and other equipment. This was because fabricating metal products and assembling them into machinery and equipment required more capital investment than did processing of wood, fibers, food stuffs, and other products of farm and forest. So, too, metalworking industries required a much larger labor force than did industries that used chemical processes. In table 1, U.S. industries are placed, according to the U.S. Census Standard Industrial Classification (SIC) system, into one of three categories based on the primary production methods used in that industry.

From the start industries that used primarily chemical processes of production were the most capital intensive, that is, had the highest ratio of capital to production workers. Industries that mechanically processed materials (other than metals) remained the most labor intensive, that is, had the lowest ratio of capital to workers; those processing metals became increasingly capital intensive. In table 1 the SIC categories are listed roughly in order of decreasing capital intensity at mid-twentieth century. The changing capital intensity of a representative industry in each of the three categories is shown in figure 1.

Rising capital intensity reflected the growing use of increasingly continuous production within a manufacturing establishment. This trend is indicated by the growth in the value added by manufacturing—that is, the difference between the cost of materials and the revenues received for the finished products. If costs of material remained the same, the value added by manufacturing increased as the flow of materials through the manufacturing plant became more continuous and faster. At the beginning of the century this throughput (that is, units of goods processed within a specific period of time), as reflected by value added in manufacturing, was already substantially greater in chemical processing industries than in mechanical processing industries. As capital replaced labor in the metal fabricating and machinery industries, the processes of production became more continuous and more capital intensive, daily throughput became larger, value added became greater, and productivity in terms of output per worker increased. At the end of the century, technological change has had a similar, although less dramatic, impact on the older labor-intensive industries that mechanically process materials other than metals. Thus, continuing technological innovation increased

Table 1.   U.S. CENSUS STANDARD INDUSTRIAL CLASSIFICATION OF U.S. MANUFACTURING INDUSTRIES

SIC Group	Industry
	Capital-Intensive Industries (Chemically Processed)
29	Petroleum and coal products
28	Chemicals and allied products
20/21	Food, tobacco, and kindred products
33	Primary metals
26	Paper and allied products
32	Stone, clay, and glass products
30	Rubber and miscellaneous plastics products
	Increasingly Capital-Intensive Industries (Mechanically Processed—Metalworking)
37	Transportation equipment
35	Nonelectrical machinery
36	Electrical and electronic equipment
38	Instruments and related products
34	Fabricated metal products
	Labor-Intensive Industries (Mechanically Processed)
27	Printing and publishing
22	Textile mill products
23	Apparel and other textile products
24	Lumber and wood products
25	Furniture and fixtures
31	Leather and leather products
39	Miscellaneous manufacturing products

SOURCES: For the Standard Industrial Classification, U.S. Office of the Budget, *The Standard Industrial Classification Manual, 1972* (1972). For the industry groupings by capital intensity, calculated from U.S. Bureau of the Census, *Historical Statistics of the United States, Colonial Times to 1970* (1975), vol. 2, series P123–176, p. 685, and series P58–67, pp. 669–680 and related tables.

the ratio of capital to labor and output per worker in all three processes of production. The result was that as output and value added increased, the number of production workers in the United States leveled off in the postwar years and began to decline in the 1980s (table 2).

The history of the changing processes of production falls into three chronological periods. The first, from the 1880s to World War I, was characterized by the transformation of existing industries and the creation of new ones that followed the completion of modern transportation and communication systems—the railroad, steamship, telegraph, and telephone. Those transformations had the greatest impact on the chemically processed industries. During the second period, between World War I and World War II, the internal combustion engine, particularly

its use in motor vehicles, created new ways of production (and reshaped existing ones) that increased capital intensity, value added by manufacturing, and, therefore, labor productivity particularly in the metalworking industries. Comparable transformations in the third period, the post–World War II era, reflected the impact of three war-engendered technological revolutions—those that created the present-day aircraft, polymer petrochemical, and electronics industries. They affected all three categories of industries.

THE 1880s TO WORLD WAR I: THE SECOND INDUSTRIAL REVOLUTION

The completion of modern transportation and communication networks quickly reshaped existing pro-

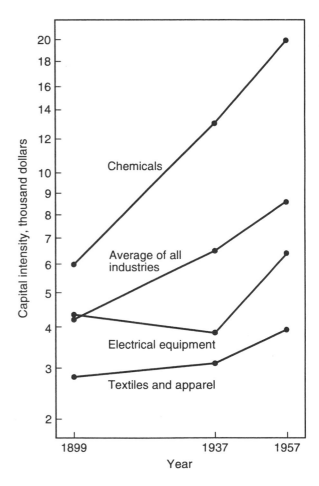

Figure 1.   Capital intensity of representative U.S. manufacturing industries, 1899, 1937, and 1957. ($1,000 manufacturing capital stock in 1929 dollars per production worker) Data from U.S. Bureau of the Census, *Historical Statistics of the United States, Colonial Times to 1970* (1975), vol. 2, series P1–12, P58–67, P123–176.

Table 2.   VALUE ADDED BY MANUFACTURE, 1899–1986[a]

Year	Capital-Intensive Industries		Metalworking Industries		Labor-Intensive Industries		Total		Production Workers (thousands)
1899	1,877	40.6%	840	21.4%	1,756	38.0%	4,823	100.0%	4,500
1937	10,817	44.2	7,142	29.1	6,638	26.7	24,497	100.0	8,560
1957	60,576	41.8	53,946	37.1	30,432	21.0	144,954	100.0	12,840
1970	119,611	40.5	118,371	40.1	57,162	19.4	295,114	100.0	13,580
1986	328,900	32.0	465,300	44.9	240,300	23.1	1,067,500	100.0	11,770

[a] For the industry groupings by capital intensity, see table 1. Data from earlier censuses were used to adjust the 1899 numbers. Dollar amounts in current million dollars.

SOURCES: U.S. Bureau of the Census, *Historical Statistics of the United States, Colonial Times to 1970* (1975), vol. 2, series P1–12, P58–67, P123–176; for 1986 from U.S. Bureau of the Census, *Annual Survey of Manufactures for 1986* (1987), tables 1 and 2.

cesses of production and the structure of the enterprises and industries that used these processes. By the 1880s the new railroad, telegraph, steamship, and cable systems made possible an unprecedented high volume of steady and regularly scheduled flows of goods and information through national and international economies. Never before had manufacturers been able to order large amounts of supplies and expect them to be delivered within, say, one week. Nor could they promise their customers comparable large-scale deliveries on a specific date. The new potential for greatly increased speed and volume of production of goods stimulated a wave of technological innovations that swept through western Europe and the United States. This wave of innovation, which took place during the last decades of the nineteenth century, created what historians have termed the second industrial revolution. (The first industrial revolution, which began in Britain in the late eighteenth century and spread to western Europe and then to the United States in the first half of the nineteenth century, was spearheaded by a new technology—the factory system of production. In textiles, leather, woodworking, metalmaking and metalworking, small shops, mills, and foundries using hand-operated machines or furnaces were replaced by factories in which workers tended batteries of machines, furnaces, or other devices powered by water and increasingly by coal-produced steam.)

In many industries, the resulting increases in output by manufacturing establishments were unprecedented. For the first time manufacturers were able to reap the benefits of the economies of scale, that is, to reduce cost per unit of output (and so enhance the value added by manufacturing) as volume increased. Such potential cost advantages of scale, however, could only be fully realized if a constant flow of material was maintained. To maintain such throughput required careful coordination of not only

the flow through the processes of production (and the more continuous the flow the better), but also the flow of input from suppliers and the flow of output to distributors and final customers.

Nevertheless, investment in production facilities large enough to exploit these advantages was not enough in itself to achieve the cost benefits of economies of scale. Two other sets of investments were necessary. Entrepreneurs organizing these activities had to create national and then international marketing and distributing organizations. They also had to recruit hierarchies of lower and middle managers to supervise production, distribution, and purchasing; and teams of top managers to monitor and coordinate the activities of the functional units and to allocate resources for the enterprise's future production and distribution.

The first firms to exploit fully the economies of scale by such three-pronged investments in production, distribution, and management had powerful advantages because those firms that followed had to build plants of comparable size, and then set up comparable national and international marketing organizations. Finally in the more technologically advanced industries, both had to establish research and development facilities to improve products and processes.

The three-pronged investment by the first movers brought into being the modern integrated industrial enterprise operated by teams of salaried managers. It also shaped the very structure of the industries in which those manufacturing enterprises operated. The capital-intensive industries were quickly dominated by a small number of large managerial enterprises that competed for market share and profit in a new oligopolistic manner. Price remained a significant competitive weapon, but these firms competed even more forcefully through functional and strategic capability—that is, by carrying out more efficiently processes of production and distribution. They did this by locating more suitable sources of supplies, providing more effective marketing services, pursuing differentiation (in branded, packaged products, primarily through advertising), undertaking systematic research and development, and moving quickly into expanding markets and out of declining ones.

The long-established labor-intensive industries were the least affected by the transportation and communications revolutions. At the beginning of the century, textiles (including apparel) and forest products (including lumber and furniture) were, next to food, the nation's largest users of capital and employers of labor. Leather and publishing and printing were far ahead of industries important later on—oil, rubber, electrical machinery, and transportation equipment—in the utilization of both capital and labor. In the older labor-intensive industries, the factory system of production had been firmly established by the mid-nineteenth century, although small handicraft shops and establishments continued to thrive.

In most factories, workers were primarily machine operators. Improved machines did increase the speed of throughput and the volume of output, but faster machinery did not substantially change existing systems of production. In cotton textiles, for example, the lighter "ring-frame" continuous spinning machinery replaced the original "mule" type, increasing output per machine-tender by one-third. The automatic Northrup loom, adopted in the 1870s, within a decade had increased the number of looms that a single worker could handle from eight to twenty-four. Similar advances increased the speed and output, as well as the cost, of equipment used in the production of wool, silk, and flax. Even more technologically complex and costly machinery made carpet production the most capital intensive industry in the textile group by the 1910s.

Despite these advances, factory production of cloth was carried out in much the same manner (i.e., sequentially) that it had been prior to completion of the railroad and telegraph networks. Raw cotton, wool, or silk was cleaned on the first floor of the factory. On the next, batteries of spinning machines spun the thread or yarn, which was then dressed and sent to the next floor. There, machines wove it into cloth, which was again dressed. The cloth, cut and folded, then went to adjacent buildings to be bleached and then dyed or tinted. In all of these textile factories, the machinery was first powered by water, then increasingly by steam. Energy was transmitted from a central source to the machines through a system of drive shafts and leather belts. After the 1890s electric power and wiring began to replace belting, and small electric motors permitted a more flexible organization and layout of the shop floor.

So, too, the production of apparel and shoes was increasingly carried out in factories equipped with new types of sewing and shoe machinery. That machinery, in turn, began to be produced in volume in the 1880s. The mechanization of shoemaking had reduced the labor costs of a pair of shoes by 1895 to one-ninth of what it had been in 1865. Reductions, although smaller, were also achieved in the cost of producing apparel, and the amount of ready-made clothing manufactured increased rapidly.

Comparable labor saving machinery was developed for the fabrication and assembly of wood products such as millwork and furniture. This facilitated the production of standardized millwork—paneling, window frames, and the like—and office and household furniture. In publishing and printing during the last years of the nineteenth century, the coming of linotype, monotype, and other fast and accurate typesetting machines again greatly reduced labor time.

As raw materials for most of these industries came from hundreds of farms or lumbering enterprises, the manufacturers continued to purchase their raw materials from middlemen. Similarly, because their products went to thousands of customers, they also sold their output to middlemen (wholesalers), who in turn sold them to retailers. In these labor-intensive machine-operated industries, most companies carried out a single function—production—and competed primarily on price and often on style.

Thus, although technological innovations did increase the volume of output of individual machines, once the machines were in place the ratio of capital to labor remained much the same. The speed of throughput (i.e., the amount of materials processed within a specific time) could be only slightly increased by improving plant design, increasing the energy used, and enlarging the size of the works. Therefore, textiles, apparel, lumber, furniture, leather, and publishing and printing remained the most labor-intensive industries.

The completion of the new railroad and telegraph systems created more opportunities to exploit scale economies in industries using chemical processes of production than in those employing mechanical ones. Their intensive use of heat and energy, the construction of larger and more efficient stills and furnaces, and the use of valves and pumps to coordinate and regulate flows increased both the capacity of plants and the speed with which materials flowed through them. Such increases in throughput were also possible in mechanical industries where the development of continuous-process machinery, more complex metalworking machines, and the careful design of the flows through the fabricating and assembling processes could vastly increase daily output.

With the adoption of the more continuous chemical and mechanical technologies, the ratio of capital to labor quickly rose. The first mover companies to make the three-pronged investment in production, distribution, and management quickly dominated their industries. They and a small number of challengers competed functionally and strategically for markets at home and abroad. Nearly all of them created marketing organizations. However, at this time they rarely integrated backwards into the production of raw materials because there was no lack of suppliers or of chemicals used in these processes.

In food, tobacco, and related products (SIC 20 and 21) the new technologies were both chemical and mechanical, although more were chemical than mechanical. The production of tobacco was transformed in the 1880s with the adoption of two continuous process machines. One machine, designed by James Bonsack, produced 120,000 cigarettes per day, as compared with 3,000 by the most dexterous handworker, and reduced costs to one-sixth their earlier level. The second machine packaged cigarettes as quickly as they were produced. James B. Duke was the first to adopt these machines but was quickly followed by four other entrepreneurs. All built national and then worldwide marketing organizations and began to compete, primarily by advertising. In 1890 the five formed a single enterprise, the American Tobacco Company.

Duke and his associates then rationalized the industry. Production units were placed under a single manufacturing department. The consolidated sales department soon marketed and distributed 5 billion cigarettes per year, first to all parts of the United States, and then worldwide. The leaf department purchased and cured tobacco in the United States and Turkey. The purchasing department bought in bulk packaging materials, machinery, and other supplies. To oversee operations, there was a single central financial and auditing department. In 1911 American Tobacco was dismembered into four companies for violations of the Sherman Antitrust Act, but the successor firms dominated the industry throughout the rest of the century, with only one successful new challenger, Philip Morris. Cigar manufacturing, on the other hand, was dominated by semiskilled hand labor until the 1920s, when a machine comparable to the Bonsack was developed for cigars.

The transformation of grain processing and marketing came somewhat more slowly. Nevertheless, as in tobacco, the first companies to make a large enough investment in production, marketing, and management to exploit fully the new scale economies (such firms as Pillsbury and Washburn-Crosby) continued to be leaders in the industry for decades. Here, the new technologies resulted from a combination of innovations. Some were borrowed from Hungarian and other European millers, others were developed in the United States. They included multiple grinding machinery, steel rollers to replace grindstones, and purifiers, aspirators, and other equipment for scraping, grading, dressing, and then packaging the flour. These "automatic, all-roller, gradual-reduction mills," as the flour companies called them, were almost continuous-processes establishments. To assure a steady flow of supplies into the mills, grain companies had buyers in rural towns and employed full-time brokers at the grain exchanges in Chicago and other midwestern cities. Nevertheless, because so much wheat was grown and the market was so big, a large number of small milling establishments continued to produce for local needs.

As Duke had done in tobacco, the grain processors packaged and branded their products. In so doing, these manufacturers took over a basic function of the wholesaler, that of dividing bulk shipments into small units to be redistributed to retailers. When packaging became part of the production process, the manufacturer rather than the wholesaler placed its brand name on the packaged product and began to advertise it. Unlike the wholesalers, who sold locally, the manufacturers advertised nationally. The wholesalers as a result suffered a loss in status. They became essentially distribution agents for the manufacturers, whose marketing departments received orders from retailers and coordinated the flow of goods to them.

The packaging revolution received another boost in 1883, when the Norton brothers, Edwin and O. W., built the first automatic-line canning factory. Their machines could solder 50 cans per minute and other machines could add tops and bottoms at 2,500 to 4,400 units per hour. On the basis of this new canning technology, which also involved new chemical food-processing techniques, Gail Borden made the large investment in production and distribution that made his firm the first mover in condensed canned milk. The Dorrances of Philadelphia did the same for Campbell Soup products; Henry John

Heinz of Pittsburgh, for his "57 varieties" of pickles, sauces, and other products; and Libby, McNeill & Libby for an enterprise that produced canned meat in Chicago.

Another packaging innovation, the mass-produced glass bottle, encouraged the development of large integrated enterprises in the distilling of grain spirits—rye and corn (Bourbon) whiskey. As with tobacco, overproduction led to the leading producers forming a single enterprise, the Whiskey Trust, which at the turn of the century became Distillers Securities. This company remained the industry's largest producer and survived the years of Prohibition (1919–1933), becoming, as National Distillers Products, the industry's leader with such well-known brands as Overholt, Old Crow, Old Taylor, and Old Grand Dad. In two other distilling industries, sugar and vegetable oil (produced from corn and cotton and linseed oil), massive output resulted in the formation of three of the six successful trusts formed in the 1880s—American Sugar, American Cotton Oil, and National Linseed.

Technological innovations in the 1880s made brewing beer even more capital-intensive than distilling whiskey. The most important were the new sterilization and preservation techniques derived from Louis Pasteur's studies, which were basic in canning as well. Innovation in brewing also included the Linde cooling compressor, steam boiling, continuous bottling methods, and temperature controlled railroad cars for transportation. By 1900, Anheuser Busch (St. Louis), Pabst, Schlitz, and Blatz (Milwaukee), and Moelin (Cincinnati) had built national distilling networks. Through intense advertising, they soon reached national markets.

The development of continuous processing in meat production followed the innovation of the refrigerated car by Gustavus Swift, which permitted the meat butchered in Chicago to be distributed to the rapidly growing cities of the Eastern Seaboard. In the mid and late 1880s, Swift and Armour (Chicago's leading meatpacker), followed by four other firms, raced to build refrigerated branch houses along railroad tracks. As the century opened, these first movers had become giant enterprises. By 1903 Swift & Company disassembled more than eight million animals per year, Armour more than seven million. By then, taking apart a steer included 78 distinct processes and 157 workers, who killed and dismembered the animals, then stored and loaded meat onto the cars. The sales departments had the critical task of adjusting daily the flow of fresh meat from packing centers at different locations to approximately two

hundred storing and selling branch houses. Armour and Swift had also become the two largest leather producers in the country and were two of the "Big Four" in fertilizers (made from bones), and Armour was a major producer of glue and abrasives. In 1902, Armour's Transportation Department operated 13,500 separate refrigerator cars, Swift's 5,900, which they used to become the nation's largest transporters and marketers of butter, eggs, poultry, and fruit, as well as beef and pork. During the next decade the two leaders and four smaller competitors expanded their European markets and pushed aside British meatpackers to become leaders in the industry in Argentina, Uruguay, and Brazil.

Although many significant sectors of food and related industries became capital intensive, others remained labor intensive. Because markets were so widespread, producers of agricultural crops so numerous, the nature of the processes so seasonal, and the other products (particularly bakery, dairy, and meat products) so perishable, SIC 20 industries remained small, local, and regional enterprises. In 1921, the first time the U.S. Census listed the group's establishments, it had far more than any other two-digit category (more than 50,000). But those firms that did make the three-pronged investment in the more continuous processing technologies dominated markets at home and moved into international markets.

By the 1880s, continuous or large-batch chemical processes were rapidly altering the methods of production for paper, glass, rubber, oil, and chemicals. In the paper industry (SIC 26 in figure 1) the transformation came with the adoption of German-developed technology to produce paper from wood rather than from rags, thus making paper a leading forest product industry. The pioneers in the new processes quickly drove those who used the old processes out of business, except those who specialized in high-quality rag papers. By the 1890s, the industry had become dominated by nine companies, and in 1898 the leaders joined to form the International Paper Company. Because the consolidated enterprise failed for a decade to rationalize production in the manner of American Tobacco, it was quickly challenged by the smaller firms. Once rationalization occurred, however, International Paper remained the industry's leader for many decades, although its market share continued to drop. Because the new processes required a steady flow of wood pulp, by 1930, 80 percent of the paper manufacturers owned their own pulp works. And because the processes required large quantities of timber and massive waterpower (both to provide cheap power and removal of waste), the American pulp and paper companies established their mills near rivers and large tracts of timber.

Leading firms soon developed full lines of products: pulp and newsprint, paperboard containers, bags and other packaging material, and then stationery and specialty papers. Only in stationery and other high-grade paper products did smaller single-function firms marketing through wholesalers continue to thrive.

The new technologies that transformed the production of plate glass, window glass, and glass containers combined another German invention—the Siemens continuous-process tank furnace—with the use of gas instead of coal. Gas heat was much superior for the glassmaking process because it greatly reduced impurities. The application of the recently developed electricity to power and control the speed of glassmaking machinery represented still another important improvement. In 1893, John Pitcairn's Pittsburgh Plate Glass Company built a large plant that incorporated these techniques to produce heavy "plate" glass for mirrors and windows for stores and other commercial and industrial establishments. In the depressed years of the 1890s, Pitcairn merged all but three major producers into his company; production was quickly rationalized, and the extensive network of sales offices and warehouses expanded. Pittsburgh Plate Glass remains today the largest glass producer in the United States.

Continuous-process technology came more slowly in the production of household window glass and glass bottles. In both, Michael Owens was the innovator. In 1912 Owens began to perfect a continuous process for pulling window glass into thin sheets, which gave his company, Libby-Owens, a critical cost advantage. Owens already had commercialized a continuous bottle-making technique, using a vacuum system to shape the bottle. Financed by E. C. Libby, he expanded production output, set up a national marketing organization, and quickly dominated the industry after 1910. A competitor was able to challenge Owens by developing a new and faster "feeder" system, but in 1929 the two bottle makers merged to become Owens-Illinois. In the 1920s, Pittsburgh Plate Glass and Libby-Illinois became competitors in both window glass and plate glass.

The other products listed by the census in "stone, clay and glass" (SIC 32 in table 1) that were produced by high-volume, capital-intensive methods were gypsum, asbestos, and abrasives, cement, and concrete products. A few large integrated firms competed oligopolistically. In other categories, bricks, tiles, ceramics, clay goods, pottery, china, tableware and kitchenware, and stone products were made by smaller firms using more labor-intensive batch methods.

Rubber and oil were still new industries in the 1880s. In rubber (SIC 30) the cost advantages of volume production were more the result of the economies of scope rather than those of scale. (Scope economies result from producing a number of items within the same establishment from the same raw materials and the same intermediate processes. An example is the production of dyes of many different colors for many different materials, pharmaceuticals and film from the same chemicals and chemical processing.) The use of different admixtures and accelerators in the rubber vulcanizing process and the different machines used to mold, extrude, and further process the rubber made it possible to produce in a single plant a wide variety of apparel (boots, gloves, and rainwear) or industrial goods (hoses, belting, flooring, and insulated materials). These factories, built in the 1880s and 1890s, also began to produce bicycle tires. By 1899, the number of workers per establishment in rubber was 130 as compared with 45 in leather and 9 in apparel. By that date the industry had become dominated by three large firms: B. F. Goodrich in apparel, Rubber Goods Manufacturing (an 1899 merger) and the United States Rubber Company (an 1890s merger) in industrial goods. In 1905 U.S. Rubber acquired Rubber Goods Manufacturing.

In oil (SIC 29), the cost advantages were those of scale rather than scope. Indeed, that industry provides the clearest illustration of the relationship between the coming of continuous-process production techniques on the one hand, and size, vertical integration, and industrial dominance on the other. The industry began in 1859, when oil was discovered in northwestern Pennsylvania. During the 1860s and 1870s, refineries rapidly increased their output by intensifying heat using a new higher-pressure "cracking" (fragmenting and isomerization of petroleum fractions) process, by using seamless wrought iron and then steel bottoms that increase the capacity and longevity of the equipment, and by improving cooling as well as heating operations. Steam power was increasingly used to move the flow of oil through the different stages of refining. By the early 1870s, a nearly continuous multidistillation process was perfected. This allowed separate end products to be distilled out at different stages of the process—first gasoline, next kerosene, and then heavy fuels and lubrication stocks—as petroleum flowed through the works. Because the primary demand until after 1900 was for kerosene, oil continued to be refined in large batches, with the products other than kerosene often being burned off or disposed of as waste.

The first entrepreneur to begin to use these new methods was John D. Rockefeller, who in 1868 completed in Cleveland, Ohio, the world's largest refinery works. By the early 1870s, it was producing one-fifth of the world's output of kerosene and its costs dropped from an average of 5 cents to under 3 cents per gallon. High volume of output permitted Rockefeller's Standard Oil Company to obtain railroad rates lower than those of competitors for its volume shipments. As the lowest cost producer with the lowest cost of transportation in the industry, Standard Oil had the leverage needed to acquire financial control of competitors. By the late 1870s, Standard Oil and the companies it controlled produced almost 90 percent of U.S. kerosene output. At the same time the capacity of refineries had been increased to between 1,500 and 2,000 barrels per day, reducing costs to 2.5 cents per gallon. Between 1879 and 1881, the Standard Oil companies constructed over 4,000 miles of pipeline connecting the oil fields to all major refineries. This assured a far greater and more certain flow of crude oil into the refineries than did railroad transportation.

In 1881, Rockefeller and his associates formed the Standard Oil Trust in order to consolidate legally the many companies that had come into their control and thereby facilitate the rationalization of the industry. Between 1882 and 1885, the Trust reduced the number of its refineries from fifty-six to twenty-three, concentrating production of kerosene in three 6,000-barrel-per-day refineries and converting other refineries for production of lubricants, paraffins, wax, and Vaseline. By 1884, the cost to the Trust of processing one gallon of crude had dropped to four-tenths of a cent. In 1884, purchasing was centralized in a single buying unit, and the rationalization of distribution quickly followed. Between 1885 and 1890 the Trust built its own fleets of railroad tank cars and oceangoing tankers, and obtained a nationwide wholesale organization. Quickly it organized comparable marketing networks overseas, often in the form of subsidiaries jointly owned with local jobbers. Integration backward into ownership of oil fields came only in the 1890s, as the Pennsylvania fields were played out and new fields in Ohio and Indiana were opened up. By 1892, to assure itself of a steady supply, Standard Oil was extracting 25 percent of the nation's crude oil.

In 1884, the Trust set up its central office at 26 Broadway in New York City where a team of middle and top managers monitored the activities of the functional departments to assure the coordination of the flow of crude and refined products through its global industrial empire. Top managers determined the enterprise's strategy of competition and growth and allocated resources. At this time, Standard's major competitors were the powerful Nobel and Rothschild enterprises in Europe, Royal Dutch in Asia, and two or three smaller firms in the United States.

But with the opening of the huge Texas and California oil fields at the turn of the century, and the coming of a new market—the motor vehicle—challengers quickly appeared. The U.S. industry was soon transformed into a modern oligopoly. By 1911, when the U.S. government dismembered Standard Oil Company for violating antitrust laws, there were already 7 other integrated oil companies besides Standard among the 200 largest American industrial enterprises.

The rapid growth of the oil, rubber, glass, paper, food, metals, textiles, and other industries led to a comparable expansion in the output of basic chemicals that were used in the production processes: caustic soda, chlorides, sulfuric and other acids, and many other chemicals. Improved techniques for production of these basic chemicals permitted the construction of larger plants with much greater output and lower costs. For example, for sulfuric acid, increased outputs lowered the cost of production from 5 cents per pound in 1867 (when production was 60,000 tons) to 1.5 cents per pound in 1882 to less than .5 cents per pound in 1900 (when one million tons was produced). By the end of the century, the ratio of capital to labor in the production of chemicals was second only to that of the still small oil industry.

In the production of iron, steel, aluminum, copper, and other primary metals, products were refined by chemical processes but shaped more by mechanical ones. During the nineteenth century, ironmaking had been improved and its output increased as coke (processed coal) replaced charcoal furnaces to transform iron ore into "pigs" of finished iron. Coal-heated reverbatory or puddling furnaces replaced the water-driven hammer, which reduced the impurities in pig iron. In the 1850s, rolling and finishing mills were built to transform pigs of iron into rails, bars, and shapes, which were then shipped to other processors for further fabrication. In the new steel mills of the 1880s and 1890s, the Bessemer converter and the open hearth furnace essentially replaced the reverbatory furnaces. The Bessemer converter could transform three to ten tons of pig iron ingots into steel with a blast of hot air, which lasted only a few minutes, thrust through the egg-shaped converter. Molten steel was then poured into ingot molds that were moved on to the rolling and finishing mills. The open hearth process, essentially a much improved puddling operation, used scrap steel as well as iron. By changing the mix of materials used and the temperature, companies could produce a variety of steels, usually of higher grade than Bessemer steel.

Andrew Carnegie was the first to build a completely new "greenfield," works specifically designed to coordinate the flow of ore and coal from the receiving yards to the blast furnaces, then to the converters, and then to the rolling and finishing mills. This establishment, the J. Edgar Thomson Works, went into full production with the completion of its initial battery of blast furnaces in 1879. In 1881 Carnegie enlarged and redesigned the nearby Homestead Works to make use of both the Bessemer and open hearth processes. In 1891, he installed a new "direct rolling process" at a third works, the Duquesne mills. By 1894, the production of these three Carnegie works totaled 1.7 million tons of steel, more than had been produced in the entire country only six years earlier.

Massive increases in throughput drove down costs and prices. Between 1880 and 1889, the price of steel rails at Pittsburgh plummeted from $67.50 to $29.25 per ton; by 1898 the price had fallen to $17.63 per ton. As output expanded and prices fell, profits rose so quickly that within a few years Carnegie became one of the nation's wealthiest individuals. Carnegie's leading competitor was the Illinois Steel Company, whose four works had an annual output of 2 million tons by the mid-1890s.

Such vast increases in throughput stimulated backward and forward integration. The two giants, Carnegie and Illinois, purchased coal mines and large ore deposits, the latter primarily in Lake Superior's rich Mesabi Range. The two firms concentrated on the production of numerous primary products—ingots, bars, rails, beams, structures, tubes, and sheet steel—and they quickly created marketing organizations to sell these products to railroads, contractors, machine makers, and other industrial customers. In the 1890s the producers of secondary steel products—wires, pipes, tinplate (a thin sheet steel coated with tin to make it rust-resistant)—began to merge into nationwide enterprises such as American Steel and Wire, American Tin Plate, American Steel Hoop, National Tube, American Sheet Steel. To be more certain of their supplies, the secondary produc-

ers began to build their own primary steelworks, and in response Carnegie threatened to begin producing secondary products. That threat led in 1901 to the formation of the United States Steel Company, the nation's first billion-dollar merger. Financed by J. P. Morgan, it united the leading primary producers, Carnegie and Federal Steel (the successor to Illinois Steel) with a number of major secondary producers.

U.S. Steel, like International Paper, was slow to consolidate the facilities and activities of its many constituent parts—a delay that gave smaller independents the opportunity to complete investments essential to become effective competitors. Once U.S. Steel's rationalization was completed, the structure of the industry remained much the same for the next half century. U.S. Steel, the dominant firm, determined prices, with smaller firms following its lead. But the smaller firms (Bethlehem, Republic, Armco, Crucible) expanded, and continued throughout the years to take market share from U.S. Steel through functional efficiency and strategic moves.

In nonferrous metals, new technologies in the 1880s and 1890s transformed one ancient industry—copper—and created a new one—aluminum. The transformation came with the development of an electrical generator that provided enough power for electrolytic reduction of smelted copper and refined alumina. In 1891 five new electrolytic copper smelters became operational, and the minimum efficient scale was so high that only twelve more smelters were built in the United States during the next 90 years (and seven of these were in operation by 1910). Five companies—Anaconda, Phelps Dodge, American Mining and Smelting, Kennecott, and Metallgesellschaft (a German firm)—dominated global as well as U.S. markets from the 1890s until well after World War II. They increasingly relied on their own sales forces to market their products. By World War II, only 10–15 percent of their primary copper products were sold through independent agents. As the postwar period opened, the four American firms produced 94 percent of the nation's output of smelted copper and 90 percent of refined copper.

Large-scale production of aluminum began with the development of a comparable electrolytic method to reduce alumina (refined bauxite). In 1888 a plant using that technology, built by two Pittsburgh entrepreneurs, Arthur Vining Davis and Alfred E. Hunt, reduced the price of refined aluminum from $12.00 to $2.00 per pound. In 1896, to achieve the full potential of the new technology, the company built a plant at Niagara Falls to utilize one of the nation's cheapest energy sources, water. With its completion, the price of aluminum dropped to 32 cents a pound.

To secure a market for their massive output, the company (which took the name of Aluminum Company of America in 1907) quickly developed a wide range of products: fittings, tubes, rods, castings, wire and cable, containers, foil, and kitchenware, which it sold through its own national and then international salesforce. Low-cost production and extensive product development had created almost insuperable barriers to entry. A potential competitor would have had to make a huge investment in facilities and develop a variety of new operating skills to be successful. Only after World War II did the monopoly become an oligopoly. Then the government, after an antitrust suit, turned over many of the war plants Alcoa had built to two other companies, Reynolds Metals and Kaiser Aluminum & Chemical, which had acquired five years of wartime experience in the production of aluminum.

The move to continuous-process production and increased capital intensity came more slowly in the shaping of metals and the making of machinery than in chemically based industries because fabricating and assembling parts into machines required a far greater amount of physical labor in each of the successive stages of production. In addition, working metal and fabricating and assembling metal parts required far more costly and complex machinery than did working nonmetal materials. Well into the twentieth century the metal-working and machinery industries remained the home of small shops producing custom-ordered equipment, usually in small batches. Nevertheless, as specialized markets grew much larger with expanding industrialization, more and more machinery firms focused on production of standardized equipment for those markets. Such firms moved toward volume output by fabricating and assembling standardized parts in large batches or even in nearly continuous sequential line production.

Of the metalworking and machinery industries, fabricated metals (SIC 34) provides a striking contrast to the capital-intensive industries in terms of size of establishments. In 1937, SIC 34 had 493,000 production workers in 8,688 establishments, an average of 56.7 workers per establishment. Primary metals, in contrast, with a work force of 792,000 in 3,245 establishments, averaged 244 workers per establishment, more than four times as many as a firm in SIC 34.

In machinery other than electrical (SIC 35), more enterprises had moved into higher volume production of standardized machines through fabricating and assembling of standardized parts. Thus the number of production workers in SIC 35 in 1937 (654,000) was 31 percent more than the number in SIC 34 and the capital expenditures of $4.1 million were nearly twice the amount. Although the number of establishments was much the same, they were concentrated in two three-digit categories, SIC 354 (metalworking), and SIC 359 (unclassified industrial machinery). (The census divides each of the two-digit Standard Industrial Classifications listed in table 1 into three- and four-digit classifications. Thus, SIC 35 includes nine three-digit classifications. For example, SIC 354 is metalworking. That classification in turn, includes nine four-digit classifications such as SIC 3541, machine tools, and SIC 3543, industrial patterns.)

Companies in SIC 35 three-digit categories (other than 354 and 359) began, during the last decades of the nineteenth century, to produce standardized products for major labor-intensive industries—textiles, shoes, lumbering, woodworking, printing, mining, and construction. Others concentrated on one major line of products such as pumps and hydraulic equipment or steam boilers, or conveyors and transmission equipment, or elevators. These products were manufactured in large batches, often shaped to customers' specialized needs. The companies built extensive salesforces and used engineers and other trained personnel to install and help maintain the equipment sold and to make arrangements for financing consumer purchases. Many also operated plants overseas. By 1914, such leaders as United Shoe Machinery, Mergenthaler Linotype, Babcock & Wilcox (boilers), Otis Elevator, Chicago Pneumatic Tool, Worthington Pump, Crown Cork & Seal, and Westinghouse Air Brake, had built manufacturing facilities abroad. Indeed, by 1914 SIC 35 included more American multinationals than did any other two-digit SIC category.

In the light machinery industries, methods of manufacturing moved closest to the continuous process developed in the chemical-based industries. This was because such industries served thousands of customers and had correspondingly long production runs. In harvesters, reapers, and other agricultural equipment; in typewriters, cash registers, adding machines, and other business equipment; and in sewing machinery, American companies had acquired by 1914 a near monopoly of international markets. By the mid-1880s each of Singer Sewing Machine's two factories, one in New Jersey and the other in Scotland, were able to produce 8,000 machines per week. By the mid-1880s McCormick Harvester made

75,000 machines annually at its plant near Chicago. In the first decade of the twentieth century, its successor, International Harvester (a 1901 merger) built large factories in Germany and Russia.

The *Census of Manufactures* published in 1882 described the system used in the mass production of sewing machines, a description that captures the essence of the new mass production in similar industries. Many different materials were used: "pig-, bar-, and sheet-iron and iron and steel wire, bar-, and sheet steel, malleable irons, Japan varnish, and power and machine supplies in general, wood for casing (largely walnut and poplar), besides a considerable range of other materials." In making the metal parts, the bulk of materials passed successively from one operating unit to another—from the foundry to the "tumbling-room, annealing, Japanning, drilling, turning, milling, grinding and polishing, ornamenting, varnishing, adjusting and proving departments." In addition, there were other metalworking departments producing tools, attachments, and needles. The "wood-working and cabinet-working departments constitute a separate and distinct manufacturer." Finally, a large assembling department was responsible for the completion of the product and its "gauging," inspection, and preparation for shipment. Factory design was continually improved to assure a smooth and scheduled flow of throughput, although the production process was not yet fully continuous. By twentieth-century standards, the movement of materials through the factory was still relatively slow. The final finishing and assembling of parts still required individual filings. Parts were standardized but not yet fully interchangeable.

As the light machinery producers moved into volume production, they created national and then worldwide wholesale organizations. They quickly discovered that existing jobbers were unable to assure that the retailers who sold their products could provide essential marketing demonstrations and service after the sale. Nor were the wholesalers able to supply the retailers with the credit necessary for purchasers to pay for the products. Moreover, the independent jobbers were slow to forward payments from the retailers to the company's corporate office—payments that were needed to meet current operating costs. Although some sewing and business machinery firms relied on their own network of retail stores, most producers of light machinery sold through networks of exclusive franchised dealers—retailers who handled their products exclusively but who could also sell related products made by other companies. Thus a McCormick Harvester dealer could sell other companies' plows, seeders, and mowers, lines that McCormick itself did not produce.

The last decades of the nineteenth century, which witnessed the transformation of many existing industries, also saw the creation of two new ones—electrical equipment and chemically produced metals and synthetic materials. Of the two the electrical equipment industry had the most immediate impact. The new electrical technology created a brand new source of light and power, a new form of urban transportation and a new way to produce metals and chemicals.

Because the electrical manufacturers sold systems for both producing and using power, they had to manufacture a number of quite different items that could be effectively used only after they had been linked together into a single system. The turbines, generators, and transformers that created electric power were large, indeed often massive, pieces of equipment. They and large electric motors, streetcars, and subway trains were made in large batch, customized processes. On the other hand, small equipment such as connectors, circuit breakers, switches, relays, fuse boxes, sockets, lamps (bulbs) and other lighting fixtures, and motors (both stationary and portable) lent themselves to more coordinated sequential volume production. Thus, production was concentrated in large works, which were designed so that different shops or factories using the same processes were able to benefit from both economies of scope (through the use of similar materials and machines) and economies of scale (by maintaining a large and steady throughput).

The first companies to make the requisite investment in these systems of production quickly dominated their industry. By the mid-1890s, little more than a decade after Thomas Edison completed the first central station in the country at Pearl Street in New York, four enterprises already dominated world markets. Two of these were American (General Electric—an 1892 merger of Thomson-Houston and Edison Electric—and Westinghouse) and two were German (Siemens and AEG). The four companies continued to dominate until after World War II.

Each of the four leaders quickly built large works and established their marketing organizations. Charles Coffin, the entrepreneur who created Thomson-Houston, constructed his first major factory in Lynn, Massachusetts, in 1884. From then until 1892, at least one new factory building was added each year to the Lynn works, for the production of generators, motors, meters and trolley cars. In those years employment at Lynn rose from 45 workers to 3,500. After Thomson-Houston merged with Edison Electric in 1892 to form General Electric (GE), the Lynn works concentrated on lighter products, while heavy machinery and engines were produced at the Edison Electric Works at Schenectady and lamp production at the Edison plant in Harrison, New Jersey. Westinghouse also concentrated production of its many products in its giant works in East Pittsburgh, Pennsylvania.

A marketing organization was more essential in this new industry than in most others because the installation and initial operations of electrical equipment by untrained workers could easily cause serious injury or death by fire or electrocution. So the first movers immediately created national and then international salesforces not only to market, but to install and service their products. Production then followed sales abroad. Even before the merger with Edison Electric in 1892, Thomson-Houston built plants abroad in both Britain and France. Westinghouse followed with works in Berlin in 1899 and then in France, Germany, Italy, and Russia. Because the equipment it sold was so costly to purchase, General Electric formed a credit company—Electric Bond & Share—to take shares of stock from the new utility companies it equipped.

The sophistication of this new physics-based technology led the companies to set up the nation's first industrial research laboratories. Before 1900, GE had laboratories at both Lynn and Schenectady that worked full time to improve the company's several lines of products and the production processes. In 1900, GE's senior executives agreed on the need for a "research laboratory that would be for the commercial application of scientific principles, and even for the discovery of those principles." To head the laboratory they hired in 1901 Willis R. Whitney, an MIT professor. Whitney's team of chemists and electrical engineers was soon working on the development of x-ray equipment, vacuum tubes, and tungsten filaments for better lighting. They were also doing research on improved plastics for insulating materials and metal alloys for equipment and wiring.

As the electrical equipment industry grew, small regional and niche firms began to produce specialized equipment, standardized replacement parts, or both. In addition, a few large companies came into being to develop and produce ancillary equipment or related electrical-based devices. The storage battery provides an excellent example of the first; the telephone the second. Because the demand for power fluctuated during the twenty-four hours of a day, utility and traction companies needed to store power to meet peak loads. Storage batteries were also needed to power telegraph, then telephone systems, police and fire alarms, and lighting in subways and trains. Here again, first mover advantages proved very powerful. The two companies that built the first large plants, created the first global marketing organizations, and then built and purchased plants in distant markets, dominated the industry worldwide until after World War II. They were Electric Storage Battery in the United States and Accumulatorem Fabrik in Germany.

Siemens and AEG, the two German leaders supplying Europe with electrical equipment, were also the first European firms to produce telephones and switching equipment. They did so in part because most of the European telephone systems were, like the telegraph, operated by national governments, which were not involved in manufacturing equipment. In the United States, on the other hand, the providers of telephone service had from the start been private companies. The leader, American Bell Company, was reorganized in 1907 and then expanded as the American Telephone & Telegraph Company. From the beginning that enterprise manufactured phones, switching, and other equipment through a subsidiary, the Western Electric Company. By 1915 its manufacturing plant in Hawthorne, Illinois, near Chicago, covered 200 acres and employed more than 17,000 workers. The company had had its Experimental Shop since the 1880s, which by the turn of the century was employing Ph.D. physicists. In 1909, the laboratory was enlarged as the Research Branch. By 1929, when its name was changed to Bell Laboratories, it employed 3,100 persons. Some 2,000 of these were on the technical staff working on radio, electronics, chemistry, magnetics, optics, applied mathematics, speech and hearing, and a wide variety of other projects. The staff was engaged both in improving existing products and processes and in developing new ones.

The coming of electricity also helped to create the modern American chemical industry. In Europe, particularly in Germany, first movers in the production and distribution of synthetic dyes, pharmaceuticals, fertilizers, and fibers (rayon) held a tremendous advantage. By the time of World War I, they dominated American as well as European markets. In the new electrolytically produced chemicals, however, Americans quickly built strong positions. Indeed this new technology gave many of the leaders in the U.S. industry their start. In 1898, Union Carbide completed a plant at Niagara Falls to produce calcium carbide and also acetylene for lighting and welding.

In 1906 a second plant was built to make silicones and ferrous-silicones, chemicals that were used in the initial processing of iron and nonferrous ores and then of metal alloys, including high-carbon ferrochrome. At about the same time, the founder of Dow Chemical, Herbert Dow, was producing chlorine electrolytically from brine in high volume at Midland, Michigan. After building a bleach plant close to optimal scale, the Dow Company began producing chloroform, carbon tetrachloride, insecticides, and fungicides. In 1907 it began making magnesium, magnesium alloys, and compounds—all electrolytically. In 1909, a third new company, American Cyanamid, built a plant at Niagara Falls, which, using a German patent, produced the first man-made fertilizers in the United States. Earlier the Solvay Process Company (a predecessor of Allied Chemical) began to produce, under a Belgian license, man-made caustic soda, an ingredient vital to the production of glass, textiles, and other chemicals.

These new chemical products were manufactured in giant plants using vast amounts of basic chemicals and electricity. In this area American enterprises pioneered in two essential production techniques. One was the use of pilot plants or semi-works to determine and test the most effective processes and the most marketable products before building a final works scaled up to optimal size. The other was termed "the unit system of production," a method of designing a plant to assure the most efficient use and monitoring of flows through the entire works. Each unit represented a single physical change in the many grinding, mixing, and evaporating processes as well as in each of the chemical or electrolytic transformations involved. This unit system of production thus provided a highly coordinated batch, often continuous-flow, process.

Because of the complexities of the production process, particularly the new electrolytic techniques, American chemical companies increasingly hired trained chemists and chemical engineers. By 1921, 30.4 percent of all the scientific personnel in U.S. industries were employed in chemicals, far more than in the second-place industry, electrical equipment, which had 7.7 percent. These chemists were involved primarily in operations, rather than in research, to improve product and process. Only the E. I. du Pont de Nemours Powder Company had set up major research and development laboratories before World War I. Others in the industry followed suit in the 1920s.

By World War I, the distinction between three basic types of industries in terms of capital expended and labor used had become well defined: labor-intensive machine-operated industries, capital-intensive chemical-based industries, and the large labor-employing but increasingly capital-intensive metal and machinery industries. These basic distinctions continued throughout the century. The more capital-intensive industries continued to be dominated by a few large firms, which continued to compete functionally and strategically in global as well as national markets.

THE INTERWAR YEARS: THE INTERNAL COMBUSTION ENGINE AND SCIENCE-BASED INDUSTRIES

In the years between World War I and World War II the transformation of production processes and the changing rank of industries in terms of labor and capital utilized reflected the impact of a new basic technology, that of the internal combustion engine and the elaboration of existing and the creation of new technologies in the chemical and electrical industries. As the twentieth century opened, the gasoline-powered internal combustion engine was just beginning to compete with steam and the new electric power as a source of energy. Its immediate and most profound impact was on transportation. After 1900, the year Ransom E. Olds demonstrated the commercial viability of the automobile by producing and selling more than 500 of his Oldsmobiles, the auto industry grew exuberantly. By 1911, 200,000 passenger cars were produced annually; by 1919, 1.5 million; by 1929, 4.5 million. Then, with the Depression, came a staggering sales drop to 1.1 million in 1932, a recovery to 3.9 million in 1937, and another fallback to 2.9 million in 1939. By 1917, of the three-digit SIC classifications, motor vehicles and equipment (SIC 371), was already ranked fifteenth in number of workers, seventh in wages, sixth in value added by manufacturing, and seventh in value of products. By 1935, twenty-one years later, it ranked third in the number of workers employed and first in the other categories.

This huge increase in output reflected the culmination of the sequential line production that was first put into place in the 1880s by the producers of agricultural equipment and other light machinery producers. The moving assembly line, perfected in 1913 at Henry Ford's Highland Park plant in Detroit, brought nearly continuous-process production to the metal and metalworking industries. The Highland Park plant used the most advanced materials, metalworking machinery, and best-practice sequential-line production systems that had been developed over the past two decades. Improved conveyors, roll-aways, and gravity slides helped speed up the flow of materials through the plant. Soon Ford engineers began to experiment with a moving line, first in assembling the flywheel magneto, then other parts of the engine, and then the entire engine. In the summer of 1913, work began on a moving assembly line to complete the chassis and the car itself. The innovation was an immediate success, throughput soared, and labor time expended on the production of a Model T dropped drastically, from 12 hours and 8 minutes in the summer of 1913 to only 2 hours and 35 minutes by the end of the year. By April 1914, Highland Park was producing 1,000 cars a day. Average labor time per car had dropped to 1 hour and 33 minutes. The resulting scale economies of throughput permitted Ford to sell his cars at far lower prices than any competitor, to pay the highest wages in the industry, and to acquire an enormous personal fortune in a very short time.

In distribution, Ford followed the pattern of the light machinery companies by setting up exclusive franchise dealers supported by an international wholesale network. The Ford organization scheduled deliveries, monitored dealers' service and repair facilities, and oversaw advertising and payments to the corporate office. In distribution, Ford carried out another impressive innovation—the branch plant, which assembled "knocked-down kits" made in Detroit. This reduced shipping expenses, while maintaining the cost advantages of scale manufacturing. By 1913, Ford had built thirteen assembly plants in the United States and one in Manchester, England. Other manufacturers soon followed Ford's example in distribution as well as production. By 1929, a total of 6,500 franchised retail dealers were selling and servicing automobiles.

In the 1920s two companies, General Motors (GM) and Chrysler, successfully challenged Ford's dominance by developing a full line of cars and light trucks—in General Motors's advertising slogan, a vehicle for "every purse and purpose." This strategy permitted the companies to exploit economies of scope by having their different end products made of much the same materials, parts, and accessories. During the Depression this spreading of costs over several product lines further reduced the ability of smaller single-line producers to compete in cost and price. In 1935 the Big Three held 90.5 percent of the domestic market.

Even before that, American automobile manufacturers had begun to dominate the world market. In 1928, 72 percent of all cars exported to foreign markets were American. In 1929, when U.S. production was 4,390,000, France's output was 210,000, Britain's 212,000, Germany's 90,000, and Japan's 24,000. All but 350 cars in Japan were assembled from General Motors and Ford knock-down kits. Subsidiaries of these two companies also accounted for a substantial share of the production of automobiles in Britain and Germany.

By this time the patterns of backward integration were changing, reflecting the availability of supplies. Ford, as the Highland Park plant came into full production, found it necessary to control nearly all parts and accessories in order to assure a steady output of 1,000 cars per day. As GM began to expand output in the 1920s, numerous small motor vehicle suppliers had already begun operation, which enabled GM's top managers to adopt an "insurance policy" strategy of controlling roughly one-third of its suppliers and purchasing the rest of its supply from independent firms. Chrysler, which did not round out its full line until 1929 with the introduction of the low-priced Plymouth, felt little pressure to integrate backwards because the Depression had drastically reduced demand and so had assured availability of supplies at reasonable prices.

The Big Three concentrated on cars and light commercial vehicles. In the production of heavier, more specialized trucks and trailers, both output and value of production were smaller. In 1929, 882,000 trucks and other units were produced as compared with 4.5 million cars. Sequential batch production remained the mode, although there was also room for smaller niche companies. Some firms did grow large by utilizing economies of both scope and scale. By 1930, White Motor and Mack Truck were among the 200 largest manufacturing companies in the United States; by 1948 so was Fruehauf Trailer. Such firms relied more than did the automobile producers on direct sales to commercial and industrial customers, and, at the manufacturing end, much more on outside suppliers.

The requirements of the automobile and truck producers, the growing demand for replacement parts and accessories plus the needs of agricultural, industrial, construction, and mining machinery makers for comparable equipment made motor vehicle parts and accessories (SIC 3714) one of the nation's largest industries. In 1935, the number of employees hired and the amount of wages paid was actually higher in this category than in the production of motor vehicles (SIC 3711). Its leaders, Borg-Warner,

Bendix, Dana, and Thompson Products, were among the nation's largest companies. By 1930, Borg-Warner, utilizing economies of scope, was producing clutches, gears, radiators, springs, chains, sprockets, heat exchange elements, and fuel pumps for a wide variety of motors and vehicles. In the 1930s it added lines for household appliance products and then produced the appliances themselves.

The automobile companies remained less diversified. Ford failed dramatically in attempts to produce tractors and airplanes. In 1921 GM decided to pull out of the tractor business because the market was so different from that of automobiles. In 1929, however, GM did purchase control of a producer of aircraft engines and bought shares in a maker of airframes and parts and accessories, primarily, in the words of president Alfred Sloan, "as a means of maintaining direct contact with developments in aviation." But GM's major success in diversification was the production of diesel locomotives. Its new plant at LaGrange, Illinois, went into full production in 1938. Once World War II was over, the diesel quickly replaced the steam locomotive on American railroads because standardized diesel locomotives assembled from standardized parts were cheaper to build and much less costly to maintain.

The internal combustion engine replaced steam power in boats and ships as well as in locomotives, but in a more evolutionary manner. Again the volume of production helped to determine the systems of production. Small outboard motors came to be made with assembly techniques, while large diesels for ocean liners and naval vessels were still custom built. The airplane was made possible by the internal combustion engine, although the aircraft industry remained tiny until the coming of World War II. In 1935, when the wholesale value of output of passenger vehicles was $1,707 million, that of the aircraft industry as a whole, including parts and accessories, was only $42.5 million.

It was the automobile, the bus, and the truck, not the airplane or ship, that transformed American life during the interwar years. In the production industries the availability of flexible truck transportation gave companies a much wider choice of location for their factories and warehouses. The automobile altered the lifestyles of American production workers, managers, and much of the rest of the population. In some cases the new transportation changed the structure of industries.

The transformation came quickly in the production and distribution of perishable foods, for example. In meatpacking it helped break the oligopoly based on railroad transportation. Small packers were able to deliver meat directly by refrigerated trucks to chain food stores. Motor transportation also permitted local dairies and bakeries to become regional in size. By the 1930s the first national dairy and bakery companies appeared.

In other industries, the internal combustion engine transformed entire product lines, particularly in agricultural and construction equipment. By 1924, International Harvester had developed a multipurpose tractor, the Farmall, that quickly drove Ford's less flexible Fordson out of the market. Harvester's major competition then came from companies in industries with closely related markets and systems of production. Its competitors included John Deere, a first mover in steel plows, whose all-purpose tractor came on the market in 1928; Caterpillar Tractor, the pioneer developer before World War I of tracked (as differentiated from wheeled) tractors, which quickly became the leader in industrial construction equipment; and Allis-Chalmers, a producer of lumber and mining machinery, which had also moved into the production of electrical equipment. In the 1930s Caterpillar, after it had established an international sales force and built plants abroad for construction equipment, turned its agricultural equipment business over to Deere. Harvester, on the other hand, which had facilities abroad before World War I, developed a line of trucks and construction equipment for overseas as well as domestic markets. These firms used sequential line production with additional moving assembly lines in a number of the assembly processes.

The rapidly expanding motor vehicle industry created a huge new market for other capital-intensive industries, including oil, rubber, glass, and metals, and brought comparable technological responses to the increased demand. In oil, the new demand for gasoline required technological innovation in both chemical and engineering technologies in order to raise the minimum efficient scale of refineries. Such scaling up involved much more than merely increasing the size of refineries. Increases in throughput and more efficient (higher octane) gasoline came from the development of new vacuum stills, continuous distillation, improved catalytic cracking, and other process innovations. Such techniques were developed by the major oil companies from innovations often developed in university chemical engineering departments. Between 1919 and 1929, refinery throughput expanded nearly 270 percent, while the number of establishments only rose 22 percent and the number of employees only 29 percent. By 1929, a daily throughput of 32,000 barrels of crude had become standard for a single refinery. By the 1930s, the petroleum industry was far and away the most capital intensive of American manufacturing industries. (Its capital intensity was 56.1 as compared with that of chemicals at 20.9, given in figure 1.) It was the third largest user of capital for production facilities, behind the two basic industries—food and primary metals.

Such expansion of production stimulated vertical integration. In order to assure uninterrupted throughput in their refineries, the twenty largest oil companies by 1937 held 96.5 percent of the nation's crude oil stocks. The shift from kerosene to gasoline as the major product plus the huge new volume of output required the construction of a completely new wholesale network of storage tanks, delivery trucks, and pumps at roadside retail service stations—at first regionally, and then nationally and internationally. Because the oil companies, like the auto and light machinery producers, preferred not to take on the costs and risks of operating these retail outlets, they either sold or leased them to franchised dealers. By 1939 only 1.7 percent of gasoline sold in the United States was marketed through company-owned outlets. Comparable, but smaller, sales organizations were built to handle the refineries' other products—kerosene, lubricants, and fuel oil—all of which were extracted in the processes of making gasoline.

In the rubber industry, the swiftly expanding demand for pneumatic tires turned the industry to exploiting economies of scale even more than those of scope. In tires, production per man-hour rose by 433 percent between 1914 and 1935, the largest for any three-digit U.S. industry. Of the six companies that came to dominate the industry, only the two leading pre-tire companies (U.S. Rubber and Goodrich) continued to make rubber apparel and industrial products as well as tires. Of the four major new tire makers, two, Firestone and Goodyear, produced original equipment for automobile and other manufacturers as well as replacements, while the other, General Tire and Fisk, concentrated on replacements alone. Firestone and Goodyear integrated backward into rubber plantations and cord-making facilities to a much greater extent than did Goodrich and United Rubber. All six companies built distribution networks at home and abroad. By 1929, independent wholesalers accounted for only 8.2 percent of all tire sales in the United States.

In glass and metals, the impact of the new motor vehicle market was somewhat less than in oil and rubber. Nevertheless, in glass the huge increases engendered by automobile demand permitted several smaller firms to challenge the first movers with a new European (the Fourcault) continuous process. These smaller firms merged in 1935 to form Furco Glass, which joined Pittsburgh Plate Glass, Owens-Illinois, and American Window Glass as one of the four major producers of nonspecialty glass. In metals the need of vehicle producers for large quantities of lighter, stronger materials stimulated innovation in light metals and alloys. It also promoted the development of both hot and cold continuous strip mills, which reduced large slabs of steel to 1/16th of an inch sheets at high speed. Here the innovations came not from U.S. Steel, the dominant firm, but from the more specialized, although large companies, such as Crucible Steel and American Rolling Mill. (They ranked 60th and 68th among the largest U.S. industrial enterprises in 1930).

Second only to the internal combustion engine as a dynamic force in U.S. production during the interwar years was the continuing application of science to industrial processes, primarily in the electrical equipment and chemical industries. During these years the electrical industry moved along the trajectory begun before 1900, and the chemical industry for the first time came into its own. Both benefited from the forced removal of the German first movers from global markets. This occurred during the four years of World War I, followed by the travail of five years of military occupation of the industrial Rhineland and Ruhr, a period also of superinflation within the German economy.

The removal of the Germans made General Electric the industry's dominant firm in global competition, followed by Westinghouse. In 1929, GE was the largest electrical manufacturer in Britain, held 25 percent of the voting shares of Germany's AEG, and had controlling interest in leading electrical manufacturers in France, Mexico, South Africa, and Japan. At home, its research and development laboratories gave it first mover advantages in x-rays and other medical equipment, in household appliances, and in radio. R&D had made GE a major player in the production of alloys, plastics, and other manmade materials.

The new product lines called for investment in both new production facilities and marketing organizations in new locations nationwide. In appliances, where the greatest growth came through the application of assembly line production, GE set up a separate "merchandising department." It provided a wholesale marketing and service network for electric-powered refrigerators, washing machines, vacuum cleaners, and space and hot water heaters. The production and distribution of x-ray equipment, alloys, and other materials were administered through different wholly owned subsidiaries. The development and then production and distribution of radio receiving and transmitting equipment was carried out through the Radio Corporation of America (RCA) formed in 1919 as a joint venture of GE, Westinghouse, and AT&T's Western Electric. In 1930 these owners sold off their interest in RCA, which then set up its own laboratories and pioneered the development of television.

Also in the interwar years, the R&D departments at GE and Westinghouse continued to improve and develop their existing products in their basic electrical power, light, and motor businesses. The research organization of AT&T's Western Electric did the same in telephones and telephone equipment. Such incremental development also brought new products. At GE, for example, the number of product lines (whose operating results were accounted for separately) rose from 10 in 1900 to 85 in 1920, to 193 in 1930, and to 281 in 1940. Thus RCA, Bell Laboratories, GE, and Westinghouse research laboratories helped to lay the scientific and technological base for the electronics revolution that was to transform the American economy after World War II.

In chemicals, the removal of German competition between 1914 and 1925 gave the American companies the start they needed to compete successfully in man-made dyes, pharmaceuticals, and fertilizers based on German technology. At the same time, they began to commercialize new products on their own. In the 1920s the major companies followed Du Pont's example by investing heavily in research and development. Like Du Pont they used a strategy of diversification based on their company-specific technological capabilities. Du Pont had seriously embarked on such a strategy even before the end of World War I in order to assure postwar use of the immense plants and technical and managerial skills that had been developed during World War I. Based on its capabilities in nitro-cellulose technologies used in making munitions, the company commercialized rayon, cellophane, photographic film, refrigerants, paints, pigments, and varnishes. For the new automobile market, it developed quick drying finishes, antifreeze, and ethyl gasoline additives. It also continued to expand the production of dyes, nitrates, ammonia, and intermediate chemicals. Dow's expanding line, based on salt chemistry, came to include a variety of chlorides, bromides, phenols, ammonias, styrene, and

magnesium. Union Carbon & Carbide (a 1917 merger headed by Union Carbide) expanded its electrochemical products, including batteries, welding and cutting materials, liquid oxygen and other gases, and metal alloys. In the 1920s it pioneered in making chemicals based on oil rather than coal feedstocks. Allied Chemical, also a merger (1921), concentrated on products based on coal tar and coal gas chemistry. Monsanto expanded its fine chemicals from saccharine to vanilla, caffeine, phenol, and specialty chemicals for the rubber industry. American Cyanamid moved from fertilizers to other organic chemicals, and in 1930 became one of the first major chemical companies to invest in pharmaceuticals. In the 1930s these major companies were beginning to exploit the science of polymer chemistry in ways that would create huge new markets after World War II. Smaller chemical enterprises expanded in much the same manner but developed fewer lines.

The strategy of diversification into technologically related products based on systematic institutionalized research and development required the chemical companies to develop new marketing organizations and to set up different research laboratories and often new production facilities. Such expansion then forced a reorganization of the enterprises' administrative structures. For example, at Du Pont, the process for producing cellophane was very similar to that for making rayon. But the finished product, which went to a very different set of industrial customers, required the creation of a wholly new marketing organization.

To coordinate and monitor the activities of the new product lines, the Du Pont Company in 1921 invented a multidivisional administrative structure—an organizational innovation of major significance. The managers of divisions were responsible for the production, distribution, R&D, as well as profit and loss for a major product line. The central corporate office monitored the current performance of the divisions and allocated resources for future activities of the divisions and the continuing growth of the enterprise as a whole. By World War II, other chemical companies had followed Du Pont's example. So too had Westinghouse, RCA, and, shortly after the war, GE. A number of firms in the food, nonelectrical machinery, and transportation equipment industries also took on a multidivisional structure as they developed new products for closely related markets.

By the coming of World War II the transformation in the processes of production stimulated by the internal combustion engine had run its course.

1143

Changes engendered by the science-based industries had taken hold. Diversified industrial enterprises, each with firms competing in several distinct markets, were becoming the norm in industries with technologically complex processes of production. The worldwide economic depression of the 1930s had temporarily reduced the output of American industrial enterprises and slowed economic growth.

AFTER WORLD WAR II: NEW TECHNOLOGIES AND THE TRANSFORMATION OF PRODUCTION

After 1939, World War II became the driving force for economic growth and industrial transformation. It had a far greater impact on American production processes than did any previous war. Its duration was much longer than that of World War I, and it was fought with far more technologically complex weapons systems.

For many major industries, particularly metals and machinery, wartime demand called for the expansion of existing facilities to produce relatively similar products. Tanks, trucks, and jeeps replaced autos and commercial vehicles on Detroit assembly lines. In 1939, because of the Depression, U.S. industrial facilities were still underutilized. But with the advent of war, industrial production quickly soared to unprecedented heights. In nonelectrical machinery, for example, the number of production workers almost doubled, from 563,000 in 1939 to 1,254,000 in 1947. And value added by manufacturing almost quadrupled from $2,037 million to $7,834 million, in current dollars.

Besides expanding existing industries, war needs created new industries and transformed older processes of production, particularly in science-based manufacturing. Overnight, the modern aircraft industry came into being. In 1939, 5,865 planes were built in the United States; in 1943, 85,433, and in 1944, 95,272. Basic innovations occurred in aircraft design, motive power, and processes of production. Particularly important for postwar developments was the jet engine, which began to appear on experimental fighter planes late in 1944. In oil refining, the needs of the air armadas for high-octane aviation gasoline brought still more innovative production techniques. That activity and the synthetic rubber program, which became vital after Japan took control of most of the world's supply of raw rubber, laid the foundations for the postwar polymer and petrochemical revolution that so changed the oil, rubber, and chemical industries. The government-sponsored

program for the development of penicillin and the expansion of the program for sulpha drugs helped bring about a postwar therapeutic revolution that transformed the pharmaceutical industry. The massive production of radio, radar, sonar, gunnery equipment, and other devices set off an electronics revolution that brought an information revolution, led by the computer. Finally, the government's Manhattan Project not only developed the bomb that ended the war with Japan, but also created a new man-made source of energy.

The modern commercial aircraft industry took form in the early postwar period. Production of military aircraft, except during the Korean and Vietnam wars, was reduced. In the years following the Korean conflict, military aircraft accounted for about one-third of total output. In the second half of the 1950s the production of commercial planes, which now had much greater carrying capacity than prewar models, averaged about 7,000 a year. In the 1960s the average came closer to 12,000 annually. By the late 1960s, most new planes were powered by jet engines and their passenger capacity had been substantially increased.

The production of these increasingly costly, technologically advanced aircraft involved sequential batch production more than continuous process techniques. It was carried on by the "project management" method of design and production that had been developed during wartime production. That is, a core team of managers with both functional and general management skills were responsible for a new or improved model from the first refinement of its design through advanced process development into the manufacturing buildup. On the other hand, engines, increasingly jet, continued to be produced more through continuous assembly line processes. Because by far the largest number of users of aircraft traveled on commercial carriers rather than individually owned craft, and because of the technological and safety factors involved in flying and parking small planes, there was little call for mass production of aircraft along the lines of automobiles and light trucks. The demand for commercial transportation soared from 5.9 billion revenue passenger miles on domestic carriers in 1946, to 30.1 billion in 1956, and to 104.2 billion in 1970.

The production of commercial aircraft and jet engines quickly became highly concentrated. Boeing, the builder of bombers—B-17, B-29, B-47, and B-52—became the first mover in postwar commercial planes by designing and producing the first commercial jet, the 707, in 1957. It then quickly made an extensive investment in production and distribution facilities, including a worldwide support system for the maintenance of its equipment. McDonnell-Douglas remained the other major player in commercial aircraft, and continued to produce military planes. The other leading aircraft producers—first Northrup and Grumman, and finally Lockheed—exited the commercial aircraft business and continued to produce military planes and aerospace products. All five aircraft builders produced a variety of parts and subassemblies. The U.S. production of engines after the war became the domain of only two enterprises—Pratt & Whitney (a division of United Technologies) and General Electric's Aircraft Engine Division. Pratt & Whitney was the first to produce the jet engine, a feat it accomplished without funding from the military; General Electric followed, but it used government funds.

War-developed missile technologies, military demands of the Cold War, and the scientific potential of space exploration created the new, largely government-funded, aerospace industry. By 1986, the production of guided missiles and space vehicles, their parts, equipment, and propulsion units employed 227,700 workers and had capital expenditures of $1.3 billion. Here, where research and particularly development costs were very high, the project management type of design and production was used even more widely than in the making of commercial aircraft.

The major aerospace enterprises were nearly all divisions of established firms. They included those of the aircraft companies just mentioned and divisions of the diversified conglomerates that had begun as aircraft producers—United Technologies (out of United Aircraft), Rockwell International (out of North American Aviation), and Martin Marietta (out of Glenn Martin). Others were divisions of auto parts and accessory makers such as Borg-Warner, TRW (out of Thompson Products), and Allied Signal (out of Bendix), all which had become large-scale producers of aircraft engines, parts, and equipment during the war. Still other aerospace players were the divisions of electrical equipment firms such as GE, Westinghouse, RCA, and Raytheon (the last was a producer of radio tubes that had enjoyed unprecedented wartime growth). For the aerospace industry, half a century of hot and cold war assured a level of government funding that gave American manufacturers a towering lead over those of other nations.

The postwar transformation of chemicals was in full swing before the new aircraft and aerospace industries had come of age, and it had a more immediate impact on the larger economy. The reshaping of the chemical industry resulted from sharp, simultaneous shifts in the industry's supply of raw materials and in the demand for its products. On the supply side, oil replaced coal as the basic raw material. The opening of the vast Persian Gulf fields and the availability of a huge tanker fleet constructed during the war supplemented the existing sources from the East Texas oil fields to provide a much cheaper, more abundant, and versatile raw material. By the mid-1950s the U.S. chemical companies had shifted from coal to refined oil and natural gas. On the demand side, the science of polymer chemistry (laboratory-produced composites of individual monomers) produced a cornucopia of new products that brought massive construction of new plants and facilities. As a result, by 1970 the chemical industry had a capital-to-labor ratio that was twice as high as that of any other SIC category except oil; and it had the largest annual capital expenditures of any of the two-digit groups.

Both the petrochemical and the polymer chemical revolutions had prewar roots. In the 1930s oil and chemical companies had begun to produce oil-based chemicals. Four oil companies—Jersey Standard, Standard of California, Shell, and Phillips—had followed Union Carbide into the production of a small number of final petrochemical products, including fertilizers and insecticides. At the same time Union Carbide pioneered the development of a polymer, polyvinyl chloride (PVC). By 1940, Du Pont had just begun to commercialize polyethylene, a polymer discovered at the U.K.'s Imperial Chemical Industries, which Du Pont received through its Patent and Process Agreement with its longtime British ally. During the war, Union Carbide had perfected without benefit of patents the processes used to produce low-density polyethylene (LDPE). In the 1930s, Dow's research on styrene led to the development of a basic monomer (liquid styrene), a polymer (polystyrene-PS), and an end product (Styrofoam). Dow also developed another oil-based chemical, vinylidene, with Saran as a versatile end product that could be extruded into pipe and tubing, injected into molded parts, made into sheets of varying thicknesses (the household Saran Wrap, for example) or woven into fabric. The wartime demand for high-octane gasoline and synthetic rubber created an unprecedented market for such oil-based feedstocks as styrene and ethylene as well as for such basic polymers as (PVC) and (PS).

After the war, the 1952 settlement of an antitrust case against Du Pont and ICI forced them to license their polyethylene process to others. At the same time, a German chemist, Karl Ziegler, invented low-pressure techniques for making high-density polyethylene (HDPE). The new process gave it a far greater number of downstream uses than the earlier (LDPE) polyethylene. It also facilitated the development of a new and very versatile polymer, polypropylene (PP). By the end of the 1950s, large works had come on stream, including those of Hercules, Dow, and Union Carbide to produce the new basic polymers (PP, HDPE, LDPE, PVC, and PS). During the 1950s and early 1960s output of these and other new chemicals increased enormously.

With the development of these polymer intermediates came a vast array of new final products that opened up huge new markets. At Du Pont, the first production of an artificial silk (nylon) and a substitute for rubber (neoprene) both began in 1939. After the war came Du Pont's polymer-based fibers (including Dacron, Orlon, and Lycra spandex), which not only replaced but also blended well with natural fibers. So did acrylic-based fibers produced by Monsanto and Rohm and Haas. By 1985 synthetics accounted for 71.6 percent of the total fiber produced in the United States. Thus, the polymer revolution transformed existing patterns in both the textile and apparel industries in obtaining, valuing, and working with their raw materials, and brought new and transformed patterns of production.

By the late 1940s, synthetic rubber had replaced natural rubber as the source of the industry's raw material. More significant in this transformation than Du Pont's neoprene was Jersey Standard's Buna S (S for styrene), which became the product of the U.S. government's wartime synthetic rubber program. Not only did new products lower the cost of raw materials, but because of the resulting scale economies, the value added in the manufacturing process quadrupled. Between 1939 and 1950 the number of production workers in the rubber industry rose from 121,000 to 146,000 workers, while the value added by manufacturing rose from $400 million to $1,620 million.

The new polymers facilitated the creation of other new industrial materials—"engineering plastics"—that could substitute for materials such as metals, glass, and paper. The result was the introduction of new packaging and wrapping materials; stronger and more impact-resistant plastics that were cheaper to fabricate than metals; materials with unprecedented insulating, adhesive, and mechanical properties; improved coatings and finishes; and lighter and stronger substitutes for glass, such as Plexiglas and

Lucite. By the 1980s, the chemical companies had cut substantially into the markets of the primary and fabricated metal producers and even more so into the makers of traditional wood and leather as well as textile goods. The production of plastics (SIC 282 and SIC 307) had become a major American industry, using huge amounts of capital and employing more workers than any traditional labor-intensive two-digit SIC groups except printing and publishing. In 1986, the plastics industry had capital expenditures of $4,186.7 million, a work force of 509,100, and its capital intensity ratio was almost three times that of fabricated metals, which had capital expenditures of $4,485 million and 1,419,500 production workers.

In agricultural markets there were new largely ammonia-based fertilizers, herbicides, pesticides, growth-regulating, and other crop-control products. From biochemistry came new medicines for humans and animals that enhanced the therapeutic revolution set off by the new antibiotics. These new end products often resulted from reshaping existing molecules and development of new polymers and other intermediates. All the new product markets expanded rapidly during the 1950s and well into the 1960s and beyond. Between 1950 and 1970, the overall market for chemicals grew at annual rates of about 2.5 times the growth rate of GNP.

The huge growth of markets and the availability of cheap, low-cost raw materials intensified the need for technological innovation to increase the minimum efficient scale of chemical plants. At first, throughput of existing plants was expanded on the basis of existing technology simply by adding another set or "train" of production processes. But merely enlarging the capacity of plants by building parallel units reduced unit costs only slightly. Based on the knowledge gained by increasing the production of gasoline in the 1920s and 1930s and again in World War II, facilities were reshaped into single-train plants.

Innovative engineering, together with increased capital investment, made possible plants with far higher minimum efficient scale and lower unit costs. This was the case, for example, at Dow Chemical's huge plant near Baton Rouge, Louisiana, completed in 1958, and also its expanded works at Freeport and Velasco on the Texas Gulf Coast. These three works produced massive quantities of feedstocks (ammonia, ethylene, vinyl chloride monomer, styrene monomer, etc.) and commodity polymer chemicals (polyethylene, polyvinylchloride, and polystyrene). They also produced more specialized chemicals such as ethylene glycol (for antifreeze), ethylene bromide (for antiknock gasoline), and perchloroethylene (for dry cleaning fluid). The final shaped plastic products were usually processed in smaller more specialized works.

The demand for these new production technologies became so great that specialized engineering firms appeared to design and construct them for chemical companies all over the world. These specialists also built works for new entrants in petrochemical-based polymers coming from the oil, paper, food, and metal industries. The resulting massive expansion of output quickly intensified international and inter-industry competition in polymer petrochemicals.

During these years of growth in the 1960s and 1970s, some leaders such as Du Pont, Monsanto, and Rohm & Haas concentrated on the production of finished products. Others, including Dow, Union Carbide, and Hercules, focused on the expansion of intermediate commodity petrochemicals. All companies continued to produce nonpolymer products. Those firms concentrating on commodity chemicals integrated backward to take control of refineries and even of oil fields. The same concern for assured supplies caused those that focused more on specialty products to maintain their production of commodity petrochemicals to use in their finished products.

As the new single-train works came on stream, output soared and competition became intense. Overcapacity was common because minimum efficient scale was so much higher than in earlier plants. With the new plants working at well below that scale, unit costs rose.

Then came the oil crises. In 1973, the oil-producing nations raised the price of oil to over $11 per barrel (it had been $1.80 in 1970) and after 1979 from $13 per barrel to $34 per barrel. The response to the fierce competition, increased production unit costs, and the sharp rise in oil prices led to one of the most significant restructurings of companies and industries that occurred in the United States during the 1970s and 1980s. Chemical firms, whose organizational capabilities had been fashioned by commercializing new products and processes sold off commodity polymer chemicals; while the oil companies, whose capabilities had always been in the exploitation of scale economies inherent in massive continuous process output, moved into or expanded their production. By 1990, this transfer, carried out through market mechanisms in which neither Wall Street financiers nor government regulators played any role of significance, had reshaped the product lines of most of the major chemical and oil companies.

By the 1990s, the oil companies dominated commodity petrochemicals and the chemical companies, using funds received from these divestitures, moved ahead in specialty polymers and other intermediates. They also focused on such end products as additives for gasoline and food, industrial coatings, enzymes, electronic chemicals, new fibers, fiber and metal composites, new engineering plastics, ceramics, imaging equipment, materials for chips and other electronic devices, pharmaceuticals, and medical equipment. By 1986, of the SIC three-digit industries, petroleum (SIC 291) still had the nation's highest capital intensity, even though it had dropped back in the ranking of capital expended. It was followed in capital intensity by industrial inorganic chemicals (SIC 286), plastics, materials, and synthetics (SIC 282) and agricultural chemicals (SIC 287).

The most successful in terms of profit and growth of the chemical group's three-digit industries, drugs (SIC 283), never became involved in the production of commodity petrochemicals. Its transformation—the therapeutic revolution—was therefore not accompanied by overproduction and crisis.

Volume production of antibiotics during World War II had created the modern pharmaceutical industry. In 1940, the first sulpha drugs had only begun to be produced commercially, and penicillin had just been discovered in Britain. War brought government-sponsored crash programs to produce both. In 1942, Merck brought out the first industrially made penicillin. Pfizer, Squibb, and other established drug firms quickly followed. By the end of the war, both sulfa and penicillin were being produced in great volume. After the war, the drug companies developed a broad range of antibiotics (such as Aureomycin and Terramycin), antihistamines, steroids, and other chemically created and produced pharmaceuticals.

Before the war, American drug companies had carried on two separate kinds of businesses. They had produced drugs in bulk, which were then sold to pharmacists to be retailed or to be mixed into doctors' prescriptions; and they had produced and marketed cosmetics, toiletries, health care, and other branded consumer products, which were usually sold over the same retail counters as their drugs.

With the coming of antibiotics and other new drugs, production became a complex chemical process rather than a simple mixing or bottling process. Marketing turned from selling in bulk or over the counter to the art of reaching the doctors who wrote the prescriptions and the hospitals where they were used. Research became far more science-based and much more costly. Those companies—Merck, Eli

Lilly, Squibb, Pfizer, Abbott, Upjohn and Smith Kline—that made the transformation successfully in the late 1940s and 1950s were still the industry's leaders in the 1990s. After the 1950s pharmaceuticals became their major business. By 1988, for all but 4 of the 13 drug companies listed among the top 200 U.S. industrials, pharmaceuticals accounted for more than half their business, and for most more than two-thirds.

As in the case of the polymer and petrochemical revolutions, the therapeutic revolution was carried out by established companies rather than by new start-ups. Large American firms competed worldwide against long-established European companies. By 1990, the Japanese had not made significant inroads in global markets in either pharmaceuticals or specialty chemicals.

World War II provided the catalyst for change in the electronics industry. Neither the huge aircraft and naval fleets nor the massive armies could have operated effectively without the new radar, sonar, and gunnery control and other electronic instruments whose development was not only perfected but which also came to be mass-produced. These new electronic devices had many postwar uses, but none was more significant than their application to the computer—the postwar period's single most important transforming product. The computer and the industries it created were to electronics what the motor vehicle had been to the internal combustion engine. Where the motor vehicle transformed modern transportation and reshaped the systems of production, the computer transformed modern communication and played a comparable role in altering ways of production.

Three wartime developments were critical to the development of the computer. Radar and sonar production accelerated the knowledge of high-frequency electronics that was essential for building high-speed circuits. New fire (gunnery) control equipment increased the knowledge of feedback techniques. Finally, the work on breaking enemy codes (and maintaining security of allied codes) led to the creation of electric analytical machines that could recognize and process symbols.

The growth of the computer industry in the 1960s and 1970s was comparable to that of the automobile in the 1910s and 1920s, and it had a similar impact on the nation's economic growth. In 1960, 6,000 large expensive mainframe computers were in operation. By 1968, there were 67,000. Growth continued with the introduction in the late 1960s of minicomputers—smaller, less costly machines for specific purposes—particularly scientific and academic. Revenues from the production of computers and the data processing industry they created rose from $1.3 billion in 1960 to $3.2 billion in 1964 to $12.8 billion in 1972—a compound annual growth rate of about 33.5 percent. The coming of the microcomputer—the personal computer—at the end of the 1970s gave the industry another huge boost. The number of microcomputers shipped by U.S. producers increased from 344,160 in 1981 to 3,290,000 in 1985. From the start, American computer companies dominated global markets. In 1981, U.S. firms had 57.7 percent of world market share, Japan was second with 13.1 percent, and France third with 9.5 percent.

In the 1950s U.S. business machine companies began to exploit the commercial possibilities of the costly giant computers initially developed for military and scientific purposes. In 1951, Remington-Rand, the nation's leading typewriter company, produced UNIVAC, the first computer designed for business uses. Other leading business machine companies—International Business Machines, Burroughs Adding Machine, National Cash Register, and also Honeywell (the nation's leading producer of industrial controls)—quickly followed. All had been the leading company in their product lines for decades. They were joined by large established firms with electronics capabilities—AT&T, General Electric, RCA, Philco, and Raytheon. The only new start-up to enter the competition was Control Data, founded by William Norris in 1957.

All these companies made substantial investments in producing and distributing new machines, but IBM was the first to make the investments that transformed it into the industry's first mover. The strategy of IBM's top managers, particularly Thomas Watson, Jr., was to reach as wide a commercial market as possible by utilizing the cost advantages of both scale and scope economies. This called for all-purpose machines, whose development demanded not only standardization (scale) but also compatibility between different but closely related products (scope). Several years of intensive investment in research and production led to the introduction in 1964 of the System 360, a broad line of compatible mainframe computers with peripherals for a wide range of uses. IBM's massive investment in research and production, the swift expansion of its domestic and international marketing organizations, and impressive increases in its management ranks gave the company a long-held dominant position.

With the single exception of Control Data, IBM's

successful mainframe competitors continued to be the business machine companies and Honeywell, all of which acquired electronics companies to improve their production and research capabilities. In contrast, the electrical/electronics companies dropped out of the business. Raytheon and General Electric sold their operations to Honeywell, RCA's computer activities were acquired by Sperry Rand (successor to Remington Rand), and Philco scrapped its computer operations soon after it was taken over by the Ford Motor Company.

Entrepreneurial start-ups played a greater role in minicomputers and microcomputers. As the established business machine companies were concentrating on developing the capabilities of the mainframe, other opportunities emerged for machines using different architectures for different markets. In minicomputers the first mover was Ken Olsen's Digital Equipment Company, where heavy investments in manufacturing for the PDP-8 line of minicomputers were accompanied by the creation of a worldwide marketing network and a sharp rise in the number of managers. Edson DeCastro, the engineer who headed the Digital team for the PDP-8, made a comparable set of investments when he left Digital in 1968 to form Data General.

In minicomputers, the most successful challenges to Digital and Data General were not entrepreneurial enterprises, but managerial companies. By 1980, Digital ranked second and Data General fourth in revenues generated by the sale of minicomputers. IBM was first, Burroughs third, and Hewlett-Packard (an established producer of electronic measuring and testing instruments) fifth.

Much the same pattern appeared in microcomputers (personal computers or PCs). By 1980, the first entrepreneurial companies to make extensive three-pronged investments—Apple Computer, Tandy, and Commodore—accounted for 72 percent of U.S. sales. Two years later, however, the three established companies—IBM, Hewlett-Packard, and the Japanese NEC—moved in and captured 35 percent of market share, driving down the entrepreneurial first movers' share to 48 percent. IBM quickly became the dominant producer of personal computers.

The rapid growth of the computer industry as a whole, as well as the special characteristics of its product, led to an explosion of opportunities in allied and ancillary industries, as had that of the motor vehicle industry four and five decades earlier. These opportunities arose primarily in the production of software and essential supplies (semiconductor chips and silicon wafers) and for service companies that developed systems to use the computer for innumerable specialized purposes. There were fewer opportunities, however, in the distribution of products and in the production of ancillary equipment than had occurred in the automobile industry.

Until the development of personal computers this was particularly true for distribution. The large marketing organizations of the mainframe and minicomputer producers sold directly to commercial, industrial, and governmental enterprises and provided the essential maintenance and services for those large and complex machines. Indeed, the major factor in the success of the business machine companies, and of IBM in particular, over their electrical/electronic rivals was the experience they had had in selling and servicing office machinery. However, selling hundreds of thousands of small, volume-produced personal computers to individuals and to a wide variety of businesses and scientific enterprises presented a new challenge, one which IBM did not take up. From the start PCs were sold by many kinds of retailers, including company-owned stores, authorized franchise dealers, franchised groups of independent retailers, super stores (carrying every kind of computer, peripheral, and supply), and mail-order houses.

The computer makers themselves continued to produce peripheral equipment (e.g., terminals, printers, tape drives, disk drives, disk files, and computer memories) as well as consumables (e.g., cards, paper, magnetic tapes, disks, and diskettes). Because the peripheral equipment could greatly expand the uses of existing machines, however, a number of small entrepreneurial firms began to produce equipment compatible with the IBM and other computers. Thus, in the 1960s such firms as Memorex and Telex began to make tape drives, disk packs, disk drives, terminals, and computer memories. But because these firms had difficulty keeping up with the continual innovations by large firms and by entrepreneurial start-ups, they were often short-lived. On the other hand, the massive output of PCs by IBM, by makers of IBM clones, and other manufacturers created a large and rapidly growing market for independent producers of peripherals.

Except for IBM and AT&T, the computer makers rarely manufactured their own basic components—microprocessors, memories, and other chips. One reason was that the availability of such supplies was relatively assured because these components were used by many other electronics-based industries, much as parts and accessories for motor vehicles were used for many other industries based on the internal combustion engine. Chips were essential, for example, in the production of telecommunications equipment, robotics, and other instruments of factory automation, and in the design, production, and operation of aircraft and aerospace equipment. The size and variety of these markets and the technological complexity of the components provided a powerful dynamic for technological innovation. Indeed, neighborhoods of small entrepreneurial firms such as those in Silicon Valley in California and along Route 128 in Massachusetts grew up to meet this demand. Therefore, most computer manufacturers seemed assured of acquiring state-of-the-art components without undertaking the high costs and risks of product development.

What most differentiated the computer from the products of the motor vehicle or any other major industry was that computers had to be programmed, and that they were used for a greater number of purposes. The production of software and the provision of computerized services became huge industries in their own right. In the beginning, the computer companies themselves wrote the software systems necessary to operate their equipment. They worked with industry groups and other users to develop major languages such as FORTRAN, BASIC, APL, and the most widely used commercial programming language, COBOL. But because the needs of computer users were so varied, hundreds of start-up enterprises began to produce software products. One of the most successful, Computer Science Corporation, in the early 1960s developed FACT, the predecessor to COBOL, and in the 1970s wrote programs for tax preparations, ticket services, accounts receivable, payrolls, and many other uses.

As the thousands of IBM Series/360s went into use in the 1960s, the production of software became a booming business. Some enterprises required little more than the ability to write programs. In these companies, 85 percent of costs were for the writing of programs, 5 percent for new program development, and 10 percent for acquiring software packages and services. This least capital-intensive of industries became an entrepreneurial heaven. By 1969, more than 2,800 software companies were in operation. The coming of the mass-produced personal computer brought another basic change. IBM turned over its major programming to a start-up company, Microsoft, which in turn licensed out programming to a hundred other software producers. Another start-up, Lotus, with its spreadsheets for financial and accounting analysis, became a multimillion dollar enterprise almost overnight, as had Microsoft.

The development of service companies or "service bureaus," as they were called, brought entrepreneurial opportunities as numerous as those in software. These companies provided services to enterprises that knew little or nothing about computers and often did not own computers. Again, the hardware producers set up their own service companies, although more slowly and to a lesser extent than they did in software. By 1966, some 700 service bureaus were generating revenues of $500 million. By 1972 the number had more than doubled to 1,500. The growth of one pioneer, Automatic Data Processing (ADP), illustrates that growth. Formed in 1948 as a processor of payrolls, it purchased its first computer from IBM in 1961. In 1964, when it ordered its first System 360, it served 500 customers. By 1975, ADP had 75,000 users in a wide variety of manufacturing, distribution, finance and insurance companies, and government agencies. In 1987, ADP was the second largest service company in the country, with $1,467.0 million in revenue, second only to TRW's credit reporting services and followed by Electronic Data Systems, which Ross Perot sold to General Motors in 1984. The fourth largest was Computer Sciences Corporation, which had been the leading software producer of the 1960s and 1970s; it now moved into production of information support and data-base management systems, and then into networks to integrate such systems for government agencies and business enterprises.

As the huge demand for software and services indicates, the computer and the information revolution it set off affected nearly every aspect of the American economy and indeed American life. All manufacturing felt its impact. In the labor-intensive industries—textiles, apparel, lumber, furniture, leather goods, books, and newspapers—computerization helped to increase value added by manufacturing (table 2) and to a lesser extent, capital intensity. Of these industries, printing and publishing changed most, with capital intensity rising from 1.0 in 1970 to 1.6 in 1986 (as compared to that of textiles and apparel, which remained about the same, figure 2). In printing and publishing, mechanical composition by linotype and monotype machines was replaced by more flexible, faster, and more accurate electronic equipment. Recently, computer graphics in composition and laser printing in production have further increased the speed of throughput and reduced the size of the labor force.

In chemically processed industries computer controls replaced workers who had moved about the plant monitoring the flow and transformation of basic

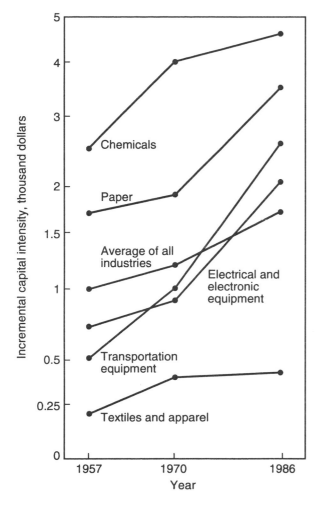

Figure 2. Annual capital intensity of representative U.S. manufacturing industries, 1957, 1970, and 1986. ($1,000 annual expenditures in 1957 dollars per production worker) Data from U.S. Bureau of the Census, *Historical Statistics of the United States, Colonial Times to 1970* (1975), vol. 2, series P1–12, P58–67, P123–176; and for 1986 from U. S. Bureau of the Census, *Annual Survey of Manufactures for 1986* (1987), tables 1 and 2.

materials (feedstocks, chemicals, and water) and checking the time, temperature, tank levels, and surge rates. In a central control room for the plant as a whole, or a major process within the plant, a small number of employees now observed on video display terminals the flows as they passed through different transforming processes. The workers in the control room took action only when computers indicated a breakdown, a slowing, or a change of flows within or between processing units.

Among these already capital-intensive industries, the new computer-based technologies had the most

effect on the paper industry, whose ratio of annual capital expenditures to labor rose from 1.9 in 1970 to 3.5 in 1986. In chemicals, the ratio increased from 2.5 in 1957 to 4.6 in 1986, in part because of the earlier rise during the polymer petrochemical transformation ("Chemicals" in figure 2). In food and cigarettes (SIC 20 and 21) the new techniques probably had a comparable impact. Their capital intensity rose steadily from 1.4 in 1957 to 2.0 in 1986. The most capital intensive of the three-digit industries in this category remained cigarettes, beverages, and grain products. But in glass, rubber and oil, computerization seems to have had only a modest effect on capital to labor ratios or value-added manufacturing. In these industries, as in chemicals, continuous process technology had been nearly perfected before the coming of the computer.

In primary metals, capital intensity actually declined between 1970 and 1986, even though computer controls were instituted for continuous casting processes and high-speed rolling mills in steel and for the smelting and rolling works in aluminum. In primary metals, the decrease in capital intensity and the sharp drop in that group's ranking as a user of capital and labor between 1970 and 1986 reflects both the replacement of metals by chemically made materials and the reduction of overall capacity in the face of foreign competition. This decline resulted in part from the failure of American steel firms to replace existing works with the new basic oxygen furnace (BOF).

In steel the BOF was the most significant postwar innovation. Using scrap rather than ore as a raw material, it had a much higher minimum efficient scale than the earlier processes. Between 1959 and 1965 Japanese producers built a number of huge greenfield BOF works with minimum efficient scale of 7 million tons. The resulting lower cost permitted them to move with strength into U.S. markets. In the 1980s small U.S. works (minimills), which used nonunion labor, produced niche products from scrap with electrical furnaces. One pioneer minimill, Nucor, made steel joists and joist girders. Another produced bars for reinforced concrete. These firms, still few in number, were able to reduce costs low enough to compete effectively in niche markets against Japanese imports and old-line American steel companies.

The metal fabricating and machinery industries were the most affected by the electronics revolution. In metal fabricating and machinery, the adoption of computer-aided design and computer-aided manufacturing (CAD/CAM) and other electronic equipment made the production processes more continuous and the industries more capital intensive. Again the impact differed for each of the metalworking groups. The effect was least in fabricated metals (SIC 34) where most of the products produced remained traditional ones. The only new electronic technologies to be widely adopted in SIC 34 were the numerically controlled (NC) machine tools—turret drills, turret lathes, planers, polishers, and the like. These machines, operated by individual workers, from the late 1960s on could be computer programmed by their users. Fabricated metals remained the home of batch processes and small machine shops. Nevertheless, the adoption of NC tools—and, in some three-digit industries such as metal forging and stamping, of computer-aided manufacturing—did increase capital expenditures and capital intensity.

In SIC 35 (machinery other than electrical), computerized machines and processes brought a greater increase in capital intensity, particularly in such three-digit SIC categories as engines and turbines and farm and construction equipment, where sequential line production had long been in operation. This was also true of SIC 38 (instruments and related products), where the ratio of capital to labor had tripled between 1957 and 1986.

But it was in electrical equipment (SIC 36) and transportation equipment (SIC 37) that the computer and the new electronic devices most dramatically moved mechanical continuous processes closest to chemical continuous processes. Between 1970 and 1986, that transformation helped to bring a threefold increase in capital intensity in SIC 36 and a fivefold increase in SIC 37 (figure 2).

The impact of the new technologies on both these groups can be best documented for SIC 371—motor vehicles and equipment. The basic layout of plants—the subassemblies and the final assembly line—remained much the same. What was new was the use of CAD/CAM, robotics and other electronic devices, and the consequent reshaping of the workers' tasks in these subassembly and final assembly lines. Robots were used primarily for welding, painting, and to a lesser extent polishing. In the assembling processes, the flows became largely computer controlled. Workers no longer carried out a single, highly specialized, repetitive task; instead they worked in teams. Their tasks were rotated, so they became knowledgeable in the handling of several different jobs. They also carried out simple machine repairs, materials ordering, quality checking of defects detected by automatic sensors, and general housekeeping. When defects were found or problems appeared, the line was immediately shut down so that the causes could be located and remedied. During the 1980s, CAD/CAM, new electronic devices, and the new methods of organizing the work force (also pioneered by Japanese automobile makers) reduced the number of workers employed and the hours spent producing an automobile. These new methods were also adopted by such leaders as John Deere and Cummins Engine in nonelectrical machinery and General Electric and Westinghouse in electrical equipment.

In electrical/electronics equipment (SIC 36) the technology of production was complex and often intricate, but required less labor and less heavy machinery than did the production of motor vehicles, commercial vehicles, industrial machinery, and aircraft. In electrical/electronics equipment, the birthplace of the computer, CAD/CAM was quickly and widely adopted. Not surprisingly, in 1986 SIC 3573 (electronic computing equipment) the ratio of capital to labor was a very high 5:1. In SIC 3674 (semiconductors and related devices) it was 7:2, the third highest of such ratios in all of the nation's four-digit categories. Only in oil refining and specialized organic chemicals was capital intensity higher. All of these ratios reflected increasingly costly investments in production facilities. For example, in the 1970s, fabricating plants for semiconductor chips cost $20 million. By the 1980s it reached $100 million, and in the early 1990s over a billion.

As this review of economic transformation and growth in the U.S. economy since 1940 emphasizes, the nation's science-based industries—chemical and electrical/electronics—have been the major driving forces for change. In these industries, basic innovations came from established business enterprises more often than from entrepreneurial start-ups. In chemicals, the commercializing of new products and processes was carried out almost wholly by large firms that had led the industry throughout the century. On the other hand, computers, the innovation that powered the postwar information revolution, were commercialized by the first movers in earlier years in the business machine industry and not, as occurred in Europe and Japan, by existing electrical enterprises. Here entrepreneurial start-ups moved into new markets with new types of computer hardware. But only those that rapidly built large enterprises continued to compete successfully in markets that were rapidly becoming global.

THE CENTRALITY OF CAPITAL-INTENSIVE INDUSTRIES

One underlying theme in the history of industrial production during the twentieth century is the replacement of human labor by machinery and other capital equipment in the processes of production. As the more capital-intensive chemical processing, metalworking, and machinery-making industries grew, their structure and the structure of companies within them acquired their modern form. These industries were quickly dominated by a small number of large firms that competed nationally and internationally in an oligopolistic manner. That is, they competed more by functional efficiency and strategic effectiveness than by price. In the older labor-intensive, machine-operated industries, smaller single function, single product enterprises continued to compete more by price, style, or by the use of highly specialized skills.

The capital-intensive industries became the core of a much larger industrial complex or nexus of interrelated medium-size and smaller business enterprises. As the first movers completed their three-pronged investment in production, distribution, and management, and as the structure of their industries jelled, the number of distributors, suppliers, equipment makers, industrial designers, consultants, and producers of replacement parts and accessories increased rapidly. So did the number of niche firms because volume production of standardized products almost always left ample room for the making of more specialized goods for smaller markets.

During the twentieth century such nexuses of large core companies and interrelated small- and medium-sized ones have been at the core of the nation's industrial growth and competitive strength. During the first two decades of the century, the industries that were transformed or created by new technologies of production provided new and expanding opportunities for investment and employment. Increasing investment in capital equipment expanded industrial demand. Expanding employment opportunities enlarged consumer demand. Thus, although machinery continued to replace labor, employment continued to grow.

The development and application of the internal combustion engine, particularly its use in the motor vehicle, continued this cycle of investment, employment, and demand through the 1920s. The number of workers in the capital-intensive, chemical-based industries and the increasingly capital-intensive metalworking and machinery industries grew substantially between 1899 and 1937, even though the Great Depression had reduced demand, output, and investment after 1929. In the three decades before the Depression, investment in R&D in terms of scientific personnel employed and funds expended was concentrated in these capital-intensive industries. Labor-intensive industries accounted for less than 5 percent of such employment and expenditures.

The United States had been the world's number one industrial producer since 1890, and by 1930 these industries helped to give it an immense lead over countries. That year, 42 percent of the world's industrial output came from the U.S., as compared to Germany's 12 percent, Britain's 9 percent, France's 7 percent, Russia's 4 percent, and Japan's 3 percent. Not surprisingly, as output and investment increased, productivity in terms of output per man-hour was much higher in the United States than in other nations.

World War II again jump-started the cycle of investment, employment, and demand, although demand remained pent up until the war's end. Then the new, war-engendered industries—aircraft and aerospace, petro/polymer chemicals, and electronics—created new industrial nexuses that continued to drive investment, output, and growth. In the 1960s and 1970s, however, as physical facilities replaced human labor, the number of production workers employed leveled off, averaging between 12 and 13 million in the 1950s and 1960s, increasing slightly in the 1970s, and then falling back to below 12 million in the mid-1980s. By 1986, fourteen of the twenty SIC groups employed fewer production workers than they had in 1957.

By the 1960s, the nations of Western Europe had largely regained their prewar economic strength, and Japan, through a massive transfer of technology, was rapidly industrializing. Industrial enterprises in both Europe and Japan quickly moved into the new industries, except for aircraft and aerospace, and created new nexuses of their own, the Europeans mainly in chemicals and the Japanese in electronics. At the same time, other enterprises moved into the mass production of motor vehicles—an industry that American firms had pioneered and had so long dominated. During and after the 1970s, increasing U.S. reliance on foreign raw materials (particularly oil), intensifying competition (particularly from Germany and Japan), and increasingly turbulent capital markets all created challenges that the U.S. industrial enterprises were striving to meet. New challenges were made even more difficult by environmental issues, a new regulatory environment, and a widening range of macroeconomic problems including inflation, changing values of the dollar, and a sharply rising national debt.

SEE ALSO Economic Performance; Infrastructure; Natural Resources; Marketing (all in this volume).

BIBLIOGRAPHY

The basic statistical sources for U.S. production are volumes from the U.S. Bureau of Census, for the years before 1970, *Historical Statistics of the United States, Colonial Times to 1970, Bicentennial Edition, Part II* (1975), chap. P, "Manufacturers," particularly Series P58–67 and P123–176; and for the years after 1970, *Annual Survey of Manufactures for 1986* (1987), "Statistics for Industry Groups and Industries: 1986 and 1985." For the period up to World War II, Alfred D. Chandler, Jr., *The Visible Hand: The Managerial Revolution in American Business* (1977), and *Scale and Scope: The Dynamics of Industrial Capitalism* (1990), provide most of the information presented here and indicate a wide variety of sources on which it is based. Harold F. Williamson, ed., *The Growth of the American Economy* (1951), chaps. 22, 24, 25, 37, and 38, provides useful additional information on the metal and machinery industries. David A. Hounshell, *From the American System of Manufacturing to Mass Production, 1800–1932* (1984), is the most valuable monograph on changing production technology before World War II.

Aside from these works, basic readings are histories of industries or biographies of industrialists. Harold Livesay, *Andrew Carnegie and the Rise of Big Business* (1984), summarizes Carnegie's accomplishments, placing them in the broader historical setting; while Joseph F. Wall, *Andrew Carnegie* (1970), describes them in much greater detail. George D. Smith, *From Monopoly to Competition: The Transformation of Alcoa* (1988), is in fact the history of the American aluminum industry. Thomas P. Navin, *Copper Management and Mining* (1988), provides useful historical information. Harold F. Williamson's coauthored two volumes, *The American Petroleum Industry: The Age of Illumination, 1859–1899* (1959), and *The Age of Energy, 1899–1959* (1963), is the best history yet written about a major American industry. Harold C. Passer, *The Electrical Manufacturers, 1875–1900: A Study in Competition, Entrepreneurship, and Technical Change* (1953), provides an outstanding analysis of the beginning of that industry. For chemicals, Alfred D. Chandler, Jr., and Stephen Salsbury, *Pierre S. du Pont and the Making of the Modern Corporation* (1971), and David A. Hounshell and John K. Smith, *Science and Corporate Strategy: Du Pont R&D, 1902–1980* (1988), provide detailed information on the U.S. industry's leaders. For automobiles, see Alfred P. Sloan, Jr., *My Years with General Motors* (1963); and Alan Nevins's coauthored three-volume biography of Henry Ford, especially vol. 2, *Ford: Expansion and Challenge, 1915–1933* (1957).

Far fewer historical studies have been written for the post–World War II years. Peter H. Spitz, *Petrochemicals: The Rise of an Industry* (1988), is indispensable for understanding the petro/polymer revolution. Peter Temin, *Taking Your Medicine: Drug Regulation in the United States* (1980), chap. 4, "The Therapeutic Revolution," is the best source on that subject. Kenneth Flamm, *Creating the Computer: Government, Industry and High Technology* (1988), supplemented by James W. Cortada, *Historical Dictionary of Data Processing: Organizations* (1987), effectively survey basic developments in the information revolution.

ECONOMIC PERFORMANCE

Richard H. K. Vietor

By the beginning of the twentieth century, the United States had surpassed the United Kingdom to become the preeminent economy in the world. Measured by gross domestic product (GDP) per person, the real output of the United States exceeded that of all other countries (figure 1). This preeminence in economic performance was to persist throughout the twentieth century, with U.S. leadership in productivity actually widening until 1950. Abundant natural resources, an immense transportation and communications infrastructure, a large internal market, and a well-balanced industrial sector all contributed to a steady rise in labor productivity, at the rate of 2.3 percent annually (figure 2). Agriculture shrunk as a percentage of national output, while manufacturing grew; services, which already dominated the economy, held steady (figure 3). Government absorbed relatively few of the nation's resources (figure 4), and Americans became net foreign investors after 1916—a position they retained until 1986 (figure 5).

World War II gave the United States a further boost, relative to all other countries. Not only were Japan and Germany smashed, but most of the victors, including the United Kingdom, France, and the Soviet Union, saw their savings, infrastructure, and human capital all severely depleted by the war. In the United States it was just the opposite: savings increased; the infrastructure expanded; labor and management skills improved; and science was significantly enhanced. By 1950, the United States stood alone: its industries dominated the globe; it held most of the world's monetary gold; it possessed a surfeit of foreign assets; and its people enjoyed an unprecedented standard of living. The so-called American Dream—job and entrepreneurial opportunities, access to college education, and ownership of homes and automobiles—now seemed feasible for a majority of Americans.

As the recovery after World War II proceeded, economic growth accelerated in most countries and international commerce expanded. Technology transfer and trade liberalization, capital accumulation, and resource exploitation combined to spur rapid growth in productivity. In the United States, productivity grew at an abnormally high rate of 2.5 percent annually between 1950 and 1973. In comparison to Japan and German, however, where productivity grew at "miracle" rates of 7 percent annually, America's position of leadership declined in relative terms. And in a few important sectors, such as steel and automobiles, Japanese productivity and international competitiveness virtually caught up with U.S. levels. The same was true, though to a lesser extent, for Germany and several other Western European countries.

After the oil price shock in 1973, real productivity growth and economic growth slowed sharply throughout the world; inflation and unemployment rose simultaneously, marking a new era of "stagflation." A series of recessions, exchange-rate fluctuations, and another oil shock (in 1979–1980) all contributed to slower growth, to budget deficits, and in the United States, to a declining ability to compete internationally. Japan and Germany seemed to adjust to these difficulties more effectively, and their economies continued toward convergence with that of the United States.

Some U.S. economic problems actually worsened in the 1980s. Although monetary and fiscal policies introduced by the Reagan administration helped alleviate inflation and restore productivity growth in manufacturing, they resulted in huge deficits in the government budget and the current account (the cash-flow portion of the balance of payments that measures exports and imports of goods, services, and factor income). By 1990, the United States had become the world's largest debtor nation. Stagnation had replaced growth, signaling the beginning of a long-term structural adjustment to the excessive debt of households, businesses, and especially government.

Because of the Unites States' economic as well

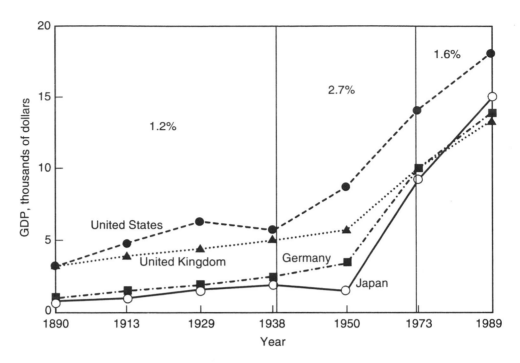

Figure 1.   Real gross domestic product per person in four countries, 1890–1989. In 1985 prices adjusted for purchasing power parity. Percentages show the annual U.S. growth rate for the three periods 1890–1938, 1938–1973, and 1973–1989. (Source: Derived from Angus Maddison, *Dynamic Forces in Capitalist Development* [1992], tables A.2 and B.4.)

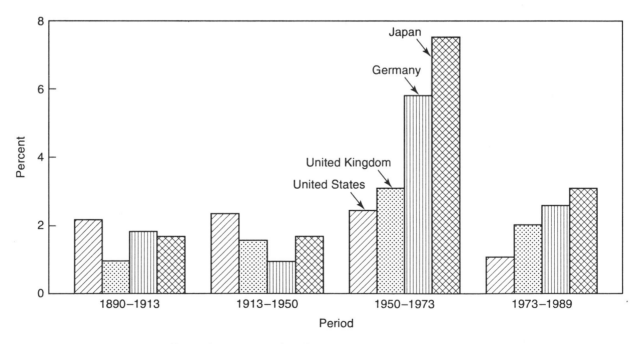

Figure 2.   Labor productivity growth in four countries, 1890–1989. Labor productivity is defined as GDP per man-hour in 1985 U.S. dollars. (Source: Derived from Angus Maddison, *Dynamic Forces in Capitalist Development* [1992], table C.11.)

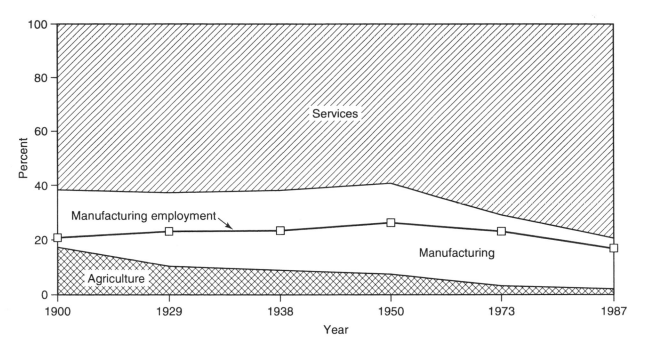

Figure 3.   Structure of the U.S. economy, 1900–1987. Services include government, finance, utilities, construction, and distribution. (Sources: *Historical Statistics of the United States; Statistical Abstract of the United States 1990.*)

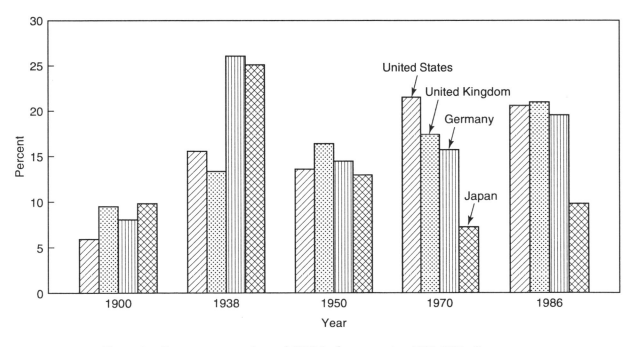

Figure 4.   Government as a share of GDP in four countries, 1900–1986. Government spending is defined in terms of national income, including state and local spending, but excluding transfers. U.S. data include public investment. (Source: *The Economist, One Hundred Years of Economic Statistics* [1989].)

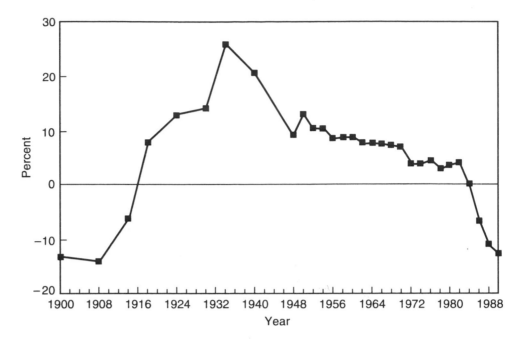

Figure 5. U.S. net foreign investment as percent of GNP, 1900–1989. (Source: *Historical Statistics of the United States*.)

as its geopolitical dominance, the twentieth century will surely be recorded in world history as the American century. Yet near the end of the century this preeminence had peaked and, in fact, had entered a sustained decline. Was the American Dream, the standard of living achieved by middle-class Americans in the 1950s and 1960s, an anomaly—a unique historical situation—or would continuing technological innovation, institutional reforms, and improved economic management cause progress to resume during the 1990s and beyond?

While this article can scarcely answer that question, it can frame the important issues by documenting and explaining the broad trends in America's economic performance since 1900. The essay is divided chronologically into three periods (1900–1938, 1938–1973, and 1973–1991), which correspond to the underlying trends in productivity growth. Dividing the century into these periods also suits several important themes that will be emphasized below: the exploitation of natural resources, the development of infrastructure, relative levels of savings and investment, the size and role of government, and the impact of the international economy on that of the United States.

THE EXPANSION OF U.S. ECONOMIC POWER, 1900–1938

At least until the United States entered World War I in 1917, private firms, private contracts, and competitive markets completely dominated the American economy. The central government's role was modest compared to those of European powers. As Alfred D. Chandler, Jr. has shown in *The Visible Hand* (1977), giant corporations, developing large-scale and vertically integrated operations, began to achieve dominance in mining, petroleum refining, steel, chemicals, rubber, and machinery. A sophisticated rail- and barge-shipping system facilitated the emergence of nationwide markets for agricultural produce, raw materials, intermediate goods, and durable goods. Mass production was integrated with mass distribution.

Mass production on a continental scale required intensive use of natural resources. In the industries whose growth Chandler documented—oil, steel, chemicals, rubber—fuel and materials contributed substantially to the value added from the manufacturing process. Even in heavy machinery, automobiles, and transport equipment, materials and energy con-

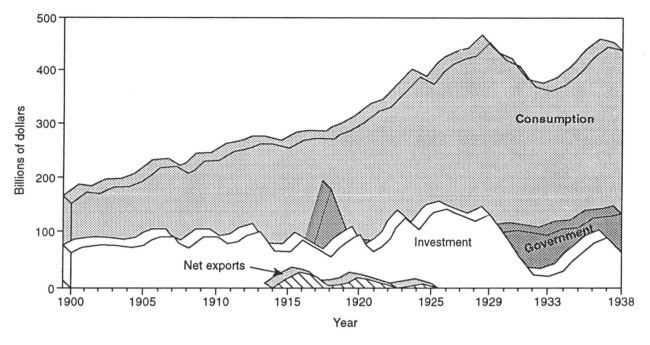

Figure 6.   Components of U.S. gross national product, 1900–1938. In constant 1982 dollars. (Source: *The Economist, One Hundred Years of Economic Statistics* [1989].)

tributed significantly. In a 1990 article, the economist Gavin Wright has suggested that the United States' rise to industrial supremacy may also have been stimulated by its mineral development. Wright offers compelling evidence that the resource intensity of American manufacturing exports (e.g., their dependence on resource inputs) increased sharply during this period, and that this was a more important factor than either labor or capital inputs.

The United States was indeed well endowed with fossil fuels, metals of all sorts, phosphates and lime, timber, agriculturally productive soil, and water. Between 1900 and 1913, real output of minerals grew at 5.6 percent annually—a much higher growth rate than was experienced by any other sector of the economy, including manufacturing. As electric power and internal combustion technologies were brought into commercial use, mineral fuels led this growth, at 6.5 percent per year. By 1913, U.S. mineral output exceeded that of any other country in coal, oil, natural gas, iron ore, copper, and phosphate, and the United States was among the top producers of most other important metals.

Yet productivity, employment, real wages, and output grew more slowly during the early years of the century. Economic growth was repeatedly disrupted by brief downturns in capital investment, triggered by financial panics in 1893, 1903, 1907, and 1914. Until World War I, prices rose at little more than 1 percent annually. Personal savings, estimated at about 15 percent of disposable income, were high relative to other nations. Figure 6 shows the components of gross national product during this period. (GNP is roughly equivalent to GDP, the standard international measure used in figure 1, except that GNP includes net factor income—interest and dividends from prior capital investments—from abroad.) Although the American economy was already dominated by consumption (64 percent), investment contributed a large share (between 19 and 23 percent) of output. Government accounted for only 11 or 12 percent of the economy, and net exports were negligible.

Agriculture, according to estimates by Robert Martin and Simon Kuznets, remained the largest sector of the prewar American economy in terms of both output and employment, but it was surpassed by manufacturing during World War I. In the years leading up to the war, infrastructure (transportation, communications, public utilities), finance, and distribution each comprised about one-ninth of the economy, while mining, construction, other services, and government all made smaller contributions (see figure 7.)

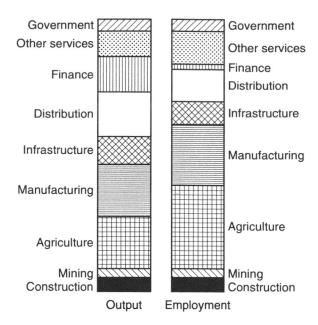

Figure 7.   Output and employment by sector, 1900–1913. Sources: Robert F. Martin, *National Income in the United States, 1799–1838* [1939] for estimates of output for 1910–1913; Simon Kuznets, *National Products since 1869* [1946].)

Until 1913–1914, when Congress created the Federal Reserve System and the Federal Trade Commission, very few economic activities were supervised by the central government. Railroad and barge transport were regulated, as were food processing and drugs; national banks were chartered by the comptroller of the currency. Because the federal budget was limited to spending on the military, the Post Office, veterans' pensions, and agriculture (figure 8), nonbudgetary activities such as the liberal dispersing of minerals, timber, and land from the huge federally owned tracts in the West had the greatest impact on economic development. State and local governments, meanwhile, spent about three times as much as the federal government. They also granted franchises, operated municipal utilities, and regulated prices and earnings of private companies in electric power, gas, street traction, banking, and insurance.

As a consequence of World War I, America's economic leadership of the international economy swelled dramatically. There were significant costs, of course: lost and disabled lives, depleted resources, wasted materials, foregone consumption, and a new debt of nearly $40 billion. But the demands for material and equipment, along with the disruption of production elsewhere in the world, gave an enormous stimulus to U.S. agriculture, processing, and manufacturing. Technological progress, quickened

by war, stimulated the development of some entirely new industries, including aviation, trucking, and radio broadcasting.

With the outbreak of war in Europe in 1914 and the availability of large loans from the United States to Great Britain and France, export demand for grains, fats, and cotton jumped sharply. Food prices also rose, and some twenty million acres were brought under production. By 1920, farm incomes had doubled from their 1914 level. Congress facilitated this effort by enacting the Smith-Lever Act, vastly expanding the Agricultural Extension Service. When the war ended, however, the drop in external demand, combined with excess capacity in agriculture and heavy industry, produced a severe deflation. Despite general economic recovery in 1922, increased mechanization, more widespread use of fertilizers, and improved farming methods kept agricultural output high and prices correspondingly low until the Great Depression.

The petroleum refining and chemical industries received a large boost from wartime demands. Higher-octane gasolines, diesel fuels, airplane fuel, and synthetic fibers were among the most dramatic advances, but significant progress was also made in steel alloys, aluminum, concrete and asphalt, machine tools, turbines, motors, generators, and a host of other products and processes. The internal combustion engine had proved itself superior for motive power: now tractors, diesel locomotives, trucks, and, above all, automobiles would stimulate a new phase of industrial growth.

New infrastructural technologies facilitated commercial expansion and economic integration. The development of seamless pipe and advances in arc welding made it feasible for companies to install large-diameter pipelines to transport natural gas and petroleum over distances of hundreds of miles. In electric power, improvements in transmission efficiency and automated controls allowed utilities to build large-scale central power stations to keep pace with the explosion of demand. Innovations in transmission and switching made nationwide long-distance telecommunications feasible. In transportation, more powerful aircraft engines and wider airframes brought the commercial aviation business into being.

Investment in infrastructure, which grew at 13 percent per year between 1922 and 1929, combined with investments in the automotive and chemicals sectors to stimulate a decade of prosperity. As figure 6 shows, real private investment during the 1920s constituted an abnormally high percent of GNP—80 percent higher than it had during the previous sixteen

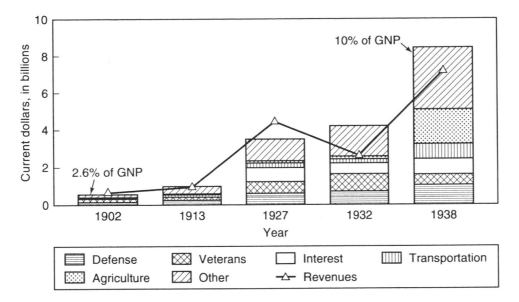

Figure 8. Federal government expenditures and revenues, 1902–1938. (Source: *Historical Statistics of the United States, Colonial Times to 1970* [1975].)

years or would over the following sixteen years. As one economist put it, "It was a concentrated flowering of investment opportunities," that created new industries and new services. Inflation was nonexistent and interest rates were low. Foreign trade grew slowly, with a positive balance. The federal government ran consistent surpluses.

In October 1929, however, panic selling on the New York Stock Exchange triggered a downturn that ultimately became the Great Depression. GNP, led by a drop in purchases of consumer durables, declined at a rate of 8.6 percent per year for the next four years. Business investment virtually collapsed, falling 74 percent by 1932. Industrial production fell a total of 63 percent, and prices fell 25 percent (figure 9). Many corporate dividend payments were suspended and bond payments were delayed. Insolvencies by the thousands swept the very sectors that had driven the previous decade's impressive growth. Worst of all, unemployment increased to 25 percent—reaching 12.8 million in 1933. Not until 1943 did the unemployment rate return to its 1929 level.

The winter of 1932–1933 is usually recalled as the time of greatest despair. In the countryside, dispossessed farmers lived in camps as they migrated west and south in search of new lives. In the cities, the unemployed milled about in the streets, burning trash to warm themselves. Many of the nation's businesses lay in ruins. Housing starts, which had exceeded 900,000 in 1925, stood at 93,000 in 1933. Throughout the Middle Atlantic states and Midwest,

plants that had once produced steel, transport equipment, machinery, and chemicals were now shuttered up. Steel mills operated at 15 percent of capacity in 1933; automobile plants at 18 percent. Numerous small utilities, without adequate financial reserves, went bankrupt all across the country. Airlines, pipelines, and nearly one hundred of the nation's railroads fell into receivership by 1933. Half the nation's coal mines were closed, and in the oil fields hundreds of small producers were shut down as prices fell to ten cents a barrel. Agricultural prices had fallen so sharply that millions of farmers could not afford to buy seed or fuel, much less pay their mortgages. The result was a nightmare of foreclosures and distress auctions. The collapse of banking was perhaps the most dramatic failure. Between 1929 and 1932, five thousand banks (more than a third of the nation's total) failed, as did hundreds of investment trusts and insurance companies. Banks became insolvent as people defaulted on mortgages and loans and withdrew their savings in order to live.

The reasons for this catastrophe were complex and are still difficult to understand. Scholars have variously attributed the crisis to inequitable income distribution, excess productive capacity, long business cycles, a speculative bubble that burst, deflationary expectations, inflexible wages and prices, banking panics, and inept monetary policy. Some analysts also blame international factors, such as adherence to the gold standard or the imposition of high tariffs in 1930. Christina Romer (1993) has provided a sensi-

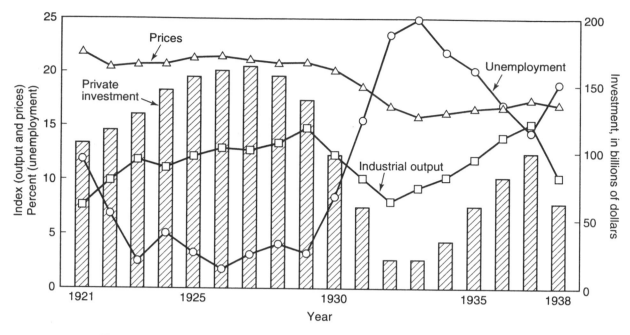

Figure 9. The Great Depression: Output, prices, unemployment, investment. Index for output and prices (left scale): 1980 = 100. Unemployment is shown in percent (left scale). Private investment is shown in billions of dollars (right scale). (Sources: *The Economist, One Hundred Years of Economic Statistics* [1989]; *Historical Statistics of the United States, Colonial Times to 1970* [1975].)

ble synthesis of these various explanations that starts with the stock market boom and the Federal Reserve's open-market sales of securities to slow speculation, a policy instituted as early as 1928. Although the higher interest rates did little to dissuade margin lending, they precipitated a contraction in the construction sector. These signals, according to Romer and others, created expectations of a deflation, expectations that further discouraged purchases of consumer durables. Then, when aggregate demand obviously began to fall, the Federal Reserve Board failed to act quickly to expand the money supply. According to the now-classic analysis of Milton Friedman and Anna Schwartz, this inaction resulted from the board's misplaced preoccupation with maintaining the gold standard. By mid-1930, with business investment shrinking fast, bank panics disrupted short-term credit for farmers and small businesses, reinforcing the downward spiral through foreclosure and bankruptcy.

At the time, people were mystified, discouraged, and angry. After a decade of prosperity and genuine optimism, this apparent failure of free enterprise undermined people's faith in competition, big business, and limited government. Despite unprecedented efforts by President Herbert Hoover to mitigate the

depression through public relief, agricultural supports, reconstruction finance, and voluntary wage and employment agreements with big business, the American market economy seemed discredited.

Since business, labor, and consumers were all incapacitated, it ultimately fell to government to act. President Franklin D. Roosevelt, a pragmatist, saw this immediately, as did business leaders in many disabled sectors. But the government and business focused on excess supply—too much productive capacity, too much inventory, for the existing demand by consumers. In England, the economist John Maynard Keynes focused on demand—a "liquidity trap" in which, despite low interest rates and abundant money, pervasive unemployment and fear had wiped out demand for goods and services. Keynes warned President Roosevelt as well as his own government that only a vigorous fiscal policy involving deficit spending by government could autonomously create the demand necessary to restart economic growth. For a time, this advice fell on deaf ears.

Taking office in 1933, Roosevelt did what seemed necessary, instituting emergency banking controls and devaluation of the dollar, stabilization of industrial prices and wages through cartelization, crop reductions, and price supports for agriculture,

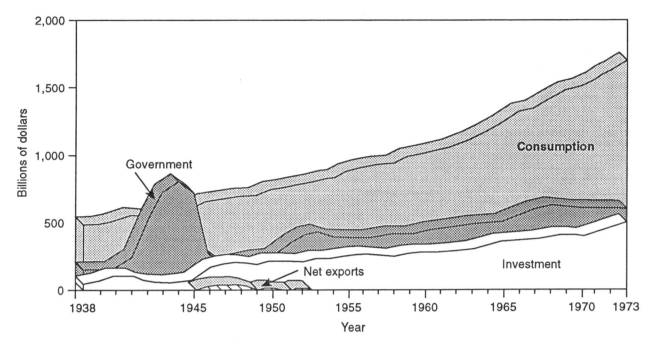

Figure 10. Components of U.S. gross national product, 1938–1973. In constant 1982 dollars. (Source: *The Economist, One Hundred Years of Economic Statistics* [1989].)

public works and welfare. Eventually, the Roosevelt administration initiated or endorsed new government controls in banking and securities, railroads, trucking, shipping and airlines, petroleum, natural gas and electric power, telecommunications, and retail trade. By 1938, competition in more than one-third of the American economy had been severely restricted by direct government regulation. But while Roosevelt did increase federal expenditures almost 100 percent in four years, deficits were held to an average of $2.9 billion (4.2 percent of average GNP)—far less than the stimulus urged by Keynes. The budget deficit actually narrowed in 1938 to less than its 1932 level. Investment and industrial production slumped, while unemployment jumped back to 19 percent.

Notwithstanding all Roosevelt's programs, the Great Depression cut deeper and lasted longer in the United States than anywhere else in the world. After dropping by 30 percent between 1929 and 1933, GNP did not fully recover until 1939. In Great Britain, by contrast, GDP declined only 5.2 percent and had recovered by 1934. In Japan, fiscal stimulus, combined with a devaluation of the yen, kept real GDP growing steadily throughout the 1930s. In Germany, where GDP had dropped by 25 percent, Hitler's massive deficit spending for mobilization restored lost ground by 1935. Only in France, where the

government adopted a restrictive monetary policy to defend the gold standard, did stagnation linger throughout the decade as in the United States.

ECONOMIC APOGEE, 1938–1973

For three and a half decades after the Great Depression, the economy of the United States grew at an annual rate of 2.7 percent per capita—twice as fast as it had earlier, or would later (figure 1). This acceleration of economic growth was triggered by an immense increase in government spending during the war (figure 10). Even after demobilization, when private consumption resumed its dominant role in the economy (62 percent of GNP), government spending continued to surpass private investment as a portion of GNP. Positive net exports made a contribution briefly during the late 1940s, but later turned to net imports. Comparing figures 6 and 10, it is readily apparent that economic activity in the post–World War II era exhibited much more stability than it had during the first third of the century. Government's larger and more active role in managing this "mixed economy" was probably the principal reason for this change.

Mobilization for World War II was an extraordinary fiscal and organizational undertaking. Between 1938 and 1945, civilian employment by the federal government jumped from 882 thousand to 3.8 million. Government expenditures jumped from less than $9 billion to $93 billion (or from 10.6 to 43.7 percent of GNP). More than half these outlays were deficit financed, adding $210 billion to a national debt that was only $37 billion in 1938. In addition to its direct spending on the military, the government made significant investments in shipbuilding, rubber, aircraft and vehicle manufacturing, uranium processing, hydroelectric power, transportation facilities, roads, and ports. Although not necessarily "efficient" in economic terms, this vast commitment of resources achieved extraordinary results. Output of processed food, chemicals, synthetic rubber, and steel tripled during the war; aluminum output increased by a factor of six; machinery production by six; and locomotive production by eight. The most spectacular gains were achieved in the manufacture of airplanes and merchant ships, whereoutput multiplied by factors of 50 and 75 respectively.

This mobilization also entailed the wholesale reorganization of the federal government and its empowerment to allocate resources, set prices, and coordinate output for all major sectors of the economy. These controls were implemented through an elaborate system of multitiered advisory groups that cooperated with the war agencies. The agencies themselves were partially staffed by business executives, so-called "dollar-a-year men," who gained new familiarity and experience with government. The work force, meanwhile, expanded by several million as women entered the industrial labor force and less skilled service workers were retrained to perform higher-value-added industrial jobs.

As the war extended into its third and fourth year, household savings mounted rapidly (from less than $2 billion in 1939 to $37 billion by 1944) because the accumulating incomes could find no outlet in consumption. During the war, certain foods and gasoline required ration cards. Civilian tires and automobiles were not produced at all, and new housing and many consumer durables were in short supply. Fears of a severe postwar recession, repeating the experience following World War I, proved unfounded because of the release of the demand that had built up during the war years. Consumption virtually exploded in 1946, and while the cutback in government did hurt GNP growth in 1946 and 1947, continued consumption, private investment for retooling, and net exports helped extend prosperity until 1949, when a mild recession did occur.

As the United States came out of the 1949 recession, it was uniquely positioned for a new era of growth. Its manufacturing capacity, augmented by the war, was huge. Military research had uncovered new technologies that held extraordinary commercial potential. Household and business savings could easily fund all the new investment needed at home, as well as much of the capital needed to rebuild Europe. The nation's expanded and newly trained labor force was ready and able to work. Its system of higher education was equipped to absorb returning veterans and to produce the graduate-level engineers, scientists, and professionals that business needed. Worldwide demand for American goods and services was limited only by lack of foreign exchange. The value of the dollar, at a record high relative to other currencies, guaranteed American purchasing power and favorable terms of trade. America's potential competitors, the former Axis powers and Allies alike, were temporarily impoverished. Everyone needed American goods and capital to rebuild after the war.

To sustain its growth during peacetime, the United States drew heavily on its abundant stocks of raw materials, labor, and capital. War had depleted, but scarcely exhausted, America's inheritance of raw materials. In the steel industry, for example, production had risen from 28 million tons in 1938 (using 2 million tons of imported ore), to 101 million tons in 1943 (with only .4 million tons of imported ore). Thus, after cumulative production of about 600 million tons during the war, it was hardly surprising that domestic prices doubled and American firms were increasingly forced to import ore—about 50 percent by the early 1970s. Import dependence in copper jumped from less than 2 percent in 1939 to 37 percent by 1949; in bauxite, from 58 percent to 70 percent; and in all the ferroalloy metals, to more than 90 percent. In the fossil fuel sector, domestic reserves of coal and natural gas were still enormous, but petroleum discoveries could not keep pace with the explosion in demand. In 1949, the United States became a net oil importer.

Although imported raw materials increasingly supplemented America's own resources in the era of postwar growth, exploitation of domestic stocks continued unabated. The boom in housing and new uses for paper and packaging stimulated demand for timber. Virgin timber, leased from federal lands, was cut more rapidly than new tree plantings could replace on a sustainable basis. Agricultural expansion for domestic consumption and for export required vast systems of irrigation, drawing increasingly from natural aquifers. Domestic reserves of petroleum and especially natural gas were rapidly depleted, in part due to government policies that restricted imports and controlled prices at artificially low levels.

The annual rate of usage for water, timber, metals, non-metallic minerals, and fuels more than doubled between 1938 and 1970; cumulative usage of these natural resources was obviously immense. The American economy appeared to be absorbing about two-fifths of the world's natural resources—mostly, although decreasingly, from domestic reserves. But since most of these resources represent a historic stock of assets simply found (or discovered at a small real cost), they should be viewed as assets on a balance sheet. Instead, their rapid depletion during this period simply augmented GNP, with no accounting for depreciation. In this sense, then, the drawdown of this inventory represents a sort of windfall for economic growth—a unique phenomenon that could never be repeated in quite the same way. By implication, America's terms of trade (i.e., the cost of its exports relative to imports) and the resource intensity of its economy would eventually have to change.

Abundant resources alone, however, hardly explain America's economic leadership and growth during the postwar era. Resources had to be effectively utilized. By the end of demobilization, the level of America's productivity was higher, relative to all other developed countries, than at any other

time in history. According to Angus Maddison's calculations of real GDP per man hour, average productivity for fifteen industrial countries (excluding the United States) was just 43 percent of the U.S. level in 1950—a larger gap than any time earlier or later in this century. Relative to Japan, Britain, and Germany, this productivity gap was even wider. As figure 11 shows, the gap in productivity between the United States and these other industrial powers had diverged since the beginning of the century.

Notwithstanding this already high absolute level, growth in total factor productivity (i.e., the ratio of outputs to all factors of production) now increased to an annual average rate of 1.53 percent for the next two decades. This rate of growth was 50 percent higher than it had been in the period since 1929, or than it would be after 1973. Labor productivity grew even faster, at 2.3 percent annually, in part, because so much capital was invested per worker.

Combined with huge gains in agriculture and the increased manufacturing scale, advances in knowledge pushed America's total factor productivity steadily higher. In his careful statistical study, *Trends in American Economic Growth, 1929–82,* Edward F. Denison attributes this overall productivity growth primarily to three factors: improvements in resource allocation (.29 percent), especially the shift

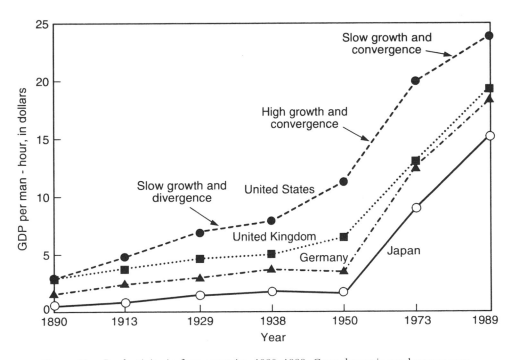

Figure 11.   Productivity in four countries, 1980–1989. Gross domestic product per man-hour in 1985 U.S. relative prices in dollars. (Source: Derived from Angus Maddison, *Dynamic Forces in Capitalist Development* [1992], table C.11.)

of agricultural workers into industry; increases from larger production units ("economies of scale," .32 percent), and above all, advances in knowledge (1.09 percent). Demographic changes (the age and sex composition of the work force), government regulation, and crime reduced this productivity by an estimated .17 percent. To estimate the contribution of knowledge, which includes both technological innovation and organizational learning, Denison and others rely on econometric studies of research and development expenditures, scientific and engineering personnel, patents, and measured diffusion rates. During the 1950s, the wartime advances in communications, electronics, power systems, machine tools, petrochemicals, and transportation all moved quickly into commercial development.

Although productivity was growing rapidly in the United States, it grew even faster in the other leading industrial economies as they benefited from technology transfer, higher savings rates, and intensive capital formation. Their productivity gap with the United States now began to narrow. In Japan, for example, labor productivity grew at 7.7 percent per year between 1950 and 1973—more than triple the U.S. rate; Germany's growth, at 6 percent, more than doubled the U.S. figure. For the fifteen leading industrial countries, according to Maddison's calculations, the productivity gap with the United States had closed by 1973 to an average rate of 2.1 percent annually.

Eventually, these more rapid gains in productivity, combined with low-cost labor (relative to the United States), protected home markets, and the export-oriented policies of Japan, Germany, France, and Italy, challenged the international competitiveness of American firms, eroded America's share of worldwide trade, and helped eliminate the positive trade balance that America had enjoyed since 1936.

The postwar reconstruction of Europe and Japan occurred in a context of relatively free trade and monetary stability sponsored by the United States. At an international conference in Bretton Woods, New Hampshire, in 1946, the Allies established a liberal economic order, with fixed exchange rates linked to the dollar, a World Bank to foster development, and an International Monetary Fund to facilitate balance-of-payments financing. In 1947, twenty-three countries meeting in Geneva negotiated a General Agreement on Tariffs and Trade (GATT), establishing historically low tariffs, a most-favored-nation reciprocity, and a system for negotiating further adjustments. Under these conditions, the growth of international trade accelerated, as did direct foreign investment by American multinational firms.

Between 1949 and 1973, U.S. merchandise ex-

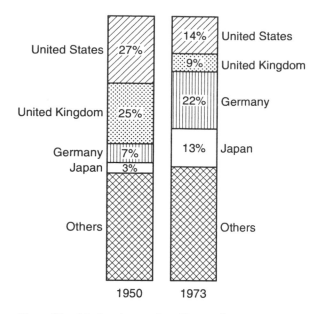

Figure 12. Market shares of world manufacturing exports, 1950 and 1973. "Others" includes France, Italy, Switzerland, and Korea, among other important exporters. (Source: R. C. O. Matthews, C. H. Feinstein, and J. C. Odling-Smee, *British Economic Growth, 1856–1973* [1982], p. 435.)

ports (in current dollars, i.e., in each year's dollars not adjusted for inflation) grew annually at 7.6 percent; imports, at 10.2 percent. The U.S. surplus in merchandise trade peaked at $6.8 billion in 1964 and generally declined thereafter, turning to a deficit in 1971. In the mid-1960s, textiles and steel became the first major industries in which net trade turned negative; they were shortly joined by transport equipment. While most other American manufacturing sectors maintained net export surpluses, their international market share dropped precipitously. Figure 12 shows shares of world trade in manufacturing. In less than two decades, the U.S. share dropped by half, displaced primarily by the gains of Japan and Germany. In fact, Germany's share substantially surpassed that of the United States (22 percent compared to 14 percent), even though Germany is a much smaller country.

Clearly, this change in relative competitiveness represented more than simply a developmental adjustment to the postwar anomaly of U.S. leadership. One cause was the nonadjustment of exchange rates under the Bretton Woods system. In his 1980 survey, William Branson showed that unit labor costs in the United States increased at a rate of 2.6 percent annually between 1950 and 1973, starting from a much higher base than those of Germany or Japan. Although their rates of increase were about the same

(Japan a little slower, Germany somewhat faster), the dollar became more and more overvalued.

The current account of the U.S. balance of payments remained generally positive throughout this period. The balance of trade in services and net investment income were positive and actually grew faster than the merchandise trade balance diminished. Travel and transportation, especially related to tourism, were consistently negative, as were net military transactions and unilateral transfers. Foreign aid, especially during the period of the Marshall Plan, and net private transfers averaged about $5 billion per year between 1950 and 1971. But finally, in 1971, the current account also turned negative.

The United States was a net capital exporter for most of the postwar era. U.S. assets abroad, primarily direct investment by American firms in Canada and Europe, grew somewhat slower than GNP, from $39 billion in 1946 to $222 billion in 1973. Foreign investments in the United States outstripped GNP growth, increasing from $15 billion to $174 billion during the same period, leaving the U.S. in a net creditor position (e.g., cumulative U.S. assets abroad minus foreign assets in the United States) of about $47 billion (about 4 percent of GNP, down from 10 percent in 1946).

As the U.S. current account surplus dissipated and capital outflows continued, foreign central banks accumulated more and more dollar reserves, for which there was insufficient private demand. After 1969, these governments, starting with the United Kingdom, began exchanging dollars for gold (at $35 an ounce). U.S. gold reserves dwindled, despite revaluations of the German mark and the French franc. By the spring of 1971, the United States retained only $12 billion in gold to back nearly $52 billion in dollar liabilities abroad. President Richard M. Nixon had urged the Japanese to import more goods and the Germans to revalue the mark, but to little avail. On 15 August 1971, Nixon renounced convertibility of the U.S. dollar, effectively taking the world off the gold standard. The Bretton Woods international monetary system, which had relied on an overvalued dollar and U.S. capital outflows to foster the recovery of Asia and Europe, was ended.

By the time President Nixon took this momentous action, the federal government had come to play a central, though decreasingly effective, role in the domestic economy as well. Government spending, even without income transfers, exceeded private investment. The government's microeconomic regulatory responsibilities had grown tremendously and now affected most sectors of the economy. And, in a significant departure from the past, the government

in 1946 had assumed primary responsibility for macroeconomic stabilization. In the Employment Act of that year, Congress articulated as national economic goals the maintenance of high incomes and full employment. It created a three-member Council of Economic Advisers (CEA) to assess the economy and make policy recommendations to the president. Following the new Keynesian concepts of managing aggregate demand with active fiscal policy, the CEA estimated the economy's potential output, based on long-term productivity growth, and recommended changes in government spending or taxation as necessary to prevent unemployment and inflation.

During the Truman and Eisenhower years, this new approach to fiscal stabilization was applied loosely but with apparent success (tax increases in 1950 to finance the Korean War and a countercyclical expansion of government spending in 1958 are often cited as examples). The zenith for Keynesian demand management came in early 1964, with the "Kennedy tax cut" (proposed by Kennedy advisers in 1963 but enacted after Lyndon Johnson had succeeded to the presidency). At a time when real output was already growing at 4 percent, this $19 billion package of cuts boosted GNP growth to 5.5 percent and lowered unemployment by 1 percent. Inflation, however, accelerated from 1.8 percent to 3.5 percent over the next two years.

Federal government expenditures, although cut back sharply after demobilization, grew steadily from 1949 on into the 1970s. Remobilization for the Korean War initiated a large, continuing stream of peacetime outlays for national security. As figure 13 shows, defense spending grew slowly, though it remained the largest element of the budget until 1971. In that year it was surpassed by spending on "human resources," a budget category that includes social security, income security, veterans' benefits, health, education, and Medicare. Collectively, these programs grew from 28 percent of outlays in 1949 to 44 percent in 1971. As figure 13 shows, when President Johnson introduced his Great Society initiatives in 1964, the slope of growth turned sharply upward; this trend continued for the next two decades. As a percentage of GNP, federal government spending doubled, to 19 percent; state and local spending accounted for another 11 percent of GNP.

The composition of revenues also changed over this period. Proceeds from individual income taxes increased, from 39 percent of the total in 1949 to 45 percent in 1973. A bigger increase, though, came from social security contributions, which rose from 9.6 percent to 25 percent of revenue. The contributions from corporate taxes and excise taxes, mean-

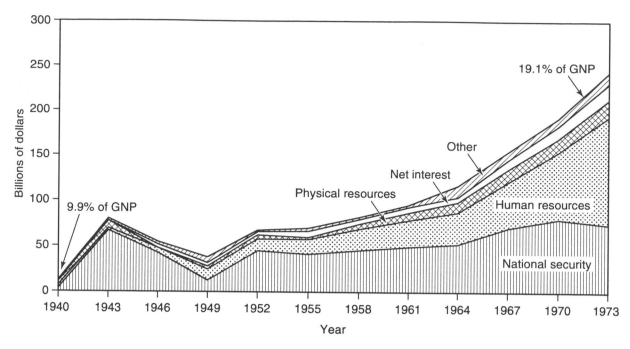

Figure 13.   Federal government outlays by function, 1940–1973. (Source: Office of Management and Budget, *Historical Tables, Budget of the United States* [1987].)

while, each dropped by half, to 15 percent and 7 percent respectively.

As significant as it was, Washington's expanded fiscal role in the macroeconomy nonetheless understated the government's overall involvement with business, labor, and the environment. During the 1950s and 1960s, independent regulatory agencies and executive-branch agencies settled down to supervising most aspects of competition and development in energy, transportation, telecommunications, and finance. Even in technically "unregulated" sectors, the federal government's enforcement of antitrust issues, labor relations, occupational health and safety standards, air and water pollution controls, and natural resource usage made its economic influence pervasive.

Some of this regulation worked well. In telecommunications, for example, a national integrated phone system provided nearly universal service by the early 1970s. Local service was better and cheaper than was the case anywhere else in the industrialized world, in part because of regulated cross subsidies from large users. The same could be said of natural gas, refined petroleum products, and electric power. The airline and commercial banking businesses also developed high-quality and widespread services. Freight railroads at least survived, and trucking actually prospered, providing high-quality, albeit costly and inefficient, transportation.

But toward the end of the 1960s and on into the mid-1970s, problems with the "mixed economy" became increasingly serious. In the transport sector, for example, economists blamed federal regulation for the worsening conditions of the nation's railroads. Excess capacity in airlines was likewise blamed on the cartel-like regulatory policies of the Civil Aeronautics Board. In telecommunications, a lack of commercial innovation was blamed on the Federal Communication Commission's policies of sheltering AT&T from competition. In banking, when market interest rates jumped in 1968, the Federal Reserve Board maintained its ceiling on deposit interest at a lower rate. This precipitated the first of several bouts of disintermediation, in which savers withdrew deposits and invested them in securities and money-market funds, eventually leading to the banking crisis of the early 1980s.

Problems in the energy sector were among the most pronounced and would eventually contribute to the oil price shock of 1973 that ended the postwar era of prosperity. In petroleum, both tax policies and quotas on oil imports had encouraged the rapid depletion of American reserves, yet without allowing prices to stimulate domestic exploration and production. In natural gas, the Federal Power Commission held real prices constant, thus stimulating demand while discouraging supply. Once America's previously discovered reserves were drawn down, gas

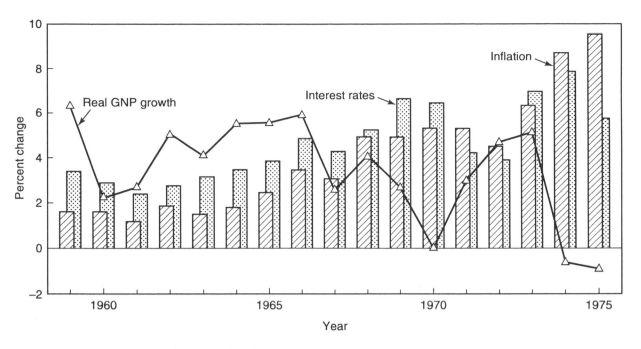

Figure 14. The onset of stagflation, 1959–1975. The era of stagflation began in 1968. The inflation rate is the GNP deflator. The interest rate is the rate on the three-month Treasury bill. (Source: *Economic Report of the President* [1992].)

shortages developed "suddenly" after 1968. Shortages of domestic oil followed in 1972.

All these problems were part of a broader change in the structure of the American economy. Accumulating rigidities in wages and prices, higher taxes that diverted savings from private investment to governmental programs for income maintenance, the unrestricted drawdown of natural resources, the accumulating effects of pollution, and the declining competitiveness of some U.S. industries were root causes of this change. The proximate cause, however, was the Johnson administration's simultaneous buildup of federal expenditures for social programs and for the war in Vietnam, and refusal to raise taxes. In 1967, the budget deficit jumped from $3 to $8 billion, and then to $25 billion in 1968. Over the next three years, as shown in figure 14, short-term interest rates and inflation nearly doubled.

In an effort to control these problems, President Nixon followed the standard advice of Keynesian economists. He asked Congress to raise taxes and reduce spending, and he encouraged slower growth of the money supply. Although GNP growth dropped sharply, inflation persisted, at a new and higher level, together with higher unemployment. These conditions marked the beginning of an era of "stagflation," with the worst yet to come.

In August 1971, as previously noted, the Nixon administration announced a package of policies designed to remedy the deteriorating trade and payments situation. Besides closing the gold window, Nixon imposed a 10 percent surcharge on imports and temporary wage and price controls. These controls, which undermined financial confidence and caused distortions in the economy, did little to alleviate inflation. By the time the mandatory controls were removed in 1973 (from everything except petroleum), inflation and interest rates had reached new heights. The value of the dollar, meanwhile, had fallen by 30 percent against the deutsche mark.

With spare capacity for petroleum production virtually exhausted in the United States, Middle Eastern countries now controlled the only remaining excess oil-producing capacity. And since oil was traded internationally in U.S. dollars, the dollar depreciation had sharply reduced the real oil revenues of Middle Eastern governments. The price correction occurred in the last quarter of 1973, when the Organization of Petroleum Exporting Countries (OPEC) unilaterally raised crude oil prices from $3 to $11.65 per barrel. Since the demand for oil was virtually inelastic in the short run, this price hike transmitted a supply shock throughout the world. Inflation accelerated, real incomes fell, and most developed economies plunged into recession.

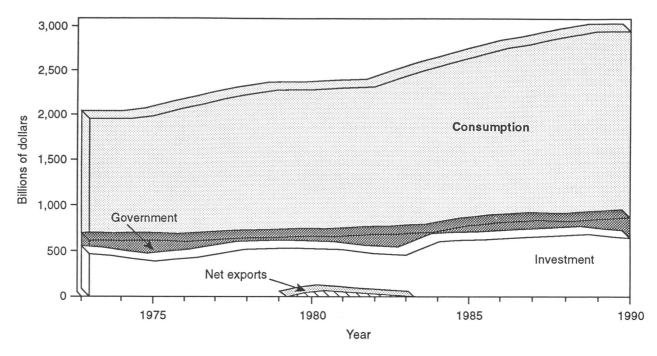

Figure 15.   Components of the gross national product, 1973–1990. In constant 1982 dollars.
(Source: *The Economist, One Hundred Years of Economic Statistics* [1989].)

DEFICITS, DEBT, AND DECLINE, 1973–1990

In the decade and a half after the first oil shock, real economic growth slowed worldwide. In the United States, growth in per capita GNP dropped by half from its earlier level (figure 1), to an annual average rate of 1.6 percent. The average rate of unemployment increased from 4.5 percent in the decade before 1973 to 7.4 percent in the decade after. Consumption and government spending in the United States, as figure 15 shows, comprised ever larger shares of the GNP; private investment and net exports shrank proportionately. Inflation, energy and environmental problems, declining manufacturing competitiveness, trade deficits, and government deficits plagued the economy. As growth in productivity stagnated, real average wages—a fundamental measure of standard of living—declined, dropping back to the level of the late 1950s (figure 16). "Malaise," as President Jimmy Carter called it in 1978, had interrupted the American Dream.

The oil shock of 1973 was scarcely the sole cause of these problems; they originated, as we have seen, in the late 1960s. But the oil shock severely aggravated inflation and induced an string of unfortunate policy responses by the federal government. Energy policy was certainly among the worst.

When OPEC quadrupled prices, Congress imposed multitiered price controls on domestic oil. In 1975, when Japan and Europe were eliminating oil-price controls, the U.S. Congress extended them for six years. Attributing shortages to a conspiracy among oil and gas companies, Congress authorized a grossly inefficient system for allocating crude oil among refiners, imposed fuel-efficiency standards on automobile manufacturers, and approved massive subsidies for coal gasification and liquefaction. The Federal Power Commission, meanwhile, held prices for natural gas below replacement costs and allocated scarce supplies among various classes of users. The Federal Trade Commission, alleging a "shared monopoly," initiated a criminal antitrust suit against the eight largest oil companies.

During this same period, worsening environmental problems forced the government to implement a series of costly regulations to control air pollution, water pollution, toxic substances, coal strip mining, and resource development on federal properties. Relying on command-and-control concepts of regulation, the Environmental Protection Agency and the Interior Department struggled to bring the worst of these problems under control. The costs of mitigation, however, were very high, especially for the resource extraction and power generation sectors. The prices of electricity, transportation, heat, light-

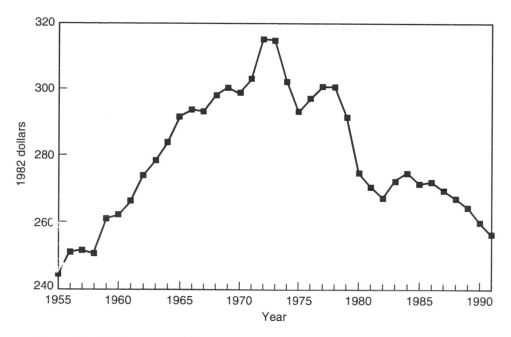

Figure 16.   Real average weekly wages, 1955–1991. (Source: *Economic Report of the Presi-dent* [1992].)

ing, water, and sewage treatment all rose sharply, aggravating inflation and inducing an angry reaction by the American public.

The sharply higher costs of fuels and of pollution controls did, however, begin to reduce the energy intensity of the American economy. As figure 17 indicates, the ratio of energy consumed to GNP declined after 1973, even though total energy consumption continued to grow. And after Congress passed the National Energy Act in 1978, even total energy consumption declined, at least through the mid-1980s. This initiative of the Carter administra-

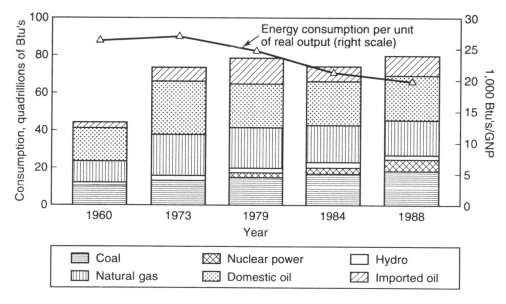

Figure 17.   U.S. energy consumption. Consumption by type of fuel is shown on the left scale in quadrillions of British thermal units. The efficiency ratio is shown on the right scale in thousands of Btu's per GNP dollar. (Source: *Statistical Abstract of the United States 1990*.)

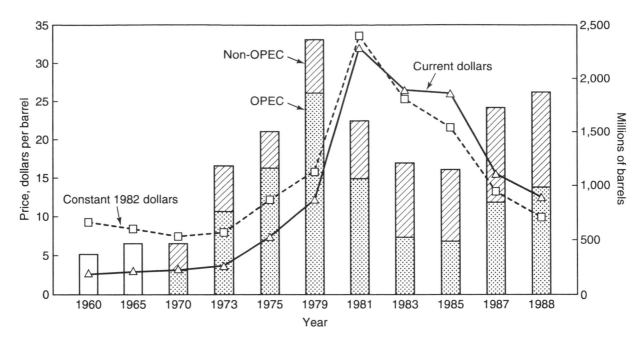

Figure 18. Petroleum prices and U.S. imports, 1960–1988. Constant price is shown in 1982 dollars. (Source: *Statistical Abstract of the United States 1990.*)

tion was designed to encourage conservation, the development of domestic oil and natural gas, and alternative energy sources. Despite imposing windfall profits taxes on domestic oil, it created tax and pricing incentives for energy efficiency and began the process of deregulating oil, natural gas, and electric power.

These reforms came none too soon. The same month that Congress passed the National Energy Act, a revolution in Iran shut down about 2.5 million barrels per day of petroleum production. With international oil markets already tight, panic purchases drove up spot-market prices and triggered a second oil shock. Over the next twenty-five months, OPEC prices ratcheted up from $13 to $34 per barrel (figure 18). Once again, real incomes were depressed worldwide, inflation soared, and tight monetary policies helped drive developed economies into recession. This time, though, high prices combined with more effective policies to induce significant responses in both supply and demand. Real oil prices, which peaked in 1981, commenced a long-term erosion that lasted until the outbreak of the Persian Gulf War in 1991.

The rise in oil prices during the 1970s contributed to a worsening problem with inflation. Import prices, because of the dollar's decline, also contributed to higher prices. Despite wage-and-price controls imposed by Nixon, the Ford administration's

public relations campaign to "whip inflation now" (WIN), and the efforts of the Carter administration's Council on Wage and Price Stability, inflation kept rising. Inflationary psychology, or expectations, seem to affect wage demands, pricing by business, and the interest rates charged by banks. Multiyear labor contracts and the indexing of federal entitlement programs to cost-of-living increases kept wages and government spending at least apace of the general inflation rate. The second oil shock, as figure 19 shows, pushed the consumer price index to a double-digit level for the first time in peacetime. Even harsh measures taken in 1980 by the Federal Reserve Board, under its new chairman, Paul Volcker, were to no avail.

The combined effects of the energy shocks and inflation almost certainly contributed to the slowdown of productivity growth in the United States and the rest of the world. The growth of labor productivity in the U.S. slowed from a rate of 2.5 percent before 1973 to a rate of 1.2 percent afterwards; between 1973 and 1981, productivity growth was especially weak—only 0.6 percent annually.

In Japan, Germany, and the United Kingdom, as figure 11 indicates, productivity growth also slowed, but not as much. Since capital investment per worker in those countries and others remained higher than in the United States, their level of labor productivity continued to converge with that of the United States

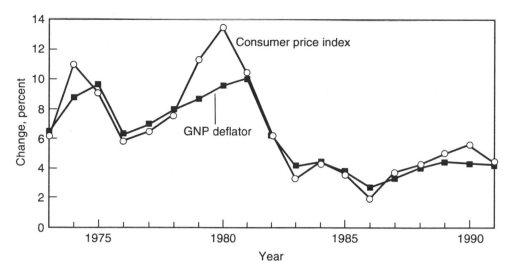

Figure 19.   Inflation and disinflation, 1973–1991. (Source: *Economic Report of the President* [1993].)

even as relative total factor productivity stabilized. Inflationary expectations and deficit spending in the United States sapped savings and pushed real interest rates higher. Private investment dropped as a share of GNP.

The U.S. labor force, meanwhile, expanded sharply. Entry into the work force by women, new immigrants, and postwar baby-boomers pushed the employment-to-population ratio from .59 in 1974 to .67 by 1989. Since new entrants were relatively less experienced and tended to enter the work force in the lower-value-added service sector, this demographic phenomenon likely had a doubly negative impact on productivity.

Instability of the business cycle, caused in part by the oil shocks and the fiscal and monetary reactions of government, repeatedly pushed actual output below potential. Capacity utilization in manufacturing, for example, averaged 87.6 percent before 1973, but just 80.3 percent between 1973 and 1989. Increased government regulation—especially environmental, occupational health and safety regulation—is seen by most economists as having reduced measured productivity growth. Not only did new regulation tend to induce inefficiencies, but the benefits of capital diverted to regulatory objectives (cleaner air, healthier workers) were generally not captured in productivity data.

These factors, according to Edward F. Denison and other economists, appear to account for about half the productivity slowdown. They attribute the remainder to misallocation of resources, intangible

work habits, slower advances in knowledge (e.g., less commercial research and development, less innovation, and fewer gains from technical education or managerial performance), and, possibly, the shift of employment from manufacturing to services. But since the effects of these so-called residuals can only be estimated, the precise causes of America's productivity slowdown remain something of a mystery.

Meanwhile, the federal government's ability to deal effectively with these problems, either in the aggregate or sector by sector, seemed to be degenerating. Slower growth meant less tax revenue relative to expanding program demands, a sure formula for chronic budget deficits. The last budget that appeared intentionally linked to the business cycle was for 1973 (fiscal year 1974), a deficit of $6 billion. Thereafter, Washington increasingly lost control of fiscal policy as an economic tool; budget deficits averaged $62 billion (or 2.9 percent of GNP) during the Ford and Carter administrations. The necessity of funding these deficits, in turn, left monetary authorities less leeway for controlling inflation.

With economic performance suffering, and with government so apparently ineffective, a political and intellectual backlash against activist government intensified during the Ford and Carter years. An emerging majority of economists deemed market forces preferable to bureaucratic control. At the micro level, this critique focused on economic regulation, especially controls that appeared to stifle potential competition. Although President Gerald Ford came to view regulation as a contributory factor to inflation, he could make little progress with its reform. But Jimmy Carter, who ran for office on an antiregulation, "anti-Washington" platform, fared considerably better. During his four years in office, Congress enacted major regulatory reforms for airlines, trucking, railroads, power generation, natural gas, and banking. Administrative actions also phased out petroleum price controls and opened up competition in telephone services.

At the macro level, the critique of government developed along two lines: a reemphasis on monetary policy, as advocated by economists from the so-called Chicago school, and greater attention to the "supply side" of the economy—that is, to productivity, capacity, savings, and investment. Since both streams of economic thinking implied a less interventionist role for government, they found immediate appeal among political conservatives and thus became the policy foundation of what came to be known as the Reagan Revolution.

"We are in the worst economic mess since the Great Depression," proclaimed President Reagan in February 1981, shortly after taking office. The so-called misery index, a combination of inflation and unemployment rates, stood at about 20 percent. Two weeks later, Reagan announced his administration's plan for economic recovery. Spending would be cut by $49 billion, regulation would be curtailed, and monetary growth would be slowed so as not to exceed the growth in real GNP. The centerpiece of the plan was a gigantic tax cut: 30 percent over three years in marginal income tax rates, with accelerated depreciation and investment tax credits for business. The cumulative reduction of tax revenues projected by the administration over six years would be nearly $700 billion. But new projected revenues, stimulated by rapid GNP growth, were to combine with the reduced expenditures to close the apparent budgetary gap.

This plan, with its optimistic assumptions, was implemented more or less intact. Congress promptly passed the Economic Recovery Tax Act of 1981, cutting personal income taxes by 25 percent and adopting the new tax credits and depreciation schedules. By September 1981, it had approved budget reductions of about $45 billion. Regulatory reforms, though, awaited further congressional action. The Federal Reserve Board, under Chairman Volcker, cooperated by sharply slowing the growth of the money supply.

Instead of growing at the projected GNP growth of 4.2 percent (for 1982), the economy plunged into recession, shrinking by 2.2 percent. Volcker's tight monetary policy, combined with sharply higher deficit financing by the government, drove real interest rates (the excess of nominal rates over expected inflation) above 8 percent for a year and a half, stifling the investment boom that was supposed to have stimulated recovery. Although the rate of inflation did drop precipitously, as figure 19 shows, the government's budget deficit, starting from a record-high level of $78 billion, nearly tripled over the next few years.

Despite the vigorous economic recovery that began in 1983 and continued through 1987, the federal budget deficit continued to grow. Expenditures' share of GNP remained about constant, but tax revenues fell. The budgetary gap peaked at 6.3 percent of GNP in 1983, shrank back to 2.9 perjycent by 1989, but was rising again towards 6 percent in the early 1990s. The Reagan administration rejected the need for significant midcourse corrections, blaming the deficits on excessive spending by Congress.

Indeed, Congress seemed incapable of capping, much less cutting, virtually any of its spending programs. Defense expenditures, which expanded to 26 percent of the budget during this period, were sacrosanct to Republicans; income transfers, taking nearly 50 percent of the budget, were sustained by Democrats. Since debt service (about 14 percent of the budget by 1988) was uncontrollable, only 10 percent of the budget represented discretionary civil expenditures that were eligible for political debate. In 1985, Congress acknowledged its own lack of political will by enacting the Gramm-Rudman-Hollings Balanced Budget Act. This law imposed a five-year schedule of deficit reductions with a system of automatic, across-the-board sequestrations if Congress failed to meet its target. Figure 20 illustrates the ineffectiveness of this approach. As soon as deficits exceeded targets, Congress made exceptions, then revised the law. A new schedule for deficit reduction, which took effect in 1988, was no more successful. In 1990, the Bush administration and Congress negotiated the Budget Enforcement Act, a new and even tougher agreement. This law capped the dollar amounts of discretionary spending and prohibited debt financing of tax reductions or increases in mandatory spending. But as the recession lingered on and the government incurred unanticipated obligations for the Persian Gulf War and the savings and loan bailout, this new regime also proved ineffective.

The consequences of this fiscal gridlock extended beyond mere operating deficits. The deficits, of course, kept on accumulating, adding up to massive debt. Figure 21 tracks the growing deficits through

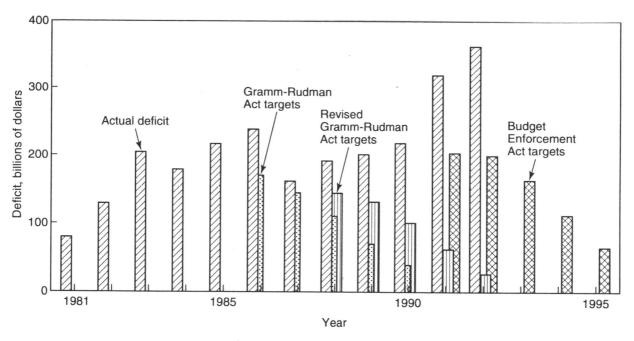

Figure 20.   Missed targets, changed targets. U.S. budget deficits and congressionally mandated reductions, 1981–1995. (Source: *Budget of the United States Government 1992.*)

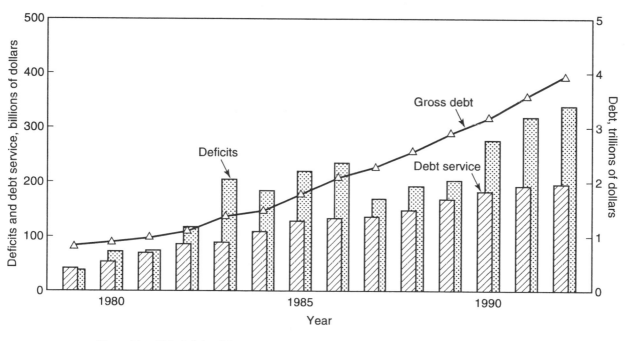

Figure 21.   U.S. deficits, debt service, and debt, 1979–1992. Deficits are on-budget deficits; they exclude Social Security. (Source: Derived from *Economic Report of the President 1993.*)

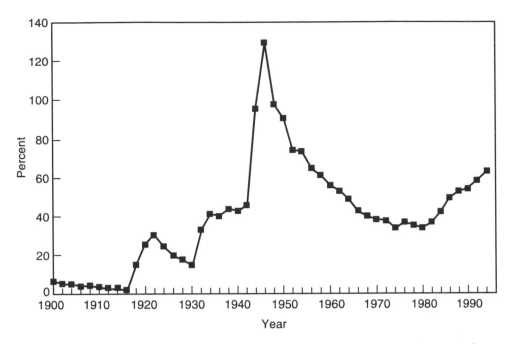

Figure 22. Federal debt as a percent of GNP, 1900–1994. (Source: *Historical Statistics of the United States, Colonial Times to 1970* [1975]; *Economic Report of the President 1993*.)

the early 1990s. The quadrupling of government debt from less than $1 trillion in 1980 to $4 trillion (about 63 percent of GNP) can be seen in figure 22. Debt service also increased steadily, reaching $200 billion for the interest on government debt held by the public. (Government trust funds, such as social security and military pensions, held about one-fourth of the debt, or $1 trillion, in Treasury securities.)

Debt service of this magnitude not only displaced other government programs but absorbed a significant portion of available domestic capital. When combined with demand for private investment in the mid-1980s and a decline in personal savings from 6.7 percent in 1981 to less than 3 percent by 1987, the burden of this debt financing led to "crowding out" of private investment through high real interest rates. Figure 23 plots the personal savings rate against the deficit, as a percentage of GNP. The difference can be viewed as the national surplus available for growth in private domestic or foreign investment (above and beyond the retained earnings of business). Despite unimpressive savings, in the 1970s this surplus at least averaged 2 percent of GNP. But in the 1980s, when savings dropped below 4 percent and deficits exceeded 4 percent, the surplus disappeared altogether. From 1985 on, net foreign borrowing was required just to cover the government's deficits.

The high real interest rates of the early 1980s had another important consequence. By stimulating demand for U.S. assets, they drove the value of the dollar up by 63 percent on a trade-weighted basis (figure 24). Not until February 1985, when the Reagan administration and other Organization for Economic Cooperation and Development (OECD) governments intervened in currency markets, did the dollar's appreciation halt, and then reverse.

The rapid rise of the dollar had a devastating impact on the competitiveness of American products. Merchandise exports dropped 15 percent and did not recover their 1981 levels (even in nominal prices) until 1987. Imports, meanwhile, jumped 27 percent before the dollar stopped appreciating in 1985, and then increased another 47 percent (despite falling oil prices) by the end of the decade. Year after year, American-based firms lost foreign sales, customer contacts, and distribution presence. Importers swamped U.S. markets. They established customer relations, developed distributor and supplier relationships, and eventually invested in manufacturing. In all but a few of America's strongest industries, U.S. competitiveness declined sharply. By the time American firms had restructured, bringing unit labor costs under control (figure 25), they faced an uphill struggle to recapture lost market share.

By stimulating consumption and raising real in-

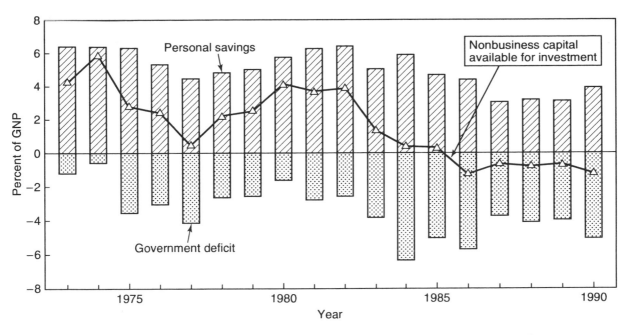

Figure 23. Savings, deficits, and "crowding out," 1973–1990. (Source: *Economic Report of the President 1992.*)

terest rates, federal deficit spending during the 1980s precipitated a structural deficit on the balance of trade and the current account. As figure 26 shows, Americans, like their government, were consuming far more than they produced. Between 1981 and 1990, the cumulative current account deficit of the United States amounted to $897 billion.

Figure 27 summarizes the effects of the Reagan-

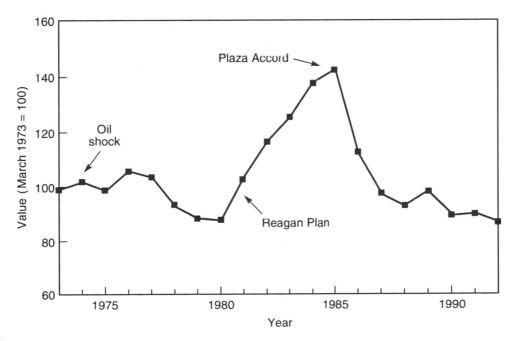

Figure 24. Exchange rates, 1973–1992. Trade-weighted valued of the U.S. dollar; March 1973 = 100. (Source: *Economic Report of the President 1993.*)

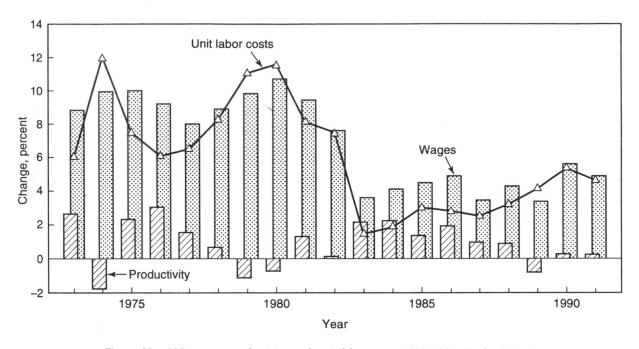

Figure 25.   U.S. wages, productivity, and unit labor costs, 1973–1991. Productivity is defined as output per hour of all persons in the business sector. (Source: *Economic Report of the President 1973.*)

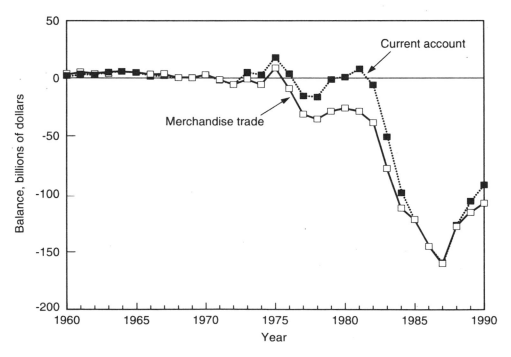

Figure 26.   U.S. international transactions: Trade and current account balance, 1960–1990. (Source: *Economic Report of the President, 1992.*)

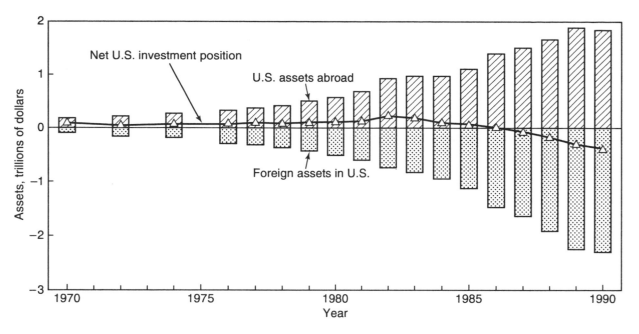

Figure 27. U.S. international investment position, 1970–1990. (Source: *Economic Report of the President 1982; Economic Report of the President 1991.*)

Bush era on the United States' position in the world economy. To finance these current account deficits, Americans had to borrow approximately $900 billion of foreign capital. Foreign assets in the United States (at estimated current cost) tripled, from $736 billion in 1982 to more than $23 trillion in 1990. Direct investment in property, plant and equipment, portfolio purchases of corporate securities, treasury bills, and foreign official reserves, each accounted for about one-fourth this amount. Although American holdings of assets abroad also increased during the 1980s, the net position declined from a surplus of $364 billion in 1982—a position accumulated over most the twentieth century—to a deficit of $362 billion in 1991. The United States had become the world's most indebted nation.

Despite a hundred years of unprecedented prosperity, economic leadership, and political dominance, the United States faced the end of the century in something of an economic hole. Its extraordinary endowment of physical assets had been diminished, though scarcely exhausted. Its environmental capacity to absorb waste and effluent was increasingly strained and required serious national attention. Its physical infrastructure and human capital were frayed and in need of revitalization. Its assets, although still immense, were now partially owned by non-Americans. And its industrial capacity, while still substantial, no longer stood alone in the world in terms of productivity, quality, or competitiveness.

When the American economy had experienced performance problems in the past, the political process introduced institutional reforms designed to redirect or restart economic progress. This was the case in the Progressive Era and once again during the New Deal. But in those earlier eras the nation was neither integrated into the larger global economy nor so heavily in debt. This time around, America was caught in a vicious cycle. Debt service was hanging over the economy, hampering investment for new growth, undermining the value of the dollar and eroding the standard of living. Foreign economies, geared more toward production than consumption, and often less democratic, competed intensely as they, too, converged on the American Dream.

SEE ALSO Economic Thought; Economic Policies; Consumption; Depressions and Recessions: The Business Cycle (all in this volume).

BIBLIOGRAPHY

For statistical data, this essay relies primarily on seven sources. *Historical Statistics of the United States, Colonial Times to 1970* (1975), compiled by the U.S. Department of Commerce, Bureau of the Census, is a two-volume standard reference that combines the most consistent time series of output and price data on every major sector of the economy with data on population, employment, finance, government, and national income. For more detailed series and for economic data since 1970, I used the Bureau of the Census's *Statistical Abstract of the United States* (1946 to 1991). For detailed, year-by-year data on the national income and product accounts, balance of payments, and money and interest rates, I used the *Economic Report of the President* (various years since 1946). For consistent budgetary data for the federal government, see Office of Management and Budget, *Historical Tables: Budget of the United States Government* (1986); for the most recent data, see Office of Management and Budget, *Budget of the United States Government FY93* (1992). For compatible international data on national income, output, and prices for Organization for Economic Cooperation and Development (OECD) countries, I used a handy volume published by the Economist Publications: *One Hundred Years of Economic Statistics* (1989). Three studies provided historical estimates and analysis of national income: Robert F. Martin, *National Income in the United States, 1799–1838* (1939); Simon Kuznets, *National Product Since 1969* (1946); and Robert E. Gallman, "Gross National Product in the United States, 1834–1909," in National Bureau of Economic Research, *Output, Employment, and Productivity in the United States After 1800* (1966).

The information on productivity and comparative sources of growth came from six sources: Edward F. Denison, *Trends in American Economic Growth, 1929–1982* (1985) provides the most consistent and detailed analysis of growth factors and the slowdown of growth that occurred in the 1970s. For analysis of productivity factors, I used John W. Kendrick, ed., *International Comparisons of Productivity and Causes of the Slowdown* (1984), and William J. Baumol, Sue Anne Batey Blackman, and Edward N. Wolff, *Productivity and American Leadership: The Long View* (1991). For the impact of technology, I benefited from Edwin Mansfield's "Technology and Productivity in the United States," in Martin Feldstein, ed., *The American Economy in Transition* (1980). For longer-term, international comparative data, I relied on the unparalleled work of Angus Maddison, including *The World Economy in the Twentieth Century* (1989), and, especially, *Dynamic Forces in Capitalist Development* (1991).

Several general economic histories provided industry-sector and business-cycle details where needed. Among these were John M. Clark, *The Costs of the World War to the American People* (1931), and Chester W. Wright, *Economic History of the United States* (1941). The most useful was the compilation of excellent analytical essays edited by Harold F. Williamson, *The Growth of the American Economy* (1951). For industry structure and the history of large corporations, I relied on the definitive study by Alfred D. Chandler, Jr., *The Visible Hand* (1977).

The Great Depression has received intense scrutiny by many economists and economic historians. Among the studies that I used were Milton Friedman and Anna J. Schwartz, *A Monetary History of the United States, 1867–1960* (1963); Michael A. Bernstein, *The Great Depression: Delayed Recovery and Economic Change in America, 1929–1939* (1987); Lester V. Chandler, *America's Greatest Depression, 1929–1941* (1970); Barry Eichengreen, *Golden Fetters: The Gold Standard and the Great Depression, 1919–1939* (1992); Christina Romer, "The Nation in Depression," *Journal of Economic Perspectives* 7, no. 2 (Spring 1993): 19–39; and Peter Temin, *Did Monetary Forces Cause the Great Depression?* (1976), and *Lessons from the Great Depression* (1989).

Several miscellaneous studies provided useful insights for this work. For an early, yet still valuable, interpretation of economic forces in the 1920s, see Robert Gordon, "Cyclical Experience in the Interwar Period: The Investment Boom of the Twenties," in National Bureau of Economic Research, *Conference on Business Cycles* (1951). For an overview of cycles in the postwar period, I used Robert J. Gordon, "Postwar Macroeconomics: The Evolution of Events and Ideas," in Martin Feldstein, ed., *The American Economy in Transition* (1980). For government macroeconomic policy in the context of the international economy, I used Michael G. Rukstad, *Macroeconomic Decision Making in the World Economy* (1989), and Herbert Stein, *Fiscal Revolution in America* (1969). For an overview and analysis of government regulation, see my article "Government Regulation of Business," in *The Cambridge Economic History of the United States* (forthcoming).

The material on energy and natural resources was drawn from several sources. An extremely thoughtful analysis is provided by Gavin Wright, "The Origins of American Industrial Success, 1879–1940," *American Economic Review* 80, no. 4 (1990): 651–668. For energy policy, see my *Energy Policy in America* (1984).

On the subject of international competitiveness, I used several studies prepared by faculty at the Harvard Business School. These included John B. Goodman, *West Germany: The Search for Stability* (1989); Bruce Scott, *Economic Strategy and Economic Performance* (1992); Bruce Scott and George Lodge, eds., *U.S. Competitiveness in the World Economy* (1985), and Thomas K. McCraw, ed., *America versus Japan* (1986).

DEPRESSIONS AND RECESSIONS:
THE BUSINESS CYCLE

Michael A. Bernstein

The economic history of the United States since the 1890s has been punctuated by several business cycles. These cycles, while varying in depth and length, all have affected the nation's political and social life. Understanding their causes remains a controversial matter for economists and historians alike. Moreover, an assessment of political events as well as international affairs in the course of this century often depends explicitly on what analytical approach was used to understand economic instability and crisis. Explanations of severe economic conditions should contribute to the historians' argument that exceptional events transform the country's political and social framework. And they should afford economists useful insights into the business cycle generally and unemployment in particular. In addition, such theoretical discussions should help analysts determine the position of American power in the twentieth-century world system with reference to the rise and decline of economic leadership and hegemony, and the more recent emergence of economic interdependence. All this analysis places extraordinary emphasis on the integration of theory, statistics, and historical evidence in constructing an understanding of America's past.

This essay is divided into three broad parts concerning theory (the first section), history (the next five sections), and some of the prospects for the American economy in the next century (the final two sections).

TRADE CYCLE THEORY

Any conception of economic instability or of cycles in economic performance must explain how, over time, markets fail to provide balanced growth. Persistent or intermittent unemployment of labor or capital are symptomatic of some difficulty in reaching what contemporary economists call equilibrium. In a capi-

talist economy characterized by a fair degree of competition in major markets, unemployment (or inflationary overemployment) of any resource should generate price changes that eliminate the distortion and "clear" the market in question. This equilibrating mechanism of modern markets may generate periodic swings in economic performance known as business or trade cycles. Obstacles to such equilibration may lead to sustained periods of instability or to depressions.

In a hypothetical simple economy in which one sector made consumption goods and another capital goods, given a particular endowment of resources and technology with a fixed population of given demographic characteristics, balanced performance would involve a virtual steady state in which the output of both sectors would be totally utilized in each production period. There would be no unemployment, of either human or produced inputs, and a simple reproduction of economic life from period to period would ensue. But the assumptions embedded in this exercise—two sector production, fixed technological and resource endowments, fixed population, and so on—belie the argument. Economies, at least capitalist economies, rarely if ever exhibit such constancy. It is this variability in the conditions affecting economic life that is the source of instability.

As population growth changes, technological know-how advances, and the composition and interaction of economic sectors is transformed, the ingredients of the growth process similarly change. Moreover, given the decentralized nature of decision making among households and firms in a capitalist economy, fluctuations in economic activity may emerge simply from the recurrent inconsistencies in coordination among numerous activities. In all these regards, cyclical volatility as well as long-term swings in economic growth are inherent in the workings of capitalist economies.

Some economic theorists and economic historians have tried to discern three general patterns in the cyclical performance of modern economies. Periodic waves of fifty years or more were examined by the Russian statistician N. D. Kondratieff in the 1930s, who argued that these long waves were associated with the introduction and dispersion of major inventions and with dramatic alterations in resource endowments resulting from such things as mineral discoveries, transportation and communication breakthroughs, and war. The Juglar cycle, a wave of approximately ten years' duration, appeared to be linked with population movements. A swing of about forty months' length—the Kitchin wave—was understood to have the appearance of a typical inventory cycle.

Simon Kuznets, Moses Abramovitz, and Richard Easterlin documented the existence of economic waves in the United States of fifteen to twenty years in length. Such swings, according to these investigators, demonstrated that in the United States and other industrialized countries economic growth throughout the nineteenth and twentieth centuries proceeded on the basis of intermittent accelerations in output growth and resource utilization. Perhaps most striking, such periods of acceleration were usually followed by serious downturns in economic activity. It seemed clear that these oscillations involved changes in resource endowments (including the size and age-composition of the population) and alterations in the intensity of resource use.

Whether secular or short-run, business cycles embody one of the central puzzles of modern economic life. Sustained (i.e., uninterrupted) economic growth requires continuing increases in investment expenditures that are large enough to make additions to productive capacity, create jobs, and expand output. In the absence of technical change, however, the rate of net investment will fall to zero as soon as the rate of increase in consumption (and hence in sales revenue) levels off. For consumption expenditures to rise consistently, there must be either enough net investment to create jobs and maintain consumer income levels or injections of spending from elsewhere in the economy such as the government, foreign trade, or from major resource discoveries or territorial expansion. This is an essential paradox of capitalist growth, and the reason why growth often takes the form of accelerations (booms) and pauses (busts). Indeed, the foundation of the mathematical theory of business cycles is found in what is known as the "accelerator model" of investment behavior.

The acceleration principle is premised on the idea that an economy's capital stock (inventory, machinery, tools, and the like) will grow when the level of output is growing. As sales for a firm increase, and thus as inventories run down and capacity is utilized at higher rates, there will be an incentive to invest in more plants and equipment, and to hire more labor to increase production and meet greater demand for the firm's product. But when sales cease to grow, or start growing at a slower rate, net investment will fall to zero as firms adjust to new economic circumstances. A reduction in the rate at which new capacity is purchased, and at which new jobs are thus created, will lead to a falling off in economic activity, or a recession. A recovery, at least in theory, will occur when the ratio between sales and capital stock rises (owing to the reduction in capital occasioned by disinvestment in the downturn) to a point where firms think it appropriate to resume net investment. Two essential concepts emerge from this fundamental characteristic of the trade cycle. It is assumed that businesspeople will seek to maintain some target ratio between the level of sales and the size of their capital stock. Furthermore, and as a consequence of this plausible behavioral assumption, sales must rise at a sufficient rate simply to keep investment level, let alone to stimulate net investment. In other words, fluctuations in consumption in capitalist economies generate undulations in investment behavior that lie behind the trade cycle. But investment itself largely determines the level of and rate of growth in consumption due to its impact on job creation and employment. Cyclical instability is, therefore, an essential and unavoidable characteristic of capitalist enterprise in particular and of capitalism in general.

Counterposed to the intermittent volatility of the real economy are perturbations in the monetary and financial system, called circulation crises and financial panics. These too can cause wide gyrations in output and employment and can even lead to general interruptions of economic activity often called, in the course of American history, "panics." What distinguishes circulation crises and financial panics from so-called real business cycles is that they have emerged independent of movements in inventory, population growth, technical change, and the like. Their propagation appears linked, in many cases, with institutional and regulatory constraints on the financial and banking sectors of the economy.

A financial crisis, in its simplest form, can emerge if there is an inadequate supply of currency in the system. If a national money supply is tied to the availability of a particular precious metal (e.g., gold or silver), fluctuations in the supply of that metal will cause changes in national output. A rapidly growing money supply will, ceteris paribus, initiate an inflationary boom as greater amounts of dollars "chase" a given output of goods and services. Conversely, if the money supply shrinks, a deflationary spiral will ensue with concomitant impacts upon output, employment, and investment. Changes in the growth rate of the money supply can occur even in a paper money system in which a central monetary authority or political events alter that growth rate over time.

In a decentralized banking system, with a hard money (i.e., precious metal) base, the potential for financial disruption is great. There exist no unambiguous lines of authority in the event that a particular region or urban area suddenly requires an increase in circulating medium. Similarly, should some banks fail owing to a deterioration in general economic conditions, poor management, or sheer bad luck, a decentralized institutional system of finance offers no mechanism by which liquidity can be restored. As banks close their doors, firms cease operations and lay off workers; households cut back consumption expenditures or substitute nonmonetary forms of exchange in their daily activities. An economic convulsion results.

Interestingly enough, circulation problems arising out of decentralized or hard money systems may be caused simply by the seasonal fluctuation of economic activity. In an agricultural economy at harvest time, for example, farmers accumulate large cash reserves as they sell their crops. At the same time, merchants, shippers, and packers require loans in order to process and move farm crops to market. Such agents often are located in cities or metropolitan areas distinct from the Farm Belts they serve, and if there is no clear channel by which farmers' cash reserves can be recycled to the banks that are financing the wholesale trade, an interruption in commerce will result.

Financial panics may also occur when and if depositors lose confidence in the security of their bank-held assets. Fractional-reserve banking, and its unique profitability and ability to stimulate economic growth, is premised on the notion that every demand deposit will not be drawn upon at once. Yet if depositors sense a lack of robustness in the banking system, a run can develop in which all deposits are in fact drawn down at the same time. In the face of such an event, individual banks must lock out their customers, and if one bank pursues this strategy, the ingredients of wholesale panic are further supplied. Such inherent fragility in the private banking system can only be compensated for by governmental institutions that establish lenders of last resort, in the form of a central or national bank, or insurance systems by which the value of all deposits is secured to some minimum. Once again, even with respect to the monetary circulation and financial mechanisms of modern economy, the possibility of crisis and volatility is ever present.

Shortfalls in national output may also occur due to reductions in the level of demand. As consumption falls, and firms' sales are reduced, a cumulative downturn may develop whereby reductions in demand cause a decrease in investment and employment, which itself furthers the decline in consumption as workers lose income. It is even possible that an economy may gravitate toward an "equilibrium" position (a state of affairs from which there seems no tendency to depart) in which significant amounts of capital and labor are unemployed. This deviation of actual from potential output may result from distortions in the price mechanism, by which adjustments in wages and prices that might bring about full employment of resources are obstructed, or from misperceptions on the part of wealth holders and workers as to the economic alternatives available to them. Capital might be hoarded, rather than productively invested, owing to a lack of confidence; labor might be withdrawn from the market in the (mistaken) impression that wages will rise in the near future. Virtual economic stagnation can be the ultimate result.

Tendencies toward underconsumption (or, its mirror image, overproduction) may be derived from short-term changes in the distribution of income or long-run transformations in the structures of capital accumulation. Downward inflexibility of prices, caused by the concentrated structure of industry or the impact of labor unions, may intensify the effective demand problem and prevent the price system from reaching a new equilibrium at full employment. On the one side, "sticky prices" limit the already constrained purchasing power of consumers. On the other, to the extent that noncompetitive pricing predominates in the capital goods sector, producers are less willing to invest in new plants and equipment. High real wages, maintained by union pressure or government policy, may further contribute to persistent disequilibrium in labor markets. Yet lowering wages in an economy with highly concentrated and thereby imperfect markets can result in a reduction in real wages as prices remain high. The effective demand crisis is thereby exacerbated. Only if price adjustments are general, economy-wide, and followed rapidly by increased investment, can a deflationary recovery process succeed.

Price inflexibility that is an outgrowth of capital concentration and imperfections in markets has especially negative implications for economic performance in the intermediate to long run. In highly concentrated industries (i.e., industries with a small number of large firms), a downturn in the business cycle may result in perverse reactions that make the slump worse. The net revenue of firms with a great deal of market power may be so attenuated in a slump that strategies of price reduction may be unfeasible. There may even be incentives to raise prices to compensate for the reduction in the volume of sales.

If price reductions do not occur when the economy-wide rate of growth declines, the necessary adjustment of sectoral rates of expansion to the aggregate rate requires reductions in individual firm's rates of capacity utilization. If industrial structure were more competitive, however, excess capacity would not result from a decline in the rate of growth; rather, prices would fall. Reductions in capacity utilization imply not only lower national income but also higher unemployment. In the presence of underutilized capacity, firms are disinclined to undertake net investment. A cumulative process will thereby be established wherein a decline in the rate of growth, by generating reductions in the rate of capacity utilization, leads to a further decline in the rate of expansion as net investment is reduced. The actions of individual firms, believing that decreases in investment might alleviate their own burden of excess capacity, merely intensify the problem economy-wide. It is this "fallacy of composition," assuming that what is good for the individual is good for the whole, that is the basis for most macroeconomic difficulties in capitalist systems.

Effective demand failures may also be generated by declines in the rate of population growth or reductions in the rate at which innovations and new technologies are introduced into the economic system. As population growth falls off (assuming some minimum level of affluence of the population as a whole), the growth of major markets such as housing, transportation, and food production also slackens. Economic growth is thereby jeopardized and may only be resumed by the introduction of new technologies and products that can absorb larger investment outlays to expand production and employment once again. If these are not forthcoming, the only solution may be some form of exogenous spending (such as governmental deficit spending) to augment consumer purchasing power.

It is also possible that in more affluent societies, an ever-increasing volume of savings is generated. Such savings may eventually find no outlets except at unrealistically low rates of interest—rates at which investors may prefer to hold their wealth in cash rather than securities, bonds, or other titles to real capital. This constitutes a monetary parallel to the real problem of a potentially vanishing set of investment and technological opportunities. In other words, at very low rates of interest, the demand for money becomes so high that it creates a "liquidity trap." As money accumulates in cash hoards, the decline in productive spending makes the downturn worse. As one distinguished macroeconomic theorist, Michal Kalecki, said: "capitalists get what they spend; workers spend what they get." If either workers' consumption spending, or capitalists' investment outlays decline, recession or depression is the result.

Compositional and structural distortions—persistent unemployment, lagging capacity utilization in major industries, and inadequate rates of net investment in a national economy—may also be the outgrowth of transformations in the composition of national product. Simple accelerator models of the business cycle fail to capture this complexity of modern economies because functional relationships between sales and investment obscure the influence of secular changes in the mix of industries constituting the national aggregate. Long-range prospects for expansion underlie the decision making associated with large investment obligations. The size and rate of growth of the relevant market are of primary concern. To the extent that firms in an industry during the trough phase of a business cycle have pessimistic expectations about their markets, a revival becomes dependent on either the creation of wholly new, promising markets (i.e., new products) or the stimulus of new expenditures from outside the industry. Highly concentrated sectors bolster the potential for economic stagnation. The reluctance to compete and drive out inefficient or high-cost producers intensifies the gloom of the environment in which enterprise plans are formulated, besides contributing to the state of depressed sales and net revenues that makes investment upturns more and more difficult.

Product innovation requires large net revenues or adequate access to external sources of funds, both of which are less available in a slump. External stimuli must be sufficiently large to have an adequate effect. Secular changes in the growth performance and potential of various industries must offset declines in certain groups with rises in others. The chance that such changes in sectoral performance will proceed smoothly is small.

Secular transitions in development involve the

decline of old and the rise of new industries. These alterations in the composition of national output tend to be discontinuous and disruptive not because of imperfections in markets but rather because of forces inherent in the accumulation of capital over time. First, the ongoing expansion of the capitalist economy is coterminous with the advance of scientific and technical knowledge that transforms production techniques, cost structures, and the availability of raw materials and creates entirely new inputs and outputs. Examples include the emergence of fossil fuels, the replacement of natural fibers with synthetics, and the rise of internal combustion as a means of locomotion. Entire industries are made obsolete or virtually so, while new ones are created. Second, the structural milieu in which product and technical changes take place is itself a product of economic growth.

The concentration and increasing specificity of capital may interfere with the movements of inputs required for smooth transitions in sectoral activity. The decline in competitive pressure in highly concentrated industries makes not only entry difficult, because of pricing strategies, but also exit. Large amounts of capital are fixed in plants and equipment, their liquidation neither encouraged by a competitive environment nor practical if the industry is in long-run decline. The hesitancy of large firms to liquidate in depressed times may also be due to a reluctance to relinquish goodwill and the technical specialization of labor and organization, and to uncertainty as to the growth potential of new markets.

Concentration of capital may lead to unequal access to investment funds, which obstructs further the possibility of easy transitions in industrial activity. Because of their past record of profitability, large enterprises have higher credit ratings and easier access to credit facilities, and are able to put up larger collateral for a loan. Equity issues by such firms are more readily financed and sold, and such firms can avoid takeovers more easily than small firms. Large firms, too, may have commonalities of interest with financial institutions through interlocking directorates. All these factors may impede the flow of capital out of old and into new sectors, thereby exacerbating the shortfalls in aggregate economic performance.

Compositional and structural change in economies may also precipitate serious unemployment problems that interfere with the achievement of full employment output. New industries may have differing capital intensities and skill requirements, relative to older sectors, that complicate (or prevent) the absorption of unemployed workers. The problem may be twofold: newer industries may not grow fast enough to provide employment opportunities for those laid off in older sectors; and even if higher growth rates are achieved, the newer industries may require different amounts and altogether different kinds of labor for their production. Structural unemployment may be the troubling and persistent consequence.

Finally, changes in the relationship of a national economy to the world economic system may also be responsible for wide fluctuations in macroeconomic behavior. A resurgence of competition from other national systems previously excluded from—or inadequately prepared for—international commerce may seriously affect the fortunes of domestic industries that have become used to doing business in protected or exclusive markets. Transformations in international currency systems, whereby a nation's monetary unit, which had previously served as *numeraire,* and its means of international transaction are rapidly integrated into a general floating currency system, will also profoundly change the performance characteristics of that economy. (A *numeraire* is that unit or commodity chosen with which to express money prices in some common index; in the case of international currency transactions, that index is usually gold. In the wake of World War II, it was the U.S. dollar.) Inflationary pressures in that nation may translate into an export boom as a currency is devalued, while deflationary patterns may yield an upswing in imports to the detriment of domestic producers. Policy flexibility and independence may also be constrained as a nation's economy becomes more integrated with economies elsewhere. Domestic changes in fiscal and monetary policy will now have international trade consequences as well. Modulations of interest rates, for example, will affect the flow of capital across national borders as investors compare rates of return in various nations.

National economic performance may also, in a mature setting, require increasing involvement of the state. Maintaining sufficient outlets for net investment expenditure might involve deficit spending to bolster effective demand; direct government purchases of goods and services (particularly of public goods such as infrastructure and defense); and government oversight of the penetration of foreign markets. These efforts might conceivably be paralleled by rising outlays by private firms on sales efforts, distribution mechanisms, and means to enhance consumer credit. While for some economic theorists, fiscal and monetary mechanisms stand as instruments of periodic countercyclical policy, for others governmental involvement in mature economies may be a permanent (and ever-increasing) feature of modern industrial systems.

In many respects, economic instability in modern states appears to be the outgrowth of coordination problems whereby the plans of private firms do not meld appropriately to maintain balanced growth over time. Business-cycle theorists have long understood that if investment decision making could be coordinated by a central authority, with aggregate demand augmented accordingly, there would not necessarily arise interruptions in the growth process. The expansion plans of one firm would be met by those of its suppliers and of its consumers, and so on. Such organization of national economic activity has most often been achieved, in capitalist settings, during wartime. The difficulty of course is that systematization of private planning by sovereign authority is inconsistent with the operation of economic systems premised upon the rights of private property.

To protect against unemployment and economic instability, the freedom to accumulate may be curtailed within the context of national planning. Yet to endorse unfettered accumulation of wealth may leave society open to divisive and potentially catastrophic political turmoil when a dramatic decrease of business activity occurs. History has shown that planned (e.g., government-controlled) systems can eradicate income volatility and unemployment, but they apparently cannot ensure adequate rates of growth in material welfare and income. Capitalist systems, by contrast, have unprecedented records when it comes to the massing of wealth and raising of living standards, but unemployment and income fluctuations cannot be eliminated except under extraordinary conditions.

RESTRUCTURING THE BANKING SYSTEM, 1890–1914

For the U.S. economy, the turn of the century presented all the promise and pitfalls of modern industrial development. While rapid economic growth generally resumed in the wake of the Civil War, except in the South, changes in industrial structure and weaknesses in the institutional setting hampered expansion during the 1890s. World market conditions were generally favorable to American interests, although agriculture (in particular the southern cotton economy) faced new competition from abroad that was both menacing and persistent. Most of all, the financial difficulties of the turn of the century epoch posed challenges for policymakers and for entrepreneurs that resulted in some far-reaching re-

forms (most significantly the Federal Reserve Act of 1913) just prior to World War I.

By the mid 1890s, American economic performance was jeopardized on the one side by falling agricultural and primary product prices. On the other, a series of local financial panics precipitated a general monetary crisis that resulted in a sustained deflation through the remainder of the decade. This first "Great Depression," as some historians have called it, created great hardship in the Farm Belt and fostered the emergence of radical movements among farmers and laborers. Continued instability through the turn of the century and, by 1907, a severe recession convinced many of the necessity for a substantive restructuring of the national financial system. Figures 1 through 3 provide a broad overview of movements in national income and product over the course of this century.

Throughout the 1890s, and during much of the nineteenth century, the periodic difficulties that emerged from the practice of fractional-reserve banking, within the context of a decentralized network, resulted in numerous panics and bank runs. In the face of these interruptions in the financial circulation, banks often suspended cash payments to depositors. In some cases, banks continued payments only up to some specified maximum daily sum. In the panic of 1907, payment suspension was frighteningly common nationwide, and the duration of such spells for many banks lasted more than two months. Scrip and other collateral instruments were used in many regions to try to compensate for the wholesale hemorrhage of the monetary system. Reductions in the supply of money, furthermore, drove the aggregate price level down. Producers, especially farmers dependent on harvest income, were particularly hard hit.

Interestingly enough, the deflationary process initiated by the turn of the century panics did not yield higher real incomes for wage earners and other consumers. Throughout the 1890s and early 1900s, a sustained merger wave resulted in an ever-increasing number of large firms that dominated the macroeconomic landscape. These oligopolies and trusts escaped the market discipline of their smaller counterparts. Sticky prices in certain major industrial markets resulted in lower real wages, and a deteriorating standard of living on the farm, as wage and farm incomes fell. As a consequence, by the end of the first decade of the new century, national politicians endorsed monetary reform.

A National Monetary Commission, established by the Aldrich-Vreeland Act of 1908, issued its final

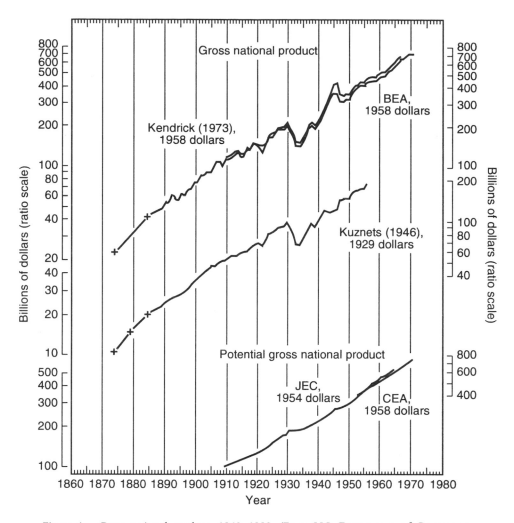

Figure 1. Gross national product, 1860–1980. (From U.S. Department of Commerce, Bureau of Economic Analysis, *Long-term Economic Growth, 1860–1970* [Washington, D.C., Government Printing Office, 1973], p. 14; NBER John Kendrick; Simon Kuznets.)

report in 1912, and Congress, inspired by its recommendations, created a Federal Reserve System—signed into law by President Woodrow Wilson the following year. With a permanent charter, the system was based upon the creation of twelve regional reserve banks that would oversee the proper growth and circulation of the national money supply. A Federal Reserve Board supervised the new system with a membership that included the secretary of the Treasury, the comptroller of the Currency, and five governors appointed by the president. Each bank had a set of directors, some of whom were chosen by the board, others by the relevant regional member banks.

It would be the task of the Reserve System to control the reserves of member banks and, thereby, modulate the supply of money circulating in the economy at large. The system, by periodically alter-

ing (through a variety of regulatory mechanisms) the amount of cash that member banks would have on reserve to loan out, could decisively alter the pace of economic activity by loosening or tightening credit. In emergencies, the system could also act as lender of last resort to avoid the suspensions and panics that had plagued the national economy in the previous century.

The creation of the Federal Reserve System solved, in the eyes of many, some of the central problems that had been responsible for the intermittent cycles of economic performance during the half-century since the Civil War. The new banking network eliminated the regional and seasonal interruptions of the financial circulation that had caused so much adversity in the past, and afforded the federal government greater control over, and awareness of

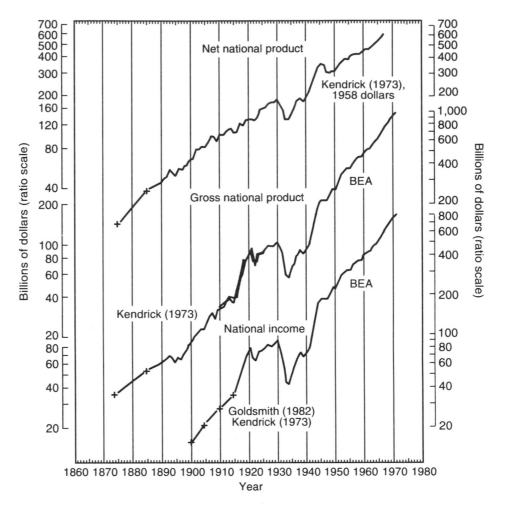

Figure 2.   National product and income, 1860–1980. (From U.S. Department of Commerce, Bureau of Economic Analysis, *Long-term Economic Growth, 1860–1970* [Washington, D.C., Government Printing Office, 1973], p. 15; NBER John Kendrick; Goldsmith.)

the growth of monetary instruments. It could not provide, however, as future events would demonstrate, sufficient safeguards against collapses in the level of effective demand or unambiguous lines of authority in the event of a general collapse in the soundness of member institutions.

THE GREAT WAR AND THE TWENTIES, 1914–1930

The Great War of 1914–1918 thrust the United States into a world leadership role in economic, military, and political terms. In some respects, the nation was not prepared—in either political or diplomatic will and means—for its new stature. Even so, the war's impacts inexorably transformed Americans' way of life in a wide variety of ways. On an economic level there was no more dramatic change than that which

occurred in America's position in the world economy. Throughout the nineteenth century—indeed, since the time of the American Revolution—the United States had been a debtor nation. The country owed more money overseas than it was owed by foreign individuals, institutions, and governments. By the time of the signing of the Versailles treaty, America had become a creditor state for the first time in its history, a status that prevailed until the 1980s.

Allied orders for war matériel and for the products of American agriculture (so necessary because of the devastation in European farming areas, east and west) cushioned the distorting impacts of wartime resource diversion and expenses. These overseas orders also contributed to the accelerating transformation in the American trade balance. Of great importance in this regard was the inflow of gold reserves, commencing in 1914, from nervous foreign individ-

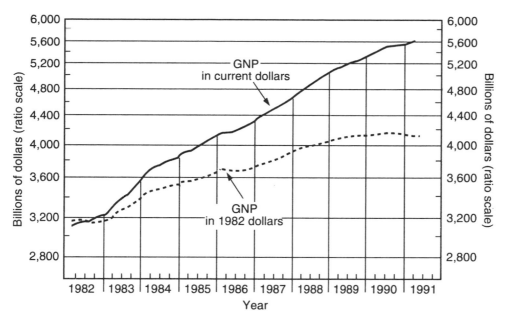

Figure 3. Gross national product, 1982–1991. (From Council of Economic Advisers, *Economic Indicators: July, 1991* [Washington, D.C., Government Printing Office, 1991], p. 1.)

uals and governments who sought a safe haven for their assets as military confrontation loomed. In 1916 alone, it is estimated that some $2 billion in gold came into the country primarily through major banks in New York City.

The performance of the American economy during World War I was quite good. Gross national product (GNP) rose approximately 22 percent (in real terms) during the war years. Demand for American industrial products increased as never before. The main expansion occurred in the chemical, machine, and metal industries that produced the weapons of war, but huge orders also went to such industries as canning, flour milling, and wool manufacturing. At the end of the war, American industrial capacity had reached levels much in excess of peacetime demand—a development that would cause difficulties in the recession of the early 1920s.

Similarly the war greatly stimulated American agriculture. By 1919, agricultural production was almost 10 percent higher than in 1913. Virtually a quarter of this enhanced output went overseas. Farmers enjoyed substantial increases in their real income as farm-gate prices rose in the face of increasing domestic and foreign demand. In many cases, such prosperity encouraged rapid investment in land, equipment, and farm buildings. Unfortunately such confidence resulted in overproduction with war's

end, and a persistent agricultural recession during the 1920s.

With the end of the Great War, federal intervention in the national economy decreased and the large number of agencies that had been created to deploy government oversight were quickly dismantled. Paralleling the rapid demobilization of the armed forces, the war economy itself quickly came to an end. While there was some political and legal debate concerning these developments, especially with respect to the repeal of labor market regulations, in the final analysis the American economy rapidly moved to a peacetime footing. Even so, the macroeconomic adjustment from war to peace was not without its tensions and frictions.

Yet the war era had a lasting legacy with respect to certain forms of governmental intervention in economic life. By the 1930s such New Deal agencies as the National Recovery Administration, the Commodity Credit Corporation, the United States Housing Administration, and the National Labor Relations Board were based on World War I models such as the War Industries Board, the Food Administration, and the Emergency Fleet Corporation. In World War II the War Production Board and numerous other war agencies were inspired as well by their World War I prototypes.

The shift from wartime to peacetime production

1191

involved a variety of difficulties. From 1920 to 1921 there was a severe but brief downturn, an anomaly in macroeconomic performance that is quite common after wars. What is so notable about the post–World War I recession is not that it occurred but rather that the lower turning point was so quickly reached. Rapid recovery arose from five proximate causes.

First, there was a strong pent-up demand for capital goods in the consumer-oriented industries which had had to wait under wartime allocative regulations for capital requirements to be met. Second, large numbers of consumers created a large demand for goods that had been unavailable during the war years. This consumption demand was tied to the third reason for the robust upturn—the accumulated savings of households (many of which had earned higher wages during wartime production and had patriotically purchased government bonds in the war-loan campaigns). Fourth, high foreign demand for U.S. output was a direct outgrowth of wartime devastation and dislocation on the European continent. And fifth, a continuation of high government spending into the early 1920s, which was linked with military outlays (owing to the time it took to demobilize) and increasing federal responsibilities that had emerged during overseas military operations.

Having weathered the 1920–1921 recession, the American economy improved later in the decade. From 1920 to 1929, total manufacturing output rose 50 percent, an aggregate figure that masks rapid rates of growth in major sectors of the economy. By 1929 the economy of the United States produced 40 percent of the world's coal; 70 percent of the world's petroleum; one-third of the world's hydroelectric power; one-half of the world's steel; and virtually all of the world's natural gas. In the same year the nation consumed more electricity than the rest of the world combined. In 1919, 6.7 million cars and 900,000 trucks were registered in the United States; ten years later the figures were 23 million cars and 3.5 million trucks. The impact that the growth of the automobile sector had on associated sectors (such as petroleum and steel) was enormous, and that broad-based development was further stimulated by a continuing increase in outlays on a national and state highway network.

These examples show that the 1920s were a period in which the American economy demonstrated great health and maturity. Yet even though the decade saw important advances in industrial output, industrial structure and technology, and in the composition of national product, it also witnessed widespread hardship in agriculture, coal mining, and textile pro-

duction, and new and precarious developments in America's international trade position.

Perhaps the most well-known symptom of the Roaring Twenties was the stock market boom. From 1921 to 1929 there were a series of booms in the issuance of new equity on the New York exchange. The stock boom was massive, exhilarating, and foolish. Margin-buying was the rule rather than the exception, and brokers allowed 75 percent to 80 percent of the value of a stock purchase to be borrowed. This was before the advent of the Securities and Exchange Commission. So confident were brokers and the public of the market's rise validating risks that transactions took on the character of a frenzy. Banks and corporations were not immune from the passions of the day; they too placed reserve funds on call in the market. When the crash came, both large firms and old pensioners would feel the pain.

American agriculture had seen better years than the 1920s. The recovery of European competitors following the Great War had removed the basis for the affluent prices of American crops (especially corn, cotton, and wheat) that had prevailed during the hostilities. And apprehension of future struggles in Europe prompted some continental governments to seek autarky with respect to agricultural produce, which further eroded the American farmers' markets. Nevertheless, because domestic consumption rose enough to counterbalance the decline in foreign demand, income in agriculture recovered by the mid-1920s and stayed level from 1925 until 1929.

Agriculture's interwar misfortunes were also linked with supply considerations. The stimulation of the World War I years had hastened not only the absolute expansion of cultivation, but also the introduction of mechanized techniques that improved per-acre yields. The substitution of gasoline for horsepower released close to 25 percent of the total acreage in crops to the production of foodstuffs rather than animal fodder—this in addition to the decrease in demand for animal feeds that the tractor initiated.

War had also brought, through its impact on the markets for agricultural output in Europe, sometimes hasty decision making that resulted in soil exhaustion and erosion. This problem, however, was not entirely the cultivators' fault, for in addition the fertilizer industry had performed poorly (in part because of the war's effect on the ocean transport of necessary nitrates and guano), and the full emergence of scientific agriculture lay in the future. Finally, trends in both transport prices and in the wages of farmhands worked to the farmer's detriment. Because the ratio of the prices received by farmers for their products to the prices they paid for consumption needs and production inputs decreased, the 1920s did not bring to the heartland the prosperity and growth-mania that they brought to the cities and industrial towns. A survey of agricultural households in 1925, for example, showed that only 10 percent of these homes had running water indoors.

Labor's fortunes also suffered after the war. Aside from the decrease in military production, shifting strength in markets and technical advances (most notably in tool and machine production) contributed to layoffs. Labor unrest was often violent, but as the decade passed, the opportunities for wage earners improved. In 1914, average annual earnings for labor were $613. By 1928, they had more than doubled. From 1922 to 1927, as the national price level fell by almost 0.1 percent per year, the real wage rose at an annual rate of approximately 2.1 percent. This increase in wages was linked with the relative calm in industrial relations that prevailed during the last half of the decade.

Labor's share in the value-added of manufacturing weakened, however, by the late 1920s. And although the doctrine of high wages had gained widespread acceptance after its introduction by Henry Ford earlier in the century, changes in income distribution and in the competitive structure of industry gave contemporaries reason for concern. Ironically and prophetically, a special commission chaired by soon-to-be president Herbert Hoover declared only months before the stock market collapse of 1929, "[u]ntil comparatively recent times, the problem of industry was to produce a sufficient quantity to supply the demand. Today the problem of industry is largely that of disposing of its products." Between 1920 and 1929, the lower 91 percent of the nonfarm population had seen its disposable per capita income fall by some 4 percent. Whether tendencies toward inadequate consumer spending by the late 1920s caused the crisis of the 1930s remains a controversial matter among economists and historians.

On the international scene, the United States became a creditor nation due in large part to the war. This fact, along with "the economic consequences of the peace," prevented the United States from pursuing economic isolation. The provisions of the Versailles treaty significantly weakened the stability of world finances. This frailty was due mainly to a dangerous arrangement by which America lent to Britain, France, and Germany, while German reparations were used by the Allies to liquidate their U.S. debts. By 1928, American banks were already wary of the

situation, but their response (to reduce the issuance of new loans to European governments) merely made the situation worse. In addition, the protectionist policies of the period not only weakened many foreign economies (since their loans could not be made good by their exports) but also hurt domestic markets by lowering the demand for U.S. exports.

There were many paradoxes of American trade policy during the 1920s. For the United States to supply increasing amounts of farm and manufacturing output to the world, massive credit had to be extended to trading partners. But greater debt, requiring as it would larger interest and principal payments by foreign borrowers, would foster potentially threatening imports to help foreign governments earn enough dollars to meet their financial obligations. Their only alternative would have been outright repudiation of their debts.

Extending credit overseas, therefore, led to conflict within the United States between bankers (whose interests favored free trade to help foreign governments pay off their liabilities) and manufacturers (who sought protection from foreign competition). Farmers were left almost entirely out of the bargain. Protectionism, deployed through the pressure of the manufacturers, and epitomized by the ill-conceived Smoot-Hawley Tariff Act of 1930, hurt agriculture by prompting retaliation by potential foreign customers. Whatever political conflicts that occurred concerning these international financial issues, however, were quickly submerged in the greatest economic crisis ever faced by the nation.

THE GREAT DEPRESSION, 1929–1939

In macroeconomic terms, the impact of the Great Depression in the United States is well known. Figures 4, 5, and 6 present data on national product, unemployment, and investment during the interwar years. From the stock market collapse in late 1929 until the mid 1930s, the physical output of goods and services contracted by 33 percent. Almost 25 percent of the labor force was idled. Capital accumulation came to a standstill. This broad outline of the nation's worst economic misfortune has been the backdrop of almost all theoretical and historical work done on the Depression.

The spectacular collapse of the stock market in New York in October 1929 did not immediately precipitate the free-fall into depression that characterized the 1930s. Indeed, in the immediate wake of the crash, many efforts were made by individual and institutional investors, J. P. Morgan most prominent

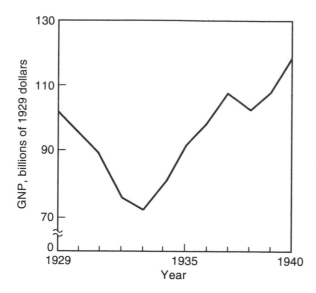

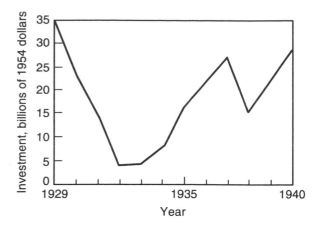

Figure 6. Gross private domestic investment, 1929–1940. (From U.S. Department of Commerce, Office of Business Economics, *U.S. Income and Output 1958* [Washington, D.C., Government Printing Office, 1959], p. 118.)

Figure 4. Gross national product, 1929–1940. (From John W. Kendrick, *Productivity Trends in the United States* [Princeton, Princeton University Press, 1961], p. 291.)

among them, to shore up the exchange with large equity purchases. Often forgotten is the fact that the stock market rallied into the early months of 1930 before declining again. While many were disturbed by the volatility of the market, there were few before mid 1930 who believed that a truly Great Depression was at hand.

What changed the situation decisively was a series of bank failures in late 1930 and early 1931. Many

banks had tied up their funds in the stock market trying to benefit from the boom, as individual investors had done. With the collapse of the market, as brokers began calling in their margin accounts, many banks were forced into bankruptcy and closed their doors to depositors as liquid assets dwindled. Failures of individual banks generated runs on other banks as depositors became nervous about the security of their accounts. Thus from the latter part of 1930 until Franklin Roosevelt's presidential inauguration in March 1933, an escalating rate of insolvencies beset the banking industry, and the nation's stock of money in circulation plummeted. These developments prompted the rapid and deep tumble of GNP that was the defining characteristic of the Great Depression.

From late 1930 to late 1933, GNP fell unrelentingly. By 1934 a slight upturn began but by 1936 this seeming recovery aborted. It was not until late 1938 and early 1939, with the coming of war in Europe and Asia, that a sustained turnaround began. Gross domestic investment fell from about 18 percent of GNP at the precrash peak in 1929 to a bit more than 5 percent by 1933. In other words, in addition to the stark falling off in national output, what distinguished the Depression of the 1930s was the almost total collapse of the investment process.

There are many theories of the causes of the Great Depression, but broadly speaking, there are three general themes that emerge from the vast amount of literature on the subject. One category of research focuses on the short-run impacts of the stock market and banking system collapse of the late 1920s and early 1930s. A second set of arguments

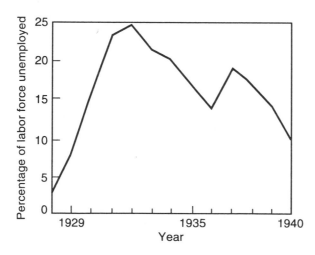

Figure 5. Aggregate unemployment (in percent), 1929–1940. (From Council of Economic Advisers, *Economic Report of the President* [Washington, D.C., Government Printing Office, 1955], p. 153.)

claims that poorly formulated and politically distorted actions of government only made worse what was in essence a typical business cycle. A third branch of scholarship takes a broader perspective and suggests that whatever started the slump in 1929, the reasons for the length and severity of the depression that followed predated and transcended the events of October 1929.

Short-run arguments about the causes of the Depression suggest that the stock market crash and the bank failures that ensued served both to reduce wealth holdings precipitously and to undercut almost fatally the confidence of investors and consumers. Businesspeople and households had both less money and less desire than ever to spend. Even with the rapid deflation of the price level from 1929 to 1933, business and consumer wealth and incomes were so radically reduced that real purchasing power was vastly diminished. With sales falling off and inventories accumulating, businesses naturally cut back investment projects. The resultant excess capacity in the economy at large generated larger waves of unemployment that, in turn, further reduced consumer buying power and the sales performance of firms. A vicious circle thus ensued from which there was seemingly no escape in the absence of powerful government intervention.

What might be called the policy-error scholarship similarly takes a short-run view of the crisis. On the one side, Keynesian critics of the New Deal found Roosevelt's spending policies too timid (indeed, in some cases, contractionary) to lead, by fiscal means, to a general recovery. On the other, monetarists faulted the apparently perverse response of the Federal Reserve Board in not coming to the aid of failing banks—which only made worse what they call the Great Contraction in the money supply. More recently, the "new macroeconomics," which emphasizes rational expectations theory and supply-side considerations, has claimed that New Deal manipulation of the private sector served only to thwart investment plans and labor market decisions—making the crisis longer-lived than necessary.

Depression theories with more of a long-run perspective tend to emphasize the fact that economic storm clouds emerged in the United States before the stock market debacle of 1929. Freight car loadings, housing starts, and other indexes of general industrial activity had turned downward well before the last quarter of 1929, some as early as 1927. As John Kenneth Galbraith said, "[c]ause and effect run from the economy to the stock market, never the reverse. Had the economy been fundamentally sound in late

1929 the effect of the great stock market crash might have been small. The shock to confidence and the loss of spending by those who were caught in the market, might soon have worn off." The long-run literature is distinctive in that it views the crash of 1929 as very much a secondary phenomenon compared to other developments in the economy that dated back to World War I or earlier.

Some investigators have argued that the distribution of national income became increasingly skewed in the 1920s. As a greater proportion of income was held by wealthier (and smaller) segments of the population, the economy's aggregate propensity to consume fell. Thus a weakness in sales, with concomitant tendencies toward reductions in investment and the layoff of labor were the result. Independent of the financial crisis initiated in 1929, underconsumption was a general problem for the interwar American economy.

Other scholars have suggested that technical change and innovations slowed in the years between the world wars. With a scarcity of outlets for new investment, the economy became increasingly frail. As firms invested in fewer new projects, the general rate of economic growth leveled off and eventually fell. What was required was the introduction of new processes, products, and techniques to stimulate firms to make net investment commitments. Robust economic growth would have been the inevitable consequence.

The "technological stagnation" theorists also found support in the arguments of those who might be called demographic pessimists. Population growth rate fell throughout the interwar period due to reduced immigration (owing essentially to public policy initiatives in the wake of the Great War) and a decrease in the domestic rate of reproduction. Slower population growth, it was held, accounted for lower rates of increase in sales especially for such important and bellwether industries as appliances, automobiles, housing, and other major durable goods. Assuming that levels of discretionary income were adequate, higher rates of population growth would have translated into stronger growth rates in national output.

Another long-term structural argument made to account for the length and severity of the depression concerned imperfect markets. Since the turn of this century, some analysts suggested, American markets—especially for labor and major manufactured goods—had become increasingly imperfect, in some cases oligopolistic. As a consequence, a downturn would not have powerful self-correcting tendencies owing to the relative rigidity of wages and prices manipulated by powerful firms and labor unions. This claim was also embraced by those who criticized New Deal industrial policy for making the Depression worse—insofar as New Deal codes and regulations tended to embolden labor unions by stipulating minimum levels for wages in most industries. With prices and wages unable to adjust to market-clearing levels, so the argument went, persistent disequilibrium in the form of idle capacity and unemployment was the consequence.

Other economists and historians have suggested that a secular transition in the terms of trade between agricultural and industrial production—both nationwide and worldwide—exacerbated the Great Depression. Their argument is that prices for primary products had been falling since World War I, while prices for manufactured goods had been rising. This left the agricultural sector in the United States, as well as primary product producing nations elsewhere, less and less able to sustain the demand for rapidly growing levels of industrial output. Ultimately a falling off in the rate of sales led to a downward spiral in the industrial economy both within the United States and throughout the world.

Investment behavior has been the least examined aspect of the Depression, yet it holds the key to understanding cyclical instability. Indeed, several economists and historians have argued that the length of the Depression and the abortive recovery of 1936–1937 were a direct result of the fact that a small recovery of consumer spending, sparked by New Deal relief policies, was not linked with an upturn in net investment. Did the investment function of the American economy of the 1930s simply disappear?

A disaggregated view of the performance of major manufacturing industries during the decade shows that this was not the case. There were large variations in the speed with which individual sectors recovered from the trough of 1933 with respect to production and investment. Certain industries seemed virtually untouched by the crash, although all suffered a bad year in 1932. Firms in the food products, tobacco products, chemicals, and petroleum industries came out of the trough relatively quickly. Those in textiles, lumber, metals, and transportation equipment did not. Indeed, within the latter group of industries certain markets did thrive after 1932, and it was only those firms committed to or moving into those markets that avoided the severe hardships of the decade. All this suggests an uneven pattern of investment resulting, at the macroeconomic level, in apparent stagnation.

To be more specific about the long-term causes of the investment failure of the 1930s, it is useful to focus on three major sources of evidence. The first of these concerns the changing nature of investment demand during the interwar decades. This information, along with a second set of data concerning alterations in the composition of final demand during the same period, shows that certain markets, and therefore industries, were in secular decline and others newly emergent at the time of the 1929 crisis. Finally, evidence concerning long-run changes in the industrial distribution of employment provides new information on the persistence of the effective demand crisis of the 1930s.

With the available data, it is possible to discern some general patterns in the capital goods demands of major manufacturing industries. These patterns demonstrate which industries were expanding and which were contracting during the interwar period. For example, an average of 2.1 percent of the total real expenditures on capital goods in the American economy was made in the processed food products sector during the 1920s. That average rose to 2.5 percent during the decade of depression. By contrast, in the textiles industry, the mean was 1.5 percent during the 1920s, and fell to 1.2 percent during the 1930s; 0.8 percent in the 1920s and 0.4 percent in the 1930s. There were dramatic increases in the average percentages for the petroleum sector, the chemicals industry, and the airplane manufacturing sector. In iron and steel production and in the automobile sector, rises were more moderate.

The precise markets in which the expanding sectors flourished were those for consumer nondurable goods, services, and newer durable products such as appliances, automobiles with luxury amenities, and communications equipment. It is typical for durable goods industries to suffer proportionately more than others during cyclical fluctuations—as consumers postpone durable goods purchases for longer periods of time. But the evidence from the interwar period suggests that a secular dynamic was at work as well—one that favored the emergence of industries producing for a more affluent population subsisting within a relatively sophisticated and fully developed infrastructure.

If trends in the composition of final demand expenditures are considered, the same pattern of interindustry variations in interwar performance emerges. The percentage of real consumer spending devoted to food, liquor, and tobacco products rose during the 1920s and 1930s; the tendency was even more dramatic when the influence of Prohibition and its repeal are taken into account. The percentage also rose in such categories as household equipment and operation, medical care and insurance, recreation, education, and welfare. The share fell for clothing and its accessories and for housing and utilities. Generally speaking, the proportion of disposable income expended on durable goods fell during the interwar period, while that spent on nondurables and services rose.

Some of the changes in consumer demand were linked with the changing occupational distribution of the labor force and with secular changes in the distribution of the national income. The proportion of white-collar workers in the economically active population rose steadily from 1900 to 1940, and these workers' earnings were roughly double those of blue-collar workers during the interwar period. Moreover, the distribution of income during the 1920s became more unequal. These factors appear to have been responsible for an increasing strength in newer, more affluent consumer markets. It is significant that not only did the Depression create proportionately more unemployment among blue-collar workers, but also the relative buying power of those who retained their jobs was magnified by the deflation generated in the wake of the crash.

A third aspect of the investment failure of the 1930s was the changing distribution of employment. Interindustry variations in rates of recovery generated an aggregate result of virtual stagnation during the 1930s. What was happening in labor markets? It appears that although certain sectors were expanding after 1932, and indeed throughout the interwar period as a whole, they nonetheless could not absorb the unemployed from the declining industries. In the tobacco products, petroleum, and chemicals industries, the relative capital intensity of new production methods was a factor.

Those sectors that were growing the fastest and that recovered after 1932 with the most vitality maintained meager shares of total employment throughout the 1930s. For example, the chemicals industry by the mid 1930s ranked twenty-fifth among all industries in its share of national employment; the petroleum sector, twenty-first; the tobacco industry, sixty-seventh; the food products firms, fourteenth. By contrast, those sectors hit hardest by the crash and slowest to recover were responsible for the predominant share of national employment in 1935. Primary metals producers ranked first; textile mills, second; lumber mills, third. Without a general rally in investment, there was little absorption of unemployment, even by the growing sectors. The persistence of unemployment made the effective demand problem worse.

This was the basis of the vicious circle of excess capacity and inadequate demand, which was, in essence, the calamity of the 1930s.

Thus a massive structural unemployment problem emerged during the 1930s that in the absence of an exogenous shock like war would have taken several years to solve. But the problem actually had emerged prior to 1929. Throughout the 1920s there had been a rather steady decline in the percentage of national employment accounted for by manufacturing and construction sectors. The same was the case for agriculture and mining. In the service industries (transportation, trade, finance, selected services, and government operations) there had been a rise. Even if there had been no crash in 1929, these trends suggest that structural unemployment would have been a major problem in the interwar period.

The problem of industrial transformation that emerged in the 1930s was quickly overcome by the advent of war. Clearly what the war provided was a twofold stimulus. First, the more mature industries of the interwar period were brought out of the doldrums by the particular demands of making war. Second, the new industries were pulled along by government orders as a result of the general increase in the GNP that fiscal spending provided, and as a result of the particular demands that such sectors could meet—the latter most notably the case for the aviation, chemicals, electronics, and petroleum industries. On the one side, mature and declining sectors were brought back to life. On the other, new industries were at last provided with the generally high level of demand that the full emergence of new products and processes required. Indeed, the war itself spawned the development of even more new industries, products, and processes. Thus did the 1940s lay in part the foundations for the prosperity of the 1950s and 1960s.

THREE DECADES OF PROSPERITY, 1940–1970

World War II achieved what the New Deal could not—economic recovery. Unemployment had decreased to only 7 percent by the time of the Japanese attack on Pearl Harbor. American entry into the war brought almost instantaneous resolution of the persistent economic difficulties of the interwar years. Rationing, federal planning, and price controls provided for the efficient and rapid diversion of resources from civilian to military production. Unemployment fell to 1.2 percent by 1944. And, while hardly inspired by specific economic concerns, President Roosevelt's "arsenal of democracy" nevertheless contained rather vivid policy lessons for economists, politicians, government officials, and the public at large.

Yet as World War II came to a close many economists and businesspeople worried about the possibility of a drop in the level of prosperity and employment to one far below that of the war. These apprehensions proved to be unwarranted. By 1946, aggregate spending did not fall and unemployment did not even reach 4 percent. Although recessions occurred between 1945 and the mid 1970s, most lasted a year or less, and none remotely approached the severity of the Great Depression of the 1930s. During these three decades American manufacturing output steadily increased with only minor setbacks. According to the Federal Reserve Board's index, manufacturing production doubled between 1945 and 1965, and tripled between 1945 and 1976.

Such robust economic performance is hardly surprising in wartime—especially when conflict is global and, with a few exceptions, kept outside of a nation's own boundaries. What is most striking about the American economic experience linked with World War II was the enduring growth and prosperity of the postwar years. Consumption and investment behavior played a major part in the great prosperity of the late 1940s and 1950s. As soon as Germany and Japan surrendered, private and foreign investment in the United States rose quickly. On the domestic side, reconversion was itself an investment stimulus. Modernization and deferred replacement projects required renewed and large deployments of funds. Profound scarcities of consumer goods, the production of which had been long postponed by wartime mobilization needs, necessitated major retooling and expansion efforts. Even fear of potentially high inflation, emerging in the wake of the dismantling of the price and wage controls of the war years, prompted many firms to move forward the date of ambitious and long-term investment projects. On the foreign side, both individuals and governments were eager to find a refuge for capital that had been in virtual hiding during the war. Along with a jump in domestic investment, therefore, a large capital inflow began in late 1945 and early 1946.

Domestic consumption was the second major component of postwar growth. Bridled demand and high household savings due to wartime shortages, rationing, and controls, coupled with the generous wage rates of the high-capacity war economy all contributed to a dramatic growth in consumer spending at war's end. The jump in disposable income was bolstered by the rapid reduction in wartime sur-

taxes and excises. And the baby boom of the wartime generation expressed itself economically in high levels of demand for significant items such as appliances, automobiles, and housing. GI bill benefits additionally increased the demand for housing and such things as educational services with associated impacts on construction and other industrial sectors.

Foreign demand for American exports grew rapidly in the immediate postwar years. In part the needs of devastated areas could only be met by the one industrial base that had been nearly untouched by war-related destruction. Explicit policy commitments to the rebuilding of Allied and occupied territories, such as the Marshall Plan in Europe, also increased the foreign market for the output of American industry. Even so, one of the most powerful influences on the impressive postwar growth of the American economy was the unique and special set of arrangements developed for international trade at the Bretton Woods Conference in 1944.

When the Allied nations' financial ministers gathered at Bretton Woods in New Hampshire, just before the war's end, they were concerned about how to reconfigure world trade and financial flows so that the disputes so characteristic of the interwar years (1919–1939) could be avoided and stability maintained. Along with the creation of an International Bank for Reconstruction and Development and of an International Monetary Fund, the conference decided to establish fixed exchanged rates between the U.S. dollar and all other internationally traded currencies. The value of the dollar was set in terms of gold at $35 per ounce, a benchmark against which the value of all other currencies was measured. As the American economy was, by far, the most powerful at the time, it was prudent and indeed necessary that its currency play such a central international role. Moreover, the other industrialized nations of the day were powerless to stop the United States from assuming this central position in world finance.

American postwar prosperity and the benefits of world economic leadership continued throughout most of the 1950s. The added fiscal stimulus of the Korean War also played a role in maintaining the high levels of growth and employment characteristic of the decade. Republican president Dwight D. Eisenhower, carrying on in the tradition of his Democratic predecessor Harry S. Truman, repeatedly committed his administration to the practice of compensatory demand management. But the prosperity of the 1950s, while robust and impressive, had nevertheless weakened by 1957. This set the stage for a new brand of economics in Washington, D.C., imbued with the doctrines of Keynesianism. From the New Frontier policies of John F. Kennedy, to the Great Society agenda of his successor Lyndon B. Johnson, through the declaration of a New Federalism by Richard M. Nixon, there ensued an era of sustained central government intervention in the nation's economic life. The self-assurance of many, but not all, of the new economists of the early 1960s, that the goal of achieving simultaneously acceptable levels of unemployment and inflation could be realized, has more recently been shattered. But throughout the 1960s and much of the 1970s, and for some even during the 1980s, the perceived obligation of government to secure overall economic stability was not seriously questioned and remained one of the more important changes of twentieth-century American economic history.

LOSS OF ECONOMIC LEADERSHIP, 1970–1990

By the 1970s, a quarter-century of American prosperity was in jeopardy. The growth rate of the GNP fell after several years of steady expansion. Unemployment rates reached disquieting levels, and the attendant downturns were persistent rather than transitory. After the dramatic rise in oil prices in 1973, the economy deteriorated. Measured in constant prices, the annual average compound growth rate of the GNP fell from 4 percent (for the period 1960–1973) to 1.8 percent (for the period 1973–1982). Annual unemployment rose from 4.8 percent of the labor force in 1973 to 8.3 percent two years later. But in 1975 a sustained recovery began as the rise in food and fuel prices slowed. As a result the inflation rate fell in the next few years from over 12 percent to between 5 and 7 percent. Nevertheless, the 1979 revolution in Iran led to significant oil price increases and an inflation rate of 16 percent during the first half of 1980. Although there was a modest upswing in late 1980, the United States by 1981–1982 experienced the worst recession since the Great Depression. The unemployment rate rose to 10 percent. The decennial average rate of unemployment was, for the 1980s, approximately 6.9 percent.

The poor macroeconomic performance of the 1970s was in fact initiated by an exogenous shock. In the wake of the Yom Kippur War of 1973, the Organization of Petroleum Exporting Countries (OPEC) instituted a series of price increases for crude oil that had disastrous consequences for the United States and other industrialized economies. The price of crude rose 12 percent in June of 1973 and then

skyrocketed with the October War in the Middle East. Oil prices rose 66 percent in October and doubled in January of 1974. From 1952 to 1965 the average inflation rate for the American economy (based on the consumer price index) stood at 1.3 percent. In the following seven years it rose to 4.1 percent, and for the decade of the seventies to 8.8 percent. For the ten years from 1972 to 1982, it is estimated that the American cost of living increased 133 percent. Poor crop yields in 1971 and 1972 due to drought conditions in the nation's agricultural regions contributed to the inflationary spiral.

The OPEC shock, while different in form, had many of the same consequences as the 1929 stock debacle. Real incomes fell dramatically. Many bank portfolios and the economic position of investors were imperiled. The confidence of consumers and investors was dealt a serious blow. Investment declined as firms became more and more hesitant and as households postponed major expenditures. Profit margins shrank as the costs of production rose. Capacity utilization and employment consequently shrank. The cumulative oil price increases of the 1970s also had a devastating impact on the American balance of payments—a $40-billion deficit in fuel imports alone by decade's end. As the GNP growth rates noted above show, the American economy fell, rose, and fell again during the rest of the 1970s. This combination of seeming economic stagnation and high inflation gave rise to a new economic label—stagflation.

There were numerous factors that forestalled recovery in the 1970s. The fiscal crisis of the Vietnam era and its related international financial development—the demise of the Bretton Woods system—fundamentally altered the relationship of the American economy to world markets. Where trading partners in the past had been content to hold their dollar reserves—essentially financing the American trade deficit—the deterioration in the value of the dollar pursuant to the war inflation and increasing political resistance abroad changed that behavior.

With the collapse of the Bretton Woods system in 1970–1971, the United States was freed from the burden of maintaining a fixed exchange rate; the resultant devaluation of the dollar improved America's export position, at least potentially, but the other consequence of the policy change was inflation. Thus on the very eve of the OPEC price explosion, the United States had already been placed in an extremely vulnerable economic position. In addition to the monetary changes, technological factors made themselves felt in the early 1970s that suggested that an industrial "retardation" was under way. This loss of international competitiveness further weakened the American economy.

As early as the 1960s, the nations devastated by World War II (most significantly Japan and the then Federal Republic of Germany) had reestablished their economic presence in world markets. They possessed an advanced technological base due to the recent rebuilding of their major industries and their relative insulation, under international treaties and agreements (exemplified by the erection of a "nuclear umbrella" by the United States), from the burdens of defense spending. Consequently, their major industries—automobiles, electronics, and steel—became powerful competitors of their American counterparts. This was the real corollary to the financial crisis precipitated by the OPEC and agricultural price increases. And it was a dramatic expression of the loss of America's leadership in the world economy as a whole.

Many scholars have focused on what they see as a managerial failure of American enterprise in the 1960s and 1970s to meet foreign competition. Certainly the case of the automobile industry suggests that American producers were locked in a kind of technological rigidity that left them exposed to the full impact of superior Japanese technology—especially when the OPEC price rise qualitatively altered the demand for cars toward lighter, more fuel-efficient vehicles. The peculiar incentives established by American tax codes, and what is often called the present-mindedness of the American corporate elite, may have been factors in this managerial failure.

But there were other factors involved in the technological deceleration of some major sectors of American industry. The stimulus afforded by World War II and the Korean conflict brought all of American industry out of the crisis of the 1930s. Indeed, it has been suggested that wartime production and the military procurement of the Cold War years were responsible for much of the prosperity of the American economy in the entire postwar era. However, while the fiscal stimulus of an enduring defense establishment may have provided a short-run fillip to national income, it may in the long run have weakened major sectors of the economy and curtailed their ability to develop and compete on an international scale.

Nowhere was the deterioration in overall American economic performance during the 1970s more apparent than in the international trade statistics. U.S. trade in manufactured goods was transformed during the 1970s. By 1977–1980 the ratio of net exports to total manufacturing trade turned negative for the first

Table 1.   U.S. TRADE IN MANUFACTURED GOODS, 1965–1980[a]

Years	Exports	Imports	Trade Ratio[b]
1965–69	20.3	16.6	0.1
1970–73	35.1	34.8	0.004
1974–76	71.7	57	0.11
1977–80	101.4	103.6	−0.01

[a] Annual averages are given in billions of dollars.
[b] Trade ratio = (exports − imports)/(exports + imports).
SOURCE: U.S. Department of Commerce, *International Economic Indicators* (September 1974 and September 1984).

time since 1940 (see tables 1 and 2). America's market share of exports of manufactures steadily decreased, and the trade performance of almost all of the major manufacturing sectors worsened. Exceptions included fields in which the United States held a virtually unassailable technological lead (such as aerospace and aviation) or where public policy had taken an active role in obstructing the worsening trend (such as leather and lumber products). Accompanying the alteration in the competitiveness of American industry in the world economy was the restructuring of the nation's

Table 2.   TRADE RATIOS FOR SELECTED INDUSTRIES, 1967 AND 1977

Industry	1967	1977	Change, 1966 to 1977
Textile mill products	−0.36	0.03	0.39
Turbine generators	0.41	0.78	0.37
Leather and leather products	−0.24	−0.02	0.22
Telephone and telegraphic equipment	0.19	0.33	0.14
Wood pulp	−0.22	−0.12	0.10
Paper and paperboard	−0.37	−0.30	0.07
Aerospace	0.80	0.82	0.02
Steel	−0.16	−0.68	−0.52
Rubber tires and tubes	−0.11	−0.51	−0.40
Apparel	−0.54	−0.86	−0.32
Machine tools	0.13	−0.12	−0.25
Photographic equipment	0.38	0.17	−0.21
Automobiles	−0.01	−0.21	−0.20
Chemicals	0.49	0.30	−0.19
House appliances	0.01	−0.14	−0.15
General industrial machinery	0.72	0.57	−0.15
Construction machinery	0.91	0.76	−0.15
Computers	0.78	0.65	−0.13
Farm machinery	0.17	0.15	−0.02

SOURCE: U.S. Department of Commerce, *Survey of Current Business: 1980, U.S. Industrial Outlook for 200 Industries with Projections for 1984.*

labor market and changes in the productivity of labor in core manufacturing industries.

As the international competitiveness of domestic industry weakened, both rates of employment and levels of labor earnings suffered in what had previously been major industrial venues. A transition to a service economy yielded relatively fewer well-paying and secure jobs than at any time since the 1930s. In 1979, 43 percent of the nonfarm labor force worked in service and retail trade. In fact, during the 1970s, these two sectors accounted for 70 percent of all the new private sector jobs created in the economy at large. Within the service sector, the growth in employment was concentrated in such activities as restaurants, hospitals, nursing homes, medical and dental offices, and business services (that ranged from personnel services and data processing to custodial operations). Employment growth in such activities as these far outpaced that in the industrial arena throughout the 1970s, and it appears that this trend continued through the 1980s.

The jobs created in these new growth areas of the contemporary American economy were quite different from those in which earlier generations had made their livings. Service workers tended to work shorter hours, and earned lower hourly wages than their peers in manufacturing. A large percentage of these positions, as well, were dead end jobs insofar as the prospects for further training and ultimate promotion to supervisory responsibility were quite limited. A vast proportion of these new jobs developed in non-union settings with lower wage levels and drastically reduced benefits compared with those of jobs in manufacturing. Not surprisingly, therefore, women and minorities (and generally younger workers) accounted for substantial shares of the employment in these newer service industries. In short, the changing structure of the national economy, linked in part with the effects of America's increasing economic interdependence with the rest of the world, led to a generation of new jobs that paid less, had less security, and offered fewer opportunities for advancement than the industrial posts that for generations had underwritten the life-cycle incomes of whole families. Of course, nostalgia about the loss of semi- and high-skilled jobs in basic industries such as automobiles and steel had to be tempered with recognition of the fact that international competition often lowered the prices for some of these major products within the United States.

The changing manner in which the U.S. economy did business with the rest of the world was perhaps the single most striking characteristic of the

period after 1980. By 1988, for example, the major export from the West Coast of the United States was wastepaper. The major imports to that coast were automobile parts, furniture, and textiles. Various American manufacturing sectors steadily shrank in size since the early 1970s when foreign competition made its presence felt in no uncertain terms. But as this process of global restructuring of commerce proceeded, many (but not all) American manufacturing firms became part of what was called the "hollowing out" of the nation's industrial base. As imports jumped 51 percent during the early 1980s, and as exports declined by about 2 percent, American firms embarked on investment strategies (in many cases stimulated by public policy) that, while individually profitable, tended to accelerate the deindustrialization trend. In 1989, for example, the General Electric Company used reserve funds to purchase $10 billion of its own stock rather than to make new acquisitions or invest in new technology with which to meet the growing competition from abroad. General Motors in 1990 operated seventeen assembly plants in Mexico that employed a total of approximately 24,000 workers. The company discussed plans to invest in an additional twelve factories in Mexico. For the year 1990, it was estimated that some 300,000 automobiles were imported from Mexico as a result of direct American corporate initiatives.

Throughout the 1980s one major sector of American industry did not suffer from atrophy—the defense industry. The presidential administration of Ronald Reagan embarked on a decade-long process of expansion in the armed services that resulted in the largest peacetime increase of American forces and weapons systems in history. By the end of the 1980s, the U.S. economy allocated close to $300 billion annually in resources to the military. Strikingly enough, the profit rate on defense contracts far outstripped that in consumer durables industries. From 1970 to 1980, the average rate of profit earned on Department of Defense contracts was about 19.4 percent, as compared with 14.4 percent in durable goods manufacturing. For the first half of the 1980s, defense industry profit rates averaged 23.3 percent, while durable goods producers managed only 10.6 percent.

The Reagan military build-up brought new and difficult pressures to bear on the American economy. Compared with most other major industrial nations, the United States committed a far greater percentage of its GNP to defense spending, approximately 6.1 percent annually by the end of the 1980s. France, for example, allocated 3.5 percent, the former Federal

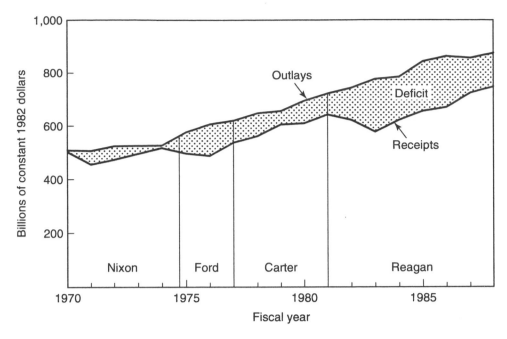

Figure 7.   Federal budget deficits, 1970–1988. (From U.S. Department of Commerce as reported in Gary M. Walton and Hugh Rockoff, *History of the American Economy* [San Diego, Harcourt Brace Jovanovich, 1990], p. 561.)

Republic of Germany 3.1 percent, and Japan a bit less than 1 percent. This development prompted some investigators to worry that the diversion of national resources to defense projects impeded the ability of American industry to increase productivity, innovate, and generally confront the overseas competition that had made such profound inroads in the world economy since the early 1970s. From the mid 1970s to the mid 1980s, American manufacturing productivity grew by roughly 2 percent as compared with 7.3 percent for Japan, 3.3 percent for West Germany, and 2.3 percent for Great Britain. While it had once seemed that defense research and production could spin off new techniques and products to benefit the private sector, some became concerned that military production had weakened domestic manufacturing by draining investment resources away from the production of "butter" to the production of "guns." To what extent these anxieties were valid constituted a new and exciting area of research for economists, economic historians, and technologists. It is important to remember that the whole idea of a peacetime military expansion following World War II had been sold to Congress and local public officials in part on the basis that resources and funding would flow to their constituencies. Military bases brought jobs to local communities and profits to local businesses. Defense spending in general also created better-paying jobs that provided higher purchasing power for the other products of domestic industry.

Rising by almost 120 percent through the 1980s, from $134 to $294.9 billion, military spending in the United States also had a profound economic impact by virtue of its contribution to a federal budget deficit and, thereby, the public debt. The cumulative federal deficit for the 1980s was approximately $2 trillion. As the budget deficit grew from 2.7 percent to 5.2 percent of GNP during Reagan's first term (1981–1985), it became clear that a substantial portion of the increase was due to increased military spending. Paralleled by a burgeoning trade deficit (that reached almost $200 billion by the end of the decade), the imbalance between federal revenues and expenditures emerged as one of the most serious challenges facing the American economy in the 1990s. The burgeoning federal deficits of recent decades are portrayed in figure 7.

PROSPECTS I: COUNTERCYCLICAL POLICY FORMULATION

From the 1890s to the Great Depression of the interwar period, countercyclical economic policy was virtually unknown. Economists were in fact limited by deep-seated intellectual prejudices in the formulation of compensatory measures. The lack of a comprehensive theory of macroeconomic behavior (prior to the advent of the Keynesian revolution) was paralleled by the absence of reliable and systematic data on the fiscal and monetary mechanisms of government. The notion of government spending itself was suspect. Budget deficits were equated with national economic ruin, and the plausible yet inaccurate analogy drawn between a family's finances and those of the state reigned supreme in economists' minds. The fallacy of composition was not yet part of the economists' lexicon.

Business cycle theory was in a similarly inchoate and uninformed state. Most economists viewed the cycle as a therapeutic cure for intermittent yet never well-explained overflows of the economic mechanism. Cycles could not be tamed, much less made obsolete. The notion of potential output and an appreciation of the losses incurred when actual national output fell below capacity (or full-employment) ceiling were yet unexplained. As a result, there was a thoroughly inadequate understanding of the process of inflation. There certainly was no conception that a slack economy would not suffer accelerating inflation under a regime of restitutive fiscal spending. Ignorance contributed to (though it does not fully explain) the virtual impotence and in some cases the unintended perversity of economic policy during the 1930s.

With the statist experience of the 1940s, and the emergence of a bipartisan commitment to aggregate demand management under the Eisenhower administration, there quickly arose a consensus regarding the benefits of fiscal activism. During the New Frontier years of John F. Kennedy's presidency, and throughout the terms of Lyndon B. Johnson, the use of the federal government's authority over taxation and monetary policy as an instrument of countercyclical control for the national economy was common and widely accepted. During the 1970s, however, the fiscal burdens of both the Vietnam War and the redistributive efforts of Johnson's Great Society programs inspired an increasing resistance to the practice of Keynesian demand management. The faltering economic performance of the late 1970s, epitomized by the very high levels of the "misery index" (the sum of the rates of inflation and unemployment), laid the foundations for a major transformation in American economic policy in the 1980s.

The emergence of so-called supply-side economics (or "Reaganomics") as a new blueprint for federal economic policy was inspired by a widespread belief that the period of American economic leadership in world affairs, the anticipated American Century of the preceding seventy-five years, might be coming to an end. Henceforth, the economic prosperity of Americans would be increasingly dependent upon developments elsewhere in a vast global marketplace. Two developments during 1978, each rooted in what were perceived to be past failures of governmental economic policies, appeared to signal the beginning of a return to policy approaches that predated the New Deal.

One was a popular movement, termed a *taxpayers' revolt*, to limit government spending and tax revenues. Prompted by some successes of this movement in state and local referendums (in particular, the passage of Proposition 13 in California in 1978 that limited property tax assessments), some national political leaders jumped on the bandwagon of economy in government in order to push proposals to limit federal employment and spending.

The second development resulted from the battering of the dollar in foreign exchange markets as holders of dollars sold them in large amounts because they feared that American economic policies would continue to cause stagflation, weak capital formation, and limited real economic growth. In response, the Federal Reserve Board moved to support the dollar through monetary stringency, and President Jimmy Carter promulgated a wide-ranging program that included voluntary guidelines for wage and price increases, further measures to support the dollar's international value, and a renewed pledge to hold down government employment and spending in order to reduce the large federal deficits of the previous decade. These developments reflected a growing belief among some national leaders and many middle-class Americans that government policies requiring ever-larger spending programs, deficit financing, and money creation (to ease the interest rate pressures that deficits would otherwise generate) were more a cause of stagflation than a solution.

Ronald Reagan's stunning landslide electoral college victory over Jimmy Carter in the 1980 presidential election signaled a (rhetorically complete yet practically partial) transition from Keynesian-style demand management to the allegedly new strategies of supply-side economic theory. Believing that the fundamental source of the problems facing the contemporary American economy had to do with supply problems rather than with demand fluctuations, the supply-side theorists focused their policy proposals on the means by which macroeconomic supply conditions might be improved. Increasing supply, it was presumed, would overcome the twin problems of stagnation and inflation that had troubled the economy since the early 1970s.

Supply-side theory focused on what were believed to be the distortions created by large government spending (and, therefore, a large governmental apparatus), high taxation of income, and inordinate governmental regulation of economic affairs. Excessive income taxation, it was argued, stifled productive effort (by discouraging overtime work, for example). It robbed individuals of the fruits of enterprise and risk-bearing. Finally, it distorted economic decision making so as to slow economic growth and create the very fiscal pressures that contributed (through the mechanism of a large federal debt and associated financial stress) to the problems of stagflation in the first instance. The solution would involve a radical reduction in taxes, a systematic shrinking of government programs and, thus, federal agency budgets, and the elimination (to the extent possible) of costly regulatory measures.

In February 1981 the newly elected Reagan administration presented its Program for Economic Recovery to the Congress. Inspired by the arguments of supply-side economists, the proposal called for the control of federal spending, the reduction or elimination of a wide variety of social entitlement and redistributive schemes dating back to the days of the New Frontier and the Great Society, and the aggressive reduction of tax rates on incomes. In particular, it called for 10 percent annual reductions in marginal income tax rates for three years beginning in summer 1981. Along with this economic platform, President Reagan's program also provided for the implementation of investment incentives for private business (by means of accelerated depreciation), the streamlining or elimination of a host of regulatory codes, and monetary stringency. The hope, along with the expectation that such measures would stimulate growth through investment, jobs creation, and greater labor productivity, was that the federal budget might be balanced by 1984 with concomitant savings on interest payments and a lessening of the loanable funds shortages caused by a massive government presence in capital markets.

By August 1981, the Economic Recovery Tax Act was made law—thereby implementing, in the form of income tax reduction, a major component of the Reagan supply-side program. Over the next three years, major cuts were made in such programs as unemployment insurance, food stamps, aid to families with dependent children, Medicaid, student loans, retirement benefits, grants for mass transportation, and benefits to import-impacted industries. Par-

alleling such transformations in fiscal policy, a strict anti-inflationary money policy was also pursued. The results were mixed. On the one side, inflation was strikingly reduced. From 9 percent in 1981, the annual rate of increase in the price level fell to 3.5 percent by the end of Reagan's first term. Unemployment, after rising to 9.7 percent in 1982, fell to about 7.5 percent in 1984–1985, and to 5 percent by the end of 1988. But, consistent with the Reagan administration's belief that an inflation threshold existed, job idleness was not pressed below the 5 percent achieved by the end of 1988. In this, the Reagan White House sharply distinguished itself from the Keynesian-style full employment commitments of both Democratic and Republican predecessors. Moreover, owing to the fiscal crisis dramatized by the extent of the federal debt, the presidential administration of Bill Clinton, as well as its immediate successors, faces certain difficulty in implementing fiscal demand management even if it wishes to do so. In this ironic sense, although the Reagan administration practiced Keynesianism in its dramatic expansion of military spending while at the same time reducing federal taxes, Reaganomics did unambiguously achieve one particular policy objective—it made the future use of Keynesian-style spending policies distinctly problematic if not impossible.

PROSPECTS II: ECONOMIC INTERDEPENDENCE AND THE END OF THE "AMERICAN CENTURY"

Far from being the dominant economic power of the day in the early 1990s, the United States became merely one member of a new set of major industrial powers. The increased interdependence created by the latest economic restructuring of the world posed both vast opportunities and difficult challenges for the American economy. U.S. policy making had to take into greater account the demands and actions of other nations. Trade performance, access to technology, productivity, and the general level of economic welfare within the United States were more affected by those of other nations. Making the transition from world economic leadership to world economic cooperation and interdependence was clearly the major task that stood before the American economy in the 1990s. Not surprisingly, this challenge left much of the American public fearful and apprehensive about the future.

Other challenges also emerged for the American economy as it approached the turn of the century. The need for job training and broader educational initiatives to improve the nation's international competitiveness became apparent. Daycare provision, increasingly important in a society where many families had two household heads earning income, also emerged on the national political agenda. Medical insurance, exceedingly costly and in 1990 unavailable to as many as 30 million Americans, potentially came to constitute, under some reform proposals, a major claim on the federal budget. Widespread substance abuse and crime, and the extraordinary financial costs of such public health problems as the AIDS epidemic all portended dramatic and difficult choices for the Congress, the executive branch, and the taxpaying public.

In addition to the general challenges afforded by foreign competition, political and economic developments around the world also had tremendous significance for the current and future performance of the American economy. The political devolution and liberalization of the former communist-bloc nations created a set of potential opportunities for American business without parallel in earlier decades. Some American firms began operations in the Russian and other Eastern European economies in the early 1990s. Meanwhile, the Commonwealth of Independent States and several of the East European nations approached the United States for massive foreign aid to assist in the transition to more privatized economic practices. The extent to which such opportunities for American overseas investment and such further demands upon the federal budget could be realized was unclear.

The changing structure of the world economy continued to pose additional challenges to the United States. Free trade pacts with Canada and Mexico had the capacity to restructure the way business was done in the Western Hemisphere. How a large American trading zone would affect industries within (and outside) the United States was hard to predict, but it was clearly possible that low-cost Mexican labor would provide a powerful competition for manufacturing and assembly activities in the United States. The continuing unification of Europe, epitomized by the reunification of Germany and the expansion of a European free trade zone, created the single largest economic entity in the world. Along with enduring discussions as to the possibility of establishing a single European currency unit, it seemed clear that continued diplomatic efforts by the European nations would succeed in counterposing to the United States, and other large economic systems, the impressive economic powers of the entire European continent. How the U.S. economy might confront such new challenges from a rapidly changing political-economic world system constituted one of the central questions for public discussion as the turn of the century approached. In this context, it was (and is) worth remembering that for over two centuries prior to World War I, Americans had always had to secure their livelihoods with constant reference to the world market. The American economic experience in the twentieth century thus appears to have been altogether unique.

SEE ALSO Wealth and Poverty; Economic Performance; Economic Policies (all in this volume).

BIBLIOGRAPHY

Some of the most classic texts in business cycle theory are Joseph A. Schumpeter, *Business Cycles: A Theoretical, Historical, and Statistical Analysis of the Capitalist Process* (1939); Wesley C. Mitchell, *Business Cycles: The Problem and its Setting* (1927); and an American Economic Association anthology, *Readings in Business Cycle Theory* (1951). For an analysis of business cycles that provides a special focus on consumption behavior, see James S. Duesenberry, *Business Cycles and Economic Growth* (1958). The relationship between long-run patterns of economic growth and decline is explored in N. D. Kondratieff, "The Long Waves in Economic Life," W. F. Stolper, trans., *Review of Economic Statistics* 17 (November 1935): 105–115. Irving Fisher, *Booms and Depressions: Some First Principles* (1932), provides one of the earliest and most systematic theoretical contributions by one of America's greatest twentieth-century economists, one of the few to come close to predicting the 1929 crash.

An extremely influential interpretation of the business cycle data collected by Nobel Memorial Prize Laureate Simon Kuznets is advanced in Moses Abramovitz, "The Nature and Significance of Kuznets Cycles," *Economic Development and Cultural Change* 9 (April 1961): 225–248. The original evidence was reported in Simon Kuznets, "Long Swings in the Growth of Population and in Related Economic Variables," *Proceedings of the American Philosophical Society* 102 (February 1958): 25–52, as well as in his *Modern Economic Growth: Rate, Structure, and Spread* (1966).

John Maynard Keynes, *The General Theory of Employment, Interest, and Money* (1936), is the most significant work in economic theory in the twentieth century, one that focuses explicitly on the performance of the macroeconomy. A related theoretical treatment is provided by Michal Kalecki, *Selected Essays on the Dynamics of the Capitalist Economy, 1933–1970* (1971). Robert A. Gordon deploys a straightforward Keynesian treatment of economic fluctuations and instability in *Business Fluctuations* (1955).

The stagnation thesis concerning American economic performance in the interwar period is most effectively presented in Alvin H. Hansen, *Full Recovery or Stagnation?* (1941). His view is dramatically confronted by the monetarist approach formulated in Milton Friedman and Anna J. Schwartz, *A Monetary History of the United States, 1867–1960* (1963). An influential article on these matters also written from a powerful anti-Keynesian perspective is Michael R. Darby, "Three-and-a-Half Million Employees Have Been Mislaid: Or, an Explanation of Unemployment, 1934–1941," *Journal of Political Economy* 84 (February 1976): 1–16. Robert E. Lucas also provides one of the core contributions to the development of the "new macroeconomics" that rejects the findings of Keynes in his "An Equilibrium Model of the Business Cycle," *Journal of Political Economy* 83 (December 1975): 1113–1144.

Finally, two central contributions to the understanding of business cycles and price and wage behavior are Paul A. Samuelson, "Interactions Between the Multiplier Analysis and the Principle of Acceleration," *Review of Economics and Statistics* 21 (May 1939): 75–78; and A. W. Phillips, "The Relation Between Unemployment and the Rate of Change in Money Wage Rates in the United Kingdom, 1861–1957," *Economica* n.s. 25 (November 1958): 283–299.

Excellent overviews of the macroeconomic trends and performance of the modern American economy are provided by Richard A. Easterlin, *Population, Labor Force, and Long Swings in Economic Growth: The American Experience* (1968); and Robert A. Gordon, *Economic Instability and Growth—The American Record* (1977). Early-twentieth-century trends in the structure of the American economy are assessed in Naomi R. Lamoreaux, *The Great Merger Movement in American Business, 1895–1904* (1985). The classic articulation of a neo-Marxist perspective on American economic performance in this century

may be found in Paul A. Baran and Paul M. Sweezy, *Monopoly Capital: An Essay on the American Economic and Social Order* (1966).

A fascinating and, in many ways, prescient assessment of the major challenges facing the U.S. economy in the post–World War I period may be found in Report of the Committee on Recent Economic Changes of the President's Conference on Unemployment, *Recent Economic Changes in the United States* (1929). George Soule provides a general survey of the economic history of the 1920s in *Prosperity Decade: From War to Depression, 1917–1929* (1947). A fine narrative of the beginnings of the Great Depression of the 1930s is John Kenneth Galbraith's *The Great Crash: 1929* (1972). Charles P. Kindleberger, *The World in Depression: 1929–1939* (1973), is the best one-volume treatment of the great economic crisis of the interwar period. A new view of the interwar crisis that looks to the impact of long-term changes in the composition of national product and expenditures is Michael A. Bernstein, *The Great Depression: Delayed Recovery and Economic Change in America, 1929–1939* (1989). The classic narrative of the first peacetime example of sustained federal intervention in the American economy is William E. Leuchtenberg, *Franklin D. Roosevelt and the New Deal, 1932–1940* (1963). Specific information concerning the post–World War II era is found in Ralph E. Freeman, ed., *Postwar Economic Trends in the United States* (1960), an excellent supplement to Harold G. Vatter's *The U.S. Economy in World War II* (1985), the only monograph available on this important subject.

The best comprehensive survey of twentieth-century national economic policy in the United States is Herbert Stein, *The Fiscal Revolution in America* (1969). Robert M. Collins, *The Business Response to Keynes: 1929–1964* (1981), is a fine exposition of the emergence of an elite bipartisan consensus regarding Keynesianism in the postwar era. An inspired argument by one of the leading architects of the Keynesian revolution in American economic policymaking in the postwar era is deployed by James Tobin in *The New Economics One Decade Older* (1974).

More recent challenges and problems facing the American economy are surveyed in R. D. Norton, "Industrial Policy and American Renewal," *Journal of Economic Literature* 24 (March 1986): 1–40; as well as in Nathan Rosenberg, *Technology and the Pursuit of Economic Growth* (1991); and Robert B. Reich, *The Next American Frontier* (1983). Alan S. Blinder, *Economic Policy and the Great Stagflation* (1979), focuses on the economic hardships and paradoxes of the 1970s; while David A. Stockman, *The Triumph of*

Politics: How the Reagan Revolution Failed (1986), examines the policy initiatives and failures of the 1980s. Paul Krugman assesses the general policy problems facing the U.S. government in recent years in *The Age of Diminished Expectations: U.S. Economic Policy in the 1990s* (1990).

Finally, some specific investigations of the causes of the contemporary weakening of the American economy may be found in William J. Baumol and Kenneth McLennan, *Productivity Growth and U.S. Competitiveness* (1985); Robert E. Baldwin, *Trade Policy in a Changing World Economy* (1989); Barry Bluestone and Bennett Harrison, *The Deindustrialization of America: Plant Closings, Community Abandonment, and the Dismantling of Basic Industries* (1982); and Robert W. Degrasse, Jr., *Military Expansion, Economic Decline: The Impact of Military Spending on U.S. Economic Performance* (1983).

CAPITAL MARKETS

George David Smith and Richard Sylla

Capital markets are the organized processes by which funds for long-term investment (or capital formation) are raised, securitized, distributed, traded, and—perhaps most important of all—valued. Historically, the major instruments of finance created and traded in capital markets have consisted of long-term government and corporate bonds, which are certificates of indebtedness, and corporate stocks, which represent ownership equity. Mortgages and other long-term loans made by banks and other lenders also qualify as capital market instruments, but in this essay we deal mainly with the traditional stock and bond securities as well as with those institutional banking functions that are involved in the creation and distribution of these securities. In any case, the distinction is of diminishing importance: modern capital markets have blurred it through the development of hybrid securities as well as securitized mortgages and other forms of loans, which, by pooling nontradable loans and then issuing tradable securities against them, increase the liquidity and negotiability of the original loans.

THE ROLE OF CAPITAL MARKETS

Capital markets are divided into primary (issuing) markets and secondary (trading) markets. Primary markets are those in which securities originate as borrowers (typically corporations and governments) contract with lenders and investors to issue securities and exchange them for money. When the contract stipulates that the borrower issuing securities will receive a specified sum from the lenders/investors, the sale of the securities is said to be underwritten—that is, guaranteed. Secondary markets are those in which securities are traded among investors after their origination. These markets, often referred to generically as the bond market and the stock market, continually value and revalue stocks and bonds and provide them with liquidity. Specific examples are the New York Stock Exchange, the over-the-counter

dealer markets in corporate stocks and bonds, and the markets for government securities—specifically U.S. Treasury bills, notes, and bonds.

How important are the capital markets in the overall scheme of economic life? Despite the great attention they receive from the broadcast and print media, their influence in the modern economy can be exaggerated. From the 1960s through the 1980s, American corporations have generated most of their capital (60 to 80 percent) from retained earnings and depreciation allowances (cash flow) and the rest from borrowing (only part of which took the form of bond issues), with little capital raised by new stock issues. Governments, moreover, despite all the talk of deficits, finance most of their activities by means of taxation rather than by issuing bonds. Academic economists are often asked for their opinions on the stock market, and most of them are puzzled by the lay interest: they consider it an economic sideshow in which old securities are merely shuffled among owners. The securities industry proper, recent government reports have noted, employs less than 1 percent of the U.S. labor force (although financial services as a whole employs a considerably larger percentage).

The capital markets might thus first appear to be a marginal affair, generating a few more dollars for corporations and governments and a few more jobs for the economy. Yet it is precisely because the capital markets are "marginal" in another, purely economic sense of the term, that they are so important. The prices of goods and services, of productive resources, and of real and financial assets are all determined at the margin—where suppliers meet demanders to determine the marginal benefits of each additional good, service, or asset as compared to its marginal costs. The results of these determinations are valuations that are indispensable to modern economic life. In the capital markets, it is the securities representing the accumulated assets and liabilities of the past—all of them, not just the fraction traded on a given day—that are valued. This, then, becomes key information for judging the performance of corporate managements as well as of those who manage government affairs. For example, the stock market values a corporation such as General Motors every day. The bond market values General Motors' outstanding debt, as well as that of the U.S. government, in like fashion. The capital markets also enable the rate of exchange between present and future values to be determined so that investors can make reasonable decisions whether to buy, sell, or hold on to corporate or government assets, and at what price.

To put it another way, capital markets are markets in financial information. Financial information is both an input into and a product of the decisions that are made in capital markets. How such information is generated, interpreted, and controlled matters greatly to the society at large. Thus the changing patterns of generating and managing financial information—including who has it or controls it, how it is processed, and who uses it—are central to understanding the historical development and regulation of capital markets.

But capital markets cannot be defined adequately in simple, static terms. Their characteristics, like those of all social processes, are contextual and dynamic. Thus if we want to know more about the nature and function of capital markets in the United States, we must address the relevant historical questions. When and why did capital markets emerge, and what were their distinctive attributes? How did the nation's capital markets come to be centered in New York, given longstanding opposition to any concentration of financial power? What was the role of the financiers who served as conduits in the capital markets in the shaping of American enterprise? More specifically, how do we account for the rise, the eclipse, and then the recent resurgence of the influence of financial capitalism over corporations? And finally, why were capital markets subject to government regulation, and what were the effects of that regulation?

In considering these questions, there are four key elements that form the thematic basis of our story. One element is largely ideological: the age-old American mistrust of concentrated financial power, a sentiment that threads through the entire fabric of American history. Related to that mistrust is a second element: the political process of regulation, which has been used, abused, and circumvented with results that were often unanticipated and unintended. The regulation of capital markets has waxed and waned over time in its effectiveness and intensity. As the twentieth century draws to a close, however, the results of regulation are uncertain. In the United States, regulation of the capital markets has served to enhance the quality and quantity of information available to investors. Regulations have also served to perpetuate a uniquely American fragmentation of power in the financial services industry. Yet, insofar as regulations have in any way influenced prices, they have, in effect, distorted the informational role of the price mechanism itself, as it is ideally supposed to work in a free market. Thus the reasons for regulation have to be carefully justified, if not morally or rationally, at least historically.

A third element of our story is information. Capital markets are fundamentally arenas in which information—a scarce good—is created, processed, and exchanged through the mechanisms of bids, offers, orders, and prices. Information is an element of capital markets that has developed in relatively linear fashion; it has spread and improved in quality over time. This has occurred in large part because of regulation, especially during and after the 1930s, but also because of improvements in information technologies.

Finally, in the twentieth century, there has been a progressive democratization of the capital markets. Participation in the markets has broadened to include wide segments of the population, the result, in large part, of the growth of such institutions as mutual and pension funds. It is true that even today, sophisticated investors or institutional participants can gain competitive advantages through superior knowledge or market power in particular investment arenas. But, on balance, anyone who is interested can enjoy timely access to the kind of high-quality information that had once been available only to small groups of wealthy bankers and their major clients.

All four elements—ideology, regulation, information, and democratization—are historically interrelated, and their interplay in the peculiar contexts of American life has resulted in an institutional arrangement that is remarkably fragmented, and yet robust, by world standards.

It is worth noting that in some ways the Wall Street institutions and markets of today seem to be exhibiting a tendency to return to the commanding positions they reached nearly a century ago. Parallels can be drawn to show that now, as then, financiers use the large pools of capital at their disposal to reshape the U.S. economic landscape; to buy, sell, and control corporations; to oversee the international flow of capital to and from the United States; and, in the process, to enrich themselves. But the road from J. P. Morgan and Kuhn, Loeb, at the turn of the century, to Drexel, Burnham, Lambert and Kohlberg, Kravis, Roberts toward its end, has gone through many twists and turns, as well as ups and downs. And while some contemporary observers argue that it has emerged rather close to where it started, the facts lead to a more complex set of conclusions. Superficial resemblances between early-century financial capitalism and more modern manifestations of financial control mask deeper changes in the basic structure of the capital markets—changes that are examined in the following pages.

THE NINETEENTH-CENTURY BACKGROUND

The basic elements of the modern American capital markets were in place at the turn of the twentieth century. The capital markets—and the institutions, organizations, and individuals that formed them—discharged large-scale and sophisticated economic functions in mobilizing, distributing, valuing, and revaluing capital. Centered then, as they are now, in New York City's Wall Street, the American capital markets operated on behalf of businesses, governments, and, for the most part, wealthy individuals. But the reach of the capital markets extended far beyond a few city blocks at the lower tip of the island of Manhattan; they extended throughout the United States and the entire world. In response to unusual or unexpected developments, the capital markets could become unglued, with prices fluctuating wildly upward and downward, the former movements generating financial euphoria and the latter sometimes culminating in worldwide financial distress and even panic.

To appreciate this state of affairs, we must review the earlier history of capital markets, which began to take shape in the United States in an economic setting vastly different from that of the industrial society of the early twentieth century. At its inception, the United States was a scattered collection of agrarian communities peopled mainly by self-sufficient farmers. Commerce engaged less than 10 percent of the population and was concentrated mainly in a few coastal cities, where there was as yet little demand for long-term capital investment. Businesses were small and proprietary. Governments at all levels of jurisdiction, except when they needed funds for emergencies or public works construction, managed most of their modest operations through current receipts from taxes and licenses. It was only later, as industrialization began to produce large-scale enterprises requiring massed capital, and as state and federal

demands increased for long-term funds to support infrastructure projects (and, in times of war, large-scale military procurement) that there evolved more specialized functions for raising capital through the issuing and sale of securities.

Although sporadic and small in volume, secondary markets for securities formed to trade primarily in debt securities. With the ratification of the Constitution, the nascent federal government's assumption and refunding of the states' and national Revolutionary War debts whetted speculative interest. By the 1790s, brokers conducted daily auctions of government bonds and bills of exchange from newly emerging state banks and the First Bank of the United States, as well as of other obligations that had the potential to rise in value. By 1792, rudimentary stock and bond exchanges were operating in New York and Philadelphia, and in 1817, the New York Stock & Exchange Board opened for business on Wall Street as a self-regulating group of traders in reputable securities. Securities that fell outside their purview were traded outdoors, "on the curbstone," the forerunner, by tradition, of the American Stock Exchange.

The establishment of the predecessors of the New York and American stock exchanges, several prestigious commercial and private banks, and such major buyers of securities as life insurance and trust companies, all in close proximity in lower Manhattan, made Wall Street the symbol of the nation's capital markets. In popular parlance, "the Street" came to represent New York's financial community as early as the 1830s, when it still competed with Boston and Philadelphia for primacy in the field.

After independence, such institutions as publicly chartered and private banking houses gradually assumed the less formal credit functions of colonial merchants. The first American banks accepted deposits, dealt in foreign and domestic exchange, issued notes that circulated as currency, made short-term loans (of less than a year's duration) to businesses for working capital, and invested in securities (long-term loans). Antebellum businesses, including commercial agricultural operations, could normally meet annual demands for working capital through the equity investments of wealthy individuals supplemented by rolling short-term credits via merchants or other unspecialized intermediaries. Such loans were secured by promissory notes or collateral in the form of claims on crops, real estate, and, only occasionally, securities.

By the mid 1830s, the American banking system—if it could be called that—was highly fragmented and uncoordinated. The antebellum United States was less a nation than a confederation of sovereign republics, or states, each jealously guarding its right to control the establishment of banks, each precluding the entry of "foreign" banks into its territory. Thus banks could not branch across state lines, and in some states they could not branch at all. Hundreds of banks not only accepted deposits and granted credit, but also issued bank notes that circulated, at varying discounts, as money. The nation as a whole had no policy or mechanism for regulating the supply of money or credit in the economy or for establishing and maintaining uniform standards for solvency and sound banking practices. On the other hand, as the nation's economy began to diversify around regional comparative advantages, the fragmented nature of the banking system served to stimulate capital market development in the larger cities, especially the major seaports, where regional banks deposited money to finance interregional trade.

The fragmented banking system rested on a substrate of libertarian sentiments, the accretion of more than a century and a half of Anglo-American ideological and political development. The sovereignty of ordinary citizens had gradually displaced the traditional claims of aristocrats, oligarchs, and theocrats. Notwithstanding the exclusion of slaves and women from the full rights of citizenship, colonial American males with different social statuses and interests—seacoast merchants, southern plantation owners, urban artisans, and the mass of yeomen farmers—were radical levelers by world standards.

The new nation's inhabitants, moreover, were a remarkably diverse people for the time. Ethnic and religious diversity and geographic sectionalism appealed to political theorists like James Madison, who argued in *The Federalist* 10 that it was precisely the factional contentiousness of American society that would prevent its political institutions from descending into tyranny. In a marketplace of contending ideas and interests, Americans could at least agree on certain fundamentals. They were united by their love of political freedom and their desire to claim their shares of the material abundance that the new nation's vast resources offered them. They were united in their hostility to anything that might hamper their individual pursuit of happiness. They were especially suspicious of centralized government and executive power, the twin evils of the ancien régime, and reinforced the factional nature of the young Republic.

The new national order reflected the continuing fear of concentrated power. It was a well-articulated, philosophically justified tendency of mind that spilled over into every organized realm of American society.

As the new nation began to industrialize, and as it hastened to integrate interregional trade, it proved politically difficult to create the kind of large, interregional financial institutions that might have made economic development more efficient than it was. Three antebellum attempts to establish a permanent central bank all foundered on the shoals of republican ideology and interest-group rivalries. Toward the end of the Revolutionary War and then later, from 1791 to 1811 and from 1816 to 1836, the central government experimented with national banks. The failures, in turn, of each of these institutions to secure rechartering as a federal central banking institution resulted from persistent worries about concentrated financial power.

Consider what happened when the nation's very first bank, the Philadelphia-based Bank of North America, was chartered by the Continental Congress in 1781. Capitalized at $400,000, the Bank's public purpose was to mobilize private credit for government needs. Although hardly a financial powerhouse, the Bank of North America was a monopoly grant, and as such it seemed to fly in the face of the spirit of egalitarianism and decentralization that suffused the new political order. Then in 1791, Congress incorporated the Bank of the United States, the purpose of which was to act as fiscal agent for the government and to stimulate private enterprise. Again, because the bank was controlled and managed by private investors, it was roundly condemned by noncommercial and agrarian interests as a rank monopoly privilege. When the bank's twenty-year charter came up for renewal in 1811, Congress failed by one vote to pass the necessary legislation.

The Second Bank of the United States was established in 1816, after war (1812–1815), rampant inflation, and the mushrooming of state-chartered banks (the number had increased from 88 to 246 in five years) created monetary chaos and a crisis in the public and private markets for credit. The Second Bank operated some sixteen branches around the country and came to perform many useful central banking functions: assisting in the management of government financial transactions, creating money through the issue of bank notes, holding international monetary reserves, and making both short- and long-term loans. Also, the Second Bank, like the first, served as a constraint on the propensity of state banks to expand credit. But bowing to political pressures from a coalition of state bankers (who could not branch across state lines), populist farmers and tradesmen (who wanted easier credit), New York bankers (who wanted their city to be the nation's financial center), and strict constructionists, Andrew Jackson vetoed Congress's renewal of the Second Bank's charter in 1832. He did so with a ringing populist indictment of what he saw as an invidious concentration of financial power in the hands of a small wealthy class that was, to make matters worse, in alliance with foreign capital. On more philosophical grounds, he argued that the bank was an unconstitutional "invasion . . . of the rights and powers of the Several States." His veto message was read widely then and thereafter to generations of schoolchildren to come, and it conferred even greater legitimacy on popular hostility against institutions of size and power. Fears of moneyed monopoly and the concentration of financial power into the hands of a few wealthy men would smolder on into the future, flaming up from time to time whenever the activities of powerful financiers were widely publicized.

There would be no central bank in the United States until the establishment, in 1913, of the Federal Reserve System. By the mid-nineteenth century, the institutional landscape of American finance featured a hodgepodge of state-chartered commercial and savings banks, as well as unchartered private banks. Only after the Civil War did the National Currency and Banking Acts of 1863–1864, along with prohibitive taxes on state bank notes (which made possible the establishment of a homogeneous paper currency), ease the financial development of a national economy. The fragmented structure of American banking, meanwhile, prolonged and reinforced the traditional flow of funds from the hinterlands to the great cities, of which New York became the most important. New York's size, its seaport, its stock exchange and call-loan markets, and its substantial number of insurance and trust companies all enhanced its position as a great "money center." The largest of the New York banks became the nation's most important agencies of credit, positioned as they were at the top of a kind of pyramided system of money reserves.

In the meantime, creative entrepreneurs began to take on capital market functions in response to growing public and private demands. Following the lapse of its federal charter, in 1836, the Second Bank of the United States pioneered private institutional investment banking functions. It marketed both government and corporate (mainly railroad) securities overseas on a commission basis. Antecedents of the modern investment banking function were also found in opportunistic middlemen, who on an occasional basis mobilized capital for canals, other internal improvements, and extraordinary government needs. In 1813, for example, the Treasury Department asked a small group of wealthy merchants to distribute bonds to raise $10 million toward the war against Great Britain. By the 1840s, commercial banks were performing investment banking functions for both public and private enterprise, albeit still on an occasional basis, alongside auctioneers, brokers, and unincorporated private bankers. Thereafter, private bankers and leading commercial bankers who could promote and engineer long-term investments became increasingly valued for their abilities to address the ad hoc complexities of particular business problems.

By the end of the Civil War, the potential scope of the capital markets had suddenly widened. A big increase in government debt (which, in the absence of taxes, had to be funded and refunded with private capital) and the development of techniques for marketing securities to large masses of people were direct consequences of the war. The application of government budget surpluses to pay down the debt put large amounts of funds in the capital markets for reinvestment in railroads—the one truly big business of the era—and other private enterprises. Even before the Civil War, the needs of railroads had already led to some widening and deepening of capital markets. No one could expect to build, let alone operate and maintain, a rail line without pooling substantial investments.

It was indeed the rapid increase in railroad construction after 1850 that called forth a new breed of investment bankers (though they were not known by the term until three decades later). Between the Civil War and the end of the century, small partnerships of private bankers in the northeastern commercial centers floated and distributed various types of railroad securities, including mortgage, equipment, and income bonds, as well as equities. They also channeled foreign investment into the United States for both railroad and government issues. (Between 1870 and 1900, foreign investment in the United States increased from $1.4 billion to $3.3 billion.) Commercial banks in New York also dealt in long-term securities. In Chicago and around the rest of the country, local commercial banks served as investment bankers for regional railroads and public projects and provided venture capital for other fledgling enterprises.

The most prominent of the new breed of private investment bankers was Jay Cooke, whose greatest coup was the sale of more than $500 million in federal bonds during the Civil War. This he accomplished through a well-coordinated network of Wall Street brokerage houses and a national sales force of some

2,500 subagents. He continued to handle most of the government's refinancing operations after the war, forging close connections with leading European firms. Cooke was the first to demonstrate the possibilities of mass marketing securities to thousands of people who had never before invested in anything. Cooke, however, went bankrupt when he found too few takers for an issue of less-than-pristine-quality railroad bonds he had promoted and then underwritten in 1873, thereby triggering one of the frequent financial panics of the nineteenth century. His undoing temporarily stalled progress toward broad public participation in the capital markets. Small investors would not be a sustaining factor in the capital markets until the 1920s.

Cooke was superseded in preeminence by John Pierpont Morgan, who vowed in the aftermath of the Cooke debacle to deal only in high-grade securities. J. P. Morgan & Company became by far the most important of a group of investment intermediaries known as the Yankee Bankers. This group of generally patrician, Anglo-Saxon, Protestant gentlemen emerged from the old Anglo-Saxon merchant communities of Boston, Philadelphia, and New York, giving rise to such firms as Kidder, Drexel, and the predecessor to J. P. Morgan, George Peabody & Company. (Peabody had migrated from Boston to London in 1835, where he played a vital role in establishing American credit abroad.) These bankers mobilized the surplus funds of foreign capitalists, particularly in England, for investment in the New World. The great Yankee Bankers typically dealt directly with only a small, elite circle of institutions and wealthy individuals.

Another distinctive group of private investment bankers emerged among well-connected German-Jewish immigrants. A few, like August Belmont, Rothschild's representative to America, arrived as bankers. Most started out as peddlers or wholesale merchants whose close international family and business ties and access to European capital enabled them to build investment houses of durable strength. In addition to Kuhn, Loeb, such firms as Seligman; Goldman, Sachs; and Lehman Brothers were in full flower in New York by the 1880s. Like the Yankee Bankers, their primary business relations seemed to operate as closed communities.

The ethnic and religious differences between the Yankee and Jewish bankers, and occasional tensions that developed around them, became an important part of the cultural milieu of Wall Street. Although these differences only rarely distorted the financial logic of syndicate-financing participation, they certainly affected hiring patterns and divided the nation's leading financiers into ethnically distinct tribes, with the Yankees erecting barricades of discrimination around their exclusive clubs and closed residential communities. To people outside the industry, the internal division of Wall Street was less problematic than the apparent coalescence of high finance around distinct tribal groups, which served only to increase the sense of the ordinary citizen's distance from the centers of economic power. The fact that one of those tribes was Jewish exacerbated the fear (among a largely anti-Semitic population) of those who had control over large sums of money—the movements of which seemed arcane and information about which was remote, if not altogether inaccessible.

THE RISE OF FINANCIAL CAPITALISM

At the turn of the century, investment bankers were still few in number, and like secular priests, they dealt in the mysteries of securities—their origination, their distribution, and their valuation. Although there had developed a common body of basic financial instruments and techniques, it was the uniqueness of each financing that made the investment banking business more of an art than a science, more an arena for highly talented craftsmen than for technicians. Entry into and survival in the inner circles of high finance required mutual confidence in the skills and reliability not just of the institutions but of the individuals who represented and sold securities. Indeed, it was the sophisticated, specialized, and personal nature of investment banking that endowed its rare practitioners with so much authority and gave them the power to exact large fees for their services. From the 1890s to 1912, the greatest of the investment bankers capitalized on their key positions in the financial affairs of the nation to exercise active control over the institutions they financed.

Before 1890, the main activity in the capital markets was in government and railroad securities, as the consolidation of the nation's proliferating railways into larger administrative systems moved apace. The railroads were the schools of high finance. Their scale and complexity brought forth modern techniques in pricing, underwriting, and syndicating securities as well as in methods for effecting corporate acquisitions and consolidations, bankruptcy rescues, and refinancings.

As bankers became more actively engaged as advisers to, and board members of, the railroads, their close relationship with the companies they financed was reassuring to the buyers of securities. Through their reputation for expertise and integrity, and their willingness to exercise ongoing fiduciary responsibility, bankers became proxies for the soundness and safety of the investments they had placed. Jacob Schiff argued that by the turn of the century, investment bankers had become more "honest in their respect for the moral obligation assumed toward those who entrusted their financial affairs to them," which in turn obliged them as a matter of professional self-interest to help nourish and protect their clients' investments over the long term. Except for the rankest short-term speculators, future deals depended on the reputation for past success, and past success meant taking care of one's security-holding clients.

In an early example of this trend, Francis Peabody of Kidder, Peabody & Company joined the board of the Santa Fe Railroad in 1871 and became chairman of its finance committee. As the Santa Fe expanded from a regional to a national organization, Kidder, Peabody floated its securities (usually in cooperation with other Boston-based banks and Baring Brothers in London), served as its transfer agent and bank of deposit, and provided financial advice to the railroad's management. When, in 1887, the Santa Fe found itself in dire straits from overexpansion, Kidder, Peabody stepped in to restructure the company's debt. The bankers imposed rigorous financial and accounting controls, reformed the company's administrative organization, and reorganized its financial structure by consolidating its outstanding bonds in such a way as to reduce its fixed charges without hurting its bondholders over the longer term. Kidder, Peabody also designed a program by which it would hold the company's stock in trust for a period of years to ensure that the reforms would be honored, while at the same time protecting the railroad from potential corporate raiders. J. P. Morgan would carry such intervention to even greater lengths in his "Morganizations" of distressed railroads over the next fifteen years. Through his conversion of bondholders to stockholders, whose interests were then protected by banker-dominated "voting trusts," Morgan brought railroad executives to heel in the service of their creditors and owners. He once found it necessary to admonish a railroad president with the curt reminder that "your roads belong to my clients." Thus did the great railroad bankers distinguish themselves from mere speculators, men like the raider and proto-greenmailer Jay Gould, who made money by manipulating securities prices and churning investments without regard for the long-term health of the underlying enterprises.

Industrial—manufacturing, processing and merchandising—companies of any size were few before the 1890s. But with the consolidation of transregional railroad and telecommunications systems arose the potential to exploit a national market for goods and services. Entrepreneurs went to work after 1873 to match the national market with the technological potential for mass production and distribution. They often did so by combining the assets of several producers, which not only reduced competition, but also made it possible to achieve lower costs through economies of scale. They then integrated forward into product distribution and backward into resource acquisition in order to achieve and protect the economies that could be realized through high-volume operations. Andrew Carnegie was rare in his desire to build his steel empire through partnership investments and retained earnings. The creation and expansion of most large corporations usually outstripped the ability of families and small groups of owner-managers to finance them, and so it became necessary to establish a market for industrial securities.

In the 1880s, a few companies in the processing industries, led by Standard Oil, devised trust arrangements to evade barriers in state law that limited one company's ability to own and control another. Formerly competing producers submitted their ownership rights to a governing trustee in exchange for trust certificates. The passage of the New Jersey Holding Company Act in 1889 effectively removed the barriers that had prevented companies from controlling other companies across state lines. Then the Sherman Antitrust Act of 1890 proscribed cartels and, by implication, the kind of trust arrangements that had developed in the oil and other processing industries in the 1880s. The political intent of the act, which was largely directed against big business, had the ironic effect of encouraging legal mergers, where trusts and less formal associational arrangements had once served. After the sharp depression of 1893–1895, all the elements were in place for a boom in the formation of ever larger industrial combinations.

Yet the market for industrial securities was regarded as extremely risky, and at the turn of the century, debt was still the preferred mode of investment. Bonds, usually mortgaged by real estate, plant, and equipment, were the primary source of capitalization among railroads, but obligations to meet the fixed charges of bonds could often lead to difficulties in hard times. This was thought, perhaps erroneously, to be even more true of industrial companies, thus driving up the cost of their debt. The alternative of industrial common equities was even more suspect.

Unlike debt, which was normally backed by liens on tangible assets, the ownership of common stock offered the less palpable promise of capital gains and uncertain dividends. In other words, common stock carried the "water" in the capitalization. To many contemporaries, this made the value of stock simply too variable and indeterminate to trust.

Corporate owners and managers, too, had motives that contributed, at least indirectly, to the relative unpopularity of industrial stock. The sale of equity threatened to dilute the control of owners, who, even if they floated stock, were seldom eager to provide the public with the kinds of information that would have made their equities seem less speculative. Professional managers did not yet see what by the 1930s would be a widely accepted fact of corporate life: that as a class, it was they who would benefit by increasing their independence from the traditional constraints of ownership.

To some extent, investment bankers were able to overcome some of the market resistance to industrial equities (and in the process allay managers' fears of dilution) by the innovative deployment of preferred stock. This financial instrument, a hybrid of equity and debt, had come into favor in railroads in the 1870s. Like bonds, preferred stock offered a predictable source of current income, paying fixed dividends; yet unlike most bonds, it could not be called in by the issuer. Sometimes preferred stock came with voting rights (the Mellons used this technique with Alcoa), but usually not. More important to investors was that the claims of preferred stockholders superseded those of common equity holders in bankruptcies, and preferred dividends were cumulative. At the turn of the century, preferred stocks typically yielded 7 percent dividends, which made their returns more attractive than government bonds at 2 percent, railroad bonds at 3 to 4 percent, and New York City mortgages at 5 percent or so. Other creative applications of financial instruments, after 1901, included the development of debentures (bonds unbacked by tangible collateral) and the increasing use of convertible bonds. Convertibles, instead of being based on mortgaged collateral, offered investors the possibility of becoming equity holders in a successful enterprise, thus enabling already indebted industrial companies to expand without reconciling prior liens.

The financial power of the most creative and expert bankers concentrated at the pinnacle of big business. The market structure of the new capital-intensive industries was moving rapidly toward oligopoly, and this was reflected in and abetted by the tendency for a relatively small group of investment bankers to control securities issues. Consider the structure of the major underwriting syndicates. Underwriting, once a simple guarantee to buy a portion of a securities issue that found no immediate market, had elaborated into a more complex sequence of functions. In their mature form, underwriting syndicates were responsible for the origination of securities (which involved determining the types, amounts, and terms), the purchase of securities from the issuer, the funding of securities (between purchase and sale), and the placement of the securities with brokers, dealers, and ultimate investors. The first three functions were the responsibility of the originating house, which for large issues was usually one of a small number of investment banks, described by Fritz Redlich as "the apex of [a] pyramid" of intermediaries that was "supported by chains of middlemen."

There was a common perception that being asked to participate in a syndicate was an offer no firm could refuse, lest it be excluded from future participations. The effect, according to no less an authority than Jacob Schiff, was to cement an alliance among a "small circle of friends" who lived by an implicit "bankers' code." In practice, the code was anticompetitive in many respects. The vaunted efficiency of the market was undercut by the degree to which bankers felt compelled to participate in what they sometimes thought were bad deals. The code also reduced competition for originations (rarely did major bankers go after one another's clients) and promoted the concentration of securities underwritings. In 1913, George F. Baker of New York's First National Bank explained to congressional investigators that for the preceding decade, every issue of corporate securities greater than $10 million was floated by syndicates led by a small group of apex firms. Mostly located in New York, these firms included J. P. Morgan; Kuhn, Loeb; the First National Bank; the National City Bank; Kidder, Peabody; and Lee, Higginson. They varied somewhat in function: Morgan and Kuhn, Loeb, the great "wholesalers," focused exclusively on underwriting, whereas Kidder, Peabody and Lee, Higginson (both Boston firms) established branch offices and retailing services. First National and National City were primarily commercial banks. Collectively and pejoratively, these alliances came to be known as the "Money Trust."

The influence of the apex firms was felt directly in the boardrooms of many of the nation's most important enterprises. In 1912, officers from just five New York banks (First National, Banker's Trust, Guaranty Trust, J. P. Morgan, and National City) were shown to hold 341 directorships in 112 companies—in banks, insurance, transportation, public utilities, manufacturing, and trading. First National's Baker, alone, held 58 seats; the Morgan partners, 72. The presence of so few bankers on so many boards, including those of competing companies, gave rise to very real conflicts of interest. Bankers on boards were at once fiduciaries to securities holders as well as fee-taking intermediaries. The result was that corporations, consumers, and securities buyers alike might be subjected to "taxes" in the form of higher securities prices and higher product prices. On the other hand, bankers had an important disciplinary role to play in the large-scale industrialization of capitalist societies. Historians have long noted that the cooperative role of the great banks of Germany and Japan in corporate governance had generally positive effects on the development of capital-intensive industries in those countries. Despite the fragmentation of the American banking system and the small-scale nature of American investment banking institutions, there is ample evidence that the few great bankers who specialized in high finance performed valuable services as directors of major U.S. corporations during their critical stages of growth at the turn of the century. If the bankers who mobilized and channeled capital to corporations could warrant to outside investors the value and quality of their investments, they could also monitor managers far more effectively and respond to a company's administrative and financial crises far more quickly than dispersed owners of securities could themselves ever hope to do.

The intervention of financiers into the corporate governance of nineteenth-century railroads extended quite naturally to the new industrial corporations of the twentieth century. This was an important development because, left to their own devices, the new class of professional managers of large industrial corporations had a general preference to retain earnings, and so they would try to shield themselves from pressures from outside equity investors who were apt to be impatient about receiving their dividends. But managers could not so easily stave off the influence of bankers, who in the formative years of big business sought not only to enforce the covenants of debt obligations but also to serve as active fiduciaries for public shareholders. Bankers might agree with managers to keep the details of corporate finances under wraps. Bankers were also likely to take a nurturing, long-term view of investments and were sympathetic to the proclivities of progressive managers for plowing back earnings for developmental projects and capital improvements. But bankers might also act to enforce the interests of owners—whose risks they represented and often shared—when managers' plans went awry. At most they could direct managers into particular paths of behavior. There is econometric evidence to support the view of pre–World War I Morgan directors that the benefits of their boardroom activities more than offset the costs of their lavish fees. According to a study by Bradford DeLong, Morgan-influenced companies "sold at higher multiples of book value than other companies, and they did so not [simply] because of the advertising value of the Morgan name, but because they earned higher returns on capital."

In other words, bankers, as active monitors of corporate enterprise, filled the breach between the increasingly dispersed owners of large-scale enterprise and the professional managers who were nominally (and legally) still the agents of the stockholders. Honest bankers, moreover, staked their names (and prospects for future business) on the soundness of the assets they represented to the public. Thus the reputations—the "character," as J. P. Morgan put it—of the great investment bankers became proxies for the soundness of investments they managed in an otherwise mysterious, changing, and volatile economy in which great corporations were becoming established as the central institutions of the new industrial order.

MATURE FINANCIAL CAPITALISM: THE U.S. STEEL CORPORATION

Consider what happened at the dawn of the "American Century." In 1901, a series of dramatic business events occurred, many of which centered on the activities of Wall Street. Railroad consolidation moved apace as J. P. Morgan & Company, Wall Street's preeminent firm, completed the merger of the Pennsylvania Coal Company with the Erie Railroad and acquired the Central Railroad of New Jersey for the Reading. Widespread market speculation in other rail securities culminated on 9 May, when two railroad banker alliances, struggling for control of the Northern Pacific Railroad, touched off one of history's more bizarre stock market panics. The Harriman–Kuhn, Loeb group and the Hill-Morgan group had secretly purchased nearly all the shares of the Northern Pacific, cornering numerous shortsellers who had sold into a rising market blissfully ignorant of the battle for corporate control that was behind the stock's rise. As the shorts scrambled to buy Northern Pacific shares, selling other companies' shares to finance the scramble, prices plummeted. Embarrassed by the unintended consequences of their battle, the contending groups reached accommodations with their panicked victims and, later in the year, with each other, when they formed a jointly owned holding company, Northern Securities.

Mergers were underway in virtually every sector of the rapidly industrializing economy, with mixed effects. Major examples of such activity can be seen in communications, transportation, and oil. AT&T relocated its parent company from Boston to New York where it could increase its capitalization and more effectively mount an offensive against smaller, more poorly financed rivals. In April, the House of Morgan purchased a steamship company (Leyland) in Europe, in an attempt to reduce competition in that industry. On the other hand, oil was discovered in Texas, which reestablished competition that had almost been eliminated in the industry by the great Standard Oil monopoly. Such events also set off heady rounds of speculation, and on the last day of April, the New York Stock Exchange posted a record daily volume of 3.3 million shares traded.

The financial markets then, even more than now, were highly sensitive to shocks, and they suffered numerous blows. Labor strikes were rampant, as workers in the new industrial order pressed for collective bargaining power. In September 1901, the assassination of President William McKinley ushered into office a regime more actively concerned with promoting the role of government in the affairs of business. In one of his first acts as president, Theodore Roosevelt launched an antitrust suit against the newly formed Northern Securities combine. Despite the inevitable volatility in the markets resulting from these occurrences, the general trend remained bullish. Over time, the federal government had also learned to make use of the capital markets and, in modest ways, to shape them in the public interest. Stimulating effects resulted from ongoing participation in the markets by the U.S. Treasury, which deployed funds accumulated from federal budget surpluses to buy back government debt. Such actions placed increasing amounts of money at Wall Street's disposal.

And yet, for the student of finance, none of the foregoing was the most remarkable news of the year. That came in February 1901 with the birth of the United States Steel Corporation. To this day, the financing of U.S. Steel ranks arguably as the deal of the century, if only because of the scale of its economic impact in the context of its time.

At the time, the U.S. economy, already the world's largest, had a gross national product of some $20 billion (about $300 billion in early 1990s purchasing power). The $1.4 billion merger that created U.S. Steel (more than $20 billion in early 1990s equivalents) was the capstone of the first great merger wave in history. Between 1897 and 1904, some 4,277 American companies consolidated into 257 corporations. But compared to all the others, the size of U.S. Steel was daunting. Its capitalization, including $550 million of 7 percent convertible preferred stock, $550 million of common stock, and $304 million of 5 percent gold bonds, was equivalent to 7 percent of the year's gross national product (a percentage that would amount to about $400 billion now, vastly larger than any 1980s merger or buyout). The valuation put on the new corporation by its promoters was astonishing; much of it seemed to consist of nothing more than "blue sky and water." It was more than twice the tangible asset valuation of the constituent properties and more than $600 million in excess of the market value of the constituent companies. So astonishing was the scale of transaction that even a well-seasoned investment banker like Isaac Seligman was moved to exclaim, "I confess it is enough to take one's breath away."

The combination of eight giant steel companies (and purchase of several more), complete with ore deposits, iron smelters, steel furnaces, fabricating plants, and connecting railways and shipping lines, demanded an unprecedented placement effort for the new corporation's securities. A large underwriting syndicate undertook the placement, in which three hundred participants agreed to guarantee $200 million of the securities. The lead bankers were J. P. Morgan & Company, whose namesake was the titan of American finance, the "Jupiter of Wall Street." Indeed, John Pierpont Morgan, the country's greatest private banker, the exemplar of sound financial judgment, and the pillar of integrity, was one of the few men in the world who could command the confidence required to pull off such an enormous scheme.

The principal seller in the deal was the great steel magnate, Andrew Carnegie, who, reflecting the views of his generation, was deeply suspicious of the entire affair. He saw little more than water in the value of U.S. Steel's stock when it was floated. Prudent and conservative to excess, he had insisted on taking his payment, all $225.6 million of it, entirely in bonds. If the combine failed, as Carnegie believed it would, he could then recover his properties, "and Pierpont and his friends will lose all their paper profits."

But Carnegie had too little faith. The new securities were placed with alacrity, so great was the investing public's confidence in a Morgan deal. When the smoke cleared, the syndicate had realized $50 million in profits (about $750 million today), fully 25 percent of the amount underwritten (a 5 to 6 percent gross spread is considered quite good for an initial public offering today). The fees, high even by "robber baron" standards, were deemed "greatly in excess of a reasonable compensation" by the new Federal Bureau of Corporations.

The House of Morgan then placed its representatives on U.S. Steel's board of directors, where the financiers would outnumber the steel executives and would therefore have a continuing influence on the giant corporation's policies, strategies, and programs.

The Morgan-led deal that created U.S. Steel was a turning point in the history of industrial securities and in the maturing of techniques in syndicate financing. Morgan and other Wall Street bankers became intimately involved with not only the creation but also the shaping and governance of big business enterprise. Indeed, for historians, the U.S. Steel episode marks the high tide of financial capitalism, a period spanning the 1890s to World War I, when bankers responsible for financing large corporations exercised extraordinary influence over corporate strategy and policy. To contemporary supporters of the transaction, the creation of U.S. Steel was just another, albeit huge, rationalization of yet another disorderly, overly competitive, underperforming industry. Its price, which anticipated a rapid and healthy stream of future earnings, reflected real gains expected from economies of scale and the elimination of "wasteful competition." To contemporary critics, the entire process—the absorption of already large companies into a mammoth combine, the seemingly inflated price of the securities, the huge profits taken by the underwriters, and the apparent influence of Wall Street on corporate governance—portended a dangerous future for American enterprise. Growing fears of the power of a financial monopoly, a Money Trust, on Wall Street led to calls for government regulation of the securities markets and financial institutions.

Government answered these calls. First the states and then, on a greater scale, the federal government would investigate, legislate, regulate, and attempt to reform the capital markets and thereby reduce Wall Street's influence on American economic life.

As a result, the aftermath of the U.S. Steel merger proved to be more than merely ironic. U.S. Steel never achieved the power its supporters had hoped for and its rivals had feared. The industry was already mature; its years of very rapid growth had subsided coincidentally with the great Carnegie's departure from the scene. Although it would remain the world's largest industrial firm for decades to come, U.S. Steel soon resorted to cartel-like techniques for setting prices, simply to sustain "reasonable" profits. The Justice Department charged U.S. Steel with monopoly practices, but the Supreme Court found, in 1920, that the company did not pose a threat to the public welfare on the ground that it lacked sufficient market power to be deemed a monopoly under the Sherman Act. By then U.S. Steel's market share had slipped to less than half and would continue to erode. By the mid-1930s the company controlled only about a third of the nation's output.

And yet the very creation of U.S. Steel ignited the smoldering resentment and fear of large institutions that had been an abiding characteristic of the American psyche since colonial times. U.S. Steel stimulated enough concern about the size and power of business corporations and enough worry about the influence of financiers over the nation's productive capacity that nothing like it would ever occur again. By the time Woodrow Wilson was sworn in as president of the United States in March 1913, the great combines of Standard Oil and American Tobacco had been sued by probusiness Republican administrations and were then broken up by the Supreme Court. J. P. Morgan died within the month, and his successors on Wall Street would never again exert the measure of control he and his partners had exercised over the nation's corporate affairs. Congressional hearings, relentless public pressure, and the looming threat of capital market regulation combined to force investment bankers to the sidelines of corporate management. The Morgan partners and other great Wall Street financiers quietly withdrew from the nation's boardrooms, sacrificing influence for a quieter, less conspicuous role in the nation's economy.

But the fact remains that the representational and oversight functions of early-twentieth-century American bankers were necessitated by the scarcity of public information on corporate performance, a condition to which the bankers themselves contributed. Corporate operating and financial data were enveloped in a shroud of secrecy that outside, or "public," investors could not penetrate. Neither formal annual reports nor independent audits were mandated by law. Reports to shareholders did not just obfuscate; they simply did not report. Such financial data as appeared publicly was flimsy at best, and almost always useless for analysis. When asked in

1899 what he thought of the stockholders' right to know about the affairs of public companies in which they invested, sugar magnate H. O. Havemeyer's reply was the very essence of a Social Darwinist's approach to investing: "Let the buyer beware; that covers the whole business. You cannot wet-nurse people. . . . They have got to wade in and get stuck and that is the way men are educated and cultivated."

PUJO AND THE MONEY TRUST

The growing presence of bankers on the boards of directors of the nation's leading firms and the apparent concentration of securities offerings among a few investment houses fanned widespread fears that Wall Street had seized control of the nation's businesses. These fears coalesced into a vigorous public debate in 1912 when Congress established the Pujo committee—so-called after its chairman, the populist Louisiana congressman Arsene Pujo—to investigate Wall Street. It was a sweeping inquiry into the affairs of money center bankers in which the committee's chief counsel, Samuel Untermyer, managed to paint a vivid, albeit distorted, tableau of the Money Trust in which he conjured up the grim specter of monopoly power in the capital markets and its alleged death grip on the nation's business. The elderly J. P. Morgan himself was called before the committee not long before his passing to endure nettlesome (some thought, literally deadly) interrogation. When Morgan explained the nature of competition among bankers, Untermyer saw conspiracy. When Morgan argued that character was the most important commodity in finance, the committee worried more about chicanery and stock manipulations. When Morgan and other bankers claimed that they had a duty to sit on corporate boards, members of the committee found conflicts of interest and abuses of power.

Concern about the activities of investment bankers merged with a parallel debate over the structure of the banking industry as a whole. The Pujo investigation served only to confirm the popular view that there was an inordinate concentration of financial authority on Wall Street, where what had become the nation's large money-center banks exercised substantial influence over the nation's supply of credit. It was true that New York City was the mecca of investment banking (see table 1), and so it was assumed that Wall Street also somehow controlled the nation's monetary assets. How could it be explained that, despite all the traditional ideological and legal

Table 1.   CONCENTRATION OF U.S. INVESTMENT BANKS (INCLUDING BRANCH OFFICES) OF MEMBERS OF THE INVESTMENT BANKERS ASSOCIATION OF AMERICA, BY CITY, 1912

City	Number
New York	108
Chicago	65
Philadelphia	31
Boston	23
Baltimore	22
St. Louis	15
Cincinnati	14
33 other cities	93
TOTAL	371

SOURCE: Vincent Carosso, *Investment Banking in America* (1971).

constraints on the power of bankers, a few New York banks had achieved so much size and power?

J. P. Morgan & Company offered a simple historical explanation of this situation. It was, they claimed, "not due to the purposes and activities of men, but primarily to the operation of our antiquated banking system which automatically compels interior banks to concentrate in New York hundreds of millions of dollars of reserve funds." It was, moreover, quite natural for "every country [to] create some one city as the great financial center." On the other hand, concerns about the concentration of funds in New York were overblown if one looked at the trend. The banking resources of New York City as a proportion of those of the United States had been declining since the turn of the century, from 23.2 percent in 1900 to 18.9 percent in 1912. Moreover, New York's largest banks were "far inferior in size to banks in the commercial capitals of much smaller countries," especially those in England, France, and Germany.

Debates over the existence of a Money Trust and its implications for the nation's banking system raged on through 1912. A year earlier, the *Wall Street Journal* had wryly suggested that if no Money Trust could be proven to exist, then one should be established right away, if only to provide an even stronger central monetary authority over the fragmented banking system of the United States. Pointing toward "the community of interest among banks" in European countries, the *Journal* echoed the sentiments of those who longed for greater rationality in the management of credit across the twenty thousand or so banks that dotted the U.S. countryside. (This was an astonishing number to Europeans, whose banking systems were far more centralized around a few large institutions.)

Left to their own devices, unregulated banks would be reckless with their credit, drive themselves into insolvency, and disrupt the efficient workings of the business economy. What was needed was more, not less, coordination in the industry.

Even the most benign explanations of how the great banks functioned and how New York had emerged as a center of finance were offensive to the traditionally power-averse sensibilities of the decentralized American body politic. Perhaps nothing so irritated ordinary citizens and populist members of Congress as the huge fees the great bankers took for their trouble. The percentages that investment bankers, in particular, plucked from the stream of corporate deals and government underwritings translated into immense personal incomes. Bankers, then as now, defended their fees as adequate compensation for the underwriting risks they assumed (even in routine cases where little risk was apparent). High fees were justified, too, by the need to attract, hold, and compensate the talents required to execute complex financial transactions (even when those talents were recruited entirely on the basis of blood and friendship). The best of the talent pool were the rare bankers who were probably worth every penny they made, persons who could not only execute sound financial deals but also provide the warranty of their worth. Speaking of his senior partner, George W. Perkins offered the Pujo committee a compelling explanation of why Morgan's seemingly privileged control of information was both right and good. Morgan had earned his position by dint of hard work, having "lived an earnest and tremendously strenuous life in the study of these questions for half a century." Thus, "if J. Pierpont Morgan should make a bond issue from the desert of Sahara and put his name on it, it would be subscribed . . . and the people [who] have bought and bought securities that his name has been put to . . . have believed that they have come out all right."

That investors in securities should come out all right was indeed a matter of the confidence one could place in men like Morgan. Investors of any kind had to rely on their trust in men who controlled virtually all the information about assets and liabilities. When grilled by Untermyer during the Pujo hearings, George F. Baker was adamant that even banks should not be forced to disclose details about their assets and liabilities. Under such conditions, he said, "business would come to a standstill." When asked why the public should "do business on confidence when it can get the facts," Baker simply responded that "the fundamental principle of banking

. . . is credit," which in his thinking was a moral, not a legal or regulatory matter.

To the Pujo committee, the fundamental principle—and problem—was power. Published in 1913, the committee's majority report identified "an established and well-defined community of interest between a few leaders of finance, created and held together through stock ownership, interlocking directorates, partnership and joint account transactions, and other forms of domination over banks, trust companies, railroads, and public service and industrial corporations, which has resulted in great and rapidly growing concentration of the control of money and credit in the hands of these few men." Louis Brandeis, himself a powerful corporate attorney and adviser to President Woodrow Wilson, followed with the publication of "Other People's Money." It appeared as a series of magazine installments (later gathered into a book), which condemned the nation's moneyed oligarchy and warned the public of the perils of big business, the evils of interlocking directorates, and the crass spectacle of greedy financiers who operated in secrecy and who took large underwriting fees while contributing little to the welfare of society. Such sentiments would reverberate throughout the twentieth century. Indeed, Brandeis's choice of title would become a staple of the popular, ironic jargon of Wall Street and was eventually coopted by the author of a popular play (later movie) that dramatized the excesses of Wall Street in the 1980s.

SECURITIES INDUSTRY STRUCTURE FROM PUJO TO THE DEPRESSION

By the time "Other People's Money" hit the newsstands in the summer of 1913, the apparent power of the then leading investment houses over corporate governance was already diminishing. In the glare of the Pujo hearings, the great bankers decided that it was the better part of valor to reduce their participation on corporate boards and to forgo attempts to take equity control of the businesses they financed. Thereafter, bankers on the boards of directors of major, complex corporations were fewer in number and, as outside directors, were increasingly less able to shape the decisions of professional managers. Other trends contributed to this outcome. As corporations grew larger and more complex, bankers could do little but acquiesce in the administrative and technical expertise of the more expert managers. Once established, moreover, well-run corporations were able to generate relatively more of the capital funds they required from retained earnings, which further reduced the bankers' leverage.

Thus after 1912, management enjoyed increasing freedom not only from owners but from bankers, as well. For better or worse, financial capitalism ceased to be a major factor in corporate governance. For decades to come, investment houses would forgo many opportunities for major equity participation in large companies, reflecting their lack of desire to absorb public criticism for a governing role they could not in any case play all that effectively.

At the same time, the apparent grip that the few great banking houses at the pinnacle of the capital markets had on the largest securities transactions was also proving to be tenuous. The reasons for this have to do with the inherently dynamic and unstable nature of the institutions that perform capital market functions.

At every stage of its history, the securities industry has been organized like a pyramid, with a few major underwriters at the top of a broadening base of both general and specialized service providers. Yet at no time has the structure of the industry or the position of firms in the competitive hierarchy been static. Particular institutions have waxed and waned in importance. Over the years, many have disappeared through mergers, others have changed their names and services, and still others have fallen into ruin, sometimes with sudden speed. Because so much of the securities business relied on particular personalities with highly specialized connections for generating business or specialized skills for executing business, the departure of key personnel could often drastically weaken a once prominent firm. Even during the brief span of the Pujo hearings, the particular group of firms at the top could not even begin to control competition in every market. The mass of small manufacturers and retailers, for example, along with municipalities and public utilities, relied mostly on regional securities underwriters and distributors, which were increasing rapidly in their numbers during this period.

In addition, the larger structural configuration within which the capital markets operated was changing profoundly. By 1913, commercial banks were insinuating themselves more aggressively into the flotation of new securities, setting up bond departments and investment banking affiliates through which they recycled corporate and individual deposits into the capital markets. This trend accelerated after World War I, when, as business profits took off, corporations turned increasingly to the securities markets for short-term as well as long-term invest-

ments, thus reducing their traditional dependency on short-term bank loans and their use of demand deposits. Even trust companies joined the fray. There emerged "full-service banks," the best model of which was the National City Bank of New York, which by the late 1920s had joined its commercial banking with the provision of trust services and the underwriting and distribution of securities on a mass scale. By 1930, almost half the new securities issues in the United States were originated by commercial banks or their affiliates, and they had become the most important factors in distribution.

Another stimulus to these institutional developments was a broadening of the demographic base of investors. Industrialization had led to rising prosperity at all levels of society. After World War I, wealth in the United States was distributed broadly, and even ordinary wage earners were able to generate savings. More people than ever were investing in stocks and bonds, their access to such instruments facilitated by new vehicles for tapping even small-scale savings. The government bond drives of World War I, an echo of Jay Cooke's campaign of half a century earlier, introduced multitudes of wage earners to the possibility of increasing their wealth through direct financial investment. When the war was over and the government reduced its debt, Wall Street institutions, some of which began to tout themselves, tellingly, as "financial department stores," developed new methods of attracting savings and financial business. During the prosperous 1920s, finance was progressively democratized in all major arenas, all the way from stock and bond investment to consumer credit. Individual investors entered the market in unprecedented numbers, with a growing desire, whetted by broadly successful issues of wartime industries, to get rich via securities, including common stocks. In the decade following the war, total corporate securities issues tripled, reaching $9.4 billion in 1929, the year when the New York Stock Exchange enjoyed its first billion-share year in trading. One year earlier, the total value of stock issues in the United States exceeded that of debt for the first time.

Thus by the 1920s, the securities markets were no longer arenas in which only the elite, moneyed classes of society risked their capital. The swelling appetite of ever larger numbers of investors for securities was fed by the rapid growth in investment firms around the country; by 1929, at least thirty-three cities had fifteen or more investment firms. Particularly important in spurring demand were the mass marketing activities of the investment affiliates of commercial banks and the growth of two other vehicles that became widely popular channels for investment in the Roaring Twenties: investment trusts and public utility holding companies. Investment trusts were sponsored by investment banks, commercial banks, investment consultants and trustees, and professional managers. Investors bought securities of the trust increasingly on credit through call loans, the risks of which were presumably reduced by the diversified basket of stocks and bonds in which the trust was invested. By 1929, there were 770 investment trusts with more than $7 billion in assets. They could make money by underwriting and distributing their own securities and also by managing their investment portfolios. And they became important receptacles for the new flotations of investment bankers.

Some public utility holding companies were organized as affiliates of engineering and electrical firms, but most, after 1920, were organized by profit-seeking investment promoters. These holding companies were largely responsible for the nation's second merger wave, which was driven by the consolidation of electrical utilities between 1923 and 1930, as the prices of utility stocks, once considered extremely risky, surpassed those of railroads. Like investment trusts, they had pyramiding features, and in some hands they were used to organize complicated, interlocking networks of ownership. Samuel Insull of Chicago created a far-flung, albeit shaky, nationwide empire of utilities that had an astonishing $2.5 billion in assets by 1930.

Inevitably, the growth of financial markets during the 1920s drew in new financiers who disregarded (if they ever knew) the codes of conduct and lacked the sense of responsibility of the great financiers of the era of financial capitalism before the war. The new, popular investment vehicles were subject to enormous abuses, through intra–holding company underwritings, through the flotation of excessively large securities issues, and through outright self-dealing, manipulation, and fraud. The general tendency of bank affiliates, utility holding companies, and investment trusts to promote and float securities without the kind of close, critical scrutiny that had been the hallmark of the great prewar investment bankers, boded ill for the country.

THE ONSET OF REGULATION

It was inevitable under such conditions that third-party—in this case, government—regulation would emerge. An institution such as National City Bank might bring the various functions of commercial and investment banking under one corporate roof, but the industry as a whole was becoming ever more fragmented, both functionally and geographically. The differentiation of investment vehicles and the broadening of participation in them by the general public posed an even more fundamental problem. It was no longer just the concentration of financial power but also its potential for widespread abuse on an ever larger scale that was important. The remedy was to establish conditions for making available more and better information so that investors could make informed decisions. J. P. Morgan saw it coming. Shortly before he died in 1913, he warned of the day "when all business will have to be done with glass pockets." At the time, there was no federal regulation of the securities market beyond the fraud provisions of the postal laws (which, to this day, remain a potent weapon in litigating securities cases). It would take another twenty years before anything like uniform standards of disclosure would be legislated into the capital markets, but regulation was aborning, nonetheless.

As noted, the Pujo hearings had important effects, but they had little immediate impact on the legal or formal regulatory framework within which the capital markets operated. The committee's recommendations to place the stock exchanges under tighter controls and to bring full disclosure standards to securities offerings came to naught, as did proposals to have the Interstate Commerce Commission supervise securities issues of railroads and to prevent interstate corporations from appointing sole agents for securities issues and from depositing their funds in private banks. Congress also ignored a recommendation that national banks be prohibited from underwriting and selling securities and that their officers be barred from participating in syndicates along with a host of other restrictions. The one arguably direct effect of Pujo on federal law was the Clayton Antitrust Act of 1914, which made it illegal for corporations to acquire stock in companies to the "substantial" detriment of competition. The act prohibited common carriers from having securities dealings with financial institutions with which they had interlocking officers or directors, and it outlawed the interlocking directorates of banks and trust companies. The atmosphere surrounding the Pujo hearings influenced the final outcome of legislation that established the Federal Reserve System. Fears of the Money Trust were partly rooted in the memory of the banking panic of 1907, a crisis resolved by the joint action of J. P. Morgan and the other money center bankers of New York, who had calmed the panic through carefully calculated shifts of pooled reserve funds to vulnerable institutions. That the nation would have to rely on the good graces of a few bankers to resolve such emergencies was enough to overcome generations of resistance to the alternative of lodging monetary authority in a central bank. But the new Federal Reserve System was itself shaped by the durable principle of federalism and the undying hostility toward private monopoly power. Congress established the system in 1913 as a decentralized organization of twelve regional banks. The intent was to prevent any further concentration of financial power in the Northeast. Unlike its early-nineteenth-century ancestors, the Federal Reserve System was constituted far more as a public than a private institution. The regional Federal Reserve banks were nominally owned by the institutions they regulated, but their oversight was effectively controlled by the government. So also was the income they earned.

The effects of the decentralized structure were as ironic as they were unintended. One immediate consequence was to help liberate the major commercial banks from their traditional conservatism. The system would have only a limited effect on the stability of most of the banks in the country, until reforms in the 1930s established a centralized board with more explicit authority over the regional branches. In the meantime, the New York branch inevitably became the most powerful and did much to advance the private interests of the money center bankers. Providing the money center banks with a lender of last resort lowered the risks of entering into the more speculative investment activities of the capital markets. A parallel consequence was that the great Wall Street financiers, stung by the attentions and allegations of the Pujo investigation, could simply retreat to lower-profile positions in public affairs. They could justifiably abdicate their responsibility for overall financial stability to the publicly controlled Federal Reserve System.

Until the Great Depression, the federal government made little attempt to involve itself in the regulation of the nation's financial markets. Government intervention came first at the state level, where attempts to penetrate the fortress of secrecy that had long surrounded the sale of securities made some headway. Perhaps inspired by the English Companies Act of 1900, which had been designed to foil those who "would sell building lots in the blue sky in fee simple," American states began crafting notification legislation to compel better disclosure of assets underlying the issue and sale of stocks and bonds. The various acts passed to this end became known collectively as blue-sky laws. In 1911, Kansas enacted a comprehensive system for registering securities and licensing investment bankers, brokers, and dealers and established an agency to enforce the laws requiring issuers of securities to file detailed financial statements on their businesses. The Kansas bank commissioner's power to approve or deny securities issues at his discretion was a radical principle, unprecedented in Anglo-American law.

Despite some early rulings by federal courts that such laws unduly interfered with individual freedoms and overburdened interstate commerce, the Supreme Court ruled, in 1917, that the states possessed the police power to enact legislation "to prevent fraud and imposition" in the securities markets within their borders. The Kansas law set in motion a series of like legislation, so that by 1933, only Nevada lacked a blue-sky law. The laws generally sought to prevent fraud at the time securities were issued by establishing registration and licensing procedures for securities and for the people dealing in them, and by setting penalties for violations. In 1921, New York made such penalties enforceable when the legislature empowered the attorney general to issue subpoenas and to seek injunctions against persons suspected of fraudulent dealings in securities.

Yet such state regulation had little impact on the basic structural characteristics of the capital markets with one notable exception: in 1905, the New York legislature's Armstrong committee investigation had revealed serious conflicts of interest among investment banks, their affiliated trust companies, and insurance companies, on whose boards investment bankers sat. Legislation was then enacted that prohibited life insurance companies from underwriting securities and from investing in corporate stock and collateral trust bonds. Seventeen states followed suit in 1908.

The blue-sky laws were basically flawed by their lack of uniformity from state to state—they varied greatly in provisions, effectiveness, and reach. Internal borders, after all, did not bound the nation's capital markets. The Investment Bankers Association (IBA), organized in 1912 to promote the ethical standards as well as the political and economic interests of the profession, lobbied for some form of national securities regulation that would bring order out of the apparent chaos created by state laws. This movement reflected a broader trend in which professionals in all walks of life promoted legal and bureaucratic solutions to national problems through "progressive" government, particularly at the federal level. The public's preference for decentralized federalism over nationalism, however, made the imposition of uniform standards from the top politically infeasible. The IBA, which represented the one interest group with the least political credibility in the matter of securities fraud, thus failed in its effort.

Other sectors of business certainly did not manifest support for national securities regulation. The executives of large corporations, in particular, had little to gain by inviting closer scrutiny of their companies' finances. As they became less powerful in the boardroom, bankers became ever more dependent upon good relations with their clients for business, relations that were based on a gentlemen's code of confidence. Corporate financial information thus continued to be jealously guarded by corporate managers and bankers alike. It was not until the Great Depression brought such overwhelming discredit to the workings of the capital markets that it became possible to establish a political consensus for national securities regulation. Only then would solid information on which valuations of the country's major corporations could be reasonably based be liberated from the executive suite.

NEW DEAL FINANCIAL REFORMS

Although Congress had been studying the country's banking problems as they developed during the first years of the 1930s, it was Herbert Hoover who launched the process of capital market reform in 1932. It was the worst year of the Great Depression, which was inseparably, if tenuously, linked to the trauma of the 1929 stock market crash, the lingering symbol of both the previous excesses and the subsequent failures of America's financial system. Warned by conservative colleagues that financiers friendly to the Democrats might try to embarrass him and damage his 1932 reelection prospects by means of short-selling bear raids on Wall Street, the Republican president issued a preemptive call for a Senate investigation of stock market practices. The Gray-Pecora investigation, so called for two of the Senate subcommittee counsels who led it, lasted for two years. Its most damaging revelations came under counsel Ferdinand Pecora during 1933 and 1934, after Hoover had already been soundly defeated for reelection by Franklin D. Roosevelt.

The Senate investigation documented what were taken to be numerous cases of financial incompetence, manipulation, fraud, and self-dealing on the part of leading financiers and financial institutions. The Gray-Pecora hearings were rife with stories about how Wall Street bankers were either duped by or had swindled their clients. In reality, the investiga-

tion uncovered little in the way of substantively illegal transgressions, but the effect of the hearings on public opinion was enormous. The nation's leading financiers began to look as inept as they were imagined to be corrupt. Charles Mitchell, head of National City Bank (then the world's largest bank) and its affiliate, National City Company, resigned during the hearings shortly after his testimony fostered allegations of his and his companies' numerous ethical transgressions, some of which appeared to border on criminality. Mitchell, humiliated, became a popular personification of financial irresponsibility, a dubious distinction he would share with many others as the decade wore on. The nation's leading financial men were rightly or wrongly scapegoated for the nation's economic ills. Great trials were held following indictments of such luminaries as the former president of the New York Stock Exchange, Richard Whitney, and the former secretary of the treasury, Andrew Mellon. Mellon escaped conviction on flimsy tax-evasion charges, but Whitney was another matter. He was convicted and jailed for having systematically embezzled from his own clients, from his yacht club, and even from the emergency gratuity fund of members of the exchange.

It was all too much for even those who had profited from the system that had fallen into disrepute. The rout of the financiers spilled over to help discredit the entire leadership of the business community. As Joseph P. Kennedy, the first chairman of the Securities and Exchange Commission, reflected on the debacle: "The belief that those in control of the corporate life of America were motivated by honesty and ideals of honorable conduct was completely shattered."

The growing litany of disclosures about corruption on Wall Street led to a renewed attempt at securities market reform on a broad front. Average citizens who had gone into the markets only to lose their money were infuriated. They had in increasing numbers committed their capital to now discredited financial fiduciaries based on scant information. What Gray-Pecora seemed to say to them was that those who controlled the information had been abusing their privileged access to it, and now everyone was paying a terrible and protracted price. Thus, amid the general banking and financial collapse and the political realignment symbolized by Roosevelt's election, it became politically feasible for the first time in history to enact securities market laws at the federal level. Under the new regime, the public could no longer be left to suffer what had once been represented to it as ordinary risk.

The New Deal would take a more paternalistic view of securities regulation and of finance in general. Most of the thinking about how to constrain the activities of financial institutions was directed toward solving the time-worn problem of the control of information. During the New Deal's first "hundred days" of legislative frenzy came the Securities Act and the Banking (Glass-Steagall) Act of 1933. The first of these required new securities offerings to be registered with the Federal Trade Commission (after 1934, with the new Securities and Exchange Commission). Issuers of new securities were required to provide prospectuses containing sufficient information from registration statements to allow potential investors to judge the value of the offerings. Issuers also had to complete registration and disclosure of new securities twenty days before they could be sold. Failure to comply entailed substantial civil liabilities.

This "truth-in-securities" act was essentially a federalization of the more stringent state blue-sky laws. It was both a response to and, in time, a promoter of the democratization of capital markets. During the 1920s, more and more bankers pursued mass marketing strategies with none of the sense of fiduciary responsibility that the elite bankers had once provided to a limited number of wealthy clients. The New Deal securities laws, by making underwriters as liable as issuing corporations for providing information to would-be investors, shifted the traditional favor of the law from issuer to shareholder and creditor interests.

To prevent conflicts of interest that might arise from combining different financial functions under one roof, the Glass-Steagall Act legislated a full separation of commercial from investment banking, and prohibited affiliations and interlocking directorships between commercial and investment banks. Banks could now either take deposits and make loans or engage in the origination and distribution of corporate securities, but not both. Commercial banks simply divested themselves of their securities affiliates, which then either went out of existence or reorganized as separate securities firms. As for the private banks, most chose to remain in the securities business. J. P. Morgan & Company, which had been the explicit political target of what was actually a "surprise last-minute insertion in the bill," opted for commercial banking, prompting some of its partners to resign and form the Morgan Stanley investment bank.

Other provisions of Glass-Steagall provided for federal deposit insurance—which for years was regarded by economists as the most significant contribution of the law—and for federal regulation of the

maximum interest rates that banks could pay on deposits (zero in the case of demand deposits). President Roosevelt had been opposed to deposit insurance, thinking that it would do little more than prop up inefficient small banks. Senator Carter Glass was opposed to it as well; his alternative was more branch banking. But unit (one-office) bankers, championed by Congressman Henry Steagall, regarded deposit insurance as a way of protecting themselves against the loosening of restrictions on branch banking, which they loathed. In the end, Glass achieved his main objective, the separation of commercial and investment banking, as well as a slight relaxation of restrictions on branch banking. And Steagall achieved his goal of near-universal deposit insurance. As for the ceilings on interest rates, they were intended to curb a supposed tendency of banks to take excessive lending risks under more competitive pricing conditions. (Curbing rates also served to reduce bankers' costs, which helped offset the increased costs of deposit insurance.)

Its supporters touted Glass-Steagall as a measure that would cure the most "obvious" financial transgressions of the time: the overspeculation and excessive risk taking that led to the Great Crash and subsequent bank failures, the apparent conflicts of interest between commercial and investment banking functions, and the flagrant abuses of fiduciary responsibilities by financiers. But the sentiments underpinning Glass-Steagall ran deeper than that. By further fragmenting financial institutions and functions, Glass-Steagall harked back to the banking controversies of the earliest decades of the American Republic. It was an echo of the continuing suspicion of concentrated financial and economic power that was manifest from those decades right down through the Pujo investigation. The specific legislative intent of the act reflected this strain of American ideology far more than any sense of newfound pragmatism about structural reform.

A year later, in 1934, the Securities Exchange Act extended the registration and full disclosure requirements to all securities already listed on stock exchanges. Those corporations whose securities were traded on exchanges were now required to register and to file annual financial reports on their operations and quarterly earnings statements. This caused a quantum improvement in the quantity and quality of information made available to the investing public, and established a need for what would become a thickly populated profession of independent corporate auditors. Information on pending shifts of corporate control was also to become public in more

Table 2. KEY TWENTIETH-CENTURY SECURITIES-INDUSTRY
REGULATORY LEGISLATION

Title	Year	Description
Kansas Blue-Sky Law	1911	The first blue-sky law: Kansas enacts a comprehensive system of licensing for the registration of securities salesmen.
Martin Act (New York)	1921	Empowered state attorney general to investigate fraudulent securities practices and to issue subpoenas and seek injunctions against suspects.
Securities Act	1933	The first federal government regulation of the securities market. Required registration of securities offerings with the Federal Trade Commission and detailed public disclosure of material financial information about issuers.
Glass-Steagall Act	1933	Required separation of investment banking (securities underwriting) from commercial banking (acceptance of deposits and lending) functions.
Securities Exchange Act	1934	Established the Securities and Exchange Commission (SEC) and required exchanges to submit rules for SEC approval. Also required companies with existing securities to disclose detailed financial information to the public.
Public Utility Holding Company Act	1935	Enabled SEC to supervise dissolutions, breakups, integrations, and capital restructurings of public utilities.
Maloney Act	1938	Authorized formation of National Association of Securities Dealers under the auspices of the SEC to oversee activities of broker-dealers in the over-the-counter market.
Trust Indenture Act	1939	Required obligers of bonds to register with SEC.
Investment Company Act	1940	Authorized SEC to oversee investment company activities.
Securities Act Amendments	1964	Required SEC registration of widely held securities and raised certification requirements for brokers.
Williams Act	1968	Required purchasers of equity to announce holdings and intentions within ten days from time accumulations reached 5 percent of a company's stock and to abide by a minimum twenty-business-day period, during which time tender offers would be open for tendering by shareholders.
Securities Investor Protection Act	1970	Established Securities Investor Protection Corporation (SIPC) to insure deposits with brokerage firms.
Employee Retirement Income Security Act	1974	Established Employee Benefit Guaranty Corporation (EBGC) to insure plan beneficiaries against loss from plan termination.
Securities Reform Act	1975	Enabled SEC to establish a national market system and strengthened authority of SEC over exchanges. Ended the practice of fixed commissions by exchanges.

SOURCES: James Burk, *Values in the Marketplace* (1988) (the table closely follow's Burk's format); Thomas McCraw, *Prophets of Regulation* (1984); Roy Smith, *The Money Wars* (1990).

timely fashion. Individuals owning more than 10 percent of a corporation's securities also had to disclose that fact as well as any subsequent transactions in those securities. All these reports and disclosures were to be made to the newly established Securities and Exchange Commission (SEC), which was also empowered to register and monitor the stock exchanges and to enforce a new ban on some manipulative trading practices as well as the regulation of others, such as short-selling.

These three laws, which were enacted within just fifteen months of each other, were the major American capital market reforms of the twentieth century (see table 2). They were soon followed by still more. The Banking Act of 1935 increased the monetary and bank regulatory powers of the Federal Reserve System and extended the Fed's power to regulate margin requirements on loans made to purchase securities. The 1935 Public Utility Holding Company Act, another of the laws directed at fragmenting private financial power, specified that a utility holding company could control only one integrated utility system. Under it, utilities were also subjected to more stringent SEC regulation than nonutilities. The Maloney Act of 1938 established rules for the over-the-counter market, leading to self-regulation by a new National Association of Securities Dealers (NASD) under SEC oversight. In the same year, an amendment to the federal bankruptcy law restricted the role of investment bankers in reorganizations of publicly held companies, an activity in which those bankers had formerly been the leading players.

The power of investment bankers was weakened further in 1939 when the Trust Indenture Act precluded them from serving as trustees for any debt securities they originated. In an earlier era, bankers had felt that it was both their duty and sound business strategy to monitor the securities they had placed. Bondholders would thereby be reassured, the reasoning went, by the bankers' ongoing involvement. But investors had long since become too suspicious of bankers for the latter to continue in that traditional role.

Finally, it was just a matter of time before investment companies (or investment trusts) would fall under regulation. In 1940 the Investment Company Act applied SEC registration and disclosure requirements to investment companies, made their investment policy changes subject to shareholder approval, and placed numerous restrictions on the participation of investment banking houses in investment company affairs. The act also restricted a mutual fund from placing more than 5 percent of its assets in the securities of any one issuer or purchasing more than 10 percent of a corporation's shares. The former provision helped ensure that the investment company would achieve portfolio diversification, and the latter prevented the investment company from having anything close to a controlling position in a corporation whose securities it had purchased. A long-term consequence of this further attenuation of the monitoring function of financial institutions over corporate managers was to diminish the affinity between the small shareholder and the ultimate object of his or her investment.

Taken as a whole, the financial reforms of 1933 to 1940 were the regulatory manifestation of the longstanding ideology opposed to concentrated power. Recall that when the Pujo investigators had pointed, in 1912–1913, to many of the same suspicious practices that would be aired again two decades later and prescribed specific legislative and structural

forms of redress, little was done to implement the recommendations. During the financial collapse and Great Depression of the 1930s, however, when forced to choose between the "evils" of high finance and big government, Americans opted for the latter. That this would be the case was evident in many statements made at the time, perhaps none so telling as that of Franklin Roosevelt, writing in 1933. "The real truth," he said, "is . . . that a financial element in the larger centers has owned the Government ever since the days of Andrew Jackson. . . . The country is going through a repetition of Jackson's fight with the Bank of the United States—only on a far bigger and broader basis." The problems addressed by the New Deal reformers, in other words, were old, familiar ones, rooted in the folklore of American politics. What had changed as a result of the economic and financial debacle of the Depression and of the exposure of fiduciary abuses in high places was the prospect of using the government to do something about them.

Thus in the 1930s, the lingering impulses of Pujo were finally translated into formal regulation in ways that exceeded anything contemplated up to that time by serious politicians. By the time the New Dealers were through, the institutions and markets of the nation's major private financial powers were embarrassed, divided up, controlled, and fundamentally altered. In the process of regulatory reform, however, the informational basis of capital market decision making was enlarged and made increasingly available to all investors by means of public disclosure of what had formerly been the privileged intelligence of corporate managers, bankers, and others to whom the managers and bankers had granted access. Two New Deal legacies—more fragmentation of finance and more information for investors—would pose new sets of problems for the capital markets and corporate boardrooms over the next half century.

TNEC AND ANTITRUST: WANING OF THE NEW DEAL FERVOR

In the wake of the New Deal reforms, the practices of investment bankers and big business in general continued to be subjected to governmental scrutiny. Political considerations were paramount in the continuing debate over the size and power of institutions in the private sector of the economy. In 1937–1938, a steep recession interrupted the economic recovery of Franklin Roosevelt's first term in office. Although later analyses of the 1937–1938 contraction established that government policies, especially the monetary policies of the Federal Reserve and the U.S. Treasury, were largely responsible for the decline, New Dealers laid the problem at the feet of big business and finance. It was they who had allegedly abused their monopoly powers to engineer the recession as a way to discredit the New Deal reforms and embarrass the administration. The president requested yet another investigation aimed at the "problem" of concentrated economic power. Congress established the Temporary National Economic Committee (TNEC), which for two years heard volumes of testimony on the structure and competitive practices of the nation's major industries.

Wall Street, possibly because it already had been thoroughly investigated and legislated into reform, received only a small part of the TNEC's attention. The brief investigation of investment banking rehashed old complaints about too much concentration in the field and debated the pros and cons of bankers serving on the boards of corporations whose securities they sold. On the other hand, the hearings devoted some discussion to what was now seen as a weakening of Wall Street's power, a consequence in part of the growing importance of "private placements" of security issues, by which a corporation could directly issue a security to insurance companies or other institutional buyers without going through the intermediation of investment bankers. Bankers argued that this development had resulted from inconveniences and risks created by SEC registration requirements; others deemed it to be evidence of the maturing of corporations who simply no longer needed banker sponsorship of their issues.

One issue aired during the TNEC investigation was that of the role of the "traditional" or "relationship" banker, the individual or institutional financier who had a longstanding relationship with a corporation, who served as its financial adviser, and who marketed the corporation's securities. This last function was normally carried out at negotiated rather than bid prices. New Deal critics viewed negotiated prices as just more evidence of abiding banker domination of corporations, of Wall Street's intractable hold over the nation's economic life. When critics argued that bankers were simply using their financial power to carve out spheres of influence by fixing prices, bankers reasoned that their relationships with their clients were the logical outcome of competition, reflecting their corporate customers' desire for stability, continuity, and responsibility. The traditional bankers, in other words, viewed their relationships with companies in much the same way a doctor might view the relationship with a patient, or an attorney with a client.

The TNEC did not settle the issue of negotiated versus competitive bids. The issue was to be debated until the Justice Department tried to settle it after World War II, when it instituted an antitrust suit against seventeen leading investment banks on charges of monopolization and conspiracy to restrain trade. The case, which was launched in 1947, droned on for six years, when Judge Harold Medina dismissed the government's charges for lack of evidence. The dismissal decisively "shattered the old myth of a Wall Street monopoly," as Vincent Carosso noted, and helped to transform the image of the investment banker into a more benign figure of authority. The entire case, moreover, had been remarkably irrelevant. By the 1950s, the investment banker wielded far less power in the nation's finances and economy than had been the case a generation earlier.

And yet, ancient and enduring suspicions about the power and privilege of Wall Street financiers would continue to hover in the ether of American ideology, only to manifest themselves again and again in the courts and in the political arena.

THE RISE OF INSTITUTIONAL INVESTORS

Public disclosure requirements vastly increased the amount of information available to capital market participants. Consider, again, the matter from the perspective of the heyday of financial capitalism, when managers and financiers kept tight control over financial information for business-strategic as well as self-interested reasons. In the more ruthlessly Darwinian business environment of the turn of the century, tight control of information could be seen to confer and protect crucial life-and-death advantages. On the other hand, who would buy the securities that corporations and bankers desired to sell if there was little or no basis for judging their worth? We have noted that financial capitalism's solution to the problem of asymmetric information—when the issuer and underwriter of securities knew much more about their worth than did the ultimate purchaser—was the integrity, the credibility, and the reputation of the intermediary. Why else were the senior Morgan partners, Jacob Schiff of Kuhn, Loeb, George F. Baker of First National, James Stillman of National City, and others like them around the turn of the century, the acknowledged titans of American finance? It was because they possessed and controlled the information relevant to their businesses. They used it, in most cases, according to the doctrine that they were working for the benefit of their clients, whether the clients were corporations issuing securities or investors who bought them.

The history of financial capitalism has in recent years inspired serious reevaluations of, as well as nostalgic longings for, the days of such paternalistic banking. It must be made clear, however, that Wall Street in the age of J. P. Morgan was hardly a democracy of money, and this is what so deeply disturbed basic American assumptions about power. Although the capital markets already had many more participants than the small group of financial titans and their usually well-to-do corporate and individual clients, small investors were left to speculate without much information. They could only try to figure out what those who controlled the information were planning or attempting to do, and then observe after the fact what the informed operators had done. This was at best second-order information, and most speculative information was of an even lower order. One might try, for example, to guess from what some speculators were doing the information they must have obtained or thought they had obtained from those who really controlled it.

Rising prosperity generated more interest and participation among ordinary citizens in the Wall Street markets. Still, most Americans saved and invested in simpler ways closer to home, for example in bank and thrift institution deposits.

Those investors who did enter the markets developed certain precepts or rules of investment applicable to a world of limited information on corporate affairs and in the absence of what later would be called security analysis. Government securities were the safest of all, because governments had powers to tax, as well as political and economic incentives, to maintain their credit. Corporate security values were best based, it was thought in the wisdom of that era, on tangible property values standing behind the securities. That is why the safest corporate securities were mortgage bonds secured by specific properties as collateral. Next came debentures based on the general credit of the enterprise. Then came preferred stocks with their set dividends and senior claims to common stock future net earnings if those dividends could not be paid. Lowest in the pecking order of investment values were common stocks, pure speculations on whatever residual earnings might be left to pay dividends or to be reinvested in the enterprise after bond, debenture, and preferred shareholders received their promised payments. This sort of analysis of common stock values inevitably led to charges

of stock watering when bankers and promoters merged and recapitalized corporations around the turn of the century.

In the 1920s, a more modern approach to investment values—one that looked more at earnings than assets—began to take firm root in the minds of investors. What had been grasped intuitively by some bankers was now being established more firmly in the literature. For example, after analyzing the limited historical records of stock prices, dividends, and corporate earnings that existed at the time, Edgar L. Smith, in a 1923 book and related articles, demonstrated that common stocks had generated greater long-term investment returns than bonds. This finding attracted considerable interest in the later 1920s, when it became clearer that corporate earnings indeed had the predicted strong relationship to dividends and stock prices.

During the 1930s the insight linking corporate earnings, dividends, and stock prices was refined to the theory, which remains generally accepted today, that a stock is worth the present discounted value of its future dividends (including its value when liquidated). Current and past earnings and dividends might therefore be relevant for estimates of future earnings and dividends, and offer some basis for the elusive problem of valuing common stocks. But, in the 1920s, as these ideas were first formulated and tested in limited ways, corporations still did not normally release information on their financial results. These informational shortcomings could foster fiduciary abuses, as the events of the later 1920s and early 1930s demonstrated.

It was only with the securities acts of the 1930s that the informational situation in capital markets was decisively altered, opening the door to a true democratization of the markets. By making more financial information available to everyone, a fundamental change occurred in the capital markets. Although far from perfect in application, the new reigning principle was that financial information, as it reflected the performance of public corporations, was no longer the domain of a small circle of bankers and their corporate clients. It was no longer reasonable to argue that bankers and corporations had a right to guard closely and control information pertinent to investment values based on Darwinian notions of competition and earned privilege.

Standardization in reporting also contributed to the democratization of information. Since the information to be made public was prescribed by the New Deal securities laws, monitored by a third-party regulatory agency (the SEC), and subjected to increasing regularization through standard accounting procedures, it could be made reliable and comparable across corporations. In response to the regulatory demand for increased information, the accounting profession mushroomed. In response to its availability, a new profession of securities analysis appeared. Retail brokerage firms—Merrill Lynch was the pioneer—employed securities analysts to prepare research reports on companies and security values for distribution at no charge to investors. Greater availability and reliability of information also led to the rating of securities by various criteria; such firms as Moody, and Standard and Poor were leaders in this field.

More important, institutional investors—insurance, investment, and trust companies as well as the newly emerging pension funds, which had diversification and economies-of-scale advantages in gathering and acting on information compared to individual investors—began to employ security analysts. And as the availability of information led institutions to increase their interest in common stock investments, the techniques for gathering information that their analysts employed over time became known generally. Scholarly and popular books on securities analysis and investment principles proliferated, as did formal and informal courses of study on these subjects. All of this reinforced the broader tendency toward democratization of the capital markets that was already underway.

Institutional investors, however, had to overcome restrictions that had been placed on their participation in the capital markets. Some were self-imposed. Traditionally, various types of banks, trust and insurance companies, pension funds (a relatively new institution in the 1930s), and investment companies had specialized in "safe and secure" bonds. This preference was often reinforced by the charters and laws under which they operated. For example, there were legal precepts and provisions preventing institutional investors from investing in stocks. For decades, state governments had been issuing legal investment lists for trustees and prohibiting certain kinds of stock investments by certain kinds of institutions, such as insurance companies. Such precepts and prohibitions were not controversial at the time they were developed. Given the limited information available and the obvious risks of investing in stocks as compared to bonds, no prudent investor of other people's money could justify putting very much of it into stocks. That, too, changed during and after the 1930s when more information on corporate finances and historical stock returns became available, when abusive stock exchange trading practices had been banned, and when interest rates and bond yields had sunk to all-time lows in American history, making stock investments relatively more attractive. By the early 1950s, trustees and institutions in state after state had sought, successfully in most instances, to broaden their allowable investments to include common stocks. By the 1960s, as stock market values continued to advance, the idea grew that it was imprudent for institutional and individual investors not to have at least some stocks in their asset portfolios.

During the prosperous post–World War II years the assets of financial institutions grew rapidly, and increasing proportions of these assets found their way into the stock market. The institutionalization of the market can be measured in different ways. Because of Glass-Steagall and other banking regulations, depository institutions have had a minimal role in the market; these institutions were and still are precluded from owning much, if any, corporate stock. The institutions that transformed U.S. equity markets after mid-century were nonbank, nondepository financial enterprises: life and general insurance companies, and especially private and public pension funds and open-end investment companies (mutual funds). Around 1950, these institutions held less than 20 percent of corporate equity, with the rest in the hands of U.S. households (mainly) and foreign owners. The institutional percentage rose to about 25 percent in the 1950s and remained around that level during the 1960s and 1970s, a period when soaring interest rates depressed stock prices. During the 1980s, the institutional percentage rose rapidly, reaching 37 percent in 1989. Preliminary estimates indicate that in the early 1990s the institutions, continuing the rapid pace of the 1980s, became the holders of roughly half of all corporate equity.

Within the main institutional categories, the changes in the portion of all corporate equity held from the start of the 1950s to the end of the 1980s were spectacular (see table 3). The greatest increase in institutional participation was in the pension funds, private and public, which owned only about 1 percent of all corporate equity in 1951 but about 25 percent of it in 1989. Next came the open-end mutual funds. The insurance companies over the four decades increased their share of total equity least; legal and regulatory restrictions on their stock investments, although somewhat relaxed, held back the insurance companies in comparison to the pension and mutual funds.

The increase in the institutional share of corporate equity in the 1950s and 1960s, from just under

Table 3. SHARE OF ALL CORPORATE EQUITY HELD BY MAJOR TYPES
OF FINANCIAL INSTITUTIONS

Year	Private Pension Funds	State and Local Government Pension Funds	Open-end Investment Companies	Life Insurance Companies	Other Insurance Companies	Totals
1951	0.8	0.0	1.7	1.3	2.3	6.1
1953	5.6	0.4	4.8	1.3	1.7	13.8
1989	17.4	7.4	6.2	3.2	2.6	36.8

SOURCES: Raymond W. Goldsmith, ed., *Institutional Investors and Corporate Stock* (1973); Board of Governors of the Federal Reserve System, *Annual Statistical Digest, 1989* (1991).

20 percent to about 25 percent, was not large compared to what happened after 1980. At the time, however, it began to strain the operating mechanisms of the stock exchanges. As can be seen in table 4, average daily trading volume on the New York Stock Exchange in 1960 was no greater than it had been in 1930, and in the interim it typically had been even lower. Between 1960 and 1965, average daily volume doubled, but even then the average trade was for only a little more than two round lots (100 shares). Then the impact of institutions became apparent. Between 1965 and 1970, the average trade almost doubled in size. More important was the increase in large-block trades, the mark of institutional participation, which soared from 3 percent of volume in 1965 to 15 percent in 1970.

By the late 1960s, these soaring trading volumes and the large-block trades of institutions swamped the capacity of even so august an institution as the New York Stock Exchange. At the time, the structure, rules, and operating procedures of the securities exchanges were throwbacks to an earlier era when individual rather than institutional trading dominated. For example, exchanges still relied on "paper" trades—that is, orders were entered, filled, and cleared by means of slips of paper. By the late 1960s, brokers were failing to settle on trades they had executed, and a number of them went bankrupt.

Congress came to the rescue in 1970 with legislation creating the Securities Investor Protection Corporation (SIPC), in order to insure customer funds placed with brokers in much the way that federal deposit insurance insured funds placed with banks. The SEC, in the meantime, was preparing its *Institutional Investor Study*. Completed in 1971, the study pointed out that many market difficulties were the result of the clash of increased institutional investment with anticompetitive exchange rules and practices, and it called for eliminating the latter.

The most conspicuous anticompetitive practice was the fixed-rate commission structure that the exchanges enforced on stock trading, which became

Table 4. VOLUME OF TRADING ON THE NEW YORK
STOCK EXCHANGE, 1900–1990

Year	Average Daily Share Volume, Millions	Average Shares Per Trade, Shares	Share of Large Block Trades, Percent
1900	0.5		
1910	0.6		
1920	0.8		
1930	3.0		
1940	4.0		
1950	2.0		
1960	3.0		
1965	6.2	224	3.1
1970	11.6	388	15.4
1975	18.6	495	16.6
1980	44.9	872	29.2
1985	109.2	1,878	51.7
1990	156.8	2,082	49.6

SOURCE: New York Stock Exchange, *Fact Book, 1991* (1991).

egregiously costly in the new world of institutional investment. Everyone knew that an order for 10,000 shares of a stock was not 100 times as costly to execute as a round lot of 100 shares, but the exchanges resisted changing the age-old fixed-commission arrangement until 1975 when the SEC, acting under pressure from the institutional investors, forced them to abandon the practice in favor of negotiated commissions driven by market forces. Congress endorsed the SEC's action in the Securities Reform Act of the same year, a measure that called for eliminating other anticompetitive practices and for moving toward a national market system of securities trading. These actions were highly stimulating to stock trading, and along with the replacement of paper trading by electronic trading they contributed directly to the huge equity trading volumes after 1975 in securities markets that were increasingly dominated by institutional investors and institutional trades.

AGENCY PROBLEMS IN MANAGERIAL CONTROL

In 1932, a lawyer, Adolf Berle, and an economist, Gardiner Means, collaborated on a seminal book, *The Modern Corporation and Private Property*. In it, the authors considered the implications of the progressive separation of ownership and control in large corporations. They observed that when the owners of an enterprise also managed and controlled it, their interest in maximizing their personal wealth and income was identical to the efficient management of the enterprise. But when ownership was separated from control, this identity of personal and business interests could easily disappear. "If we are to assume that the desire for *personal profit* is the prime force motivating control," Berle and Means wrote, "we must conclude that the interests of control are different from and often radically opposed to those of ownership; that the owners most emphatically will not be served by a profit-seeking controlling group. In the operation of the corporation, the controlling group even if they own a large block of stock, can serve their own pockets better by profiting at the expense of the company than by making profits for it." In short, the modern corporation presented what has come to be known as a principal-agent problem: the agents (the managers) may well have incentives to manage corporations opportunistically in their personal interests rather than in the interests of the principals (the owners). In the bygone world of financial capitalism, the solution to the principal-agent problem was to have bankers ensure that corporate managers were

acting in the interests of the creditors and the shareholders to whom the bankers had sold the corporation's securities. But by the 1970s, the bankers had long been in retreat and were unlikely to reassert their power.

The chief beneficiaries of this political reallocation of economic power, aside from the new bureaucrats in government who were charged with carrying out the reforms, were the corporate managers. They benefited from the resolution of a longstanding issue—a gray area in law and practice—concerning whether commercial banks could own corporate stock and possibly exercise some control over the corporations that issued it. The New Deal reforms decided the matter; they could not. Moreover, managerial power was enhanced by the legal fragmentation of banks and other financial institutions and by the fragmentation of the portfolios of institutional investors through explicit restrictions on how much and what kinds of corporate securities the institutions could own. There was a less explicit implication of the reforms that would be continually reiterated: financial institutions were not to gather, and certainly not to exercise, controlling interests in the corporations whose securities they might own.

The result of these written and unwritten rules in the post–World War II era was to free corporate managers from a traditional and potential source of monitoring and discipline—namely, large financial institutions that owned their securities. This created a wide berth for managerial opportunism. The countervailing forces that existed (including those of the revivified and newly organized mass labor movement) were certainly less focused and weaker than control based on financial power. And even within the corporate governance structure, where a board of directors in principle might exercise control by proxy, managers could coopt the process. Managers frequently made themselves directors and for all practical purposes appointed and compensated "outside" directors who often owned relatively little stock in the companies they were directing. Moreover, the size of modern corporations and the wide distribution of their stock militated against the formation of effective disgruntled stockholder coalitions and proxy wars. When such a contest did occur—the 1955 Montgomery Ward proxy war pitting chairman Sewell Avery against outsider Louis Wolfson, for example—it attracted attention mainly because it was an exception rather than the rule. Under such circumstances, stockholders of large corporations were left to express their dissatisfaction with management by selling their shares. Only if large numbers of them

Table 5.   INDIVIDUAL SHAREHOLDERS, 1930–1985

Year	Number, Millions	Percent of Population
1930	9–11	7.3–8.9
1947	5.4	3.7
1965	20.1	10.3
1975	25.3	11.9
1985	47.0	20.2

SOURCE: James Burk, *Values in the Marketplace* (1988).

did so in concert would the share price be likely to fall to the point where outside investors would have incentives to take over a corporation and install more effective managers. But even this simple mechanism had been blunted by the New Deal reforms that had further fragmented financial institutions and then restricted them from taking controlling positions in corporations.

Despite the restrictions, financial institutions began to grow by leaps and bounds during the post–World War II era, all the while increasing their holdings of corporate stock. Increased disclosure of corporate information had made stock ownership more attractive to institutions as well as to individuals. Individual participation in the equity markets nearly trebled between World War II and the mid-1960s and more than doubled again in the next twenty years (see table 5). And in any case, during the first two postwar decades (roughly 1945 to 1965), there was little concern in the markets about corporate mismanagement and little notice of the potential for self-aggrandizing behavior by corporate executives. The robust performance of the American economy, which was reflected in the rapidly rising value of corporate equity, redounded to the favor of corporate managers, who were held in high public esteem. This was the era of the Organization Man triumphant, the quiet hero of the "Golden Age" of American corporate enterprise. Other leading industrial economies, those of America's allies as well as its former enemies, had been crippled for so long by depression and war that to get back on their feet they needed what the United States alone had in abundance: capital, technology, and managerial expertise. But as their economies—particularly those of Western Europe and Japan—gradually recovered, chinks in the armor of seemingly invincible American corporations became all too evident.

Serious problems of managerial opportunism became glaringly obvious in the "conglomerate" movement of the 1960s—the third merger wave in American history. A new hybrid strain of corporate financial manager made end runs around antitrust regulations by engineering mergers and acquisitions of companies in unrelated industries. Such mergers were justified on grounds of diversification, synergy, and economies of scope, and some did achieve results in accordance with those precepts. But too much of the activity involved little more than attempts to realize profits through tax loopholes and accounting games. The exploitation of cash flows to build corporate empires that often made no structural sense also "justified" larger managerial salaries and perquisites. This, in turn, helped fuel a long spiral of increases in executive compensation throughout the corporate economy. When many of the more spectacular diversified corporate combines that were created between 1968 and 1972 went awry, because they were either overleveraged or impossible to administer efficiently, they had to be undone piecemeal or wholesale in later years. The problems created by all the restructuring (which often diverted funds from more productive uses) would look even worse when the managers of the nation's "center corporations" were challenged by more efficient global competitors in the late 1970s and 1980s. By the 1980s, American executives came under fire for having underinvested in new technologies, for having failed to address needed labor reforms, and for having ignored their customers' concerns about the cost and quality of goods and services.

In the wake of—and not altogether unrelated to—problems arising from corporate merger activity, the federal government moved to protect the pension rights of corporate employees. Not all the growing pension obligations of corporations were fully funded, and if a corporation were to become bankrupt, the unfunded liabilities—or at least part of them—might never be paid. Responding to this concern, Congress enacted the Employee Retirement Income Security Act (ERISA) of 1974. Under ERISA's terms, the government established the Pension Benefit Guaranty Corporation as an insurer of unfunded pension liabilities in corporate-sponsored plans. In return for assuming this obligation, ERISA laid down precepts for pension fund management that called for wide diversification of portfolios to preserve principal and minimize the risks of large losses.

In responding to problems, actual and potential, arising from the increasing importance of private pension funds, ERISA provided a firmer foundation for their continued growth, which turned out to be spectacular. But the investment precepts that came with ERISA reflected the durable American ideology of financial fragmentation, the belief that financial institutions should not be allowed to exert control over nonfinancial businesses. Yet even without ERISA's provisions, this would not have been much of a threat so long as corporate executives continued to oversee the managers of their pension funds. These executives naturally took a dim view of any pension fund activism that exerted pressure on corporate managers in the name of stockholders' rights.

Two basic trends that flowed out of the New Deal reforms were by now on a collision course. Regulatory reinforcement of the fragmentation of American financial institutions had served, on the one hand, to enhance the independence of corporate management. At the same time, regulations that had required corporations and intermediaries to provide more financial and operating information for anyone who was interested had promoted a progressively broader participation in the equity markets. This occurred both through more direct investments by individuals and, increasingly, through indirect individual participation in such institutional stockholders as pension and mutual funds. Nonbank financial institutions, which possessed comparative advantages in gathering, processing, and using this information, were the prime beneficiaries. The tension between these two legacies of the New Deal reforms—the enhancement of corporate managerial independence and the increased powers of institutionalized finance (which now represented the interests of ever growing numbers of Americans)—was moving toward the breaking point.

FINANCIAL CAPITALISM RESURGENT?

At the start of the 1980s, indices of American stock prices were at levels not much different from those of the mid 1960s. Many factors contributed to this dismal performance. On the macroeconomic level, the cumulative social and economic costs of the Great Society and the Vietnam War were enormous, furnishing evidence that the reach of American policymakers greatly exceeded their grasp. By the mid 1970s, the nation was beset by rampant inflation, soaring interest rates, the political scandals of Watergate, and the first of two oil price shocks. Governmental finances were complicated by a rising national debt, as defense and social welfare expenditures outpaced even inflation-driven increases in tax revenues. Americans demanded ever more services from government, but also opposed its growth and the tax increases to support it. After the Bretton Woods international fixed-exchange-rate monetary system put in place at the end of World War II collapsed in

1971, the international value of the dollar fell. To make matters worse, government policies toward business, which had been largely dictated by the geopolitical requirements of the Cold War, ignored or in some cases badly distorted the progress of investment and innovation in the economy's center industries.

At the microeconomic level, increasing competition from abroad for American domestic as well as overseas markets had dislocating effects on the country's major manufacturing industries, in which many corporations suffered from chronic mismanagement. The cumulative effects of executive timidity, underinvestment in innovation, wasteful empire-building, and inefficient administration severely damaged such key American industries as autos, steel, and consumer electronics. Market shares eroded—in some cases vanished—under the onslaught of better-managed foreign firms. Institutional investors—banks, insurance companies, mutual and pension funds, and other pools of capital—likewise suffered from the lower returns that reflected the problems of American industry. Although these institutions, representing ever more people, collectively financed and owned a growing proportion of corporate America, they remained so fragmented by regulatory legacies that few thought they could do much directly to influence or discipline underperforming managers.

Or could they? The long-depressed stock markets of the early 1980s featured many bargains in corporate assets. Once exposed, gaps between actual and potential corporate values provided incentives for financial entrepreneurs to find ways of closing them. Recognition of such gaps also gave ambitious corporate managers incentives to buy up all or parts of their firms from the absentee owner-shareholders. With greater ownership stakes, the managers could then strive to improve returns on these assets and hence improve their market value. In too many cases, however, managers simply used excess cash to build empires through acquisitions that were often ill-conceived or unrelated to their ability to manage them, instead of investing in new productive facilities or paying out more dividends to shareholders.

The result of all this activity was a new merger wave—the fourth in American history. This one involved a remarkable variety of transactions, ranging from cross-company acquisitions to internal management buyouts, to a variety of deals, both friendly and hostile, led by third parties. What generally characterized the 1980s merger wave was its extraordinary use of debt financing to acquire, restructure, and often dismantle corporate assets. Over the course of the decade, the number of mergers and acquisitions approached 30,000, with a total value well in excess of $1 trillion. The annual number of deals peaked at more than 4,000 in 1986, and 1988 was the peak year in total value—$227 billion. Between 1980 and 1988, 178 deals of more than $1 billion each were consummated, peaking at 42 such deals in 1988. That was the year of the largest single transaction in modern corporate history. The $24.7 billion leveraged buyout of RJR–Nabisco by an investor group organized by Kohlberg Kravis Roberts & Company (KKR) upset the conventional wisdom that some companies, no matter how poorly valued, were simply too big to be taken over.

Perhaps the single most important financial innovation in this period was the leveraged buyout (LBO), perfected by specialized financial firms such as KKR, Forstmann-Little, Clayton & Dubilier, and Gibbons, Green, and van Amerongen. A typical LBO operation was made up of (1) a general partner who sponsored and supervised the LBO (these, firms such as KKR, were the entrepreneurs of the process); (2) the limited partners who provided the equity capital to finance the LBO transaction (typically a group of institutional investors); and (3) the LBO management team, persons who might or might not have been managers of the bought-out properties, but who usually held large equity stakes in them after the restructuring. By borrowing most of the money to finance buyouts, these three parties to the LBO operation stood to make handsome returns on their highly leveraged equity investments. Most of the buyout firms were new to Wall Street—KKR, for instance, was organized in 1976 after its founding partners had first pioneered in LBO financings at the Wall Street firm of Bear, Stearns. Their important entrepreneurial achievement was to mobilize the huge but fragmented pools of capital held by institutional investors to accomplish what these institutions themselves were precluded from doing on their own by laws and regulations.

In addition to new organizations, new methods of financing also emerged. In the 1970s, at the investment house of Drexel, Burnham, Lambert, a young bond trader named Michael Milken pioneered new applications for low-rated, high-yield securities. A Wharton MBA, Milken had discovered what others in the financial community had overlooked in the academic literature, particularly in W. Braddock Hickman's 1958 study *Corporate Bond Quality and Investor Experience*. Hickman's findings were simply that investors who bought "low-quality," high-yielding bonds during the first half of the century had

earned returns that more than compensated for the higher risks they assumed when they bought such securities in preference to higher-rated issues. To sell these so-called junk bonds, which he had first used to finance poorly rated entrepreneurial firms, Milken assembled what would become a powerful distribution network. He accomplished this by convincing others of the validity of Hickman's conclusions while picking good targets for investment. Soon he established a loyal following of smaller insurance companies and mutual funds that were hungry for alternatives to the low stock market returns of the 1970s. He later brought in some savings and loan institutions (S&Ls), whose fundraising and investment options had been widened by deregulation in 1980 and 1982. As a result of rising interest rates and heavy losses of savings deposits to the new money-market funds, many of the S&Ls jumped at this newly available opportunity to earn higher investment returns than their mortgage portfolios allowed.

By the mid-1980s, Milken had shifted his strategy from one of primarily financing undercapitalized firms to one that provided junk bond leveraging for larger-scale corporate takeovers. Other firms—including such established houses as the giant brokerage house of Merrill Lynch and the bond-trading house of Salomon Brothers—set up their own junk-bond operations, so that corporate raiders, ambitious managers, and LBO firms alike could now mobilize debt capital quickly and on an unprecedented scale.

In the meantime, the corporate raider had become a fixture in the American economy. Raiders such as T. Boone Pickens, Carl Icahn, and James Goldsmith were initially little-known, self-made, financial opportunists who ferreted out "undervalued" target companies, lined up debt financing, and then made tender offers that existing shareholders found difficult to refuse. They themselves were not managers and perhaps had no desire even to be owners. Their game was often no more than to accumulate threatening positions in a target company's stock in order to extract "greenmail" from terrified executives who would surely lose their jobs in a successful takeover. This happened when boards of directors that were captive to sitting managers agreed to buy back raiders' shares at premiums thinly disguised as "fees for services."

Corporate executives and their captive boards soon devised new methods for fending off hostile takeovers. The most famous was the "poison pill," a generic term for any plan under which a company threatened by a takeover could increase its outstanding shares and sell them to "old" shareholders at a "concessionary price." Raiders were intentionally excluded from these ownership-diluting bargains. The poison pill reversed the discrimination in the pricing of stock that the raiders had been seeking, and accordingly it raised the costs of a takeover bid. Key executives also persuaded their boards to grant them "golden parachutes," handsome payments should they be unseated in a takeover. The justification was that golden parachutes would make managers more objective in their consideration of tender offers, which would work to the benefit of the shareholders. Others, however, saw nothing more in these schemes than artificial increases in the costs of buying and selling companies. As more management time and corporate resources went into devising ways to fend off hostile takeovers, the raiders countered by arguing that their activities rendered society a service. One of them, Carl Icahn, wrote in the Sunday *New York Times Magazine* in January 1989 that takeovers were the cure "for a disease that is destroying American productivity: gross and widespread incompetent management." The role of the raider, he said, was "to unseat corporate bureaucracies, control runaway costs and make America competitive again."

By the early 1990s, academicians and stock analysts agreed that the changes of the 1980s in many cases did create more efficient companies and did prod managers to higher performance in virtually every sector of the private economy. It is nonetheless difficult to sort out the degree to which better corporate performance was caused or inspired by the management buyouts and hostile takeovers of that decade. Other factors, such as foreign competition, new technology transfer, and generational changes in management, also played a part. Numerous studies, including those done at the Federal Reserve, supported the view that the restructurings of the takeover boom were beneficial to the economy, but the extent of the gain was still not clear. In a 1991 study, Michael Jensen, an academic proponent of the restructurings, estimated the value they created for bought-out shareholders, from 1976 to 1990, at $650 billion, or more than a third of the $1.8 trillion value of the transactions. On the other hand, the general level of stock prices roughly tripled over the same period, so perhaps only an undetermined fraction of these gains could be attributed to restructuring activities. Since not all of the restructurings were successful, the gains of bought-out shareholders were offset to an extent—perhaps 5 to 10 percent—by losses from high-yield bond defaults and those of other creditors.

In purely financial terms, many of the corporate restructurings were spectacular in recouping corporate values that had been lost by inefficient management and in creating new shareholder wealth. The 1985 LBO of the unwieldy conglomerate Beatrice, for instance, recouped about $1 billion of shareholder value after KKR took over the company and broke it up into operations that could stand better on their own. The gigantic 1988 LBO of RJR–Nabisco was estimated just three years later to have added $17 billion to the wealth of the investors who both sold and bought it, while improving the overall operating performance of the company. Prebuyout shareholders alone reaped capital gains of more than $13 billion from the deal.

Key to the long-term success of buyout firms was their ability to make positive contributions to corporate policies, strategies, and operations. Their rewards came not only from the fees and capital gains generated by the deals themselves but also from the further, long-term gains realized from improved performance of the restructured companies. These gains came when the buyout partners got to know their businesses well enough to make sound resource allocation decisions, to install and promote better executive managers, and then to keep a watchful eye on their performance. Gains would also arise if the buyout specialists ensured that executive managers themselves held enough equity in the businesses to have a direct financial stake in improved performance. This meant, among other things, that managers of mature businesses would have to demonstrate their ability to take the sometimes counterintuitive step of shrinking, rather than growing, their companies into better health. They would often have to be willing to abandon comfortable strategies and methods that had served American business in the past in order to compete in a radically changing environment. At least one buyout firm, Kelso & Company, which pioneered the Employee Stock Ownership Plan (ESOP) in the 1970s, subsequently established an investment partnership that actually imposed a new operating regimen, "demand flow manufacturing," on many of the companies it financed. In these ways, LBO restructurings served to restore in many corporations a mode of financial capitalism the likes of which had not been seen since Morgan's era before World War I.

Still, as in all merger waves, there were the inevitable problems and abuses that went far beyond the dubious greenmail tactics of the corporate raiders. Many companies saw their stock prices manipulated by outright fraud. And the leveraging of corporate capital ran on to excess. Good firms had their businesses disrupted, even destroyed, in the wake of overpriced buyouts that served only to enrich exiting stockholders and those who arranged the deals. Not all buyout firms were as skilled as KKR at packaging deals and then reforming companies. Not all junk-bond financiers proved as deft at identifying good investment prospects as Milken's Drexel operation, which enjoyed fantastic success but also slipped into some bad errors of judgment and integrity as time went on. The employees and community stakeholders of bought-out companies that later went into default on their bonds—as happened with the buyouts of the drug chain Revco, the convenience-store franchiser Southland, and the trucking firm Fruehauf—were certainly worse off after the deals than they had been before. And raider Carl Icahn eventually proved that he could not manage an airline any better than his predecessors at TWA, once he had taken over that company. In 1989, Gibbons, Green, and its financier, First Boston, failed to find takers for bonds on a $450 million bridge loan after a successful but overpriced bid for the sprawling empire of the Ohio Mattress Company. Robert Campeau's miscalculated purchases of retailers Federated Department Stores and Allied Stores slipped into bankruptcy when operating performance was insufficient to service the debt interest. And UAL's (United Airlines) $6.75 billion employee-led buyout failed to win backing, after poor structuring of the deal by its banks. By the end of 1989, Milken had been indicted and the once-soaring junk-bond market slipped into depression. The takeover boom had come to an end.

By then, even the more successful deals were coming under widespread criticism. The dislocations caused by takeovers and restructurings, along with mounting evidence of fraud in the financial markets, brought politics roaring back into the financial arena and reignited old ideological passions. Even earlier, a political outcome was that corporate managers who felt threatened by the prospects of takeover activity were able successfully to lobby state legislatures to enact more stringent antitakeover laws than those that dated back to the Williams Act of 1968 (see table 2). Deeply rooted American suspicions of Wall Street's financial power made such appeals plausible and even welcome.

The American public in the meantime was deluged by an outpouring of newspaper and magazine articles, books, movies, television documentaries, even plays that depicted financiers as money-grubbing, antisocial brats. A new generation of muckraking best-sellers—with titles such as *The Predators' Ball, Barbarians at the Gate, The Money Machine,* and

Den of Thieves—reflected the prevailing attitude. Such fictional characters as novelist Tom Wolfe's rich but feckless bond trader, Sherman McCoy, who proved that he could not function in the "real world" of common people, and the manipulative financier, Gordon Gekko, who announced "Greed is good" in the movie *Wall Street,* gave sharp definition to the images that financiers evoked in the minds of most Americans.

Life imitated art, as federal court dockets were filled with cases charging greed and corruption by investment bankers and their clients. A Wall Street icon, Ivan Boesky, and a rising star, Martin Siegel, were convicted of insider trading, and the spectacular career of Michael Milken was cut short after his conviction on charges of securities fraud and stock manipulation. It all seemed to prove that even the wealthiest financiers could not be trusted. Enhanced by modern mass media technologies, the real and fictional exposés revealed the 1980s to be a "Bonfire of the Vanities," to use Tom Wolfe's title for the era. But this was just a reprise of an old song. The vilification of financiers and Wall Street embodied historically familiar themes, echoed and reechoed from the time of the American Revolution through the eras of Biddle and Jackson, Morgan and Pujo, and Mitchell and Roosevelt.

Doubts about the soundness of the financial system were abetted by the spectacular crash of stock prices in October 1987 and by the minicrash two years later. Massive losses incurred by federally insured S&Ls during the 1980s added fuel to the bonfire, leaving taxpayers to cover the government-insured losses at the end of the decade. To be sure, any ill effects of corporate restructurings and the "S&L debacle" were only dimly related. The S&L problem was mostly one of real-estate loan defaults, largely the result of mismatched assets and liabilities in the inflationary environment of the 1970s and then exacerbated by badly planned deregulation in the 1980s. But a number of S&Ls had bought junk bonds, so their problems and Wall Street's were linked in the public mind.

Once again, the government applied the brakes to what had been an accelerating trend toward deregulation in the capital markets. Since the 1970s, major commercial banking institutions, Citicorp and Chase Manhattan Bank, for example, had made some progress in obtaining relaxations of Glass-Steagall's rigid barriers between investment and commercial banking. In 1991, the U.S. Treasury unveiled a plan for "Modernizing the Financial System" along lines that would encourage the developing attempts of large banks and other financial firms to re-create the pre-1930s-style full-service, "financial department stores." These efforts got nowhere that year in Congress. Attempts by Salomon Brothers to rig bids in the U.S. government bond market also helped to shelve plans for further liberalization of banking and securities market regulations. For Wall Street, however, none of these developments, adverse though they were, came anywhere close to the debacle it had suffered during the 1930s. Events suggested, if anything, that the power of financial capitalism was on the increase. Consider the dramatic change that took place in the first three years of the 1990s. Throughout the 1980s, there were few attempts by institutional investors to exercise influence over the policies of corporate managers. Those great intermediary institutions—the pension and mutual funds—did little to represent the interests of the owners of corporate stocks. They did not debate management decisions or seek seats on corporate boards, and they refrained from actively monitoring corporate managers' performance. By 1993, however, institutional activism was directly responsible for instigating reforms in the nation's largest companies. Pressure from institutional shareholders led to the ousters of chief executives at General Motors, IBM, and American Express, each one a company in need of reform, each one a traditional bastion of managerial control. Corporate boards began to take more seriously the concerns of their institutional investors, who in turn found it profitable, over the long run, to behave more like owners than mere holders of stock. Without threats of corporate raids or buyouts, institutional shareholders finally began to show corporate managements that they could exercise the latent prerogatives of dissatisfied owners who wanted to keep, not sell, their companies. An overriding lesson of the 1980s merger wave was that the owners of capital through their representatives, financial intermediaries, could once again have a positive, disciplinary role to play in corporate performance.

THE FUTURE

Financial capitalism, once thought to be dead, reasserted itself in the American corporate economy of the 1980s and 1990s. Whether this development will prove to be more than a temporary aberration is uncertain. Will the central capital market community identified with Wall Street be forced again to retreat, as after Pujo, or be beaten down and reined in, as during the New Deal? Will there be another passage of decades until a new opportunity arises for it to reassert the creative-destructive powers of finance in economic affairs? Will American financial history continue to repeat itself, or at least continue, in Mark Twain's words, to rhyme?

Clearly the issues raised by this historical survey merit more study and debate. A lingering hostility to concentrated financial power has been present in the United States from the outset, suggesting that more repetition, more rhyming, lies ahead. But there are also reasons to doubt that this pattern will continue, or at least that it should continue. Looking back, we can see that the role and impact of American financiers and financial institutions evolved substantially from their primitive beginnings after the Revolution to the time of J. P. Morgan and the high tide of financial capitalism. They changed even more rapidly by the time of Charles Mitchell and the New Deal and transformed themselves even more radically from the 1930s to the modern era of Michael Milken, KKR, and Salomon Brothers. Putting it that way might suggest that capital markets have changed for the worse, but in more fundamental ways they have clearly changed for the better.

Today more financial information is available more readily than ever to all capital market participants. Computer and telecommunications technologies provide open and speedy access to the capital markets, liberating trading in securities from traditional constraints of time and place. Methods of interpreting and using financial information have improved so much that some of the methodologists have even won Nobel Prizes for their work. There has, in other words, been a distinct trend favoring increased dissemination of financial information and a broadening sophistication in its use by masses of investors. This has happened because of the more general trend toward democratization of finance and financial institutions. As a result of these developments there is a stark contrast between J. Pierpont Morgan's financial world at the turn of the century and that of the present day. Although Morgan evokes considerable nostalgia among historians and practitioners of finance alike, it is important to remember that he (and others like him) wielded great financial power by virtue of privileged access to information. By keeping the information to himself and his partners, Morgan used it in sometimes stupendous and mystifying ways for the benefit of a limited number of large corporations and wealthy investors. How suspicious it all must have seemed to the mass of people and their representatives in political life!

Thanks to increasingly strict disclosure rules, modern institutional as well as individual investors have relatively free access to the sorts of financial and corporate information that were once considered privileged data by privileged bankers. No longer, for instance, can even acquisitions of more than 5 percent of a corporation's stock be made without full public disclosure. Thanks to disclosure and other rules regulating their businesses, institutional investors have to keep both their clients and the regulators well informed about their activities, investment policies, and financial results.

And who, after all, are the clients of these institutions, the banks and trust companies, the insurance companies, the mutual funds, and the pension funds? Thanks to the growth and wider distribution of wealth, and to the progressive democratization of finance, the clients are now proportionally more people than ever before. And the financial institutions that intermediate individual and household investments are also more diverse and numerous than before. Indeed, political and social presumptions about finance have been so altered since the turn of the century that everyone is now entitled, at least in law and in theory, to equal access to financial information. Any attempt to "corner information," any privileged use of information on an "insider" basis, is necessarily illegal or unethical, or both. The implications of these changes are historically profound.

These new circumstances challenge the ideological presumption that financial institutions should be fragmented. They likewise challenge the presumption that financiers—now institutions more than individuals—should be prevented from exerting control over the managements of corporations whose securities they hold and manage in the interests of their client-investors. The laws and regulations that implement these presumptions foster the tendency of corporate executives to deploy assets belonging to others for their own personal goals. If financial capitalism has now evolved toward what has been called "pension fund socialism," in which the masses are coming to own the means of production, should financial regulation continue to advance the separation of ownership and control in the corporate sector? Or should it be altered in the direction of bringing ownership and control closer together? In an increasingly global economy should American capital markets continue to operate under regulatory controls that enforce fragmentation of institutional structures while most major industrial countries operate under lesser constraints? If the informational practices of other countries—which are now generally less open than American standards—begin to converge with those of the United States, a likely result would be that U.S. financial institutions would lose global and even domestic market shares. By failing to adjust old ideologies and regulations to new realities of a global marketplace, the United States could be in danger of converting one of its historical competitive advantages—efficient capital markets of great breadth and depth—into a competitive liability.

However the questions may be answered in time, one thing is certain for the near-term future. The abiding influences of American culture, as they are reflected in power-averse ideologies and fragmented political structures, will continue to influence the course of development of domestic and, by extension, global capital markets for some time to come.

SEE ALSO Taxation; Economic Policies; Economic Performance (all in this volume).

BIBLIOGRAPHY

Basic scholarly surveys of the twentieth-century history of American banking and other financial intermediaries are Fritz Redlich, *The Molding of American Banking: Men and Ideas* (1947, 1951); Herman E. Krooss and Martin R. Blyn, *A History of Financial Intermediaries* (1971); Vincent P. Carosso, *Investment Banking in America* (1970); and the lively though somewhat skewed popular history by James Grant, *Money of the Mind: Borrowing and Lending in America from the Civil War to Michael Milken* (1992). For the nineteenth-century background, see Richard Sylla, *The American Capital Market, 1846–1914* (1975); and Bray Hammond, *Banks and Politics in America: From the Revolution to the Civil War* (1957).

These surveys can be rewardingly supplemented by such older works as Arthur Dewing, *Corporate Promotion and Reorganizations* (1924); Louis Brandeis's famous polemic, *Other People's Money and How the Bankers Use It* (1914); and Adolph Berle and Gardiner Means, *The Modern Corporation and Private Property* (1932), the classic analysis of the progressive separation of ownership and control in American business. For an update on the same theme, see Michael C. Jensen, "Corporate Control and the Politics of Finance," *Journal of Applied Corporate Finance* 4 (Summer 1991): 13; George P. Baker, "Beatrice: A Study in the Creation and Destruction of Value," *Journal of Finance* 47 (July 1992): 1081–1119; and Allen Kaufman and Ernest Englander, "Kohlberg Kravis Roberts & Co. and the Challenge to Managerial Capitalism," *Business and Economic History* 2d ser., 21 (1992): 97.

On information problems, see Jonathan Barron Baskin, "The Development of Corporate Financial Markets in Britain and the United States, 1600–1914: Overcoming Asymmetric Information," *Business History Review* 62 (Summer 1968): 199–237; J. Bradford DeLong, "Did J. P. Morgan's Men Add Value? An Economist's Perspective on Financial Capitalism," in Peter Temin, ed., *Inside the Business Enterprise: Historical Perspectives on the Use of Information* (1991); David F. Hawkins, "The Development of Modern Financial Reporting Practices among American Manufacturing Corporations," *Business History Review* 37 (Autumn 1963): 145–162; and a government study by the Office of Technology Assessment, U.S. Congress, *Electronic Bulls and Bears: U.S. Securities Markets and Information Technology* (1990).

Useful works on regulation are the collection of essays in Samuel L. Hayes, III, ed., *Wall Street and Regulation* (1987); James Burk, *Values in the Market Place: The Stock Market under Federal Securities Law* (1988), which contains a wealth of statistical data; and Joel Seligman, *The Transformation of Wall Street: The History of the Securities and Exchange Commission and Modern Corporate Finance* (1982). Combining analysis of legal and regulatory developments with larger ideological issues are Thomas C. McCraw, *Prophets of Regulation: Charles Francis Adams, Louis D. Brandeis, James A. Landis and Alfred E. Kahn* (1984); Mark J. Roe, "Political and Legal Constraints on Ownership and Control of Public Companies," *Journal of Financial Economics* 27 (1990): 7–41; and, by the same author, "A Political Theory of American Corporate Finance," *Columbia Law Review* 91 (January 1991): 10–67.

For the economic and social background of the New Deal reforms, see John Kenneth Galbraith, *The Great Crash* (1972); Eugene N. White, *The Regulation and Reform of the American Banking System, 1900–1929* (1983); Gary M. Walton, *Regulatory Change in an Atmosphere of Crisis* (1979); and John Brooks, *Once in Golconda: A True Drama of Wall Street, 1920–1938* (1969).

Good specialized works on aspects of capital market developments include Thomas R. Navin and Marian V. Sears, "The Rise of a Market for Industrial Securities, 1887–1902," *Business History Review* 29 (Summer 1995): 105; Samuel L. Hayes, III, A. Michael Spence, and David Van Praag Marks, *Competition in the Investment Banking Industry* (1983), ch. 1; and Ralph L. Nelson, *Merger Movements in American Industry: 1895–1956* (1959).

Histories of particular institutions that place the firms in their broader contexts are Ronald Chernow's expansive *The House of Morgan* (1991), which includes excellent biographical material on George Peabody and three generations of Morgans from Junius to J. P., Jr.; Robert Sobel's lively histories, *The Big Board: A History of the New York Stock Market* (1965) and *The Life and Times of Dillon Read* (1991); Vincent P. Carosso, *More than a Century of Investment Banking: The Kidder, Peabody & Co. Story* (1974); and Harold van B. Cleveland and Thomas Huertas, *Citibank, 1812–1970* (1985).

Useful biographies of bankers include Frederick Lewis Allen, *The Great Pierpont Morgan* (1949); Cyrus Adler, *Jacob H. Schiff: His Life and Letters*, 2 vols. (1929); and the essays on Morgan and E. H. Harriman in Jonathan Hughes, *The Vital Few: The Entrepreneur & American Economic Progress*, 2d ed. (1986).

FOREIGN TRADE AND FOREIGN INVESTMENT

Mira Wilkins

In 1900 the United States was an economic giant in the international arena; its industrial output was greater than that of any other nation. U.S. foreign trade (exports plus imports) was in dollar volume second only to that of Great Britain, the most important trading country; since 1894 the United States had been a net exporter of goods each year. During most of the twentieth century, the United States continued (in dollar volume of commerce) to rank among the world's foremost trading nations. It remained a net exporter of goods every year from 1900 to 1970, but, with the exception of two years, was transformed into a net importer of goods from 1971 onward.

Until World War I, the nation was a net debtor in international accounts; that is, foreigners had larger investments in the United States than U.S. residents had abroad. The United States attracted more foreign capital than any other single country, making it the world's premier debtor nation. That status changed dramatically during World War I, from which the United States emerged as a significant creditor. It continued as a net creditor in international accounts—with foreigners owing more to Americans than Americans owed to foreigners—until the late 1980s, when once more the United States became a debtor nation. By the early 1990s the country had returned to its pre–World War I position as the world's greatest debtor nation.

The composition of U.S. trade changed over the course of the twentieth century. In 1900 the country was a net exporter of agricultural products; this persisted until 1921 (with the exception of two years). During the interwar period and on to 1955, the United States was generally an importer of agricultural products. After 1960, the balance was once again reversed, and the United States became a regular net exporter of agricultural commodities. From 1900 to 1937 (one year excluded), raw cotton was the nation's largest single export. From 1900 to 1924 (five years aside), the country's largest single import was sugar. Not until the 1960s did wheat and then corn and soybeans far exceed raw cotton as the nation's most prominent agricultural exports. (During the 1970s and 1980s, corn, soybeans, and wheat jockeyed for first place.) Regarding nonprecious mineral resources, the United States was a net exporter during most years of the first four decades of the century; subsequently, it was a net importer.

Throughout the twentieth century, U.S. international trade in manufactured goods (including processed food, intermediate products, and finished manufactures) surpassed U.S. trade in crude raw materials and unprocessed food. While the latter two categories constituted 41 percent of merchandise exports and 48 percent of imports in 1900, both percentages dropped during the course of the century. By 1970 these primary commodities represented only 17 percent of merchandise exports and 17 percent of imports. While the pattern of imports changed in the next decades (with the sizable crude oil imports in the 1970s), the percentages of crude raw materials and food in American trade followed a declining trend (for example, in 1990 the share was down to 13 percent for merchandise exports and 17 percent for imports). The growing importance of manufactured products in trade was highlighted in 1938 when, by value, "machinery" replaced raw cotton as the country's single largest export. In 1990, machinery was still the single greatest export, although the product mix under that rubric had changed significantly, reflecting developments in U.S. technology. Key imports have also varied over the decades: sugar never regained first place after 1924; crude rubber ranked at the top for several years, to be replaced from 1928 to 1938 by forest products, principally paper and pulp from Canada; for most years, coffee led from 1945 to 1956. From 1957 onward, petroleum and petroleum products—largely crude oil but some refined petroleum products as well—assumed major importance as imports (automotive imports did exceed oil imports from 1967 to 1973). With high oil prices in the 1970s, petroleum and petroleum products ranked supreme, reaching about 32 percent of all U.S. imports in 1980. After 1985 automotive imports overtook petroleum and petroleum products, and the country had become a sizable importer of capital goods. Indeed, gradually from the 1960s on, America became a major importer of a truly broad range of manufactured products that in the past the country had exported.

Merchandise trade figures exclude service-sector, or "invisible," commerce. Invisibles comprise transportation, travel, insurance, and the return on intangible assets; the definition often also includes the income on U.S. investments abroad and on foreign investments in the United States. Using this broader classification, in 1900 the United States had a negative balance in service-sector trade—a balance that was offset by the positive merchandise trade balance. By contrast, since 1971 the U.S. deficit in the merchandise trade balance has been reduced by the favorable balance in the service-sector trade. U.S. service-sector exports have become relatively more important over the course of the century.

The direction of U.S. trade has also shifted. In 1900, the United Kingdom was the country's foremost trading partner in both merchandise exports and imports. With a few exceptional years, Britain held first place as the destination for U.S. exports, until 1945. In 1946, Canada replaced the United Kingdom to become the preeminent market for U.S. exports—and it remained so in the early 1990s. By 1961, Japan had surpassed the United Kingdom, assuming second place as a recipient of American exports.

As a source for U.S. merchandise imports, Britain was in premier rank only through 1916. America's imports from Canada surpassed those from the United Kingdom in 1917, and Canada held first place until 1985, when Japanese merchandise imports into the United States pushed Canada into second place; Canada resumed its first-place position in 1990. (Japan had moved into second place in terms of U.S. imports in 1960.) Overall, the United Kingdom's early prominence in U.S. trade was eclipsed first by U.S.-Canadian and more recently by U.S.-Japanese trade.

Patterns of foreign investments have likewise shifted over the decades. Foreign investments can be short- or long-term, portfolio or direct. They can involve private-sector or governmental transactions. All trade must be paid for, and payments typically require short-term credits. Short-term foreign investments are often related to trade finance and tend to be highly volatile.

Long-term foreign investments can be either portfolio or direct investments. Portfolio investments, which can be in equity or debt, are associated with international finance. Foreign portfolio investors look for a high return combined with safety and Americans investing abroad seek a higher return than that available at home. In each case the investor has no direct interest in the operations of the business or the government whose securities are acquired—except, of course, that the investor wants businesses to be profitable and government borrowers to be responsible. Portfolio investors do not wish to intervene in running foreign businesses or governments, and interventions only occur when something goes wrong and the recipient of the invested capital is not fulfilling its obligations.

By contrast, direct investments are made by individuals or, more often, by companies with the aim of obtaining returns through the supervision of business operations abroad. Multinational corporations make the most important direct investments. Returns from direct investments come not only from the financial inputs but also from the package of business attributes transferred over borders. The intangible organizational, technological, and goodwill assets moved internationally may be (and usually are) more consequential than the ones reflected in the financial flows. Motivations for, patterns of, and pace of foreign direct investments differ from those of portfolio investments. And, because the contribution of foreign direct investors is more than merely financial, statistics on the size of foreign direct investments generally understate the overall impact of multinational corporations, which extends beyond the recorded value of the investments.

Governments borrow and lend internationally, and make direct investments abroad through government-owned enterprises. U.S. government bonds are held abroad, and the U.S. government sells its paper beyond the U.S. borders to finance domestic deficits. Foreign investors in U.S. government securities are portfolio investors in the United States. The U.S. government has also participated in lending abroad, usually to foreign governments. While this lending is in the main politically (rather than strictly financially) motivated, the U.S. government has expected borrowers to meet their obligations, and, while the definitional fit is not exact, a U.S. government loan can be classified as a portfolio investment. Many foreign governments have made and held portfolio investments in the United States, in corporate as well as government securities (thus, for example, Arab governments in the 1970s invested oil surpluses in a portfolio of American securities, and the British government has at various times held American corporate securities, particularly those acquired in connection with its financing of the two world wars). Foreign government-owned companies have made direct investments in the United States. In addition, foreign governments have raised money in America, issuing bonds (sold to U.S. portfolio investors), borrowing from banks, as well as borrowing from the U.S. government.

The size and mix of inward and outward private long-term portfolio and direct investments has changed substantially during the course of the twentieth century, as has the importance of governments as lenders and borrowers. Each category of foreign investment has its own complex history. During the twentieth century, portfolio investments both coming into and going out of the United States have typically (but not exclusively) been denominated in dollars. By contrast, U.S. outward and inward direct investments create obligations usually denominated in the currencies of the host country, although this is not necessarily the case when there is debt financing of the direct investments. Annual capital flow figures fluctuate wildly and, for many technical reasons do not provide a basis for calculating the overall levels of international investments.

In the period before 1914 when the United States was a net debtor nation, inward portfolio investments were far greater than inward direct investments. In the period from 1900 to 1914, little U.S. federal, state, or local government paper was held outside the United States; the major stakes in the country were in private-sector investments. Obligations were usually denominated in dollars. As for the smaller American investments abroad during the period 1900–1914, the bulk were direct investments by U.S. multinational corporations, although there were also some portfolio holdings.

During World War I the investment pattern underwent a metamorphosis. The U.S. government made huge loans to the Allied powers—loans that dwarfed private investments, although U.S. banks and businesses also made large new portfolio and direct investments abroad. Meanwhile, foreign investments in America declined as foreigners sold securities to transfer their monies into their own domestic war issues and as German investments in the United States were sequestered by the Alien Property Custodian. By war's end the United States had become a creditor nation.

In the 1920s, Germany became a significant borrower in the United States. Through the interwar period, the United States remained a creditor nation, with its citizens and companies engaging in sizable foreign portfolio and direct investments. America maintained its creditor status in the 1930s, despite major delinquencies in American loans (payments stopped on practically all the big U.S. government World War I loans, and many private loans went into default) and despite an influx of foreign, especially portfolio, investment into the United States from investors seeking safety and security.

During and after World War II, the United States' participation in the global economy grew. The 1950s and 1960s saw an immense expansion by U.S. multinational corporations, including both those that had long been internationally active and many newcomers. At the same time, European, Canadian, and (more slowly) Japanese portfolio and direct investments in the United States rose, investments far overshadowed by U.S.-owned businesses abroad. Until the 1970s, U.S. direct investments abroad typically surpassed U.S. outward portfolio investments (except during the dozen or so years following World War I, before the major defaults of the 1930s). In the 1970s this pattern changed with the vast enlargement of indebtedness of developing countries.

In the 1970s and 1980s, foreign portfolio and direct investments coming into the United States rose so rapidly that by the late 1980s such investments exceeded U.S. investments abroad, transforming the United States into a net debtor. As had historically been the case, incoming portfolio investments continued to be larger than inward direct investments in the United States. A substantial part of the swelling U.S. government deficit was financed from abroad. Most American portfolio investment obligations to foreigners were denominated in dollars, as in the past. In addition, in the 1970s, 1980s, and 1990s foreign multinationals developed a highly conspicuous presence in the United States, effectively internationalizing domestic banking and industry.

What is the connection between the foreign trade and investment patterns as described above? Because much short-term investment has been linked with trade finance, the relationship between trade and short-term investments is usually obvious: the larger the trade, the more short-term investments. But this connection may be less valid during the 1970s, 1980s, and 1990s, when numerous short-term investments (sometimes, to complicate matters, in long-term securities) were made to hedge and to speculate on currency fluctuations. The relationship between long-term foreign portfolio investments and trade patterns is far less transparent, and the nature of the interaction between foreign direct investments and trade is highly controversial. In some years, long-term portfolio investments and trade went in tandem. In others, the opposite was true. It has been argued, on the one hand, that foreign direct investment substitutes for (reduces) exports and, on the other hand, that it encourages (complements) exports.

Another salient point is that, throughout the twentieth century, a sizable portion of U.S. merchandise trade—exports and imports—involved transactions by, and often totally within, multinational corporations. Regrettably, figures on this subject are not available before 1977. For that year, however, the data show that 54 percent of U.S. export trade and 56 percent of U.S. import trade was conducted by U.S.-headquartered and foreign multinational corporations. (Qualitative evidence indicates that the percentages would probably have been much higher in the 1960s than in the 1970s.) These percentages fell slightly in the 1980s. For the years since 1977 for which figures are available, intracompany merchandise trade ranged from a high of 41 percent of total U.S. exports in 1985 to a low of 32 percent in 1988. Intracompany trade hovered between 42 percent of U.S. imports in 1977 and 40 percent in 1988. It is likely that multinational corporations participate in an even higher share of international service-sector transactions.

Technology transfers have been, and remain a significant aspect of foreign trade and investment. Throughout the twentieth century, multinational corporations have been vital conduits for the movement of the new technologies. Overall statistical data on this aspect of commerce are lean, but numerous individual case studies provide ample evidence of the crucial role of multinationals in technology exports and imports.

THE OPENING OF THE CENTURY, 1900–1914

In 1900 the United States had the world's largest industrial output. Although American companies produced principally for the domestic market, which was already the world's greatest, the dollar volume of American international trade was also large, ranking second only to that of Great Britain. U.S. exports represented roughly 6 percent of gross national product (GNP), imports about 4 percent. America's giant industries, sheltered in the late nineteenth century by a high protective tariff, had increasingly substituted domestic production for imports. The 1897 Dingley tariff was the highest to that time in American history, and by 1900 finished manufactured goods accounted for only 25 percent of all U.S. imports.

As has been stated, in 1900, the United States was a net exporter of goods. Raw cotton was the largest single export, but the country also sold a range of innovative manufactured products to foreign markets. Between 1900 and 1914, the dollar value (in current dollars) of U.S. finished manufactured exports more than doubled, while all U.S. merchandise exports rose, from $1.4 billion to $2.3 billion. Manufactured exports consisted of such mass-produced goods as sewing machines, harvesters, and by 1914, automobiles. American goods were highly competitive in world markets. The United Kingdom, still committed to free trade, was the largest single destination for U.S. exports.

Woodrow Wilson was elected president in 1912 on a platform that included lower tariff duties, and the 1913 Tariff Act saw a reduction in these imposts. By this time, American manufacturers did not need protection. U.S. merchandise imports rose from $850 million to $1.9 billion between 1900 and 1914, a faster increase than that for exports (although imports continued to be far below exports). Most U.S. foreign commerce (exports and imports) in these years were financed with sterling acceptances and carried on British ships. While the merchandise trade balance was positive, the United States had a negative balance in its service-sector trade throughout the period from 1900 to 1914.

During these years, the United States remained a debtor nation in world accounts. No other country was a greater recipient of the exported capital of the United Kingdom, Holland, and Germany. Investors from Britain constituted the largest group of foreign investors in the United States. Foreign investments in America had a material impact on economic growth. U.S. railroads had been financed in significant measure by foreign investors, who still owned sizable quantities of railroad stocks and bonds. One-quarter of the common stock in America's biggest corporation, U.S. Steel, was held abroad in 1914. Most of these inward foreign investments were portfolio stakes in private-sector activities. While some debt was denominated in foreign currencies, dollar-denominated obligations predominated. There were also important inward foreign direct investments; already, many European multinationals had business stakes in the United States, made both because tariffs had blocked their imports and because they wished to participate in the huge and growing American market. In a number of instances, these multinationals transferred new technology (e.g., in rayon, dyes, and radio) to the United States.

Meanwhile, as for outward foreign portfolio investments from the United States, major New York banks were beginning to issue foreign loans and to participate in loans issued internationally. These banks had long maintained transatlantic contacts and had first gained experience by mediating capital transactions into the United States; they utilized the knowledge they thereby accumulated in the new business of capital export.

Far more significant, however, was that many of the most prominent American industrial enterprises were extending themselves internationally. Companies such as Singer Sewing Machine, Standard Oil of New Jersey, Western Electric, General Electric, Westinghouse, National Cash Register, and Ford Motor Company were making business investments outside the United States. For example, Ford, formed in 1903, exported the sixth car it built. By 1904, it had established a factory in Canada; by 1914 it was manufacturing in England and was investing elsewhere overseas. And Ford was not atypical. Thus, even while the United States was a giant recipient of capital from abroad, its companies were undertaking foreign direct investments and spreading American technologies to the rest of the world. In 1901, one British writer noted that the chief new features of London life—telephones, portable cameras, phonographs, electric streetcars, typewriters—all came from America. They came via both exports and direct investments.

Many of the U.S. direct investments abroad were made by national and, now, multinational firms. Others were by individuals and by companies set up on a bilateral basis to do business in Mexico, Canada, or the Caribbean. In 1900, Mexico attracted more U.S. foreign direct investment than any other country. By 1914, as a consequence of the nationalization of the Mexican railroads and the Mexican revolution, Canada had assumed first place as host to the spillover of American business investments.

By the outbreak of World War I in Europe in 1914, the United States was a large participant in international trade. Exports represented about 6 percent of the U.S. GNP; imports a little less than 5 percent. More important, the United States was the world's most important recipient of inward foreign investment. The more than $7 billion long-term in-

vestment in the United States from abroad equaled almost 20 percent of the U.S. GNP. Inward foreign investment had contributed to the country's prosperity. The stage was being set for the United States to reverse its net debtor position and to become a creditor in international accounts.

THE TWO WORLD WARS AND THE INTERWAR YEARS, 1914–1945

The United States assumed a new role in the world economy during World War I. As a percentage of GNP, U.S. exports were higher in 1916 (11.5 percent) than at any time during the entire twentieth century. Yet, during that same year the United States abandoned its 1913 commitment to freer trade, and tariffs rose. In dollar value, exports (largely to meet European postwar recovery needs) peaked in 1920 and did not again reach that level until 1943. U.S. tariffs increased slightly in the 1920s; then, in 1930, with the Smoot-Hawley Act, tariff duties soared. Imports and exports fell. In 1934, the Roosevelt administration attempted to lower duties and to enlarge international trade, but the worldwide depression and other nations' autarchic policies, along with bloc trading, created conditions not conducive to U.S. export development. Meanwhile, the existing U.S. tariffs and the malaise in the American economy discouraged import growth. Trade expansion resumed only with World War II.

During World War I, the interwar period, and World War II, fluctuations in value notwithstanding, U.S. exports always exceeded imports. From 1922 to 1941, exports as a percentage of GNP ranged from a high of 5.4 percent (1925) to a low of 2.8 percent (1932); from 1931 to 1939, exports never exceeded 3.7 percent of GNP. Imports were even less significant, ranging from a high of 4.5 percent of GNP (1926) to a low of 2.3 percent (1932, 1938). From 1931 to 1939, except in 1937, when they were 3.4 percent of GNP, imports moved within the range of 2.3 to 2.9 percent of GNP. During World War II, exports became relatively more important and imports relatively less.

America became a net creditor in international accounts during World War I. After U.S. entry into the war in 1917, U.S. government lending to the Allied powers became extensive, and the problems of foreign governments' wartime debts to the United States shadowed the U.S. economy during the 1920s. These huge intergovernmental loans were in the main repudiated in the early 1930s. Meanwhile, U.S. banks had also become deeply involved in sponsoring foreign securities issues, a process that continued and mounted in the 1920s. Likewise, during World War I and particularly in the 1920s, American multinationals expanded globally on an unprecedented scale, in some instances joining international cartels. Foreign investment in the United States, which had declined in absolute terms during World War I, started to revive in the 1920s. Despite the many defaults on American-made loans in the 1930s and despite a new and great influx of capital into the country during that decade, the United States remained a net creditor, and its creditor position grew greatly during World War II.

World War I broke out in Europe in the summer of 1914. America did not enter until 1917. U.S. exports swelled from $2.3 billion in 1914 to $6 billion in 1918, the last year of the war. Wartime demand for American products in Europe and the need to fill markets formerly served by Europeans were responsible for the surge. Imports into the United States rose more slowly, from $1.9 billion in 1914 to $3 billion in 1918. But because prices approximately doubled during the war, the dollar increase in imports actually represented a volume decline. There were two reasons for this: wartime obstacles to trade and new U.S. tariffs. Behind the tariff walls, U.S. domestic production substituted for imports, particularly in the chemical industry.

World War I saw a sizable expansion of U.S. long-term investments abroad and a reduction, in absolute terms, in foreign investments in the United States. Most notably, by the end of 1918 U.S. government lending to the Allied powers reached $7.6 billion (and would continue to grow). The level of private portfolio investments abroad was $2.5 billion, while outward direct investments equaled $3.6 billion. This brought total long-term outward U.S. foreign investments to $13.7 billion at the end of 1918—up from $3.5 billion as of 30 June 1914. (Losses to American investors due to expropriations after the Russian revolution and sequestrations by the German enemy were more than offset by the formidable growth.)

By contrast, foreign investment in the United States fell during the war years from a total of $7.1 billion (30 June 1914) to $3 billion (31 December 1918). The decline occurred because Europeans sold American securities to finance the war and because the Alien Property Custodian took over "enemy," principally German, properties in the United States (these assets were far larger than U.S. interests in Germany).

Since the dawn of the new century, the United States had been the world's premier industrial nation.

It emerged from World War I with no physical damage, a new economic prowess, a strong currency, and as a creditor nation in world accounts. Now New York vied with London for the leading role as the world's financial center.

U.S. exports continued to increase in 1919 and 1920, meeting the needs of European recovery. Peaking at $8 billion in 1920, exports then fell dramatically in 1921 and 1922 since in Europe funds to buy American goods were not available. From 1923 to 1929, U.S. exports gradually recovered, reaching $5.1 billion in 1929, but this was not even the 1916 level. U.S. imports also grew in 1919–1920, peaking in 1920 at $5.3 billion; in 1921 they plunged even more than exports (the severe recession in America, probably more than the Emergency Tariff of 1921, was responsible). Despite the 1922 tariff, imports rose slightly that year and during the rest of the 1920s fluctuated in the range of $3.6 to $4.4 billion.

Right after the war, there was an immense optimism about the prospects for U.S. exports. In 1918 Congress passed the Webb-Pomerene Act, which exempted combinations of exporting firms from antitrust prosecution; in 1919 it passed the Edge Act, which authorized American national banks to set up subsidiaries for international transactions. In New York, the immediate postwar period saw the widespread introduction of dollar acceptances, with the goal of moving the financing of U.S. international trade into American hands.

American bankers began to issue bonds for long-term foreign financing on an unprecedented scale. Europeans and then Latin Americans proved eager customers. As the 1920s progressed, U.S. lending abroad soared, including substantial loans to Germany to stabilize the mark and to help Germany meet its postwar reparation obligations. In the peak year, 1927, foreign capital issues (exclusive of refunding issues) in the United States were $1.3 billion. Toward the end of the 1920s, the quality of foreign issues declined as American bankers competed with one another for investment opportunities. All this lending was done by the private sector; the U.S. government's wartime loans were completed a few years after the war. The debt, however, remained and the U.S. government expected the Allied governments to pay interest and principal due.

Meanwhile, American multinationals were expanding globally. Leading U.S. industrials enlarged their business abroad. Companies went to developing countries and to Canada for raw materials; they also established operations abroad—in Europe, Canada, and elsewhere—to assemble, to package, and to manufacture. There were large foreign investments in public utilities. Some U.S. companies joined with prominent firms in foreign countries to divide world markets; many did not. Everywhere these multinationals served as conduits for the dispersion of U.S. technological expertise.

In the main, U.S. portfolio investment and U.S. direct investment abroad were remarkably separate activities. Only when banks are included as multinationals is something of a convergence observable. Not until the Federal Reserve Act was passed (December 1913) were national banks allowed to establish branches overseas. In 1913, there had existed only 26 foreign branches of American incorporated commercial banking institutions. By 1920 that number had soared to 181, including 81 branches of newly established American foreign banking corporations, organized primarily to finance international trade. With the dropoff in trade in the early 1920s, however, all 81 closed down. As of June 1926, American-incorporated commercial banks had 107 branches abroad, of which 84 were associated with National City Bank (which aided and assisted other American multinationals). Also, a number of American private banks in London and Paris were joined by partnership linkages; these banks negotiated on behalf of American issuers and arranged for foreign and American issues to be traded abroad as well as in the United States.

While the amount of foreign investment in America had declined during World War I, it had by no means evaporated. Foreign direct investors in America, unable to get financing from abroad, had turned to U.S. financial markets for assistance. After the war, restrictions on capital exports were commonplace in Europe. These impeded some new investments, although the U.S. capital market was always available to the inward foreign direct investors. As New York became an international financial center, foreign banks wanted a presence there, and by 1918, twenty-four foreign banks had licensed agencies in New York; the number rose to thirty-eight in 1923.

Before World War I, the New York Stock Exchange had been a domestic market. Now, with America's new role as a creditor, the New York stock market began listing foreign bonds (and to a lesser extent stock). In the immediate postwar years, foreign exchange restrictions abroad meant an enhanced relative position for New York. Finance in America became ever more cosmopolitan. As wartime and postwar restraints on capital exports were slowly dismantled abroad, foreign investors resumed their in-

terest in American securities; in addition, they traded in New York in foreign securities (those issued in dollars for foreign governments and corporations). By the mid-1920s, with the pound once more tied to gold, with normalcy seemingly restored, British investors actively bought and sold American (and foreign) securities traded in New York. In the last years of the 1920s, as values spiraled on the New York stock market, foreign investors joined the buying spree. As in times past, foreign portfolio investments exceeded foreign direct investments in the United States. Some Europeans made direct investments in the United States to obtain financing for their businesses abroad. The industrial prowess of the country meant that many European multinationals had no competitive advantage, yet some foreign leaders—Dunlop, Michelin, I. G. Farben, the predecessors of Ciba-Geigy, Unilever (Lever Brothers), Saint Gobain, Courtaulds, and Shell, for example—did produce in America in the 1920s. Some of the German companies that had been taken over during World War I were able to resume business in the United States. And, particularly in the chemical and rayon industries, there was an inward transfer of technology.

During the 1920s, international businesses developed strategic alliances, joint ventures, and patent licensing arrangements; though such ways of working together were not unprecedented, they became far more extensive than previously. The interrelationships between and among American, European, and Canadian businesses were often highly complex, with literally thousands of agreements covering individual products. In many cases, these connections stimulated technological interchanges to and from the United States. Agreements to divide world markets and to exchange technology meant that since prior reservations of national markets were made, companies had incentives to share their technological innovations over the borders. Because U.S. antitrust law forbade cartels, these accords were tailored to conform with American legal requirements as then perceived.

Scholars have debated the nature of U.S. economic policies in the 1920s. For instance, were the policies internationalist or isolationist? Clearly, the U.S. rejection of the Treaty of Versailles and the United States' failure to join the League of Nations demonstrated Americans' unwillingness to take part in an international community. Some scholars have argued, however, that because U.S. policymakers participated in the formulation, if not directly in the financing, of the Dawes and Young plans (to help Germany control inflation, stabilize the mark, return to and stay on the gold standard, and pay reparations) and because leading American international bankers had the ear of officials in Washington, U.S. economic policy was internationalist in orientation. These scholars maintain, moreover, that U.S. endorsement of the Open Door policy was designed to encourage U.S. trade and investment abroad and thus represented an outlook that was far from insular.

On the other hand, those who persist in the belief that U.S. economic policies were parochial note that U.S. international economic involvement had little to do with international cooperation. They stress that the policies were shaped by a desire to return to the normal, self-regulating, prewar system of stable currencies based on the gold standard. They argue that the United States intended to keep tariffs high and to let the private sector finance the Dawes and Young plans. The Commerce Department opposed American multinationals' building plants abroad for fear this would deprive Americans of jobs. U.S. policymakers favored outward foreign direct investments only when they provided an immediate aid to the domestic economy, such as the spurring of U.S. exports, or the provision of more oil supplies. In addition, U.S. policy did not look kindly on foreign investment in the United States; indeed, in one vital industry, radios, a 1920 policy resulted in the forced sale by the British Marconi Company of its direct investments in the company that became Radio Corporation of America. Still, whatever the interpretation of U.S. government policies, no controversy exists on the matter that America itself was indisputably involved in the world economy, through foreign trade and, especially, international investments.

Indeed, when the boom of the 1920s ended, this international economic participation made it easy for Americans to blame outsiders for what went wrong at home. Many contemporaries saw foreigners as responsible for the crash of 1929, withdrawing their monies from the New York stock market. Others concluded that the World War I peace settlement and its aftermath provided the cause for the 1929–1933 economic downturn. In order to safeguard domestic jobs, Congress enacted the highest tariff ever, passing the Smoot-Hawley Act in 1930. As expected, U.S. imports fell, but exports also plummeted, which was particularly damaging since the country was a net exporter. By 1932, both imports and exports had fallen to merely 30 percent of their 1929 level. Compounding the problem, U.S. lending abroad, which had slowed before the crash, virtually stopped in its aftermath. Thus, foreigners had few dollars either gained through their trade with the United States or through borrowing. Accordingly, they raised their own tariffs and added other restrictions on their imports. Meanwhile, President Herbert Hoover maintained the gold-based dollar, while more countries devalued their currencies, leading to the dollar's becoming relatively overvalued. This further contributed to the shrinking American exports.

As economic conditions worldwide deteriorated and as U.S. lending abroad was curtailed, many foreign borrowers defaulted. American businesses cut back on new direct investments abroad. In June 1931 Hoover recommended a one-year moratorium on German reparation payments when it was clear that the Germans could not meet their responsibilities. Germany's inability to pay reparations meant that the Allies could not make payments to the United States on their large wartime intergovernmental debts, so the moratorium extended to such obligations as well. This "one-year" moratorium in fact stretched forever, with the U.S. government eventually having to write off nearly all its World War I loans.

By the time President Franklin D. Roosevelt took office in 1933, the domestic and world economy lay in deep depression. The condition of the international economy meant that it could not serve as an engine to aid American economic growth. Practically everywhere nations had erected, or were erecting, new barriers to trade—not merely tariffs but a whole collection of quotas and exchange controls. Output had dropped practically everywhere; trade had fallen even faster. Investment was universally at risk. Those foreign investors who remained in the U.S. stock market saw a sharp attrition in the value of their holdings. Some foreign direct investors in America closed their plants, unable to survive the economic adversity. Although there was new outward and inward direct investment in manufacturing by multinationals that could not reach markets through exports, such stakes were relatively few and did little to offset the general downturn in international investment.

One of Roosevelt's first actions was to devalue the dollar, making U.S. goods more competitive on world markets. In 1934, Congress passed the Reciprocal Trade Agreements Act, seeking to reduce tariffs. That same year, Congress authorized two Export-Import Banks (later merged into one), with the goal of spurring U.S. exports. Such measures notwithstanding, trade remained sluggish since nations around the world lacked the foreign exchange with which to buy imports. The United States was unable to counter effectively worldwide tendencies toward autarky and bloc trading. Instead, U.S. policymakers concentrated on designing domestic solutions to relieve domestic distress.

International lending by Americans did not revive. In 1934 Congress passed the Johnson Act, which forbade loans to governments that had defaulted on intergovernmental debts. Americans now had cause to reflect on the perils of being a creditor nation. In such an unattractive international climate, most U.S. multinationals held back on new activities. The major exceptions were the American oil companies. In 1938, they participated in the important new oil discoveries in Saudi Arabia and Kuwait. That same year, however, Mexico nationalized the operations of foreign oil companies there—the most important expropriation since the Russian revolution.

During the years 1934–1939, there was a steady flow of foreign capital into the United States. This "hot money" went primarily into portfolio investments. Despite the Depression, the United States was politically stable, rendering investments in America more secure than they were elsewhere. Also, the price of gold, then $35 per ounce, was considered high, leading foreigners to sell gold to the U.S. government for dollars. These dollars became the basis for investment in the United States. Americans generally felt threatened by the inflow of gold and foreign capital fearing that it would be destabilizing—that securities could be as easily sold as bought. Economists discussed what they called "abnormal" capital flows: capital, which was "supposed" to move from richer to poorer nations, was now flowing *into* the United States, which, though injured by the Depression, remained, comparatively speaking, a rich country.

Americans of the 1930s nursed deep suspicions about the rest of world. The United States had a long tradition of wanting to separate itself from Old World problems and quarrels, and the new distrust fit into, and was reinforced by, that well-established mold. Fascism in Germany and Italy, communism in Russia, militarism in Japan, and the civil war in Spain all strengthened the widely held sentiment that America should divorce itself from the mess outside its boundaries. The America First movement gathered adherents. And, as the New Deal tackled the economic difficulties at home, international banks and big businesses (many of which were multinationals) became political targets. America's international lending practices were judged to be corrupting. The Nye Committee, for example, accused international bankers of having gotten cozy with the British during World War I, helping to push the United States into the war. Initially, with the National Industrial Recovery Act of 1933, the Roosevelt administration had been prepared to suspend antitrust investigations to encourage businessmen to work together to save the economy. After the downturn in 1938, however, the government completely reversed this policy: antitrust concerns were reactivated and big business, including many of America's major multinationals, came under fire. The contacts that these businesses had made with foreign cartels in the 1920s seemed particularly harmful.

When war in Europe started in September 1939, new trade and investment restrictions abroad supplemented those earlier imposed. Yet the war did mean that foreign orders for American goods began to rise. The United States did not enter the war until December 1941, and in the two years of neutrality American attitudes gradually shifted from isolationism to a strong antagonism to German militarism and support of the Allies.

In 1939 U.S. exports stood at $3.1 billion; in 1940 they had risen to $3.9 billion. New U.S. sympathy with the Allied cause and the financing provided in the Lend-Lease program (enacted in March 1941) helped push U.S. exports higher—to $5 billion in 1941. With improvements in the nation's domestic economy, U.S. imports also increased, from $2.3 billion in 1939 to $3.2 billion in 1941.

With monies provided through the Reconstruction Finance Corporation and the Lend-Lease program in 1941, the U.S. government once more participated in international lending. To do so however, the United States had to get around the Johnson Act of 1934 and the neutrality laws of the 1930s. During the period in which the United States remained neutral (1939–1941), American bankers were backstage rather than principal actors. A number of U.S. industrials were tarred because of their associations with the German company I. G. Farben. Thus, even while U.S. isolationist views receded and the probability that America would enter the war grew, hostile attacks on international business continued and, indeed, accelerated. Big businesses were accused of having impeded America's war effort because of their ties with German companies that were in turn perceived as proxies for the German government.

Foreign investment in the United States grew from 1939 to 1941, with "safety" being the prime motive. When the Germans moved into Denmark, Norway, Holland, Belgium, and France in the spring of 1940, the U.S. government froze the American assets of residents of these occupied countries to prevent them from being used by the Germans. In June 1941 assets of other major continental European countries (including Germany, Switzerland, and the Soviet Union) were frozen, and in July 1941 Japanese and Chinese assets were also blocked.

Meanwhile, as U.S. plans for Lend-Lease went forward in early 1941, and as President Roosevelt and Secretary of the Treasury Henry Morgenthau sought public approval, some questioned how the United States could justify aid to the British when there were British assets in the United States. As a result, at the insistence of the U.S. government, the British government forced one of the largest British direct investors, Courtaulds, to divest its important rayon operations in the United States as a symbol of British willingness to make sacrifices. The British also took steps, again under U.S. government pressure, to sell or to pledge other British portfolio and direct investments in the United States in exchange for their borrowings.

The new U.S. loans were structured in a very different way from the World War I credits so as not to create a postwar burden. On 14 August 1941, Roosevelt and British Prime Minister Winston Churchill issued the Atlantic Charter, a joint statement on broad postwar goals and plans for international economic cooperation. By September, fifteen countries had endorsed the principles set down in the Atlantic Charter. Thus, even before U.S. entry into the war, American policymakers had begun to think about the role America would play in the postwar world economy.

Especially after Pearl Harbor, the rest of the world became much less "alien" to the average American. Americans went to fight abroad. Radio broadcasts told families at home what was happening overseas. "March of Time" newsreels brought Americans pictures from around the globe. Exports contributed to the war boom in the U.S. economy. Exports skyrocketed from 1942 to 1944 to meet the wartime requirements of the Allies. (By 1944, U.S. exports had reached $14 billion, a higher dollar amount than ever before in history.) U.S. imports also rose (though in 1944 they were still a mere $3.9 billion—lower than in 1925–1929).

Export growth was assisted by the formidable involvement of the U.S. government in the war effort. Under the rubric of unilateral transfers (foreign aid and military spending), U.S. government support of the Allies amounted to $32.6 billion for the three years 1942–1944. This figure soars over private foreign portfolio or direct investments in either direction—outward or inward. Taking into account many ups and downs, net U.S. business abroad basically stayed stable during the war years, so the great overall expansion of the American economy was accompanied by a relative decline in the importance of American business abroad. Bankers devoted their attention to U.S. war bonds, shying away from international lending. Inward foreign investment, at war's end, was probably smaller than before Pearl Harbor. During the war all enemy investment had been sequestered; some foreign investments had become domestic as owners immigrated to the United States; and there had been little new inflow, although the market value of existing foreign investments in the United States had risen.

Much more important, however, than the private international investment transactions during the war years was the new consensus in the United States that the country now had to have a major role in the international arena. The U.S. government had pledged its participation in shaping the postwar world economy. Unlike after World War I, the country would now accept international responsibility. Those planning the peace carefully studied the aftermath of World War I to avoid repeating that baneful history. America played host to Allied leaders at the Bretton Woods Conference in New Hampshire in 1944, which resulted in the formation of the International Monetary Fund and the International Bank for Reconstruction and Development (the World Bank), both to be headquartered in Washington, D.C. In the design for the postwar monetary system, the dollar would be the central currency. In San Francisco in 1945, plans were consummated for the United Nations, and again the United States took the lead, becoming the permanent host country to the international organization.

AFTER WORLD WAR II, 1945–1970

The United States emerged from the war with a prosperous domestic economy. The nation's global hegemony was unchallenged, for around the world both victorious and defeated nations lay in ruins. The United States was the world's foremost industrial, financial, and military power. Technological innovations were the norm. The U.S. government became a strong advocate of an open economy, favoring freer trade and capital movement. The government's attitude toward participation in shaping the world order was entirely different from that of the post–World War I era: no one in 1945 wanted to return to the prewar status quo. Americans recognized that the world economy would not right itself automatically or with only minor interventions. America had to take the initiative in aiding and assisting worldwide economic reconstruction. And practically everyone was convinced that Americans would gain from the restoration of a healthy global economy.

The ravages of war were enormous. And, to make matters more difficult, as the United States formulated its policies for the peace, the Cold War began. Would France and Italy go communist? What about Greece and Turkey? The Soviet Union occupied much of Eastern Europe; communism was on the rise in China. America was convinced that poverty and communism went in tandem.

Multilateral aid by the International Bank for Reconstruction and Development (the World Bank) proved inadequate for European recovery, and American foreign aid mounted to fill the gap. The Marshall Plan provided mammoth assistance to Europe. Decisions were made in Washington to help Germany and Japan rebuild their economies—on a democratic basis—to avoid a vindictive peace that might lead to a third world war. The United States wanted noncommunist, friendly Germany and Japan as allies in the future.

The United States also sought to encourage the stabilization of foreign currencies. Convinced that international trade would not revive if there were not a functioning payments system and a stable monetary order, the International Monetary Fund took steps to help countries select the right values for their currencies and to maintain stability. Under the Anglo-American Agreement (ratified by Congress in July 1946), the United States canceled all British obligations under wartime Lend-Lease and extended a $3.75 billion line of credit to help Britain resume currency convertibility. The United States also participated in the General Agreement on Tariffs and Trade (GATT, effective January 1948), whose purpose was to lower barriers to international trade.

In the immediate postwar years, dollars were in short supply around the world. U.S. foreign aid provided dollars so that others could purchase American goods. Likewise, the U.S. government urged American business to take part in reconstructing Europe by investing abroad. Later, it would encourage companies to invest throughout the world (communist countries excepted). American policymakers took for granted that U.S. participation in a healthy world economy was in America's interest, both political and economic.

The atomic bomb had made the world a smaller, more dangerous place, and the success of U.S. postwar strategies seemed imperative. Air travel had also made the world seem more compact. Communications had become easier: television gave Americans an increasing awareness of what was happening outside the country. And the Korean War, which began in 1950, alerted Americans to the importance of having allies in Asia as well as in Europe.

With America's aid and encouragement, Europe and Japan rapidly recovered during the 1950s and 1960s. West Germany and Japan emerged from occupation in 1952. Former enemies (West Germany and France) worked together toward a unified Europe. The Treaty of Rome (1957) established the six-member European Economic Community (the Common Market). The first efforts to obtain currency convertibility by the major countries had been unsuccessful, but they began to bear fruit by the late 1950s. In addition, around the globe, the British, French, Dutch, and Belgian empires were carved into independent nations. Everywhere the United States supported development—with foreign aid programs, with the 1960s Alliance for Progress in Latin America, and with the endorsement of decolonization. The Cold War influenced U.S. policy throughout the period. American economic goals seemed to be met as world trade and investment revived—at least among noncommunist countries. The economies of the communist countries—the Soviet Union and Eastern Europe, China, North Korea, and, in the 1960s, Cuba—were long to remain separate.

Immediately after the war, America's role in world trade became critical, as U.S. exports aided recovery in western Europe. U.S. imports rose from $4.1 billion in 1945 to $8.8 billion in 1950, providing the dollars with which the world, in turn, could purchase American goods. Canada continued to be the United States' single largest trading partner in both exports and imports, and Americans took this close relationship for granted. Considered as a whole, however, Europe comprised the larger market for American exports.

In the immediate postwar years, U.S. businesses were cautious about expanding internationally. Prosperity at home meant that domestic demand for goods was high. Moreover, since restrictions on foreign exchange remained the norm in many countries and since profit remittances were often blocked, few American companies wanted to risk making overseas investments. Beginning in 1948, the U.S. government offered limited investment guarantees to encourage U.S. businesses to invest in Europe. The United States also supported American companies' efforts to develop oil in Saudi Arabia, in order to provide energy supplies to Europe. To permit American oil companies to cooperate in the Middle East, antitrust rules were relaxed—a major concession since antitrust litigation, briefly suspended during the war, had been renewed, with international businesses among the principal defendants. Some large U.S. businesses under antitrust attack felt particularly hesitant about expansion abroad. Nonetheless, gradually U.S. companies began to pay more attention to international business. By 1950 the book value of U.S. direct investments abroad totaled about $11.8 billion. Not surprisingly, Canada attracted the greatest share of U.S. direct investment ($3.6 billion), more than all of Europe. U.S. banks, however, demonstrated little interest in foreign lending. Rather, the world depended on U.S. government aid and credits, and, to a far lesser extent, on the World Bank.

Foreign portfolio investments in the United States seem to have been higher than most people at the time realized. Treasury Department and Federal Reserve figures indicate that foreign ownership of American securities totaled $7.4 billion in 1950 ($4.3 billion in U.S. Treasuries, $200 million in corporate bonds, and $2.9 billion in corporate equities). This represented about 2.3 percent of all outstanding American securities. Undoubtedly, some of this investment was in short-term holdings, and the holdings in U.S. Treasuries seem to have included official foreign government as well as private investment. The Department of Commerce estimated inward foreign direct investments at $3.4 billion at the end of 1950, with the major investments from British and Canadian sources. At this time, however, foreign investments in the United States were among the last things on most Americans' minds.

The 1950s and 1960s saw an expanding world economy aided by the revival of world trade and investment. Barriers to trade and investment began to erode in western industrial countries. Slowly, the currencies of major industrial nations became convertible and obstacles to payments began to dissipate. GATT-sponsored "rounds" (negotiations) encouraged leading nations to move toward freer trade.

The United States was always in the forefront of these developments. Its currency had been convertible throughout. In 1962, Congress cut U.S. tariff duties sharply. America was secure in its industrial capabilities and could afford to set the example for the rest of the world. Throughout the 1950s and 1960s, the United States remained a net exporter of merchandise. Yet, in the 1960s, as U.S. economic growth accelerated and as the country's tariffs were reduced, imports mounted and gradually the giant U.S. trade surplus began to shrink. As a percentage of GNP, exports and imports were higher than during most of the 1920s and in the 1930s, but lower than in the years before World War I.

The 1950s and 1960s saw vibrant technological progress and an enormous proliferation of new products in the United States. Economic growth occurred worldwide. Facilities were modernized in many countries, and foreign enterprises grew more competitive. At first, a sizable share of new U.S. imports were in products such as textiles and steel, and economists noted that these were in the "less research-oriented" industries. America's overall commitment to freer trade notwithstanding, protectionist sentiments arose in these sectors. American policymakers yielded on a patchwork basis to these pressures, requesting voluntary export restraints in certain industries from U.S. trading partners. The United States remained a net exporter of textiles until 1954 and of iron and steel products until 1962. The increase in steel imports seemed especially troublesome, since steel was a basic U.S. industry (U.S. Steel had for many years been America's largest corporation).

As the United States became open to imports and became a net importer of many consumer goods, average Americans began to purchase a variety of products made abroad. In a range of consumer goods (excluding for the moment, automobiles) for which the United States had long been a net exporter, the country had become a net importer as early as 1959. And in automobiles, an industry that America had dominated throughout most of the twentieth century, the country became a net importer in 1968. Soon the imports would become formidable.

The United States became ever more involved in the world economy through the activities of U.S. multinational corporations. By the mid-1950s but especially in the 1960s, corporate caution about international expansion evaporated and American companies eagerly invested abroad. Once the United States had been a mineral-rich nation, but, coal excepted, this no longer seemed to be the case. American multinationals now made large investments in new resources throughout the developing world, bringing vast quantities of copper, bauxite, iron ore, and oil into international trade. Oil multinationals discovered and developed new oil supplies. By the 1960s the low price of abundant oil meant that, for the first time in history, countries around the world used more oil than coal. Cheap oil spurred global economic growth.

American companies extended themselves into Europe, where they saw promising new opportunities, particularly after the establishment of the European Common Market and the relaxation of currency controls. American exports often were not competitive, and U.S. companies had to invest abroad to reach their foreign customers. By the early 1960s, American companies were making large investments in Common Market countries; they were experienced in doing business in the United States' large domestic economy, and when an important part of western Europe became one market, technologies that emphasized economies of scale were highly appropriate. American multinationals offered both producer and consumer goods, and grew rapidly in the newly thriving Europe, contributing to the European prosperity.

American businesses participated in the industrialization of the rest of the world. As Brazil and other less-developed countries industrialized, they adopted import substitution policies. Barriers to trade stopped U.S. multinationals from exporting to these markets; thus, they invested in these countries, assisting in the industrialization process.

Everywhere they invested, whether in developed or developing nations, U.S. companies became conduits for the dispersion of America's formidable technological achievements. This was true even where the investment was small: Japan carefully curbed the entry of American multinationals but encouraged licensing arrangements whereby Japanese firms got the advantages of American know-how. The Japanese rapidly employed, modified, and improved on this technology.

The first commercial jet crossed the Atlantic in 1958. Jet travel quickly became universal, transforming the management of multinational enterprise. Coordination and control over great distances was facilitated; it was no longer a major proposition for a company to send managers abroad.

By the 1960s, American multinationals' impact on the world economy was extraordinary. Their role was far more important than that of exports or U.S. outward private portfolio investment. Banks such as the predecessor to Citibank had spread worldwide as multinational enterprises, serving corporate clients and to some extent host-country markets. There was some foreign lending by American banks, but it was not extensive. (U.S. policies came to restrict outgoing private portfolio investments.)

While American multinationals—industrials and, to a lesser extent, banks—were creating global operations, foreign investments in the United States had quietly and unobtrusively been increasing. As in the past, in the 1950s and 1960s inward portfolio investments exceeded inward direct investments. The rise in inward foreign investments was uneven, at first

principally in U.S. public debt securities and then, by the late 1960s, in U.S. equities. And, as America prospered and foreign nations' restrictions on capital exports were relaxed, European and, gradually, Japanese multinationals saw new business opportunities in the United States. A foreign multinational could, moreover, always expand in the United States based on borrowing in this country, so capital export restrictions were not necessarily germane. As American imports, especially those from Japan, rose, foreign multinationals, particularly Japanese companies, recognized that they needed to establish distribution systems to sell their goods in the United States. Although this did not involve large investments, it offered entry and familiarity with the U.S. market.

Foreign banks were among the foreign multinationals coming into the United States; most established themselves in New York City. In 1961, New York State changed its banking laws to allow foreign banks to set up branches (that is, to accept domestic deposits), encouraging the enlargement of foreign banking in the United States. Since the United States was the world's greatest creditor nation, foreign banks desired a presence in that nation's financial capital. Japanese multinational banks that had been in California before World War II reestablished themselves in San Francisco and Los Angeles, and, of course, in New York.

As America became more deeply involved in the world economy through trade and investment, American policymakers became concerned about the nation's balance of payments. Even though the country remained a net exporter of goods during the 1960s, the nation's balance of payments showed chronic deficits. The causes were multiple, including the spending on the Vietnam War, foreign aid, and multinational enterprises' massive expansion abroad. Europe, which had been short on dollars in the immediate postwar years, by the 1960s had a surfeit of dollars.

A number of U.S. measures were adopted to cope with the balance-of-payments deficits. In 1962, the United States issued the so-called Roosa bonds. Denominated in foreign currencies and designed to be sold abroad, they resulted in an increase in foreign investment in U.S. government securities. The Interest Equalization Tax (IET), enacted in 1964, sought to discourage U.S. investment abroad. Since most such stakes were direct investments and not motivated by interest-rate considerations, the law had little overall impact; it does appear, however, to have reduced some outgoing private portfolio investments. In 1965 President Lyndon B. Johnson introduced a voluntary balance-of-payments program. He urged the largest U.S. multinationals to improve their individual balance of payments by raising exports, bringing back more income from abroad, and slowing the outflow of capital. These and other measures notwithstanding, balance-of-payments deficits persisted, and on 1 January 1968, President Johnson imposed mandatory controls on the outflow of all U.S. direct investment, as well as controls over the reinvestment of U.S. business profits earned abroad—the first such measures in American history. The aim was not to limit U.S. foreign direct investment, but to curb its negative balance-of-payments effects. U.S. businesses could borrow abroad for expansion outside the country—and they did so. Moreover, since the U.S. government wanted to encourage private investments rather than to depend on foreign aid to developing nations, the regulations exempted U.S. direct investments in these countries.

With the U.S. balance-of-payments deficits, the world became awash with dollars. Because the dollar was overvalued, American exports were often not competitive. Rather than send the dollars back to the United States, international money managers participated in a "Eurodollar" market. Dollars (and soon other currencies) were borrowed and lent in the European currency markets, where transactions were not subject to U.S. regulations. Thus, when Johnson imposed restrictions on outgoing U.S. direct investments in 1968, American companies were easily able to turn to the Eurodollar market.

Overall, the 1960s was a prosperous decade. American multinationals contributed to worldwide growth. Cheap oil, brought into commerce by U.S. and European multinationals, was aiding industrialization on a global scale. The benefits were widely diffused. World prosperity served as an engine for individual nations' growth, including that of the United States. The U.S. balance-of-payments deficit financed world economic advancement.

THE ERA OF UNCERTAINTIES, 1971–1994

By the time Richard M. Nixon was elected president in 1968, many Americans had become unhappy about their nation's role in the world. American "leadership" had led to military involvement in Vietnam. While U.S. exports still exceeded imports, the gap was narrowing rapidly. Concerns over America's competitive position rose as European and Japanese industrial capacity grew. In those sectors where U.S. imports were largest, talk of protectionism became more common, contrasting sharply with the country's immediate postwar consensus in support of freer trade. U.S. balance-of-payments problems seemed intractable.

In 1971, when it appeared that U.S. merchandise imports would exceed exports for the first time in the twentieth century, Nixon surprised the world by unilaterally devaluing the dollar. The Bretton Woods system of stable exchange rates had established a process by which every nation in the world could devalue its currency—except the United States. In 1944 no one had anticipated that this would ever be necessary. After the "Nixon shock," the United States made attempts to set a new value on the dollar and to restore the system. This proved impossible, and in 1973 the world moved into a new monetary era of floating exchange rates. No longer was the dollar the centerpiece of the international monetary system; indeed, there was no key currency.

Many economists assumed that fluctuating exchange rates would eliminate deficits in the U.S. balance of payments and that the dollar would find a level where U.S. trade would be in balance. American exports would automatically become competitive again, or so the theory went. This did not happen. From 1971 through the early 1990s (1973 and 1975 excepted), the United States had a deficit in its trade accounts.

Three other events in 1973 also symbolized America's relative loss of stature. One was the defeat in Vietnam. No longer was the country seen as invincible. The second was the enlargement of the Common Market (the European Community): the six original members were joined by the United Kingdom, Ireland, and Denmark. This development foreshadowed an even stronger Europe. The third event was the decision of the Organization of Petroleum Exporting Countries (OPEC) to raise oil prices.

This last event had truly profound economic consequences—for the United States and the world. Oil was a uniquely important product. The worldwide economic growth of the 1960s had been fueled by cheap oil. The American and the world economy depended on this energy source. For reasons related to supply and demand, oil prices began to rise in the early 1970s. In the fall of 1973 and then again in January 1974, OPEC pushed up the price of crude oil almost fourfold.

High oil prices worsened America's trade deficit, stimulated inflation, and caused a worldwide reallocation of wealth. The major oil-exporting nations became so wealthy that they purchased the oilfields within their boundaries from the American multinationals. OPEC's action emboldened other developing countries to try to hike the prices of bauxite, bananas, copper, and other commodities. Increasingly, these countries insisted that their resources be owned nationally rather than by American (or other foreign) companies. Wealthy oil-exporting nations had large dollar surpluses, some of which flowed into the United States, prompting concern that "the Arabs were buying America." Some of these monies were recycled into Third World debt by American and European banks, and developing countries welcomed the newly available funds. At the end of the 1970s, OPEC raised oil prices even higher. By then, with inflation rampant worldwide, U.S. policymakers pushed up interest rates and the debt costs of developing countries escalated. By the early 1980s, the latter were defaulting.

Meanwhile, with inflation out of control in the United States, American imports had skyrocketed—not only oil but also consumer goods, particularly automobiles. American cars in the 1960s had become gas-guzzlers; new high oil prices meant that the smaller cars made abroad suddenly became especially attractive to U.S. consumers.

At the same time that U.S. merchandise imports rose, there was a sizable increase in inward portfolio and direct investments in the United States. Monies from OPEC countries and from newly wealthy individuals worldwide flowed in, mainly as portfolio investments. Yet inward foreign direct investments also expanded as the possibility of U.S. protectionism, stimulated by the greater imports, encouraged such stakes. Moreover, foreign multinationals were looking for stability in a world of fluctuating exchange rates, and investments in America gave them more flexibility and less vulnerability. In addition, jobs-hungry state governments sought out inward investments by foreign multinationals. Foreign banks felt it ever more critical to be in America.

In the 1980s oil prices dropped, and U.S. inflation was controlled. The dollar strengthened in the middle of the decade, but then its value fell again. Through all of this, the U.S. trade deficit persisted; and foreign portfolio and direct investments in the United States continued to rise. Particularly notable were the growing involvements of Japanese investors. The increase in foreign investments in the United States meant that in the late 1980s America became a debtor nation in world accounts—in fact, it became, as in the years before World War I, the world's largest debtor nation.

All the while, American investments abroad remained large, with U.S. multinationals continuing to do a sizable business in foreign countries. In the 1980s the European Community increased from nine

to twelve member states, and plans for "Europe-1992" (and the European Union) developed. U.S. companies wanted to be poised to take advantage of the potential. As the 1980s ended, the failure of communism and the close of the Cold War meant the opening up of formerly communist countries to investments, with these countries seeking to attract American multinationals. As the 1980s had progressed and the 1990s began, developing countries that in the 1970s had expropriated American properties and excoriated U.S. multinationals now sought to lure the same American companies. The United Nations Centre for Transnational Corporations applauded foreign direct investment as an engine of growth. In addition, American international bank lending grew; debts were rescheduled and stretched out, and new loans were made. Finance continued to be a global activity. Technology made it easy for Americans and foreigners to move funds internationally to take advantage of investment opportunities. Despite America's new debtor-nation status, U.S. multinationals and U.S. lending retained great significance in the world economy.

The years 1971–1974 represented a watershed in the post–World War II era. The collapse of the Bretton Woods system jarred the entire world economy. Because the devalued dollar was expected to cope with the U.S. payments deficit, in 1973 Nixon removed U.S. restrictions on outward foreign direct investment. U.S. multinationals refunded debts incurred in Europe with a sizable outflow of American capital.

OPEC's hiking of oil prices was perceived by many Americans as part of a conspiracy between OPEC nations and U.S. multinationals—and the latter came under investigation in the United States. To some critics, the global reach of mighty U.S. transnational corporations seemed an improper extension of U.S. power. In 1974, their action spurred by OPEC's success, developing nations united in their advocacy of a New International Economic Order that would not be dominated by the United States. Part of their agenda involved confronting U.S. multinational corporations.

The devaluation of the dollar made American properties and securities cheaper for foreigners to buy and, like a rising tariff, increased the price of imported goods for Americans. Because, at least initially, it seemed that foreign imports would be less competitive, many foreign multinationals made investments in production in the United States.

"Stagflation," the combination of economic stagnation and inflation, became the norm in America during the 1970s. Floating exchange rates generated uncertainty. From 1974 to 1981 (with the exception of 1975), America was a net importer of goods. The United States' commitment to free trade tottered as oil and consumer goods came in from abroad. By 1977, foreign oil represented 30 percent of American imports and 44 percent of U.S. oil consumption. Imports from Japan—particularly automobiles and electronics products—became conspicuous. As Americans tried to conserve oil, more automobiles were imported since foreign cars were more fuel efficient. Then came the Iranian revolution and the Iran-Iraq War, and oil prices soared, with prices doubling in 1979 alone.

A profound change in the composition of U.S. investment abroad also occurred during the 1970s. Because of the wealth generated by OPEC-induced high prices, nations increasingly acquired their own crude oil producing properties. Thus, in 1970, the seven major international oil companies (five of them U.S.-headquartered) produced 68.9 percent of the world's crude oil (outside the United States and communist countries), while host-country oil companies were responsible for only 8.4 percent (other international oil companies produced 22.7 percent). By 1979, however, an almost complete reversal had occurred; the seven majors accounted for only 23.9 percent of production, with other international oil companies producing 7.4 percent, and state-owned host-country companies producing 68.7 percent of the total.

So, too, many other raw material properties moved from the ownership of American multinationals to the control of host states, often through expropriation rather than through purchase. Given the risk, U.S. companies became reluctant to make sizable investments in developing countries and turned toward opportunities in Europe. A trend that had been apparent for years accelerated in the 1970s: in 1950, a mere 15 percent of U.S. direct investment abroad had been in Europe; by 1960 that figure had risen to 20 percent. By 1970 it stood at 31 percent, and by 1980, 66 percent.

In the 1970s, as the oil countries' wealth increased, OPEC investors looked for high returns. American banks took their deposits and recycled the monies into loans, many of which were redirected to developing countries. American banks became involved in loans to developing countries as never before in history. (The situation differed from that of the 1920s, when bonds were sold to the public; now the lending was done by the banks from their abundant resources.) For many developing countries,

the loans seemed an excellent alternative to investments by multinationals, for the funds usually went to government borrowers and lenders did not expect control. Yet, as interest rates soared at decade's end, the burden of carrying the debt also rose sharply. Developing countries were forced to borrow more—not for productive purposes, but to pay the interest on prior debt. For the first time since the 1920s, American outgoing portfolio investments assumed major importance.

During the 1970s, attention focused on the steadily growing foreign investment in the United States. The inward investments were both portfolio and direct ones, though portfolio investments constituted the larger share. The amount and percentage of U.S. public debt held by foreign investors multiplied, topping 30 percent of the debt outstanding in 1977. This was a percentage that had not been seen in America since the first half of the nineteenth century. "Carter bonds"—that is, U.S. debt denominated in foreign currencies—encouraged this trend. Investment advisers often placed OPEC investors' surpluses in U.S. Treasuries. And as interest rates in the United States rose at decade's end, more monies from abroad flowed into corporate bonds.

Foreign multinationals also enlarged their American business. The U.S. market was immense, and companies that feared emerging U.S. protectionist sentiments invested in production to meet the demand. Whether because of voluntary export restrictions or in response to charges of dumping, foreign multinationals believed it prudent to make their products within the United States. Japanese consumer electronics firms made new investments in manufacturing. Japanese semiconductor companies (some of them the same as in consumer electronics) invested in factories in America. And then came the motorcycle companies. Japanese direct investment in the United States as a percentage of the total inward direct investment had been a mere 1.3 percent in 1974; by 1980, it was 7.7 percent. American consumers had no way of knowing whether the products they were buying were imported from Japan or produced by a Japanese firm in America. Foreign multinationals that invested in the United States in distribution and manufacturing were joined by multinational foreign banks; in addition, a number of foreign investors were seeing new opportunities in U.S. real estate. Of all the foreign multinationals in America in the 1970s, British businesses remained the most important, but companies from many nations were making new investments.

The rise in inward foreign investments spurred

Congress to pass laws to monitor the inflow. An interagency Committee on Foreign Investment in the United States (CFIUS) was established in 1975 to review investments that "might have major implications for United States national interests." Special concerns were voiced over foreign-government-owned companies in America.

New studies of all multinational activities showed that a sizable share of America's international trade was not "arms' length"—that is, between independent buyers and sellers. Instead, integrated multinational enterprises, American and foreign, handled a large amount of trade within their own firms. This trade was not only in end products, but also in intermediate goods and technology. None of this, of course, was new; what was novel was the increasing awareness of the extent of such intracompany commerce. American trade policies had typically been based on bilateral considerations, and to a large extent policies continued to be divorced from investment issues. The complexities of multilateral intracompany trade added new dimensions to the considerations.

As American banks moved abroad and foreign banks came to America, bank regulators became more conscious of (and nervous over) the global aspects of finance. The Eurodollar market, which lay outside American regulators' control, had emerged in the 1960s. Now, with the explosion of OPEC "petrodollars," the Eurodollar market commanded new attention. Foreign banks in the United States, moreover, could engage in multistate activities forbidden their American counterparts. In the United States, pressures arose to break down the walls preventing interstate banking. The International Banking Act of 1978 was an attempt to give American banks the same advantages as their foreign counterparts in the U.S. market. In the 1970s, Federal Reserve officials began to cooperate to an unprecedented extent with foreign central bankers.

Ezra Vogel's *Japan as Number One* published in 1979, startled Americans. Weak U.S. economic performance during the decade had prompted economists to debate the country's competitive position. The United States no longer stood alone as an industrial giant. Economists such as Lester Thurow were describing the U.S. economy as one that "no longer performed." In the 1950s and 1960s, Americans had lost rank in textiles and steel. Now, economists' concerns concentrated on the research-intensive, high-technology industries. So, too, growing automobile imports could no longer be dismissed as a temporary, niche-market phenomenon. The U.S. automobile industry, once the nation's pride and joy, in the 1970s

seemed unresponsive even to domestic requirements. Inflation and fluctuating currencies made it hard to measure the country's global competitive stature. Nonetheless, despite rising protectionist views within the country, when the GATT Tokyo Round concluded in 1979, the United States agreed to lower tariffs by 30 percent, the European Community by 27 percent, and Japan by 22 percent. (See figure 1 for an overview of U.S. tariff duties since the 1890s.) The United States still felt sufficiently secure to take the lead in freeing up world trade. The United States was now wide open to imports.

As the 1980s began, U.S. inflation was brought under control by a strong dose of high interest rates and an induced recession. The victory over inflation was sustained by lower oil prices and by new competition from imports as well as by the presence of foreign multinationals in America.

At the end of the 1970s, the Carter administration had inaugurated the process of deregulation, which accelerated during the Reagan years. The Reagan administration fervently attacked large-scale government intervention in the economy. In the mid-1980s, the dollar rose in value, becoming stronger than before the Nixon shock, and then fell sharply. Dollar fluctuations continued on a downward path into the early 1990s. By 1992, the dollar had reached new lows against the German mark and the Japanese yen. The uncertainties of the 1980s and early 1990s notwithstanding, trade and international investment increased. Companies learned to hedge against currency variations. Foreign direct investments—inward and outward—could also assist in mitigating the negative effects of currency instability.

The United States continued to be a net importer of goods throughout the 1980s and early 1990s. Even as the trade deficit loomed ever larger, the U.S. generally continued to endorse free trade, while frequently introducing or threatening patchwork, ad hoc protectionist measures. In 1988, Congress passed the Omnibus Trade and Competitiveness Act (also called the Trade Expansion Act). A provision in it, known as "Super 301" (the 1974 trade act, section 301, had been the weaker precedent), gave the U.S. trade representative the authority to look into "unreasonable and discriminatory" barriers to U.S. exports and to identify unfair traders and appropriate U.S. imports on which to retaliate. Several countries (including Japan and Brazil) were targeted. Yet, overall, the U.S. market remained open and consumer choices were responsible for the enlarged trade.

In the immediate aftermath of the sharp rise in oil prices in 1979 (which came to be known as OPEC

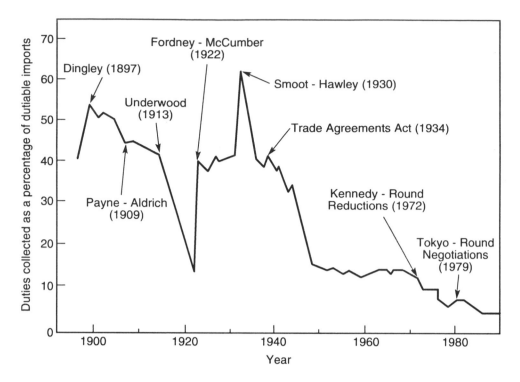

Figure 1. U.S. Tariff duties, 1895–1990. (Source: Adapted from Richard G. Lipsey et al., *Economics,* 9th ed. [1990].)

II), Americans made efforts to conserve energy, to develop domestic oil resources and energy alternatives, and to lower the country's need for oil imports. Yet as oil prices had dropped in the 1980s, these measures appeared less necessary, and it once again seemed to make economic sense to import cheap oil. By the start of 1990s, imported oil accounted for 50 percent of U.S. consumption—even higher than the 44 percent in 1977, when President Jimmy Carter had warned about national dependence on foreign oil. In 1992 Congress passed an energy bill, seeking to reduce this American reliance on foreign oil, but the problem had less urgency than in the 1970s. Low oil prices and the greater diversity of imports meant that at the start of the 1990s oil imports accounted for only about 10 to 13 percent of total imports, compared to 30 percent in the 1970s and 32 percent in 1980. By the late 1980s, merchandise imports from Japan, Canada, West Germany, Taiwan, Mexico, and South Korea were greater than those from the United Kingdom or from any individual OPEC country. By 1990 imports, which now represented a very wide range of products, had reached 9 percent of U.S. GNP; exports represented just over 7 percent. Industries became international. During the 1980s, imports penetrated basic Ameri-

can industries. Table 1 gives U.S. factories' share of the U.S. market in specified industries. Despite the new production by foreign-owned firms in this country, the shares captured by imports rose.

While America remained a net importer of goods, it also became a sizable net importer of capital, and in the late 1980s, America became a debtor nation in world accounts. Some economists criticized the statistics, arguing that the numbers mixed apples and oranges (historical with current values) and

Table 1. U.S. FACTORIES' SHARE OF U.S. MARKET, 1979 AND 1989[a]

Industry	1979	1989
Telephone equipment ($16.5 billion)	95%	81%
Computers ($61.6 billion)	94	66
Semiconductors ($15.8 billion)	90	67
Industrial machinery ($37.8 billion)	95	83
Color television ($5 billion)	92	74
Apparel ($69.5 billion)	86	74
Machine tools ($3.4 billion)	77	54

[a] Figures in parenthesis refer to 1989 shipments; data include production by foreign-owned U.S. factories in 1979 and 1989.
SOURCE: Edmund Faltermayer, "Is 'Made in the USA' Fading Away?" *Fortune* (24 September 1990): 64.

pointing out that important U.S. direct investments abroad remained larger than foreign direct investments in the United States. Pressure grew to make the statistics more meaningful and in 1989 revised figures on foreign direct investments, using current and market values, increased the recorded amount of U.S. business investments abroad, thus reducing the extent of America's negative international position. The new statistics shifted forward the date when America became a debtor in international accounts. But, statistical manipulations notwithstanding, America by the late 1980s was unquestionably a debtor nation in world accounts.

Much of the 1980s was devoted to working out the difficulties springing from large-scale defaults by developing countries during the early years of the decade. U.S. bank regulators wanted to be sure that these bad loans did not undermine the solvency of major American banks. Debt extensions, rescheduling, and new loans ultimately brought the level of Latin American debt (in current dollars) higher in the early 1990s than it had been in the early 1980s. Regarding other outward foreign portfolio investments, when U.S. interest rates dropped sharply in the early 1990s, portfolio managers devised global equity and global income funds. With these, the American public participated in U.S. outward foreign portfolio investments through familiar investment conduits.

In 1990 Canada remained the largest single national recipient of U.S. direct investments. American multinationals retained but often restructured their interests in Europe. Despite the difficulties of operating there, new U.S. direct investments were being made in Japan. Roughly 75 percent of U.S. outward direct investment in 1990 was in developed countries, yet by the late 1980s and early 1990s many developing countries, hurt by their experiences with foreign debt, were trying to attract direct investments by American multinationals. Attitudes had gone through a sea change, partly because of the success of Asian "tigers," such as Singapore, which had remained open to foreign multinationals all along, and partly because of the end of the Cold War.

For decades, developing countries had sought U.S. aid and attention by threatening to align themselves with the communist bloc. With the dissolution of the Soviet Union, however, developing nations looked more eagerly toward foreign (U.S., European, and Japanese) multinationals, lest their interests be neglected in the new global environment. The poor track record of centrally planned economies provided yet another reason that developing countries' attitude

toward multinationals had become more favorable. During the 1980s and early 1990s, many nations embarked on deregulation, privatization, and greater reliance on market forces. They invited U.S. multinationals to participate in their more open economies. The same was true in eastern Europe and the states of the former Soviet Union.

As these profound changes in the world economy influenced U.S. outward investments, inward foreign investments in America mounted rapidly; as in the past, portfolio investments accounted for a greater portion than did direct investments. In 1980, Japan had passed a foreign exchange control law that allowed Japanese nationals to make major investments abroad. Japanese banks and insurance companies promptly did so, undertaking portfolio investments in the United States, where they could obtain higher returns than at home. While the percentages of U.S. public debt held abroad do not appear to have reached the heights of the 1970s, as the size of America's domestic deficit ballooned in the 1980s, foreign (particularly Japanese) investors bought ever larger quantities of U.S. Treasury bonds. Foreign purchasers of such securities helped America finance its swelling domestic deficit. But when U.S. interest rates fell in the late 1980s and early 1990s, these investors retreated.

Foreign investors in the United States played a part in the flamboyant financial world of the 1980s, with its leveraged buyouts and junk bonds. As a percentage of American corporate debt, foreign holdings appear to have peaked at about 14 percent in 1986. Foreign holdings of American equities rose steadily in the 1980s, although until the last half of the decade they represented less than 5 percent of the stock outstanding (a level that they barely crept above).

So large had foreign portfolio investments (especially those in U.S. Treasury issues) in the United States become by the late 1980s that questions arose whether the United States could still pursue an independent monetary policy. Foreign investors' divestments reportedly played a causal role in the sharp downturn in the stock market in October 1987, when the Dow-Jones Industrial Average plunged by more than five hundred points. In the early 1990s, as discussions went forward in the United States about lowering interest rates to stimulate the domestic economy, people began to fear a massive exodus of foreign monies would ensue. Interest rates did in fact fall greatly, and there was a sizable outflow. Even so, interest rates continued to be lowered. American monetary policy was constrained but not undermined by the presence of foreign investors. Nonetheless, the participation of foreign investors continued to create uneasiness in the United States, mitigated only partly by the reassuring awareness that most of America's foreign obligations were denominated in dollars. This meant that as foreign investors abandoned the dollar (and the dollar depreciated in value), they hurt themselves as long as they retained any dollar holdings. In the recent past, some U.S. debt had been denominated in foreign currencies: the Roosa bonds of 1962, the Carter bonds of the 1970s, and, in the 1980s, the Eurobonds and even yen bonds offered by certain government agencies. On the whole, however, most of America's foreign obligations were dollar-denominated, making the country invulnerable to one set of uncertainties that faced most other international debtors: when the dollar's value fell, America's international debt stayed the same.

As inward foreign *direct* investments climbed in the 1980s, many U.S. industries became thoroughly international. This was especially true of the electronics, automobile, rubber tire, and pharmaceutical industries, as well as the communications and media sector (from film studios to magazine publishing). It became impossible to consider many American "domestic" industries without including the part played by foreign companies in those industries. In some instances, automobiles for example, the presence of formidable foreign rivals inside America's borders prompted U.S. companies to improve their production technologies and the quality of their products. In the 1980s, for the first time in U.S. history Japanese firms began manufacturing cars at plants in the United States. American consumers obtained the benefits of the new competition.

At the end of the 1980s, measured by book value of direct investments, British multinationals retained first place among the foreign multinationals in the United States. Japanese stakes had escalated rapidly, however, and, measured by the size of nonbank affiliates' assets and total sales, the Japanese had by the late 1980s surpassed the British. Also, Japanese ownership of bank assets in the United States was far greater than that of the British.

The American economy has always been so large that figures on foreign affiliates' share of U.S. manufacturing assets or U.S. employment in manufacturing have tended to obscure the significant role of foreign direct investment in more narrowly defined sectors. Yet, by 1989, foreign affiliates did own 16.8 percent of U.S. manufacturing assets and provided 11 percent of U.S. jobs in manufacturing. Foreign direct investments in the banking sector were even more dramatic. In 1990, U.S. financial affiliates of foreign banks and bank holding companies held 21.2 percent of the assets of all U.S. banks. These rising foreign investments in America were what had transformed the United States in the late 1980s into the world's greatest debtor nation.

America's new status as a net importer of both goods and capital had a profound impact on the domestic economy. The country's basic industries felt the competition. A net 1.2 million manufacturing jobs were lost in the 1980s, as U.S. firms closed noncompetitive and obsolete plants and became more efficient in their production methods. Of these 1.2 million jobs, fully 500,000 were among apparel and textile workers, though jobs were likewise lost in steel and in the electronics and automobile industries. Foreign multinationals in these sectors opened modern facilities in the United States—plants that utilized the latest process technologies and required fewer production workers than did American-owned plants in the same industries.

The framework of public policy considerations altered. At the Uruguay Round of GATT (started in 1986), the United States pressed for liberalization of the service-sector trade, where the country still had a positive balance. There were new discussions of TRIPS (trade-related intellectual property rights) and TRIMS (trade-related investment matters). For years, the Uruguay Round floundered, but was eventually completed in 1993. The final GATT agreement would lower worldwide trade barriers (124 nations agreed to cut tariffs by one-third), required signatories to protect intellectual property, reduced many nontariff restrictions on trade, and set up a new trade organization, the World Trade Organization, to administer the agreement. While critics charged that if the United States joined the WTO, this would jeopardize U.S. sovereignty, in November 1994 Congress approved the GATT agreement and the proposed WTO. Meanwhile, on a bilateral basis, American policymakers pushed Japan to lower nontariff barriers to American exports. The deficit in U.S.-Japanese trade was particularly large, and the rise of Japan as a formidable rival posed many policy challenges. The ratification of GATT would be helpful in opening the Japanese market.

On a regional basis, Americans took new steps toward trade liberalization. As the European Community moved toward greater integration (and the European Union emerged), Americans sought a counterpart in the Western Hemisphere with the U.S.-Canadian Free Trade Agreement of 1988 and the North American Free Trade Agreement of 1992 (NAFTA, ratified in 1993). The United States in the early 1990s participated in APEC—the Asia Pacific Economic Cooperation group. These involvements—as now with most "trade" arrangements—affected both trade and investment patterns, increasing the amounts of cross-border interactions. Many Americans, especially those losing their jobs to imports, feared the "export" of jobs and the import of goods made by cheap labor, and thus no longer endorsed freer trade. Critics wondered whether the U.S. postwar policy of trade liberalization had been in the nation's interest. However, both the Bush and Clinton administrations recognized the gains that stood to be made from unimpeded global trade. Protectionist measures would continue to be taken; yet as in past years, these were ad hoc, sector-specific, and often based on charges that other nations were unfairly "dumping" goods in the United States, that is, selling deliberately underpriced goods simply in order to gain market share. The Clinton administration endorsed *free* trade but only if it were *fair,* and it placed a new emphasis on developing industrial policy that included a "fair" (i.e., reciprocal) trade policy. At the same time, its strong support of NAFTA and GATT and its participation in APEC meant a continuation of the postwar commitment to more open trade.

With the exception of some national-security sectors (including shipping and airlines, broadcasting, nuclear energy, and defense), American policy throughout the post–World War II years had been wide open to inward foreign direct investments. State governments actively encouraged the entry of foreign multinationals, viewing foreign direct investment as a means of bringing economic growth, jobs, and tax revenues. They feted the newcomers. Yet as Japanese direct investment mounted in the 1980s, considerable ambivalence arose. And when investments were made in highly symbolic properties such as Rockefeller Center and Columbia Pictures, "Japan-bashing" intensified. Moreover, concern mounted that foreign multinationals in the United States did not pay their fair share of U.S. taxes. On the other hand, as the Cold War ended, some of the policies on national security changed; America became even more open to inward foreign investment.

American policymakers had for many years assumed that monopolies would "crystalize" if government did not intervene to break them up. But as technology changed rapidly, both domestically and internationally, in the 1980s there were numerous opportunities for competition in both new and older industries. International businesses, long vulnerable to U.S. antitrust action, found in the 1980s that they could form alliances and join in partial relations with foreign-owned firms without being subject to attack. The relaxation of antitrust enforcement in the 1980s had a significant effect on international business relationships.

In banking and finance, U.S. policymakers came to recognize the necessity of fostering cooperation among bank regulators around the world and setting international standards for safety and soundness. Such views were incorporated into the 1991 Foreign Bank Supervision Enhancement Act and the discussions of the Basel international standards for bank capital. What emerged in the 1980s and early 1990s was a broad policy recognition that what happened in the world economy mattered to America.

THE UNITED STATES AND THE WORLD ECONOMY

The United States has been intimately involved in the world economy—through trade, investments, and technology transfers—throughout the twentieth century. This engagement fluctuated in magnitude and changed in nature. American participation shifted as the size and characteristics of the U.S. economy evolved. At the start of the century, the United States was the industrial leader of the world. A half-century later, after the massive destruction to its rivals caused by World War II, America's global industrial prowess was without peer. In absolute and relative terms, American leadership was more secure than it had been five decades earlier. Yet, as European nations and Japan recovered, the United States faced strong competitors abroad. So, too, as industrialization spread globally, the number of countries playing an important role in world trade and investment rose. In absolute terms, America in the 1990s remained an industrial giant; in relative terms, its position was far less dominant than in 1950.

The United States was deeply, significantly involved in the international economy throughout the century. But, except during those episodes when foreigners were blamed for shortcomings at home, the sheer size of the domestic economy and America's isolation between two oceans made it easy for most Americans to remain oblivious to the United States' international economic interactions. Even after World War II, when communications and transportation were rapidly improving, when average Americans were learning more and more about the outside world, and when there was strong public support for the Marshall Plan, a core belief survived that somehow the U.S. domestic economy was impervious to international influence. The general perception that America was the influencer but not itself importantly affected (much less transformed) by the global economy persisted into the 1960s.

By the 1970s, however, when the United States had become a net importer of goods, foreign products were a part of every American's daily life. Americans were wearing Italian shoes, sitting in front of Japanese television sets, and driving German (and Japanese) cars. Overnight, a very personal awareness of America's role in the world emerged.

When Americans talk about encouraging trade, they often concentrate on exports—and the jobs that exports generate. Yet there are two sides to the trade coin, and for average Americans exports are, in the main, an abstraction; imports, by contrast, are very visible. Thus, as imports have risen in volume and as a percentage of GNP, Americans have paid increasing attention to the international economy.

Imports have two effects: they give consumers new choices, and they may compete with goods made at home and thus may cause the loss of jobs in particular industries. This second effect has historically generated the most publicity. In recent years, imports as a percentage of gross national product have been higher than at any other time in the twentieth century.

Despite policymakers' almost myopic focus on trade, however, imports are overshadowed by the immense amount of foreign capital in the United States today. While ratios on trade, and on the level of foreign investments vis-à-vis GNP, are not analogous, they are, nonetheless, useful for comparison, demonstrating how vital it is to devote attention to investment relationships. (See table 2 for a comparison of export/import and investment figures.)

In the early years of the century, America's manufactured products were highly competitive in global markets. Although a debtor nation, the United States was a net exporter of goods. By the 1990s, the United States was not only once again a net importer of capital, it was also a net importer of goods. This status has stimulated some very difficult questions. Do the figures imply American decline or even senility? How are they to be explained? Are they cause for worry, and, if so, why?

The economic historian Gavin Wright has suggested that America's competitive advantage during the early twentieth century was based on cheap, nonreproducible mineral resources and that the loss of advantage has come with the need to import raw

Table 2.   U.S. EXPORTS, IMPORTS, OUTWARD AND INWARD FOREIGN INVESTMENTS, 1914 AND 1990[a]

	1914	1990
U.S. exports	6%	7%
U.S. imports	5	9
U.S. outward foreign investments (portfolio and direct)[b]	10	15[c]
Foreign investments in the U.S. (portfolio and direct)[b]	20	25

[a] Exports, imports, and investments are measured as percentage of gross national product.

[b] Foreign investment figures in the numerator are stock data. In the 1990 figures, the level of direct investment is valued at current cost. The percentage estimates on investments are rough approximations.

[c] This figure probably understates the level of both long-term outward foreign portfolio and direct investments.

materials. Other economists, notably Robert Lipsey, have pointed out that American companies abroad continue to be sizable exporters and that this betokens competitive strength even though the nation's share in world exports has declined. Perhaps, they suggest, we should look at a nation's companies rather than at the nation as a geographical entity when studying its competitive advantage and competitive vitality.

Some macroeconomists who look solely at the United States' low domestic savings and investment rates feel that these factors should be given priority over the foreign trade and investment deficits, and that policies directed at the former problems will solve the latter. Other writers, such as Robert Reich, argue that work at home matters most: America is strong if foreign investors are providing Americans with jobs. On such a view, production within the country's borders is much more important than domestic competitive vigor.

Some economists maintain that manufacturing is so essential that American industry should be fostered and protected. Then there are those economists who insist that America's problems lie abroad, not at home; that foreign nations (particularly Japan) discriminate unfairly against American goods and investors; that the United States must insist on reciprocity and, if necessary, retaliate against market protection abroad.

Still others believe that the mature American economy has inevitably shifted toward services, that the America of the 1990s has advantages in research-oriented services, and that domestic manufacturing is less important than sustaining America's comparative advantages in human capital and in service exports.

Some macroeconomists see net capital inflows as beneficial as long as the capital goes to productive purposes. Because American obligations are mainly denominated in dollars, the United States maintains its sovereignty and there is no basis for serious concern. Others argue that large inward foreign investments are in fact a consequence and proof of America's strength.

Yet other economists change the argument's focus and insist that it is wrong to look at the U.S. economy in national terms. On this view, global economic growth is much more crucial, and America will thrive with the development of the international economy, just as it has always prospered when the world economy is expanding and healthy. Specialization, with the resulting gains from trade and investment, will be to everyone's advantage even though certain U.S. industries may be hurt in the process and even though the United States' relative position may decline. America has no monopoly on technological innovation, and international interactions make progress achieved by foreign industry available for Americans to absorb, adapt, and use for further innovation. According to this argument, American producers gain from the new global rivalry, which challenges domestic automobile, steel, and electronics makers to become more competitive, and U.S. consumers are rewarded by global competition, obtaining higher quality, cheaper, and more varied goods.

On the other side, some counter that America must look out for America first. Proponents of this view push for a domestic industrial policy and believe that too much international interchange always weakens fiscal and monetary policy instruments. On this view, foreigners in America rob the country of homegrown technology and undermine its competitive power through unfair competition ("dumping" goods and selling products made by low-paid foreign workers). A loss of jobs in the United States equals a loss of income for consumption. These economists, and their supporters, argue that the open world economy exposes America to the perils of fluctuating exchange rates and price explosions in vital sectors (oil, for example) and that the possible withdrawal of foreign capital always threatens to leave the country helpless and dependent. National security considerations require that the United States be able to provide for its own basic needs.

Environmentalists have added their views to those of the economists, expressing fears that lowering barriers to trade exacerbates businesses' cost-consciousness, thus impeding the pursuit of sound environmental policies. Environmentalists see trade and foreign investment policies as subordinate to, not separate from, ecological ones, and often argue strongly against the expansion of free trade.

Some aspects of the debate about America's role in the world economy are novel, particularly the ideas of the environmentalists. Many others have long been part of the domestic dialogue, surfacing periodically. The controversies, however, become ever more important as private-sector international economic engagements have come to affect the domestic economy in a manner unprecedented in the twentieth century. In the 1990s not only were the size and scope of America's participation in the world economy greater than in the past, but truly unique was the widespread awareness of the significant impact of the rest of the world on Americans' daily lives.

SEE ALSO America and the World Economy; The National-Security State; Foreign Policy (all in volume II); Economic Performance (in this volume).

BIBLIOGRAPHY

No comprehensive history of America's foreign-trade patterns exists, but mention should be made of Robert E. Lipsey's many contributions, as well as those of Raymond Vernon and Louis Wells on trade and direct investments. On U.S. tariff policy, see the classic by F. W. Taussig, *The Tariff History of the United States* (8th rev. ed., 1931; reprint, 1964), which goes only through the tariff of 1930. Neither is there a general history of U.S. portfolio investments abroad; the large literature on this subject is distinct from that on U.S. business abroad. On the latter, see Mira Wilkins, *The Emergence of Multinational Enterprise: American Business Abroad from the Colonial Era to 1914* (1970), and *The Maturing of Multinational Enterprise: American Business Abroad from 1914 to 1970* (1974). Alfred Chandler's work on the growth of American business deals with multinational enterprise. For foreign investment in the United States (portfolio and direct), see Mira Wilkins, *The History of Foreign Investment in the United States to 1914* (1989), and the sequel, covering 1914 to 1994, which is in process. I know of no single historical study on short-term and long-term portfolio and direct international investments, and their relations to foreign trade, although much has been written on the subject.

Note on sources: trade figures in this essay are in current dollars, that is, they are not adjusted for inflation, and are from published U.S. government statistics. Since different government sources provide different figures, I have chosen the most plausible, specifying what is being measured. The foreign investment data (also in current dollars) are from both government statistics and my own research.

ECONOMIC POLICIES

Ellis W. Hawley

American economic policy in the twentieth century has followed patterns characteristic of other industrialized nations. Many of the forces shaping policy elsewhere have also been at work in America, and in the policy output there are similar concerns about the abuses of economic power, similar efforts to deal with market and community failure, similar interplays between elitist and populist impulses, and similar conflicts between capitalist, socialist, and corporatist ideals. Yet in other respects the policy-making and administrative apparatus erected in the United States has unique characteristics and has produced a unique blend of policy prescriptions, tensions, and compromises. America entered the twentieth century with an underdeveloped administrative state, a business structure acquiring managerial capacities without parallel elsewhere, and deeply entrenched historical commitments to the values of individualism, democracy, federalism, and the rule of law. In these respects it was an exceptional nation, and this affected the policy choices that it made to deal with twentieth-century capitalism and the social disruptions that accompanied it.

In particular, the heritage with which America entered the twentieth century tended to marginalize the kind of dirigiste, socialist, and antimodernist prescriptions that gained substantial followings in other capitalist societies. America was a land largely without the imperial bureaucracies, Marxist-inspired labor movements, and "old regime" institutions from which such prescriptions emerged. Its threatened and discontented groups tended to seek fuller realization of liberal ideals rather than seeing liberalism as inimical to their interests. The result was the development of a uniquely American version of the interventionist state. In America the presumption has been that an expanding array of antitrust agencies, regulatory commissions, regulative associations, and statist compensations could produce the kind of liberal economic behavior that served the nation as a whole. The central policy goal has been the creation of a properly regulated market as the instrument to achieve economic and social improvement and a stronger position internationally. Because departures from this goal have been limited and temporary, policy debate and interest-group struggle have revolved primarily around three matters. One has been competing definitions of "good" market behavior. The others have been competing designs for the needed compensatory action and competing views of the proper regulatory roles of the antitrust agency, the public commission, and the public-spirited association.

What follows is a description of how America's unique version of the interventionist state was built and used, how its policy output changed through time, and how it was occasionally challenged by those who disputed the need for it or its adequacy for dealing with the nation's economic problems. The story can be divided logically into five chronological phases. Following a brief look at the new economy and policy heritage as they existed in 1900, the account will focus first on the pre-1917 era of progressive reform. It will then examine in turn the era of World War I and Republican ascendancy, the era of the New Deal and World War II, the era of the corporate commonwealth from 1949 to 1968, and the post-1960s era of unsettled issues and shifting models. Much of the policy produced by America's interventionist state was marked by incoherence, contradiction, vacillation, and the fragmentation characteristic of interest-group politics. Yet enduring principles, visions, cultural commitments, and power relationships also entered into the making of policy choices and helped to give the policy output a degree of continuity and unity.

THE NEW ECONOMY AND THE POLICY HERITAGE

As the United States entered the twentieth century, many of its citizens worried about the changes that had taken place in its economy over the last two decades of the nineteenth century. Most noticeable and most worrisome was the transition from family-owned businesses producing for restricted markets to centralized, bureaucratic corporations producing for large-scale markets. Small businessmen, industrial laborers, and the nation's farmers, it seemed, were all being pushed to the sidelines or into roles that involved major losses of independence and opportunity. In response to cries of alarm about an economy that could undermine the basis for republican governance and virtue, Congress established a national forum for discussion, study, and the airing of grievances. In 1898 it created the United States Industrial Commission, consisting of ten members of Congress plus nine presidential appointees from civil life, and eventually with an extensive staff of administrators and economic experts. The commission ended its work in 1902 and by that time had produced a nineteen-volume report. In its publications, it dealt not only with the changing business structure but also with the labor, farm, and immigration problems and how they were related to what commission member James H. Kyle called a "new and strange industrialism."

The Industrial Commission's reports documented in detail what others were saying about a new kind of economy. From the unprecedented burst of industrial reorganization and consolidation that swept the country from 1897 to 1902 had come a new array of business structures that in the name of efficiency and progress were implementing a virtual "revolution" in production and distribution methods. At the same time a growing industrial labor force fed by massive immigration had given a new edge to labor relations and to demands that collective bargaining replace individual contracts, while a new and more businesslike agriculture was dealing harshly with those who lacked the requisite capital and skills. Accompanying the process was a growing gap between the needs and implications of this new economy and the governmental system and social norms inherited from the past. America, the commission concluded, needed more knowledge and more government to adjust to and secure the benefits of the new economy. In its recommendations it stressed particularly the desirability of federal licensing for large corporations and national standards to reduce excessive diversity in state legislation.

In conducting its studies and formulating its recommendations, the commission relied heavily on the pro–big business ideas of such scholars as Jeremiah W. Jenks of Cornell University. It embraced in particular the view that the new economy represented natural progress toward a higher civilization in which government would have to assume new responsibilities, especially for the protection and beneficial use of invested capital. Yet the commission's view reflected only one of several attitudes in the corporate world. Some corporate apologists believed the new economy was developing its own forms of market discipline and common law, which could not be improved upon by greater governmental intervention. Others believed that a developing sense of corporate stewardship and philanthropic obligation was rendering any new form of governmental action unnecessary. The steel magnate, Andrew Carnegie, for example, argued that Americans should accept and welcome the survival of the fittest in their business system, provided that the fittest also accepted a responsibility to use their wealth and power for social improvement. In the union of the two lay the potential for a continuation of both material and spiritual progress.

There was, however, growing support for governmental intervention in the popular press, from those speaking for small business, rural, and labor interests, and from "new school" economists who had broken with classical theory. In these quarters, the belief was that the new business structures were undermining the conditions that had allowed market transactions, community norms, and minimal government to provide both order and liberty. They were creating instead a new order, if not a "new feudalism," marked by economic exploitation, social injustice, political corruption, dependent relationships, and recurrent crises. They were producing a society clearly at odds with the republican and liberal values to which America was supposed to be dedicated. And, although such critics often conceded a need for greater efficiency, stability, and technical progress, they argued that the degree to which big business provided these was greatly exaggerated, and that there were ways to have them without tolerating the abuses attendant upon unregulated corporate concentration. A new state could be built that would allow America to combine growing abundance and security with the preservation of liberty, democracy, and opportunity.

These opponents of corporate giantism, however, were more united in their perception of the evils involved than they were in their remedial prescriptions. Small business owners wanted not only curbs on big business but also protection from labor monopolies and support for their own associations and community structures. Farmers and laborers disagreed with each other and among themselves about the type of intervention that should be undertaken. A new middle class of professional and technical specialists leaned toward technocratic solutions but disagreed about how these could be reconciled with democracy and individualism. And a diverse body of economic thinkers offered differing views on the extent to which group formation and voluntary agreements could reduce the need for governmental control. Complicating matters was a general unwillingness to scrap the essentials of America's nineteenth-century political state of parties, courts, and strong local units. Only a few critics and reformers wanted a regulatory structure in which these older safeguards of freedom would be abolished.

What most critics agreed upon was that the policies operating in 1900 had worked to strengthen big business rather than curb or control it. Such was the case, they said, with the tariff protection, which culminated in the Dingley Tariff of 1897, and with the "sound money" system, which was rooted in the gold standard and national bank charters. Such was also the case with a public lands policy that encouraged rapid private exploitation, and a Court-produced constitutional law that had turned the due process clause into a defense of corporate property rights. Although the Interstate Commerce Act of 1887, the Sherman Antitrust Act of 1890, and a number of state regulatory and antitrust laws were on the books, the resulting regulatory commissions had been reduced to impotence by adverse court decisions, and efforts to implement the antitrust laws had fared badly. These statutes, regulations, and court decisions had succeeded primarily in diverting business consolidation away from loose combinations into tighter ones. Citing *Ohio* v. *Standard Oil Co. of Ohio* (1892), *United States* v. *E. C. Knight* (1895), and *United States* v. *Trans-Missouri Freight Association* (1897), corporate lawyers could assure their clients that combination was still possible. It could be done legally through asset acquisitions and holding companies, especially in the manufacturing sector and when undertaken for purposes of vertical integration.

By 1900, support for reform measures in each of these policy areas was growing. The labor upheavals of the 1880s and the "populist revolt" of the 1890s had failed to produce a major new party on the political left, but both the Republican and Democratic parties were developing "progressive" wings. As they did so, they became increasingly responsive to middle-class critics of the new economy and increasingly inclined to back a regime of intervention purporting to create and preserve "fair" markets and fair market behavior. In theory, such a regime could produce an increasingly efficient, stable, and progressive capitalism in which socially virtuous conduct would also be suitably rewarded. Among backers of the idea it was becoming an article of faith that fuller middle-class participation in politics would yield a "progressive statecraft" capable of determining what was "fair" and "good" and acting on that determination.

Even as these reform initiatives emerged, however, another vision also claiming to be progressive was emerging from the corporate world and offering designs for a government that could assist the new economy in developing its own enlightened mechanisms of self-regulation. A growing group of corporate leaders saw the need for banking and monetary reform and for more effective methods of market stabilization. Many also saw the need for a new educational and incentive system that could steer the working and older middle classes into their "proper" places in a corporate order. Because some despaired of achieving these things on their own, particularly in view of the interventionism of local governments sensitive to anticorporate attitudes, the idea of using a reformed government for the purpose began moving to the fore. As articulated in numerous conferences, in the recommendations of agencies such as the Industrial Commission, and in the program espoused by the newly formed National Civic Federation, the idea was to reform American government along corporate lines and then to use its new and more businesslike bureaus to help fill the perceived institutional gaps in the private sector. For some the model was what the Germans had achieved in their marketing, labor, and educational systems; for others a corporatist ideal of using the state to create an extra-political system of organized cooperation served to inspire and guide the initiatives undertaken.

Thus, from both the corporate world and its critics came ideologies justifying governmental expansion and intervention as essential for continued economic progress. Despite the differing ideas of progress, both ideological streams envisioned an enlarged government that entrusted more of its power to a properly trained administrative elite. The "progressive state," in other words, would acquire its capacity to provide needed regulation and institution building by becoming in larger measure an administrative state. It would ground its operations more in applied social science and less in struggles for partisan, group, and individual advantage. And while preserving the "liberal state" of the nineteenth century, it would rely on an enlightened bureaucracy interacting with an increasingly rational citizenry as the instruments needed to reconcile inherited values with modern needs.

Building a new administrative state, however, would prove an arduous task. The efforts to do so coexisted with a persisting legacy of antibureaucratic values that could be invoked by legislators, judges, local officials, and private associations reluctant to accept the roles that progressives would now assign them. Compromise was necessary to establish administrative units capable of coexistence with the older governmental order, and in practice compromise usually meant fragmented and narrowly constrained bureaucratic authority with the bureaucrats forced in some measure to function as interest-group politicians. An interventionist state with an expanded and more powerful executive branch gradually took shape, but it was notably deficient in administrative resources, heavily dependent upon private and local resources for implementing its policies, still subject to frustrating vetoes from older forms of institutional authority, and still susceptible to the corrupt misuse of its powers. These features provided its opponents with much grist for their continuing antistatist critique. But the assumptions and constraints propelling American state-building along this peculiar path were remarkably enduring.

The path taken worked to bring, in the words of political scientist Stephen Skowronek, both "a narrowing of the political alternatives and an obfuscation of the distinctions among them." On the one hand, progressive claims and promises helped to undercut and marginalize the analyses and prescriptions being offered by socialists, populists, and national planners. On the other, the progressive tendency to transform political issues into technical ones worked to obscure what was at stake and to satisfy those who were uncomfortable making stark choices between a corporate order and a democratic one. In operation, progressivism did not allow the new economy to develop on its own and find ways to govern itself nor did it attempt to destroy the new business system as a threat to democratic individualism and republican governance. On the contrary, it produced a new governing apparatus that in turn helped make the United States both a pioneer in the development of managerial capitalism and a nation uniquely committed by law to preserving opportunity, fairness, and virtue in the marketplace.

THE QUEST FOR A PROGRESSIVE POLITICAL ECONOMY, 1900–1916

The quest for a progressive regulatory apparatus began on the state and local levels, particularly apparent in the growth of state and municipal commissions that took over some of the policy-making chores of legislative committees. These commissions were supposed to operate as apolitical and expert tribunals devoted to the pursuit of the public interest. In sectors of the economy where competitive markets had allegedly failed and could not be expected to work—areas, in other words, of "natural monopoly," chronic outbursts of "destructive competition," or market transactions involving "gross unfairness"—commission regulation was to provide "fair returns" on "fair value." It would thereby become a surrogate for the lost discipline of a market system. From 1900 to 1916, other states followed the lead of Massachusetts, Wisconsin, and New York in transforming the primitive administrative products of earlier encounters with the railroads into complex public bureaucracies charged with supervising and regulating an array of transportation, utility, and natural resource industries. In addition, the apparatus sprouted arms empowered to bring greater "fairness" to agricultural and labor markets, protect smaller businesses from "predatory" and "unfair" competitive methods, safeguard consumers from harmful products, and assist professional groups in enforcing ethical standards. Yet the evolution of expert commissions remained slow and uneven because republican ideals remained strong and most of the resources for bureaucratization had developed in the private sector. From the beginning, heavy reliance on a collaborating network of legislative committees, local officials, sympathetic judges, and "public-spirited" private partners became a central feature of the apparatus. In practice, this reliance tended to undercut its apolitical pretenses and make it susceptible to "capture" by those being regulated.

As progressive reformers saw it, moreover, the apparatus was seriously defective because it lacked uniformity from state to state and it was unable to deal with problems of national scope. What was achieved in one state could be undone or rendered ineffective by policies adopted in others or by legal interpretations that reserved the regulation of interstate commerce to the federal government. Consequently, both corporate and anticorporate groups soon advocated and helped to build a federal regulatory apparatus that in theory could supplement that on the state and local levels. It could, as they saw it, deal with problems that the latter was incapable of addressing and help to bring greater coherence and rationality to regulation as a whole. By 1916 the United States had not only a National Conference of Commissioners engaged in promoting "model" state legislation and administration but also an expanding system of federal grants-in-aid geared to national standards and an expanding federal bureaucracy with its own regulatory commissions and collaborative networks.

One component of the new federal apparatus was mainly a product of the Industrial Commission's recommendations. These had not led to federal licensing of corporations. But they had produced a Bureau of Corporations whose experts conducted detailed investigations of corporate practice and sought a "reasonable" antitrust law under which administrators could distinguish between "good" and "bad" trusts and secure more of the former. This was also the policy goal of President Theodore Roosevelt in the years from 1903 to 1909. And after the Supreme Court held the Sherman Act applicable to tight combinations, as it did in *Northern Securities Co.* v. *United States* (1904) and *Swift & Co.* v. *United States* (1905), the idea of a revised antitrust law had considerable support in the corporate world. Under Roosevelt legislation to implement it failed, and under President William Howard Taft a number of Roosevelt's "good" trusts were subjected to prosecution. But in the period from 1911 to 1914 a version of the idea triumphed. In *Standard Oil Co. of New Jersey* v. *United States* (1911) and *United States* v. *American Tobacco Co.* (1911), the Supreme Court enunciated a "rule of reason" limiting the application of the Sherman Act to "unreasonable" restraints of trade, and in 1914 Congress enacted the Clayton and Federal Trade Commission (FTC) acts, which established a new commission and outlawed practices that decreased competition. The new FTC absorbed the Bureau of Corporations, continued the investigations into corporate practice, and took action to halt what the FTC itself determined to be "unfair methods of competition."

Ostensibly, these antitrust settlements implemented Woodrow Wilson's 1912 platform of a New Freedom rather than Theodore Roosevelt's platform of a New Nationalism. Thus, the official goal was "regulated competition" rather than "regulated monopoly." But the distinction between reasonable and monopolistic restraints was difficult to conceptualize, and the "rule of reason" became in practice an elastic concept subject to continuing pressures for expansion and contraction. The settlements, moreover, tended to institutionalize and perpetuate tensions that lawmakers were unable to resolve. The new commission was left heavily dependent on sympathetic judges and Justice Department prosecutors. The law was expected to achieve both economic efficiency and moralized market transactions, but these goals were less compatible than the theory of "regulated compe-

tition" assumed. And put in place were an apparatus and body of law that were used not only to promote competition as a way to enhance productivity and consumer welfare but also to protect small competitors from larger rivals and sponsor an anticompetitive system of industrial self-government.

Another feature of the new regulatory apparatus that showed the limits of government by commission was that portion concerned with making tariff and trade policy. By 1908 consumer concern with the rising cost of living, arguments linking the tariff to the growth of trusts, and pressure from particular export and import interests had combined to create strong demands for tariff reform. Prominent among the reformers were advocates of an apolitical and expert tariff commission that could take the issue out of politics and produce "reasonable" and "fair" schedules of benefit to America as a whole. Yet in the making of the Payne-Aldrich Tariff in 1909 and the Underwood Tariff in 1913, much political wheeling and dealing was in evidence. For the Underwood Tariff, President Wilson was able to muster a coalition that lowered rates substantially and shifted more of the revenue burden to a new federal income tax, but his recommendation for a tariff commission did not become law. Not until 1916 was such a commission established and then only to provide expert data and advice for congressional consideration. It had no power to regulate imports and no control over the assistance that the State and Commerce departments were providing to export interests.

A counterpart to antitrust and tariff reform could be found in monetary reform. Strong pressure for monetary reform dated particularly from the Panic of 1907, which had revealed in dramatic fashion the inability of the banking and currency system to meet changing business needs. The political situation, however, was such that neither the privately owned central bank proposed by a National Monetary Commission, nor the regional system of government banks desired by agricultural interests, nor the regulatory bureaucracy envisioned by some progressives could be established. Instead, the Federal Reserve Act of 1913 created a blend of public and private regulation—an "intersect," in the words of economist Kenneth Boulding—and entrusted it with limited powers to manage banking reserves and a money supply based on commercial paper as well as gold. Although nominally headed by a new administrative agency, the Federal Reserve Board, the system was heavily reliant on twelve privately owned Federal Reserve Banks. Its power was further constrained by the persistence of state banking regulated by state agencies. Its defenders viewed it as a way to combine public control with private efficiency and by doing so to correct the irrational behavior that led to monetary feasts and famines. But its capacities along these lines remained to be demonstrated.

Meanwhile, even as progressive reformers created such agencies as the Federal Trade Commission, the Tariff Commission, and the Federal Reserve System, they were also working to create a regulatory apparatus through which the national government could deal with the problems posed by "natural monopolies" and market-generated threats to public health and safety. Through legislation in 1903, 1906, 1910, and 1913, the Interstate Commerce Commission (ICC) was transformed from an impotent collector of data to an agency empowered to fix rates, control competitive practices, and regulate corporate financing in the railroad industry. It also acquired new powers over petroleum pipelines, interstate telephone and telegraph traffic, and the cable industry. Following passage of the Meat Inspection and Pure Food and Drug acts in 1906, the Department of Agriculture established bureaucracies engaged in providing new forms of consumer protection. Yet again, these bureaucratic growths were left heavily reliant on sympathetic judges, friendly congressional committees, and collaborative local and private agencies. They were not parts of an autonomous administrative state. Often their policy output was better explained by interest-group influence than by rational assessment of national need. Railroad rate-fixing, in particular, became a shipper-dominated activity, with arguments about the need for capital improvements usually ignored in ICC decisions.

Another problem addressed by builders of a new regulatory apparatus was the wastage, misallocation, and premature exhaustion of natural resources. This early environmental movement was heightened by concerns about the closing of the frontier. Again, as in other major policy areas, progressive reformers worked against various kinds of resistance to shift decision making away from an older set of institutions to an administrative and professional elite imbued with the ideals of scientific management. Their success was far from complete, however. Resource management remained a fragmented enterprise in which interest-group politics, sectional conflict, and clashes between aesthetic and utilitarian values continued to shape policy outputs. The National Conservation Commission was merely a temporary study group established in the wake of a 1908 White House Conference on Conservation. And progressives were forced to settle for such partial successes as the new Forest Service developed under Gifford Pinchot, the

U.S. Reclamation Service developed under Frederick Newell, and limited presidential actions to establish federal resource preserves.

The federal regulatory apparatus that had been constructed by 1916 also included new bureaucracies engaged in limited modification of agricultural and labor markets. The Department of Agriculture, with support from business-minded farm groups, members of Congress from rural areas, and the previously established land-grant college system, had become a promoter of "scientific agriculture" and a provider of new marketing and educational services. A new Federal Farm Loan System, established in 1916, placed the federal government in the business of providing rural credit. New labor legislation empowered agencies in the Department of Labor to operate conciliation, employment, and statistical services. And still other agencies were empowered to halt interstate trade in goods produced by child labor and enforce hour, wage, and safety standards in the railroad and shipping industries. The nation as yet had no Federal Farm Board; its Commission on Industrial Relations was merely another temporary study group (operative from 1912 to 1915); and its system for regulating the practices of labor unions still operated, for the most part, through the courts. But an apparatus similar to those in other policy areas was in the making, and the bureaucrats involved, especially in the Department of Agriculture, were developing a comparable degree of discretionary autonomy.

By 1916 the nation was also moving toward the view that "good" farm and labor organizations, like "good" trusts and professional societies, could become vital parts of the needed regulatory apparatus. This idea still encountered much resistance, particularly from organizations such as the National Association of Manufacturers, with its constituency of smaller business firms, and from judges trained in a law of contractual individualism. The idea also came in different forms; one scenario viewed such farm and labor organizations as units in an emerging "economic government" while another envisioned them as units in a collective bargaining system from which all Americans would benefit. But indicative of the direction of that policy was the inclusion of limited antitrust exemptions for such groups in the Clayton Antitrust Act. Similarly indicative were the tendencies to include representatives from these groups in policy study agencies and then to recognize the groups as responsible bodies to which regulatory and bargaining power could properly be entrusted. The still largely unsettled question was: What constituted the "good" organization in each field?

In important respects, the quest for the regulatory state envisioned in progressive prescriptions fell short, leaving would-be alterers of economic behavior with an apparatus that required effective use of political and lawyerly skills as well as administrative ones. Yet the theory of how to secure a properly functioning economy remained remarkably intact. The answer lay neither in socialism, national planning, nor laissez-faire, but rather in a regulation of the market system that would remedy the failures apparent in its production of financial panic, monopoly power, and social disintegration. Through interventions that would secure "good" behavior at the microeconomic level, it was believed, one could ensure "good" behavior on the part of the economy as a whole. And the reigning assumption was that this could be done through piecemeal action. Undertaken in separate spheres and at different levels and loosely coordinated by a mixture of expert knowledge, political bargaining, and constitutional law, such action could provide the needed intervention while preventing its abuse.

Defenders of this so-called American system, moreover, pointed to the economy's gains in productivity, output, and better business practice as proof that the system was working. It was a system, they claimed, that allowed America's workplaces and markets to undergo a continuing technological and organizational evolution that promised to provide greater abundance for all. Although critics continued to expound on the burdens of government and the contradictions of capitalism, most Americans were convinced that impressive strides had been made toward a political economy that combined the energies and efficiencies of capitalist markets with an appropriate mix of republican governance and the administrative state. Some even argued that these developments were saving America from European statism as well as from the destructive side of the new economy.

THE GREAT WAR AND THE NEW ECONOMIC ERA, 1917–1932

As of 1916, however, America's new regulatory apparatus was not readily adaptable to solving the economic problems produced by modern warfare. This became glaringly apparent when the nation entered World War I. To a remarkable extent the experience of coping with a war crisis and its legacies steered American state-building and its economic policy output into new channels in the years from 1917 to 1932. The mobilization experience produced new structures and visions that continued to affect policy

debates and choices throughout the period. Demobilization followed patterns that closed off some options and opened others. Efforts to return to normalcy developed alongside and in tension with efforts to apply the war's lessons concerning the need for managerial organization and rationality. When prosperity failed in 1929, the war experience would become a prime source of ideas for meeting another national crisis. During the period, America did not do away with the regulatory apparatus developed earlier. It did, however, supplement the apparatus with new mechanisms based on war-altered perceptions of how market failures could best be overcome.

Entry into the war and the accompanying decision to raise a large army for combat in Europe created a demand for war materials that could not be met through purchases in existing markets. Market transactions by themselves were incapable of providing the needed goods, services, and manpower, at least within the time or at the price levels thought reasonable or without severe and debilitating social disruptions. The resulting search for a market substitute quickly led to mobilization and use of governmental and private power to create a mixture of controls and incentives thought capable of meeting the special needs of a nation engaged in making the world "safe for democracy." An apparatus emerged through which soldiers were conscripted, prices and wages administered, "wastes" and "risks" of competitive behavior reduced, organizational formation guided and coordinated, and patriotism harnessed in ways that allowed it to function as a substitute for market incentives.

The central problem in creating such an apparatus was the underdeveloped nature of the American administrative state. It lacked the kinds of administrative resources and capacities that existed in the other major belligerent countries. But for these resources and capacities, too, a substitute was found. In part this was achieved by transforming existing agencies into instruments of war management or entrusting administrative tasks to the military. In much greater part it was achieved by calling the administrative resources of the private sector into national service and making them a major component of the new managerial and regulatory apparatus. Under such agencies as the Food Administration, the War Industries Board, the War Trade Board, and the Fuel Administration, a parallel structure of commodity divisions and industrial committees gradually emerged. The former were staffed by businessmen on leave to perform government service, the latter by industrial representatives. This interlocking structure, along with its counterparts for war finance and war labor policy, became the core of America's substitute for an administrative state. The regular agencies of government remained relatively small. The expansion of governmental operation was limited to the railroad, shipping, and telecommunications industries, and even in these "nationalization" typically involved the conversion of existing private managements into public operating agencies.

Not everyone was satisfied with the policies that emerged from the wartime apparatus. Some businessmen chafed under irksome restrictions. Some labor groups denied that wages and working conditions were being fairly determined. Some farmers complained about business domination of the Food Administration and presidential favoritism to southern interests. A variety of taxpayer and consumer groups deplored the mix of tax and price increases being used to pay for the unprecedented federal expenditures. Despite these complaints, the effects of patriotism, information management, and settlements achieved through special commissions, tribunals, and integrators helped the apparatus work tolerably well. For the duration of the war, it produced economic behavior that brought forth the growing stream of men, money, and matériel essential to an Allied victory. At war's end, its reputation for success was such that a number of administrators wanted to adapt major segments of the wartime system to the tasks of postwar reconstruction and peacetime economic management. In late 1918 and early 1919 there appeared a number of designs for a Peace Industries Board, a peacetime Council of Industrial Progress, a permanent National Labor Board, and a new Industrial Cabinet modeled on Wilson's War Council.

Efforts to implement these designs, however, failed to win presidential, congressional, public, or major interest-group support. Campaigns to legalize progressive forms of cartelization, build permanent structures of labor-management-government cooperation, and adapt wartime developments to the tasks of informed economic and social management all foundered. Much of the nation's policy-making apparatus instead came under the control of those bent upon restoring traditional arrangements and branding any departures from them as politically and socially subversive. In both major parties the progressive wings responsible for prewar state-building were overwhelmed by their conservative rivals. Patriotism was harnessed not to visions of cooperative action and administered progress, but to campaigns for ridding the country of profiteers, radical subversives, un-American ethnic groups, and an unnecessarily burdensome government. By 1920 it was clear that designs to graft the war state onto that built by progressive reformers had been at least temporarily blocked. If a new capacity for economic and social management was to be developed, a goal to which a number of former war administrators and technocratic professionals still subscribed, then that capacity would have to emerge from the corporate world. It must come through the utilization of corporate and philanthropic resources rather than from the political world now in charge of developing state resources.

The elections in 1920 brought an even fuller eclipse of political progressivism. By the time the elections were held, the economy had gone through a speculative boom into its worst slump since the 1890s, but those who thought bolder programs of statist intervention were the cure for these economic ills fared badly at the polls. The prescriptions applied by the conservative victors at the polls called either for a return to the normalcy of pre-progressive times or for a new and more businesslike progressivism designed to assist the corporate world in developing the managerial institutions needed by a progressive nation. In the new cabinet appointed by President Warren G. Harding in 1921, Secretary of the Treasury Andrew Mellon and Secretary of Commerce Herbert Hoover symbolized these two sides of a policy mix. Both Mellon's aim of normalcy and Hoover's of a businesslike progressivism were soon associated with economic recovery and the emergence of what was widely heralded as the world's most successful economy.

At the core of Mellonism, as it was applied from 1921 through 1928, was a tax policy intended to remove the burden of government on the economically successful and by so doing to stimulate economic development. This was the aim of the Mellon tax plan of 1921. Despite continuing resistance from and compromises with congressional progressives, the plan's supporters were eventually successful in securing major reductions in the federal income, inheritance, and business profits taxes. In addition, Mellonism brought a new federal budgeting system, higher protective tariffs, and a more businesslike attitude toward the provision of public goods, all of which were seen as ways to foster enterprise. Although most historians attributed the economic boom of the period to technological innovations rather than to Mellonist policy prescriptions, the coincidence of lower taxes, rising revenues, and steady reductions in the federal debt enabled Mellon and his supporters to claim validation for their prescriptions and predictions. By the late 1920s, Mellon was being hailed as the greatest secretary of the Treasury since Alexander Hamilton.

At the core of Hooverism, on the other hand, was a vision of economic and social improvement through the organized application of an expanding managerial science. Where Mellon saw burdens to be lifted, Hoover saw organizational and informational gaps to be filled. Under his direction, the Department of Commerce sought to fill them by linking itself to administrative resources in the private sector, much as the war agencies had done in 1917 and 1918, and then mounting campaigns that coupled social scientific inquiry with consensus building and organized cooperative action. Launched with much fanfare were campaigns for standardization and simplification, trade promotion, control of the business cycle, constructive as opposed to destructive competition, better business statistics, and a variety of social betterment projects. In the eyes of some, Hoover's operations were on their way to providing a substitute for the progressive state. They were fostering the formation of new units of economic self-government that could take over the regulative tasks no longer assignable to the market. And while numerous businessmen resisted such organizational efforts, enough of the business community was responsive to create the impression of a "new capitalism" reforming itself through industrial statesmanship and associational action. By the late 1920s, Hoover had become the "Great Engineer" in an age that idealized engineering principles. He and Mellon were hailed as co-authors of the nation's economic success story. As Hoover prepared to run for president in 1928, he was being credited with helping America organize its way out of the postwar depression and into a new economic era that promised permanent growth and prosperity.

Meanwhile, as Mellonism and Hooverism gained support, the regulatory apparatus erected by prewar progressives came under attack. Gradually it was reshaped along lines more consonant with the new policy environment. Antitrust law became tolerant of monopoly power and then of a wide range of associational activities. Utility and natural resource regulation moved into more cooperative modes, with larger roles for industrial self-regulation. The Tariff Commission, which in 1922 acquired the power to recommend schedule changes to be implemented by the president, became an instrument for securing greater tariff protection rather than freer trade. The Federal Reserve System came under the domination of the Federal Reserve Bank of New York and tended to embrace the goals of international bankers rather

than those concerned with domestic economic management. And prewar efforts to strengthen the market position of laborers and farmers gave way to antilabor court decisions, an equation of open shops and company unions with the American way, and the Hooverization of large segments of the Labor and Agriculture departments. Political progressives in Congress protested these developments strongly. But they lacked the power to change the new policy outputs or to override the presidential vetoes that blocked such congressionally approved measures as those authorizing agricultural price supports and federal development of the Tennessee River. The progressives' contribution to the policy mix consisted chiefly of expanded farm credits, limited investigative harassment of the meat and power trusts, and occasional blockage of measures desired by the Republican administration.

Moreover, new additions made to the American regulatory apparatus were usually in line with the new faith in business-government collaboration and public-spirited industrial self-government. This was true, for example, of the regulatory agencies established under the Grain Futures Act of 1922, the Alaskan Salmon Act of 1924, the Air Commerce Act of 1926, and the Radio Act of 1927. It was true on the state and local levels of the controls over real estate development. And it was equally true of the Federal Farm Board established under the Agricultural Marketing Act of 1929. Intended to implement Hoover's solution for alleviating persistent agricultural distress, the board's central goal was to organize and nurture agricultural associations that could bring order and rationality to farm markets. In the apparatus that existed by 1929, the roles envisioned for antitrust agencies and public commissions had shrunk substantially, while those envisioned for private and quasi-private associations had become a good deal larger.

Had economic expansion continued, the regulatory apparatus being built in the private sector might have become even more firmly established as the American solution to problems created by economic change. But the stock market crash of 1929, followed by the onset of the Great Depression, created conditions at marked variance with the promises of permanently growing prosperity. It became apparent that the apparatus was unable to prevent the kind of speculative excesses that had turned past economic booms into economic busts. It simply could not generate the compensatory spending envisioned in Hoover's schemes of business cycle control. It proved unsuited to the task of correcting serious market malfunctions, and without power to meet its expected social obligations. Thus, it came under attack as one of the sources of national economic difficulty. Critics were soon offering a variety of recovery programs calling for new kinds of regulatory machinery. And moving into the policy void was a discordant amalgam of market restorers, quasi-socialist planners, anticorporate populists and progressives, and spokesmen for a compulsory associationalism resembling the schemes articulated by European corporatists.

By 1932, as depression conditions worsened, Hooverism was thoroughly discredited as the path to future economic progress. In 1929 President Hoover had rejected Mellon's advice to liquidate everything. Instead, Hoover set out to short-circuit the business cycle through actions compatible with his own political philosophy. Initially, he sought to sustain and expand spending through increased public works, easier money, farm price supports, and business organizations pledged to maintain wage rates and undertake new investment programs. Subsequently, he devised a second program aimed at reversing economic decline abroad, restoring business confidence, and reestablishing the credit flows needed to put idle resources to work. As a part of this, he finally recommended and secured the creation of a Reconstruction Finance Corporation, modeled on the War Finance Corporation. In mid-1932 he sponsored a new network of cooperative industrial committees, charged them with the tasks of unfreezing credit and creating jobs, and invoked other war analogies to enlist public support. But recovery did not ensue, and Hoover remained highly resistant to the calls of his critics for instruments powerful enough to wage and win a real war against depression conditions. Reaching for these, he insisted, would destroy the whole basis for future economic and social progress. But a majority of Americans did not agree, as his overwhelming defeat in the election of 1932 showed.

As Americans awaited the inauguration of president-elect Franklin D. Roosevelt, they could look back on sixteen years during which economic policies had been strongly influenced by the nation's experience during World War I. From that experience had come both a vision of managerial prowess and a resurgent anti-statism. The result had been a policy mix initially credited with producing the world's most successful economy and subsequently blamed for a worldwide economic breakdown. The influence of that experience was not at an end. During his presidency, Hoover had increasingly clothed his efforts to deal with the depression in war metaphors. And to an even greater extent, such metaphors would help to justify the policy innovations and state-building of Roosevelt's New Deal.

THE NEW DEAL ORDER AND ITS LEGITIMATION, 1933–1948

In the history of U.S. economic policy, the period from 1933 through 1948 was a time of numerous innovations. To meet the crises of the Great Depression and World War II, American policymakers provided the nation with a new array of administered and regulated markets, social safety nets, and government-operated economic compensators. All of this represented a major change. Yet in the political economy that eventually emerged and gained legitimacy, there were also strong elements of persistence and continuity. The thrusts toward corporatist, socialist, and neopopulist prescriptions were all contained and turned back, leaving intact the American form of managerial capitalism and much of the regulatory apparatus previously erected by progressive reformers and New Era rationalizers. The new roles created in the 1933–1948 period for farm and labor associations, public finance agencies, and a military-industrial complex were all logical extensions of actions taken prior to 1933. Remaining very much alive were the anti-statist and antibureaucratic traditions. In practice, this meant that the American administrative state remained fragmented and constrained, still with little capacity for central planning and still heavily reliant on local and private administrative resources. Franklin Roosevelt was an innovator, but he also brought with him Wilsonian progressivism, the World War I experience, and New Era associationalism.

This mix was clearly evident in the laws and programs that emerged from the special session of Congress that Roosevelt convened in March 1933. Given top priority were emergency measures intended to salvage the banking system, provide additional federal resources for debt and unemployment relief, and sustain the government's capacity to tax and borrow. Also enacted were two major recovery measures that gained support as complex mixtures of progressive interventionism, warlike mobilization, and New Era associationalism. Under the National Industrial Recovery Act of June 1933, the workings of business and labor markets were to be realigned in accordance with national needs by suspension of the antitrust laws and erection in their place of a system of government-sanctioned "codes of fair competition" negotiated with and largely administered through business associations. The result could be interpreted as a logical expansion of the progressive concern with keeping competition "fair," as a resurrection of the apparatus once associated with the War Industries Board, or as the logical outcome of the industrial self-government encouraged by Hoover's Department of Commerce. Similarly, under the Agricultural Adjustment Act of May 1933, the workings of farm markets were to be reshaped through a system of producer allotments and fair price supports negotiated with and largely administered through organized farm groups. Again, it was possible to see this as the logical culmination of Wilsonian state-building, as the resurrection of a less business-minded Food Administration, or as the necessary outcome of earlier efforts to achieve orderly marketing through agricultural associations.

The New Deal's initial recovery theories, however, proved faulty in practice. In operation, the new array of codes, allotments, price supports, and protective trade barriers tended to reduce production and idle more resources rather than create the basis for renewed expansion. Efforts to counteract this tendency through public works spending were also too limited to be effective. And as depressed conditions persisted, the recovery programs became the targets of mounting criticism, both from disillusioned businessmen and farmers and from labor, consumer, and small business interests. By 1935 the system administered by the Agricultural Adjustment Administration had created enough benefits for commercial farmers to make itself politically viable. But the system administered by the National Recovery Administration (NRA) had few supporters remaining, and there was little disposition to revive it when the Supreme Court, in *Schechter Poultry Corp.* v. *United States* (May 1935), ruled its legal foundations unconstitutional. Remnants of the NRA codes would survive in trade association programs, in special laws directed against chain stores, and in legislation seeking to "stabilize" elements of the oil, coal, securities, and transportation industries. But the theory of recovery planning through a "concert of interests" had been discredited and the way opened for a theory that would seek recovery through a pluralistic "balance of interests."

Consequently, the "second New Deal," which emerged in 1934 and produced a new cluster of laws and programs in 1935, undertook to reduce and constrain corporate power rather than to enlist it in a battle against the nation's economic ills. The abuses of power on Wall Street, in the airline and shipping industries, and by the holding-company systems in the electrical power industry all received legislative attention. A new revenue act levied special taxes on corporate "bigness" and the super-rich. The Wagner-Connery National Labor Relations Act of 1935 implemented a policy of fostering strong independent unions. And under new social legislation in 1935, most notably the Relief and Recovery Act and the Social Security Act, the federal government assumed new responsibilities for social insurance, unemployment relief, and assistance to the handicapped. In theory, the mix of business controls, enhanced labor power, greater social security, and renewed "pump-priming" through works projects and lending programs was supposed to restore the "balance" necessary to generate new flows of consumer and investment spending. But in practice, such a balance proved elusive. Under the laws associated with the second New Deal, unionization came to the mass-production industries, an American version of the welfare state became established, and the regulatory apparatus acquired new appendages. But the economic upturn of 1936 and early 1937 quickly reversed when the pump-priming operations were halted.

As the recession of 1937 deepened, conservative critics blamed it on the New Deal and called for liberating business from the new burdens imposed by government. The Roosevelt administration was torn between competing prescriptions for remedial action. Calls for antitrust action to deal with monopolist conspiracies vied for attention with new designs for national economic planning, either through an expanded administrative state or through a new business-government-labor partnership. More significant, the recession had undercut the rationale for economic pump-priming and produced heated debate between those who wanted to trim federal budgets to induce more private spending and those who believed that economic maturation had created a system in which compensatory spending by public agencies had become permanently necessary. Secretary of the Treasury Henry Morgenthau argued strongly for cutting the budget. But at the Federal Reserve Board, chaired by Utah banker Marriner Eccles, a group of economists had embraced the macroeconomic theories of John Maynard Keynes. These advisers favored a resumption of large-scale public spending and its subsequent management to maintain effective demand at a full employment level.

In the third New Deal of 1938, Roosevelt opted for new antitrust and spending measures. Another Relief and Recovery Act provided some $3 billion to put the federal spending and lending agencies back into business. A major new investigative agency, the Temporary National Economic Committee, was created to study the extent and abuses of monopoly power. To some it appeared as an updated version of the Industrial Commission of 1898. And following Thurman Arnold's appointment to head the Antitrust Division, the Sherman Act was revived as an instrument for dealing with undesirable restraints of trade. Between 1938 and 1941 the division initiated nearly as many cases as had been initiated in the entire history of the Sherman Act prior to 1938. National economic policy was moving away from attempts at detailed administration of "failed" markets. Yet the congressional session of 1938 also produced another Agricultural Adjustment Act, a new Fair Labor Standards Act, and new legislation for the aviation, natural gas, advertising, and drug industries—all involving further expansions of the federal regulatory apparatus. And if Roosevelt had been successful, it also would have produced new and stronger planning instruments. He tried but failed to secure a planning-oriented reorganization of the executive branch and a new set of regional planning agencies modeled on the Tennessee Valley Authority, which he had helped to create in 1933.

Congress, intent upon reasserting its prerogatives, proved strongly resistant to the idea that America needed a managerial state capable of generating and implementing national economic plans. Nor was Congress ready to accept the need for a permanent stream of compensatory spending to be managed in the interest of full employment and stable prices. In 1939 the Roosevelt administration did use Keynesian arguments to urge the approval of new public works appropriations, but it failed to secure what it requested. As the economy entered another slump, the debate over whether the situation called for more or less public spending took on even greater intensity.

In a sense, war quickly settled the debate. By 1941 the new rearmament and lend-lease programs were providing a sort of public works expenditure that conservatives could support. And once the United States became a full-scale belligerent in World War II, a new managerial apparatus resembling that of World War I became the means for mobilizing idle resources and channeling them into the production and use of nationally needed goods. Once again the administrative structures of the private sector were called into national service. The result was a new array of public-private partnerships operating under the auspices of such agencies as the War Production Board, the National War Labor Board, the Office of Price Administration, and the Office of War Mobilization. Again this administrative machinery was used to reshape the workings of labor, capital,

commodity, and consumer markets. Again the growth of the state was rendered palatable by stressing its temporary nature and the extent to which it was facilitating needed social action rather than implementing a command system. In addition, operation of the new warfare state succeeded in bringing forth the desired flow of war goods. By 1944 the United States was producing twice as much war matériel as all its enemies combined, and it was doing so while twelve million workers were in the armed forces and while the economy was also producing more civilian goods than in 1939. Seemingly, the wartime system had succeeded where the New Deal had failed, and again there was hope in some quarters that some of it could be adapted to peacetime purposes.

By war's end New Deal reformism had been contained in ways that reduced its threat to the managerial institutions of the private sector. Antitrust action was becoming a form of regulation useful for maintaining the existing system rather than for dissolving or redistributing economic power. Labor radicalism was fading as radicals lost out to the builders of a regulatory unionism adaptable to managerial purposes. Radical Keynesianism, which had aroused fears of an ever-growing public sector managed by public servants in the interests of macroeconomic stability, was yielding to a commercial variety that envisioned variations in taxes as the prime managerial tools. And cradle-to-grave welfare statism, although embodied in wartime legislative proposals, was losing support. It was being replaced by employer-based welfarism under which corporate management could exercise considerable control over a major component of social spending. The New Deal State, shorn of its potential to implement anticorporate designs and equipped with new mechanisms to facilitate business-government cooperation, had by 1945 become a more suitable partner for business elites.

In the immediate postwar period, it was not always clear that a new partnership was taking root because the potential partners were at odds over tax, social, labor, and reconversion policy. The result was heated rhetoric in which the Truman administration was charged with seeking power for antibusiness bureaucrats and corporate elites were accused of being unregenerate enemies of a virtuous people. Despite the rhetoric, the period's policy output consisted of legislation that preserved and built upon what the New Deal state had become by 1945. The Employment Act of 1946 accepted Keynesian thinking and made macroeconomic management a federal responsibility, although it gave little managerial power to the economic council that it established. The Taft-

Hartley Act of 1947 coupled the New Deal guarantees of labor rights with management-desired curbs on union behavior. The Revenue Act of 1948 symbolized an abandonment of redistributionist designs. The welfare measures of 1949 and 1950 produced only minor adjustments in the social security, labor standards, and housing programs. Only in the area of antitrust, where a reinvigorated Antitrust Division under Wendell Berge tried to shape a "new Sherman Act" aimed at oligopolistic industries, did it seem that the state might be harnessed to anticorporate purposes. But by 1950 this effort was fading, its small business supporters having been appeased by an expanded system of small business aids and by legislation to prevent anticompetitive mergers.

As these accommodations were being worked out, efforts to preserve and build upon wartime arrangements were producing a new structure of business advisory councils and governmental jobs that were more or less reserved for businessmen on leave from the private sector. Such arrangements were especially noticeable in the government-industry relationships established by key bureaus and divisions in the Interior, State, Commerce, and Defense departments. They were noticeable as well in new foreign aid programs, in the quasi-governmental status enjoyed by big business's newly established Committee for Economic Development, and in the elaborate advisory structures used by the National Security Resources Board and the Council of Economic Advisers. The dominant trend was toward making these links stronger rather than weaker. As the decade of the 1940s drew to a close, a pragmatic centrism willing to accept and work within existing structures of power was gaining ground in both corporate and political circles. Business and government, as one commentator put it, were again preparing themselves to "go steady."

As President Truman began his second administration, he could take credit for helping to preserve and legitimize much of the New Deal regulatory and welfare apparatus. Yet he also had presided over the exhaustion of the New Deal's potential for bringing a radical redistribution of economic power and benefits. By doing so, he had helped to lay the groundwork for a new system of economic governance in which important regulatory and welfare duties would be openly entrusted to the large-scale economic organizations of the private sector. In Western Europe, the depression and war experiences had paved the way for an era in which socialist parties, nationalization strategies, and statist planners played leading roles in redirecting capitalist development

into more socially desirable paths. But in the United States this was not the case. Americans sought instead to achieve a socially responsible capitalism through the building of a "corporate commonwealth" allegedly capable of preserving the freedoms, competencies, and incentives that a "socialist commonwealth" or a "managerial state" would destroy.

THE ERA OF THE CORPORATE COMMONWEALTH, 1949–1968

In 1949 America's postwar economy suffered a relatively severe slump, calling into question some of the optimism about future economic growth. But again a military buildup helped to increase aggregate demand. After 1949 the nation entered a period of economic expansion that led many commentators to conclude that it had found workable solutions to the problems of capitalist crises and corporate power. It had combined market-based incentives and disciplines with beneficial economic governance through a mixture of public and private institutions. The result was a new capitalism characterized by workable competition, organizational checks and balances, and socially responsible economic leaders capable of devising and implementing a nationally beneficial "social contract." The United States had become, it was said, the land of the "middle way" or "vital center." The nation's institutional development enabled its business people to seize the opportunities available for industry and market building without creating the imbalances that could undermine further expansion. The country had built on its depression and war experiences in ways that were helping it to realize the dreams of New Era leaders in the 1920s. The proof lay in an economy that kept growing in size and productivity, in its worldwide reputation for efficiency and managerial innovation, and in the goods and services that it made available for mass consumption, social housekeeping, and the defense of the free world.

One indication that the era of New Deal reformism was giving way to a period dominated by the ideal of a corporate commonwealth came in the Truman administration's response to the slump of 1949. Significantly, the recession was not blamed on abuses of business power or maldistributions of income. Nor was it seen as proof that more of the investment function must be taken over by the federal government. Instead, it was tackled through educational and organizational measures intended to rebuild "confidence" within the private sector and assist it to undertake countercyclical investment.

"Under our system," President Truman declared, "private and public economic policies go hand in hand." They had to be blended to achieve maximum effectiveness, and through this blend America might continue to have a "new frontier" of economic expansion. Both Truman and his leading economic advisers believed that the key to stable growth was an organized "mutuality" committing interest groups to a national perspective and shared responsibility for keeping the economy running. And the efforts to build this, said chairman of the Council of Economic Advisers Leon Keyserling in June 1950, had been a major factor in containing and reversing the first serious downturn of the postwar period.

In December 1949 the anti-recession program also produced a new Committee on Business and Government Relations, chaired by Secretary of Commerce Charles Sawyer and including among its members the attorney general and the chairmen of the Federal Trade Commission and the Council of Economic Advisers. The initiative for its formation came from Sawyer and Keyserling, both of whom believed that governmental policies needed remolding as a means of promoting the enlightened business community that was needed for future growth. Throughout 1950, the committee studied ways of sharing managerial responsibility and of putting anti-trust enforcement and federal regulation on a "cooperative" as opposed to a "compulsive" basis. As commentators noted, the Truman Administration's Fair Deal seemed increasingly inclined to put its faith in an expansion of public-spirited private government rather than in additions to America's administrative state.

The impetus toward business-government cooperation received another boost when the United States became involved in the Korean War. In late 1950, by working with the Chamber of Commerce, the American Trade Association Executives, and the National Association of Manufacturers, Sawyer's Commerce Department established an elaborate network of industrial advisory committees that assisted in the allocation of war orders and controlled materials. A new Office of Defense Mobilization, headed by General Electric's Charles E. Wilson, also became an instrument for expanding governmental positions held by businessmen on leave from the private sector. And initially, efforts to control inflation were designed to be implemented through voluntary guidelines and collaborative committees. Later in the war, as price and wage controls became mandatory and increasingly irksome, and when Truman tried unsuccessfully to impose a labor settlement on the steel

industry, the new partnership seemed in danger of dissolving. But this danger evaporated when Dwight D. Eisenhower was elected president in 1952. As early as 1949, Eisenhower had been extolling the virtues of "cooperative effort" as the way to curb bureaucratic growth and prevent governmental despotism. By 1953 he was ready to build on the new foundations for business-government collaboration that had been laid during Truman's second administration.

One policy area in which Eisenhower's administration built upon earlier trends was that of antitrust. In the immediate postwar period, the Antitrust Division had used the Sherman Act to attack oligopolistic market structures. In cases involving the tobacco, railroad, and motion picture industries it had enjoyed enough success to arouse fears that existing legal shields against reckless structural reformers and neo-populist politicians were about to be removed. After 1949, however, the Truman administration had quickly backed away from the implications of such action. The Anti-Merger Act of 1950 was directed against future mergers, not existing combines. Meanwhile, "bigness" was extolled for its ability to lower costs and enhance social and national security. And in seeking through its Committee on Business and Government Relations to put antitrust on a more cooperative basis, the administration set the stage for the National Committee to Study the Antitrust Laws, appointed by Attorney General Herbert Brownell in 1953. From it came a 1955 report congratulating the nation for maintaining a kind of competition that allowed modern business to function effectively. For the balance of the decade, federal antitrust authorities busied themselves with marginal cases and cooperative consultations aimed at curbing cartel-like behavior rather than reducing corporate power. The committee's report, said Sen. Estes Kefauver (D-Tenn.), amounted to a "gigantic brief for the non-enforcement of the antitrust laws." But Kefauver's own subsequent efforts to arouse congressional and public interest in the issue had little effect on a policy geared to system maintenance rather than structural reform.

As antitrust activity was marginalized, Eisenhower's administration also tried to build the "cooperative unit" that in its view could curb "creeping socialism," keep mass and partisan politics within proper bounds, and demonstrate the capacities of an enlightened private sector for national service. Invoking the image of swollen and incompetent government, it moved to trim budgets, scrap price and wage controls, privatize governmental business operations, and transfer offshore oil lands to state control.

Yet at the same time, it championed welfare policies that retained and built upon the New Deal and Fair Deal measures. It continued to expand the national security state that had begun growing rapidly during the Korean War; and it continued to accept managerial responsibilities that it sought to discharge through new linkages to responsible wielders of private power. The latter policy was apparent in the "stag dinners" with business executives, through which Eisenhower sought to build and coordinate corporate statesmanship; in the growth and stabilization programs that linked Keynesian strategies to the salesmanship of the Advertising Council and the Committee for Economic Development; and most graphically in the new and expanded machinery for extra-governmental arrangements that was added to numerous federal departments.

By the mid-1950s, for example, the Interior, Labor, Agriculture, and Justice departments had adopted cooperative modes. In practice this meant larger regulatory and developmental roles for private associations, councils, and consortia. The Defense Department had also established close relations with a number of partners, both in industry and in American science and engineering. In the Commerce Department, where Charles Sawyer had laid the groundwork, Eisenhower's appointees had proceeded to take over and build upon the Korean War committees. They were now linked to industry divisions headed by volunteer experts, and were used to help administer a number of efficiency and informational programs in which local business groups served as a cooperative field service. This arrangement, according to Rep. Emmanuel Celler (D-N.Y.), amounted to an improper and undemocratic delegation of public power to private groups. But after hearings before Celler's House Antitrust Subcommittee, the only changes made were to put civil servants in charge of the industry divisions and relegate business volunteers to the status of assistants.

"Partnership" was also in vogue in the industrial sectors operating under regulatory commissions. In such areas as transportation, communications, energy, and finance, federal and state agencies worked with the companies that they regulated to fashion a durable accommodation aimed at fostering orderly growth along familiar, predictable lines. The results were considered highly satisfactory by most contemporary commentators. They included a modern airline industry whose service and prices were the envy of the industrial world and a mass communications system without parallel in any other nation. And beyond this they included a petroleum industry that was fueling national growth with cheap and abundant energy, an electrical power industry that served the masses while steadily lowering its unit costs, and a banking system that was both security conscious and remarkably successful in meeting the nation's growing demand for credit and financial services. Most Americans no longer considered any of these areas to be policy problems. But some were perturbed by the effects that regulatory policy choices were having on the markets for coal and railroad passenger service, and a few argued that the regulatory system administered by the Interstate Commerce Commission had become obsolete and was doing the nation more harm than good.

By 1960 the Democrats were talking about the need for stimulating speedier growth and facilitating adjustment to technological change. But most of them accepted the general outlines of the corporate commonwealth as being the "American way." In the economic programs pushed by President John F. Kennedy the reliance on private-sector agencies remained an important component of America's system of economic governance. The primary goal of fiscal and monetary policy was expanded private investment rather than new public goods. The emphasis on antitrust enforcement and regulatory rule-making remained cooperative rather than confrontational. The Commerce Department's network of industrial committees and councils underwent further expansion, and under new laws for trade promotion, area redevelopment, and manpower retraining a similar emphasis on public-private partnerships quickly appeared. In addition, voluntary price and wage guidelines based on assumptions of corporate statesmanship amenable to national guidance, were supposed to curb inflationary wage-price spirals that could erode purchasing power. Despite the acrimony generated by Kennedy's pressures on guideline violators, especially on the steel industry in 1962, the general drift of policy was toward a more formalized corporate commonwealth rather than an expansion of public power into domains that were privately governed. Some Kennedyites thought highly of the "indicative planning" system then in operation in France. As of 1963 some had hopes of nudging American business into cooperating in a similar planning process.

In the mid-1960s, moreover, accelerated economic growth indicated that America's unique regulatory apparatus was more successful than ever. America, it was claimed, had found a superior way both to deal with specific market failures and to apply the macroeconomic prescriptions of Keynesianism.

And the achievement, it was also claimed, was producing a growth dividend that could be used for social improvements and enhanced national security. By 1966 President Lyndon B. Johnson had not only made new commitments abroad but also had secured much new social legislation intended to build a Great Society. Not since the New Deal had there been a similar expansion in federal welfare programs. Yet these were mostly divorced from concerns about economic malperformance, and Johnson's cultivation of business groups as enlightened partners seemed largely successful in convincing them that they had nothing to fear from this type of statist expansion. The expansion, it was assumed, could be paid for from the growth increment. It could therefore leave the workings of the economy and its regulators undisturbed, and in this way could speed social progress without endangering economic gains.

Johnson also assumed that the expanding war in Vietnam could be fought without the unpopular anti-inflation measures used during the Korean War. For this, however, the growth dividend proved insufficient. The result by 1968 was an overheated economy in which rising prices, credit crunches, and trade imbalances generated growing discontent and produced recriminatory finger-pointing that rapidly began to erode the earlier policy consensus. As the decade drew to a close, a variety of voices began to urge alternatives to the established system of economic governance: the political right; a resurgent movement for national economic planning; a new anticorporate left utilizing both Marxist and populist analyses; and an emerging antigrowth movement concerned with the limits and costs of growth. Popular faith in the underlying assumptions of the established system—especially in the beneficence of corporate power, the success of regulatory intervention, the wisdom of economic experts, and the desirability of growth—was shaken as it had not been since the Great Depression. As consensual support evaporated, the way lay open for intense new policy debates. These debates reconsidered the relative roles assigned to market and nonmarket coordination, how much of the latter could be entrusted to private groups, and the extent to which the government's portion should be shielded from the pressures of mass and partisan politics.

For a generation Americans had believed that the regulatory apparatus created by piecemeal reform and the maturation of modern organizational institutions had made possible the emergence of a new type of capitalism. This American-style system had remained "free" yet was no longer plagued by the instabilities, disorders, and excesses once thought to be the price of freedom. But in the 1960s many citizens had begun to see the apparatus as undemocratic, dehumanizing, and exploitative. It was yielding a policy product inferior to what could be achieved by some other system. A variety of nostrums were put forward: freer markets, more planning, more community and citizen action, and new and more powerful regulatory commissions. When the economy began to waver under the stresses that resulted from Johnson's military and social programs, the ranks of those finding fault with the American system of market interventions began to swell rapidly. The political and ideological consensus that had sustained the growth and workings of America's version of a corporate commonwealth was disappearing. The nation was about to enter a new era of policy debates that would leave its economic wisdom unsettled and its guiding regulatory models in almost continual flux.

UNSETTLED WISDOM AND SHIFTING MODELS, 1969–1994

In the era of the corporate commonwealth, which some had seen as the beginnings of an American century, the national economy had become a marvel of growth, productivity, rising living standards, and competitiveness in international markets. But after 1968 it became a trouble-ridden economy, plagued by weakening productivity, managerial stodginess, new international competitors, difficulties in securing vital raw materials, and a growing imperviousness to the Keynesian levers that were supposed to keep employment full and prices stable. The world economy that it had dominated since 1945 was changing; Japan and Western Europe were forging their own versions of managerial capitalism and the nations that produced raw materials were beginning to assert their own national interests. It seemed that new strategies and institutions were required to deal with the changing economic environment. Yet these were slow to emerge from either the political or the corporate world. Instead, the nation became mired in bitter policy debates reminiscent of those in the 1890s and 1930s. As policy veered between competing models of a better regulatory regime, the additions to and changes in the regulatory apparatus remained under attack and were subject to uncertain futures. A great nation, one commentator noted, could have no weakness more devastating than an inability to define the role of government in its economy, and in the quarter-century that followed 1969 the United States had great difficulty doing so.

In 1969 newly inaugurated president Richard M. Nixon sought a monetary solution to the problem of worsening inflation. To his surprise, however, the impact of slowed monetary growth fell more on output than on prices. By 1970 the economy was in a state of "stagflation" marked by mounting unemployment, stagnating production, growing trade imbalances, and rising prices all at the same time. To break the irrational inflationary expectations believed responsible, Nixon decided upon a New Economic Policy featuring wage-price controls, tax incentives, import surcharges, and severance of the dollar from gold. Launched in 1971, the new policy enjoyed some initial success, but in 1973, when Nixon tried to put the controls on a more voluntary basis, they proved too weak. They could not deal with a new surge of inflation powered by world food shortages and by the restrictive actions of the Organization of Petroleum Exporting Countries. In 1974 the controls were abandoned as a hopeless failure, and in the debates that followed different lessons were soon being drawn from the whole experience. For some it demonstrated the folly of trying to interfere with market forces. For others it seemed a botched attempt to reestablish public-private cooperation. Still others regarded it as a bungled opportunity to build much needed planning institutions.

The period of Nixon's experimentation with price and wage controls was also a period during which the "new regulationists" concerned with environmental issues, occupational health and safety, consumer protection, and job discrimination made substantial progress toward adding a major new component to the nation's regulatory apparatus. Growing rapidly under legislation passed in the early 1970s were such agencies as the Occupational Safety and Health Administration, the Consumer Products Safety Commission, and the Environmental Protection Agency. Expanding too were the controls over personnel practices administered by the Equal Employment Opportunity Commission. Moving to the fore in much of this activity was an anticorporate outlook uncharacteristic of either the older industry-specific regulation or the beginning of the new regulation in the 1960s. In the eyes of a growing group of protesters within the corporate world, the growth of such regulation amounted to a "second managerial revolution." The new movement seemed to be shifting power from professional business managers to anticorporate bureaucrats and in the process to be destroying the cooperative and managerial machinery

through which the nation's new economic problems might be solved.

As the new regulation grew, the old also came under strong attack as having been captured by regulated industries and their political henchmen and used by its captors to sustain exploitative and wasteful operations. One branch of the consumer activist movement urged "market restoration" as a remedy. By the mid-1970s it had joined forces with laissez-faire fundamentalists and neoclassical economic analysts to call for regulatory reform that would reintroduce competition to correct the situation. The political world, despite the resistance offered by targeted industries, proved receptive. The Nixon administration responded with studies of potential deregulation in the transportation field. President Gerald R. Ford and Sen. Edward M. Kennedy advocated the idea, symbolizing its appeal in both conservative and liberal circles. By the end of Ford's administration, Congress was considering a variety of bills to deregulate the airlines, the railroad and trucking industries, the communications and banking fields, and various other areas where commission regulation had once been seen as advancing the public interest.

In addition, critics were attacking the kind of regulation provided by the nation's antitrust agencies. On one side, neoclassical economic analysts performed studies purporting to show that antitrust had served primarily to protect the backward and inefficient and to perpetuate antimodernist nonsense. On the other side, a vocal group of neopopulists pointed to the failure of antitrust law, as currently interpreted and enforced, to deal with corporate threats to republican values. The law, they claimed, had failed to prevent the new concentrations of corporate power apparent in conglomerate mergers, multinational firms, and newly oligopolized markets. The need, this second group said, was for new laws that could be used to promote deconcentration and industrial restructuring. By 1975 some of their proposals were being seriously considered in Congress. Legislation to break up the leading oil firms came close to passage, and extensive hearings were held on an "industrial reorganization" bill through which Sen. Philip Hart (D-Mich.) proposed to limit market shares and dismember corporate giants. In 1976 Congress settled for an Antitrust Improvements Act that merely made investigation and litigation somewhat easier, but outright trustbusting was no longer being summarily dismissed. Cooperative enforcement was being subordinated to adversarial action and a consumer protection mission. For the first time in years, antitrust prosecutors were making limited attempts to restructure some of the nation's corporate giants. Receiving much publicity were the major new "structural relief" cases against International Business Machines and American Telephone and Telegraph.

During Jimmy Carter's presidency, these efforts to reshape the regulatory apparatus continued, producing legislation that introduced more competition into the transportation and banking industries, added new environmental controls, and established new incentives for energy conservation and production. In addition, Congress passed the Humphrey-Hawkins Act of 1978 exhorting the government to promote full employment and balanced growth. And responding to worsening stagflation, Carter installed a new set of wage-price guidelines that were supposed to work in conjunction with new packages of fiscal stimulants and constraints. But the policy output lacked coherence. The debates over what could be done through market restoration, economic planning, or new kinds of selective market intervention grew even more intense. As the problems of stagflation and declining competitiveness worsened, the faith that policymakers had placed in Keynesian prescriptions, piecemeal regulation, and corporate management continued to erode. Symbolic of the changing climate were a new fascination with the Japanese and West German systems, a huge bail-out loan for the Chrysler Corporation, and the establishment of new think tanks devoted to critiquing the economic thought allegedly responsible for the nation's plight.

In the corporate world, concerns focused primarily on ways to contain and reduce the costs of the new regulation. This was the objective of an increasingly successful business counteroffensive led by the newly established Business Roundtable. But some corporate leaders also longed for a new era of business-government cooperation in which they could work with public officials to build the coordinative institutions that were becoming indispensable for a modern capitalist order. America, they said, needed to create its own version of the institutions that were responsible for Japan's economic success. By the late 1970s, their thinking had become part of a "reindustrialization" movement that was also attracting support from liberal academics, groups concerned with saving jobs in the Rust Belt of the industrial Northeast and Midwest, and leading officials in the Carter administration. In September 1980 Carter announced a new "economic revitalization" program envisioning, in the words of *Newsweek,* a "made-in-America version of the government-business partnership in productive Japan." Business reaction, however, was not enthusiastic. Most business

groups ended up supporting the Republicans, led by Ronald Reagan and offering, along with traditional anti-statism, a "supply-side economics" that would achieve revitalization through tax and budget policies reminiscent of those associated with Andrew Mellon in the 1920s.

In 1981, fresh from his resounding electoral victory over Carter, President Reagan was able to translate much of the program he advocated into major changes in public policy. The Revenue Act of 1981 very sharply reduced personal income taxes and other levies in ways called for by supply-side theory. A new budget reduced social expenditures while increasing those for defense. And in line with the prescriptions of Reagan's monetarist and deregulationist supporters, further actions were taken to slow monetary growth and relax many of the regulatory rules about which business groups had been complaining. In theory, this application of "Reaganomics" was supposed to check inflation while producing a robust growth fueled by the release of entrepreneurial energies. But instead, the year 1982 brought a severe recession marked by the highest unemployment rate since the Great Depression. Federal deficits mounted, and credit stringencies forced many farmers, builders, and small businessmen into bankruptcy. Reagan's response was to urge Americans to stay the course, but Congress was in no mood to do so as the year ended.

One indication of congressional sentiment was a new budget battle involving the "take back" of some of the tax and spending cuts. Another was considerable congressional support for the reindustrialization idea, which was being advanced now as "industrial policy." In 1982 and 1983 this idea won the endorsement of a number of prominent Democratic politicians and was the subject of extended hearings before congressional committees. The movement produced an array of bills calling for such institutions as a national council on industrial competitiveness, subcouncils in the major industries, and special banks to assist new industrial development. Neither "take back" nor "industrial policy," however, succeeded in destroying the core of Reagan's economic program or the political base upon which it rested. When the economy turned up in 1983 and 1984, this time with the earlier inflationary expectations broken, the president could claim victory. Although his critics downplayed the effects of the supply-side revolution and attributed the upturn to increases in military spending, improvements in the oil situation, and mounting indebtedness to foreign capitalists, Reagan could and did claim to have released economic forces that were transforming a stagnating economy into a booming one. He was overwhelmingly reelected in the election of 1984.

Meanwhile, the Reaganites and their opponents were battling toward a stalemate on the issue of reconstructing America's regulatory apparatus. Market restoration continued to be the order of the day in finance, telecommunications, transportation, and energy production. Laissez-faire also became the new policy of the antitrust agencies, especially in regard to the kind of mergers that had long been prevented under the Anti-Merger Act of 1950. And efforts continued to scrap or "marketize" the more costly features of the new environmental, safety, and employment regulation. Yet the markets restored were the kind that soon produced speculative excesses and failing financial institutions, small-town decay and crumbling union agreements, and a "vulture capitalism" conducted through hostile takeover bids. In addition, there were eroding safety and reliability standards and higher rates for such things as local telephone service and transportation to less densely populated areas. Movements for "re-regulation" quickly appeared, and intense lobbying by environmental groups soon brought the Reagan campaign against environmental protection to a halt. Business groups might oppose such controls as too costly in an era of growing competitive pressures from abroad, but they reflected a continuing social demand for clean air, soil, and water that had not been altered by the new faith in market forces.

Whether or not market restoration was responsible, the economic growth rate did speed up in the mid-1980s. Yet even as output and employment expanded, several features of the boom seemed to be piling up trouble for the future. For example, social "entitlement" spending remained higher and new investment lower than the Reaganites had anticipated. One result was unprecedented budget deficits, which not only posed a threat to the normal workings of capital markets but also shifted substantial bills to future generations, meanwhile making Keynesian compensators unworkable. Deficits were being financed by massive borrowing from abroad, a practice that by 1987 had transformed the United States from the leading creditor to the world's largest debtor nation. Economic growth was following patterns that produced expanding clusters of high- and low-paying jobs while destroying the kind of well-paying positions once held by the middle and industrial working classes. For all of these reasons, Reaganomics failed to build the kind of consensus that had supported the New Era system in the 1920s or Eisenhower's American Era in the 1950s. Under President George

Bush, who upon taking over in 1989 promised to preserve the Reagan Revolution, this failure became even more evident. Efforts to reduce the deficit through tax increases alienated the Reaganites while the workings of Reagan-style market restoration, especially as they affected the job structure and the distribution of wealth and income, created new demands for making the market's output fairer and more socially beneficial.

By 1991, as a new recession made it difficult to handle the debts and commitments built up in the 1980s, the functioning of the economy had become a central factor in eroding Bush's popularity and political base. In 1992 poor economic performance was one of the major issues that helped Bill Clinton win the White House. But whether his administration would open the way to a more equitably shared and less debt-ridden growth, achieved through new coordinative and regulatory institutions and new programs of public investment, remained to be seen. Efforts to move in this direction encountered strong resistance that forced numerous concessions and compromises. The persistence of fierce controversy indicated that the era of unsettled wisdom about the role of government in the economy and what was needed in the way of regulatory reform had not yet ended.

AT THE CENTURY'S CLOSE

As the twentieth century drew to a close, it was apparent that the interactions between America's corporate economy and its liberal-democratic polity had produced much that had parallels in other advanced industrial democracies. America had developed, although in limited forms, its own versions of the welfare state, corporatist ordering mechanisms, government-directed operations, and populist rituals that had helped to produce viable political economies elsewhere. Yet America also remained unique in the faith that its leaders and citizens continued to place in market forces. The nation as a whole still seemed to believe that a proper mix of antitrust agencies, regulatory commissions, regulative associations, and governmental compensators would correct market failures and keep a market system operating in ways that furthered national and social progress. Its policymakers, over the course of the century, had disagreed about the shape and makeup of this regulatory mix, and consensuses that had been reached on the matter had failed to endure when economic performance fell below a threshold of expectations. But the groups that envisioned and worked for alternatives to a regulated corporate capitalism had been marginalized quite early and had remained in that condition. Despite repeated critiques of policy fragmentation, incoherence, and shortsightedness, America had remained without the kind of integrative policy institutions that would enable it to recognize the interrelated nature of its economic problems and implement coherent, system-wide solutions. It had refused to move along the path toward capitalist planning and central guidance of economic development taken by some of its major international competitors.

Whether the United States needed to move along this path also remained a matter of considerable debate among those analyzing the American political economy and its workings in the 1990s. Some argued strongly that such integrative machinery had become essential if corporate organization, labor-management relations, and the industrial and job structures were to be readjusted in ways essential to better economic performance. But others believed that a better answer lay in more market restoration or in greater democratization of existing institutions. And continuing to block the path leading to institutions of integration and guidance was a polity and political culture still deeply committed to the dispersion and division of power. Numerous powers of veto persisted within the government, and most policymakers seemed to believe that piecemeal action to deal with demonstrated market failures was still the way to have both freedom and order. If the development of integrative machinery was America's "next frontier," its conquest would not be easy.

SEE ALSO Economic Thought; Economic Performance; Consumption; Depressions and Recessions: The Business Cycle (all in this volume).

BIBLIOGRAPHY

The best overall account, especially good on the interactions between corporate and government development is Louis Galambos and Joseph Pratt, *The Rise of the Corporate Commonwealth: United States Business and Public Policy in the 20th Century* (1988). Also valuable are the overall accounts of regulation, antitrust activity, and macroeconomic policy found respectively in Thomas K. McCraw, *Prophets of Regulation: Charles Francis Adams, Louis D. Brandeis, James M. Landis, Alfred E. Kahn* (1984); Tony Freyer, *Regulating Big Business: Antitrust in Great Britain and America, 1880–1980* (1992), and Anthony S. Campagna, *U.S. National Economic Policy, 1917–1985* (1987). The best overall treatments of energy policy are in John G. Clark, *Energy and the Federal Government: Fossil Fuel Policies, 1900–1945* (1987) and Richard Vietor, *Energy Policy in America since 1945: A Study in Business-Government Relations* (1984). Two collections of insightful essays on the changing patterns of business-government relations and regulatory activity are Joseph R. Frese and Jacob Judd, eds. *Business and Government: Essays in Twentieth-Century Cooperation and Confrontation* (1985) and Thomas K. McCraw, ed., *Regulation in Perspective: Historical Essays* (1981).

American economic policy in the period from 1900 to 1933 has received extensive treatment. Among the works essential for understanding it are:

Morton Keller, *Regulating a New Economy: Public Policy and Economic Change in America, 1900–1933* (1990), providing a detailed survey with emphasis on the themes of persistence and pluralism; Martin J. Sklar, *The Corporate Reconstruction of American Capitalism, 1890–1916: The Market, the Law, and Politics* (1988), which argues persuasively that modern America was formed by an intersection of reform and corporatizing impulses; Stephen Skowronek, *Building a New American State: The Expansion of National Administrative Capacities, 1877–1920* (1982), providing the best analysis of the process through which America's peculiar version of a national administrative state was negotiated; James Weinstein, *The Corporate Ideal in the Liberal State, 1900–1918* (1968), focusing on the role of corporate interests in shaping America's response to economic change: Robert Wiebe, *The Search for Order, 1877–1920* (1967), an influential and now widely accepted reinterpretation of progressivism; Olivier Zunz, *Making America Corporate, 1870–1920* (1990), a path-breaking account of the new corporate middle class and its role in remaking America's system of economic governance; and Samuel P. Hays, *Conservation and the Gospel of Efficiency: The Progressive Conservation Movement, 1890–1920* (1959). Also indispensable for an understanding of developments in 1917 and 1918 is Robert D. Cuff, *The War Industries Board: Business-*

Government Relations during World War I (1973). And offering revised views of policy developments during the 1920s and the Hoover administration are Ellis W. Hawley, *The Great War and the Search for a Modern Order: A History of the American People and Their Institutions, 1917–1933* (1979); Robert Himmelberg, *The Origins of the National Recovery Administration: Business, Government, and the Trade Association Issue, 1921–1933* (1976); and Guy Alchon, *The Invisible Hand of Planning: Capitalism, Social Science, and the State in the 1920s* (1985).

The coming of the New Deal system and its subsequent evolution into the corporate commonwealth of the 1950s and 1960s have also received extensive treatment. Ellis W. Hawley, *The New Deal and the Problem of Monopoly: A Study in Economic Ambivalence* (1966) focuses on the confused search for new coordinative and managerial tools during the New Deal years. Steve Fraser and Gary Gestle, eds., *The Rise and Fall of the New Deal Order, 1930–1980* (1989) contains essays exploring the failure of the New Deal to fulfill its democratic potential. And other aspects of the New Deal's policy heritage are explored in Robert Collins, *The Business Response to Keynes, 1929–1964* (1981); Otis L. Graham, *Toward a Planned Society: From Roosevelt to Nixon* (1976); and

Kim McQuaid, *Big Business and Presidential Power: From FDR to Reagan* (1982). The latter focuses particularly on the kind of political economics acted upon by the leaders of the nation's largest corporations, as does McQuaid's *Uneasy Partners: Big Business in American Politics, 1945–1990* (1994). For policy developments after World War II, Murray Weidenbaum, *The Modern Public Sector* (1969) is excellent; and essential for understanding the economic policies of the 1950s is Robert Griffith, "Dwight D. Eisenhower and the Corporate Commonwealth," *American Historical Review* 87 (February 1982): 87–122.

For more recent policy developments, the most illuminating works are Martha Derthick and Paul Quirk, *The Politics of Deregulation* (1985); Benjamin Friedman, *Day of Reckoning: The Consequences of American Economic Policy under Reagan and after* (1988), on the adverse side of the "Reagan Revolution"; and Samuel P. Hays, *Beauty, Health, and Permanence: Environmental Politics in the United States, 1955–1985* (1987). Also important for its essays on post-1960 policy debates and decisions is Robert H. Bremner, Gary W. Reichard, and Richard J. Hopkins, eds., *American Choices: Social Dilemmas and Public Policy since 1960* (1986).

ECONOMIC THOUGHT

Jack High

Academic economics in the United States achieved its first noteworthy advances in the 1880s and 1890s. Prior to that time, economics was taught as part of moral philosophy, usually to the detriment of both disciplines. As late as 1880, there were only a dozen or so full-time economists in the United States, and the country had not produced anyone remotely comparable to Adam Smith in Great Britain or Jean Baptiste Say in France.

FORGING A NEW PROFESSION, 1880–1900

Once the subject got underway professionally (the American Economic Association was formed in 1885), internal wrangling over scientific method and economic policy produced deep divisions among economists. One group, led by Charles Dunbar of Harvard and the astronomer-economist Simon Newcomb of Johns Hopkins, approved of the deductive method and the general policy of laissez faire that had been passed on to American economic thought from Great Britain and France. Another group, led by Richard Ely, a cofounder of the American Economic Association, was intent on driving deductive theory and laissez-faire policy from academic discussion.

The controversy, which was at times bitter, weakened a fledgling profession. Because of it, Ely fled Johns Hopkins for the University of Wisconsin, but even there he had to defend himself against charges that he was a socialist. In 1892 he was forced out as secretary of the American Economic Association. Nor was Ely the only casualty. Newcomb, who had produced, according to Joseph Schumpeter, "the outstanding performance of American general economics" in the late nineteenth century, gave up economics almost entirely. Dunbar's attitude symbolized that of many prominent economists; he refused to join the American Economic Association until the influence of Ely had been removed. When Ely resigned in 1892, Dunbar accepted the presidency of

the association. None of this divisive controversy helped the image of economics, yet it was in this setting that Americans labored to establish a respectable profession.

Despite the rancor over policy and method, by 1900 U.S. economists had secured a beachhead for their science as a distinct discipline. In their hands, economics became a practical science that embodied both theory and history. Moreover, although economists contributed as informed experts to policy debate, their pronouncements on policy were not to be confused with their purely scientific work. American economists drew a line between science and policy. Economists were helped in their endeavor to establish a profession by a lively public interest in economic subjects. Monetary policy and the tariff had interested Americans since the beginning of the Republic. After the Civil War, labor and trusts were added to the list of hotly debated subjects, thanks to the rise of big business and an urban working class. American economists were also helped by an extraordinarily fruitful period of economic theorizing in Europe.

Between 1870 and 1900, economic theory underwent a sea change in the Western world. The theory of value expounded by such classical economists as Adam Smith, David Ricardo, and Karl Marx was turned on its head. Instead of labor imparting value to consumers' goods, as the labor theory of value supposed, it was consumer demand that gave value to labor, and to land and capital as well. This shift in value theory, commonly known as the marginal revolution, took place in two steps. First, economists established a causal connection between the utility of a consumers' good and its price. Second, they established a causal connection between the price of a consumers' good and the prices of the producers' goods that made it.

The connection between utility and consumers' goods was demonstrated independently in the 1870s by three European economists—William Stanley Jevons in England, Carl Menger in Austria, and Leon

Walras in France. At the time, academic economics in America was just getting underway. Not until 1892, when Irving Fisher published his *Mathematical Investigations into the Theory of Value and Prices*, did American economists make any recognized contribution to utility theory. Fisher, along with the Italian sociologist Vilfredo Pareto, was the first to establish relationships between utility and price using ordinal utility (that is, the comparative ranking of utility levels) rather than cardinal utility (the quantitative measurement of something called a util). As it turned out, Fisher was ahead of his time; ordinal utility theory was not widely adopted among English-speaking economists until the 1930s. Even today, a century after its publication, Fisher's *Investigations* still strikes the reader as modern; with few additions, it could be used in contemporary economics courses.

The second step of the marginal revolution—establishing the principles that determine the prices of land, labor, and capital—did not occur until the 1890s, two decades after the beginnings of the revolution in utility theory. By this time American economists had absorbed marginalist principles and they made a significant contribution. In a series of articles, but especially in his renowned *The Distribution of Wealth* (1899), John Bates Clark brought the pricing of all factors of production under a single explanation, now known as marginal productivity theory.

Clark's theoretical achievement was to relate the payment for factors to their productivity. He demonstrated that, in a perfectly adjusted economy, each worker will be paid the monetary value of what he or she produces. This law does not hold exactly in practice, of course, but competitive pressures approximate the result. If a worker is paid less than the value of what he or she produces, a rival employer can earn a profit by offering a higher wage. If a worker is paid more than such value, the resulting loss to the employer induces the offer of a lower wage. Thus, assuming mobility of labor, the competitive bidding of employers leads to workers being paid approximately the value of what they produce. Clark applied this same reasoning to capital and land, thus bringing factor pricing under a single law.

Clark was noted for his humanitarian impulses, and he placed great social weight on his result. In *The Distribution of Wealth* he wrote, "A plan of living that should force men to leave in their employers' hands anything that by right of creation is theirs, would be an institutional robbery." Clark's marginal productivity theory showed that workers were not forced to leave the value of what they created in the hands of capitalists. Hence, concluded Clark, the law

of factor pricing justifies the "right of society to exist in its present form."

Clark violated the precept that science and ethics should be kept separate, and Schumpeter and other economists have criticized him for it. But Clark's emphasis on ethical questions seems appropriate for the time in which he wrote. The exploitation of labor by capital was a common concern in the United States, as it was elsewhere. Labor unrest had reached crisis proportions in the eighties and nineties. The McCormick strike of 1886, the Haymarket bombing and subsequent sham trials of the same year, the Homestead (1892) and Pullman (1894) strikes were characterized by violence, brutality, and tragic death. The attempt to bring the combined force of economics and ethics to bear on such explosive disputes should hardly be condemned on the grounds that science was being sullied.

Clark was not the only American economist to develop the marginal productivity theory. Stuart Wood, the first person to get an American doctoral degree in economics (he attended Harvard), published an impressive contribution in the *Quarterly Journal of Economics* in 1888. European economists, especially Philip Wicksteed in Great Britain and Knut Wicksell in Sweden, also developed the theory independently of Clark. But even European economists recognized Clark as the preeminent contributor to marginal productivity theory.

Institutional economics, a strain of thought apart from and in large measure opposed to marginal utility theory, had its origins in the work of Thorstein Veblen. Veblen, a student of Clark, objected to the mechanical nature of the new theory. In "Why Is Economics Not an Evolutionary Science?", published in the July 1898 issue of the *Quarterly Journal of Economics*, he derided the economic man of marginal utility theory as a "lightning calculator of pleasures and pains, who oscillates like a homogeneous globule of desire for happiness under the impulse of stimuli that shift him about the area, but leave him intact. . . . Self-poised in elemental space, he spins symmetrically about his own spiritual axis until the parallelogram of forces bears down upon him, whereupon he follows the line of the resultant." Veblen did not object to theory per se, but he thought that evolutionary biology, not Newtonian physics, was the appropriate model for economics. To Veblen, economic life was a process of cumulative change, much like the evolution of species.

Besides their contributions to the corpus of marginal theory, American economists began to produce some excellent historical studies: Frank Taussig's *Tariff*

History of the United States (1885), Charles Dunbar's *Chapters on the Theory and History of Banking* (1891), and David A. Wells's *Recent Economic Changes* (1889). Edwin R. A. Seligman's *The Economic Interpretation of History* (1902) became a classic statement of the place of economic motivation in historical interpretation.

Monetary bimetallism and the rise of trusts were the policy issues that occupied the attention of economists on the eve of the twentieth century. A fall in the price of silver had begun in the 1870s, when Germany switched from a silver to a gold standard. United States silver producers began to call on the government to mint silver and exchange silver dollars at 16 to 1 for gold dollars. This policy would have contributed to inflation, which was favored by farmers and some labor groups but opposed by bankers, merchants, and industrialists. Thus bimetallism, the simultaneous circulation of both gold and silver money at a 16:1 exchange ratio, became a heated political controversy in the United States. According to the historian Edward C. Kirkland, minting silver "was preached in every schoolhouse, on street corners, in hired halls, and at farmers' picnics." William Jennings Bryan took up the cause, and made it the main point of contention in his unsuccessful presidential bid against William McKinley in 1896.

Economists joined the fray, and most of them took the side of gold. J. Laurence Laughlin engaged in a running debate with an enterprising pamphleteer, William H. Harvey, otherwise known as Professor Coin. The debate symbolized the controversy at large. Laughlin was chairman of the economics department at the University of Chicago and represented the viewpoint of the academic and commercial establishment. He steadfastly advocated a gold standard. Harvey was a populist and represented the viewpoint of farmers and other chronic debtors. He championed the cause of silver. But some prominent economists took the side of bimetallism. Francis Walker, president of the Massachusetts Institute of Technology, broke with his colleagues and presented a scholarly case for silver in *International Bimetallism* (1896). Walker made it clear that bimetallism had a long history in international trade, and was defensible both theoretically and practically. Bimetallism was not merely the policy of cranks and wild-eyed reformers, as its opponents often charged. Yet Elisha B. Andrews, the president of Brown University, was dismissed for taking the side of silver. Academic freedom was not yet an operating principle in American universities.

By the turn of the century, large corporations had appeared on the American economic landscape, first in the shape of railroads, then as industrial enterprises. Their size, gargantuan by comparison to that of earlier firms, naturally attracted the attention of the rising economics profession. Arthur Hadley, who later became president of Yale, cogently analyzed the economics of the railroad industry in *Railroad Transportation* (1885). Hadley emphasized that, because permanent investments were high relative to operating expenses, competition could be ruinous to the profits of the roads. As giant firms spread into petroleum, chemicals, sugar, tobacco, and other industries, the implications of large-scale organization were avidly studied and debated. Henry Carter Adams's *The Relation of the State to Industrial Action* (1887) laid out principles under which the government should regulate the play of competitive forces. Adams, who taught at the University of Michigan and later did excellent statistical studies at the Interstate Commerce Commission, emphasized that competitive forces would not properly function in industries with significant scale economies. For these situations he urged that regulation should supplant, or at least supplement, competition. His book became the classic economic rationale for government regulation.

In 1899 Congress established the United States Industrial Commission to study the growing influence of trusts. Headed by Jeremiah Jenks, a respected economist from Cornell, the commission studied industries that had organized themselves into combinations of large firms. The commission concluded that the formation of trusts initially raised prices, but that over time prices fell and wages rose in large-scale industries. The work of the Industrial Commission was the first occasion on which a number of economists had assembled under the aegis of federal government to study a national issue. The result was a report notable for its careful collection of facts and sophisticated use of theory.

AMERICAN ECONOMICS COMES OF AGE, 1900–1920

By 1900, economics in the United States was a picture of health and promise. The American Economic Association (AEA) had begun to rise above its petty factionalism. Its membership stood at 802, up from 182 in 1886. The profession had three well-established academic journals: the *Quarterly Journal of Economics*, edited at Harvard; the *Political Science Quarterly*, edited at Columbia; and the *Journal of Political Econ-*

omy, edited at Chicago. In 1911 the AEA itself began issuing the *American Economic Review.*

Academic economics had spread from coast to coast by 1900, although it was noticeably stronger in the East, where economists had served as presidents of Yale, MIT, and Brown. These universities, along with Cornell, Harvard, Columbia, Pennsylvania, and Johns Hopkins, led developments on the eastern seaboard. Chicago, Wisconsin, and Michigan had strong departments in the Midwest. Stanford was the flagship of the West.

Owing to the increasing demand for economics courses at the college level, many books on economic principles appeared between 1900 and 1920. Several were outstanding models of analysis and exposition. These works laid bare the underlying logic of the science, illustrated general principles with concrete examples, and engaged the reader with a scholarly and lucid style. Authors of the texts had reached a consensus on a scientific method that included both induction and deduction, and had thus achieved a balance between theory and history. Nearly a century after they were written, these works, each written by an American master, remain excellent sources for the beginning student to learn economics: Frank A. Fetter, *Economic Principles* (1904); Edwin R. A. Seligman, *Principles of Economics* (1909); Irving Fisher, *Elementary Principles of Economics* (1910); Frank Taussig, *Principles of Economics* (1911); Herbert Davenport, *Economics of Enterprise* (1913); and Henry Seager, *Principles of Economics* (1913). All these volumes contained the essentials of theory, and each had a distinctive emphasis. Taussig's book contained an exceptional treatment of international trade, Fisher's of capital and income. Davenport stressed the role of the entrepreneur. Fetter made a fundamental contribution to the theory of interest.

Several important subjects, however, remained underdeveloped. Monetary theory and business cycle analysis still had not been integrated into marginalist thinking. Neither had the theory of interest or the theory of profit, both of which are crucial to any theory of distribution.

The theory of interest is an old subject in Western thought. Aristotle thought that money lending was barren of productive value; Thomas Aquinas condemned interest taking as a sin. The classical economists were more tolerant; they classified interest as a separate and legitimate kind of income. Laborers earned wages, landowners earned rent, capitalists earned interest. The classical economists believed that each kind of income was fixed by a different economic law.

With the emergence of marginalism, payments to productive agents—whether workers, land, or capital goods—were subsumed under the single principle of marginal productivity. These payments were still labeled by different names, but to call the payment to capital goods "interest" invited confusion. A farmer might call his payment for the use of land "rent," and for hired labor "wages." But he would not call his payment for use of a tractor "interest." Interest is, in fact, a kind of income different from rent and its level is determined by a principle different from that of marginal productivity. Recognition of this point, and the development of an explanation for interest consistent with the marginal theory of distribution, was achieved primarily by Frank Fetter and Irving Fisher.

Fetter and Fisher argued that interest payments on loans reflect an underlying "time-value." Consumers and producers place a higher value on present economic goods than on future economic goods. Wheat today is worth more than wheat a year from now. A forest whose timber is ready for harvest now is worth more than a forest whose timber has just been planted. Time-value results in the discounting of future goods. Capital valuation is the discounting process applied to future income streams. An orchard, a plow, or a building will sell for the "present value" of the future income stream it is expected to yield. Time-value most commonly manifests itself in the loan market. Loans exchange present for future goods. The borrower receives money, which gives an immediate command over goods. The lender gives up immediate command, but asks in return a larger command over future goods. The premium paid for present over future goods is the rate of interest. (In practice, the interest rate on loans also will reflect the risk of not being repaid, and the danger of fluctuations in the value of money. Only where these risks are negligible will the rate of interest reflect pure time-value.)

Although the Fetter-Fisher theory of interest stirred up a heated debate, and was accepted by the profession only partially, it modified prevailing distribution theory in an elegant way. According to marginal productivity theory, the payment to factors precisely exhausts the value of the product. If the totality of productive agents produces goods worth $1 million, and each worker and each parcel of land and each capital good is paid the value of its marginal product, then total factor payments will sum to exactly $1 million. If this is true, however, nothing remains for the payment of interest.

Fetter solved this puzzle by pointing out that

time-value applies to the payment of factors, just as it applies to the borrowing of money. A worker producing goods for immediate consumption will be paid the full value of his or her marginal product. But a worker who plants the seed for next year's crop will be paid only the discounted value of the marginal product. The difference between the discounted value and the value at maturity is precisely the rate of interest, just as it is in the case of bonds or any other good that involves a present value calculation.

While American economists incorporated interest theory into marginalist thought during the first decades of the twentieth century, they were less successful at reconciling monetary theory and marginalism. Monetary theory was the subject of lively controversy, most of which centered around the "quantity theory of money." Simon Newcomb, in his *Principles of Political Economy* (1886), had formulated an "equation of societary circulation," which expressed the basic idea of the quantity theory: that there is a direct, quantifiable link between the supply of money and the price level. Irving Fisher gave impetus to the quantity theory in *The Purchasing Power of Money* (1911). Fisher presented what became the standard version of quantity equation, $MV = PT$, where M represents the total stock of money in an economy, V its velocity of circulation (i.e., the times per year the average dollar was spent), P a price index, and T the number of trades per year. Fisher devoted careful attention to the measurement of his aggregate numbers, and he thereby became one of the profession's leading contributors to index numbers.

Fisher's opponents criticized the quantity theory on several grounds. Henry Parker Willis, a student of J. Laurence Laughlin who would later play an instrumental role in setting up the Federal Reserve System, characterized Fisher's equation as "empty and truismatic." Laughlin himself objected to the assumption of static equilibrium on which the equation was based. Most importantly, critics objected to the theory's one-sidedness. The quantity theory paid almost exclusive attention to the supply of money, thus implicitly ignoring the demand for money. Quantity theorists made no attempt to incorporate monetary theory into the general schema of marginal utility that had recently revolutionized professional thinking.

The most notable attempt to bring monetary theory within the orbit of general value theory was made by Benjamin Anderson, a Harvard economist who left the academy to become chief economist for the Chase Bank in New York. In *Social Value* (1911), Anderson had gone some way toward integrating marginal utility theory into a theory of institutions. He argued that marginal valuation took place in an already established system of social value. This established system was the result of the past evolution of social institutions. Anderson's book, *The Value of Money* (1917), analyzed the evolution of money as a social institution. The value of money (or, to put it another way, the price level) depended on the *past* evolution of the monetary system and the *present* valuations by agents in that system. Anderson's analysis attracted a great deal of attention at the time he wrote, but he exerted little long-term influence over the development of monetary theory. To this day, monetary theory has not been fully integrated into the general theory of value.

The study of business cycles also lay outside the orbit of general value theory during the first two decades of the century, and has remained so since. The two most notable contributors to the study of cycles were Henry L. Moore and Wesley C. Mitchell, both of Columbia.

The usual method of business cycle study has been to formulate generalizations based on statistical correlation, with little regard paid to marginal utility or to price theory in general. Using this method, Moore's *Economic Cycles* (1914) established the dubious proposition that rainfall cycles cause business cycles. Moore collected rainfall data in the Ohio Valley from 1838 to 1910, and fit a harmonic function to the data using the statistical method of least squares. He found a close correlation between rainfall and the size of the grain crops. His crucial finding, however, was an inverse correlation between crop output and industrial output. During the periods that production of crops increased and agricultural prices fell, industrial output decreased and unemployment rose. Conversely, during the periods that production of crops decreased, industrial output and overall employment increased. Moore concluded that "the fundamental, persistent cause of the cycles in the activity of industry and of the cycles of general prices is the cyclical movement in the yield per acre of the crops." Moore was a respected economist known for his advocacy of the mathematical method in economics, and he has often been saluted as a pioneer in the use of statistics. Yet his dubious conclusions illustrate the dangers of substituting statistics for the commonsense "literary economics" that he himself derided.

Wesley Clair Mitchell was less impressive than Moore in his use of mathematics, but far more comprehensive and compelling in his presentation of statistics and his treatment of theory. In his landmark

Business Cycles (1913), Mitchell used a remarkably wide variety of statistics from the United States, England, France, and Germany to trace the ebb and flow of the price system from 1890 through 1911. He recorded the output fluctuations in retail goods, industrial production, farm products, and securities. He showed how the prices of consumers' goods, raw materials, partially finished goods, wages, agricultural products, interest rates, bonds, and stocks rose and fell through the two decades. He also examined the activity of banks, and found that the circulation of notes, clearing operations, and the ratio of cash to deposits exhibited cyclical movements corresponding to the rhythms of trade.

From his close statistical studies, Mitchell fashioned the following descriptive analysis of the business cycle. At the beginning stages of an upturn, prices rise faster than costs. The prospect of profits looks promising. Interest rates are low and credit is readily available, so businesses expand. But during the expansion costs begin to outstrip prices. Wages rise, especially during the latter stages of the boom. The increased borrowing pushes up interest rates. Prospects for profits begin to dim. Businesses cut back and some fail. Firms' inability to repay their loans causes the banks to retrench. A credit crunch, and often a financial panic, follow. Prices, interest rates, and employment begin to fall. A downturn is now underway. But just as the boom in business activity does not last, neither does the fall. The decreased demand forces interest rates and costs down. Pockets of profit opportunity begin to appear. Some businesses begin to expand. Their increased activity spreads to customers and suppliers. The economy is once again in the beginning stages of an upturn.

Mitchell attributed business cycles to economists' and policymakers' failure to master the intricate workings of the monetary economy. His observation, while true, does not really answer the central question of the business cycle as he framed it. If profits drive the economy, why do profit-seeking businessmen, en masse, undertake projects that lose money? Nor did Mitchell devote much space to remedies, although he briefly endorsed the banking reforms embodied in the Federal Reserve Act of 1913, and he approved of counter-cyclical spending by government. Overall, the mystery of business cycles remains one of the principal puzzles of capitalist economies.

Another development in American economics during the first two decades of the twentieth century was institutionalism. As noted earlier, its leading spokesman, Thorstein Veblen, modeled his economics more along the lines of biology than of mechanical

equilibrium. In two of his most celebrated books, *The Theory of the Leisure Class* (1899) and *The Theory of Business Enterprise* (1904), he sharply distinguished the "machine culture" from the "business culture." He saw modern Western economies as theaters of conflict between the two.

The machine culture, according to Veblen, grows out of modern production processes. Machine production (by which Veblen simply meant modern industry) depends on the scientific outlook of engineers, chemists, and other experts, with their systematic knowledge of causal forces, quantitative precision, uniformity, and temporal coordination. By contrast, the business culture grows out of commercial transactions. Business life focuses on purchase and sale, speculation, and pecuniary gain. It is based on law and the conventions of property rather than on modern science and engineering. It concentrates on short-term control, price fluctuations, and the profitable resale of securities.

These two cultures, the machine and the business, inculcate different habits of thought in their respective members. The machine culture creates matter-of-factness and concern for cause and effect in the material world. It breaks down respect for convention and authority. "Broadly," wrote Veblen "the machine discipline acts to disintegrate the institutional heritage of all degrees of antiquity and authenticity." The business culture, on the other hand, is based on the conventions of property and natural rights. It depends on morality and law rather than on facts and quantities. The law, especially the common law as it has come down to us from England, is primarily concerned with precedent. It is backward looking and conservative, the very opposite of the machine culture. The result, said Veblen, is "an appreciable and widening difference between the habits of life of the two classes," so that, eventually, "the two classes come to have an increasing difficulty in understanding one another and appreciating one another's convictions, ideals, capacities, and shortcomings." Veblen believed that the business culture would ultimately lose the contest; the machine can do without business, but business cannot do without the machine.

Veblen's analysis stood in sharp contrast to the conventional economics of his day. More dynamic than marginal theory, it stressed the evolution of cultural norms and their influence on individual behavior. He searched for causal linkages between today's economic life and tomorrow's. Because of the complexity of the subject matter, his causal linkages were usually tenuous; they could not reasonably be characterized as economic laws. Yet Veblen's analysis was realistic. It displayed a vast knowledge of history and culture, and it addressed economic life as it was, not as some ethereal abstraction. The attempt to forge a close connection between economic analysis and actual conditions has been a hallmark of institutional economics since the time of Veblen.

Two of the main policy subjects with which economists involved themselves during the first two decades of the twentieth century were trusts and banking.

At the century's turn, in the midst of a great merger wave, three books appeared on trusts. Jeremiah Jenks's *The Trust Problem* (1900) and John Bates Clark's *The Control of Trusts* (1901) presented big business in a favorable light. Jenks and Clark thought that trusts captured efficiencies of production without unduly exploiting their monopoly power. Clark emphasized the ability of potential competition to control the abuses of large firms. Using a line of argument similar to one that Joseph Schumpeter would later make famous, Clark wrote, "the large and efficient mill that has not yet been built is a regulator of prices in advance of its existence."

Based on his work with the U.S. Industrial Commission, Jenks presented price and wage data for industries involved in the manufacture of sugar, kerosene, spirits, tin-plate, and wire— five industries run by large industrial combinations. Between 1880 and 1900, prices fell and wages rose in all five industries. Jenks attributed this result to the higher productivity per worker under the trust organization. Neither Clark nor Jenks recommended trust-busting. Like most economists of the period, they opposed the Sherman Antitrust Act. They favored more modest policies that would address specific evils. Jenks advocated publicity as a remedy for the abuses of the trusts. Clark wanted to prohibit predatory pricing, price discrimination, and exclusive dealing contracts. He believed that such practices enabled large firms to put small yet efficient rivals out of business. Clark and Jenks worked with the National Civic Federation to draft trust legislation; their views were reflected in the Clayton Act and the Federal Trade Commission Act, both of which were signed into law in 1914.

Richard Ely, in *Monopolies and Trusts* (1902), thought that trusts were more culpable of abusing monopoly power than did Clark and Jenks. Where abuses could not be curbed by regulation, he advocated government ownership, especially of utilities. Ely's viewpoint, which was shared by many prominent economists, including the conservatively minded Frank Taussig, was the subject of an in-depth study sponsored by the National Civic Federation in 1905. A bipartisan committee studied at first-hand publicly and privately owned utilities in the United States and England. The committee issued a massive three-volume report, *Municipal and Private Operation of Public Utilities* (1907), which found corruption in both government-owned and government-regulated utilities. The only difference seemed to lie in who benefited from the corruption.

Interest in banking and its reform was stimulated by the Panic of 1907. Panics and subsequent depressions were of course nothing new in the United States; they had occurred in 1819, 1837, 1857, 1873, and 1893. But the Panic of 1907 was particularly severe, and Congress took stronger action than usual. The House of Representatives established the Pujo Committee (named for its chairman, Arsène Pujo of Louisiana) to investigate the role of a "money trust" in causing panics. In 1908 the Aldrich-Vreeland Act created a National Monetary Commission, whose chairman was influential Republican Senator Nelson Aldrich of Rhode Island, to investigate banking reform. In 1910 Aldrich introduced a bill to establish a central bank, but the change from a Republican to a Democratic administration in 1912 led to the bill's defeat. In March 1912 a House Committee, led by Democrat Carter Glass of Virginia, introduced its own bill, which became the Federal Reserve Act of 1913.

Meanwhile, economists exhibited keen interest in reform of the national banking system. Alone among industrial nations, the United States had no central bank, thanks to the enduring hostility of the populace toward concentrated power. Nearly all economists criticized the existing system for its inelastic currency, which contributed to financial panics. Since most of the reserves of smaller banks were held by large New York banks, who invested them in the stock market, a heavy demand for funds by farmers could trigger a selling off in the stock market. To avoid this problem of an inelastic currency, to which the Panic of 1907 was attributed, economists favored the creation of a central bank.

J. Laurence Laughlin of the University of Chicago and his former student, H. Parker Willis, were heavily involved in banking reform. When the Aldrich plan of 1910 was proposed, Laughlin served as chairman of the National Citizens' League, a group of Chicago businessmen formed to promote the bill. Representative Carter Glass appointed Willis as economic expert to his banking subcommittee, which drew up the bill that became the Federal Reserve Act. The act established a strong central bank whose duty was to strengthen credit, create a currency more responsive to the needs of trade, and prevent financial panics and economic depressions. Economists heaped praise on it at the time of its passage. Not until the experience of 1930s was it evident how inadequate, even disruptive, a central bank could be if it pursued the wrong policies.

If we take 1920 as a vantage point and look back over the progress of economic thought in the United States, we see an impressive development. Within the space of fifty years, economic theory had grown from a pale intellectual imitation of its European counterpart, taught mostly in theology departments, to an independent science at the leading edge of theory internationally. American economists could point with pride to a corpus of theory that they had helped to develop. Names such as Clark, Fisher, Fetter, Mitchell, Taussig, and Veblen were respected throughout Europe. Several U.S. economics departments ranked among the best in the world. Economists were increasingly called upon to help solve problems of policy. Several had served in important positions during World War I. As both an academic discipline and a practical science economics in the United States had come of age.

DEVELOPMENT, DISSENT, AND DEPRESSION, 1920–1940

In the twenties and thirties, basic economic theory did not advance as rapidly or as broadly as it had done over the previous decades: in part because many leading economists felt satisfied with the main tenets of marginalist doctrine, but also because of the growth of the institutionalist movement and its critical attitudes toward marginalism. The institutionalists, though a diverse group, were united in their desire for more realism in economic theory. The institutionalist movement included Veblen, with his evolutionary bent, and Mitchell with his statistical one. It included Walton Hale Hamilton, who had an extraordinarily wide range of interests (he contributed seventeen articles to the *Encyclopedia of the Social Sciences* (1938) on subjects ranging from competition to celibacy). It included Rexford Guy Tugwell, an advocate of government planning who would become part of Roosevelt's brain trust, and Gardiner C. Means, whose work with Adolf Berle would raise troublesome questions about the functioning of corporate enterprise.

Perhaps the most important of all the institutionalists was John R. Commons. Commons, a student of Ely, had published his first economics book, *The*

Distribution of Wealth, in 1893. It was a contribution to marginalist theory, and Commons never displayed the disdain for marginalism that other institutionalists did; still, he thought that economic theory needed a base broader than marginal utility. *The Legal Foundations of Capitalism* (1924) and *Institutional Economics* (1934) works were long, detailed expeditions into the history of economic and legal thought, from which Commons emerged with some suggestive theoretical ideas. Commons attempted to broaden economic theory by making the transaction, rather than the individual, the unit of analysis. A transaction required an underlying system of property and two or more individuals who exchanged legal title to goods. This focus on the transaction immediately expanded economics into a consideration of the legal system and government. In Commons's view transactions were embedded in a set of customs, which imposed rules on individual conduct. These institutions were often economic organizations—"going concerns," as Commons called them. To Commons, business firms, labor unions, and bureaucracies have their own stated purposes and rules of conduct that discipline individual action.

Institutionalists typically paid close attention to the effects of the legal system on economics. This attention to law and economics led to one of the most influential contributions of the interwar years, *The Modern Corporation and Private Property* (1932), written by Adolf Berle, an attorney and member of Roosevelt's brain trust, and Gardiner C. Means, an economist from Columbia University.

With a wealth of legal and statistical detail, Berle and Means delineated the problems associated with separating the ownership of the modern corporation from its control. This separation created the possibility of managers pursuing their own interests at the expense of stockholders. As a solution to this problem, Berle and Means advanced the proposition that common law should treat the corporation as a trust. Whoever controlled the direction of the firm had to exercise a fiduciary responsibility to the stockholders. All decisions of the board of directors and principal officers of the corporation should be taken with the goal of looking out for the well-being of the stockholders and the public at large.

Berle and Means raised an issue that later attracted a great deal of attention under the rubric of principal-agent theory. This line of inquiry examined the various incentives that managers (the agents) face in carrying out the interests of stockholders (the principals). Such scholars as Henry Manne, Michael Jensen, William Meckling, and Oliver Williamson have studied the business firm from this point of view. Although modern scholars have often disagreed with the solutions offered by Berle and Means, the problems they raised have endured because of their importance to modern economies.

Even if the advance of economic theory in general was not as prominent in the interwar years as it had previously been, there were some noteworthy individual contributions, particularly those of Frank Knight and Edward Chamberlin. Knight's work, *Risk, Uncertainty, and Profit* (1921), tackled a troublesome problem of income distribution, the source of business profits. Clark, Fetter, and Fisher had worked out a theoretical explanation for payments to land, labor, and capital goods, and also for the payment of interest to lenders of capital. But this theory assumed an equilibrium condition in which there were no profits. In equilibrium, prices are fully adjusted so that it is impossible to "buy low and sell high." Knight undertook a close examination of the conditions of equilibrium, as a hypothetical exercise, so that he could understand the underlying causes of profits, which were a distinctly disequilibrium phenomenon. Building on the work of Clark and of Frederick B. Hawley, a businessman with a keen interest in economics, Knight developed a theory of profits based on "uncertainty."

Knight drew a distinction between risk and uncertainty. Risk is quantifiable, as in the actuarial tables used by insurance companies. But the "risk" surrounding economic events is often not quantifiable. Knowledge is too incomplete and the future is too shrouded in mystery to construct probability distributions. According to Knight, this kind of incomplete knowledge, which he labeled uncertainty, opens up profit opportunities. Those who are better able to judge the future and to shape its events can earn profits. Judgment, creativity, and leadership become valuable attributes of business management; profit is their reward.

Knight's work provided economists an opportunity for transforming the static "laws" of marginal productivity theory into a dynamic theory of enterprise. Unfortunately, they did not take it. In an ironic twist of twentieth-century theory, economists concentrated their attention, not on Knight's theory of profit, but on his refinements to equilibrium theory. Knight made a signal contribution to the theory of equilibrium through his rigorous analysis of perfect competition, because he wanted to contrast the imaginary world of equilibrium with the real world of business enterprise. For Knight, perfect competition theory was merely a prelude, which his contemporaries mistook for the symphony. Knight became a powerful voice in pre–World War II economics, but his profit theory has never been widely accepted in the profession.

It was largely in reaction to the unrealistic nature of perfect competition that Edward Chamberlin of Harvard wrote his *Theory of Monopolistic Competition* (1933). Chamberlin objected to the idea that competition consisted of innumerable small firms selling identical products. He pointed to competition among the few, for which he used the term *oligopoly*. He drew attention to the many ways in which firms compete by differentiating their products. Brand names, favorable location, and customer loyalty give firms, in Chamberlin's view, small islands of monopoly power. Monopolistic elements mean that firms have some control over price and product quality, something they do not have in the perfectly competitive industries of orthodox theory.

Monopolistic competition became the subject of a great deal of discussion during the thirties and forties. It took its place alongside perfect competition and monopoly in economic analysis. These three theoretical constructs gave impetus to an emerging theory of industrial organization, which placed great importance on the number of firms in an industry. The basic reasoning, as later developed by Chamberlin's colleagues at Harvard, Edward S. Mason and Joe S. Bain, was that the number of firms in an industry (its structure) determined the conduct of those firms, which in turn determined the efficiency of the industry (its performance). This became known as the "structure-conduct-performance" approach to industrial organization, which dominated the field in the post World War II era.

Despite the influence of Chamberlin's work, monopolistic competition did not displace perfect competition to the extent that Chamberlin had hoped. Partly this resulted from the graphics and mathematics of Chamberlin's analysis, which were complicated and clumsy compared to those of perfect competition and monopoly. The perfectly competitive notion of "given price" was central to the existence proofs of general equilibrium theory. A second reason for Chamberlin's circumscribed influence was the simultaneous appearance of a similar product, *The Theory of Imperfect Competition* (1933), by the British economist Joan Robinson. Robinson's book placed far more weight than Chamberlin's on the marginal revenue curve, which became one of the most widely used analytical tools of modern economics. Credit for exploiting this device rightly went to Robinson (although it was apparently first derived by an American economist, Theodore Yntema, in the December 1928 issue of the *Journal of Political Economy*).

American economists showed an interest in business cycle theory during the twenties and produced some suggestive contributions, but nothing definitive. Mitchell remained the towering figure in the field, and in 1927 he issued an expanded version of his *Business Cycles*, but without any fundamentally new insights into causes or remedies. Alvin Hansen's *Cycles of Prosperity and Depression* (1921) was perhaps the best contribution to cycle theory by a U.S. economist. Hansen emphasized problems in the operation of the banking system as a leading cause of cycles. When banks increase purchasing power through credit expansion to business, Hansen argued, purchasing power is redistributed from wage earners to entrepreneurs. Altered purchasing power changes demand, reconfigures prices, and increases profits and production. However, this increase cannot be sustained, and when the credit expansion stops, profits and production experience a sharp decline. "Here," wrote Hansen, "may be found the fundamental cause of the business cycle."

The idea that the seeds of depression are sown in expansionary banking policy constituted an important and none too obvious contribution to business cycle theory. Irving Fisher had said something similar, briefly, in *The Rate of Interest* (1906). Frank Fetter, in a long paper entitled "Interest Theory and Price Movements" delivered at the American Economic Association meetings in 1926, offered a similar model. Fetter's paper also went a long way toward integrating business cycle theory with marginal economics.

Had any of these economists offered a portent of trouble ahead, or even if they had pressed their analysis with a criticism of monetary policy during the twenties, their theoretical work might have gained a great deal of attention during the depressed thirties. But none did. Fetter was silent about the implications of his model for the American economy. Hansen, in his *Business-Cycle Theory* (1927) even speculated that cycles would become less violent as time went on. Fisher, in a speech to the New York Men's Credit Association on 21 October 1929, said, "I cannot see that the present shakedown is going to be a collapse." Predictions such as these reveal just how unexpected the Great Depression was even to the very best professional economists. As things worsened year after year, the Depression created an atmosphere of doubt in which many economic reforms were proposed.

Comprehensive government planning of the economy was widely discussed during the thirties. Such planning during World War I had convinced many economists that centralized direction was feasible. The most respected economist to advocate government planning was Rexford Guy Tugwell of Columbia, who argued in *The Industrial Discipline and the Governmental Arts* (1933) that government allocation of investment capital, based on a comprehensive national economic plan, would prevent depressions. Popularizers such as George Soule and Stuart Chase also claimed that central planning would eliminate depressions and unemployment. Most professional economists, including J. M. Clark, Alvin Hansen, Frank H. Knight, and Sumner H. Slichter, counseled the public not to expect too much from planning. In the *Harvard Business Review* for 1935, Slichter analyzed a plan for national consumption drawn up in 1934 by a group of experts. The plan proposed to increase consumption of movies, men's bathrobes, and women's dresses by one-third to one-half, and to reduce consumption of breakfast cereals, nuts, biscuits, cake, and macaroni by similar amounts. Slichter ridiculed the arbitrary nature of such plans and predicted that agencies charged with administering them would become targets of special interest groups.

Public work projects were also advocated as a means of preventing depressions. Economists urged the government to build up a reserve fund during prosperous years that could be used to finance public works during depressed years. The *American Economic Review* of December 1934 reported favorably on Adolf Hitler's use of public works to reduce unemployment and stimulate the German economy. Social insurance for workers was also advanced as a way of alleviating the worst effects of depressions.

Aside from economists' opposition to high tariffs (over one thousand signed a petition urging Herbert Hoover to oppose the Smoot-Hawley tariff of 1930), there was little agreement on either the causes of or cures for the Depression. The thirties were years of doubt and soul searching for the profession. John Maurice Clark urged humility on his fellow economists in his presidential address to the American Economic Association in 1935. The aged and distinguished Frank Taussig expressed bafflement so deep as to be almost embarrassing in "Doctors, Economists, and the Depression," published in *Harper's Magazine* (1932). According to Taussig, the complexity of the subject, the inability to experiment, and the "wavering and incalculable behavior" of mankind prevented economists from knowing what caused the Depression or how to cure it. Taussig could only implore his readers to wait, assuring them that depressions ended, for reasons as mysterious as they started. Not until American economists became persuaded by John Maynard Keynes's *General Theory of Employment, Interest, and Money* (1936) did they again feel some confidence about how to prevent severe depressions.

HEGEMONY OF SORTS, 1940–1970

The war period, if we include a margin of a few years on either side, was a watershed in American economics. From this time onward, economic theory ascended to a position of preeminence within the profession, and U.S. economists led the world in the development of theory. Two-thirds of the Nobel prizes in economics, which began in 1968, have gone to economists at U.S. universities. The ascendancy of American economics is partly attributable to the influx of foreign-born and trained economists—Joseph Schumpeter, Ludwig Mises, Abba Lerner, Wassily Leontief, Franco Modigliani, and Gerard Debreu are a few of the illustrious figures who moved from European to U.S. universities during the turbulent thirties and forties. But others—Kenneth Arrow, James Buchanan, Milton Friedman, Paul Samuelson, George Stigler, and James Tobin—who were to become just as respected, were native-born and educated.

Two theoretical developments mark the postwar divide—the rise of mathematical economics (including econometrics) and the ascendancy of Keynesianism. Mathematical economics was not unknown before World War II. The Econometric Society was formed in Cleveland in December 1930. The society's goal, according to its constitution, was "the advancement of economic theory in its relation to statistics and mathematics." Two years later, in January 1933, it began publication of *Econometrica*. As already mentioned, Simon Newcomb, Irving Fisher, and Henry Moore had applied mathematics to economics in the late nineteenth and early twentieth centuries. Moreover, those who were to later contribute so influentially to mathematical economics began to publish in the twenties and thirties, so one could argue that the seeds of change were sown prior to World War II, as the historian of economic thought A. W. Coats has done.

Nevertheless, mathematical economics was not part of the common domain of the economics profession prior to World War II. The *American Economic Review*, for example, in the years 1915, 1925, and 1935, had a total of three articles with equations.

This amounted to 4 percent of the articles for those years. In the 1940s, mathematical articles began to increase markedly. In 1945, eight of twenty-seven articles, or 30 percent, contained equations; in 1955, 43 percent did, and in 1965 the figure rose to 80 percent. Nor do simple percentages do justice to the progress of mathematics between 1940 and 1970. The complexity of the mathematics changed from relatively simple algebra to differentiation, integration, axiomatic set theory, topology, and multiple regression analysis.

If one were to identify a particular work that marked the arrival of mathematical economics in the United States, it would be Paul A. Samuelson's *Foundations of Economic Analysis*, published in 1947. The book ranged over nearly the whole of economic theory—equilibrium conditions, comparative statics, cost and production, consumer behavior, welfare theory, index numbers, Keynesian economics, and monetary theory. Samuelson showed a masterful command of multivariate calculus (both differential and integral), matrix algebra, and differential equations. Despite his disclaimer that "the pure mathematician will recognize all too readily the essentially elementary character of the tools used," the pure economist must have been dazzled by it all. Samuelson left no doubt that a wide range of economic problems were amenable to mathematical treatment.

Samuelson could rightly claim that his tools were elementary to the professional mathematician. Not so with the economists who developed general equilibrium theory in the postwar years. These economists, led by Kenneth Arrow and Gerard Debreu, undertook to show that a decentralized, competitive economy, even one with millions of economic agents, could achieve an equilibrium. The idea was to start with a set of consumers and producers, each with well-specified utility and production functions, and to demonstrate, using the economic assumption that everyone acts in his own self-interest, that there exists a set of prices for which all markets will simultaneously clear.

The attempt to prove the existence of a general equilibrium was an exciting intellectual journey that had started in France with the publication of Leon Walras's *Elements of Pure Economics* (1874) and had traveled through Europe, where Enrico Barone and Vilfredo Pareto (Italy), Francis Ysidro Edgeworth (England), and Gustav Cassell (Sweden) contributed. Gifted mathematicians such as Abraham Wald and Karl Menger (the son of the economist) took up the subject in 1930s Austria. The research culminated in the United States when Arrow and Debreu published the "Existence of an Equilibrium for a Competitive Economy" in the July 1954 issue of *Econometrica*.

Once the existence of equilibrium had been proved mathematically, general equilibrium theorists turned to refining and extending their results. Two outstanding works in this tradition are Gerard Debreu's *Theory of Value* (1959) and Kenneth Arrow and Frank Hahn's *General Competitive Analysis* (1971). The latter book also demonstrated the conditions under which disequilibrium prices would converge to their equilibrium values. The restrictive assumptions required for convergence eventually led some economists to doubt that general equilibrium had much relevance for actual economies. At the time, however, the pioneers of general equilibrium theory were focused on a complex mathematical problem—proving the existence of a general equilibrium—the solution of which ranks as one of the most impressive achievements in the history of mathematical economics.

The second landmark development of post-war economics in the United States began in Britain, with the publication of John Maynard Keynes's *General Theory of Employment, Interest, and Money* in 1936. The initial American reception of this work was not auspicious. Jacob Viner of the University of Chicago and Alvin Hansen of Harvard, the latter of whom would later become a tireless advocate of Keynes's ideas, both gave the *General Theory* tepid reviews. Frank Knight's evaluation in the *Canadian Journal of Economics and Political Science* was positively harsh. Knight declared that the book contributed nothing of theoretical value, but thought that "perhaps its wild overstatement may serve to emphasize some factors which have been relatively neglected." From this inauspicious beginning, Keynesianism grew to dominate macroeconomic theory and policy in the fifties and sixties. Then, in an astonishing reversal, Keynesianism lost influence even faster than it had acquired it. The Keynesian episode is a curious story that demonstrates both the power and the vulnerability of academic economics.

Keynesian analysis exhibited three interrelated characteristics. First, Keynes aggregated the economy into four markets—output, labor, bond, and money. Second, he introduced the idea of an "unemployment equilibrium," a situation in which aggregate demand in the output market is insufficient to eliminate excess supply in the labor or capital markets; in fact, Keynes believed that in the long run capitalist economies would reach a point where the capital stock would no longer grow and there would be large-scale unemployment. Third, he argued that

government actions, such as inflation or public works, would increase employment and the capital stock when the market failed to do so.

As Keynesian ideas were studied and developed in the United States, statistical models and evidence played a key role. Lawrence Klein of the University of Pennsylvania, for example, used Keynesian theory to develop aggregated models of economic forecasting. Through these models, Klein pioneered in the development of statistical techniques and simulated solutions. Meanwhile, James Tobin of Yale combined time-series and cross-sectional data to estimate Keynes's consumption function for the American economy. His work resulted in a new technique called Tobin analysis. Both Klein and Tobin would later receive Nobel prizes for their advancement of Keynesian economics.

The central piece of evidence confirming Keynesian theory was the Phillips Curve, a statistical relationship named after British statistician A. W. Phillips that seemed to demonstrate an inverse correlation between inflation and unemployment. Increasing one would lower the other, and vice-versa, so that if market activity resulted in too much unemployment, government could lower the level by increasing the money supply. On the policy side, the Keynesian belief that government should control the level of unemployment was embodied in the Employment Act of 1946, which created the Council of Economic Advisers. The high point of Keynesian policy activism occurred in 1964, when the Kennedy-Johnson tax cut programs stimulated the economy and reduced unemployment, just as the Keynesian advisers of these presidents, Walter Heller and James Tobin, had predicted would happen.

Although mathematical economics and Keynesianism gained a commanding position in economic theory between 1940 and 1970, several economists produced influential work that pushed against one or the other of these main tides. Joseph Schumpeter's *Capitalism, Socialism, and Democracy* (1942) achieved the status of a classic that was nevertheless read by large numbers of people. Eschewing the mathematical method and criticizing head-on the doctrines of perfect competition and Keynesian stagnation, Schumpeter laid out his vision of the modern economic process.

Describing capitalism as a "perennial gale of creative destruction," he emphasized the incessant forces of change in the market economy. In Schumpeter's model of capitalism, the lure of profits stimulates entrepreneurs to seek out new markets, to discover new production techniques, to offer new goods, and to try new methods of organization. The evolutionary process of change, not the static world of perfect competition, constituted the core of capitalist reality in Schumpeter's vision.

Drawing on his vast store of historical knowledge and his deep understanding of economic theory, Schumpeter argued that the capitalist process is an engine of unparalleled productivity. Yet he predicted the downfall of capitalism, not because it would fail to deliver the goods, but because it would succeed too well. In an increasingly wealthy society, entrepreneurship would become less important. The man of affairs, who can get things done, would command less respect. Large enterprises would erode the political influence of the small trader. Ultimately, the polity would lose its respect for private property and independence. Schumpeter, like Veblen, concluded that the culture of modern capitalism moves inexorably to undermine its own institutions.

Another influential economist who stood outside the analytical mainstream was John Kenneth Galbraith. Where most of the profession spoke increasingly to itself, Galbraith spoke to the public. While the profession as a whole turned toward mathematics, Galbraith used his matchless prose style as a sharp polemical weapon. In *American Capitalism* (1952), *The Affluent Society* (1958), and *The New Industrial State* (1967), Galbraith set forth his vision of the economy. In his portrayal, the growth of complex technology played a crucial role. Modern technology required a commitment to research and development, to minute specialization, and to long lead times and planning. The small firms of traditional economic theory were incapable of undertaking these commitments. Large corporations and government involvement were required. Galbraith attempted to reformulate economic theory to take account of these institutional changes.

"Countervailing power" was one of the ideas that Galbraith introduced in his attempt to incorporate modern conditions into theory. Countervailing power meant that the strength of large corporations would be offset by the growth of other large institutions. If, for example, large steel firms exerted power over the hiring of labor, then workers would counter by forming a large and equally powerful union. If large food manufacturers exercise their economic muscle by charging high prices to grocers, then the latter would respond through the buying power of large chain stores. Modern economic life, in Galbraith's view, is a series of moves and countermoves by large and powerful institutions. This approach to economics was radically different from the mathematical development of general equilibrium theory under atomistic competition.

Another set of ideas that grew up outside the orthodoxy of postwar economics has come to be known as the Chicago school. Milton Friedman pushed especially hard against the prevailing tide of Keynesianism in the fifties and sixties. Almost single-handedly, he restored the quantity theory of money to an influential position in economics. A brilliant statistician, Friedman recast the quantity equation in terms that were comparable to Keynesian equations and amenable to econometric techniques, so that the effectiveness of the two theories could be statistically compared. Friedman was able to demonstrate that the quantity of money was far more important to the general functioning of the economy than Keynesians had believed, and he eventually changed the balance of opinion within the profession. Friedman went on to conclude that monetary authorities should follow a fixed rule in controlling the quantity of money. The role of monetary policy was to prevent money from becoming a source of disturbance to the normal functioning of the economy. Unlike the Keynesians, who had argued that the Great Depression resulted from an errant market, Friedman and Anna Schwarz, in their massive *Monetary History of the United States* (1962), argued that the tragically misguided policies of the Federal Reserve Board during the thirties contributed significantly to the depth and duration of the economic collapse.

By the 1960s, American economists began to extend their analysis into other fields of inquiry, notably law and political science. Economists had always paid attention to the content of particular laws that directly affect economic behavior, such as antitrust and public utility law. But the "law and economics" movement that developed in the 1960s and 1970s was based much more on price theory than previous work had been. It focused on economic forces at work in the evolution of law, and it evaluated various legal arrangements using a standard of economic efficiency.

Ronald Coase, a British-born economist who taught in the law school at the University of Chicago, was a pivotal figure in the development of law and economics. His article, "Problem of Social Cost" (1961), provided a powerful stimulus into inquiry between economics and legal arrangements. In 1958 he helped to launch (and for many years he edited) the *Journal of Law and Economics*, which was a major forum for this kind of research. The most unswerving application of economics to the law has come from Richard Posner, who has served as both professor of law at Chicago and as a federal judge. Posner's analysis of negligence well illustrates his overall approach. Rather than place the responsibility for accidents on the persons who cause damage, as strict liability would do, Posner would place it on the persons who can avoid accidents most easily. This is economically efficient in the same sense that it is efficient to have low-cost firms manufacture consumers' products. Posner's book, *Economic Analysis of Law* (1972), is a tour de force, covering property law, contract law, antitrust, regulation, corporate law, and constitutional law, all in the pure light of economic efficiency.

Meanwhile, the "public choice" school also rose to prominence by extending economics to another discipline, this time political science. James Buchanan and Gordon Tullock's classic work, *The Calculus of Consent* (1962), justified government on economic as opposed to moral grounds. Government, they argued, can provide public goods at lower cost than can private organizations. Consequently, persons interested in nothing but their own self-interest will institute government. In a democracy these same people will also impose various checks, so that government itself does not beget more costs than benefits. Anthony Downs's *An Economic Theory of Democracy* (1957) modeled political parties as vote maximizers and voters as utility maximizers. Government policies are thus the result of two competitive processes—(1) competition between parties striving to maximize votes so as to stay in office, and (2) competition between voters striving to reap the benefits of legislation. This mode of analysis challenged the accepted view that government activity furthers some vague public interest; rather it focused attention on the operation of economic self-interest within the public domain.

While economics extended its methods and principles to fields usually reserved for the other social sciences, the discipline also became narrower in important ways. For example, mathematical economics and Keynesianism had a curious effect on the subdiscipline of economic history in postwar America. From the nineteenth century through the 1930s, history had been essential fare for the American economist, who placed high value on both abstract theory and concrete economic events. In the 1940s, however, the increased attention to mathematics, statistics, and macroeconomics began to crowd history out of the professional journals and out of the curriculum. Throughout the forties and fifties, there was a noticeable decline in historical study by economists.

In the 1960s, however, the interest in history returned in new garb, transformed by mathematics and statistics. This new economic history, as it was called, cast historical propositions into a form testable through various econometric techniques. Pioneers in the field, which included William Parker, Douglass North, Donald McCloskey, and Robert Fogel, and Stanley Engerman, gathered large amounts of statistical data, which they applied primarily to issues in American history. The effects of the Navigation Acts on American colonial trade, the profitability of slavery, and the contribution of the railroad to American economic growth were among the subjects addressed using statistical techniques. North and Fogel were awarded the Nobel prize for their work.

The methods and often the conclusions of the "cliometricians," differed sharply from those of traditional historians. The new historians claimed that they were bringing science to bear on historical issues, many of which seemed to be unresolvable through traditional historiography. Despite the epic debate among historians, the new approach did little to restore history to its former prominence within the economics profession. The new economic history became a subdiscipline within economics, but has not become a part of the general training of economists. Douglass North attributed economists' lack of interest in the new history to its derivative nature. The new historians were doing exactly what economists were doing, but, in North's words, "with dead issues rather than live ones and with data of generally poorer quality."

One of the few historians to navigate a successful middle course between cliometrics on one side and traditional historiography on the other was Alfred D. Chandler, Jr. His intensive studies of the rise of big business in America, culminating in the Pulitzer prize-winning book, *The Visible Hand* (1977), demonstrated that theory, history, and statistics could be successfully combined without using advanced mathematics.

CRISIS, 1970 AND AFTER

The hegemony of Keynesianism and general equilibrium theory began to break apart around 1970. The problem started in macroeconomics, with the collapse of the Phillips curve. As mentioned earlier, this curve plotted the relationship between unemployment and inflation. It was, according to Keynesian theory and statistical evidence, a stable inverse relationship that could be beneficially manipulated by government policymakers. If unemployment started to increase, the government, through monetary policy, could reduce it by inflating a little. If inflation started to climb too fast, government could reduce it at the expense of some jobs. Maintaining a proper adjustment between inflation and unemployment was the legitimate and fairly simple task of government. It was one of the ways in which, according to Keynesian economics, government balanced an unstable economy.

In the 1970s, the Phillips curve went awry. A century of statistics had demonstrated that the curve sloped downward, that is, as inflation increased, unemployment decreased. Now it began to slope upward. Inflation and unemployment increased together, something that was decidedly not supposed to happen. But even this perverse "stagflation" did not hold steady. Applied to the actual experience of the American economy in the 1970s, the curve began to bend back on itself, then took a sharp dive downward, leveled off, and started an upward climb again. What was once a stable relationship on which government policies could be based began to resemble a roller-coaster ride.

Economists were quick to respond to the aberrant Phillips curve. They accused the practitioners of macroeconomics with a failure to root their propositions in the solid soil of microeconomics. But basing macroeconomics in microtheory proved to be no easy matter. The microeconomics of general equilibrium theory—no matter how precise the assumptions, no matter how tight the logic—left little room for the subjects with which macroeconomics dealt. In general microeconomic equilibrium, there is no unemployment. All markets clear for all time. Nor is there scope for inflation. The system does not contain money. Instead, all calculations are made in units of a "numeraire," which can be any good in the economy, guppies as well as gold. So far is general equilibrium theory from describing what goes on in actual economies that one prominent macroeconomist, Robert Clower, called it elegant "science fiction."

Thus began the search for a macroeconomics based on microeconomics, and for a microeconomics serviceable for developing macroeconomic principles. Economists produced a great deal of research in this area. The seventies were years of foment, soul-searching, and experimentation in economics. The most influential research applied to economics another branch of mathematics: probability theory. Especially noteworthy were rational expectations theory and search theory. Rational expectations theorists such as Robert Lucas and Thomas Sargent argued that government monetary policies could influence employment or output only to the extent that these policies were not anticipated by businessmen and

workers. For example, if inflationary policy had the effect of lowering real wage rates, and thus increasing employment, it would do so only for a time. Eventually, workers would catch on to the fact that their wages had been lowered and would reduce the amount of labor they supplied. In the long run, therefore, government could not increase employment. Naturally, the new macroeconomics, as it was called, had some sharp criticisms for activist Keynesian policies.

Search theorists, such as George Stigler and Armen Alchian, argued that markets were characterized, not by a single price for each good, but by price distributions. These economists argued that workers would look for higher wage offers until the costs of the search outweighed the expected benefits. During the period of search, workers would remain unemployed because they found it advantageous to do so. This line of inquiry, which was based on the premise that a spotty knowledge of market conditions could be modeled as a probability distribution, sent its probes into nearly every corner of economic theory. The "economics of information" became a major area of research in the seventies and eighties.

Several other doctrines also gained ground during these years of disquiet. Yet there is little in these various doctrines that would unite them into a coherent alternative to traditional theory. The adherents of these doctrines have in common only a conviction that their theory is superior to the orthodoxy, and usually to other heterodoxies as well.

Institutional economics remained the largest and best established of the heterodoxies. In its modern form, institutionalism consists of two strands, one emanating from Veblen, the other from Commons. The Veblen branch underscores the importance of technological change in shaping economic life. The Commons branch emphasizes the ways in which legal rulings and other institutions shape economic behavior. Both strands unite in stressing the evolutionary and historical aspects of modern economies. They place much less importance on prices, and much more on law and custom, than does traditional economic theory. In 1963, the institutionalists founded the Association for Evolutionary Economics and in 1967 began publishing the *Journal of Economic Issues*. Under the editorship of Warren Samuels of Michigan State University, this journal became a focal point for research in the institutionalist tradition.

Another strand of heterodoxy that gained adherents in the postseventies era was "Austrian" economics. This set of ideas originally grew up around Carl

Menger at the University of Vienna, but migrated to the United States after Hitler's Anschluss of Austria in 1937. After World War II, Ludwig Mises, who moved to New York University, and Friedrich Hayek, who taught for a time at the University of Chicago, were especially influential in America. Unlike the institutionalists, the modern Austrians have not been critical of marginal economics per se, but they have criticized the direction it has taken. Murray Rothbard's *Man, Economy, and State* (1962), faulted neoclassical theory for its preoccupation with mathematics, and presented an encyclopedic nonmathematical restatement of economic principles based on marginal analysis. His work is a self-conscious throwback to the treatises of the pre–World War I era. Israel Kirzner's *Competition and Entrepreneurship* (1973) criticized neoclassical theory for its preoccupation with perfect competition, which neglected the importance of the entrepreneur in economic life. Kirzner integrated entrepreneurial action into neoclassical economics, and his work has been accepted by orthodox economists to a much greater extent than other Austrian or institutionalist writing.

Marxist economics was another strand of thought that gained influence because of the theoretical discord of the seventies. Despite its enormous influence throughout the rest of the world, Marxism never really caught on with American economists. Not until the depression years of the thirties did American economics produce any first-rate Marxist thinkers. In 1942 Paul Sweezy, who was American-born and educated (except for a stint at the London School of Economics), published *The Theory of Capitalist Development*, which applied Marxian economics to conditions in America. Most notable was Sweezy's presentation of an underconsumptionist theory of business depressions. In 1966 Sweezy coauthored, with Paul Baran, a Russian immigrant educated in the United States, *Monopoly Capital*, a book that further applied Marxian thought to modern conditions. Baran and Sweezy argued that, in a mature market economy dominated by large firms, capital accumulation exceeds the opportunity for profitable investment. In their model, the imbalance would lead ultimately to stagnation of the economy. Published during a period of increasing dissatisfaction with American public policy, especially the war in Vietnam, *Monopoly Capital* caught the imagination of a number of young scholars. In 1968 they formed the Union of Radical Political Economists, which began publication of the *Review of Radical Political Economics*, a journal devoted to Marxian thought. Meanwhile, the veteran Sweezy continued to edit the *Monthly Review*, a publication with which he first became associated in 1949, into the nineties.

One of the most enterprising of the research programs to come out of the failure of Keynesianism was a searching re-interpretation of Keynesian theory itself. Paul Samuelson wrote of *The General Theory* in *Econometrica* (1946), "It is a badly written book, poorly organized. . . . It is arrogant, bad-tempered, polemical, and not overly-generous in its acknowledgements. It abounds in mares' nests and confusions." As orthodox Keynesianism broke down, there was much room for reinterpreting and developing Keynes's ideas. This activity became a minor growth industry under the rubric of post-Keynesian economics.

A pioneering effort at reinterpretation came from Axel Leijonhufvud of the University of California at Los Angeles. In his treatise, *On Keynesian Economics and the Economics of Keynes* (1968), Leijonhufvud claimed that the traditional Keynesian income-expenditure model missed the essential features of Keynes's system, for in fact, Keynes's general model was one of disequilibrium, filled with uncertainty and groping. In unusual times, such as the Great Depression, traditional profit and loss calculations could seriously mislead businessmen, and the economy as a whole would therefore not function as it did in normal times. A stream of books and articles on post-Keynesian thought appeared during the seventies and eighties. The *Journal of Post-Keynesian Economics*, edited by Paul Davidson and Sidney Weintraub (until his death in 1983), provided the main forum for this research.

Another alternative to perfectly competitive theory that emerged after the 1970s was game theory. The kernel of this line of thinking is straightforward. Two or more players array themselves against one another, either to cooperate or to compete. Each has a set of strategies he can employ, and for each pair of strategies, there is a pay-off to each player. The object of the game is to choose those actions that will maximize the expected pay-off.

The beginnings of the theory in economics date from 1944, when John von Neumann and Oskar Morgenstern, both at Princeton University, published *The Theory of Games and Economic Behavior*. Although it quickly attracted the attention of specialists, its use did not become widespread for a long time, partly because perfect competition theory held sway. (Perfect competition, where everyone in the market takes price as given, removes most of the conflict from economic situations. Bargaining between producers and consumers, or strategic interactions between producers, has no place in a perfectly competitive world.) During the 1950s and 1960s, game theory grew increasingly popular, helped by a lucid mathematical treatment by R. Duncan Luce and Howard Raiffa in *Games and Decisions* (1957), and by an intuitively appealing, nonmathematical treatment by Thomas Schelling in *The Strategy of Conflict* (1960). In 1984 Robert Axelrod's *Evolution of Cooperation* applied game theory to the development of institutions, explaining cultural norms as solutions to various applications of the prisoners' dilemma. The use of game theory is now common and growing, especially in the field of industrial organization.

In general, issues of proper scientific method began to attract more attention in the 1980s, as evidenced by the appearance of new journals such as *Economics and Philosophy* and *Methodus*. A change in the accepted methods of scientific study appeared to be underway by the early 1990s. Logical positivism seemed to be losing ground to other methods that were more consistent with current thinking in the philosophy of science. The most forceful critic of the official methodology in economics was Donald McCloskey. Arguing that positivism is obsolete in philosophy, that falsification is seldom decisive, that reliable prediction is impossible, and that economists do not practice what they preach anyway, McCloskey urged economists to widen their methodological horizons. His *Rhetoric of Economics* (1985) presented a series of eloquent pleas for abandoning all rules of method except honesty, civility, and concern for truth.

Hermeneutics, advocated by the German philosopher Hans-Georg Gadamer, also began a modest penetration of the American economics profession, as evidenced by Don Lavoie's *Hermeneutics and Economics* (1991). This approach has a strong empirical bent, in that it studies the ways in which scientists actually practice their professions. Lavoie was especially critical of the importance given to mathematics and statistics. He argued that this kind of emphasis unduly narrowed economics, driving out, among other things, traditional historiography, with its concern for original documents and up-close examination of events.

RETROSPECT AND PROSPECT

Clearly, economics has become a difficult subject to master. At the beginning of the century, any interested lay person could comprehend the professional journals and the economics treatises. By 1950 this was no longer true. Paul Samuelson's *Foundations of Economic Analysis* (1947) and Ludwig Mises's *Human Action* (1949) are daunting treatises. In 1989, it took the average economics student six and a half years of graduate study to earn a doctoral degree.

Despite the increasing difficulty of economics over the century, the profession has grown in size, visibility, and prestige. Membership in the American Economic Association is a telling index: 800 in 1900, 3,000 in 1930, 7,000 in 1950, then a very rapid growth to 19,000 in 1970, followed by a leveling off—there were 20,000 members in 1990.

The rising number of economists, along with the profession's first commandment, "thou shalt publish," has resulted in a vastly increased number of journals. Whereas only three academic economics journals were published in the United States in 1900, almost twenty were in circulation in 1960, and about eighty-five by the early 1990s. Most of these specialized in a particular field. The ratio of journals to members of the American Economic Association was actually about the same in 1990 as it was in 1900, roughly 1 per 250 members.

One of the unanticipated developments of American economics was the extent to which economists have became public figures. Of course, economists had always played a role in policy formation, through their counsels to politicians and their popular writings. Allyn Young and Frank Taussig, for example, accompanied President Woodrow Wilson to the Versailles Peace Conference in 1919. Rexford Guy Tugwell became one of FDR's braintrusters in the thirties. But prior to World War II, no American economist became a celebrity, with the possible exception of Irving Fisher, who was an indefatigable crusader for the prohibition of alcoholic beverages as well as for sound money.

After the war, Paul Samuelson and Milton Friedman became household names through their columns in *Newsweek*. John Kenneth Galbraith became a best-selling author and the star of a public television series, as did Friedman. Such stardom reflects the inherent importance of economic issues and the prominence given to them by the public.

Another noteworthy feature of American economics has been its rich variety. A profession that can encompass Commons's institutionalist-oriented *Legal Foundations of Capitalism* and Arrow and Hahn's highly mathematical *General Competitive Analysis* is very broad indeed. The variety of economic thought in America reflects the size of the country's population and the diversity of its public opinion. Despite the dominance of mathematical economics, various nonmathematical schools survive, as evidenced by the institutionalists, post-Keynesians, Austrians, and Marxists.

The collapse of socialist economies in Europe during the late 1980s and early 1990s may portend another important change in American economic thought during the next generation. With few exceptions, economists did not realize that centrally planned economies would ultimately collapse, any more than they predicted the Great Depression of the 1930s. Ludwig Mises had argued as early as 1919 that socialism would ultimately fail because modern economies were too complex to be directed by a central plan. For most economists, however, Oskar Lange, a Polish economist who taught for a time at the University of Chicago, decisively refuted Mises's argument in the 1930s. Using the perfectly competitive model, Lange constructed fairly straightforward rules for formulating and revising central plans. This use of the perfectly competitive model turned out to be highly misleading, suggesting that the theory of competition, which lies at the core of modern economic theory, needs a fundamental reworking.

Part of the problem with modern economic thought may well have been too much reliance on mathematical methods. Concern with technique seemed to crowd out concern for reality. This defect became especially evident in the professional education of graduate students. In *The Making of an Economist* (1989), David Colander and Arjo Klamer surveyed graduate students at leading universities: 98 percent of these students believed that excellence in mathematics was important to professional success, while only 25 percent believed that a knowledge of the economy was important. It is hard to avoid the conclusion that academic economics had become, in the eyes of its future practitioners, a ritualistic dance of equations unrelated to significant economic reality. As these graduates move into positions of authority within society, mathematical economics will become more vulnerable to attack. Should future economists choose to reorient their discipline toward its traditional roots in history and philosophy, they will be helped by trends in the philosophy of science, trends which place less emphasis on learning formal technique and more on cultivating judgment and wisdom. How much the situation will change, or what form the change might take, is of course impossible to say.

What the historian can say with confidence is that the intellectual and social processes by which economists have established their ideas have been filled with frustrating conflict, wrong turns, missed opportunities, abstruse expression, fads and fancies, unnecessary narrowness, and unwarranted imperialism. Nevertheless, these processes have produced a robust body of principles that are indispensable to understanding modern social life.

SEE ALSO Economic Policies; Economic Performance; Consumption; Depressions and Recessions: The Business Cycle (all in this volume).

BIBLIOGRAPHY

Joseph Dorfman, *The Economic Mind in American Civilization,* 5 vols. (1946–1959), offers the most comprehensive account of American economics up to 1933. Joseph Schumpeter's *History of Economic Analysis* (1954) is a masterwork on the history of economic thought; little space is devoted to U.S. economists, but that little is well worth reading. Paul A. Samuelson, "Economic Thought and the New Industrialism," in Arthur M. Schlesinger, Jr. and Morton White, eds., *Paths of American Thought* (1963), identifies some distinctive elements in American economics.

William J. Barber, ed., *Breaking the Academic Mold* (1988), chronicles the establishment and progress of economics departments in American universities. A. W. Coats gives a fine account of the formation and activities of American economists' oldest and largest professional organization in a series of three articles: "The First Two Decades of the American Economic Association," *American Economic Review* 50 (September 1960): 555–574; "The American Economic Association, 1904–29," *American Economic Review* 54 (June 1964): 261–285; "The American Economic Association and the Economics Profession," *Journal of Economic Literature* 23 (December 1985): 1697–1727. Also of interest is "The Current 'Crisis' in Economics in Historical Perspective," in the *Nebraska Journal of Economics and Business* 16 (Summer 1977): 3–16. Coats provides a general overview of U.S. developments in "Economic Thought," *Encyclopedia of American Economic History,* vol. 1, ed. Glenn Porter (1980): 468–483. Mary Furner, *Advocacy and Objectivity* (1975), presents a thoroughly researched account of the social science profession's coming of age in America.

Thomas DiLorenzo and Jack C. High, "Antitrust and Competition, Historically Considered," *Economic Inquiry* 26 (July 1988): 423–435, document U.S. economists' early opposition to the Sherman Antitrust Act. Edwin R. A. Seligman, "Economics in the United States," in *Essays in Economics* (1925), is an annotated bibliography of American economics up to the 1920s. John Maurice Clark, "Past Accomplishments and Present Prospects of American Economics," *American Economic Review* 26 (March 1936): 1–11, presents an interesting assessment of economics in the mid-1930s. Thomas K. McCraw, "Berle and Means," *Reviews in American History* 16 (December 1990): 578–596, proffers reflective insight into the origins, content, and influences of *The Modern Corporation.* Paul T. Homan, "Economics in the War Period," *American Economic Review* 36 (December 1946): 855–871, surveys U.S. economists' writings and service in government during World War II.

Mark Blaug, *Great Economists Since Keynes* (1971), masterfully sketches vignettes of prominent modern economists. William Breit and Roger Ransom, *The Academic Scribblers,* rev. ed. (1982), offer short essays, aimed at the layperson, on modern American economists that influenced policy. John Eatwell et al., eds., *The New Palgrave Dictionary of Economics,* 4 vols. (1987), present essays of varying length on important American economists and economic subjects. Alan Gruchy, *Modern Economic Thought: The American Contribution* (1947), sympathetically renders the ideas of prominent American institutionalists.

Melvin W. Reder, "Chicago Economics: Permanence and Change," *Journal of Economic Literature* 20 (March 1982): 1–38, tells what the Chicago school is and is not; Reder is himself an eminent member of the school. Warren J. Samuels, ed., *The Chicago School of Political Economy* (1976), presents essays in which institutionalists criticize, and occasionally praise, Chicago school economics.

E. Roy Weintraub, "On the Existence of a Competitive Equilibrium: 1930–1954," *Journal of Economic Literature* 21 (March 1983): 1–39, gives an authoritative account, complete with proofs, of the development of general equilibrium theory. C. G. Velanovski, *The New Law and Economics* (1982), presents an historical account of the modern law and economics movement. Ann Krueger et al., *Journal of Economic Literature* 29 (September 1991), present the results of a comprehensive study of graduate economics education in America sponsored by the American Economic Association.

TAXATION

W. Elliot Brownlee

Government, and the tax system that fuels it, have grown dramatically in the United States during the twentieth century. The public sector grew even more rapidly than the swiftly expanding economy as a whole. Government expenditures—the sum of purchases of goods and services and transfer payments—at all levels of government increased from 7 to 8 percent of gross national product prior to World War I to nearly 40 percent by the 1970s.

THE CONTEXT: TRENDS IN THE GROWTH OF GOVERNMENT

This stunning increase took place in a largely discontinuous fashion; it was primarily the cumulative result of several rather discrete transitions. Each transition accompanied a major emergency in national life, such as a great war (including the Cold War) or a severe economic depression. The emergencies appear to have had an upward ratchet effect, in that after each crisis, government spending stabilized at levels substantially higher than those that prevailed before the crisis.

Several other trends were associated with the growth in the relative scale of the public sector. First, governmental activity became more centralized. Public-sector expenditures were about two-thirds of state and local expenditures in 1902, but less than one-third of state and local in 1970. Within the nonfederal public sector, local spending accounted for nearly 90 percent of total spending in 1902, but less than 50 percent in 1970. The growth of the federal government was most rapid during World War I, the New Deal decade of the 1930s, and World War II, while the growth of state government was most pronounced during the 1920s and 1960s.

Second, spending on health and welfare services and defense grew. In 1902 the expenditures required for general administration—running the State, Treasury, and Commerce departments, for example—dominated federal spending, and the costs of operating the postal service took nearly one-fourth of the budget. By 1990, general administration costs had shrunk to roughly one-third of the budget. Meanwhile, expenditures on health and welfare services had increased from virtually nothing at the beginning of the century to nearly one-third of the federal budget. Defense spending took about the same share of federal expenditures in 1990 that it had in 1902, but from the 1940s into the 1970s it had accounted for over 40 percent of federal spending.

Finally, the nation's tax system relied increasingly on corporate and personal income taxation (table 1). The role of income tax revenues grew swiftly between 1913 and the 1920s, declined as the Great Depression shrank the income tax base, then soared during World War II, from 19.4 percent of all U.S. tax revenues in 1940 to 54.1 percent in 1950, and continued to grow, although at a reduced rate, until the 1980s. The heavy reliance on income taxation in the twentieth century distinguished the tax system of the United States from that of most other industrial nations. Even by the late 1980s, the United States relied more heavily on income taxation than did the other major industrial nations, except for Canada and Japan, which employed a highly productive corporate income tax (table 2). In contrast, the other industrial nations, with the exception of Japan, made far greater use of sales taxes, particularly national value-added taxes.

No comprehensive explanation accounts for this stunning set of transitions. Economists have found some associations between the growth of public spending and economic factors such as the growth in per capita incomes; increases in population; the tendency for the demand for public services to remain high even in the face of increasing costs of those services; and the social costs associated with urbanization, industrialization, and greater complexity in social organization. But these statistical associations account, at best, for no more than half of the

Table 1. TOTAL U.S. REVENUES BY TYPE OF TAX

Year	Income Taxes, Percent	Sales Taxes, Percent	Property Taxes, Percent	User Charges and Miscellaneous, Percent
1902	0.0	37.5	51.4	11.1
1913	1.5	29.5	58.7	10.3
1927	24.3	16.5	50.0	9.2
1932	14.5	18.6	56.2	10.7
1936	15.8	32.0	38.7	13.5
1940	19.4	32.4	34.9	13.3
1950	54.1	25.4	14.4	6.1
1960	58.2	21.6	14.5	5.7
1970	59.2	20.9	14.6	5.3
1980	63.4	19.5	11.9	5.2
1983	59.3	20.4	13.4	6.9
1990	56.7	21.1	11.6	10.6

SOURCES: Department of the Treasury, Office of State and Local Finance, "Federal-State-Local Relations" (September 1985): 47–49; Department of Commerce, *Survey of Current Business* 72 (March 1992): 10.

growth in public spending during the twentieth century. No such set of narrowly defined economic factors can explain the centralization of government, the shifts in governmental functions, and the changes in the structure of public finance. Understanding the transitions depends more heavily on an appreciation of fundamental shifts in civic values than on consideration of economic factors. Understanding these shifts in civic values, in turn, requires understanding of their institutional context: the workings of politics and political institutions and the impact on those institutions of externally driven social crises.

FROM STABILITY TO CRISIS AND CHAOS

The period of the American Revolution and the formation of the U.S. Constitution reveals much about the ideology and culture underlying American taxation. Eighteenth-century Americans displayed a preference for direct taxation—primarily the taxation of property—to try to make taxation hurt, which would in turn retard the growth of government. Some of the resistance to taxation grew out of traditional liberal thought. This line of thinking emphasized individualism, celebrated the pursuit of private self-interest and financial gain, and regarded with suspicion governmental initiatives that might impede the search for individual gain. The era of the early republic presents much evidence to support the view that America was, and is, a society of profit-maximizing tax resisters. Then, as now, in large numbers, Americans cheated, evaded taxes, exploited the tax codes' loopholes, migrated to low-tax havens, and sought political groups and representatives committed to reducing taxes.

Table 2. REVENUE BY TYPE OF TAX IN MAJOR INDUSTRIAL NATIONS, 1987

Country	Personal Income Tax, Percent	Corporate Income Tax, Percent	Goods and Services Taxes, Percent
United States	36.2	8.1	16.7
Canada	38.7	8.0	29.8
France	12.7	5.2	29.3
Germany	29.0	5.0	25.4
Japan	24.0	22.9	12.9
Netherlands	19.7	7.7	26.0
Sweden	37.2	4.1	24.1
Switzerland	34.0	6.2	19.1
United Kingdom	26.6	10.6	31.4

SOURCE: *OECD Statistics on the Member Countries in Figures,* Supplement to the *OECD Observer* no. 164 (June/July 1990).

But the nation has another side to its ideological history—one with roots in the same formative era. Even then, traditional liberalism did not hold sway, unopposed or unqualified. Historians now agree that the central language of the Revolution contained not only Lockean liberalism, with its emphasis on private rights, but also classical republicanism, or civic humanism, that stressed communal responsibilities. These ideas focused on the threat of corruption to public order, the dangers of commercialism, and the need to foster public virtue. The Founders (and even Adam Smith) held these ideas of classical republicanism in tension with those of liberalism.

Commitments to civic humanism could create pressure for higher, rather than lower, taxes. For example, the ideal of a harmonious republic of citizens equal before the law created demands for taxes to destroy islands of privilege by taxing the privileged more heavily. That ideal also embraced the notion that taxpaying was one of the normal obligations of a citizenry bound together in a republic by ties of affection and respect. This thinking went further, emphasizing the direct relationship between wealth and responsibility to support government and public order. It embraced enlightened self-interest and included "ability to pay" as a criterion in determining patterns of taxation. In his first canon of taxation, Adam Smith (in *Wealth of Nations*) declared that "the subjects of every state ought to contribute towards the support of the government, as nearly as possible, in proportion to their respective abilities."

Article I, section 9, of the Constitution severely limited taxation by specifying that "No capitation or other direct tax shall be laid, unless in proportion to the census." With this provision, the founders of the republic intended to limit the power of the national government to impose property taxes. But this limitation was not a victory for liberalism so much as for civic humanism. The limitation reflected the fact that the framers of the Constitution thought about taxation in the context of the corruption of the British Parliament and monarchy, and worried about the potential for similar abuse by the new federal government. They believed that local control was necessary for the equitable operation of the property tax. The federal government, they feared, might abuse the tax to attack certain categories of property (such as slaves), to favor town dwellers over farmers, or to punish a particular section of the country.

The constitutional limitation also reflected the fear of factionalism that James Madison, a civic humanist, expressed in *Federalist* 10. He predicted that "the most common and durable source of factions" would be "the various and unequal distribution of property." He concluded that the issue of taxation, more than any other, created an opportunity and temptation for "a predominant party to trample on the rules of justice." Moreover, the intent of the constitutional limitation was not to deny the new republic the resources it needed. Indeed, a central hope of Madison, Alexander Hamilton, and the other supporters of the Constitution was that the new central government, in contrast to the government of the Articles of Confederation, would have the taxing power that was required for a strong and meaningful nation.

Thus, even with the limitation, the Constitution left the way open for the new federal government to raise the tax revenues it needed, through indirect taxes such as tariffs (import duties). Such taxes worked, both politically and financially. When tariff rates were low, they won popularity. Low tariffs were productive of revenue; they were inexpensive to collect; they were widely diffused; they seemed to tax extravagant living; and they were useful in economic diplomacy. Low and moderate tariffs allowed the leaders of the early republic to limit the political divisiveness of taxation. In their effort to create a unified and just republic, the early American leaders used relatively low tariffs to prevent tax issues from arousing the disruptive forces of factionalism.

The major wars and depressions that began with the Civil War and continued into the twentieth century shattered the tax system of the early republic. Invariably the mobilization for emergencies, beginning with the Civil War, required new or higher taxes and therefore forced thoroughgoing reexamination of finance options. The search for tax revenues has stimulated political conflict over national values and intensified ideological and distributional divisions within American society. The conflict over taxation was always severely turbulent. Constitutional restrictions, the structure of party government, ideas and ideologies, professional expertise, technology, the distribution of wealth, and international forces all affected the course of tax policy during these periods of political upheaval. But historical contingency and political entrepreneurs also played crucial roles. Consequently the flow of tax policy was chaotic during the century and a half of intermittent total war and national crisis.

Under these pressures, the fundamental character of the tax system changed during each national emergency, each time with major redistributional consequences. At the same time, the emergencies, and the reconstructed revenue systems they fostered, expanded the capacity of the federal government for acquiring resources. In creating more robust systems of taxation, each of the crises created new opportunities for proponents of expanded government programs to advance their interests without resorting to the costly political process of raising taxes. Thus, the profound transformation of the nation's public revenue systems during periods of national emergencies has tended to facilitate the growth of government even after the emergencies were over.

THE CIVIL WAR AND THE HIGH-TARIFF SYSTEM

The first of the national emergencies that transformed government and its revenue systems was the Civil War. The war was the nation's first modern war in the sense of requiring enormous capital outlays. The need for capital demanded an unprecedented program of emergency taxation. The Republicans, who had ridden into power on the sectional crisis of the 1850s, introduced a high-tariff system. That system became the centerpiece of an ambitious new program of national economic policy and nation-building. The great increase in tariffs was also a stunning victory for economic nationalism and protectionism. The introduction of high tariffs during the Civil War initiated a political process of making tax protection, tax incentives, and tax subsidies important—and, indeed, permanent—elements in the nation's political economy. In part through these aspects of the high tariff system, the Republicans turned the tax system into the promoter of big government and of party rule.

The high tariffs were placed on items of everyday consumption and were therefore regressive, meaning that they tended to tax people with lower incomes at higher rates than those with higher incomes. Nonetheless, support for high tariffs was broad and diverse. This support continued to be powerful well into the twentieth century—until at least the passage of the Reciprocal Trade Agreements Act of 1934, and even beyond.

American business and workers liked the regulatory effects of the tariff system. Manufacturers welcomed the protection they believed the tariffs afforded them against foreign competitors. Beginning in the 1870s and 1880s, manufacturers were especially enthusiastic about the high-tariff system because it allowed them to build national marketing organizations free of worries about disruptions caused by European competitors. The high tariffs provided benefits not so much to the infant industries

favored by Adam Smith as to giant American corporations that were integrating vertically and gaining a long-term advantage over European competitors who were restricted to smaller markets. Supportive as well were many American bankers, who were interested in facilitating the flow of European capital to America. They appreciated how the high-tariff system worked to pay off the public debt to Europeans. Finally, high tariffs seemed to benefit workers who feared competition from lower-wage labor in Europe, Latin America, and Asia.

The high-tariff system won approval as well because of the new government programs it supported: transfer payments, public works, and military initiatives. Republican governments used tariffs to fund the nation's first major system of social insurance: an ambitious program of pensions and disability benefits for Union veterans. As the pensions grew increasingly generous during the 1870s and 1880s, they became a central element in the strength of the Republican party, and continued to be important politically and economically into the twentieth century. In addition, community leaders throughout the North became accustomed to feeding from what became known as the "pork barrel"—the annual Rivers and Harbors bill that the tariff revenues funded. During the 1880s and 1890s, tariffs funded the creation of the large battle fleet the United States needed to become a world power. Also supporting tariffs were the bond holders of the Union government. The tariffs provided the revenues to repay the bond holders, and did so without substantially increasing their tax burden.

In the post–Civil War period, the Democratic party challenged Republican power with a biting critique of the tariff. Drawing on the ideals of the American Revolution and the early republic, the Democrats attacked special privilege, monopoly power, and public corruption. With an assault on the tariff as the "mother of trusts" and the primary engine of a Republican program of subsidizing giant corporations, the Democrats appealed to farmers, southerners, middle-class consumers, and small businesspeople for support. At the national level, the two competing political parties based their identities on sharply conflicting ideological views of the tariff, and of taxation in general. Those identities would shape revenue policy until World War II. The Republicans' high-tariff system and the Democrats' response to it had polarized the parties on issues of taxation. These issues would exacerbate class conflict for nearly a century.

After the Civil War, taxation at the state and local level, which traditionally consisted of the property (primarily real estate) tax, also entered a period of turbulence. Before the Civil War, as commerce had expanded and the industrial revolution gathered force, Jacksonian reformers had gradually extended the scope of property taxation, trying to tax all forms of wealth. In most states they had created a general property tax designed to reach not only real estate, tools, equipment, and furnishings, but also intangible personal property such as cash, credits, notes, stocks, bonds, and mortgages. Most states had added to their constitutions provisions for universality (requiring that all property be taxed) and uniformity (requiring that properties of equal value be taxed at the same rate).

By 1900, however, it became clear that the structure of the economy had changed so significantly that the general property tax was failing to live up to its egalitarian promise of taxing all wealth at the same rate. For one thing, existing administrative structures often relied heavily on self-assessment. This method proved inadequate to expose and determine the value of cash, credits, notes, stocks, bonds, and mortgages, especially in the nation's largest cities. Then, too, assessment procedures were insensitive to changes in price level. This meant that the property tax became increasingly burdensome during the economic crises of the late nineteenth century and the long-term decline in prices that ensued after the Civil War. The increased burden was especially great for farmers and small businesspeople, and they became a major force for a new wave of property-tax reform during the twentieth century.

EARLY TWENTIETH-CENTURY PROGRESSIVE POLICY INITIATIVES

The severe economic depression of the 1890s, the growing force of industrialization, and the Progressive movement they helped spawn led to a process of tax reform. At the state and local level, governments began to develop the modern property tax, with its standardized assessment practices and its focus on real estate. At the same time, state governments designed new taxes such as franchise taxes, utility taxes, and even income taxes. At the federal level, the passage of the Sixteenth Amendment in 1913 and the enactment of federal income taxation established the foundation for the modern revenue system of the federal government.

The adoption of the federal income tax had far more to do with the search for social justice than with the quest for an elastic source of revenue. It was driven primarily by democratic statism, an impulse to use the instruments of state power to promote a democratic social order. The goal was to use the taxing power of the federal government to restructure the distribution of income and wealth. This redistributional democratic statism was a major theme uniting many of the important initiatives of the federal government undertaken before World War II. It was, in part, a new kind of liberalism, a realignment of classic nineteenth-century liberalism and the commonwealth tradition of early republicanism (which had included a distrust of commerce). Democratic statists regarded themselves as applying the ideals of the American Revolution to the new conditions of industrial society. While the strategy remained one of liberating individual energies by providing a social order of abundant opportunity, the tactics had changed. To the new liberals, the state had become a necessary instrument and ally, not an enemy.

The departures in tax policy of the early twentieth century had their foundation not only in the ideological heritage of the American Revolution but also in the terrible depression of the mid-1890s. The severity and length of that depression fueled popular enthusiasm for restructuring the nation's revenue system. Economic distress stimulated movements by Populists and champions of Henry George's single tax for social justice through taxation. These converging movements came to focus on the progressive income tax, bringing about the enactment of a modest federal income tax in 1894 (in the Wilson-Gorman Tariff). Central to the appeal of the income tax movement was the argument that the tax would reallocate fiscal burdens according to ability to pay and would help restore a virtuous republic free of concentrations of economic power. What was truly radical about the movement for progressive income taxation was the goal of basing the entire tax system on taxing the largest incomes and corporate profits. Income tax champions argued that their tax would not touch the wages and salaries of ordinary people but would, instead, attack unearned profits and monopoly power. Those who had faced expropriation would now do the expropriating.

In competition with democratic statism for control of America's reform energies, however, was a more conservative vision, one that historians have described as progressive capitalism or corporate liberalism. Reformers of this persuasion emphasized government encouragement of cooperation and philanthropy among individuals and corporations. In contrast to democratic statists, corporate liberals looked with admiration on the efficiency of the modern corporation and the investment system. To them, increased government intervention in the marketplace was desirable only if necessary to resolve conflicts or defuse resistance that would otherwise inhibit economic growth.

Democratic statism and corporate liberalism were similar in that they represented efforts to bring a greater degree of order to industrial society. Both approaches to reform sought to strengthen national institutions; both were supported by some elements from each party; and both fueled the so-called Progressive movement. This movement, exemplified by Republican President Theodore Roosevelt and Democratic President Woodrow Wilson, included bipartisan support for greater governmental interventions in the economy, particularly with regard to the regulation of business. Democratic statism and corporate liberalism merged to advance the development of federal railroad regulation, the creation of the Federal Reserve system (1913), and the passage of the Federal Trade Commission and Clayton Antitrust acts (1914). They merged also behind the use of taxation as a regulatory device, as a mechanism to deter or punish behavior that undermined a republican order. Progressives continued the policy of taxing tobacco and alcohol at high rates. They also invoked the federal taxing power to regulate grain and cotton futures, the production of white phosphorous matches, the consumption of narcotics, and even the employment of child labor.

Democratic statism and liberal capitalism were slow, however, to unite in support of a major tax program for funding the federal government. Consequently, the federal income tax movement progressed sluggishly until World War I.

Prior to the war, Republican leaders preferred continued reliance on tariffs or the adoption of national sales taxes. Democratic leaders focused on tariff reform. Unlike the Republicans, they had generally favored small government. Thus, they were reluctant to create any new taxes, even if they were more equitable than the tariffs. However, in 1896 the Democratic party embraced income taxation in response to the rising tide of populism and an unpopular Supreme Court ruling. In 1895, in *Pollock* v. *Farmer's Loan and Trust Co.*, the Court decided that the very modest income tax of the Wilson-Gorman Tariff of 1894 violated Article I, section 9, of the Constitution.

The Court ruling, coupled with the national victories of the Republican party that began in 1896, delayed the adoption of the federal income tax. But popular support for income taxation continued to grow, even within the Republican party. In 1909,

reform leaders in Congress from both parties finally united to send the Sixteenth Amendment, legalizing a federal income tax, to the states for ratification. But it was not until 1913 that ratification prevailed, carried forward during its critical phase by the presidential election of 1912. In that campaign, popular enthusiasm for federal policies designed to attack monopoly power reached an all-time high.

Even with growing support for income taxation, the revenue legislation enacted in 1913 was only a modest step forward. Virtually no proponent of the tax within the government believed that the income tax would become a major, let alone a dominant, source of revenue. Even the supporters of income taxation were uncertain how the income tax would work. The Underwood Tariff of 1913 established the income tax at the "normal" rate of 1 percent on both individual and corporate incomes, with a high exemption excusing virtually all middle-class Americans from the tax. Meanwhile, the tariff system continued to produce revenue; it was, in fact, even more productive because the Wilson administration's reductions in tariff rates stimulated trade and actually increased tariff revenues.

While federal policy before World War I shifted only gradually toward increased taxation, with an emphasis on social justice, state and local tax policy changed more rapidly, as states and localities faced needs for substantial new revenues. The process of urbanization accelerated in the first decade of the century, and cities had to invest more in parks, schools, hospitals, transit systems, waterworks, and sewers. State governments, too, faced new revenue needs. Beginning in the first decade of the new century, they increased their regulation of wages, hours, and other working conditions. States also increased their investments in higher education and began to aid localities in the financing of schools and roads.

The growing fiscal pressure on state and local governments stimulated efforts to reform the general property taxes that were at the core of most governments' revenue systems. Rather than abandon the taxes, most states and cities tried to make property taxes work more effectively in order to capitalize on the recent enormous growth of real estate values.

To make the assessment of property values more efficient, governments gradually abandoned the Jacksonian effort to assess the value of all property. Instead, they either excluded from taxation difficult-to-assess categories of property—particularly those of an intangible nature—or classified property into categories according to the difficulty of assessment and then taxed them at different rates. At the same time, state governments moved vigorously to improve the assessment of real estate, particularly at the local level. States created tax commissions and boards of equalization, staffed them with tax experts, gave them power over local assessment procedures and the appointment of assessors, and charged the boards with ensuring a more uniform assessment of real estate at its market value. Most state governments began to take themselves out the enterprise of property taxation. They did so because county governments, which almost always retained control of the assessment process, competitively undervalued property to reduce their state taxes. Meanwhile, states began to develop their own specialized sources of revenue. In 1911, Wisconsin led the way by adopting the first modern income tax, which included a stringently administered 6 percent tax on corporate income.

The transformations of tax systems between the 1880s and World War I were based, for the first time, on analyses provided by professional economists. Experts within the newly forming economics profession developed a lively curiosity about state and local tax issues. After 1900, led by experts like Edwin R. A. Seligman of Columbia University and Thomas S. Adams of the University of Wisconsin and Yale University, economists increasingly served state and local governments as consultants and members of tax commissions. In 1907, to enhance their status and influence within both the public and private sectors, those economists with an interest in tax issues joined with state and local tax administrators, and with accountants and tax lawyers, to organize the National Tax Association. The organizers declared that their intention was to "formulate and announce . . . the best informed economic thought and ripest administrative experience available for the correct guidance of public opinion, [and] legislative and administration action on all questions pertaining to taxation." Through their analysis of public finance and of the general property tax in particular, these economists, on the one hand, assisted state and local governments in capitalizing on their property-tax base. On the other hand, they worked with corporate and individual taxpayers to establish a more predictable and equitable system of state and local taxation.

THE CRISIS OF WORLD WAR I, 1916–1921

The financial demands of World War I, set in the context of redistributional politics, increased the pace of tax reform far beyond the leisurely rate that corporate liberals would have preferred. In fact, it produced a brand-new tax regime. This new tax system was the most significant domestic initiative to emerge from the war. The process began in 1916 when President Wilson and Secretary of the Treasury William G. McAdoo made the single most important financial decision of the war. They chose to cooperate with a group of insurgent Democrats in arranging wartime finance on the basis of highly progressive taxation. Led by Congressman Claude Kitchin of North Carolina, who chaired the House Ways and Means Committee, the insurgent Democrats attacked concentrations of wealth, special privilege, and public corruption. The group held enough power to insist that if preparedness, and later the war effort, were to move forward, it would do so only on their financial terms. They embraced taxation as an important means to achieve social justice according to the humanistic ideals of the early republic. Redistributional taxation then became a major element of the Wilson administration's program for steering between socialism and unmediated capitalism.

The war provided an opportunity for Democratic progressives to focus the wartime debate over taxation on one of the most fundamental and sensitive economic issues in modern America: What stake does society have in corporate profits? More specifically, the question became one of whether the modern corporation was the central engine of productivity, which tax policy should reinforce, or an economic predator, which tax policy could and should tame. The outcome of the debate was that the nation embraced a new tax system: soak-the-rich income taxation.

During this period of crisis, one in which the pressure of fighting a modern war coincided with powerful demands to break the hold of corporate privilege, Woodrow Wilson and the Democratic party turned Republican fiscal policy on its head. The Democrats embraced a tax policy that they claimed, just as the Republicans had claimed for their tariff system, would sustain a powerful state and economic prosperity. But, unlike the Republicans' tariff system, the new tax policy of the Democrats assaulted, rather than protected, the privileges associated with corporate wealth.

The Democratic tax program, implemented in the wartime Revenue Acts, transformed the experimental, rather tentative income tax into the foremost instrument of federal taxation. Their program introduced federal estate taxation. It imposed the first significant taxation of corporate profits and personal incomes, but rejected a mass-based income tax—one that would have fallen most heavily on wages and salaries. It also adopted the concept of taxing corporate excess profits. America was the only World War I belligerent to place excess-profits taxation—a graduated tax on all business profits above a "normal" rate of return—at the center of wartime finance. Excess-profits taxation turned out to be responsible for most of the tax revenues raised by the federal government during the war, accounting for a larger share of total revenues than in any other belligerent nation.

The income tax, with excess-profits taxation at its core, outraged business leaders. Redistributional taxation, along with the wartime strengthening of the Treasury (including the Bureau of Internal Revenue, the forerunner to the Internal Revenue Service [IRS]), posed a long-term strategic threat to the nation's corporations. Most severely threatened were the largest corporations, which believed their financial autonomy to be in jeopardy. In addition, the new tax system threatened to empower, as never before, the federal government, which was now under the control of distinctly egalitarian forces. Indeed, no other single issue aroused so much corporate hostility to the Wilson administration as did the financing of the war. The resulting conflict between advocates of democratic statist, soak-the-rich taxation, on the one hand, and business leaders, on the other hand, would rage for more than two decades.

Despite the damage to business confidence, the Wilson administration and congressional Democratic leaders went forward with excess-profits taxation. They did so in part because they shared Claude Kitchin's ideal of using taxation to restructure the economy according to nineteenth-century liberal ideals. They assumed that the largest corporations exercised inordinate control over wealth and that a money trust dominated the allocation of capital. For Wilson and McAdoo, the tax program, with its promise to tax monopoly power, seemed to constitute an attractive new dimension to their New Freedom approach to the emancipation of business. Wartime public finance was based on the taxation of assets that democratic statists regarded as ill-gotten or socially dangerous, comparable to the rents from the land monopolies that Henry George and his followers had wished to tax. In fact, both Wilson and McAdoo entertained explicit single-tax ideas as they developed their tax-reform program.

Party government also played a crucial role in the tax decisions of the Wilson administration. Wilson and McAdoo knew they could have easily engineered passage of a much less progressive tax system—one that would have relied more heavily on consumption taxes and mass-based income taxes—in cooperation with Republicans and a minority of conservative Democrats. But they also knew that this would have betrayed both the heritage and the current program of their political party. After all, their party had strong traditions of representing the disadvantaged, of hostility to a strong central government as the instrument of privilege, of opposition to the taxation of consumption, and of support for public policies designed to widen access to economic opportunity. Failure to adopt a highly progressive and reconstructive tax program would have had serious consequences for Wilson and McAdoo. Such failure would have bitterly divided their party. It would have spoiled their opportunities for attracting Republican progressives to their party and destroyed their strong partnership with congressional Democrats. This was a partnership that both Wilson and McAdoo regarded as necessary for the effective advancement of national administration.

Closely related to the Wilson administration's tax program was its sale of bonds to middle-class Americans. Rather than tax middle-class Americans at high levels, the Wilson administration employed a voluntary program to mobilize their savings, which McAdoo called "capitalizing patriotism." He attempted to persuade Americans to change their economic behavior: to reduce consumption, increase savings, and become creditors of the state. After the conclusion of the war, he hoped, the middle-class bond holders would be repaid by tax dollars raised from corporations and the wealthiest Americans.

Selling the high-priced bonds directly to average Americans on a multibillion-dollar scale required sales campaigns far greater in scope than those anywhere else in the world. Largely through trial and error, the Wilson administration formulated a vast array of state-controlled national marketing techniques, including the sophisticated analysis of national income and savings. Financing by the new Federal Reserve system, which McAdoo turned into an arm of the Treasury to facilitate borrowing for bond sales, was important, but not as important as McAdoo's efforts to shift private savings into bonds. In the course of four "liberty loans," Secretary McAdoo and the Treasury expanded the federal government's and the nation's knowledge of the social basis of capital markets. Informed by its own systematic investigations and armed with modern techniques of mass communication, the Treasury placed its loans deep in the middle class—far deeper than it had during the Civil War or than European governments had done in World War I. In the third liberty loan campaign (conducted in April 1918), at least half of all American families subscribed. The borrowing stimulated a large increase in voluntary saving, just as McAdoo and the Treasury had hoped.

The implications of Wilson's program of public finance for the department of Treasury were very broad. The complex and ambitious program of taxing and borrowing required a vast expansion of the Treasury's administrative capacity. The department developed many of its central attributes during World War I. During the war, the Federal Reserve system functioned as an agency of the Treasury, facilitating bond sales and providing business information on a national scale. The other major arm of the Treasury at that time was the Bureau of Internal Revenue, whose personnel increased from 4,000 to 15,800 between 1913 and 1920. The bureau was reorganized along multifunctional lines, with clear specifications of responsibilities and chains of command.

During this period an exceptionally capable team assembled by McAdoo was running the Treasury—the kind of team that in the future would characterize the Treasury at its best. It employed businesslike methods and demonstrated intellectual flexibility, entrepreneurship, and institutional diversity. Lacking an adequate civil service, McAdoo fashioned within the Treasury the kind of organization the political scientist Hugh Heclo has called (in "The State and America's Higher Civil Service," 1982) an "informal political technocracy," or a "loose grouping of people where the lines of policy, politics, and administration merge in a complex jumble of bodies." This was an early example of what would become a typical expression of America's unique form of a higher civil service.

The Treasury group served as the Wilson administration's primary instrument for learning about financial policy and its social implications, shaping the definition of financial issues and administration programs, and mobilizing support for those programs. The group developed a significant degree of autonomy and provided the necessary means for McAdoo to form and dominate networks that linked competing centers of power within the federal government, and linked the government with civil society. Because McAdoo had formed such a group, he was able to design and implement a financial policy with clear social objectives. Under his leadership, the Treasury avoided falling under the control either of competing centers of power within the government, or of groups outside the government. Consequently, the Treasury escaped the disarray that befell much of the Wilson administration's mobilization effort.

Wilsonian democratic statism finally succumbed to a business counterattack. In 1918, corporate leaders and Republicans found an opening, when President Wilson tried to make a case for doubling taxes. Using vigorous antitax, antigovernment campaigns throughout the nation, and antisouthern campaigns in the West, Republicans gained control of Congress. Then, in 1920, they rode to a presidential victory during an economic depression. The Democratic party of Woodrow Wilson had failed to do what the Republican party of Abraham Lincoln had done: establish long-term control of the federal government and create a new party system.

Although defeated politically, the Wilson administration had proved that the American state—despite its apparent weakness—was capable of fighting a sustained, capital-intensive war. Progressive taxation and the sale of "the war for democracy" to the American people through the bond drives had built that popular support and mobilized resources on a vast scale. These wartime efforts contributed significantly to an expansion of the federal government's political authority—by increasing the government's ability to use democratic politics to acquire resources for national defense and the waging of war.

THE CONSOLIDATION OF THE 1920s

The Republican regime that assumed control of the federal government in 1921 did much to roll back the democratic statism of the Wilson presidency. The three successive Republican administrations, under the financial leadership of their secretary of the Treasury, Andrew Mellon (1921–1932), adopted a new financial strategy: reduce the power of the state, protect capital markets, but find ways of mediating class conflict.

On the one hand, Mellon attacked the most redistributional parts of the wartime tax system. His revenue measures abolished the excess-profits tax (in 1921), made the individual income tax much less progressive, and established the preferential taxation of capital gains. The soak-the-rich strategy remained, but only at reduced rates, with major loopholes, and with its sharp anticorporate edge dulled. Within the Treasury, the primary tax adviser, the Yale University economist Thomas S. Adams, advocated reducing the rate of progression but eliminating the deductions introduced by Mellon, and integrating corporate and individual income taxation. He failed to win support from Secretary Mellon.

On the other hand, Mellon protected income taxation against the threat posed by leading Republicans who wanted to replace it with a national sales tax. Mellon persuaded corporations and the wealthiest individuals to accept, instead, limited progressive income taxation and the principle of ability to pay. This approach would, Mellon told them, demonstrate their civic responsibility and defuse radical attacks on capital. Mellon's strategy might be described as the pursuit of enlightened self-interest: corporate liberalism, in contrast to Woodrow Wilson's democratic statism.

Mellon consolidated the flow of income tax revenues into the Treasury. The portion of general revenues provided to the federal government by indirect taxes (mainly through the tariff system) fell from almost 75 percent in 1902 to about 25 percent in the 1920s; meanwhile, income tax revenues increased and accounted for nearly 50 percent of the general revenues of the federal government. (The remaining 25 percent consisted of other taxes, such as gift and estate taxes, and, most significantly, postal revenues.)

Mellon also continued the work of the Wilson administration to strengthen the Treasury. He promoted the passage of the Budget and Accounting Act of 1921, which created the first national budget system and delegated administration of this budget to the Treasury. The act established presidential responsibility for preparing a comprehensive budget, rather than simply assembling and transmitting departmental requests. It created two important agencies: the Bureau of the Budget—located within the Treasury—to assist in budget preparation, and the General Accounting Office to conduct independent audits of the federal government.

Mellon also attempted to strengthen the Treasury by transforming it into a nonpartisan agency. On one level, his goal was to insulate it from pressure from Democratic Congresses. In his 1924 book, *Taxation: The People's Business,* Mellon explained that "tax revision should never be made the football either of partisan or class politics but should be worked out by those who have made a careful study of the subject in its larger aspects and are prepared to recommend the course which, in the end, will prove for the country's best interest." Mellon was interested in more than scientific policy making, however. He also wanted to ensure that the Treasury worked within the context of conservative assumptions about the state and about corporate power.

While the federal government sought domestic order by reinforcing private investment in the 1920s, state and local governments were virtually alone in providing human services. Local governments faced the welfare needs associated with the severe economic depression of 1920–1921, and the depressed conditions that continued throughout the 1920s in much of the nation's agricultural and mining industries. State governments responded to citizens' increasing demands for schools and highways. Consequently, state governments became the most swiftly growing level of government during the 1920s.

Citizens' increasing expectations of their local and state governments, coupled with the pressures that depression conditions placed on property taxation, led states to complete the process of narrowing property taxation to real estate and leaving it largely to local governments. In addition, states introduced some new revenue elements that they have relied on ever since: sales taxes, user charges, and special taxes on corporations and incomes. In 1902, states were getting about 53 percent of their tax revenues from property taxation; by 1927, they raised only about 23 percent from that source. Of the new taxes, those on sales were the most dynamic. Their share of state tax revenues increased from 18 percent in 1902 and 1913 to 27 percent in 1927 and 38 percent in 1932.

Despite the regressive nature of sales taxation, egalitarian impulses were responsible for its expansion. Its proponents believed that it would help restore the uniformity of taxation that had been lost with the decline of general property taxation. Sales taxes would, they argued, reach personal property, especially the increasing volume of consumer durable goods. As states experimented with sales taxation, they discovered that it was efficient to administer because businesses shared in the expense of collection. Moreover, the public reacted calmly to revenue taken through sales taxation, for several reasons. Payments were rendered in small increments; the sales taxes had a high degree of horizontal equity; and many people believed they could avoid such taxes through prudent living. Also, during the 1920s, state tax commissions and panels of experts began to study the economic impact of sales and other taxes, and convinced policymakers that sales taxes were less inimical to economic growth than property or income taxes. In particular, the experts appreciated the less direct impact that sales taxes had on savings and investment.

States turned to user charges as a practical response to the need for the huge revenues required to pay for the building of highway systems. State building of highways accelerated during the 1920s, leading to disputes among farmers, truckers, automobile clubs (representing passenger-car owners), taxpayers' associations (representing various categories of real estate owners), and railroads over who should pay for the highways. The agricultural depression of the 1920s hardened the resistance of farmers to new taxes. In response, states adopted vehicle registration fees, license fees, and gasoline taxes, all of which were designed to allocate the costs of highways to the users.

States aimed their special taxes at the property that the general property tax had failed to reach. These substitute taxes included inheritance taxes; a variety of special taxes on banks, utilities (including the ad valorem taxation of railroad assets), and insurance companies; and modest personal income taxes. By 1930, the state income taxes accounted for only about 10 percent of state tax revenues.

During the 1920s, local, state, and federal governments established a clear division of tax labor. The federal government specialized in income taxation because of its equity and elasticity. State governments specialized in sales taxation because of its economy of collection and lack of political controversy, and because of the states' limited access to property taxation and income taxation. Local governments specialized in real estate taxation because it was the only practical system of taxation available, and because localities believed they needed control over an important local revenue source.

THE CRISIS OF THE GREAT DEPRESSION ERA

The nation's worst economic collapse, the Great Depression, shook Americans' faith in their economic system. It convinced many that the flaws in the nation's economy were fundamental in character, and required a restructuring of national public policy along democratic statist lines that would include a measure of tax reform.

The Republican administration of Herbert Hoover (1929–1933) was the first to respond to the national emergency. Judged by the standards of the day, Hoover was an economic activist, as he manipulated tax rates to stimulate investment and reduce unemployment. In effect, Hoover began to extend the scope of corporate liberalism to include fiscal activism.

Hoover began his innovative program soon after the stock market crash in 1929. As part of what was, between 1929 and 1931, an expansive fiscal policy, he and Congress cut taxes payable in 1930. In October 1931, however, the Federal Reserve system produced a monetary contraction that severely limited the ability of the nation's banking system to meet domestic demands for currency and credit. Hoover

feared competition between government and private borrowers, a consequent increase in the long-term interest rate, and an inhibition of private investment. Also, he believed that wavering confidence in the dollar within foreign quarters stemmed in part from the persistent deficits of his administration. Consequently, in December 1931, Hoover invoked a new phase of his fiscal policy—the phase that has left the most lasting impression in the public's memory. He asked Congress for tax increases that promised to raise revenues by one-third. The Revenue Act of 1932 raised income tax rates and was the largest peacetime tax increase in the nation's history. Along with the monetary contraction, it worsened the depression and contributed to Franklin D. Roosevelt's electoral victory in 1932.

In its first hundred days, the Democratic administration of Franklin Roosevelt quickly moved beyond the corporate liberalism of Herbert Hoover to apply the coercive power of government to the tasks of relief and economic recovery. But the New Deal brought no immediate fiscal innovations. Roosevelt tried to adhere to his 1932 campaign pledge to balance the federal budget, a task that for three years the administration of Herbert Hoover had been unable to accomplish. In 1933, Roosevelt warned Congress that "too often in recent history liberal governments have been wrecked on the rocks of loose fiscal policy." In fact, until 1938, Roosevelt continued to state his belief that a balanced budget was important as a means of fostering the confidence of the public—especially of business—in government, thereby encouraging investment and economic recovery. Meanwhile, he read the polls that suggested that the vast majority of Americans, even during the 1936 campaign, wished him to balance the budget.

Budget balancing, however, was not easy. New Deal programs were often expensive, so that financing them while balancing the budget would have required much larger tax revenues. Faced with a tax base shrunken by depression conditions, Roosevelt and Congress could obtain new revenues only by massive increases in tax rates or by the introduction of substantial new taxes. They recognized that if they raised taxes sufficiently to balance the budget in the short run, they would probably make the depression even worse. Consequently, they accepted some deficit spending as necessary, and during his first term Roosevelt asserted in every budget message that the deficits would disappear along with the depression. In fact, federal deficits grew from $2.6 billion in 1933 to $4.4 billion in 1936, or over 40 percent of 1936 federal expenditures.

On matters of taxation, Roosevelt was clearly in the democratic statist tradition. Like Woodrow Wilson before him, he was personally devoted to both balanced budgets and redistributional taxation. Roosevelt believed deeply in soak-the-rich taxation, which shifted the tax burden to the wealthiest individuals and corporations. Nonetheless, prior to 1935, Roosevelt moved slowly in promoting progressive redistribution. Even in 1935, Roosevelt advocated employee payroll taxes as the primary means of financing Social Security.

Roosevelt had good political reasons for moving slowly on a radical tax agenda. For one thing, his highest priority was raising revenues for new programs, and he was wary of business opposition to these programs. He was often willing to accept regressive taxes to head off such opposition. Also, his secretary of the Treasury, Henry Morgenthau, Jr., required time to rebuild—after the twelve years of Republican leadership—a Treasury staff willing to undertake the work of devising new progressive taxes that would be effective in raising revenue. In addition, Roosevelt was worried that if economic recovery failed, business would be able to convince the public that progressive tax policy had been to blame. Finally, in the case of social security taxation, Roosevelt thought of social security as an insurance system in which the taxes paid by middle-class people were premiums that established investments.

In 1939 Roosevelt and Congress replaced social security's individual equity with a welfare element; they redistributed funds within the system and introduced pay-as-you-go financing. But they continued to use insurance terminology in explaining the system to the public. Roosevelt's advertising campaign limited pressure from the public on the federal government to monitor and report on the viability of the system. Roosevelt believed that "with those taxes in there, no damn politician can ever scrap my social security program." He succeeded, probably beyond his wildest expectations.

In 1935, Roosevelt shifted tax policy in a more statist direction as he responded to growing challenges from the Left, particularly Huey Long's "Share Our Wealth" movement. Through the Revenue Act of 1935, Roosevelt resumed vigorous redistributional taxation. He called for a graduated tax on corporations to check the growth of monopoly, a tax on the dividends that holding companies received from corporations they controlled, surtaxes to raise the maximum income tax rate on individuals from 63 to 79 percent, and a tax on inheritances to be imposed in addition to federal estate taxation. In 1936 only about 2 million American households—out of a total of 32 million—owed any federal income tax.

In his message to Congress preceding the Revenue Act of 1935, Roosevelt declared that accumulations of wealth meant "great and undesirable concentration of control in relatively few individuals over the employment and welfare of many, many others." Later, the president explained that his purpose was "not to destroy wealth, but to create a broader range of opportunity, to restrain the growth of unwholesome and sterile accumulations and to lay the burdens of Government where they can best be carried." Roosevelt justified his tax reform program in terms of both its inherent equity and its ability to liberate the energies of individuals and small corporations, which would advance recovery.

Congress gave Roosevelt much of the tax reform he wanted in the Revenue Act of 1935. Roosevelt now believed that he would not have to request any further new taxes until after the presidential election of 1936. But in early 1936, the Supreme Court's invalidation of the Agricultural Adjustment Act's processing tax and Congress's override of Roosevelt's veto of a bonus bill for World War I veterans threatened to create a substantial increase in the federal deficit. In response, Roosevelt asked Congress to pass a revenue-raising measure that he expected to have even more redistributional significance than the Revenue Act of 1935: an undistributed profits tax.

Roosevelt's new proposal for taxing corporations was to eliminate the existing taxes on corporate income, capital stock, and excess profits and replace them with a tax on retained earnings—the profits that corporations did not distribute to their stockholders. The tax would be graduated according to the proportion of the profits that were undistributed. Roosevelt and Secretary of the Treasury Morgenthau believed that the measure would fight both tax avoidance and the concentration of corporate power. Corporations, they were convinced, deliberately retained profits to avoid the taxation of dividends under the individual income tax. Further, they believed that the largest corporations had the power to retain greater shares of surpluses than did small companies. The surpluses, they were certain, gave large corporations an unfair competitive advantage by reducing their need to borrow new capital. Moreover, Roosevelt and Morgenthau thought that large corporations often reinvested their surpluses unwisely. The undistributed profits tax would provide a powerful incentive to corporations to distribute their profits to their shareholders. Those shareholders, in turn, would generate large revenues for the government by paying high surtaxes.

In proposing and crafting these taxes, Treasury experts dug into their archives for inspiration. Most influential was their discovery of Thomas S. Adams's 1919 proposal for an undistributed-profits tax, one that he had favored as a replacement for excess-profits taxation and as a tax that would place corporations and partnerships on a more equal basis.

Congress enacted the corporate measure, which was, along with the excess-profits tax, the most radical tax ever enacted by the federal government. In the Revenue Act of 1937, Congress further tightened the income tax. It increased taxation of personal holding companies, limited deductions for corporate yachts and country estates, restricted deductions for losses from sales or exchanges of property, reduced incentives for the creation of multiple trusts, and eliminated favors for nonresident taxpayers. Roosevelt intended to continue his reform program in 1938. He planned to increase the undistributed profits tax, to establish a graduated tax on capital gains, and to tax the income from federal, state, and local bonds.

These plans, more than any other dimension of the New Deal, aroused fear and hostility on the part of large corporations. Quite correctly, they viewed Roosevelt's tax program as a threat to their control over capital and their latitude for financial planning. There is no evidence that capital went on strike, as many New Dealers, who noticed a lag in business investment, charged. But business did seize the political opening created by the recession of 1937–1938 and Roosevelt's unsuccessful court fight in 1937. Conservative Democrats broke with the president and argued that tax cuts were necessary to restore business confidence. In 1938, a coalition of Republicans and conservative Democrats ended New Deal tax reform by pushing through Congress a measure that gutted the tax on undistributed profits and discarded the graduated corporate income tax. Roosevelt, respecting the strength of the opposition, decided not to veto the bill. Instead, he allowed the Revenue Act of 1938 to become law without his signature and denounced it as the "abandonment of a important principle of American taxation," namely taxation according to ability to pay. In 1939, Congress eradicated the undistributed-profits tax and formally canceled New Deal tax reform.

Tax reform was not the only casualty in 1937–1938; economic recovery was another. Roosevelt could not ignore the strong likelihood that restrictive fiscal policy had contributed to the sharp recession of 1937–1938. Consequently, he listened more closely to a group of government officials, scattered across the Works Progress Administration (WPA), the Department of Agriculture, and the Federal Reserve, who pressed upon him the ideas of John Maynard Keynes. There is no evidence that any of these officials—the most important of whom were Harry Hopkins, Henry Wallace, and Marriner Eccles—ever convinced Roosevelt of their view that deficits would be needed permanently in order to maintain full employment. But, in 1938, Roosevelt did shift fiscal policy into line with Keynesian policy and used a Keynesian argument to justify what he had done. He explained to Congress that his large increases in expenditures, unaccompanied by tax increases, would add "to the purchasing power of the Nation."

State and local governments also contributed to the nation's fiscal policy throughout the Great Depression. During the early years of the Depression, state governments increased spending for unemployment relief. They did so primarily through subventions to local governments, who faced sharply declining property tax revenues, soaring rates of default, and even popular revolts, including a tax strike in Chicago. States acquired the necessary resources by increasing sales taxes and reducing spending on highways and schools. State constitutions, however, limited deficit finance, and new state and municipal bonds were extremely difficult to market. As the Depression worsened in 1931 and 1932, state and local governments found it impossible to conduct business as usual and still balance their budgets. They began adopting more drastic economies, scaling back total expenditures in 1931, and sharply contracting them in 1933 and 1934. State governments welcomed federal funding of unemployment relief and public works, although they resisted requirements for state matching funds. When economic recovery advanced, particularly in 1936 and 1938, state and local governments resumed spending on public works and education and once again increased their total outlays.

Sharp increases in tax rates, however, erased any stimulative effect of increased state and local spending. State and local governments had pushed up tax rates every year between 1929 and 1933, and they maintained those high levels until 1936, when they raised them even further. State governments increased the scope and rates of their sales taxes until, in 1940, they were raising most of their funds through such levies. By 1940, consumer taxes—on gasoline, tobacco, liquor, soft drinks, and oleomargarine—produced $1.1 billion, while the new general retail sales taxes, which thirty-three states adopted between 1932 and 1937, produced $500 million. Meanwhile, local governments increased their effective rates of property taxation. Assisting state and local governments were two different forces: a good-government movement that promoted conscientious taxpaying, and the New Deal's Home Owners' Loan Corporation (HOLC), which required borrowers to pay off back taxes as a condition for receiving subsidized mortgage loans. As a consequence of the 1933–1939 tax increases, state and local governments would have had huge budget surpluses if the economy had been at full employment. In fact, these surpluses were large enough to offset the expansive effects of federal deficits in all but two of those seven years.

With the Roosevelt administration's embrace of deficit spending as a positive good came further centralization of budgetary control. The Reorganization Act of 1939 created the Executive Office of the President (EOP), transferred to it the Bureau of the Budget (from Treasury), and the National Resources Planning Board (from Interior). The act also established the Office of Emergency Management within the EOP. To encourage public support of the act, Congress emphasized the goal of reducing expenditures through coordination and elimination of overlapping agencies. But the primary purpose of the Reorganization Act was to increase presidential control over a greatly expanded executive branch. A crucial part of the president's new capability was enhanced access to economic expertise.

The Reorganization Act of 1939 advanced the victory of Keynesianism. By 1939, veteran economists in government service had become more partial to deficits than they had been in 1933 or in 1937. These experts had begun to discover in the writings of Keynes an economic rationale for their political position. Augmenting the ranks of these government economists during 1939 and 1940 were academic economists who supported the New Deal for the first time. They enthusiastically embraced Keynesian ideas. Some were senior economists who used Keynes to support their own longstanding beliefs that economic stagnation was inevitable without permanent deficits or drastic income redistribution. Among them was Alvin Hansen, who came to Washington in 1940 as an adviser to the Federal Reserve and the National Resources Planning Board. Others were younger, and had been weaned on Keynes's *General Theory*. These economists staffed agencies such as the Bureau of the Budget and the Division of Industrial Economics within the Department of Commerce.

While the general public was less enthusiastic than these economists were about sustained deficits, by 1938 the Roosevelt administration had established a consensus that the federal government should avoid adopting restrictive fiscal policies (such as the Hoover administration's tax increase of 1932) during recession or depression conditions. The public at large had grown more accustomed to, if not enthusiastically in favor of, continued deficits to manage economic recovery. Through the medium of the New Deal, the nation had institutionalized the expansion of spending programs during economic reversals. This was so despite the fact that the federal government had not developed a clearly defined strategy of spending and deficits; no federal agency was capable of specifying reliable techniques and magnitudes.

WORLD WAR II: ANOTHER CRISIS

During World War II, the Roosevelt administration and Congress shifted national priorities dramatically toward prosecuting the war effort. Preventing inflation, rather than curing depression, became the major fiscal problem. Roosevelt sought to avoid the excessive inflation that great deficits had helped cause during and after World War I.

The pressures for inflation, however, were enormous. Energized by Pearl Harbor, governmental expenditures soared and continued to increase through 1945. These expenditures represented a more massive shift of resources from peacetime to wartime needs than was the case during World War I. The average level of federal expenditures from 1942 through 1945 amounted to roughly half of national product, more than twice the average ratio during World War I. In addition, the shift of resources was faster and more prolonged.

Learning from the experience of financing World War I, Roosevelt and Congress agreed that the government should impose price controls and rationing of very scarce goods. In addition, they decided that Congress should raise taxes significantly to pay for wartime spending and to prevent consumers from bidding up prices in competition with the government. Because of new tax revenues, the federal deficit, after increasing from $6.2 billion in 1941 to $57.4 billion in 1943, held at about the 1943 level for the remainder of the war.

The choice of the specific taxes was, however, a matter of severe contention. Roosevelt revived the reform ambitions that Congress had crushed in 1938. Like Wilson and McAdoo in 1916–1917, he and Secretary of the Treasury Henry Morgenthau preferred to finance the war with taxes that bore heavily on business and upper-income groups. In 1941 Morgenthau now proposed taxing away all corporate profits above a 6 percent rate of return. Roosevelt went further: "In time of this grave national danger, when all excess income should go to win the war," he told a joint session of Congress in 1942, "no American citizen ought to have a net income, after he has paid his taxes, of more than $25,000."

But such radical war-tax proposals faced two major obstacles. One was the opposition from a diverse group of military planners, foreign-policy strategists, financial leaders, and economists. Throughout the turbulence of the 1920s and 1930s, these experts had studied the economic lessons of World War I, and its aftermath. This group of experts, now wishing to mobilize even greater resources, more smoothly and predictably than had been done during World War I, and with less inflation, promoted a policy of mass-based income taxation—an income tax that focused on wages and salaries.

The second obstacle to Roosevelt's wartime proposals was, in sharp contrast with Wilson's war experience, powerful congressional opposition. Many members of Congress, including leading Democrats, worried that Morgenthau's plan would handicap corporations in coping with the economic slump expected to follow the war.

Ignoring Roosevelt, Congress instituted what became the basis of a new tax regime—a broadly based income tax. Because of significant reductions in personal exemptions, huge revenues flowed from the taxation of wages and salaries. The number of individual taxpayers grew from 3.9 million in 1939 to 42.6 million in 1945, and federal income tax collections over the period leaped from $2.2 billion to $35.1 billion. Membership in the community of taxpayers, as law professors Stanley Surrey and William Warren put it, "spread from the country club district down to the railroad tracks and then over the *other* side of the tracks." Mass taxation had replaced class taxation. At the same time, the federal government came to dominate the nation's revenue system. In 1940, federal income tax had accounted for only 16 percent of the taxes collected by all levels of government; by 1950 the federal income tax produced over 51 percent of all collections.

Mass taxation succeeded, in part, because of the popularity of the war effort. In contrast to World War I mobilization, it was not necessary to leverage popular support for the war by enacting a highly redistributional tax system. Most Americans concluded that their nation's security was at stake, and the Roosevelt administration used the propaganda machinery at its command to persuade the millions of new taxpayers that they ought to pay.

The Treasury, its Bureau of Internal Revenue, and the Office of War Information launched a massive propaganda campaign. In the campaign, they invoked the same calls for patriotism and civic responsibility that the Wilson administration had used so effectively during World War I. The Treasury commissioned Irving Berlin to write a song for the effort entitled "I Paid My Income Tax Today." The Treasury sent recordings of the song to radio stations and asked Danny Kaye to tour New York night clubs with the song. The Treasury also commissioned a Disney animated short, "The New Spirit," which starred Donald Duck. Informed by the radio that it is "your privilege, not just your duty . . . to help your government by paying your tax and paying it promptly," Donald gathered the supplies necessary to fill in his return (including a bottle of aspirin). He found the job easier and, with the exemptions and credits for his three nephews, less painful than he anticipated. The film ended with Donald traveling to Washington to pay his tax in person, and to see how tax revenues were transformed into the arsenal of democracy. In early 1942, over 32 million people in 12,000 theaters watched "The New Spirit."

In crafting its advertising campaign, the Roosevelt administration recognized that a successful mass-based income tax must rely heavily on voluntary cooperation. And, the success of the income tax demonstrated once again the financial power of democratic government.

The structure of the new tax was as important as propaganda in winning middle-class support. General deductions (for example, for interest on home mortgages and for payments of state and local taxes) sweetened the new tax system for the middle class. Moreover, middle-class taxpayers preferred the mass-based income tax to a national sales tax, which many corporate leaders favored and promoted. Furthermore, fear of a renewed depression made the public more tolerant of taxation that was favorable to the corporations and corporate privilege. However naive this leniency may have seemed to radical New Dealers, it expressed a widely shared commitment to the pursuit of enlightened self-interest. In the same spirit, during World War II many New Deal legislators favored the mass-based income tax as the best way to ensure a flow of revenues to support federal programs of social justice. Finally, the introduction of payroll withholding took much of the sting out of taxpaying.

During the fight over withholding, adopted in the Revenue Act of 1943, Congress prevailed over Roosevelt. The president noted that the act would, because of the phasing in of withholding, forgive an entire year's tax liability, and he concluded that the lion's share of the benefits of forgiveness would go to the wealthy. He therefore denounced the bill as "not a tax bill but a tax relief bill, providing relief not for the needy but for the greedy." He vetoed the bill but, for the first time in history, Congress overrode a presidential veto of a revenue act. The humiliating defeat led Roosevelt to accept mass-based income taxation without further discord. The new tax system essentially ended the conflict that had begun during World War I between business advocates and progressives over soak-the-rich income taxation.

BIPARTISAN GOVERNMENT, 1946–1980

The experience of World War II, following so closely on the heels of the Great Depression, helped produce a popular, bipartisan consensus of support for the basic shifts in national policy that the Roosevelt administration had engineered. In the realm of domestic fiscal policy, World War II institutionalized structural Keynesianism. Mass-based income taxation had kept wartime deficits under control but the deficits were still far larger than any before. The conjunction of great deficits and dramatic economic expansion converted many Americans to the faith that great deficits not only had produced the economic expansion of World War II, ending the Great Depression, but also were required for sustained prosperity in peacetime.

Among the converted were a growing number of businesspeople, represented by the Committee for Economic Development, who came to view periodic deficits as a way to tame the business cycle without undermining the investment system. In effect, Keynesianism had become the culmination of corporate liberalism (or progressive capitalism) and its search for social order. A consequence of the emerging Keynesian consensus fostered by the New Deal and World War II was congressional passage of the Employment Act of 1946. The act declared the federal government's central responsibility for managing the level of employment. It created the Council of Economic Advisers to provide economic advice that was expert and independent. It also formally embodied a central objective of the New Deal: to embrace human values as the context for setting and evaluating fiscal policy.

The combination of mass-based income taxation for general revenues, a regressive payroll tax for social insurance, and sustained deficit spending, survived during the postwar era as the central means of financing the federal government. As part of the process, the two major parties, for the first time since the early nineteenth century, reached agreement on the essential elements of the nation's fiscal policy. Some important differences remained between the two parties, but both agreed on a few central points: protecting corporate financial structures from assaults like the taxation of retained earnings, using fiscal policy in the cause of economic stabilization, providing an elastic source of revenue for national defense, continuing the New Deal's insurance premium approach to funding the social security system, and eschewing national sales taxation.

The general decline of partisanship after World War II no doubt contributed to the convergence of the two parties on fiscal policy, but the convergence on tax policy was actually rather one-sided. It was mainly the product of a shift in direction by the Democratic party. In the postwar era, Democrats largely abandoned taxation as an instrument to mobilize class interests. While presidents Kennedy and Johnson continued to support tax reforms, such as the taxation of capital gains at death, they also advocated tax cuts and did so with language that was reminiscent of Andrew Mellon's. In 1964, Congress responded to Johnson's call for a tax cut "to increase our national income and Federal revenues" by slashing taxes in the face of large deficits. The Council of Economic Advisers agreed and sanctioned the 1964 cuts, which were especially generous to corporations and wealthy Americans in that they cut capital gains taxes and allowed more generous depreciation allowances. Thus, Democrats helped the Republican party finish the job it had begun during the 1920s: taking both the partisan sting and the redistributional threat out of taxation. The shift in the tax policy favored by the Democratic party was part of its more general shift—one begun after 1937, accelerated during World War II, and completed in the Kennedy-Johnson era—that meant abandoning democratic statism and embracing corporate liberalism. This shift had expanded the Democratic party's intellectual scope, and political potency, by incorporating Keynesian countercyclical policies.

The bipartisan consensus ushered in an era of buoyant public finance that lasted until the 1980s. The policies that produced the revenues were nearly invisible, far removed from the contested turf of partisan politics. With little public debate, and with bipartisan agreement, the federal government consistently raised social security tax rates. The combined employer and employee tax rates equaled 3 percent in 1950, 6 percent in 1960, 9.6 percent in 1970, 12.26

percent in 1980, and 15.3 percent by 1990. The higher tax rates, as well as increases in the tax base, produced an increase in social security taxes from less than 1 percent of gross national product (GNP) in the late 1940s to over 7 percent by the late 1970s. With this funding, social security payments increased from $472 million in 1946 (less than 1 percent of GNP) to $105 billion in 1979 (about 4.3 percent of GNP).

Even less visible was the role of persistent inflation, which peaked first in the late 1940s, then resumed during the late 1960s, and continued throughout the 1970s. Accelerating inflation expedited federal finance in two important ways.

First, inflation reduced the value of outstanding debt, particularly in the years just after World War II. The federal debt as a percentage of GNP had reached an all-time high following World War II—nearly 90 percent. The unexpected nature of the acceleration in price increases after the war helped push real interest rates on the debt to extremely low, even negative, levels. With low interest rates, and with surging tax revenues, the federal government's interest payments fell to under 14 percent of general revenues during the 1940s and then fell even lower, remaining under 10 percent until the heavy borrowing of the 1980s.

Second, accelerating inflation meant that increasing numbers of families moved into higher tax brackets faster than their real income increased. In effect, this bracket creep raised individual tax rates, and meant that the federal government could often respond positively to requests for new programs without enacting politically damaging tax increases.

The highly elastic revenue system of the federal government paid for the strategic defense programs of the Cold War, and, without any general or permanent increases in income taxation, also for the mobilizations for the Korean and Vietnam wars. But, except during these two wars, the size of the defense budget relative to GNP tended to decline through the 1970s. Thus the increases in federal revenues went largely for the expansion of domestic programs.

The most rapid growth in federal programs over the period between the end of World War II and 1980 was in education, welfare, health services (including Medicare), and urban redevelopment. In addition, the inflation-driven increases permitted income tax reductions or new tax expenditures—tax preferences in the form of special exclusions, deductions, and credits hidden in the tax code. These tax expenditures became increasingly popular in the 1960s and 1970s for several reasons. Democrats became attracted to

them as ways to accomplish their social goals—such as the promotion of home ownership embedded in the deduction of mortgage interest—without having to make large and politically difficult direct expenditures of funds. And some Democrats and Republicans found self-serving political benefits in hiding expenditure programs from public scrutiny. Meanwhile, taxpayers aggressively sought preferential treatment within the tax code in order to offset the effects of bracket creep.

During the 1960s and 1970s, the strong income tax revenues also allowed a substantial increase in the channeling of federal revenues to state and local governments through indirect methods: grants-in-aid and revenue sharing. The federal government had begun grants to the states during the 1860s and 1870s for specific purposes, largely agricultural research and education. As early as 1914, with the Smith-Lever Act's support for agricultural extension, the federal government had introduced the modern system of grants-in-aid, which included matching requirements, formulas for distribution between the states, and monitoring of states' expenditure plans. During the New Deal such federal grants increased, accounting for as much as 13 percent of state and local revenues. Federal grants declined in importance during the 1940s, increased modestly during the 1950s, and then grew swiftly during the 1960s and 1970s. In these decades, revenue sharing—federal subsidies to state and local governments without programmatic strings—dominated. By 1974, more than 20 percent of state and local revenues came from federal aid.

The federal transfers represented a recognition of the increasing demands on state and local governments for services. They amounted to a kind of tax relief to state and local governments. Following World War II, state and local tax receipts had increased even more rapidly than had federal taxes. State and local taxes almost doubled as a percentage of GNP, rising to almost 10 percent of GNP by 1972. State income taxes increased in importance over the entire postwar period, but increases in state sales taxation and local property taxes dominated the growth in state and local revenues.

Beginning in the late 1970s, state and local governments became popular targets of general attacks on the growth of government. The movement was founded on concerns about the rising costs of government, widespread doubts about the effectiveness of governmental solutions to social problems, dissatisfaction over the quality of public services, and distrust of legislatures.

This movement against government growth gained its most dramatic expression in a 1978 taxpayers' revolt in California. In a referendum, California's voters approved Proposition 13, amending the state's constitution to limit the property-tax rate to 1 percent of market value, and to require a two-thirds majority of each house of the legislature to enact any new taxes. Stimulated by the success of Proposition 13, coalitions similar to the one that had formed in California—a combination of small homeowners and owners of commercial property trying to reduce their tax bills, conservatives attacking welfare, liberals seeking a more progressive tax system, and people simply striking out at modern life—formed in a number of other states. The measures they framed were not as drastic as Proposition 13, but all were in its spirit and most survived state-level referenda and court challenges.

Opposition to government spending and taxing quickly reached the federal level. Tax reform gathered momentum, winning support in diverse quarters. Conservatives focused on bracket creep while liberal tax experts exposed the inequities resulting from increasing exemptions and deductions. Two liberal tax experts, law professor Stanley Surrey and economist Joseph Pechman, were especially influential. In 1968, Surrey, as assistant secretary of the Treasury, introduced the organizing concept of tax expenditures. He and Pechman helped the Treasury articulate its position that the government should pursue social goals openly, through direct expenditures. They worked from within the Treasury to highlight the massive size of the hidden tax expenditures, and to underscore the kind of economic inefficiencies and distortions they introduced. In 1974, the Congressional Budget Act acknowledged the importance of the tax expenditure concept and advanced the debate by requiring the annual publication of a tax expenditure budget. Subsequently, the Congressional Budget Office estimated that in 1967 tax expenditures cost the federal government nearly $37 billion (equal to 21 percent of federal expenditures), and that the total cost had soared to $327 billion by 1984 (equal to 35 percent of federal expenditures).

As a presidential candidate in 1976, Jimmy Carter responded to growing pubic discontent by describing the American tax system as a disgrace. He promised to make the federal income tax more progressive and to avoid "a piecemeal approach to change." But during his first two years in office, Carter found himself embroiled in piecemeal change and frustrated in his efforts to reduce the taxes of lower-income families. Congress insisted on avoiding tax cuts that might stimulate consumption and inflation, and concentrated instead on seeking ways of stimulating business investment to encourage productivity and discourage inflation. Congress prevailed, and President Carter reluctantly signed the Revenue Act of 1978, which provided only minimal tax relief and simplification for individuals while it offered generous cuts in capital gains and business taxes.

While Congress failed to enact reform during the Carter administration, it did seriously consider a new tax—a value-added tax on consumption—as part of a possible comprehensive overhaul of the federal tax system. For each transaction in the chain of production, the tax would apply a small levy to the value added in that step—the difference between the sale price of the product or service and the costs of the goods and services purchased to create the product or service. France adopted a value-added tax as early as 1954, and between 1967 and 1973 all of the members of the European Economic Community, including Great Britain, adopted it as their standard form of sales taxation.

In 1978 Senator Russell Long, chair of the Senate Finance Committee, proposed substituting value-added taxation for income and social security taxes. Then Al Ullman, a Democratic representative from Oregon and chair of the House Ways and Means Committee, introduced a concrete plan to move in that direction. For the first time since 1940, Congress looked closely at comprehensive taxation of consumption.

Ullman's proposed Tax Reconstruction Act of 1980 was probably the most radical approach to tax reform seriously considered by Congress since World War II. However, liberals were worried about its regressivity, and conservatives, including business leaders, argued that the new tax would encourage the growth of government. Together, they prevented the bill from coming to a vote. Meanwhile, Oregon voters, disliking the prospect of a new tax on consumption, ended Ullman's congressional career. Once again, just as at earlier junctures, the federal government stopped short of encouraging savings and investment through the comprehensive taxation of consumption. Only the high-tariff system of the late nineteenth century stands as a possible exception to this pattern. But the motivation for that system had little to do with the stimulation of savings; it was aimed more directly at the manipulation of international prices of manufactured goods and labor.

THE REAGAN "REVOLUTION," 1981–1992

The buoyant-revenue era ended quickly during the 1980s. Some signs of its demise had been apparent in the late 1970s. Most notably, the Federal Reserve had begun to attack inflation, pushing interest rates well above the rate of inflation. Also, Republicans and Democrats had joined in supporting increases in defense expenditures relative to GNP, thus closing out the post-Vietnam peace dividends. But the major changes were brought about by the Reagan "revolution"—implementation of the new priorities set by the election of Ronald Reagan in 1980, namely the reduction of taxes, a sharp increase in defense expenditures, and a reduction in domestic programs.

The Reagan administration undertook the reduction of taxes through the 1981 passage of the Economic Recovery Tax Act of 1981 (ERTA). ERTA was made possible by Republican control of the Senate, conservative domination of the House, and growing popular enthusiasm for tax cutting. The president and some of his supporters rationalized the tax cutting as supply-side stimulation of the economy. ERTA was one of the most dramatic shifts in tax policy since World War I. Its key provisions—its indexing of rates for inflation and its severe slashing of personal and business taxes—ensured that the era of dynamic federal revenues would end. ERTA reduced the role of the income tax in the nation's revenue system for the first time since the Great Depression. By 1990, indexing alone had reduced federal revenues by about $180 billion a year, and the ERTA rate reductions cost the Treasury an additional $80 billion annually. Meanwhile, income tax revenues as a share of all federal taxes declined from 63 percent in 1980 to 57 percent in 1990. Thus, by the early 1980s, largely as a consequence of ERTA, politically low-cost means of increasing revenues had vanished. For the moment, the Reagan revolution appeared to have succeeded in breaking the upward ratchet effect of federal taxation.

With the losses in revenue as a consequence of ERTA, the Reagan administration incurred unprecedented deficits. They were roughly the size of the ERTA reductions in revenue. ERTA had failed to provide the supply-side benefits Reagan had predicted and the Reagan administration was unable to cut back federal expenditures. In fact, Reagan began a massive defense buildup. The resulting deficits more than tripled the national debt between 1980 and 1990, when it reached the astronomical sum of $3.3 trillion. Meanwhile, interest payments on the debt rose from 15 to 18 percent of federal expenditures.

The mushrooming interest charges, restriction of discretionary spending, and increasing dependence on foreign creditors significantly weakened the federal government.

The Federal Reserve Board, led by its chair, Paul Volcker, had to impose an unusually restrictive monetary policy to contain the inflationary pressures of the massive deficits, and to keep interest rates sufficiently high to attract foreign capital to finance the deficits. This monetary policy, however, reinforced the tendency of the large federal borrowing to crowd out private borrowers. Among the crowded-out borrowers were those who would have put the nation's savings to more productive use. Thus the conjunction of fiscal policy and monetary policy contributed heavily to the slowdown of the nation's economic productivity during the 1980s.

In response to the deficits, Congress took extraordinary action. It passed the Gramm-Rudman-Hollings Act in 1985, which imposed automatic spending reductions (but not tax increases) whenever the deficit exceeded prescribed levels. This act also placed previously off-budget expenditures in a unified federal budget. These expenditures had grown since World War I and had escalated during the 1970s and 1980s. By 1985, they had reached nearly one-quarter of all federal outlays. In 1987, Congress took social security trust funds off budget, while including their income and expenditures in calculating Gramm-Rudman deficit targets. Meanwhile, beginning in 1983, the social security funds began to produce surpluses, which the federal government used to help finance its deficits. Gramm-Rudman had some disciplinary effect, but deficits have continued to increase into the 1990s.

During 1984 and 1985, while the deficit crisis mounted, both the Reagan administration and congressional Democrats, supported by Treasury staff, began scouting the income tax system to find areas requiring structural reform. They edged into a competitive scramble to occupy the high ground of tax reform. The consequence of this process was the passage of tax legislation even more dramatic than ERTA—the Tax Reform Act of 1986.

Like ERTA and the tax reforms of the 1920s, the 1986 measure was initiated by Republicans seeking to reduce the taxes on wealth. But the tax reform process in 1986 differed from its predecessors. First, the Republican administration in 1986 had new and different goals; it was more interested in improving economic incentives for enterprise capitalism than in protecting corporate bureaucracies or the real-estate industry. Corporations received major tax increases in 1986, and the real-estate industry was a major loser. Second, the writing of the 1986 act included substantial Democratic participation. In fact, both Sen. Daniel Patrick Moynihan and Sen. Bill Bradley, who had studied the role of Stanley Surrey within the Treasury, took crucial, creative parts in the drama. Third, these political entrepreneurs successfully championed a position never previously associated with either of the two major parties: focusing reform of the income tax on broadening its income base and creating a more uniform—a more horizontally equitable—tax even at the expense of sacrificing the tax's progressive rate structure. They succeeded in part because the fiscal environment had become vastly different from that of the 1920s, or even of the 1960s and 1970s. In the new environment of huge deficits, Congress could no longer enact reform bills that provided tax reductions to particular groups at the cost of reducing the overall level of taxation. Nor could Congress any longer rely on inflation-driven tax increases to finance tax reductions. Because of the deficit crisis, every reduction in tax rates or increase in a tax loophole had to be paid for through a reduction in another loophole elsewhere in the tax code.

The passage of the Tax Reform Act of 1986 came as a nearly complete surprise to tax experts, most of all to the political scientists who believed in the powerful sway of grinding interest-group pluralism. They had not realized to what extent taxes were up for grabs. The act left major winners and losers in its wake. It eliminated some important tax expenditures that had favored the middle class—those that had subsidized consumer interest payments, state and local taxes, and long-term capital gains—and repealed the investment tax credit for corporations. But the act also provided some important benefits for both lower- and upper-income groups. Sharp increases in the personal exemption and the standard deduction favored taxpayers in the lowest income brackets. Reductions in the rates on the top brackets, and the cut in the top corporate rate from 48 percent to 34 percent, favored the wealthiest taxpayers. By attacking special deductions and credits, the act moved toward eliminating tax-based privilege and reaffirming the duties of citizenship. It preserved the standards of progressivity and ability to pay while promoting efficiency and uniformity. During the late 1980s and early 1990s, Congress took no further steps toward reducing deductions and broadening the base of income taxation, but it did leave essentially intact the terms of the 1986 tax reform.

The 1980s saw major changes in federal taxation

that disrupted the post–World War II policy equilibrium. The income tax system was in as much flux as it had been during the 1940s, and from the turmoil emerged the possibility of a new fiscal environment. Joseph Pechman emphasized that the 1986 reform act significantly strengthened the base for income taxation by eliminating tax shelters. He estimated that a very modest increase in rates, as little as three percentage points across the board, could raise as much as $100 billion a year.

AT CENTURY'S END

The presidential administration of Bill Clinton may bring another major episode of governmental reform during which citizens' expectations of their government rise rather than fall. Every such reform episode in the past has manifested increased expectations of the nation's tax system, and has brought various combinations of tax reforms and tax increases. There is no reason to believe that a reform movement during the 1990s would be any different. During the 1990s, Americans may consider the complex tangle of federal deficits, poverty, degradation of social infrastructure (including education), competitive weaknesses, and environmental destruction to have reached the level of a national emergency. If they do, they will probably call for a new system of federal taxation, just as they have in the past in times of crisis.

A new system might include major new taxes—for example, an expenditure tax, or one or both of the two measures discussed prominently by the Clinton administration during its first year: an energy-consumption tax or a value-added tax. These or other new taxes might replace old ones, such as the social security payroll tax. A new system might involve further reform of income taxation along the lines established in 1986. But whatever tax system might emerge, a prerequisite for change is a restoration of public trust in the federal government—the kind of trust that enabled the federal government to finance World War II using the mass-based income tax. Historical experience indicates that establishing this trust will require two elements. The first is a shift toward greater progressivity in the rate structure of the total tax system. The second is persuading the public that the national government deserves greater support, that it is making worthy efforts to solve the nation's structural problems. Until both of these changes occur, campaign phrases like George Bush's 1988 promise: "Read my lips. No new taxes!" will continue to attract support not only from business and the wealthy but also from the swelling numbers of middle- and low-income families who are alienated from politics and government. During the 1980s they came to agree with the pronouncement of hotel magnate and convicted tax-evader Leona Helmsley that "only the little people pay taxes," and they saw little evidence that the federal government was effectively solving the nation's structural problems.

In addition, a tax-reforming administration must be alert for the moments in which key players may be willing to change their minds. The Clinton administration would do well to listen to the advice of Thomas S. Adams, the most important economist in the Treasury between 1917 and 1933. He told the American Economic Association in his 1927 presidential address that although class politics heavily shaped taxation, he found that on many tax issues "a majority of legislators and voters are unaffected and disinterested; they may cast their votes as a more or less disinterested jury." And, "in the adoption of tax legislation there come zero hours, when the zeal of the narrowly selfish flags." The challenge that

Adams saw was for experts, and for politicians, to take advantage of such openings. "There are thus many important tax problems," he declared, "which may be settled on the broad basis of equity and sound public policy, if one is wise and ingenious enough to find the right solution."

The history of American public finance suggests that administrations are able to take advantage of the opportunities identified by Adams for what political scientists have called "social learning." Administrations must approach tax reform in a comprehensive fashion, articulate the goals of reform in ways that rise above the interests of particular groups, and organize the process of reform to insulate experts from political pressure. In the politics of tax reform, conflict has always been severe, and the outcome uncertain. But out of this turbulence, the wisest tax policies have been shaped by politicians and experts who, despite their immersion in a grinding political process, learned how to define a transcendent public interest.

SEE ALSO The Presidency; The Constitution; Congress; Federalism; Social Welfare (all in volume I); Economic Thought; Economic Policies; Capital Markets (all in this volume).

BIBLIOGRAPHY

The development of American taxation since the Civil War has recently attracted substantial scholarship, but historians have left the topic largely to political scientists and economists. Most influential among the political scientists writing tax history is John Witte. His book, *The Politics and Development of the Federal Income Tax* (1985), stresses the grinding of interest-group competition within fragmented political structures. He argues that through an incremental process of shaping legislation, economic interest groups have created complex webs of special programs, preferential rates of taxation, and tax expenditures. The inspiration for Witte's model, which is commonly described as pluralist, was the legislative gridlock of the 1970s.

The most comprehensive alternative to a pluralist interpretation remains an older "progressive" history of federal tax policy: Sidney Ratner's *American Taxation: Its History as a Social Force in Democracy* (1942); revised as *Taxation and Democracy in America* (1967). Ratner argues that the history of taxation in the United States has been a struggle between "the thrust

for social justice and the counterthrust for private gain." The historian John D. Buenker reinforces and supplements Ratner's interpretation of the social roots of the income tax movement by identifying the contribution of urban Democrats to the ratification of the Sixteenth Amendment; see John D. Buenker, *The Income Tax and the Progressive Era* (1985). Evidence with regard to support for income taxation within the urban middle classes is found in historian C. K. Yearly's *The Money Machines: The Breakdown and Reform of Governmental and Party Finance in the North, 1860–1920* (1970).

A "capitalist state" interpretation turns the Progressive view on its head by arguing that corporations and the wealthiest Americans were responsible for enacting the income tax, and that they did so to protect the investment system and their own power; see legal historian Robert Stanley's *Dimensions of Law in the Service of Order: Origins of the Federal Income Tax, 1861–1913* (1993).

Two economists advance a fourth interpretation—a "neoconservative" one—of the origins of income taxation. Ben Baack and Edward J. Ray claim, based on correlations between legislative voting behavior and the geographic distribution of federal spending, that "the current issue of the impact of special-interest politics on our national well-being has its roots in the bias of discretionary federal spending at the turn of the century"; see Baack and Ray, "The Political Economy of the Origin and Development of the Federal Income Tax," in *Emergence of the Modern Political Economy: Research in Economic History,* ed. Robert Higgs (1985). More generally, neoconservative tax histories dwell on how interest groups of "tax-eaters," to use John C. Calhoun's phrase, have used the income tax to undermine traditional American resistance to taxpaying and establish the state in twentieth-century America.

For a fifth approach, which treats the state as an autonomous actor and looks closely at the role of ideas and actors within government, see W. Elliot Brownlee, "Wilson and Financing the Modern State: The Revenue Act of 1916," *Proceedings of the American Philosophical Society* (1985); Brownlee, "Economists and the Formation of the Modern Tax System in the United States: The World War I Crisis," in *The State and Economic Knowledge: The American and British Experience,* ed. Mary O. Furner and Barry E. Supple (1990); and Brownlee, "Social Investigation and Political Learning in the Financing of World War I," in *The State and Social Investigation in Britain and the United States,* ed. Lacey and Furner (1993). In contrast, economist Charles Gilbert advocates a pluralist interpretation of World War I finance in his *American Financing of World War I* (1970).

The economist Herbert Stein also brings the state back into the history of taxation. His book, *The Fiscal Revolution in America* (1969), is the leading history of the development of the modern fiscal policy and thinking, especially within the Hoover and Roosevelt administrations. For a contrasting capitalist-state interpretation of Hoover's tax policies, and the tax policies of the Republicans during the 1920s, see Ronald Frederick King, "From Redistributive to Hegemonic Logic: The Transformation of American Tax Politics, 1894–1963," *Politics and Society* 12, no.1 (1983). King argues that Mellon introduced a "hegemonic tax logic" into national politics and policy.

The historian Mark Leff carries the capitalist-state interpretation of national tax politics into the New Deal era, arguing that Franklin D. Roosevelt looked only for symbolic victories in tax reform and was never willing to take on the power of the wealthiest Americans by undertaking a serious program of income and wealth redistribution; see Leff,

The Limits of Symbolic Reform: The New Deal and Taxation (1984). For a neoconservative study of tax policy during the New Deal, see David Beito, *Tax Payers in Revolt: Tax Resistance during the Great Depression* (1989).

We have no in-depth history of World War II taxation, but the legal historian Carolyn C. Jones offers graphic descriptions of the advertising campaigns employed by the federal government during World War II to sell income taxation to the masses; see Jones, "Class Tax to Mass Tax: The Role of Propaganda in the Expansion of the Income Tax During World War II," *Buffalo Law Review* 37, no. 3 (1989).

Various political scientists reinforce John Witte's pluralist interpretation of taxation's development since World War II. Thomas J. Reese, for example, provides a compelling analysis of the influence of bureaucratic complexity in *The Politics of Taxation* (1980), particularly on the congressional side, in shaping tax policy during the 1960s and 1970s.

Ronald F. King has put more flesh on the bones of his capitalist-state theory with a history of the way in which the Kennedy administration employed investment-tax subsidies. By virtue of the way it mobilized such subsides to reconcile the potentially conflicting interests of business and labor, the Kennedy administration was, according to King, "the quintessential presidency of the postwar American regime;" *Money, Time and Politics: Investment Tax Subsidies and American Democracy* (1993). For a discussion of the politics of corporate taxation that is more sensitive than King's to the differences within American business along sectoral lines, and to the autonomous power of the state, see Cathie J. Martin, *Shifting the Burden: The Struggle over Growth and Corporate Taxation* (1991).

The history of the Reagan tax reforms is well documented and analyzed. *Showdown at Gucci Gulch: Lawmakers, Lobbyists, and the Unlikely Triumph of Tax Reform* (1987), by Jeffrey H. Birnbaum and Alan S. Murray, is a history of the Tax Reform Act of 1986 by two *Wall Street Journal* reporters. Some political scientists use the 1986 act as evidence to buttress their argument that a "new politics of reform" has now replaced interest-group pluralism; see Timothy J. Conlan, Margaret T. Wrightson, and David R. Beam, *Taxing Choices: The Politics of Tax Reform* (1990). The economist Eugene Steuerle, who was an influential Treasury official in the Reagan administration, offers insightful analysis in his book, *The Tax Decade, 1981–1990* (1992), stressing the influence of the changing economic environment on tax policy.

THE INFRASTRUCTURE

William R. Childs

Any economy, whether local, urban, regional, national, or international, contains within its overall structure an infrastructure. Although an infrastructure is often taken for granted (*infra* connotes below or inferior as well as within), it supports the basic exchanges of products and services and thereby enables the economy to function. In the twentieth century, the infrastructure of the United States has supported a remarkable expansion of the largest national economy in the world.

Scholars of infrastructure usually focus on the physical structures of energy, communications, and transport systems within and between urban areas, and on the policies behind the construction of these structures. Other urban services, such as water and waste removal, are sometimes included. This essay adds housing to the list, since residential construction and related policies interact with and support energy, communications, and transport systems.

Infrastructures encourage expansion of business enterprise, enhance national wealth, and improve living standards. In the twentieth century, the industrialized nations have experienced a mix of successes and failures in these infrastructure-related areas. For example, at the end of this century, France has a fine passenger-train system that is not fully utilized and a highly touted computerized telecommunications system that cannot easily be adapted to innovations. Japan also has efficient high-speed rail service, but its highway system is badly clogged with excess traffic and its housing falls far short of the standard one would expect of an economic superpower.

The first section of this essay compares the factors behind American infrastructure development with those of other industrial nations. The second section reviews the evolution of the American infrastructure up to the twentieth century. The bulk of the essay then traces the policies behind and statistical results of infrastructure development during three periods: 1900 to 1940, World War II, and 1945 to the present.

Private enterprise has constructed most of the American infrastructure, but government aid in some form has always contributed to the process. In the twentieth century, government promotion has increased. The American infrastructure has evolved in an ad hoc manner, without overall direction and coordination, in large measure because of American ideological commitment to private enterprise and aversion to government planning. Perhaps because of this uncoordinated mixed private-public pattern, the infrastructure has been flexible and resilient in responding to economic changes. Although not all Americans have shared in the increased living standards (some indeed have been systematically excluded), business expansion and increased national wealth have benefited a growing number of Americans throughout most of the century.

FACTORS OF INFRASTRUCTURE DEVELOPMENT

Four forces—geographic size, population density, political economy, and technology—drive infrastructure developments.

The first two, geography and population, shape the scale and scope of a national infrastructure. Comparisons of the geographic sizes and population densities of economic competitors can be revealing (table 1).

The United States constitutes about 7 percent of the world's total area. It is less than one-half the size of the former Soviet Union, nearly twice as large as Europe, and twenty-five times the size of Japan. The United Kingdom is about equal in size to Indiana plus Illinois; France would fit inside Texas; and the former West Germany would fit inside North and South Dakota. The United Kingdom, France, Japan, and Germany together would fit inside Alaska, with nearly 70,000 square miles left over. Mexico is only slightly larger than Alaska, Arkansas, and Louisiana combined. Japan could fit inside Ohio, New York, and Pennsylvania, and is smaller than Montana.

Table 1.   FIVE INDUSTRIAL COUNTRIES COMPARED, 1990

Country	Area, Millions of Square Miles	Population, Millions	Population Density, Persons per Square Mile
United States	3.60	250	69
Soviet Union	8.60	291	34
China	3.70	1,120	302
Canada	3.80	26	7
Japan	0.14	124	860

SOURCE: *Statistical Abstract of the United States* (1991).

Japan's 860 persons per square mile seems to contrast sharply with America's 69. But some areas of the United States support much heavier population densities than others. The density of the Northeast's Boston–New York–Washington corridor resembles that of Japan. But Ohio and Texas, each with a substantial total population, have very much lower population densities than does Japan. Thus, infrastructures will develop differently in the Northeast than in the Midwest and Southwest. Generally different ratios of geographic size to population totals shape national infrastructures differently.

The quality, quantity, and availability of natural resources, the accessibility of natural routes to other markets, and the pace of population increase also vary from one country to another and affect infrastructure development. Most of America's competitors have a smaller geographic base, fewer or lower quality natural resources, and many more or else many fewer people. The sheer size of America's land mass and the vast amount of it that is suitable for agriculture and human habitation contrast sharply with other nations. Australia, the former Soviet Union, and Canada consist of much land—desert and frozen tundra—that is simply not conducive to agricultural pursuits or city building.

The third force is political economy. As the twentieth century comes to a close, policy analysts and the media are drawing attention to America's infrastructure and how it might develop in the twenty-first century. This discussion has continued debates that were begun during the formative years of the republic, two hundred years ago. Alexander Hamilton and Thomas Jefferson represent differing American views of that early period toward political economy, or government promotion and regulation of the economy. *Internal improvements* was the eighteenth- and nineteenth-century term for infrastructure. Discussions on this subject, taking place as they have within a political economy dedicated to enhancing private capitalist enterprise and democratic decision making, have centered on striking the proper balance between private and public contributions. While private enterprise has dominated economic development throughout American history, local, state, and national governments have contributed significantly to the process.

Most other industrialized nations have approached infrastructure policy in a very different manner from the American pattern. Either the national government has owned and managed most elements of the infrastructure, or government and business have closely cooperated with one another to plan and construct infrastructures. In the American experience, by contrast, antagonisms between business and government and among businesses have prevented the emergence of coherent and coordinated economic and industrial policies.

Additionally, Americans have had access to abundant resources and for most of their history have remained relatively aloof from conflicts in other regions of the world. They have been free to improve their standards of living and create great national wealth in ways that have consumed a disproportionate share of the world's natural resources. One way in which Americans have been more intensive consumers of natural resources is in their consumption of energy (table 2). In the United States, fewer people use more energy to produce the largest domestic market in the world.

These numbers also reveal a positive trend: Americans have been wasting less and producing more. During the last third of the twentieth century, American values have been changing. Some social critics have suggested that this reflects a period of transformation from abundance to scarcity. Whether that is the primary force or even true (at various times the twentieth-century world economy has been awash in surpluses of petroleum and thirsty for new supplies even as abundant coal sources wait to be mined), or whether Americans have become embarrassed by their abundance, is arguable. The point is that values have been changing and that this has affected the political economy of infrastructure.

Table 2. ENERGY CONSUMPTION AND POPULATION AS PERCENTAGES OF WORLD TOTALS

Country	Energy Consumption, Percent				Population, Percent, 1990
	1960	1970	1980	1988	
United States	37.1	34.4	27.7	24.5	4.7
Japan	2.4	5.2	5.1	4.8	2.2
Europe	26.5	26.7	25.1	21.9	9.4
South America	2.0	2.2	2.9	3.0	5.6

SOURCE: *Statistical Abstract of the United States* (1991).

Some scholars have argued that geography, population, and political economy do not shape infrastructure developments as much as the fourth force, technology, does. They view technology as an independent variable that is transferable across national boundaries. In this view, infrastructures are machine-like and develop in similar spatial and temporal patterns in all countries. This essay suggests, in contrast, that technology depends on and interacts with the other factors.

THE EVOLUTION OF THE AMERICAN INFRASTRUCTURE

Modern national economies function through much more extensive, complex, and interconnected infrastructures than did ancient civilizations. In the United States, the necessity for and the ability to construct large-scale systems appeared during the nineteenth century. Population increased from 31 million in 1860 to nearly 92 million in 1910. Industrialists adopted major transformations in energy, communications, and transport systems to serve the need for increased power and speed in manufacturing and distribution. Before mid-century, they used coal as the primary energy source, a rudimentary but efficient mail system for communication, and canals and rivers for transportation, to fashion a growing urban-national infrastructure. But only when they adopted the railroads and the telegraph and telephone were they able to create an internal national market, which soon extended American manufacturing and commercial activities around the world.

From the industrial-driven base, Americans shaped the urban-national infrastructure to serve the consumer culture that has marked much of the twentieth century. Especially after 1910, a new generation of primary energy systems and innovations in communication and transportation filled in gaps left by the industrializing process. The basic urban-industrial connection remained, but became more complicated. Population growth shifted from the older developed areas to the newly developing regions of the South, Southwest, and West. The flexibility of the American infrastructure accommodated these changes, sustained national mobilization during two world wars, and supported the emergence of the United States into a position of economic dominance and political leadership in the post–World War II world.

All of this evolved through choices made in the economic markets and in local and national political arenas. Significantly, Americans constructed their infrastructure without the benefit of the bureaucratic legacy which underlay the mercantile experience of older established nation states like England and France and of Japan, with its more recently developing economic potential. American systems builders first drew from and improved designs that had been developed in the United Kingdom and continental Europe during the eighteenth and nineteenth centuries. The American mixture of private-public policy making and a growing complexity in the interactions between social and technological forces in the political economy shaped the twentieth-century United States infrastructure in ways different from the European and industrial antecedents.

THE INFRASTRUCTURE AT THE TURN OF THE CENTURY

In the late nineteenth century, more American businesses changed their operations to serve the growing consumer markets in the cities and the countryside. Mail-order catalog firms and urban department stores, for example, had to respond quickly to sudden shifts in consumer tastes, which they themselves were simultaneously helping to shape. This required more production, faster communication, and quicker transportation. Electricity and natural gas were cleaner, more powerful, and more versatile than coal-steam power. The telephone offered businesses even more opportunities to control fast-changing business conditions than did the telegraph. By the 1910s the internal-combustion engine, fueled by petroleum (the emerging primary energy source), enabled motor trucks to begin supplanting horse-drawn delivery wagons in the cities and the surrounding countryside. The interaction of these innovations with older systems and other innovations to come (airplane, radio) underlies much of the history of the infrastructure.

Between 1890 and 1920, American cities grew tremendously. Increased numbers of immigrant laborers, an emerging middle class of business managers, and a growing number of clerks and secretaries accounted for the growth and the new emphasis on consumerism. By 1920, a majority of the nearly 106 million Americans lived in urban areas. As their wages improved, white-collar workers and skilled laborers moved away from the crowded urban cores into outlying suburban areas. This in turn created demand for expanded housing construction and the extension of urban transit and other services.

City governments, having won reforms that released them from longstanding state government controls, spent heavily on infrastructure construction from the mid-1890s to about 1914. Municipal construction and management supplanted the older, privately run transit, water, and refuse systems that had predominated in nineteenth-century American cities. With the rise in expenditures came some efforts to plan and coordinate services, but the dominant trend was growth that followed market forces. New infrastructures appeared first in business centers, then in upper-class neighborhoods, followed by middle-class and eventually lower-middle-class areas. Rural areas and poor urban neighborhoods lagged far behind.

There were important exceptions to the trend toward municipal ownership and management of urban services. One was housing, which remained an essentially private enterprise well into the twentieth century. Building-and-loan associations, which appeared before the Civil War, enabled workers to save for downpayments on houses costing between $1,000 and $5,000 in 1900. Commercial banks, beginning hesitantly in the 1890s, but participating more avidly after 1915, offered short-term mortgages. Consequently, home ownership increased, from 38 percent of single-family dwellings in 1910 to 64 percent in 1987 (table 3).

Generally, housing trends during this period reflected unfettered market forces at work. At the turn of the century, many cities began requiring that certain standards be met in construction of multifamily dwellings, but often these laws were not enforced. Only when the Great Depression undermined longstanding underpinnings of housing construction and finance did the industry request government help. Nationally funded subsidies and tax policies have since promoted private construction. Private and public funds spent to construct multi-family housing projects for poor Americans, however, have remained a small percentage of housing investments throughout the century.

Other exceptions to municipal ownership and management of infrastructures in 1910 could be found in the new energy and communication systems. These services not only enhanced the quality of urban life, but also connected city dwellers to the rest of the national economy. Electricity, fuel oil, and natural gas competed to supplant coal as the primary energy source for motive power, lighting, heating, and cooking. (Electric power, of course, relied largely on older power sources, water and coal, to run the steam engines—and, later, the steam turbines—that created the electricity.)

While private investment and management of electric power systems have remained the rule throughout the century, the debate over whether electric power systems should be public or private continued well into the 1930s. Private and industrial electric power plants represented 97 percent of total production in 1920. Over the next half-century, municipal, national, and cooperative ventures whittled away the previous nearly complete dominance of private power. Still, in 1987, private and industrial ownership totaled 78.8 percent (table 4).

Electricity had been touted in the late nineteenth century as a technology that would disperse industry and population across the nation and thus eliminate many problems associated with crowded cities. In

Table 3.   OWNER-OCCUPIED AND RENTER-OCCUPIED HOUSING UNITS (NONFARM), PERCENT, 1910–1991

Year	Owner-Occupied	Renter-Occupied
1910	38	62
1920	41	59
1930	46	54
1940	41	59
1950	53	47
1970	62	38
1987	64	36
1991	64	36

Sources: *Historical Statistics of the United States* (1976); *Statistical Abstract of the United States* (1991, 1994).

Table 4. ELECTRIC ENERGY: POWER-PLANT OWNERSHIP
AND PRODUCTION OF ELECTRICITY, 1920–1990

| Year | Electric Ownership, Percent of Total Production | | | Total Production, Billions of kw/h |
	Private and Industrial	Cooperative and Municipal	Federal and Other	
1920	97	2.4	0.6	57
1930	96	3	1	115
1940	91	3	5	180
1950	84	4	12	389
1960	79	5	16	844
1970	79	6	15	1,640
1980	78[a]	12	10	2,286
1987	79[a]	13	8	2,572
1990	78	13	8	2,808

[a] 1980, 1987, and 1990 numbers are for investor-owned utilities.
SOURCES: *Historical Statistics of the United States* (1975); *Statistical Abstract of the United States* (1990, 1994).

fact, the opposite happened. For example, in Chicago Samuel Insull and the technicians he hired developed an efficient system of electric generation—the largest in the world in 1910—that attracted more concentration of industrial activity to the Chicago area, not less. Urban-based industry has used more electricity than have either residential or commercial establishments throughout the century; not until 1969 did the combined use by residential and commercial establishments exceed consumption by industry, which has remained concentrated in the cities.

For petroleum and its uses, the 1910s marked a time of transition. Kerosene, machine oils, and natural gas for urban street lighting had sustained the formative years of the oil and gas industry. By 1910, however, electricity was supplanting kerosene and natural gas for lighting. Crude-oil producers turned to refining gasoline to serve the new automobiles. Natural-gas firms encountered a more troubled transition, and development of large-scale gas fields and pipeline systems lay years in the future.

The regulation of municipal services and other industrial enterprises, which began in the late nineteenth century, greatly affected the evolutionary patterns of these enterprises during the twentieth century. The new urban infrastructures, or utilities, were capital intensive. Before service could begin, large amounts of investment were required to construct production plants and install distribution lines. Because utilities operated most efficiently if developed through large-scale business structures, they tended to be monopolies—and American ideology generally abhors monopoly and concentrated power of any kind. Consumers demanded protection from mo-

nopolistic practices. Thus, regulatory bodies (city councils, state boards) began to monitor the utilities. These agencies adjudicated consumer complaints arising from private management decisions concerning service and rates. (Because local and state governments granted charters and rights of eminent domain to the utilities, they could, following Anglo-American legal traditions, regulate private enterprise.)

Some Americans in 1910 preferred that the government own and manage the new electric and natural gas utilities, and a few municipal governments in fact did just this. Even here, however, fears of concentrated economic power, coupled with lobbying by private utility managers who distrusted municipal controls, led to the establishment of state agencies that regulated both the municipally owned and privately owned utilities. National ownership and management of utility enterprises did not exist in 1910. The national government did not become directly involved until the 1930s.

Although they are clearly a form of transportation, pipelines are best understood within the context of the economic development of the oil and natural gas industries. At the turn of the century, one large firm, Standard Oil of New Jersey, controlled 90 percent of the 6,800 miles of interstate crude-oil pipelines. In 1906, in large measure as a response to Standard's position, the national government extended supervisory controls over interstate pipelines. Yet, national regulation of pipelines did not restrict private investment and development to the extent found in the natural gas industry or railways (discussed below). Instead, the discovery of new fields quickly undermined Standard's dominance.

In 1910 the telephone was evolving rapidly into regional markets connected to national and international markets. The telephone (wire transmission of voice) represented a logical extension of the telegraph (wire transmission of data—words, numbers), which had grown alongside the railways. The telephone increased the speed and accuracy with which communication took place, not only within business districts and between neighborhoods, but also across regional and national markets. In 1899, there were 13 telephones per 1,000 people. By 1910 that had increased to 82 per 1,000, and Bell Telephone companies handled on the average day 18,000 local calls and 602 long distance calls (independent firms handled 17,000 local and 260 long distance calls). In 1920, 35 percent of American households had a telephone; this figure rose to 90 percent by the 1970s.

The telephone, like electricity and natural gas (but for different reasons), became a private utility subject to government regulation. Managers of the largest telephone utility, AT&T, shrewdly encouraged the view that the national telephone system was a natural monopoly that required national regulation. Under government regulation, the telephone company rapidly expanded, free of distracting competitors.

The most prominent aspect of the national infrastructure in 1910 was the railway network, consisting of 352,000 miles of track. The railroads had spurred industrial development and urban and suburban growth. In the nineteenth century, local, state, and national government had encouraged railway construction through charters, rights of eminent domain, and land grants. But, contrary to patterns in other countries, early railway construction occurred primarily through private investment and management.

Like urban utilities, railways were extremely capital intensive. Seven railway systems emerged from stages of competition, combination, and consolidation in the late nineteenth and early twentieth centuries to comprise the bulk of the national network in 1910. Although in great need of capital to fund refurbishment of the systems, the railways appeared to have a good future ahead of them. They were the transport mode of choice for most manufactured goods, and for raw and processed agricultural products. They had a lucrative express business and a growing passenger service. They were, however, constrained in their ability to respond rapidly to changing economic and demographic trends. Physically, it was difficult to move old track or build new track to meet new consumer trends. Government regulation also restrained the railways. Begun in the

states in the 1870s and at the national level in the late 1880s, railway regulation had by 1910 evolved to the point that most important management decisions were made only after negotiations with regulatory commissions had been completed.

In fact, the railroads in 1910 represented a mature industry during a period of basic transformation in the national economy. Their managers struggled with a variety of problems in addition to regulation. The national government supported an old technology (water transport) and new ones as well (buses and trucks). The usual restraints found in mature industries (management and labor resistance to change) also hindered effective responses. While theoretically the new transport technologies (especially trucking) could have been integrated with the railways, and while there was some movement to coordinate the different transport modes to ensure that each one performed the tasks for which it was best suited, integration and coordination came about haphazardly and infrequently. Partly in consequence, the private railways lost much of their high-valued freight to trucks by 1940 and nearly all of the passenger services to automobiles, buses, and airlines by 1970.

By the 1910s, most of the basic innovations and the general outlines of government policy that supported infrastructure development for the first half of the twentieth century were in place. Housing was expanding into the suburbs. Pipelines and wires connected new energy sources to manufacturing and urban centers, and communication was enhanced by telephones (and soon, radio transmission). Municipalities controlled transit, water, and refuse systems. Meanwhile, local subsidies and state supervision supplemented the private ownership and management of other utilities. The national government became more involved, mainly after 1930, but it engaged in far less direct investment and control than did governments in other industrialized nations. A mixed private-public system, with more emphasis on the private than the public, formed the context of infrastructure development in the United States.

THE INFRASTRUCTURE, 1910–1940

Growth in population, from nearly 92 million in 1910 to nearly 132 million in 1940, underlay the growing consumer economy. Refinements in existing infrastructures and development of new technologies interacted with this demographic growth. Private, municipal, and state contributions funded most urban and national systems until the 1930s. The national government contributed minimal financial aid and ineffectively attempted to coordinate standards. Beginning in the Depression decade and continuing through World War II and beyond, the national government took a more active role.

The increased national role resulted in part from unprecedented economic shocks brought on by the succession of World War I, a sharp postwar depression (1920–1921), followed by nearly a decade of prosperity (1921–1929) and then a decade of wide and deep depression (1930–1940). Growing awareness that local and state resources could not meet new modern problems and that prosperity was tied to the international economy led Americans, in a halting fashion, to engage the national government in economic policy making more than ever before. Yet the national government never planned and coordinated the economy. Attempts to coordinate individual systems were made, but most of these failed.

American involvement in World War I greatly affected developments in the U.S. infrastructure for the rest of the century. In some cities, the war required vast new housing. In many others, the war exposed inadequate terminal facilities and street systems. Nationally, the war spurred regionalization of electric power, expansion of petroleum production and telecommunications, and extension of state and national highway development. Although the war highlighted the centrality of the railways in the economy, it also furnished a glimpse of the future importance of trucks and airplanes.

In urban America after 1910, increased paving of streets, extension of streetcar lines, conversion from coal to electric and natural gas energy production, and expansion of telephone services reflected the interaction of new technologies with changing demographics and the economic shift to consumerism. Changes in transportation and energy usage reflected changing standards of health from that which had marked early industrialism in American cities. Waste from horses, plus smoke from coal-fired stoves, furnaces, and manufacturing plants, had made life in the city unhealthy and at times unbearable. When people improved their incomes, they often moved to the suburbs, away from the sources of these pollutants. They brought with them new conveniences based on relatively less-polluting technologies.

With the automobile becoming more available to middle-class and working people, and with the motor truck replacing horse-drawn wagons on urban streets, traffic congestion became a major problem. Cities had been designed for pedestrians and horses, not autos and trucks. Early responses included improving access between suburban homes and central

business districts by constructing parkways, which were multilaned roads with access limited mainly to the endpoints. These roads reflected attempts of designers to enhance urban life by channeling travel through "rural" areas, but they benefited mainly the upper classes who could afford to live in the suburbs.

Most improvements in urban motor transportation involved hard-surfacing of existing roads, which helped eliminate congestion problems in the worst weather, but did not solve many other urban problems. The exception to this general pattern occurred in the West, where urban centers were only then being constructed and where the automobile influenced new designs for urban highways. In most urban areas, bonds, taxes, and special assessments funded municipal expenditures for improved urban roads. Between 1910 and 1930, only expenditures for education exceeded those for urban road development.

Mass-transit systems had enhanced intra-urban transportation since the 1830s. Despite the paving of municipal and rural roads and the growth in automobile sales, mass transit within and between urban areas remained an important portion of the nation's transit system for the first half of the twentieth century. The streetcar facilitated movement between home, work, retail establishments, and amusement parks. First horse-drawn, then electric streetcar (trolley) systems spread throughout urban neighborhoods and contiguous suburbs. Nearly 30,000 miles of streetcar tracks existed in 1903. More people rode trolleys in the 1920s than ever before, with ridership totals reaching a peak in 1923 at 15.7 billion riders. Trolley patronage only slowly declined as buses and autos gained prominence. Meanwhile, interurban railways connected cities. Private firms also operated most of this track mileage. Commuter track mileage peaked in 1934 at 28,500 miles. Surface railways carried 7.5 billion passengers in 1936 and this ridership reached its peak in 1944 at 9.5 billion.

These mass-transit systems became less important, however, because financial scandals and new technologies created problems that private managers could not overcome without help from public officials, which was not forthcoming. Those officials supported hard-surfacing of streets and rural roads, which enabled the automobile's cousin, the motor bus, to contribute to the demise of streetcars and interurban railways. Between the mid-1920s and the mid-1950s, a General Motors subsidiary assumed operation of over 100 streetcar lines across the nation and replaced the streetcars with buses. Motor buses increased ridership from 404 million in 1922, to 2.5 billion in 1930, to a peak 10.2 billion in 1949. The automobile did not fully overtake mass transit as the transport mode of choice until after World War II.

In the area of housing, 100 percent of the yearly values of new residential unit construction between 1915 and 1929, except for a brief government program in 1918–1919, was traceable to private investment. The percentage of owner-occupied homes increased from 38.4 percent in 1910 to 46 percent by 1930. Municipal governments, through extension of transit, water, and other services to outlying areas, encouraged suburban development.

A minority of real estate brokers, beginning in the 1910s, had pushed their industry to give more attention to the design of new communities. Specifications for location and widths of streets and placement of underground utility services marked this private-public program in urban-suburban design. The coordinated planning idea met much resistance, however, and was not widely adopted. With more government aid to housing in the 1930s came increased support for planning, but the pre-1920s trend toward ad hoc development that followed real estate market forces predominated. The few planned communities actually built benefited only upper and upper-middle income wage earners.

Even though private investment continued to dominate housing construction, the Depression decade marked a revolution of sorts in national government involvement in housing. Two programs, one targeted for private and another for public housing, were initiated under the crisis conditions. The Home Owners Loan Corporation (HOLC), an emergency program (1933–1936), furnished short-term help to homeowners facing foreclosure. Together, the HOLC and the Federal Housing Authority (FHA), which Congress created under the 1934 National Housing Act, changed the way in which large numbers of Americans purchased houses. Instead of large downpayments and balloon notes, eligible home buyers could now put very little down and pay a long-term, low-interest mortgage. The differences between the lower FHA mortgage rates and the market rate were paid by the government. The white middle class in the suburbs benefited most from this program. Discriminatory aspects of the FHA program diverted funds from inner cities and often withheld them from black Americans. Public policy thus accelerated housing construction in the suburbs and the migration of whites from the inner cities.

The FHA joined other programs—the Federal Home Loan Bank Board (1932), the Federal Savings and Loan Insurance Corporation (1933), and the Federal National Mortgage Association (1938)—as national aids to banking and construction firms engaged in the housing industry. And they aided suburban development in the way they distributed the funds. All these New Deal programs, however, had insufficient impact in the 1930s. The Great Depression was so severe that nonfarm housing units occupied by owners actually decreased from 46 percent in 1930 to 41.4 percent in 1940. But these housing policies begun under the New Deal had profound effects during the post–World War II period.

Between 1910 and 1940, Americans increasingly equipped their homes with new consumer items, many of which operated best with electricity (radios, irons, refrigerators), or natural gas (cooking stoves and heating furnaces). Initially more expensive and more complex than their coal-fired predecessors, electric power and natural gas services expanded because they offered cleaner operations that reduced pollution and because they were advertised as "modern conveniences." Use of electricity and natural gas did seem to improve the health of urban dwellers. During the 1919 flu epidemic, hospitals heated with natural gas suffered lower rates of patient deaths than those heated with coal or wood. Overall, these energy utilities diffused in a similar pattern: first, they served inner-city business districts, then affluent neighborhoods, and finally all sections of the city and outlying suburbs. Rural Americans did not receive these services in large numbers until the national government encouraged expansion in the late 1930s and 1940s.

Increased investment resulted in a sustained increase in production of electric energy until 1929. Large investments in the 1920s underwrote the construction of regional systems. Electric utilities suffered reduced investments during the 1930s, in large measure because of reduced industrial activity and perhaps as a response to disclosure of some financial chicanery. New investment did occur, though at lower levels. Electricity was needed for some enterprises that actually expanded during the Depression, such as oil production, which required electric motors to operate pumping machinery. Electric energy production began to decline in 1930, hitting a low of 99 billion kw/h in 1932, and did not recover to 1929 levels until 1935 (119 billion kw/h). (See table 5 for 1915–1990 private investment expenditures for utilities.)

Ownership patterns of energy production changed only a little; the preponderance of private ownership remained. New competition appeared when the national government sponsored the Tennessee Valley Authority (TVA) in 1933, and rural

Table 5. INVESTMENT EXPENDITURES FOR NEW PRIVATE CONSTRUCTION OF PUBLIC UTILITIES, MILLIONS OF DOLLARS,[a] 1915–1990

Year	Electricity	Natural Gas	Telephone and Telegraph	Petroleum Pipelines
1915[a]	540	250	150	100
1920	750	215	230	100
1925	1,400	550	460	160
1930	1,260	620	800	90
1935	300	170	150	65
1940	870	275	300	90
1945	620	370	250	100
1950	1,880	1,300	570	290
1960	2,000	1,100	1,100	130
1970	5,800	1,700	3,000	300
1980[b]	16,000	5,000	7,800	800
1985[b]	16,000	5,200	8,400	300
1990[b]	12,900	5,400	9,600	400

SOURCE: *Historical Statistics of the United States: Colonial Times to 1970* (1976); *Statistical Abstract of the United States* (1992).
[a] Figures for 1915–1950 in 1957–1959 dollars.
[b] Figures for 1980–1990 in current dollars.

cooperatives and the Bonneville Power Administration later in the decade.

The public power competition, particularly TVA, not only accelerated overall growth patterns, but also inaugurated a new development phase in the evolution of electric light and power. After the 1930s, more and more electric generating systems were tied into regional economic development plans. Dams were constructed not only to generate electricity, but also to improve flood controls, establish recreational facilities, and produce fertilizers for farmers. Thus, as an old infrastructure was maturing, some aspects of it took on new purposes.

Along with these changes in urban and regional utilities came expansion of communication systems. The telephone allowed direct and instantaneous contact between customer, retailer, and producer. It enabled producers to respond quickly to shifts in consumer preferences. Growth of the telephone infrastructure was dramatic (table 6).

Increase in miles of wire tells only part of the story of communications infrastructure development. For instance, it says nothing about radio broadcasting, which had appeared early in the century. World War I highlighted the usefulness of radio broadcasting. Ironically, contrary to the literal meaning of the term *broadcasting*, government officials expected the new technology to be limited to only a few usable bands. In 1912 the national government restricted certain bands for government use only and required licenses for anyone desiring to send radio signals. By 1923, over five hundred licenses had been issued and

many of these were granted to commercial enterprises. Even though the early years of commercial broadcasting focused on local audiences, the idea of nationwide networks of radio stations appeared before it was technically possible to link stations (AT&T was the first to establish a network of stations, in 1926). By 1930, several networks had been established and 3.75 million households had radios. Broadcasters initially resisted sending advertisements over the radio waves because such direct selling appeared unseemly.

The structure of the national broadcast industry, however, forced changes in advertising. As with the utilities, scale economies operated in radio broadcast-

Table 6. TELEPHONE-WIRE INFRASTRUCTURE, 1920–1990

Year	Wire Mileage, Thousands of Miles
1920	30,112
1930	81,128
1940	96,000[a]
1950	153,440
1960	336,470
1970	628,000
1980	1,131,000
1987	1,371,000
1989	1,502,000
1990	1,528,000

[a] Estimated.
SOURCES: *Historical Statistics of the United States* (1976); *Statistical Abstract of the United States* (1991, 1994).

ing. Given the need for advertising to pay operating costs and the numerous local stations involved, station managers and advertising executives preferred dealing with large-scale national networks to arrange for and sell advertising. National ads were more efficient for the radio stations and more effective for national manufacturers and their ad agencies. The radio then became a convenient advertising medium for the consumer society.

By the end of the 1920s, after a complex interaction of technology, economics, and management decisions in the private sector, the communications businesses had been divided into telegraphy (transmission of data over wire); telephony (transmission of voice over wire); and broadcast (transmission of electronic data and voice through the airwaves to all receiving stations). AT&T was not allowed to cross over into data transmission or broadcast services. Instead, it vertically integrated its operation to control all aspects of the voice transmission business, from manufacturing equipment to providing local and long distance services. The national government sanctioned these private agreements in the 1926 Federal Radio Act and in 1928 established the Federal Radio Commission (FRC) to monitor the communications industry. The Federal Communications Commission (FCC) replaced the FRC in 1934.

In deciding whether to grant a request for licenses to broadcast, the FCC was guided by three general values. The commission's decisions reflected the belief in free and open access to information, the desire to serve the local needs of a broadcast station's audience, and the usual American practice of protecting existing businesses from new competition. There was no overall plan, however. In tying itself to local values and to stations already in operation, the FCC tended to restrain the spread of broadcasting and the development of innovations. Even when the technology of radio broadcasting improved and more frequencies became usable, the FCC continued its conservative policy.

National transportation developments also underwent immense changes between 1910 and 1940, with the decade of the 1930s marking a significant transition period. Much of the action focused on surface transportation. The airline industry developed more slowly, even though governments promoted it.

In this period, as throughout American history as a whole, water transport received sustained financial help from the national government. One of the most prominent national programs involved construction of the Panama Canal, which opened in

Table 7.   INTERNAL WATERBORNE TONNAGE AND FEDERAL EXPENDITURES FOR RIVERS AND HARBORS, 1900–1988

Year	Tonnage Transported, Millions of Tons	Federal Expenditures, Millions of Dollars
1900	na	19
1924	352	62
1930	406	74
1940	497	107
1950	651	190
1960	760	801
1970	951	895
1980	1,078	2,229
1988	1,112	3,111

SOURCES: *Historical Statistics of the United States* (1976); *Statistical Abstract of the United States* (1990, 1991).

August 1914. Not only did the government spend monies to improve inland waterways and harbors (usually without charging the water carriers any user fees), it also protected water carriers by restricting competitors' (railways' and trucks') rate decreases to the levels that water carriers charged. Over all, government promotion sustained an infrastructure that had showed signs in the nineteenth century of disappearing altogether in the face of new competition from the faster railroads. The overall record of federal expenditures for waterways is shown in table 7.

Meanwhile, railways in the period 1910 to 1940 faced very severe problems, many of which derived from the maturing of the industry. At first, the railways focused on improving service, especially passenger travel. Success in reducing the weight of trains and the use of diesel-electric locomotives increased speeds to 120 mph. Cross-country service benefited as travel times between cities were reduced by 20 to 40 percent. (In 1930 passenger trains took only three days to travel from New York City to Los Angeles.) Total track miles increased from 352,000 in 1910 to nearly 430,000 in 1930. From that point forward, total mileage decreased. By the middle of the twentieth century, it appeared that railways would not be able to retain their market share, much less expand services. National regulation, competition from trucks and buses, local resistance to abandonment of low-profit service, and lack of coordination with other transport modes led to the relative decline of the railways' profitability and importance to the economy.

The Great Depression exacerbated these developments, as American transportation suffered from overcapacity. Between 1933 and 1936, the federal government attempted to coordinate railway operations, but private management resistance and competition from buses, trucks, and waterways (all of which national policies protected) forestalled efficiency. Buses and trucks, with cartel-like regulation established in 1935, continued to make inroads into railway revenues and to contribute to overcapacity. Congress called for coordination of all competing transport modes in the Transportation Act of 1940, but that did not occur. The entire transportation system would have become more efficient had coordination materialized, but ideological fears of economic concentration, a historical commitment to support all modes of transport, and concerns for alleviating high levels of unemployment undermined the drive for efficiency. (As it turned out, this example of American economic waste proved fortuitous during World War II.)

Development of America's highways, supported by government policies, also contributed to the railroads' decline. Ironically, the initial impetus for improving highways, late in the nineteenth century, had come from farmers and railway executives who wanted better connections between farm and depot. As it turned out, the more highways were surfaced, the more autos and motor trucks appeared to use them. The relative decline of the railroads seemed almost inevitable.

World War I had spurred development of highway transportation modes in two ways. Military use illustrated the commercial applications of the new motor truck, which stimulated manufacturers to increase production. Then, because of the unforeseen early end of the war, a surplus of trucks accumulated in 1919 and were given to state highway departments to use in building roads. Highway construction took place through cooperative relations between the Federal Bureau of Roads and state highway departments. The main emphasis in highway infrastructure development for the next thirty years was building hard-surface rural roads and extending and paving municipal streets.

Although some policy advocates wanted a coordinated approach that would systematically tie urban road and mass transit systems to the national, secondary, and rural road systems, they were unable to effect such a scheme. Professional engineering groups' focus on efficiency in inter-city transportation combined with local and state politics to forestall coordination of urban and highway transportation systems. Despite the lack of centralized planning, however, the upgrading of existing highways created a flexible road system that supported the continued expansion of motor trucking and pleasure car driving.

Most of the highway mileage constructed in the first half of the twentieth century was paid for by user fees (licenses and fuel taxes) collected by state and federal government agencies. In 1916, when federal-aid development began, the states furnished more funds than did the federal government. During the period 1917 to 1921, federal expenditures totaled $95 million (43 percent of the total), the states' expenditures $127 million (57 percent). During the 1920s, total expenditures showed no sustained increase and no substantial change in the sharing of costs. In 1930, the federal government spent $100 million (42 percent), the states $137 million (58 percent). The designated federal highway system grew only from 169,000 miles in 1923 to 194,000 miles in 1930.

Expenditures for federal-aid highways increased during the Depression decade, though the year-to-year pattern was erratic and totals were less than one might expect, given the need for jobs. The important change came in the division of funds between the national and state governments, with the former taking on more of the burden (table 8). In 1933 the national government spent $223 million (84 percent) to the states' $41 million (16 percent); in 1937, of a total of $521 million, the national government spent $348 million (67 percent, down from 1933, but still greater than in 1930) and the states $173 million (33 percent). The total number of miles designated for the federal system increased to 227,000.

Hard-surfacing and the gradual development of a national system of highways for the most part followed preestablished roadways, which had developed from the earliest turnpike and railway routes. The improved roadways encouraged increased use of autos and trucks, even during the Depression. By the end of the 1930s, in fact, the highway system could no longer efficiently handle the increased number of motor vehicles that used it. If motor vehicle numbers continued to increase, the policy of improving existing roadways would have to change; new roads would have to be laid out.

In contrast, air travel was slow to develop. The airplane had been introduced in the first decade of the century. Identified as a potential component in modern warfare during World War I, in the 1920s and 1930s it became an object of fascination in American culture. In 1930, just as the railways reduced to three days the time of travel between New York City and Los Angeles, the airlines flew the distance in thirty-six hours. Even then, the airlines languished, unable to attract enough revenues to offset costs.

Table 8.   FEDERAL-AID HIGHWAY SYSTEMS CONSTRUCTION AND FUNDING[a] AND TOTAL ROAD MILEAGE, 1917–1970

Year	Miles Completed During Year,[b] Thousands	Source of Funds, Millions of Dollars[c]		Total Miles Designated as Part of Federal System, Thousands	Total Miles Surfaced and Unsurfaced, Thousands
		National	State		
1917–1921	13	95	130	na	3,160
1925	11	100	120	180	3,246
1930	10	100	140	190	3,259
1931	16	230	100	200	3,291
1940	11	150	120	235	3,287
1945	3	80	25	300	3,319
1950	20	390	360	640	3,313
1960	21	2,270	990	870	3,546
1970	11	3,520	1,110	895	3,730

[a] Includes primary system throughout, secondary systems beginning in 1942, and interstate system beginning in 1951.
[b] Miles completed during year includes new and rebuilt.
[c] Funds actually spent.
SOURCE: *Historical Statistics of the United States: Colonial Times to 1970* (1976).

Many characteristics of the airline industry paralleled those of other infrastructures: it was capital intensive and required the hiring of very skilled labor. Like water transport, the airline industry existed in large measure because government subsidized and promoted it. Local and state governments furnished the airports (not until the 1970s were the airlines required to pay user fees). Initially the national government subsidized airline development with lucrative mail contracts. Then, in 1938, Congress established the Civil Aeronautics Authority (later, Civil Aeronautics Board, or CAB) to exert national regulatory control over the emerging airline industry. The result was an oligopolistic, cartel-like industry that was stable but sluggish in growth.

Joining airlines, trucks, and autos in hastening the decline of the railroads between 1910 and 1940 was the petroleum pipeline. As the petroleum industry expanded during the 1920s, so too did its underground transport network. Pipelines were extremely capital intensive. Some pipeline companies were subsidiaries of petroleum production firms; others were common carriers selling their service to more than one company. This conflict between private firms and common carriers, together with the fact that pipelines depended on state-granted franchises and rights of eminent domain, led to regulation. Before the 1930s, pipelines were subject mostly to state regulations. The expansion of petroleum production during the Depression decade, however, prompted the national government to increase its regulatory vigilance, as it did with railways, trucks, and airlines. Even then, government regulation of oil pipelines

did not interfere very much with private-sector decisions.

Between 1910 and 1940, the evolution of the overall industrial and consumer infrastructures took place against a shifting economic background: first war, then sharp postwar recession, then a decade of prosperity, and finally a decade of deep depression. Geographic and population forces, along with new technologies, fostered widespread expansion of new energy, communication, and transportation systems, even as some older ones declined in importance. National government involvement was much more apparent in 1940 than it had been in 1910, but this did not signal a reversal of American reliance on private investment. Nor did it result in coordinated policies or less wasteful developments. Government promotion and regulation favored some infrastructures over others (electric over natural gas; water, autos, trucks, and airlines over railways). But this was the result of democratic politics, not responses to technological determinism or commitment to systematic coordination within and between infrastructure types. National policy was not forcefully directed from Washington.

WORLD WAR II

In conjunction with the New Deal, World War II marked a widespread acceptance among Americans of more national government involvement in the economy. The national budget increased from less than $10 billion in 1941 to over $98 billion by the end of the war (current dollars). Government respon-

Table 9. FEDERAL HOUSING-FINANCE PROGRAMS AND NEW PUBLIC RESIDENTIAL CONSTRUCTION, IN MILLIONS OF DOLLARS PER YEAR, 1935–1988[a]

Year	Loans[b] FHA[c]	Loans[b] VA[d]	Advances Outstanding at Federal, Home Loan Banks[e]	Value of New Public Residential Construction
1935	96		87	9
1940	800		200	200
1945	500	200	200	80
1950	3,600	3,000	800	350
1955	3,200	7,200	1,400	270
1960	5,300	2,000	2,000	700
1965	8,100	2,700	6,000	600
1970	11,400	3,400	10,600	1,100
	Mortgage Debt Outstanding Secured by Federal and Related Agencies[e]			
1980	34,000			1,650
1988	251,000			1,500

[a] Figures for 1935–1970 in 1957–1959 dollars; figures for 1980–1988 in constant (1982) dollars.
[b] Loans made with government agency guarantee.
[c] Includes new and existing homes and projects; FHA, Federal Housing Authority.
[d] VA, Veterans Administration.
[e] Loans outstanding at end of year.
SOURCES: *Historical Statistics of the United States* (1976); *Statistical Abstract of the United States* (1992).

sibility for macroeconomic issues, such as controlling inflation, and for microeconomic programs, including promotion of old and new industries, expanded almost across the board. Government spending for mobilization raised the economy out of the Depression.

For the most part, the existing infrastructures proved adequate to the needs of wartime mobilization. The overcapacity of the 1930s became a blessing in the 1940s. In housing, petroleum pipelines, and telecommunications, prewar patterns accelerated. In some cases, however, mobilization interrupted prewar trends. After the war, the railway industry's future did not look as bright as it had during the war. Mass transit reached its peak in 1944 and helped hide from view the inadequacy of the highway system. For trucking, buses, and water carriers, the war experience increased revenues, but decreased market share.

The national government assumed more responsibility than it had during World War I for furnishing housing in areas unprepared for mobilization. The South, Midwest, and West Coast benefited the most from construction of vast military barracks and housing for workers. National funds also aided municipalities in constructing city administration buildings. Private investment in housing still predominated, but national government programs stimulated housing activity as well. This national commitment continued after the war (table 9). The 1930s decline in the number of owner-occupied housing units was re-

versed. National public housing programs existed, but they embraced only a few and were ineffective in helping low-income Americans improve their economic or social status.

Wartime necessity led to a major national government contribution to the petroleum pipeline industry and a consequent shift in its structure. In 1941 and 1942, shipments of petroleum, vital to the war effort, were lost to Axis submarine attacks along the Atlantic and Gulf coasts. In addition to coordinating more railway and truck shipments, the national government between 1942 and 1944 sponsored the construction of two major pipelines. They transformed the method by which petroleum and natural gas were delivered to the East Coast. At the end of 1941, only 4 percent of the oil delivered to the East Coast had been delivered by pipeline. By 1945, the Big Inch pipeline (1,254 miles long) carried 50 percent of all crude oil from east Texas to the East Coast. The Little Inch (1,475 miles long) carried gasoline and other refined products from the Gulf Coast to the East Coast. After the war, the government sold both lines to private companies, which converted both to natural gas pipelines. This vastly improved the potential growth of natural gas in the postwar period. Government regulation, however, prevented the industry from meeting that potential (table 10).

Electric light and power systems proved adequate to support the war. Massive amounts of electric power required for the atomic bomb project

Table 10. PETROLEUM AND NATURAL GAS PIPELINE
INFRASTRUCTURE, 1921–1987

Year	Petroleum Miles of Pipeline	Barrels Transported, Millions Crude	Refined	Natural Gas, Miles of Pipeline
1921	55,260	na	na	na
1933	93,724	538	29	66,000[a]
1940	100,156	890	72	310,670[b]
1950	128,589	1,500	300	387,470
1960	151,968	2,200	900	632,130
1970	175,735	3,600	2,400	913,000[c]
1980	172,700	6,400	4,200	1,052,000[c]
1987	167,900	6,300	4,900	1,151,000[c]

[a] Estimated.
[b] Figure is for 1945.
[c] Includes field and gathering, transmission, and distribution.
SOURCES: *Historical Statistics of the United States* (1976); *Statistical Abstract of the United States* (1962, 1990).

prompted expansion of TVA's production. TVA and other federal projects increased production from 8.6 billion kw/h in 1940 to a high point in 1944 of 28.9 billion kw/h. Total utility and industrial production increased from 119 billion kw/h in 1939 to a peak in 1944 of 279.5 billion kw/h.

Technological developments shaped to military needs laid the groundwork for changing the telecommunications infrastructure in the postwar period. Military-induced research and development broadened the use of microwave broadcasting, which was superior to radio and television broadcasting. Microwave broadcasts transmitted more data signals more clearly with less chance of interference. Other technological developments, particularly in computers, also expanded opportunities for postwar telecommunications.

The war experience temporarily reversed the fortunes of the railways and, ironically, presented false signals about future growth. Despite rising labor costs during the war, the railroads' net income remained at high levels through 1945 for both freight and passenger traffic. Railways increased their share of freight hauling from 63 percent of intercity traffic in 1940 to a high point of 73 percent in 1943. Increased load factors in both carload and less-than-carload shipments improved productivity. Government employees traveling about the country, massive troop movements, restrictions on automobile travel through gas rationing, and the prohibition on automobile manufacturing caused an increase in wartime rail passenger business to four times the 1930s levels.

During the war only pipelines received direct government aid; all other transport modes improved volume because of increased war-related business. While trucks lost market share, from 10 percent in 1941 to a low point of 5 percent in 1944, they hauled an all-time high in 1941 of 81 billion ton-miles. The 67 billion ton-miles hauled in 1945 still topped the 62 billion ton-miles in 1940. Inland waterways also lost share, dropping from 17 percent in 1941 to 13 percent in 1943 and 1944, but gained in volume, from 118 billion ton-miles in 1940 to 143 ton-miles in 1945. Oil pipelines, after a drop between 1941 and 1942, from 8.4 percent to 7.7 percent of the market, gained share by 1945, to nearly 12 percent.

Meanwhile, national and state funds spent for highway construction declined. The retrenchment actually began in 1938 and reached a low point in 1945 of only $101 million (75 percent national, 25 percent state). At the same time, wartime responsibilities prompted a growing emphasis on creating a national highway system. The total number of miles designated for the federal highway system increased from 235,000 in 1940 to 368,000 by 1944.

Even before the United States entered the war, trends in airline travel suggested a coming spurt of business growth. In 1940, passenger revenues were twice the mail revenues of airlines. The war further prepared airlines for a postwar boom. The military had trained thousands of pilots and technological developments had improved the speed, size, and comfort of airplanes.

World War II revealed that most American infrastructures were ready for very heavy demands, despite the uncoordinated programs of the preceding de-

1344

cades. Those that were prepared, particularly the railways and highways, survived for some time with reduced investments. Those that were not, such as housing and petroleum pipelines, were infused with massive government funding. Meanwhile, however, the war experience hid from view transformations under way in the infrastructure mix that not only undergirded but also haunted economic developments during the last half of the twentieth century.

POSTWAR PERIOD TO THE 1990s

The twenty-five year period from 1945 to 1970 was characterized by stupendous economic growth. Pent-up consumer demand from the war years ushered in an age of unprecedented affluence in America. The shifting of jobs and people to the South and West continued. Government policies contributed to a widening of the white middle class and to the celebrated baby boom. The GI bill of 1944, for example, promised to the 16 million veterans and their families educational subsidies, job training programs, and start-up funds for small business enterprises. Infrastructure development followed patterns that had been visible before the war. The major difference was that the national government increased the number of programs and the funding levels. But it still did not coordinate those programs. And private efforts still outstripped government aid.

The twenty-year period that followed, from the early 1970s to the early 1990s, was a much less affluent era. Overall economic growth slowed. Demographic shifts of population increase to the South, Southwest, and West continued. But infrastructure policies in these areas did not always keep pace with the growth. Older urban areas suffered from reduced populations and a smaller tax base as suburbs continued to draw more affluent whites and a growing number of affluent blacks. Highway and housing policies implemented in the 1950s and 1960s encouraged these patterns. In addition, fighting a war in Vietnam and a war on poverty at home in the 1960s and early 1970s strained the national budget. Two energy price shocks (1973, 1979) combined with these other forces to create an extended period of stagflation in which prices and interest rates remained high even as economic growth remained stagnant. In the 1980s, the national debt reached unprecedented levels. In a situation of chronic deficits, national government funds for new construction and maintenance were cut back. Expenditures did not keep pace with inflation or even with the rate of growth of the gross national product. Increases in local and state funding made up some but not all of the reduced federal funds.

Meanwhile, American cultural values underwent some significant changes that led to national policies that, on the one hand, intensified government regulation of business and, on the other hand, reduced government interference in business choices. The civil rights revolution and the environmental movement challenged long-held assumptions that resulted in stepped-up national government regulation of business hiring practices and polluting activities. Even as the national government became more involved in everyday business affairs through these social and environmental controls, it began to lessen its interference in economic choices in the marketplace by deregulating specific infrastructure industries—telecommunications and transportation, and to a lesser degree natural gas.

Despite these changes, and perhaps in response to them, infrastructure policies revealed a flexibility that began to accommodate the changing economy and culture. The adaptations to change were not perfect; they have not solved all the problems. There is certainly much more to do in the twenty-first century.

Housing policies continued prewar trends and took on new urgency with the baby boom. The national population increased from 132 million in 1940 to 250 million in 1990. Planning of suburban communities remained the exception in housing development. White homeowners continued to receive a disproportionate share of FHA funds and highest-income white homeowners received the biggest benefits through mortgage-interest tax exemptions. Veterans Administration loans and FHA loans supported the explosion of middle-class suburbs, which in turn required funds for transport and municipal services.

While Congress reflected some of the revitalized concern for social welfare in America and passed statutes to increase public housing, it never really made a strong commitment in actual funds allocated. The Housing Act of 1949 called for a six-year program in which 135,000 public housing units would be constructed every year, for a total of 810,000 units. Less than one quarter of the proposed total were actually built. By the 1960s, what public housing programs existed were under attack. Critics claimed the projects had been managed inefficiently. More to the point, poor designs, inflation, declining incomes of tenants, confused policy goals, and the absence of programs through which tenants could become homeowners had made public housing unpopular.

The Kennedy administration and, to a greater extent, the Johnson administration attempted to alter the direction of housing policy but with little positive effect. The earlier programs had targeted only the very poorest of the working poor, leaving out those who earned incomes that were over the government-imposed limits, but well below the level required to obtain adequate housing. The new programs targeted those not helped by the FHA, VA, or earlier public housing programs. Johnson succeeded in getting Congress to authorize rent-subsidy programs for these Americans, but the funds actually spent did not help many of those who needed help in achieving the American dream of owning a house.

Housing policy shifted again in the 1970s, but the results matched earlier patterns. Local, state, and national programs offered tax incentives to developers, and local officials were given more flexibility to plan and construct housing for needy Americans. But unforeseen aspects of this shift made it less encompassing than had been intended. Developers built units in the suburbs to house more American elderly than ever before, but mostly white elderly inhabited these new structures; black elderly and young poor Americans of all races were excluded. Tax policies and national-local revenue-sharing subsidies targeted specifically at revitalizing the urban cores helped such cities as Baltimore, Pittsburgh, Atlanta, and Seattle rebuild decimated areas. This gentrification of former slums revitalized some residential and business districts, but displaced the poor who had lived in the slums and left them no place to turn.

Changes in the energy infrastructure proved especially turbulent, yet energy was more flexible and successful in responding to change than was the public housing infrastructure. During the last half of the century, managers of light and power systems faced confusing times. In part, assumptions based on past experience misled the power planners. Utilities projected construction needs based on two assumptions: (1) continued population growth and demand trends and (2) continued cheap energy costs. Neither assumption proved reliable. Demand for electricity did triple between the 1960s and 1990s, as Americans continued to flock to air-conditioned facilities in sunbelt areas and as all-electric homes were constructed. Americans had enjoyed for much of the century the lowest energy costs in the world. After 1970, however, for a multitude of reasons, energy costs increased dramatically. Even though the higher rates remained well below those in most other countries, they still slowed the growth of demand and undermined the need for new construction of power plants. Higher rates led to research in alternative energy sources and to improved conservation programs.

The national government engaged in no new TVA-type projects, but it did encourage research into and expansion of nuclear power plants. But this latest technology did not diffuse throughout the economy as predicted. Numerous cultural and technological problems delayed, and perhaps permanently retarded, the use of nuclear energy. Nuclear power's association with weapons of mass destruction, the unwillingness of industry and government leaders to discuss candidly the real dangers in the technology, the 1979 accident at Three Mile Island in Pennsylvania, and the problem of disposing of spent nuclear fuel have all curtailed its development in the United States. In addition, American competitive ideology, plus numerous regulatory changes in safety requirements, tended to encourage the development of various designs; no one generic nuclear plant design was adopted. Over 100 plants were constructed between 1960 and 1989. Nuclear's percent of total electric utility generation increased from 0.4 percent in 1965 to 11 percent in 1980, and to 20 percent in 1990. Nonetheless, more units had been planned. Cost overruns, brought on by design problems, poor safety programs, government regulations, and inflation, plagued the industry and slowed growth. Numerous plants were abandoned or reconverted to coal-fired or natural gas plants. The loss of investment dollars and the added costs of conversions reverberated throughout the economy.

Meanwhile, natural gas utilities expanded. Between 1946 and 1959, the industry added 350,000 miles of pipelines, which was a 530 percent increase over the mileage constructed during the period 1933–1945. By the 1960s, natural gas had become the nation's sixth largest industry and at last appeared to be fulfilling the promise it had shown for so long. Yet this surge of growth was not to last. Shortages of natural gas supplies appeared in the 1970s. Some utilities could not serve all customers adequately during short-term weather-induced increases in demand such as heat waves and cold snaps.

Government policies tracing back to the late 1930s and private sector mistakes combined to create this crisis. In 1938 Congress had placed natural gas pipelines under the supervision of the Federal Power Commission (FPC). Conflict over the level of rates and over whether state agencies or the FPC had control over those rates created uncertainty. As a result, for the next two decades, expansion of natural gas services was slower than it might otherwise have

Table 11.   ENERGY PRODUCTION: MARKET SHARE OF
ENERGY SOURCES, 1960–1990

Year	Market Share, Percent				Electric Production by Nuclear Plants	Number of Nuclear Plants
	Coal	Petroleum	Natural Gas	Other[a]		
1960	26	36	34	4	na[b]	
1970	23	33	39	5	1.4	18
1980	29	28	34	9	11.0	70
1988	32	26	30	12	19.5	108
1990	33	23	30	14	20.6[c]	111[c]

[a] Includes geothermal, hydro, wind, and solar power, and, in 1960, nuclear.
[b] Nuclear power included in other figure for 1960.
[c] Preliminary.
SOURCE: *Statistical Abstract of the United States* (1991).

been. Because natural gas firms had to locate new sources to ensure continued service, they believed funds for exploration should be included in the rates charged. The question of how expensive it was to locate new sources (not every well drilled yielded gas) pitted the regulators against natural gas companies; the regulators won. The FPC pegged prices too low, which retarded exploration for new natural gas reserves. The private sector mistakenly based long-term gas supply contracts on projections of continued low costs of drilling. But the new gas fields to be discovered lay deeper in the earth, which increased the costs of exploration. Some deregulation of prices and new efforts to encourage use of natural gas in automobiles in the 1980s and early 1990s have brightened the industry's prospects, however.

While natural gas policy haltingly developed and nuclear energy failed to emerge as predicted, oil and gasoline continued to dominate the energy infrastructure mix. Particularly in the Northeast, fuel oil remained a significant source of home heating. And gasoline, of course, powered the automobile culture that symbolized the American consumer culture.

Events in the world political economy after 1945 interacted with domestic energy source patterns to create an energy crisis in the 1970s. Oil supplies in the Mideast, discovered in the 1930s and 1940s, were so huge that, even with transportation costs, a barrel of Mideast oil delivered to the United States cost much less than a barrel of U.S. oil. Given the price difference, oil imports into the United States steadily increased. By the early 1970s, Americans were importing over 50 percent of the crude oil they used. Exploration for domestic reserves of crude declined. In 1973 and again in the late 1970s, political events in the Mideast led to sharp rises in the cost of imported oil. Prices rose and spot shortages disrupted

daily lives. While the higher prices reinvigorated the domestic petroleum infrastructure, they also contributed to the stagflation that had gripped the economy.

Meanwhile, reflecting a flexibility inherent in America's vast cache of natural resources, coal made a comeback in the energy mix (see table 11). Coal increased its market share percentage of energy sources produced and consumed, while petroleum and natural gas lost share. These changes emerged even as the Alaskan pipeline, completed in 1977, brought into play the North Slope crude oil find, and environmental concerns about energy pollution, particularly from high-sulfur coal emissions, increased.

One of the major cultural shifts that occurred during the postwar era was the environmental movement. The waste perpetrated by previous generations was no longer acceptable. The environmental movement had more positive than negative impacts on the energy infrastructure, and, though unintentionally, helped revitalize the railways. It is true that environmental protests helped delay construction of the 800-mile Alaskan pipeline, which was in part developed to reduce dependence on imported oil. And it is true that environmental lobbyists blocked construction of hydroelectric plants and nuclear projects. But poor management also delayed the Alaskan project and it is not altogether clear that the other projects were necessary. Meanwhile, in conjunction with stagflation and other economic changes, environmental groups have promoted conservation programs, more efficient uses of electricity, and diversification of energy sources.

A certain flexibility exists in the energy-production equation. As production of petroleum decreased, the use of coal and alternative fuels increased (see table 11 above). For the most part between 1971 and

1986 consumption patterns paralleled production figures; production fell each year except in 1976–1980 and consumption fell from 1974 to 1976 and from 1980 to 1985. Americans have exhibited the ability to reduce production and consumption. And they have done so even as their population increased and even as the political economy failed to develop coordinated policies.

Continued haphazard policy making did bring some interesting changes in the energy infrastructure that underscored the energy system's flexibility in responding to change. In the early 1990s, many local, state, and national agencies, along with some private firms, converted their motor vehicle fleets to autos and trucks fueled by natural gas, an energy source much cleaner than gasoline and about 50 percent cheaper. Utility managers revived the concept of interregional sharing of electric grids that had begun back in the 1920s. Cooperation between generating regions made existing power plants more efficient and better able to service peak demand periods. The demand for new construction dropped; older plants could be scrapped or, alternatively, refurbished to be made more efficient.

Utility managers also altered regional mixes of energy sources. For example, between the mid-1960s and the mid-1980s, the Middle Atlantic states reduced the use of coal from 64 to 45 percent of total fuel requirements. During the same period, the south Atlantic region balanced its reliance on coal with 25 percent nuclear power. In 1963, the mountain states relied on hydropower for 45 percent of their electric production, a rather high percentage in an arid region. By 1985, and despite increased population, hydropower generation there had been reduced to 22 percent. New England had a balanced mixture of power sources in the early 1990s, yet the flexibility implied by this balance was compromised by the region's reliance on imported oil for its fuel oil. In terms of optimum mixes of energy sources, much remained to be done across the United States.

Shifts in fuel mixes reflected responses more to economic and policy changes than to technological innovations. Between 1963 and 1985, some regions responded to environmental rules by switching to low-sulfur coal mined in the western states: the west south-central states increased their coal use to 45 percent of total fuel consumption, the mountain states to 74 percent, and the west north-central states to 75 percent. Other regions, however, responded to environmental rules with enhanced technology. For example, a few Midwest electric power firms developed more environmentally friendly and eco-nomically efficient production units that burned high-sulfur coal. This latter move, while not necessarily economically the best option available, represents utilities' responses to regional economics: the use of the technology made it possible for high-sulfur coal miners to keep their jobs.

Changes in the communications infrastructure reflected patterns similar to those in energy. That is, the changes were by-products of the uncoordinated interaction of market forces, political action, and technology. Diffusion of new communications technologies after World War II was delayed in part by lack of market receptivity and in part by government regulatory policies that tended to separate systems rather than encourage cross-fertilization and integration. Television developed commercially only in the 1950s. In 1950, 104 commercial broadcast television stations reached 3.9 million households; by 1990, 1,092 stations reached 98 percent of American households. The FCC restricted development to three national networks and local channel distribution to twelve, even though the technology could handle many more channels. By the 1960s, however, technological and market changes began to force regulatory changes.

Initially, CATV (Community Antenna Television, or cable television) extended television markets by collecting weak signals into an antenna and distributing a boosted signal through cable wire (developed by AT&T in the 1930s) to customers who were unable to receive the weak signal. Television networks appreciated this service. Cable television was also capable of collecting and distributing signals from far away, and this brought potential competition that the networks did not want. Although it was clearly a new technology that enhanced not only the national market but also the clarity of televised pictures, cable television diffused only slowly into the national market. The FCC, convinced that cable represented a threat to local programming, restricted cable expansion in the 1950s and 1960s. In 1955, 400 cable systems served 150,000 homes; by 1970, 2,500 systems served only 4.5 million homes. After 1970, however, spurred on by relaxation of broadcast regulation—if controlled somewhat by local agencies—cable television exploded across the national landscape (see table 12).

In the late 1950s and early 1960s technological development clashed with government restraints. Research efforts at the National Aeronautics and Space Administration (NASA) produced satellites capable of transmitting data, voice, and video from points all around the globe. AT&T argued before

Table 12. RADIO, TELEVISION, AND CABLE TELEVISION, 1921–1990

Year	Radio		Television		Cable Television	
	Stations	Households, Thousands	Stations	Households, Thousands	Systems	Households, Thousands
1921	1	NA	0	0	0	0
1925	571	2,750	0	0	0	0
1930	618	13,750	0	0	0	0
1940	847	28,500	0	0	0	0
1950	2,835	40,700	104	3,875	0	0
1960	4,224	50,193	579	45,750	640	650
1970	6,519	62,000	677	59,550	2,490	4,500
1980	7,871	a	734	76,000	4,225	15,500
1990	9,379	a	1,092	b	9,575	50,000

[a] In 1980 and 1989, 99.0 percent of households had radios.
[b] In 1990, 98.2 percent of households had televisions.
SOURCES: *Historical Statistics of the United States* (1976); *Statistical Abstract of the United States* (1994).

the FCC that, as the regulated telecommunications monopoly, it should be granted exclusive rights over satellite communications. Given the national government's investment in the new technology, however, others argued that a competitive system should be established. In 1962 Congress compromised and created COMSAT, a firm with 50 percent of its assets owned by common carriers like AT&T (AT&T controlled 25 percent) and 50 percent owned by the public. (Many manufacturers of satellite communications equipment bought the public shares.) Significantly, COMSAT carried only international communications; it did not carry domestic messages nor did it engage in ground-based communications. This division continued the earlier regulatory policy in which communications firms were prohibited from entering different modes of transmission.

AT&T's inability to furnish enough capacity to carry the increased traffic in communication of data, voice, and video forced the FCC to allow private networks to circumvent the common carrier system. Ironically, this placed AT&T at a competitive disadvantage. Because the telephone company enjoyed regulatory protection, it had been prohibited from competing with the new technologies, especially in the design and manufacture of computers. This restriction, plus the advent of private satellite communications later in the 1960s, joined with continued antitrust concerns about AT&T to force the telephone company to respond or be left behind in the rapidly changing telecommunications markets. Effective in 1984, AT&T agreed to relinquish its regulated monopoly status in exchange for more freedom to compete in the new telecommunications markets.

Deregulation facilitated rapid development of new national and global markets in telecommunications. By the 1980s the innovations in communications and computers touched a broad range of societal issues, including the nature of work, social relationships, population concentrations, the operation of stock and bond markets, and intrusions into private lives. Perhaps not since the railroad had a technological innovation resulted in such fundamental challenges to prevailing political-economic cultures.

The transportation industries underwent less dramatic changes than did the telecommunications industries, but the transport infrastructure continued to serve the economy well. Passenger trends during World War II misguided railroad decisions in the postwar period. The statistics for passenger miles in 1947, for example, suggested that despite the drop-off in military travel and competition from buses and autos, growth was to continue, for in that year the railways hauled half again as many passengers as they had in 1929—and they did so more efficiently, with 29 percent fewer track miles devoted to passenger service. This led railway management to invest a billion dollars in improvements during the late 1940s. During that same period, however, buses and autos took about 10 billion passenger miles from the railways (autos increased the number of passenger miles during this period by 70 billion). Airlines, which increased their intercity mileage by 2 billion miles in the late 1940s, accounted for much of the 3 billion passenger-miles lost by the railways in long-distance passenger travel. Railway passenger-miles fell off greatly after 1950, from 6.4 percent of all intercity passenger traffic to under 1.0 percent by 1970 (see table 15 below).

Table 13.   INTERCITY FREIGHT TRAFFIC BY
TYPE OF TRANSPORT, PERCENT OF
TONNAGE, 1939–1990[a]

Year	Railroads	Motor	Inland Water Transport	Oil Pipelines
1939	64.4	9.2	16.7	9.7
1940	63.2	9.5	18.1	9.1
1945	68.6	6.2	13.3	11.8
1950	57.4	15.8	14.9	11.8
1960	44.7	21.5	16.6	17.2
1970	39.8	21.3	16.5	22.3
1980	37.5	22.3	16.4	23.6
1990	37.5	25.8	16.2	20.2

[a] Airlines carried some freight and that accounts for totals less than 100 percent.

SOURCE: *Historical Statistics of the United States: Colonial Times to 1970* (1976); *Statistical Abstract of the United States* (1992).

Postwar pressures on railway passenger commuter and long-distance passenger services led to a shift from private to public management of railway passenger services. By the 1960s metropolitan public-private organizations had taken over commuter services. In 1971 the national government relieved the railways of the burden of long-distance passenger services. The National Railroad Passenger Corporation, Amtrak, owned the equipment, but operated across the country through track rights granted by the private railroad firms. One exception to this rule involved the Boston-to-Washington corridor. Amtrak owned the track and operating rights in that heavy-traffic area and made its only profit there.

The story of railway freight hauling in the second half of the twentieth century is one of decline followed by an unpredicted revival. This turn of events reflects nicely some of the overall characteristics of America's infrastructure: the flexibility inherent in the national economy, the growing complexity of

interconnections between systems, and the continuing importance of both the private and public sectors in determining economic policies.

Railways lost market share in freight hauling, dropping from a high point of 72.5 percent in 1943 to 57.4 percent by 1950, and to 39.8 percent in 1970 (the level in 1940). Railway productivity, however, improved, in large measure because managers invested in diesel-electric locomotives and encouraged more efficient loading techniques, including containerization and piggy-back operations (truck trailers on flat railroad cars). These efforts helped slow the railroads' loss of market share after 1970 (table 13).

Mergers also underlay the increased efficiencies in railway hauling. Except in the West, railway holdings became more concentrated. From 1,100 private firms in the mid-1940s, the industry shrank to 680 firms by 1972. In 1972, in every region but the West, one firm earned most of the revenue. Fears of concentration that had elicited railway regulation a century before, however, were muted in the late twentieth century, probably because of the existence of so many competing transport modes.

In 1980 U.S. rail systems constituted 29 percent of all railway trackage in the world. They conducted twice the work on two-thirds the mileage that had existed in 1916. With environmental legislation encouraging the use of low-sulfur coal, railroads increased revenues by hauling western coal to other areas of the country. As deregulation loosened government controls, private investment increased and the rail networks were refurbished (see table 14). Railway freight revenues, $11 billion in 1970, averaged over $25 billion per year during the 1980s. This mature industry was still very significant indeed to the nation's economy.

All the other transport modes were also important to the transport infrastructure. Significantly,

Table 14.   FEDERAL TRANSPORTATION OUTLAYS AND PRIVATE
RAILROAD INVESTMENT[a] 1970–1988

Year	Federal Transportation Outlays as Percentage of Total Federal Outlays	Federal Outlays for Transportation				Private Railway Investment
		Ground[b]	Air	Water	Other	
1970	3.6	4,700	1,400	900	26	360
1975	3.3	7,000	2,400	1,400	74	na
1980	3.6	15,300	3,700	2,200	104	950
1985	2.7	17,600	4,900	3,200	137	3,460
1988	2.6	18,100	5,900	3,100	116	2,650

[a] Dollar amounts in millions.
[b] User fees included.
SOURCE: *Statistical Abstract of the United States* (1990).

water carriers retained a relatively steady percentage of the tonnage hauled in the postwar era to the 1990s (see table 13). (Generally, of course, the value of waterborne tonnage is less than for the other carriers; yet, some petroleum products are hauled by water and their value would be higher than, say, wheat hauled by railroads.) Starting with 16.7 percent of the tonnage hauled in 1939, water carriers reached a low point of 13.3 percent in 1945, rebounded by 1955 to 1939 levels, and held 16.5 percent of the intercity freight market in 1970. In 1990 they still carried 15.6 percent of the tonnage. Public funds supported the inland, coastal, and Great Lakes water carriers (see table 14). The opening of the St. Lawrence Seaway in 1959, along with local private-public efforts to make terminal facilities more efficient, sustained the percentage of intercity freight hauled by water carriers. In addition to the steady 16 percent of traffic tonnage hauled, water carriers contributed to local economies. For example, activity at the Port of Houston softened the blow to that city's economy during the oil bust of the late 1980s.

Except for the railways, all freight haulers improved their market share between 1945 and the 1990s. In one sense, airlines have taken over very little of the intercity freight business. From less than 0.05 percent in 1958, airlines in 1970 carried only 0.2 percent in 1970. Yet the vast expansion of two-day and overnight mail and small package service, formerly the express business the railways hauled, relied heavily on airplanes. In 1973, Federal Express inaugurated this kind of service and by 1986 five other firms had entered the business. This development enabled retail establishments to serve a large customer base (worldwide) at relatively low cost. The use of airlines for transporting small packages and even larger shipments is still expanding in the 1990s.

Highway transportation undercut railway operations and did so in part with government encouragement. From 1946 to 1967, funds for federal aid to highways increased: from $147 million in 1946 (58.5 percent federal, 41.5 percent state) to $4 billion in 1967 (78 percent federal, 22 percent state). By 1950 there were 644,000 miles of national highways plus 1.6 million miles of state and local paved or gravel roads. An automobile could travel from New York City to Los Angeles in 72 hours. Yet, highway construction continued the earlier policy of hard-surfacing existing roads. New road construction lagged behind the growth of the economy and the rising numbers of automobiles.

Overcrowded highways, particularly in the Northeast and Middle Atlantic states, elicited a profu-

sion of state-controlled toll roads. This not only hampered ease of travel, but also increased expenses for commercial and pleasure drivers alike. In the 1950s, lobbying by a diverse coalition of highway engineers, trucking and union leaders, auto clubs, and big-city mayors convinced Congress and President Dwight D. Eisenhower to federalize the construction of a national highway system. Appeals to national defense needs, based in part on the recent mobilization for the Korean War, also helped bring about the Federal-Aid Highway Act of 1956 (the Interstate Highway Act).

The act initially called for 40,500 miles of new highways. Unlike earlier programs, which improved existing routes and were funded solely through user taxes, the new interstate system was funded with general funds as well. Sharing of the funding was on a 90-to-10 basis, with the federal government assuming the larger obligation. Thickness of the concrete, width and grades of the roadbed, and other details came from studies conducted by engineers from the Federal Bureau of Public Roads. The system's designs were based partly on trucking needs and engineers' intentions to connect national transport networks to urban road networks. Unintended results materialized, however, as the system was constructed. Older relationships between urban cores and suburban areas were undermined. "Loops" around the cities helped truckers avoid congestion, but also created incentives for businesses to move away from urban cores. Once-thriving business districts deteriorated and racially segregated groups, created in part through housing policies as described above, appeared to be trapped by the physical barriers of the new freeways.

The loop system underscored attempts to deal with the decades-old problem of motor vehicle congestion in urban areas. But the new interstate designs also created traffic patterns that made alternative mass transit systems difficult to plan and very expensive to construct. A few mass-transit programs appeared, but they were overshadowed by the American commitment to super highways and to the individual freedom reflected in automobile use. National government funds for mass transit paled in comparison to allocations for road development. In 1989, for example, federal grants to state and local governments from the Highway Trust Fund totaled $13.5 billion, while grants for urban mass transportation projects totaled $3.5 billion.

In contrast to the effects of the earlier highway programs, the new interstates and connections did not increase the percentage of intercity passenger

Table 15.   DOMESTIC INTERCITY PASSENGER TRAFFIC, PERCENT OF TOTAL VOLUME, 1950–1990[a]

Year	Autos	Buses	Airlines	Railways
1950	86.2	5.2	2.0	6.4
1955	89.0	3.6	3.2	4.0
1960	90.1	2.5	4.3	2.8
1970	86.9	2.1	10.0	0.9
1980	83.5	1.7	14.1	0.7
1990	80.8	1.1	17.4	0.6

[a] Inland waterways carried some passengers.
SOURCE: *Historical Statistics of the United States: Colonial Times to 1970* (1976); *Statistical Abstract of the United States* (1992).

travel occurring by highway. Between 1950 and 1960, the yearly percentage of intercity passenger travel by automobile did increase, but the interstate system was just being constructed (see table 15). The total passenger-miles also increased (from 438 billion auto passenger-miles to 1 trillion) during this period. Bus traffic, however, declined as a percentage and in the aggregate (from 26 to 25 billion passenger-miles). After 1960, both automobiles and buses lost shares of the intercity passenger market to the airlines.

By 1967, 887,000 miles of highway had been designated as part of the national highway system. The American highway infrastructure was by far the largest in the world. In the late 1980s, it was servicing 170 million vehicles. Only 10 percent of the total 3.9 million miles was not surfaced. Most of the 42,000 miles of the interstate system had been completed; nearly 20 percent of auto traffic and about 50 percent of truck traffic (by ton-mile) used the interstate system. The new system affected many kinds of business decisions. For example, Japanese automakers located their American assembly plants in close proximity to interstates to serve the just-in-time production process and the delivery of new cars to nearby concentrations of population.

By the 1980s, however, deterioration of the highway system threatened the system's continued usefulness. By the mid-1980s, reports noted that nearly 45 percent of all American highway bridges were structurally deficient or obsolete. Political fears of high national budget deficits helped create this situation, for funds available from user taxes that were earmarked for maintenance were not always spent, so that these surplus funds could be counted against the deficit. In 1985, for example, executive-branch agencies did not spend over $4 billion that was available for maintenance.

Air traffic underwent the greatest change of all

transport modes during the last half of the twentieth century. As noted earlier, airlines had received quite a bit of help from government sources, through regulation of competition and the construction of airports (see table 16)—and, like water carriers, but unlike trucks and buses, airlines did not pay user fees until the 1970s.

Air passenger-miles increased by 31 percent from 1947 to 1950, and by 148 percent from 1950 to 1955. By the late 1950s, jet engines, larger planes, and business-class service had lured more customers. But plane accidents in 1959 and 1960, labor disputes, and increased fares slowed growth in the early 1960s. Passenger-miles increased by only 15 percent between 1959 and 1962.

Critics of CAB regulation gained prominence in the political arena when they cited market theory to argue that CAB controls restricted competition and innovation and should be relaxed if the airline industry was to serve adequately America's growing economic needs. Then came a series of changes similar to those that occurred in telecommunications. In 1978 Congress passed the Airline Deregulation Act, which increased the pace of a trend the CAB itself recently had been supporting toward reducing the barriers to entry for new competitors. More entries did occur after 1978, but intense competition, even in a growing market, meant that many of these new firms could not survive. Commuter airlines, which as expected attempted to fill in niches created when larger carriers adjusted their air routes to maximize trunkline efficiencies, totaled 214 in 1980 and reached a peak of 246 the following year. By 1988 this number had decreased to 163.

The deregulation of airlines spurred another trend that predated 1978: in order to reduce costs

Table 16.   AIRPORTS AND FUNDING, 1927–1970

Year	Airports	Airport Funding,[a] Millions of Dollars	
		Federal	Local and State
1927	1,036	na	na
1930	1,782	na	na
1940	2,331	na	na
1947	5,759	68	74
1950	6,403	165	177
1960	6,881	573	611
1970	11,261	1,199	1,254

[a] Cumulative.
SOURCE: *Historical Statistics of the United States* (1976).

and fill more airline seats, airlines developed a system of hubs and spokes. By routing airplanes, including some commuters, from a variety of cities to one hub city, airlines could bring passengers with the same destination but different origins together to fill one larger plane. Thus, the passenger-load factor (the percentage of available seats actually occupied) increased from 49.7 percent in 1970 to 62.5 percent in 1988. Increased fuel efficiencies also resulted, from 13.1 passenger-miles per gallon in 1970 to 28 in 1987. As with railways in the late nineteenth century, the airlines in the last decade of the twentieth century apparently face an extended period of competition, combination, and consolidation.

POLITICAL AND ECONOMIC CONTEXTS

The United States is the youngest of the major modern industrialized nation-states. At the start of the twentieth century, just over one hundred years after its founding, it was the leading agricultural, industrial, and mining economy in the world. It had overtaken nations that had a one-half century head start in industrialization. Its vast geographic expanse, rich in numerous natural resources, held great potential for increasing economic wealth and improving living standards.

Two hundred years after its founding, the American economy, though covering a smaller geographic area than Canada, was worth seven times the value of the economies of Canada and Mexico combined. Serving a population of almost 250 million in 1990, the nation's transformed infrastructures supported the post-industrial, service-oriented political economy of the wealthiest nation in the world.

But economic growth had not been evenly distributed in the United States. Living standards varied widely by geographic region, class, and race. Some regions suffered from economic decline while others prospered. Previously upwardly-mobile groups were moving backward. Some previously static groups were improving, but others that had been declining were deteriorating at a faster rate than before. Other nation-states were doing better than the United States in areas such as per capita wealth, rates of infant mortality, and highway death rates. The infrastructure did not cause these mixed results as much as it mirrored other factors in the American political economy that did cause them.

The American infrastructure evolved within a mixed economic system that relied primarily on private investment and management decisions, but also thrived because of contingent help from local, state, and national governments. This process and its results in America contrast sharply with those in other countries.

It is illuminating, for example, to compare American policies toward nuclear electric generation and high-speed rail transportation systems with those in France and Japan. In 1987, 17.7 percent of U.S. electricity production came from nuclear plants. In all of western Europe, 26 percent of electricity production came from nuclear plants, with France having the highest percentage at 59 percent, Italy the lowest at 4 percent. Japan produced 21 percent of its electric energy with nuclear plants. Still, total generating capacity and actual generation of electricity by nuclear plants in the United States exceeded that of any other country. In 1987, the United States had nuclear-generated gross capacity of nearly 100 million kilowatts and generated 481 billion kw/h; the next highest producer was France, with 52 million kilowatts of capacity and 266 billion kw/h generated.

Differences in the interaction between political economies and technology in these countries explains the relatively low percentage of American nuclear generation and the virtual cessation of new construction of U.S. nuclear power plants late in the twentieth century. The cooperative aspect of business-government relations in France and Japan enabled each country to develop one generic design, involving relatively small generating units. In the United States, however, mutual private sector–government involvement led to the development of numerous designs and larger-capacity plants. American regulators faced great difficulty in monitoring so many different designs. Then, too, environmental protests led to delays and increased construction costs. It was not the regulation, but rather the political-economic interaction with nuclear technology that stymied the American nuclear industry.

Policies toward high-speed passenger trains have also developed differently in the United States. American high-speed rail enthusiasts, pointing to examples in Europe and Japan, noted that these systems could relieve congested highways, reduce highway death tolls, connect the nation's airports to metropolitan areas, complete the efficiencies of the emerging global airline systems, and decrease the negative impact of autos and airplanes on the environment. Systems proposed in Florida, Ohio, and Texas met resistance, however. When public funds were required, state governments demurred. Farmers complained that the systems would interrupt agricultural operations. Environmentalists alleged that plant and animal species would be endangered. No one, it seemed, could convincingly predict which markets would be served.

Similar differences of opinion lay behind problems in responding to the deteriorating state of America's urban and transport infrastructures. No doubt influenced by high national deficits and overwhelmed state budgets, some argued that future infrastructures should be designed and paid for on the basis of economic efficiency formulas. Mirroring the logic behind the deregulation movement, policy analysts argued that those who benefited from the new systems should pay most of their costs. (Automated devices would record who used a system and when, and would send a bill to the user.) Efficiency proponents appeared oblivious to the key problems that have bedeviled American policymakers since the time of Jefferson and Hamilton: how to assess the costs and benefits of infrastructure construction for private business and the general welfare; how to reconcile American values of freedom and liberty with the desire for efficiency; how to ensure that as many people as possible will benefit from economic growth.

Who benefits and how much, for example, from the interstate highway system? Who is harmed? Does it matter whether the manufacturer, the trucker, or the retailer pays higher taxes? Do not all Americans benefit from highways that are efficiently maintained?

How would an automated system determine which vehicle hauled the most productive individual(s)? Perhaps the efficiency approach may cost more in the long run. Perhaps the historical approach of combining user fees with general taxes should be retained.

What is clear from these issues and the foregoing overview is this: the United States in the twentieth century has continued to rest its economic policies on concepts of competition, free enterprise, and negative government born in the eighteenth century. Americans have not been unbending, however. They have called upon governments to help free enterprise. During the last third of the twentieth century, they have also shown a flexibility that has enabled them to adapt to new cultural values that reject some wasteful practices of the past. As the debates over infrastructures continue into the next century, policymakers will have to take into account historical parameters. They will have to acknowledge the rigidities and the flexibilities in the American system. They will have to understand how the contingencies of history—wars, depressions, prosperous times, changing values—have sustained the continuities and given birth to the discontinuities. Only in this manner will they uphold the historical flexibility of America's infrastructure, even as they modify the wasteful aspects of it and try to include more citizens in the benefits deriving from it.

See Also Conservation and the Environment; Natural Resources; Industrial Production; Distribution; Consumption (all in this volume).

BIBLIOGRAPHY

Two major and readily accessible sources, *Historical Statistics of the United States: From Colonial Times to 1970* (1976) and *Statistical Abstract of the U.S.* (1957–1992), anchored this essay. Because the two works do not always approach the same topics in ways that enable the researcher to make easy comparisons, the references to other sources found in each are indispensable to those desiring more detail. Statistics only show, they do not explain, and thus they should be supplemented with other sources.

Arnulf Grubler, *The Rise and Fall of Infrastructures: Dynamics of Evolution and Technological Change in Transport* (Heidelberg, 1990), offers statistical analyses to bolster the argument that technology determines the evolutionary pattern of infrastructures, a position contrary to the one offered in this essay. Raymond S. Hartman and David R. Wheeler, "Schumpeterian Waves of Innovation and Infrastructure Development in Great Britain and the United States: The Kondratieff Cycle Revisited," *Research in Economic History* 4 (1979): 37–85, falls into the same camp as Grubler.

Because infrastructures make cities functional and tie cities to one another, urban studies provide essential information. Jesse H. Ausubel and Robert Herman, eds., *Cities and Their Vital Systems: Infrastructure Past, Present, and Future* (1988), contains several useful essays and the volume as a whole is intended to foster thinking about urban systems within large categories, from the impact on the individual to the connections to global infrastructures. Joel A. Tarr, "The Evolution of the Urban Infrastructure in the Nineteenth and Twentieth Centuries," *Perspectives on Urban Infrastruc-*

ture, Royce Hanson, ed. (1984), pp. 4–66, offers more information on the nineteenth century and points out how little we actually understand about infrastructure. Tarr and Gabriel Dupuy, eds., *Technology and the Rise of the Networked City in Europe and America* (1988), compares urban infrastructure diffusion patterns; see especially Mark H. Rose, "Urban Gas and Electric Systems and Social Change, 1900–1940."

Kenneth T. Jackson, *Crabgrass Frontier: The Suburbanization of the United States* (1985), contains a wealth of insights and facts relevant to urban development, especially to housing. Marc A. Weiss, *The Rise of the Community Builders: The American Real Estate Industry and Urban Land Planning* (1987), documents the private-public cooperative movement that merged with government programs in the 1930s to stimulate suburban developments. Daniel R. Mandelker and Roger Montgomery, eds., *Housing in America: Problems and Perspectives* (1973), contains numerous essays on housing topics, including policies and subsidies, markets, technology, land, and race. R. Allen Hays, *The Federal Government and Urban Housing: Ideology and Change in Public Policy* (1985), though focused on the 1970s, includes useful information on the contours of national policies toward housing since the 1930s.

For studies of energy infrastructure, one should begin with Thomas P. Hughes, *Networks of Power: Electrification in Western Society, 1880–1930* (1983), for it is a classic comparative analysis of the emergence of electrical power systems in the United States, the United Kingdom, and Germany that shows how technology interacts with culture and geography. John G. Clark, *The Political Economy of World Energy: A Twentieth Century Perspective* (1990), furnishes a statistics-laden yet informative overview of energy developments worldwide during the twentieth century. Clark's *Energy and the Federal Government: Fossil Fuel Policies, 1900–1946* (1987), reveals just how uncoordinated energy policy was during the first half of the twentieth century. Richard H. K. Vietor, *Energy Policy in America since 1945: A Study of Business-Government Relations* (1984) is an insightful analysis of the chaotic and uncoordinated U.S. energy policy after World War II. Arthur M. Johnson, *Petroleum Pipelines and Public Policy, 1906–1959* (1967) remains the standard work on business-government relations and pipeline regulation. George H. Daniels and Mark H. Rose, eds., *Energy and Transport: Historical Perspectives on Policy Issues* (1982), contains essays

that analyze the interaction of technology with economic and social factors and the interaction between two infrastructures, energy and transport.

There are relatively more works on transport infrastructure. Alfred D. Chandler, *The Visible Hand* (1977), shows how the railroads established a national transport infrastructure by 1900. Mark S. Foster, *From Streetcar to Super Highway: American City Planners and Urban Transportation, 1900–1940* (1981), chronicles the early history of the interactions of engineering principles and politics in urban-national road transport systems. Mark H. Rose, *Interstate: Express Highway Politics, 1941–1956* (1990), shows how the diffusion of the automobile interacted with political-economic developments to bring about the Interstate Highway Act. Bruce E. Seely, *Building the American Highway System: Engineers as Policy Makers* (1987), covers some of the same ground as Rose, but gives special emphasis to the role engineers played in highway development, thus showing how complicated infrastructure history is. George Fox Mott, ed., *Transportation Century* (1966), presents a mid-twentieth-century look at transport developments, including an essay on water transport. William R. Childs, *Trucking and the Public Interest: The Emergence of Federal Regulation, 1914–1940* (1985), shows how the flexibility of motor trucking contributed to the mid-century decline of railways. Kent T. Healy, *Performance of the U.S. Railroads since World War II: A Quarter Century of Private Operation* (1985), is an indispensable source for understanding the decline and rebirth of railroading.

While some of the urban studies noted above contain sections on communications, Robert B. Horwitz, *The Irony of Regulatory Reform: The Deregulation of American Telecommunications* (1989), furnishes an overview of the evolution of the national communications infrastructure. Peter Temin, with Louis Galambos, *The Fall of the Bell System* (1987), also reveals the complex, interrelated contexts in which telecommunications infrastructure changed. Roger L. Kemp, ed., *America's Infrastructure: Problems and Prospects* (1986), is representative of the critical analyses of infrastructure that appeared in the late twentieth century. John Atlee Kouwenhoven, *The Beer Can by the Highway: Essays on What's American about America* (1988), in the title essay, suggests how "waste" may have shaped American society, and thereby makes a sobering suggestion about future infrastructure policy making.

CONSERVATION AND THE ENVIRONMENT

Arthur F. McEvoy

Conservation of the environment and natural resources has been as important to the development of the United States in the twentieth century as the conquest of frontier lands was in the three centuries of Euro-American settlement that preceded it. Through the seventeenth, eighteenth, and nineteenth centuries the sheer extent of the land, the vast wealth of its resources, and the relative scarcity of labor and capital available to exploit them were the key challenges to economic life in the New World. They were powerful determinants of American politics and culture, as well. After 1890, when the Bureau of the Census announced the closing of the American frontier, the environmental challenge facing Americans began to shift from one of development to one of conservation. Regulating access to resources became a chief concern of government: resource conservation not only demanded new forms of government intervention in the economy but called forth new ways of thinking about the world and the place of people in it.

More is involved in a country's environmental history than just political struggles over conservation or what its leading intellectuals think and write about Nature. The structure of the nation's economy depends critically on the natural resources available to it. Every industrial activity has some ecological impact; pollution and resource depletion are the best examples. Economic production thus takes place under ecological conditions that the economy itself creates, at least in part. Likewise, people's ideas about Nature take shape partly from their experience in the world. Someone living in an industrial society will necessarily have different ideas about Nature from those of a medieval peasant or an aboriginal hunter-gatherer. But people also have the power to imagine how they wish the world would be and to make Nature over in their image of it: they can tame rivers, replace forests with farmsteads, and so on. The history of human society in the natural environment, then, consists of a complex system of interaction among ecology, economic activity, and culture.

Societies and the natural environments of which they are a part evolve together, as whole systems. Just like natural communities, human societies endure only if their environments remain in a condition that will provide them with the resources they need to live. The United States at the turn of the twentieth century faced radically changed environmental conditions with a social order profoundly influenced by several hundred years of expansion across an extremely wealthy but lightly defended frontier. America's effort to adapt to its changed ecological circumstances—an effort that manifested itself in the country's economy, its science, its politics, and its culture—did much to direct the course of social change in the twentieth century.

The most powerful stimulus to American conservation was the closure of the frontier. In 1893, Frederick Jackson Turner explained this tectonic change in a paper entitled "The Significance of the Frontier in American History." Turner was a historian at the University of Wisconsin and one of several influential figures in American environmentalism who came from southern Wisconsin. "The existence of an area of free land, its continuous recession, and the advance of American settlement westward," Turner claimed, "explain American development." Americans' individualism, the distinctiveness of their society from that of Europe, and their peculiar form of nationalist democracy were, Turner thought, attributable to the experience of settling the westward-moving frontier. The end of that movement, Turner concluded, had "closed the first period of American history."

Turner's essay was a complex structure of myth, nostalgia, and analysis. In one sense it was no more than a retelling of a creation story that Turner had in no way invented; his was merely the Homeric version. It resonates with nostalgia for lost innocence and a quiet foreboding for what Turner saw as a European-style future of urban crowding, corporate concentration, and class warfare in the United States. As historical analysis it was deeply flawed, ascribing too much determinative power to the natural environment and ignoring such important contributions to U.S. history as those of urban society, European culture, and Native American resistance to Euro-American advancement. Still, the Turner thesis remains the cornerstone of American historiography because it captures the central importance of open spaces and abundant resources to the country's history. More important, it remains the most coherent and powerful statement of what many Americans think distinguishes their culture from that of other nations: cheap and plentiful natural resources, freedom to prospect the public domain, and opportunity to escape the ills of civilization through travel to new and "unspoiled" places. The frontier icon is one of the most powerful in American culture and exerted a powerful influence over subsequent thought and action about environment and resource conservation. The twentieth century has seen two outbursts of organized public enthusiasm for environment and resource conservation: the "conservation" movement between 1890 and 1920 and the "environmental" movement that began in the 1960s. The two movements had much in common, including many of the institutions, symbols, and strategies that the first wave brought into being and that survived to figure prominently in the second. They shared, as well, a sense of limits, of a closing frontier, motivating participants in each of them to urge better care of the natural environment. Conservation and environment played a less visible role between the world wars, although Franklin Delano Roosevelt's New Deal carried forward many of the earlier movement's programs and ideals. Most important, the New Deal leavened Progressive conservation with the concern for social justice that later distinguished post–World War II environmentalism from its turn-of-the-century ancestor.

PROGRESSIVE CONSERVATION, 1890–1917

Conservation was one of many different reform programs that, together, constituted turn-of-the-century Progressivism. In many ways, conservation was the Progressive Era's most characteristic movement and an important fount of symbols and strategies for its sister programs. Progressive conservation came in three distinguishable stages. The first, between 1890 and 1901, saw a steady increase in public awareness of conservation issues, primarily as they concerned forests, water, and wildlife. This period saw the creation of bureaucratic agencies in the federal government to regulate access to those resources; the most significant were the Forest Service, the National Park Service, and the Federal Bureau of Reclamation. During the second phase, between 1901 and 1908, conservationists articulated their social vision in its most coherent form under the leadership of President Theodore Roosevelt. Between 1908 and 1920, the third phase of the movement gradually declined as it got down to the business of working in government.

Conservation was an attractive, highly manipulable metaphor that could garner political support for a great many social programs, but which could also obscure significant differences between alternative visions of how to allocate resources and how actually to carry policies out. It is generally useful to describe the turn-of-the-century conservation movement in terms of a dichotomy between its two most important wings. "Conservationists" proper were utilitarian in outlook, favoring the rational development and professional management of natural resources by scientific experts working for powerful, centralized government agencies. Their chief spokesperson was Gifford Pinchot, who ran the U.S. Forest Service under Presidents Roosevelt and Taft. The other wing consisted of "preservationists" who wished to protect pristine natural environments from all economic use; their chief oracle and patron saint was John Muir. Although preservationists cooperated with conservationists in establishing the National Forest system, they later broke with their utilitarian rivals and found a bureaucratic home in the Park Service.

Like any substantial social movement, the preservationist wing of the first conservation movement gathered together a number of different interest groups, with sometimes conflicting values, ideologies, and tactics. One subgroup consisted of wilderness devotees like Muir, driven by their spiritual regard for Nature and their conviction that contact with undeveloped environments was essential to a person's character development. Another included natural scientists for whom wilderness was an irreplaceable source of knowledge about the world. There were, also, well-to-do hunters and sportspeople, some of whom recognized the link between nature preservation and continued access to game animals, others of whom were Social Darwinists who thought wilderness experience essential for cultivating the vigorous, masterful character required of the ruling Anglo-Saxon race. Theodore Roosevelt was an important symbol of this sub-group, although he made his biggest contributions to the utilitarian wing of the early conservation movement. Yet another group under the preservationist tent consisted of fem-

John Muir at the annual Sierra Club outing to Yosemite, July or August 1907. Photograph by F. M. Fultz. COURTESY SIERRA CLUB PICTORIAL COLLECTIONS, BANCROFT LIBRARY, UNIVERSITY OF CALIFORNIA, BERKELEY.

inists or members of reform groups like the American Civic Association, who pressed for park development in the cities as well as in the wilderness. These used conservation as a convenient metaphor for social progress generally. Many preservationist groups combined two or more of these motives, more or less comfortably.

One thing that tied the different strands of preservationism together was an awareness of closure, of the end of the frontier. For many, vanishing wilderness symbolized the problems of urbanization, corporate concentration, and the emergence of class warfare—all of which threatened the traditional American, Turnerian values of independence, industry, and mobility. The real wilderness, it seemed, was in the cities, described in Theodore Dreiser's *An American Tragedy* (1925) or Upton Sinclair's *The Jungle* (1906), and not in the expanses of the West, now the more benign for having been cleared of their earlier tenants.

The movement had a significant strain of racism and Social Darwinism, composed as it was of upper-class and professional people worried about threats to their traditional social leadership. Then, as later in the century, preservationism contained a strong element of anti-modernism, even though many of its adherents were well-to-do and benefited from the modern order as much as anyone. Preservationists conformed to the "mugwump" social type—social critics who enjoyed high social standing, social reformers inspired by romantic visions of the past. Whatever their motives, however, the preservationists lent immense energy to turn-of-the-century conservationism and made possible what gains it did achieve. Their religious commitment to the movement and their anti-utilitarianism made them formidable opponents to developers. Preservation's inspiration and chief spokesperson was John Muir, who retained a devoted following through the end of the twentieth century. Born in Scotland in 1838, Muir emigrated with his family to Wisconsin at the age of eleven. His family broke the wilderness and established a pioneer farm: he saw the forest cleared and the last of the local natives disappear, saw the clouds of passenger pigeons and the hunters who would later extinguish them. A skilled mechanic and inventor, Muir attended college at the University of Wisconsin, where a professor introduced him to the transcendentalism of Emerson and Thoreau. Following an industrial accident that cost him the sight of one eye, Muir abandoned his city trade. After completing a hike from the upper Midwest to the Gulf of Mexico, Muir moved to California in 1868 and wandered into the Sierra, where he found a job at a sawmill in the Yosemite Valley. In 1890, at the behest of Robert Underwood Johnson, Muir began writing about Yosemite for the *Century* magazine and galvanized the movement to make the valley into a national park. Congress established the park that year, largely according to Muir's specifications. In 1892, Muir, along with a number of academics from Stanford and the University of California at Berkeley, organized the Sierra Club. He served as the club's president until his death twenty-two years later.

Muir was primarily interested in preserving the nation's wilderness areas for their own sake, although he frequently brought such utilitarian arguments as watershed protection to bear on behalf of the campaign. In alliance with Gifford Pinchot and the utilitarian wing of the movement, Muir and his followers scored some impressive early victories. Congress passed a statute in 1891 that allowed the president to withdraw public lands from sale for use as forest preserves; set-asides began under President Harrison and increased rapidly after the turn of the century under Theodore Roosevelt and his successor, William Howard Taft. The 1891 statute made no reference to developing the resources of the forest reserves; the Forest Service Organic Act of 1897, however, made multiple use of forest resources the governing principle of the new system. At this point, when Pinchot made clear that he favored using the forests for grazing, mining, and lumbering, as well as for more passive uses such as watershed protection and wilderness preservation, Muir broke with him forever. Muir thereafter abjured utilitarian arguments and wrote only in terms of nature-worship and the preservation of wilderness for its own sake.

The movement achieved other significant victories in its first decade. In 1903, Theodore Roosevelt issued an executive order setting aside a refuge in Florida for pelicans, which were being hunted for their feathers. Pelican Island became the first national wildlife refuge; the pelicans themselves would become major actors in the revival of environmentalism after World War II. The disappearance of whales, bison, passenger pigeons, and countless fisheries and game animals had made wildlife a national issue by the end of the nineteenth century. Many states had established fish and game commissions in the decades since the Civil War but could do little to prevent poaching and interstate traffic in meat, feathers, and other wildlife products. In 1900, however, Rep. John D. Lacey (R-Iowa) engineered passage of a federal statute prohibiting interstate shipment of wildlife killed in violation of the laws of the state in which they were taken. One of the first instances in which Congress exercised its power to police commercial traffic in a particular commodity, the Lacey Act gave national effect to state wildlife regulations and did much to aid in their enforcement. Lacey was also instrumental in the passage of the Antiquities Act of 1906, which gave the president authority to set aside land for the purpose of establishing national monuments. At Muir's behest, Roosevelt used this statute to create Grand Canyon National Monument in 1908.

The other wing of the first conservation movement followed a more utilitarian line of thinking than that of Muir and the preservationists. Appropriating the name conservationists, these people were also spurred into action by the closure of the frontier. Their goal, however, was to ensure the "wise use" of natural resources in the future. Two historical experiences were key in formulating the consciousness of this wing of the movement. The first was the astonishing rapacity with which industry had stripped Michigan and Wisconsin of their forests in the 1870s and 1880s in order to build the transcontinental railroads and the plains civilization to which they gave birth. Much as later politicians worried about dwindling oil supplies, Theodore Roosevelt pointed to an impending "timber famine" and pushed the government to bring what forests remained in the public domain under rational control.

The second of utilitarian conservationism's formative experiences was the challenge of developing the arid lands of the Southwest. By the end of the nineteenth century, this was the only land of any extent that remained open for settlement. Making this land productive, however, would require government planning and scientific management of the region's critical resource, water. The explorer John Wesley Powell, who in 1869 had been the first Euro-American to traverse the Grand Canyon, said so in his 1878 *Report on the Lands of the Arid Region of the United States.* Powell's protégé, W. J. McGee, was Theodore Roosevelt's chief spokesperson for multiple-use water management, including irrigation, hydroelectric power generation, flood control, and navigation. Timber management and water development, then, were the organizing tasks of utilitarian conservation.

The utilitarian and preservationist wings of the first conservation movement both drew their inspiration from the end of the frontier. Whereas preservation had deep roots in the early nineteenth-century romanticism of Emerson and Thoreau, however, utilitarian conservation stemmed from tectonic changes in the structure of American society and political economy at the turn of the twentieth. These included, first, significant centralization in the social order due to the emergence of a nationalized mass market for consumer goods, concentration of economic power under the control of huge, integrated corporations, and a corresponding loss of local autonomy. Industrial maturity made the nation's economy and politics increasingly interdependent. While many Americans sensed that their lives were increasingly controlled by faraway strangers, it encouraged others (largely the faraway strangers) to believe that engineers and social planners might conquer hitherto intractable social problems like poverty, destructive competition in business, and resource depletion.

The second change that paved the way for utilitarian conservation was the vastly increased importance of applied science and technology, particularly in economic production. Scientists and other professional people organized themselves into national as-

Pulling Stumps in the Wisconsin Cutover District. COURTESY UNIVERSITY OF WISCONSIN–MADISON DIVISION OF ARCHIVES.

sociations and moved into government in force to supervise the management of social processes. The professional foresters and hydrologists who spearheaded the conservation movement exemplified this change, but similar processes took place at the same time in all areas of government and in private business as well. Resource depletion was a dramatic symbol of the many social problems that confronted the advanced, interdependent industrial society of the late nineteenth century. It made clear to all that the invisible hand of the market would henceforth need guidance from the visible hand of centralized, scientific expertise.

The most troubled resources were wildlife, grasslands, and, especially, timber and water; conservation ideology grew out of government efforts to deal with them. National consumption of timber for fuel and construction reached its peak about 1900, by which time Americans had cleared vast areas of the continent of its trees. Pioneers simply burned a good share of this timber to clear their land for plowing. The pace of cutting had even increased toward the end of the nineteenth century as industry made new and more efficient tools available to the lumber industry. The most spectacular clearing took place in the Great

Lakes states, particularly Wisconsin and Michigan. Here, land policy, tax laws, and many other political factors contributed to wasteful cutting, partly to encourage rapid development of the resource and partly on the theory that the highest use of any land was for farming. In the northern lake states, however, the thin soil leached quickly and failed to provide good yields to the thousands of farmers who came to the pinelands in the wake of the sawmills. By the end of the 1880s, poverty and soil erosion were taking hold in Wisconsin and the other lake states; many farmers went broke and ownership of the land gravitated to big companies with the capital to sustain it.

A small but very articulate group of professional foresters had been warning Congress since the 1870s that if cutting in the lake states continued at current rates, the forest would disappear entirely in only a few years. Here, the sometimes misleading tactic of extrapolating from current rates of use to predict imminent famine—one of timber, in this case— helped galvanize popular support for the professional foresters' political agenda. The 1891 act that allowed the president to reserve land for national forests, for example, had been intended only to prevent fraud and to slow the disbursement of public lands into private hands. The foresters' lobby, however, engineered the inclusion of their rider with little public notice or debate. The multiple-use provisions of the 1897 act, which permanently alienated Muir and his followers from the utilitarians, entered the law in much the same way. Still, the national forests were the proving ground for the sustained-yield, multiple-use concept of resource management that Gifford Pinchot brought to fruition during the administration of President Theodore Roosevelt.

The experiences of homesteaders in the High Plains were as catalytic for Progressive Era water policy as the clearing of the lake states pinelands was for timber policy. The two decades after the end of the Civil War, those in which the U.S. industrial revolution gained full steam and the clearing of the pinelands began, also saw thousands of farmers settle in western Nebraska, Kansas, and the Dakotas, many of them occupying the land for free under the Homestead Act. These lands, west of the 100th meridian, are normally semiarid; but the 1870s and 1880s were unusually wet decades and homesteaders could grow their crops without the aid of irrigation. Drought, severe winters, and insect plagues brought the easy times to an abrupt close after the mid-1880s, however, and by the turn of the century some two-thirds of the dry-land farmers in the High Plains had abandoned their homesteads and moved on, many to Canada. The explorer John Wesley Powell and his followers concluded that only government-sponsored collectives could build and manage the irrigation works that would see arid-lands farmers through dry times as well as wet.

Great Plains cattle grazing offered a particularly gruesome manifestation of the problems that unmanaged, uncontrolled access to the public domain brought with it at the end of the nineteenth century. As Indians and bison had disappeared from the plains between 1860 and 1890, the range rapidly filled with cattle owned by large, highly capitalized companies based on the East Coast or even in England. These cattle grazed on the public range for free, unlimited in their numbers by any public authority. There ensued a classic "commons tragedy," in which resources shared in common but exploited by competing individuals were inevitably overharvested to the ultimate ruin of all. The open-range system worked well on the high plains so long as the climate remained wet, but the onset of bad weather in the mid-1880s brought disaster. The winter of 1886–1887 was particularly harsh, and thousands of animals perished in what became known as the great die-up. The few cattle firms that survived learned to manage their

herds more carefully, limiting their numbers on the summer range and feeding them on irrigated farms in the winter. Like the professional foresters, cattle growers became very interested in having government regulate grazing scientifically, both on the public grasslands and in the national forests.

Theodore Roosevelt—"that damned cowboy," to one of his detractors—made conservation the cornerstone of national policy after he became president in 1901. Water reclamation was the first conservation issue to draw serious attention from the new administration. A federal program for promoting irrigation in the arid West seemed essential, given the failure of private as well as state efforts to muster and manage the huge amounts of capital required for such undertakings. Inspired by Powell's *Arid Lands* report, Roosevelt put his weight behind the efforts of Rep. Francis G. Newlands (D) of Nevada. The Newlands Reclamation Act of 1902 became the centerpiece of federal water policy and would remain in force through the rest of the century.

The Newlands Act set up a scheme whereby the federal government would build and operate reservoirs to conserve runoff. The act established a Reclamation Service in the U.S. Geological Survey, which became the U.S. Bureau of Reclamation (BuRec) in the Department of the Interior in 1907. Centralizing authority to build and manage the projects in the federal government meant that expert planning and economic efficiency, rather than political logrolling, would determine where the projects would go. The act also intended that small farmers would be the projects' main beneficiaries, and so initially limited eligibility for federal water to farms of 80 acres or less and later to those of a maximum 160 acres. BuRec never enforced the acreage-limitation provisions of the law, however, and large-scale, corporate farms became the principal beneficiaries of the Newlands Act. Water sales were supposed to pay for the projects over the long run, but the government sold its water so cheaply—as little as one-tenth its market price—that the projects never did pay for themselves as promised.

Just as Turner's frontier myth envisioned a transformation of wilderness into independent small farms, as if all the world were south central Wisconsin, the Newlands Act made no provision for the role of cities in the allocation of federal water or in western development generally. Mayor Fred Eaton of Los Angeles occupied this vacuum in the 1920s, when he persuaded BuRec to let his city take precedence over local farmers in a huge project the bureau had planned for the Owens Valley, northeast of the

1362

city. In the meantime the city's agents secretly bought up land in the valley so as to protect the city's rights to the water. When BuRec eventually abandoned the project, the city piped the water out of the valley, leaving local farmers high, dry, and out of business. Southern California water politics later inspired Raymond Chandler's novel, *The Big Sleep* (1939), and Roman Polanski's film, *Chinatown* (1974).

Private land speculation was everywhere a significant barrier to the Newlands Act's Turnerian vision of small farms and agrarian democracy. In the time it took the government to plan and build its reclamation projects, private landowners with enough capital to invest frequently bought up as much of the irrigable land near the projects as they could. By the time the projects began delivering water, much of the target land was already privately owned in lots substantially bigger than the 160-acre homesteads that Senator Newlands had envisioned, setting the stage for a century of struggle between large landowners and the government. Westerners saw the ostensibly democratic Newlands Act as a license for federal bureaucrats to make decisions affecting their livelihoods without giving them any say in the process. Political democracy and economic efficiency, it seemed, were not necessarily one and the same thing.

Forest policy was the second main theater of Progressive Era conservation and the one that defined it ideologically and politically. The national forests had begun simply as a means of forestalling the destruction of federally held timbered lands, by withdrawing them from public sale. Cutover slopes also tended to promote flooding and soil erosion. Watershed protection was therefore an ancillary benefit of the reserves and was passive enough a "use" that both utilitarian conservationists and preservationists like Muir could endorse it as justification for withdrawing the lands. The split within the movement came when the president's authority to create the national forests was politically secure and the executive branch got down to the business of actually managing them.

Roosevelt selected Gifford Pinchot to do the job, appointing him director of the Division of Forestry in the Agriculture Department. Pinchot had come from a wealthy family that had donated the money to establish a forestry school at Yale. After studying forestry himself in Germany, he had returned to the United States with a plan to apply the German model of centralized state ownership and scientific management to American forests. The Forestry Division, for its part, had started out as a typical USDA research agency, with no control over forest management per

se: as public lands, the forests themselves were still under the jurisdiction of the Department of the Interior. Congress had only authorized the Division of Forestry to develop new and more efficient uses of wood, to sponsor demonstration projects, and to encourage private parties like the railroads to see to their own timber needs by planting their own forests. None of these projects was particularly successful.

Pinchot, however, was a gifted bureaucratic imperialist, and his utilitarian vision was perfectly in tune with Roosevelt's ideas about Progressive reform generally. In 1905, Pinchot engineered the transfer of the national forests from the Department of the Interior to his division at USDA, where they remained thereafter. By 1908, he had built up a staff of 1,500, including a cadre of young, idealistic technocrats who exercised centralized, expert control over some 150 million acres of national forest. The Forest Service self-consciously set the tone for Progressive conservation. Declaring itself above politics, it became the mainspring of scientific, utilitarian policymaking—the very model of a Progressive government agency. Pinchot and his energetic lieutenants perfected the concept of "sustained-yield, multiple-use" management as they integrated timber production in the national forests with watershed protection, mining, grazing, and later recreation. First and foremost, however, the national forests were to ensure a supply of timber to the economy. "Wise use" meant that production would have priority over wilderness preservation for aesthetic purposes, as Muir's followers wanted, or over preservation of habitat for wildlife, as the sport-hunting interests wanted. Fire suppression was an ecologically dubious idea because it allowed brush and deadfall to accumulate in the forests, creating the danger of much more serious fires sometime in the future. It nonetheless became the cornerstone of Forest Service management policy; it eventually bequeathed to American culture one of its most powerful environmental icons, Smokey the Bear.

As conservation became a national mania between 1900 and 1910, Pinchot's Forest Service most clearly symbolized the movement's ideals and tactics. Like his sponsor, Theodore Roosevelt, Pinchot presented his case for centralized, technocratic management of natural resources in democratic terms. His version of the Benthamite formula, "the greatest good for the greatest number over the longest time," was to him the only reasonable guide to policymaking, in conservation or any other area. In this, Pinchotian conservation embodied the soul of progressivism: scientific management, long-term planning, and centralized management were organizing principles of reform—not only in resources management but in business and many other areas of public life, as well.

The urban middle and professional classes who provided Progressivism with its strongest support wished to control the social changes that advancing technology and corporate concentration brought with them. Sharing Turner's unease about the shape of the new century, they hoped to use modern methods of expert planning and centralized control to sustain the older, individualistic, agrarian ideals that Turner had pointed to as essentially American. Conservation rhetoric and ideology quickly spread from natural resources to many other policy areas. Above all, conservation meant replacing the older pull-and-haul of market bargaining and political dealmaking with newer methods based on modern science, technology, and bureaucratic efficiency. Progressive Era conservationists accomplished a great deal, chiefly by way of slowing the plunder of the public lands and by creating the institutional framework within which resources might in the future be managed rationally. But contradictions between the Progressive conservationists' democratic ends and their bureaucratic means became apparent almost as soon as they got down to work.

The Pinchotian devotion to scientific utilitarianism did not insulate conservation from politics. Pinchot and Roosevelt tried to use government to correct the wastefulness and shortsightedness that big business demonstrated in its use of resources. Neither was opposed to monopoly per se; both drew a distinction between "good," or socially responsible monopolies and "bad" ones. Pinchot, therefore, got along very well with Weyerhaueser, Louisiana Pacific, and the other big timber companies, all of which shared Pinchot's preference for higher lumber prices and for long-run stability in the industry. On behalf of the big cattle growers, who were interested in restricting access to public grazing lands and in managing them scientifically, Pinchot became the chief advocate of permitting grazing in the national forests. To the chagrin of John Muir, whose defense of Yosemite had originally been motivated by the abuses of sheepherders and their "wooly locusts," grazing gradually became the most economically significant use of the national forests.

Progressive, utilitarian conservation reached its zenith toward the end of Theodore Roosevelt's administration. In 1907, the administration inaugurated the Inland Waterways Commission, which was to bring multiple-use watershed planning to the Co-lumbia, the Mississippi, the Tennessee, and other major river basins. Representative Newlands sponsored the administration's bill, which would have empowered a presidential board of experts to study water problems, build projects, and coordinate the activities of all government water resource agencies. In 1908, Roosevelt staged a conference of state governors, leading public figures, and representatives of national professional organizations to discuss the scientific, social, and moral aspects of conservation. John Muir was conspicuously uninvited. Little came of the conference, however, except an unsuccessful recommendation that Congress endow a national conservation commission and several new presidential commissions to deal with rural life, efficiency in government, and other subjects. The imperial but ambiguous logic of conservation had by this point extended so far as to lose both its focus and its political power.

Although William Howard Taft had pledged to continue Roosevelt's conservation program after becoming president in 1909, he was a good deal more conservative than his predecessor and less willing to push beyond the bounds of traditional constitutionalism in order to further the Progressive agenda. A more traditional Republican than Roosevelt, Taft instinctively favored private initiative over government involvement in the economy. His secretary of the Interior, Richard A. Ballinger, aroused Pinchot's ire by pushing to release more lands and reservoir sites for private, as opposed to government, development. For his part, Ballinger opposed Pinchot's campaign to extend Forest Service authority over timberlands on Indian reservations, which were nominally the domain of the Department of the Interior. In 1910, finally, Pinchot lost his job at the Forest Service in a controversy with Ballinger over the sale of Alaskan coal lands to private developers. This last battle was highly publicized and did much to enshrine Pinchot as a friend of the people, in opposition to the "special interests," and to cement Progressive conservation's ambiguous synthesis between efficiency and democracy.

All the theoretical and political contradictions in early-twentieth-century conservation came into play in the decade-long controversy over Hetch Hetchy, a remote valley of the Tuolumne River in the Sierra Nevada north of Yosemite Park in California. Hetch Hetchy was California's first big water project: the city of San Francisco had earlier proposed damming the Tuolumne to provide the Bay Area with water. Although the Department of the Interior initially denied the application, it reversed itself after the earthquake and fire of 1906 dramatized the city's need for a dependable municipal water supply. Muir and the Sierra Club immediately launched a national campaign to save the valley. Prodevelopment interests, particularly in San Francisco, were outraged at the "hoggish and mushy aesthetes," the "long-haired men and short-haired women" who stood with the lunatic Muir in the way of the city's safety and progress. The Hetch Hetchy conflict was the first contest between preservation and development that centered on a specific tract of land; it established the pattern for a series of such struggles over reclamation projects in the coming decades.

This first battle ended in a loss for the preservationists. The city won the contest by adding recreation to the list of multiple uses that the project would ostensibly serve. Presenting the public with artists' conceptions of hiking trails and campgrounds along the shore of the proposed reservoir, developers argued that damming the Tuolumne would make Hetch Hetchy Valley more beautiful, not less, and would in any case make it accessible to greater numbers of people. Here, the democratic and utilitarian arguments of the developers easily coopted the aesthetic position of the preservationists: parks became a cheap and effective compromise for development. Congress finally authorized the Hetch Hetchy project in 1914; a brokenhearted Muir died that year.

The Hetch Hetchy project turned out to be a colossal blunder, requiring twenty years and double the projected cost to develop. In the meantime Oakland, across the bay, found a cheaper source of water and built its own project at lower cost. The developers had promised to sell power from the Hetch Hetchy installation only to municipal utilities, but later transferred the electricity to the Pacific Gas and Electric Company for sale to San Francisco consumers. The reservoir itself, sold to the voters as a potential park, turned out to be ugly in the extreme. Later environmentalists, to prevent other water projects from going forward, effectively contrasted the developers' visionary drawings with photographs of the dreary reality that Hetch Hetchy came to be.

Hetch Hetchy also galvanized national support for the preservation movement, which secured the establishment of a National Park Service in 1916: where the Forest Service had become a laboratory for utilitarian conservation, the Park Service became the preservationists' bastion. The Park Service's first director was Stephen Mather, a self-made millionaire and sportsperson. Mather's first challenge was to resist the encroachment of the Forest Service, which wished to incorporate the new agency under its own supervision. The Park Service became part of the Department of the Interior, though rivalry between the two agencies persisted throughout the century. The rivalry was not altogether unhealthy. Following the Park Service's example, the Forest Service began its own recreational programs in the 1920s, and in the 1930s began to set aside wilderness areas in remote parts of the national forests. In the 1980s, competing Park Service and Forest Service efforts to rehabilitate lands devastated by the eruption of Mount St. Helens in Washington provided a valuable experiment in forest ecology.

Mather was usually as conservative in his tactics as Pinchot had been aggressive. He would not nominate an area for inclusion in the parks system, for example, unless its scenic value so outweighed potential competing uses of the land as to guarantee its successful inclusion and its later protection from encroachment. In one of his early victories, Mather kept the Forest Service away from what became Glacier National Park and then agreed with the Great Northern Railroad to build a hotel in the park to promote tourism there. When the railroad's permit to operate its sawmill in the park expired, however, Mather preempted the company's campaign to extend its cutting privileges by gathering his rangers together and dynamiting the mill. This was an early instance of a long-standing, if controversial, tradition in American environmentalism that became known as monkeywrenching.

In a way, the Park Service was closer kin to the Forest Service than the bitter rivalry between Pinchot's utilitarians and Muir's preservationists in general might suggest. Both wished to save what little remained of the frontier that in some way had made the United States what it was. At bottom, in spite of Muir's genuine appreciation of Nature for its own sake, the Park Service differed from its rival not over the value of utilitarianism per se but over which values should be more heavily weighted in the utilitarian calculus that both of them used. Pinchotians favored the industrial use of resources; Sierra Clubbers and their ilk wished to see the land devoted to sightseeing recreation. Both are economic uses, as later theorists would point out. By the end of the century, overcrowding and overdevelopment would threaten the national parks no less than overgrazing and clearcutting endangered the national forests.

The successful establishment of the Park Service notwithstanding, the loss of Hetch Hetchy in 1913 marked the decline of the first conservation movement. Popular support for Pinchot and for Theodore Roosevelt fell off rapidly after the latter's unsuccessful third-party campaign for the presidency in 1912 and after developments in Europe distracted public attention away from natural resources and the environment. After World War I, the utilitarian wing of the movement dwindled to a handful of people headquartered in the Forest Service, while preservationist groups like the Sierra Club and California's Save-the-Redwoods League continued their activities outside of politics and government. Conservation had accomplished much in a short time, shielding great expanses of land from destruction and firmly establishing nature protection and resources management as government responsibilities. Not the least of the movement's contributions was that it epitomized the new importance of scientific planning and economic rationality in public affairs. The conservationist response to the frontier's closing thus worked a significant and permanent change in the American political culture.

NEW DEAL CONSERVATION, 1917–1950

The challenges that faced the United States in the period between 1917 and 1950 were more strictly economic than environmental: encouraging production to fight two world wars and the intervening economic collapse took precedence over preserving and husbanding natural resources. The period between the slow demise of the first conservation movement during the World War I and the slow emergence of a new, "environmental" movement after the World War II was, therefore, largely a time of consolidating and elaborating the political changes that came with Progressive Era conservation.

The period was not without significant ecological developments, of course. The most important was that fossil fuels replaced wood as the country's main source of energy. In many ways petroleum opened a new kind of frontier that promised much the same kind of limitless growth that the old one had. Fossil energy catalyzed a host of changes in the relationships among the country's economy, society, and environment. Automobile transportation more closely linked rural with urban areas. Trucks and fertilizers transformed not only the American diet but the ecological impact of its agriculture. Plastics, antibiotics, and pesticides—all manufactured from petrochemicals—not only presented new kinds of pollution problems but created the material conditions for significant changes in scientific thought about the relationship between humans and their natural environment. Timber, agriculture, and other extractive industries, meanwhile, never recovered

from the postwar recession of 1918–1921. The Dust Bowl of the 1930s made clear to all the persistence of serious imbalances between the economy and its resource base. The interwar period had two important things in common with its predecessor, however: its most important conservationist politician was a Roosevelt, and its most articulate environmental theoretician came from south central Wisconsin.

Agriculture—the production of a community's subsistence from the land—is the point at which the nation's social and economic practices interact most intimately with its natural environment. The independent, small-scale, diversified farm was the organizing principle of Jeffersonian political ideology and of nineteenth-century U.S. public-lands policy. It was the *telos,* the endpoint, to which Turner's progression from wilderness to civilization tended. Agriculture generated two of the twentieth century's most significant environmental problems—the Dust Bowl of the 1930s and the DDT crisis that catalyzed the reemergence of popular environmentalism after World War II. If agriculture was the leading edge of nineteenth-century economic and ecological change, it was the sector most thoroughly and characteristically transformed by fossil energy in the twentieth.

Farm technology changed radically in the interwar period. Where agricultural growth had for most of the country's history been extensive—generated by the addition of new land under crops—after World War I growth was intensive, brought about by technological change that let farmers produce more crops from a given area of land. Mechanization of American agriculture had begun in the mid-nineteenth century with the introduction of such labor-saving devices as mechanical reapers. But until the gasoline tractor, most farm machinery relied on horsepower and thus did little to change the ecology of farming. Experiments with steam engines on farms generally proved unsuccessful. The gasoline tractor, introduced by Ford, permitted a massive infusion of new resources to agriculture and transformed the relationship between American farmers and the land. Where there had been only 17,000 tractors on U.S. farms at the beginning of World War I, there were 246,000 by 1920.

First and foremost, internal combustion revolutionized the demography of American agriculture by displacing its work force. In 1900, some 60 percent of the U.S. population lived in rural areas. The number of workers in agriculture peaked in 1916. During that decade, however, the share of the country's population living in rural areas dipped below 50 percent and has declined steadily since then. By 1970, fewer than 4 percent of Americans supplied food, not only to the rest of the country but to many people in foreign countries as well. Average farm size increased at the same time, from 155 acres in 1935 to 380 acres in 1970. In the 1980s, fewer than 5 percent of all American farms contained well over half of the country's productive farmland.

Mechanization also led to significant changes in the nation's diet. Although Americans maintained roughly the same intake of calories in the late twentieth century as they had in 1900, more vitamins and more fresh fruits and vegetables (delivered by truck to urban markets) greatly improved the population's nutrition. In the 1980s, on the other hand, average Americans ate only about half as much grain and vegetables as their turn-of-the-century predecessors. Consumption of poultry tripled between 1900 and 1980 and increased sharply thereafter as many Americans tried to reduce the amount of fat in their diets. Beef consumption nearly doubled in the decades after World War II, to about 120 pounds per person per year in the 1980s. Whereas most of the people in the world took about 70 percent of their dietary protein from vegetables and grain, Americans in the 1980s derived 69 percent of their protein from animal sources.

These developments entailed drastic changes in the ecology of American farms. Most farm animals eat grain, just as people do. While modern Americans consume about 150 pounds of grain per capita each year, it takes another 2,200 pounds of grain to grow the livestock that produce the eggs, meat, and dairy products, that an average American consumes. In terms of its biomass, or weight of living tissue, the modern American livestock population outweighs the human population by about four to one. The amount of waste that these animals produce in a year is equivalent to that of a population of over 2 billion human beings. Nineteenth-century farms tended to recycle what relatively little animal waste they produced; their mechanized, specialized twentieth-century successors were less likely to do so. Greater inputs of energy to farming here corresponded to greater outputs, not only of animal protein but of animal waste and other pollutants as well.

Intensive agriculture brought with it a host of technological developments, all of which had important ecological impacts. Intensive livestock production requires vaccines and antibiotics to control disease. A USDA scientist developed a vaccine for hog cholera in 1913, for example, which cut pork growers' losses to disease by half within a few years.

By the 1980s, American farm animals consumed more antibiotics than did American people. Crop losses were controlled by selective breeding and, increasingly, through the use of synthetic pesticides. A German chemist invented DDT, the most important of these, in 1894, although it was not until just before World War II that the Swiss chemical firm Geigy established its potential for killing unwanted insects.

Most important in the interwar period was the development of chemical fertilizer. In 1913, a German scientist developed a process that used enormous quantities of electrical energy to manufacture ammonia by synthesizing hydrogen and nitrogen. The main raw material for modern fertilizer production is natural gas, like petroleum a fossil fuel. After World War II fertilizer manufacture became the fourth-largest primary industry in the United States, after petroleum, steel, and cement. In the 1980s the United States used the equivalent of 200,000 barrels of oil each day in the production of ammonia-based fertilizers. The manufacture of pesticides, likewise, requires enormous amounts of fossil fuel, both in the energy required to manufacture them and in the petroleum feedstocks that make up the raw materials that go into them. All these changes—in farm mechanization, agronomy, and farm chemistry—developed in tandem. Together, they created a new frontier of petroleum-based development for American agriculture that was not unlike the frontier of land that had fed its growth in earlier times.

During the interwar period, then, American farmers built an agro-ecosystem of plants and animals specifically bred for their ability to turn water and petroleum into food, to be harvested mechanically and trucked to distant markets. The environmental impacts of these changes were tremendous. Most dramatic was the change in energy consumption. Agriculture accounts for about 12 percent of the modern American energy budget, including not only fuel to drive tractors and other farm machinery but also for irrigation, for the production of fertilizers and pesticides, and for the transportation, processing, and storage of food products. In 1910, American farmers, on average, used one calorie of energy in the form of fuel and animal power to produce each calorie of food energy. By the 1980s American farmers consumed eight or nine times as much energy in fuel as they produced in food. A group at Cornell University estimated that producing one acre of American corn required the energy equivalent of eighty-six gallons of gasoline.

Intensive agriculture accounts for about 85 percent of the consumptive water use in the U.S. economy. Only about 10 percent of the country's total acreage under crops is irrigated, but that share of the land produces more than one-fourth of all the nation's crops. Most of this takes place in the West, where state and federal government reclamation projects supply water to farms at significantly subsidized prices. Other farms rely on fossil water, mined from underground aquifers: because this water is free for the taking it tends to be used inefficiently, like water reclaimed from western watersheds. Aquifers in the Central Valley of California and underneath the southern Great Plains have been seriously depleted as farmers draw water out of them faster than natural flow can replenish them. The intensive use of water and of agricultural chemicals has interacted to generate significant pollution problems. Half or more of the fertilizers and pesticides applied to crops simply washes away into the nation's watersheds, percolates into groundwater, or degrades into the soil, increasing its salinity and reducing productivity.

Soil erosion in the Great Plains was the most dramatic environmental manifestation of the interwar period's mechanized, energy-intensive agro-ecology. Mechanical tilling and chemical fertilization produces short-term gains in mineral fertility and farm profits, but damages the structure of the soil and promotes erosion. In the first few decades after the turn of the century, American farmers moved again onto the plains to produce wheat with the aid of the new farm machinery. They were encouraged, much as the dry farmers of the 1870s and 1880s had been, by a long run of wet seasons that produced good yields, for a time. Strong markets for American wheat between the outbreak of World War I and the end of the 1920s led them on. The USDA, eager to boost productivity and profits in an industry that remained troubled through the 1920s, actively encouraged plains farmers to mechanize and to put as much land under crops as possible.

The bill came due after 1933, as the cyclical climate of the plains turned hot and dry again, crops failed, and windstorms began to raise the unprotected topsoil into huge dust storms that blackened the sky all the way to the East Coast and far out to sea. Livestock died by the thousands, just as they had in the harsh winters of the 1880s. Eventually the Dust Bowl, one of the most spectacular ecological disasters in human history, covered the dry plains from western Texas all the way north through Oklahoma, Kansas, Nebraska, Colorado, and Wyoming. Once again plains farmers abandoned their lands and migrated, many to take up jobs as migrant laborers in the irrigated factory farms of California. The drought

and windstorms of the 1930s were natural phenomena, to which the plants and animals that inhabited the plains before the advent of modern agriculture had adapted over the long run. The Dust Bowl, however, was an artifact of American agriculture and government policy that encouraged its expansion into an environment to which it was maladapted and where the potential costs of that maladaptation were very high.

Franklin Delano Roosevelt became president in 1933, just as drought and wind began to destroy plains agriculture. The New Deal brought conservation and environment once again into national politics, after nearly two decades of inattention. The younger Roosevelt began a renewed effort to realize the goals of the Progressive Era conservation movement. He also reinvigorated the alliance between conservation and reform politics that his elder cousin had tried to cement but which had dissolved after he left power. Pinchot's utilitarian followers had simply assumed that utilitarian resource management would automatically lead to "the greatest good for the greatest number." New Dealers, in contrast, took a deliberate interest in forging the link between social justice and the conservation of natural resources. The necessary bond between the two was most evident in agriculture.

Although he was not the hunter and cowboy that Theodore Roosevelt had been, FDR was a committed conservationist and experienced in conservation politics. He had some experience with Pinchot and the Forest Service while serving as assistant secretary of the Navy under President Wilson. Forced by polio to retire from public life in the early 1920s, he spent much of his time reforesting his estate at Hyde Park, New York. Following his encounter with Pinchot, FDR developed a political theory of conservation that accounted for the relations among politics, economics, and resource management in a much more coherent and sophisticated way than that of his Progressive Era predecessors. He thought that if private timber companies continued to clear the nation's forests in the name of individual liberty, the whole country would eventually suffer from the erosion, flooding, and economic devastation that they left behind them in the lake states and in large parts of the West.

Pointing to the communitarian, cooperative aspects of frontier life that Turner had mentioned but underemphasized, Roosevelt insisted that individualistic competition was useful to the public good only up to a certain point. Beyond that point, cooperation and state regulation for the common good had to take over. Roosevelt took these principles, which he saw in Pinchot's programs for reclamation and forest management, and applied them to a range of reform efforts in education, industrial policy, transportation, and so on, wider than the Progressives had ever imagined. In essence, FDR broadened his predecessors' utilitarian calculus to include social justice and participatory democracy in addition to the economic profit that Pinchot had assumed led automatically to the public good. At the core of his ideology, however, was conservation as he had learned it from Theodore Roosevelt, Gifford Pinchot, and their allies: in 1936, accused of instinctively approaching all social problems in terms of timber, land, and water, Roosevelt replied, "I must plead guilty to that charge."

Farms were near the heart of most of Roosevelt's conservation initiatives. One of his favorites was a plan to plant millions of trees to form a "shelterbelt" a hundred miles wide along the 100th meridian from Canada to Mexico. Although the program was much-ridiculed at the time, windbreaks are an effective way to prevent local erosion. Plains farmers discovered this to their chagrin when, in the 1980s, many cut down their windbreaks so as to put more land under crops. During the 1930s the shelterbelt program helped some 33,000 farmers plant windbreaks: strung together, they would have stretched for 18,000 miles. In addition, the administration bought up cutover and eroded lands in the lake states and in the South and turned them over to the Forest Service for planting. The New Deal brought Pinchotian conservation to the grasslands of the high plains in the Taylor Grazing Act of 1934, which brought sustained-yield management under permit, on the Forest Service model, to cattle grazing on the public lands.

Another of Roosevelt's pet programs was the Civilian Conservation Corps (CCC), which brought together New Deal public works and Progressive Era resource development. During the 1930s, the CCC provided minimum-wage jobs for 2 million young men planting trees, thinning old forests, and stocking waterways with fish. The program built wildlife shelters, dug irrigation canals, and restored parks and national monuments. For the Forest Service, CCC workers fought fires, cut fire trails, and built lodges and lookout towers. Some of their projects survive today as models of the distinctive New Deal style of architecture, including the lodges at Starved Rock in Illinois, and Timberline, near Mount Hood in Oregon. The CCC, which Gov. Edmund G. Brown, Jr., revived as a California state agency in the 1970s, brilliantly combined conservationist and social-jus-

tice values, synthesizing the New Deal's welfare-state, public-works philosophy with the Pinchotian urge to cultivate Nature and make it useful to people.

The New Deal also resurrected Progressive Era plans for multiple-use watershed development. The pilot project was the Tennessee Valley Authority (TVA). The Tennessee Valley covers parts of seven states. In the Depression decade it was an economic wasteland, troubled by depleted farmland, rampant erosion, chronic flooding, and intractable poverty. Old-line Progressives in Congress, under the leadership of Sen. George Norris, had been working for a decade or more to use federal authority to revive the region. The Wilson administration had built a dam at Muscle Shoals, Alabama, to generate power for the manufacture of explosives for the Army. Norris and Roosevelt placed the Muscle Shoals project at the center of a vast, multi-purpose watershed development project.

Under the TVA plan for regional development, the dam at Muscle Shoals was to generate power for farms and to make fertilizer. Income from sales of power would pay for improvements to flood control and navigation, soil conservation, and reforestation. TVA brought great strides in adult education to this traditionally underdeveloped region and began significant experiments in local-community control over economic planning and development. Roosevelt had dreams of applying the TVA model to all the major watersheds in the country; though he made a start in the Columbia River basin in the Pacific Northwest, the plan ran aground on the opposition of such private interests as electric utilities, the American Farm Bureau Federation, and the Army Corps of Engineers. Most of TVA's social-welfare and multiple-use aspects gradually withered, and eventually Congress cut off funds for further watershed development. Eventually, TVA amounted to little more than a state-operated power and fertilizer company, and not a very conservation-minded one, at that: the Tellico Dam, which handed an early setback to the Endangered Species Act in the 1970s, was a TVA project.

Perhaps the most characteristic New Deal conservation efforts, however, were those of the Soil Conservation Service in the U.S. Department of Agriculture. Under FDR's Agriculture secretary, Henry A. Wallace, the USDA became the most innovative and progressive arm of the federal government. At Agriculture, Wallace supervised a cadre of lieutenants that included Rexford G. Tugwell, Robert Marshall, Howard Zahniser, and Hugh Hammond Bennett. Marshall was a protégé of Gifford Pinchot. He and Zahniser, however, were devoted to the wilderness and were admirers of John Muir, and both of them distinguished themselves in the Wilderness Society after leaving government service. Bennett's domain was the Soil Conservation Service, established by Congress in 1935 as dust from the plains states rained down on the seat of the national government.

Bennett was no less a visionary than Pinchot had been in his day. Under his charismatic leadership, the Soil Conservation Service operated demonstration farms and nurseries, sponsored research in conservation and agronomy, and instructed tens of thousands of farmers in such techniques as crop rotation, contour plowing, and the use of fertilizers and nitrogen-enhancing grasses to rebuild damaged soil. While he was as much a prophet of technological progress as Pinchot had been, Bennett was more committed to participatory democracy: for him, economic and political self-determination for farmers and soil conservation were inextricably linked. Erosion, according to another USDA official, was "one of the symptoms of some deep maladjustments between the soil and its farming system. . . . Frequently we find weak plant cover and declining soil fertility resulting from unstable economic conditions, bad tenure relationships, overcrowded land, poverty, disease, and wars." In particular, Bennett's program for small-watershed reclamation incorporated all of the multipurpose goals of TVA in a context of small-scale, localized agrarian democracy. Because it circumvented not only the private authority of the American Farm Bureau Federation but also the political interests vested in the land-grant colleges and their extension services, the Soil Conservation Service aroused a storm of political opposition. By the early 1950s, it had gone the way of TVA, deprived of funds and shorn of its politically dangerous programs by a conservative Congress.

The New Deal achieved many of the goals of earlier conservationists, chiefly by overcoming political obstacles to the kinds of government intervention that conservation sometimes required. In some ways it carried conservation ideology several steps beyond that of the Progressives, by recognizing that politics were integral to the relationship between society and its natural environment: social justice and participatory democracy were, therefore, essential components of a successful conservation program rather than ancillary byproducts as Pinchot, McGee, and the others had assumed. Many of the New Deal's most innovative programs, however—TVA and the Soil Conservation Service foremost among them—aroused serious opposition because their benefits were social rather than economic. They accrued to large numbers of people with little political power instead of to small, well-organized interest groups like the Farm Bureau. Their benefits were difficult to translate into dollars to be earned in a time of economic depression. If conservation meant saving resources from short-sighted exploitation for immediate profit, a government devoted first and foremost to short-term economic growth could be only a half-hearted ally, no matter how lofty its purposes.

In the realm of politics, then, the utilitarian strain of conservation remained dominant through the interwar period. This was partly because the nation's paramount concerns—winning two world wars and rebuilding a shattered economy—were material in nature. In addition, the era's dominant political figure—FDR—was a pragmatist who concentrated on improving the economic management of resources rather than the aesthetic and spiritual concerns that had motivated Muir and his followers. A great deal of private activity took place during the period, however: while the Sierra Club became little more than a social club for wealthy California outdoorspeople, such groups as the Wilderness Society and the Audubon Society kept Muir's legacy alive. A few philanthropists, notably John D. Rockefeller, Jr., quietly invested their energy and their fortunes in wilderness preservation. Sportspeople's groups such as the National Wildlife Federation and the Izaak Walton League, meanwhile, promoted wildlife conservation so as to ensure steady supplies of fish and game for their use. This side of the movement, however, remained in the background between 1917 and 1950. Nor did the period see the kind of advances in environmental thinking that Muir and his followers had lent to the Progressive Era.

There was, however, one exception. If FDR was interwar conservation's most important politician, Aldo Leopold was its signal theoretician. Leopold, a wildlife biologist trained in the Pinchotian tradition, abandoned it later in life and became one of the great prophets of twentieth-century environmentalism. He had attended the Forestry School at Yale and worked for Pinchot's Forest Service until the late 1920s. There, he witnessed one of utilitarian conservation's greatest disasters, in the Kaibab National Forest in northern Arizona. The Theodore Roosevelt administration had designated the area as a national game preserve. Intending to promote a supply of deer for hunting in good Pinchotian fashion, the Forest Service set about exterminating wolves and other predators as fast as it could. Initial results were good: the population of deer in the Kaibab Forest rocketed from 4,000 in 1906 to 100,000 by 1924. At that point, however, the deer outstripped their own resources and began to starve. Sixty thousand of them died in the winters of 1924–1925 and 1925–1926; by 1939 the population was down to 10,000 and the overgrazed forest habitat was in ruins. As an object lesson in predator-prey relationships, the Kaibab catastrophe was a crucial event in the history of ecology and of environmentalism.

It also made a profound impression on Leopold. He later recalled a moment of spiritual awakening when, looking into the dying eyes of a wolf he had just shot, he realized the arrogance of sorting animal species into "crops" to be cultivated and "pests" to be exterminated. Shortly afterward, he joined the Izaak Walton League and became a cofounder of the Wilderness Society. In 1933, he joined the faculty of the University of Wisconsin as the nation's first professor of wildlife management. He also purchased an abandoned, cutover farm nearby, a few miles from where John Muir's family had broken the wilderness for their homestead nearly a century before, and spent his spare time reforesting the property, much as FDR had done at Hyde Park in New York. Leopold lost his life fighting a fire in 1948, but left behind a collection of essays he had distilled from his observations and experiences on the farm. Published the following year as *A Sand County Almanac,* the book quickly became one of American environmentalism's most influential texts.

Like Muir, Leopold was uncomfortable with the materialism of Progressive conservation. Influenced by a strain of Russian mysticism that taught him to see spirituality and consciousness in all Nature, Leopold abandoned the Western tradition of separating spirit from matter and humankind from Nature. The profound reconciliation with the immanent but unknowable spirit in Nature that suffuses *A Sand County Almanac* distinguishes the book from the heroic, manic striving of Muir's writings. Different from Muir, too, was Leopold's comfort with the human cultivation of Nature. Unlike Muir, who sought meaning and essence only where no human mark was visible, Leopold found the divine in the daily, routine interaction with the world that was part of rural life. What Leopold called "the land ethic" or "thinking like a mountain" meant knitting together work, worship, and the world on a day-to-day basis.

Leopold thus synthesized the spirituality of Muir and the materialism of Pinchot in a way that distinguished him from others of his time but also, in many ways, made him the best exemplar of interwar environmental thought and action. His essential message, one of tolerance for other forms of life, brought together Muir's reverence for Nature and Pinchot's willingness to cultivate it. But Leopold retained neither the preservationists' thinly veiled sociophobia nor the narrow-minded economism of what he derided as "state college agriculture." In many ways this tolerance compared with the political benevolence of Franklin Roosevelt, who in his own way brought turn-of-the-century conservationism out of the study and into the real world. Leopold's was not yet a fully modern environmentalism, however. Just as the New Deal brought conservation and democratic politics together but neglected the sacred aspects of Nature, Leopold joined contemplation and cultivation but retained a Muir-like political asceticism. It was not until after 1960 that Rachel Carson and those who followed her brought together Nature, production, and politics to create a new and fundamentally different kind of environmentalism.

POSTWAR ENVIRONMENTALISM, 1950–1990

Public concern for the natural environment flowered again in the decades after 1950. The nationwide celebration of Earth Day on 22 April 1970 marked the moment of self-awareness for the new "environmental" movement. Environmentalism, however, had roots in fundamental developments that had been reworking relationships among Nature, the economy, and popular consciousness since the end of World War II. Like its turn-of-the-century predecessor, postwar environmentalism worked a transformation in American society and politics that went far beyond issues of ecology and resources management alone. Progressive Era conservation had fundamentally been a reaction to the multifaceted challenges that faced the United States with the closing of its western frontier. Environmentalism, similarly, responded to concerns about the planet's ability to sustain the economic intensification that had begun with the shift from organic to fossil energy at the beginning of the century.

The end of World War II brought significant changes in the ecology of American life that laid the material basis for the new environmentalism. The energy-intensification of agriculture continued as before, but with an important difference. Where before the war energy-intensification had primarily meant mechanizing farm tasks, after 1950 new petrochemical inputs came in the form of fertilizers and pesticides, which subsidized the growth of the crops themselves. Energy-intensification had yielded steady increases in farm productivity between 1910 and 1950; after 1950, however, steadily increasing inputs of chemical energy brought steadily decreasing marginal returns in yield. They also brought increases in pollution and soil degradation. After DDT proved effective against unwanted insects during the war, for example, use of this long-lived poison grew exponentially until, by the time the U.S. government banned its domestic use in 1972, it pervaded the global environment on land and sea and from pole to pole. Growing awareness of pollution from fossil fuels and disruptions in the world oil market in the 1970s suggested that the era of petroleum-based expansion was coming to an end, much as the era of frontier expansion had come to an end in the 1890s.

Pesticides were but one manifestation of a revolution in industrial chemistry that took place during and after World War II. New processes made possible the large-scale manufacture of detergents, synthetic fibers, plastics, and antibiotics, in addition to DDT and other pesticides. These products brought with them significant changes in the ecology of American life. In addition to creating their own enormous demand for petroleum as raw material and for manufacturing, synthetics made possible cheap, disposable packaging and products and thus vastly increased the amount of garbage that the economy generated. Detergents and other synthetics also differed from earlier products in that they were frequently impervious to biodegradation at best and sometimes positively dangerous as pollutants.

Still more powerful in its impact on global ecology and popular consciousness was the unleashing of a new form of energy, nuclear fission. In many ways the explosion of the first atomic bomb in 1945 was the defining moment of the century's second half. Not least of the bomb's effects on American life was the introduction of a new and highly dangerous form of pollution in the form of radioactive fallout from nuclear bombs and the byproducts from the "peaceful" use of nuclear energy to generate electricity. In the late 1950s and early 1960s scientists publicized threats to human health from both DDT and nuclear fallout. The fact that both of these pollutants became hazardous to people after working their way through the environment gave Americans a powerful double lesson in ecology and its relevance to their lives. Environmental politics suddenly became much more immediate, personal, and hence socially transformative than they had ever been during the Progressive Era.

Social changes in the aftermath of World War II interacted with ecological ones to prepare the ground for the new environmentalism. Internationally, World War II brought the end of the European empires. Subsequent economic and demographic changes in former colonies dramatically increased the drain on the world's natural resources and the burden of pollution on its natural systems. At home, a booming economy raised American standards of living and public education to levels unprecedented in human history. Rising standards of living led many more people than before to value outdoor recreation in "natural" settings, particularly as mass ownership of automobiles enabled people of most social classes to travel long distances on vacation. For a time, between their introduction in the 1940s and the onset of the AIDS epidemic in the 1980s, synthetic antibiotics all but eliminated infectious disease as a serious threat to public health. Removal of this threat increased people's attention to the effects on their well-being of unhealthy lifestyles and of environmental pollution. Changes in popular understanding about Nature came from advances in science and technology: computer science and ecology, particularly, were important sources of new ways of thinking about society, just as economics had been in the Progressive Era.

What characterized postwar environmentalism, then, was a synergy among ecology, political economy, and popular consciousness that had been beyond the reach of earlier conservationists, whether of the preservationist or the utilitarian variety. The tremendous increase in the intensity of interaction between human society and the natural environment that the postwar era brought with it so highlighted the interdependence between the two as to lead people to understand Nature and their place in it in a new and different way. Environmentalism became both a symbol and a catalyst for systemic changes that were transforming the whole of American life, just as it had at the turn of the century. Each of the four decades between 1950 and 1990 manifested its own, characteristic environmental politics. Altogether, the developments of the century's second half may well amount to a revolution in Western culture and ecology.

The twentieth century's second great conservationist wave began in the 1950s with a revival of preservationist activism led by latter-day followers of John Muir. Muir's influence had waned steadily since the early years of the century, and the Democratic administrations of 1933–1953 had developed a mixed record on parks and wilderness. Less concerned with preservation than with putting people to work, the New Deal sponsored a lot of watershed reclamation in the old, Progressive mold. Hydropower development did significant damage to the fisheries of the Columbia River when Grand Coulee Dam closed off the upper reaches of the basin to running salmon, although other projects along the river were careful to include hatcheries and fish ladders in their installations. Shasta Dam in California, on the other hand, had benefited the Sacramento Basin salmon resource by ensuring a steady flow of cold, clean water into the river below. The New Deal also authorized Everglades National Park in 1934 and Cape Hatteras National Seashore three years later. These were the first parks set aside strictly for wildlife and wilderness preservation, as opposed to their scenic or recreational value. The Eisenhower administration, however, was openly hostile: it shifted resources out of federal conservation agencies, opened wildlife refuges to oil and gas exploration, and began a new phase of aggressive watershed reclamation. The last endeavor sparked a revival of the wilderness preservation movement and reintroduced John Muir to the popular culture after several decades in the shadow of utilitarian conservation.

Eisenhower's secretary of the Interior, who oversaw both the Bureau of Reclamation and the National Park Service, was an Oregon automobile dealer named Douglas McKay, who became known as "Giveaway McKay" for the eagerness with which he authorized public and private development on Interior Department lands. In the late 1940s BuRec had drawn up plans for a water-storage project in the upper Colorado Basin that included a dam at Echo Park, inside the Dinosaur National Monument in northwestern Colorado. The dam would have inundated large stretches of the hitherto unspoiled canyons of the Green and Yampa Rivers. A coalition of conservation groups, including the Sierra Club, the Wilderness Society, and the Audubon Society, had managed to forestall the development, despite President Truman's inclination to go forward with it. The Eisenhower administration, however, immediately submitted to Congress a new authorization for the project.

Directing the fight against the Echo Park project was the Wilderness Society, led by the New Dealer Howard Zahniser, and the Sierra Club, which had recently come under the control of a new cadre consisting of the photographer Ansel Adams, Richard Leonard, a lawyer, and David Brower. Brower was a particularly aggressive leader, so charismatic that his admirers described him as a reincarnated (but politically more sophisticated) John Muir. One of Brower's and Adams's main contributions to environmental politics was the use of photography: in 1953,

Brower rafted through the Echo Park site, taking photographs that he later displayed to Congress alongside pictures of the ruined Hetch Hetchy Valley. He collaborated with the publisher Alfred A. Knopf to produce a book of essays and photographs on Dinosaur Monument, prominently featuring drawings of what had been promised for Hetch Hetchy and, for comparison, photographs of the result. The campaign was successful, and in 1955 the Colorado Project became law with a proviso stipulating that no construction would take place at Dinosaur or any other Park Service installation.

The Sierra Club and its allies lost a similar fight to save the Glen Canyon on the Colorado River from inundation several years later. In the wake of that defeat Brower produced the first of many Sierra Club books, *The Place No One Knew,* containing Eliot Porter's photographs of the lost canyon interlaced with epigraphs from Thoreau, Muir, and others. Like Adams's famous 1948 photoessay on the Sierra Nevada, *Yosemite and the Range of Light,* the Porter book and those that followed it hewed closely to Muir's preservationist ideology. The photographs are ascetic, almost abstract in their clarity and texture: they contain not a trace of human habitation. Uncompromising preservation in Muir's tradition was an effective strategy for forestalling reclamation projects, given the social and demographic changes of the post–World War II period; Sierra Club campaigns and publications helped save the Grand Canyon from inundation and were instrumental in securing the passage of the Wilderness Act of 1964 and the Wild and Scenic Rivers Act of 1968.

Where struggles to save the western wilderness created the modern environmental lobby group, a similar struggle in the developed East bequeathed to the world the environmental lawyer. Historically, the courts had not been friendly to environmental issues because the damage done by polluters and developers typically falls on great numbers of people, none of whom suffers enough to claim standing to sue, much less win against an opponent for whom the benefits of development are typically tangible, measurable, and substantial. This began to change in the 1960s. One early suit was *Scenic Hudson Preservation Conference* v. *Federal Power Commission,* which reached the federal court of appeals in New York in 1966. Victor Yannacone, a lawyer, sued to prevent Consolidated Edison from building a hydroelectric project on a particularly scenic part of the Hudson River north of New York City. Yannacone won: the substance of the ruling was that the Power Commission had failed to account for damage to scenic, aesthetic, or environmental values in planning the project. Yannacone's tactical innovation, which the court approved, was to allege that a coalition of pressure groups could sue in court to force normally prodevelopment government agencies to attend in good faith to environmental values. The Sierra Club used the tactic six years later in the U.S. Supreme Court case of *Sierra Club* v. *Morton,* which stopped plans to build a ski resort in the Sierra Nevada on the grounds that club members would lose the benefit of their wilderness experience were the development to go forward.

While the tactics of these postwar lobbyists and lawyers might have been modern, their ideology plainly echoed that of turn-of-the-century preservationists. Their supporters were primarily well-to-do people who could afford to visit parks and wilderness areas and who had the resources to support campaigns to preserve them. Like Muir, they appreciated wilderness areas primarily for their aesthetic value and sought to keep them in pristine condition. Like turn-of-the-century preservationists, they drew criticism for being "hoggish and mushy aesthetes" who cared more for their recreation than for the welfare of working people less well-off than they. The criticism was unfair in most cases; still, later environmental groups concentrated on issues, such as pollution and workplace safety, that were more likely to benefit a broader spectrum of people. However narrow their particular interests, these latter-day followers of Muir reactivated environmental politics in the 1950s and 1960s, beginning a process that would eventually affect much of American life.

Post–World War II conservation broke away from its turn-of-the-century predecessor as an increasing number of natural scientists began joining its ranks. The significant technological changes that transformed the American economy after World War II, particularly nuclear energy, industrial chemistry, and automation, not only wrought fundamental changes in the ecology of the planet; they also gave people new conceptual tools with which to understand the ways in which energy and materials moved through the environment. These changes brought scientists themselves into government and politics in a new way, as policy issues became increasingly technical. World War II had been a boon to high-technology business. Wartime research introduced great advances in electronics, physics, oceanography, and other fields. Bringing scientists into government in this way inevitably drew public attention to the social impact of science and technology after the war.

As scientists assumed increased importance in policy making within government, some of them took up environmental politics outside the government as an alternative. Aldo Leopold had developed a sharp critique of government resource policy after he left the Forest Service, but avoided direct involvement in political action. After 1950, in contrast, scientists from all parts of the political spectrum agitated for environmental reform. Some were traditional Socialists like Barry Commoner, whose organization of the St. Louis Committee for Nuclear Information in 1958 was one of the first explicitly political organizations of scientists. Rachel Carson occupied a place nearer the political center, though her antipesticide campaign presaged in many ways the significant contribution to environmentalism that feminist politics would make after 1970. Still others took positions on environmental issues that had conservative implications. One of these was the biologist Garrett Hardin, whose article, "The Tragedy of the Commons," became a canonical text in modern environmentalism. Following in the footsteps of Muir's disciples, these scientists contributed a second element to the new environmentalism that distinguished it from the old.

Nuclear fallout provided the public with its first object lesson on relationships between postwar technology and the environment. Here, the leader was Barry Commoner, a biologist who had worked in the Navy's campaign against insect-borne diseases during the war and had been impressed by the unexpected effects of DDT on the fish and reptile species he studied. After the war, he helped the Navy develop programs for the peacetime use of nuclear energy and was instrumental in the creation of the Atomic Energy Commission in 1946. In the mid-1950s scientists began talking among themselves about radioactive fallout from atmospheric testing of nuclear weapons. By the end of the decade, newspapers regularly printed maps tracking clouds of fallout from particular explosions as they made their way around the globe. Strontium 90, a common element in the fallout, aroused particular alarm because it has the same chemical valence as calcium: American parents took a very powerful lesson in ecology from reports about how radioactive strontium moved from explosion to atmosphere, to rain, to grass, to dairy cattle, and finally into their children's milk.

Commoner turned this new kind of environmental concern into political action. Using the St. Louis Committee for Nuclear Information as a base, Commoner joined the chemist Linus Pauling and others in agitating for a ban on the atmospheric testing of nuclear weapons. The Atmospheric Test Ban Treaty became reality in 1963; Pauling won the Nobel Peace Prize for his contribution to the campaign. Commoner remained at the forefront of left-wing environmentalism thereafter. He published his book, *Losing Ground,* in 1971 and even ran for president in 1980. His main strategy was to underscore the social impacts of science and technology, insisting that environmental problems were not the inevitable byproducts of affluence or population growth but rather stemmed from the political choices that went into the development of harmful technologies. One of the earliest scientists to take up environmental politics, Commoner remained for decades one of the leading exemplars of this new kind of environmental activist.

Although she took up activism less willingly than Commoner, the marine biologist Rachel Carson was probably more responsible than any other individual for the emergence of the new environmentalism of the 1960s and 1970s. Carson was one of two women scientists who worked for the U.S. Fish and Wildlife Service in the 1940s. Like Commoner, she had noticed the dangers of DDT during the war and its aftermath; she was also deeply impressed by the atomic bomb and gradually developed a powerful political critique of lethal technology. She came back to DDT in 1958 when she read a letter to a Boston newspaper from a woman protesting that recent aerial spraying of DDT had killed a number of songbirds on her property. *Silent Spring* appeared in 1962; its impact was immediate and profound.

Unlike *A Sand County Almanac* or Muir's writings on the Sierra Nevada, *Silent Spring* was very carefully organized and written for political impact. Carson pointedly drew the comparison between DDT and nuclear fallout, which had already seized the public's attention. Pesticides and nuclear weapons were both examples of the kind of totalitarian approach to one's enemies, in agriculture or in international politics, that had motivated Hitler's campaign against European Jewry. The environmental problems that pesticides brought with them were, however, only a symptom of a deeper maladjustment in modern attitudes toward science, humankind, and nature. Pesticides were clumsy, "chemical blunderbusses" that belonged to the "Neanderthal" age of technology. Carson advocated replacing them with environmentally sensitive, selective biological and natural controls.

Silent Spring's political contribution was to draw explicitly the links between DDT and what Leopold had called state college agriculture. It was not just the technology that was hazardous; DDT was only one manifestation of the collaboration among the chemical industry, the government, and the universi-

ties that made chemical-intensive agriculture possible. Controversy over the book raged through the rest of the 1960s. Finally, in 1972, after California biologists linked DDT to serious declines in populations of pelicans and other seabirds, the federal government banned most domestic production and uses of DDT. Four year later, the Toxic Substances Control Act of 1976 banned all twelve of the most toxic pesticides named in *Silent Spring.*

Carson had done more than anyone else to educate the public about pollution and the environment. She tied the philosophical, and especially the political, aspects of dangerous technology to their environmental effects. Her most important contribution to the developing public consciousness was to bring public health into the equation. Muir had recognized no categories in nature: while he had little use for people, he was able to knit himself at least together with Nature in a single, pulsating harmony. In general, however, conservationists before Carson had mostly concerned themselves with nonhuman nature and with society only indirectly, if at all. Carson closed that gap, demonstrating clearly the important links among ecology, political economy, and consciousness. Above all, Rachel Carson triggered the political and cultural transformation that changed conservation into environmentalism.

Environmentally minded scientists used physics and chemistry to promote public awareness of the environmental problems associated with nuclear energy in the late fifties and pesticides in the early sixties. In the late sixties, economics contributed the conceptual underpinnings for a burgeoning concern with the so-called population explosion. The leading theorist here was Paul Ehrlich, a Stanford biologist. Ehrlich's address to the Sierra Club on population problems in 1967 led a few years later to the publication of his book, *The Population Bomb.* Recalling the nineteenth-century British economist Thomas Malthus, Ehrlich claimed that uncontrolled population growth was the root cause of most of humankind's environmental problems and concluded that only rigorous birth control—preferably through individual choice, but under state compulsion if need be—could save humanity from overpopulation and eventual catastrophe.

While Ehrlich was a political liberal and later distinguished himself as an opponent of the Reagan administration's nuclear weapons program, his flirtation with Malthus had profoundly conservative political implications. These became clear with the publication in 1968 of an article by Garrett Hardin, another California biologist, called "The Tragedy of the Commons." Hardin's article popularized a body of scholarship on the economics of property rights that had been developing since 1950. The central claim was that, where resources are shared in common, competing individuals rush to take as much as they can out of the common pool before others do, leading inevitably to the eventual ruin both of the resources and of the community. Hardin described the planet's capacity to sustain human life as just such a common pool: the Earth's resources were finite, he claimed, and unlimited license to breed was leading the human race to eventual disaster. "The Tragedy of the Commons" quickly became canon. Environmentalists used the model to explain all kinds of environmental problems, from overpopulation to air pollution to wildlife depletion to the overcrowding of the national parks. Energy shortages in the 1970s seemed to confirm the impending scarcity that Hardin and his followers predicted; public interest in energy conservation and recycling increased greatly as a result.

Hardin and other "limits to growth" theorists—the term comes from a 1972 report by the Club of Rome that forecast the depletion of the planet's resources at current rates of growth—advocated government restrictions on childbearing and counseled against international support for countries in Asia and Africa that were afflicted by overpopulation and famine. Representatives of such countries attacked this strain of environmentalism as a right-wing conspiracy to deny them the benefits of economic growth. Barry Commoner and other left-leaning environmentalists, meanwhile, argued that population control was just another technical fix like DDT. It ignored the social and political roots of overpopulation, they reasoned, while it served the interests of the wealthy and powerful at the expense of those on whom the burdens of the policy were to fall.

The energy crisis that followed the formation of the international petroleum cartel, OPEC, in the early 1970s led some environmentalists to focus on the economics of American energy use. In a series of articles in the ultra-Establishment journal *Foreign Affairs,* Amory Lovins and his colleagues analyzed the economic and environmental consequences of what they called the hard path of development based on fossil and nuclear energy. Efficiency and conservation, they argued, were the country's largest and cheapest remaining sources of energy. Echoing Carson's political critique, Lovins showed how petroleum and nuclear energy were not only inefficient and ecologically destructive but brought with them political consequences that ranged from corporate concentration to a dangerously powerful national-security apparatus. Soft paths like conservation and renewable-energy resources were not only more sustainable in the long run but more democratic as well. Energy strategists like Lovins used economics to increase public awareness of environmental problems just as the population theorists did, although with radically different political implications.

Two decades of increasing agitation over environmental issues, from parks to pesticides to population and petroleum, finally bore fruit in a burst of reform legislation between 1969 and 1976. This new wave of federal regulation transformed American politics to an extent not seen since the Progressive Era and the New Deal. In many ways the new wave of lawmaking was the offspring of the civil rights and peace movements of the 1960s. The antiwar movement, particularly, contributed a great deal of energy and talent to environmentalism as the Vietnam War came to an end for most Americans in the early 1970s. A clutch of new environmental lobby-and-litigation groups came into being in the late sixties and early seventies, including the Natural Resources Defense Council, the Environmental Defense Fund, Friends of the Earth, and the League of Conservation Voters.

Just as conservation had provided controlling metaphors and organizing principles for Progressive Era reform, ecology characterized the reforms of the 1970s and distinguished the new wave from its predecessors. Where Progressive and New Deal reforms typically aimed at particular industries like banking or broadcasting or aviation, the statutes of the 1970s addressed broad-ranging social issues such as health, safety, and the environment as they appeared across the whole economy. Environmentalism emphasized the interrelatedness of social, economic, and ecological problems. It synthesized spirituality, science, politics, and economics into a very broad, systematic critique of the American political economy. That critique now surfaced in reforms aimed at many different social problems.

The first of the new statutes was the National Environmental Policy Act (NEPA) of 1969, passed in the wake of a series of ecological disasters that focused public demands for environmental protection. The wreck of the oil tanker *Torrey Canyon* spilled 119,000 tons of crude oil into the English Channel in 1967. In 1969, another chemical spill caused a section of the Cuyahoga River in Ohio to catch fire. The same year an oil well off the southern California coast blew out and ruined miles of beaches near Santa Barbara, causing the deaths of thousands of seabirds and marine mammals.

NEPA was a pathbreaking piece of legislation that amounted to a Magna Carta of the environmental movement. Fundamentally, NEPA directed agencies of the federal government to revise their procedures so as to safeguard environmental values in all their activities. The Senate bill had contained a potentially revolutionary provision that recognized "a fundamental and inalienable right to a healthful environment," but this language was softened in the final version. NEPA's most important provision required government agencies to submit environmental impact statements (EIS) for all major projects. The EIS was a new kind of legal instrument that both forced agencies to plan for the environmental consequences of their activities and gave citizens the opportunity to challenge their findings. NEPA thus greatly increased the power of environmental activists to intervene in public policymaking for resources and the environment. NEPA also enhanced the role in government of the new Environmental Protection Agency: under NEPA, the agency had the authority to review and comment on the environmental impact of federal policymaking across a wide area. Other new environmental laws allowed citizen suits to force agencies to do their jobs, while the federal courts continued to enhanced citizen powers to challenge government activity.

All the many varieties of environmentalism that had been developing since 1950 came together on Earth Day, 22 April 1970. The idea for a nationwide environmental teach-in, a tactic borrowed from the antiwar movement, originated in the office of the Senate's most active environmentalist, Gaylord Nelson of (naturally enough) Wisconsin. Earth Day was marked by speeches and demonstrations in cities and on campuses all over the nation. It marked the coming to maturity and self-awareness of the new environmental movement and led in turn to a series of environmental statutes, including the Clean Air Amendments of 1970, the Federal Water Pollution Control Amendments of 1972 (later renamed the Clean Water Act), and the Endangered Species Act of 1973. Many of these statutes strengthened legislation already on the books with tougher standards, new procedures, and citizen-suit provisions. They amounted, however, to a significant change in the American political economy. Their systemic approach to environmental problems, focus on diffused social costs, and especially the priority they gave to such intangible values as species preservation, open space, and risk-avoidance, all distinguished the post-1970 statutes from the reforms of the Progressive Era and the New Deal.

This outpouring of political change was all the more remarkable because it took place in a time of continued antiwar unrest and under a Republican administration nominally committed to freeing business activity from government supervision. The political energy behind it also generated reform in other areas as well—occupational health and safety, consumer-product safety, and traffic safety, as well as those aimed at more strictly environmental problems. Just as conservation had provided the model for political reform in the Progressive Era, environmental ideas and tactics shaped both the substance and the procedure of reform in areas only remotely related to ecology.

The country could not sustain the political energy of the early seventies for long, however. The pace of legislation dropped off sharply after the recession of 1974–1975, although Congress passed the Resource Conservation and Recovery Act to control the disposal of hazardous materials in 1976 and reauthorized the Clean Air Act the following year. A scandal involving a toxic-waste dump at Love Canal in New York spurred Congress to pass the Comprehensive Environmental Response, Compensation, and Liability Act of 1980, which established the Superfund for cleaning up old toxic sites. Still, environmentalism had changed American politics irrevocably: the Reagan Republicans came into power in 1981 believing that they had a mandate to dismantle Superfund, the Endangered Species Act, and the other reforms of the 1970s, but found that their efforts to do so only strengthened popular support for environmental protection.

The 1980s brought an elaboration and exfoliation of environmental culture that was all the more remarkable given the generally conservative context of the decade's politics. Groups like the Sierra Club continued to grow in spite of systematic efforts in the executive branch and the courts to roll back the environmental gains of the previous decade. Environmentalism's steady progress into the popular culture created alliances that would have seemed strange to the organizers of Earth Day. Advertising agencies, for example, found a strong demand among consumers for recycled or otherwise environmentally sound products. A telling example of ecology's secure place in the culture was a 1990 agreement between the Environmental Defense Fund and McDonald's Corporation to cooperate in research aimed at reducing the amount of waste generated in the company's restaurants. EDF took no money for the project, while McDonald's foreswore any effort to control the EDF's work and agreed not to use the project in its advertising. Mainstream environmental groups achieved a level of political respectability that their predecessors could hardly have imagined. At the same time, new tactics and theories developed vigorously.

One change that came over the environmental movement after the mid-1970s was a significant broadening of its demography. Environmentalism had traditionally been the preserve of middle- and upper-class white men, although feminist groups had been active in Progressive Era reform and many participated in the conservationist initiatives of the time. Rachel Carson had not written self-consciously from a woman's perspective, although the near-total domination of her profession by men at the time may have made it easier for her to leave government service for full-time nature-writing. Later feminists would recognize clearly a feminine voice in her concern for relationships between living things in any event. Certainly there was no shortage of sexism in the vicious opposition that *Silent Spring* aroused in the chemical industry. In the 1980s, however, feminists learned that they had much in common with the political ecology movement and thereafter contributed a distinctive voice to environmentalism. Such feminist writers as Mary Daly, Carolyn Merchant, and Susan Griffin made important contributions to social/environmental theory while some groups, particularly in the antinuclear movement, explicitly avowed a feminist critique of environmental problems. The agitation at Love Canal, which led to the passage of the Superfund legislation, was quite distinctly a localized movement of mothers on behalf of their children's safety.

African American groups had shown little enthusiasm for ecology in the 1960s and 1970s, although this began to change as environmentalism finally began to address workplace hazards, public health, and other problems of so-called built environments. By the 1980s, the Congressional Black Caucus was the most consistently proenvironment organization in the federal government.

American Indians, particularly, assumed a central role in environmental politics. Indians had long been a powerful symbol of the lost frontier, patronizing though the conservationists' use of the Indian icon might be. Once tribal governments established some power to control natural resources in their territories, however, Indians became powerful and creative environmental players in their own right and on their own behalf. Court decisions in the 1970s gave control over a significant shares of the Pacific Northwest salmon industry to the Yakima, Puyallup, and other Native American groups. Groups in other parts of the country won similar victories by bringing together civil rights and environmental politics. The fact that Indian reservations lay scattered all across the country, many of them at key points in sensitive ecological systems, forced state and national lawmakers to cooperate with the tribes in developing new, more localized and participatory approaches to managing wildlife, water, grassland, and other resources.

Postwar environmentalists brought a new set of tactics to the movement, from the Sierra Club's effective use of wilderness photography in the 1950s to the teams of scientists and litigators that the Environmental Defense Fund and the Natural Resources Defense Council developed in the 1970s. Other groups borrowed more aggressive, direct-action methods from the civil rights and antiwar movements of the 1960s. The Canadian group Greenpeace outfitted a ship, the *Rainbow Warrior*, to harass high-seas whalers and to interdict nuclear testing in the South Pacific. Greenpeace commandos in small rubber boats staged amphibious landings at a southern California nuclear plant in the 1970s and once even invaded the Soviet Union to protest that country's whaling operations.

A 1976 novel by Edward Abbey, *The Monkey-Wrench Gang*, popularized a new term for sabotage directed against logging and reclamation projects in the West. In 1985, Dave Foreman of the group EarthFirst! compiled a how-to guide for environmental saboteurs entitled *Eco-Defense: A Field Guide to Monkeywrenching*. Foreman's followers chained themselves to trees in old-growth forests scheduled for logging and drove spikes into standing timber so as to damage the loggers' machinery. Foreman's politics were ambiguous and controversial. Earth First! adopted the direct-action tactics of the most radical black and antiwar movements of the 1960s, but followed the most reactionary of the population economists in urging that starving nations be left to their fates. Tree-spiking threatened lumber workers with serious injury and brought a good deal of public outrage down upon Foreman's group. Foreman's defenders, in turn, claimed that protecting the last remains of original forest demanded radical measures. They further maintained that the notorious danger of timber work was as much a product of the industry's disregard for safety as it was of environmentalist monkeywrenching.

The 1980s saw the development of a new philosophical approach to environmentalism, Deep Ecology. Its first exponent was a Norwegian philosopher, Arne Naess, who held that all life forms had as much right to live as human beings did. Another contribu-

The Earth from space. This photograph of the earth, taken by the Apollo 17 astronauts in December 1972, was a great spur to environmentalism in the 1970s. COURTESY NASA.

tor to the theory of Deep Ecology was a British chemist, James Lovelock. Lovelock had made a fortune by patenting a device for assaying gas molecules at extremely low concentrations that proved to be an important tool in space exploration. In 1979, he published *Gaia: A New Look at Life on Earth*. The book, named after the Greek goddess of the Earth, made the claim that all life on the Earth consists of one great, self-regulating planetary organism. That organism, Lovelock thought, consisted not only of every living creature but also of many things that people normally think of as nonliving: the atmosphere, the oceans, and the planet itself.

Biologists since Darwin had typically understood life as something that adapts to but is essentially separate from its physical and chemical environments. Lovelock challenged that idea. To explain his hypothesis, Lovelock pointed out that the Earth's atmosphere, unlike that of Mars and other "dead" planets, is chemically unstable: full of oxygen, methane, and other active gases that would normally react with each other until they reached equilibrium. Life, taken as a whole, maintains that instability. Earth's atmosphere, Lovelock reasoned, is thus both necessary for and produced by life. The conclusion was that living things and their chemical and physical environments make up a coherent, interdependent, self-regulating, living whole. Lovelock's Gaia hypothesis drew a wide range of reaction, from skepticism from his scientific colleagues to eager acceptance by EarthFirst! and other groups on the environmental left.

Like Turner's hypothesis about the influence of the frontier on American history, the Gaia hypothesis is an extremely creative one, important perhaps as much for the debate that it engenders about humankind's relationship with the natural world as for its intrinsic scientific value. Over the 1980s, at any rate, it encouraged scientists to think and write about the interdependence of life, climate, and geology much more than they had done previously. If Gaia's main lesson is that one ought not to draw neat distinctions between life and nonlife, it fit with the main course of development in modern environmental thought, which was steadily to break down distinctions between humans and the nonhuman world. Since 1950 wilderness advocates like David Brower, scientists like Rachel Carson and Barry Commoner, and the political activists of the 1970s had all worked to dissolve the boundaries between ecology, political economy, and popular consciousness: in that sense, Gaia was only a late and intellectually creative step along the way.

THE ENVIRONMENTAL REVOLUTION IN AMERICAN CULTURE

Environmental thought and policy have played a central role in the development of twentieth-century American capitalism. Americans have always known that the natural wealth of the continent they took over from the Indians was crucial to their economic development and their cultural identity. It was not, however, until the end of the frontier forced them to confront the fact that their resources were finite after all that they began to think systematically about the relationship between their society and its nonhuman environment. Since the seventeenth century, capitalism has been a profoundly progressive form of social organization that incorporated particular concepts of the relationships between political economy, ecology, and consciousness. By the twentieth century it had given humankind the technical capacity, at least, to end privation on the planet. In the United States, particularly, it also encouraged the liberation of humankind's potential to understand the world and to cultivate it for the good of all.

Capitalism thrived, however, under a particular set of ecological conditions—those of the frontier. The physical conditions that supported the expansion of European society in the United States came to an end in the 1890s, although Americans found in artificial forms of energy a temporary substitute for unlimited supplies of new land. Since the 1890s, American politics and social thought have in significant measure revolved around the problem of adapting traditional forms of economic production and social organization to the new order of things.

Progressive Era conservation was fundamentally a struggle to come to grips with the sea change announced by Frederick Jackson Turner. As Turner put it, their challenge was to bring what was best about frontier culture into the modern era. Preservationists like John Muir believed that protecting what little remained of undeveloped Nature was crucial to the spiritual well-being of individual Americans. Gifford Pinchot and the other utilitarian conservationists, in contrast, tried to harness new theories in economics and politics that emerged from advanced industrial society to the conservation of natural resources, especially timber and water. Interdependence and central planning were the key concepts. After developing them first in the context of resources management, the Progressives applied the conservationist way of thinking to a range of other social problems, from education to social welfare. If the Progressives tended to neglect such intangible values as participatory democracy and aesthetics, they at least brought a halt to the profligacy that had devastated huge areas of the country.

Franklin D. Roosevelt and the other New Dealers faced, above all, the challenge of rebuilding a capitalist economy that had nearly destroyed itself. They thus borrowed more from Pinchot's utilitarian approach than from the asceticism and spirituality of Muir. In the TVA and other plans for rehabilitating the nation's agricultural sector, they brought scientific policymaking and central planning to levels that the Progressives could hardly have imagined. They also, however, realized that sustainable resource use and social democracy were interdependent. At its best, as in the Soil Conservation Service, the New Deal linked self-determination for those who worked the land with intelligent community control over production in a way that Turner might well have approved. Aldo Leopold, though trained in the Pinchotian tradition, brought an appreciation of Nature for its own sake more into line with life in society than Muir had found possible.

Fundamental changes in ecology, economic production, and social thought interacted to bring about the birth of a new and radically different form of environmentalism in the post–World War II era. What distinguished the new movement from the old was the close integration, in thought and action, of natural science, politics, and spirituality. Wilderness preservationists rehabilitated the ideology of John Muir, but with a new political sophistication learned from experience in the New Deal. Scientists like Rachel Carson translated their awareness of the dangers of postwar technology into popular language and catalyzed social reform in a way that Leopold could not or would not do. Social activists from the 1960s, finally, brought the new movement to maturity on Earth Day, 1970, and in the remarkable burst of lawmaking for resources and environment that followed it.

The reform wave of the 1970s lasted no longer than those of the Progressive Era and the New Deal, but it worked no less fundamental a change in the American political order. As before, environmental concepts and strategies dominated policymaking not only for natural resources but also for a wide range of social problems. As before, new ideas about nature both stemmed from changes in social experience and suggested ways in which to harmonize the social order more closely with the facts of life as people knew them. By the twentieth century's last decade the ideas and habits of environmentalism had apparently worked their way into the culture thoroughly and irrevocably. The frontier may have been officially closed in 1890, but coming to terms with it, economically, politically, and culturally, required much of the country's social energy for the entire twentieth century.

SEE ALSO Infrastructure; Natural Resources; Consumption (all in this volume); Leisure and Recreation (volume IV).

BIBLIOGRAPHY

Frederick Jackson Turner's essay is reprinted in Turner, *The Significance of the Frontier in American History* (1985), among other places. For an environmental perspective on the history of the West, see Donald Worster, *Under Western Skies: Nature and History in the American West* (1992). Alfred W. Crosby, *Ecological Imperialism: The Biological Expansion of Europe, 900–1900* (1987), is an excellent treatment of the frontier process in general, from an ecological perspective.

There are a number of good treatments of environmental politics in the United States. Samuel P. Hays, *Conservation and the Gospel of Efficiency: The Progressive Conservation Movement, 1890–1920* (1959), shows how conservation lay at the heart of Progressive reform, and his *Beauty, Health, and Permanence: Environmental Politics in the United States, 1955–1985* (1989), treats the emergence of modern environmentalism. One of the best general histories of twentieth-century environmentalism, from the preservationist perspective, is Stephen Fox, *John Muir and His Legacy: The American Conservation Movement* (1981). Donald Fleming, "The Roots of the New Conservation Movement," *Perspectives in American History* 6 (1972): 3–179, traces the intellectual history of modern environmentalism. Roderick Nash, *Wilderness and the American Mind* (1967), is a standard text on American attitudes toward the environment. Alfred Runte, *National Parks: The American Experience* (1979), is a good history of the national park system.

The starting point for the study of environmental ideas is Donald Worster, *Nature's Economy: A History of Ecological Ideas* (1985); see also his *The Wealth of Nature: Environmental History and the Ecological Imagination* (1993). Carolyn Merchant, *The Death of Nature: Women, Ecology, and the Scientific Revolution* (1980), not only captures the essence of modern Western culture's approach to the environment but highlights the crucial but frequently ignored significance of gender in relations between humankind and the natural world. Some of the most sophisticated theoretical work on ecology and social change may be found in Carolyn Merchant, *Ecological Revolutions: Nature, Gender, and Science in New England* (1989), and Laurence Tribe, "Ways Not to Think about Plastic Trees: New Foundations for Environmental Law," *Yale Law Journal* 83 (1974): 1315–1348.

Donald Worster, ed., "A Round Table: Environmental History," *Journal of American History* 76 (1990): 1087–1147, is a good introduction to environmental historiography; and Donald Worster, ed., *The Ends of the Earth: Perspectives on Modern Environmental History* (1989), contains a selection of recent work as well as excellent discussions of the field by Worster himself. Worster's *Dust Bowl: The Southern Plains in the 1930s* (1982), and William Cronon, *Nature's Metropolis: Chicago and the Great West, 1848–1893* (1991), are examples of some of the best work in the field.

Frances Cairncross, *Costing the Earth: The Challenge for Governments, the Opportunities for Business* (1992), is a good treatment of current environmental problems from a highly economistic point of view. Robert Pogue Harrison, *Forests: The Shadow of Civilization* (1992), is a lyrical exercise in literary criticism. Al Gore, *Earth in the Balance: Healing the Global Environment* (1992), is interesting not only because its author is the highest elected official in the world to write coherently on the environment, but also because the book manifests so many different strains of American environmental culture.

Canonical texts in American environmentalism, most of which were mentioned here, include George Perkins Marsh, *Man and Nature: Or Physical Geography* (1865). Edwin Way Teale, ed., *The Wilderness World of John Muir* (1975), is a good collection of Muir's writing. Gifford Pinchot, *Breaking New Ground* (1987), is a history of conservation written by its chief architect. Aldo Leopold's main work is *A Sand County Almanac: And Sketches Here and There* (1949). Ansel Adams, *Yosemite and the Range of Light* (1982), captures the photographer's vision of the Sierra Nevada and is an excellent companion to Muir's writing. John McPhee, *Encounters with the Archdruid* (1971), is a good introduction to the life and thought of David Brower. Rachel Carson, *Silent Spring* (1962), may be the most important text in the canon. Garrett Hardin's provocative article, "The Tragedy of the Commons," appeared in *Science* 162 (1968): 1243–1248. See also Paul Ehrlich, *The Population Bomb* (1975). Barry Commoner, *The Closing Circle* (1971), presents the left-wing case for environmentalism and against Hardin. The core text for energy politics is Amory B. Lovins, "Energy Strategy: The Road Not Taken?" *Foreign Affairs* 55 (1976): 65–96. Dave Foreman and Bill Haywood, eds., *Eco-Defense: A Field Guide to Monkeywrenching* (1985), is an artifact of the movement as well as a how-to manual. Finally, an introduction to Deep Ecology may be had in James Lovelock, *Gaia: A New Look at Life on Earth* (1987).

NATURAL RESOURCES

Gavin Wright

The United States has long been rich in natural resources, an abundance that has had a profound influence on the country's prosperity and economic preeminence in the world. The term *natural* may imply that these resources have the character of gifts to the economy, and therefore that the country has been the beneficiary of extraordinary good fortune in its endowment of land, forests, and minerals. To a very considerable degree, however, American natural resource abundance was manmade, or "socially constructed." Although the temperate-zone regions of the country were blessed with naturally fertile soils, the expansion of cropland throughout the nineteenth century required an arduous struggle to clear these lands of their original forest. The further extensions of agriculture during the twentieth century have been possible only with the aid of artificial irrigation and other forms of human intervention. As agricultural technologies have become more sophisticated, production has soared even while inputs of labor and land have contracted.

The development of the country's endowment of minerals was no more natural than was that of its farmland. American world leadership in industrial minerals emerged in historical time, as much a part of the process of economic development as was the rise of mechanized agriculture and manufacturing. The centrality of minerals to the American economy peaked in the first quarter of the twentieth century. Since then, the economy has steadily moved away from its earlier reliance on domestic resources, although important legacies of its resource-using history remain, chiefly in patterns of land-use and household behavior. The change is partly attributable to depletion of domestic supplies, but is more fully explained by the decline in transportation costs and other barriers to international trade, the development of mineral deposits around the world, and the rise of science-based technologies not tightly bound to the location of resources. The country's shift to the status of net resource importer is often viewed with alarm, but it does not have decisive economic consequences in the modern world. Environmental issues are now more likely to be an appropriate focus of emerging concern.

CONCEPTS AND THEMES

By longstanding convention in economics, the factors of production are grouped into three categories: labor, capital, and land. The last of these is understood to refer not just to soil but to all inputs into the economy not produced by human activity. Among these natural resources, it is also conventional to make a distinction between renewable and nonrenewable resources: the latter are those taken from the earth and not replaced, like coal or iron ore; the former are those animal and vegetable substances capable of replacing themselves or being replaced, like trees or livestock. According to another venerable and intuitively plausible doctrine, it would seem obvious that nonrenewable resources will become scarcer over the course of time, because they are ultimately fixed in quantity and will inevitably become exhausted. A line of economic analysis has examined the terms and rate at which this exhaustion will occur, beginning with Harold Hotelling's classic 1931 article, "The Economics of Exhaustible Resources." If one applies this logic to American history, which from the settlers' perspective began with a vast untouched continent at the disposal of a small population, it is not surprising to find that economic activity centered heavily on the use of natural resources at first and then gradually changed.

A little intuition can be a dangerous thing, however, because the facts of history have confounded this scenario many times over. The long-term relative price trend of virtually all useful nonrenewable materials has been downward, as shown in a 1963 study by Harold J. Barnett and Chandler Morse, and continues so in the 1990s. Ironically, the natural resources that have become increasingly scarce have been the renewable ones, such as timber and various types of wildlife. The American economy has become less closely tied to mineral supplies, but this has not been the result of resource exhaustion and rising prices. Evidently something is lacking in the intuitive notion of resource exhaustion as a guide to history.

According to E. A. Wrigley (1988), a crucial dimension of the eighteenth-century industrial revolution was the development of mineral-using technologies, which released industry from the constraints of the "organic economy." So long as energy had to be obtained from vegetable sources such as timber, its supply was either limited to an annual harvest or subject to rising costs as it came from greater and greater distances. The replacement of wood by coal, however, opened up for human use a vast inventory of already-stored energy, an inventory known to be abundant in England. Because mineral deposits were geographically concentrated, moreover, specialized transportation systems could carry these materials to appropriately located establishments for use. Cheap, concentrated energy thus served to relax geographic limits on the scale of production and to increase the return on fixed investment in all sectors. To a considerable degree, the trans-national technological developments of the nineteenth century represented an elaboration and refinement of these basic principles.

From the perspective of 1800, however, many of the practices of European settlers in North America represented a step backward. American farmers with their abundance of land were indifferent to the intensive, yield-enhancing methods that Europeans considered "scientific agriculture." At the same time, America was not thought to have any significant deposits of valuable minerals. Both Adam Smith and Benjamin Franklin observed that North America had no mines, or at least "none that are at present supposed to be worth the working," according to Smith. So the United States relied on imports of British coal until the 1820s. The absence of coal, however, was compensated by an abundance of wood. And timber was not only plentiful but readily available because it was a byproduct of the ongoing process of clearing forests for farmland. Nineteenth-century Americans adapted their technologies and consumption patterns to the use of wood to an extent unmatched in the world at that time. But reliance on wood fuels consigned industries to what were then outmoded technologies, such as charcoal-using iron foundries. According to Alfred Chandler (1972), it was not until the opening of the anthracite fields of eastern Pennsylvania that large-scale, steam-powered factories were feasible in America. The emergence of the United States as the world's leading mineral producer came later, between the Civil War and World War I.

The next section of this essay examines agriculture, first among the so-called primary sectors of the economy, tracing the transition from input-based expansion in the nineteenth century to technology-driven productivity growth in the twentieth. Attention shifts to minerals in the next sections, which recount first the expansion of that sector and its links to industrialization, and then the causes and consequences of the shift to external sources of minerals. The last two sections take up two notable case studies: petroleum, the last and most dramatic example of America's resource-centered history; and forests and the timber industry, whose history interacts with that of minerals and exhibits a long transition from "mining" to "farming."

TWENTIETH-CENTURY AMERICAN AGRICULTURE

American agricultural production has grown continually since the early nineteenth century, but the character of the resources generating that growth has dramatically changed. In the nineteenth century, the increased output of crops largely followed the expansion of farm acreage, as settlers moved westward and occupied the best natural farmland in the nation. Labor productivity grew by two- to fourfold, in part because of migration onto better farmland but mainly because of the adoption of mechanical technologies in the major northern field crops, greatly expanding the acreage that a single farm worker could cultivate and harvest. These trends continued into the twentieth century, as animal power gave way to tractors, but they could not go on indefinitely. By 1910, the best farmland was under cultivation; total harvested acreage peaked in 1930 and has declined modestly since then. Hours of labor in agriculture ceased to grow early in the century, and since World War II they have fallen to a small fraction of what they once were (figure 1). Continued output growth has been driven not by traditional resources but by rising inputs of machinery, fertilizer, chemicals, irrigation, and new scientifically developed forms of feed and seed.

Yields per acre, which showed almost no upward trend prior to the 1930s, have doubled or tripled since then in nearly all the major crops (figure 2). The most spectacular example is hybrid corn: the new seeds were first adopted in Iowa between 1933 and 1935, and by

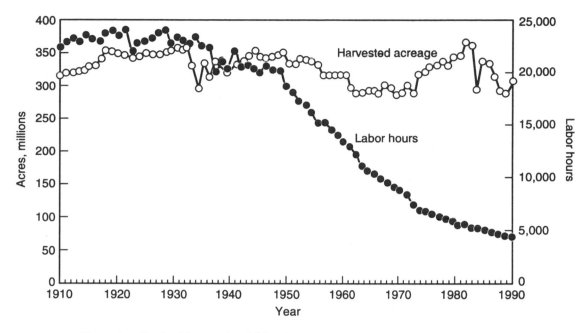

Figure 1. Cropland harvested and labor hours in U.S. agriculture, 1910–1990. Source: U.S. Department of Agriculture, Economic Research Service, *Economic Indicators of the Farm Sector* (1982); U.S. Dept. of Commerce, Bureau of the Census, *Agricultural Statistics* (1991).

1959 accounted for 95 percent of corn planted nationwide, increasing yields from the historic level of 25 bushels per acre to 62 between 1960 and 1964, and to more than 100 in the 1980s. The yield increases in other crops were only slightly less impressive. Part of the impact derived from the complementarity between improved strains and greater use of fertilizer. The use of commercial fertilizer accelerated after

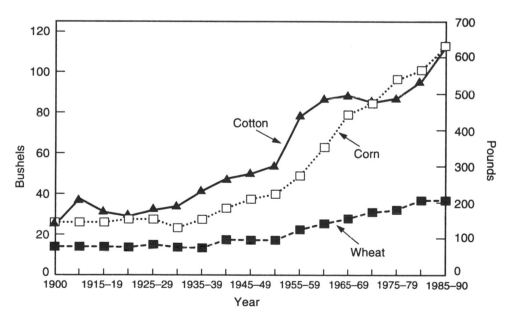

Figure 2. Wheat, corn, and cotton, yields per acre, 1900–1990. Source: *Historical Statistics of the United States* (1970); U.S. Dept. of Commerce, Bureau of the Census, *Agricultural Statistics* (1991).

World War II, in part because of technological breakthroughs and cost reductions in the fertilizer industry itself. Increased attention to yields and soils was also encouraged by government farm programs, which limited acreage in particular crops.

These technological trends have had a dramatic counterpart in the human experience of farming. Although agriculture is still one of the great strengths of the American economy, it no longer provides employment for substantial numbers of the country's labor force. The share of persons engaged in agricultural production fell from more than 35 percent in 1900 to less than 3 percent in 1990. The incidence of tenancy has declined, and the typical modern American farmer is now a part-timer, earning the majority of his or her income elsewhere. Farms today are not only large but highly specialized and commercial. They supply not much more of their own household needs (e.g., milk, chickens, fruits and vegetables) than the national average. The demise of the traditional farm as a family enterprise has often been painful, although in the postwar era many were able to retire on favorable terms because of the appreciated value of their real estate.

As in many other areas of life, the South was a special case. In the cotton and tobacco belts, mechanization was long delayed, and living standards remained far below those prevailing elsewhere in the country. In the Deep South, early in the century, the predominant organizational form was not the family farm but the plantation, with distinctive labor institutions (primarily sharecropping) operating within a system of racial segregation. Although labor was mobile within the sector, the agricultural population was largely isolated from outside opportunities. The regional gap was so great that the South accounted for more than half the nation's farm population in 1910, though it produced only 30 percent of the gross value of farm products. The first major outmigration from southern agriculture began during World War I, but the decisive break did not come until World War II, and the final blow was the introduction of the first commercially successful mechanical cotton picker by International Harvester in 1949. As the result of mechanization, increased yields per acre, and competition from synthetic fibers as well as new producers elsewhere in the world, cotton acreage in the South declined precipitously, from 23 million in 1930 to 3 million in 1982. Southern corn acreage fell by a similar amount. About half of the displaced cotton-corn acreage shifted into other crops, mainly soybeans; the remainder is now forestland.

Although American agricultural history has many economic, political, and social dimensions, the topic here is how this history relates to natural resources. Has production been limited by the growing scarcity of farmland, the supply of which is fixed by nature? Worse yet, has the rise of output been possible only because the country has drawn down stocks of natural resources such as groundwater? Has the use of chemical fertilizers and pesticides inflicted lasting damage on the environment, damage that increasingly sophisticated biotechnologies may only worsen?

The first of these questions is the easiest to answer. It is difficult to maintain that agricultural production has been or will be severely constrained by a shortage of cropland. Acreage harvested is well below its historical peak, and much land formerly in crops has reverted to forest. The U.S. Conservation Service estimates that for every hundred acres presently in cropland, there are thirty-six acres of potential cropland of roughly comparable quality. Earlier analyses of the dangers of soil erosion are now known to have exaggerated the magnitude of losses, while underestimating the recuperative powers of the soil. In any case, the increased yields per acre are undeniable. It is true that the value of farmland has increased over the twentieth century, but it is also true that the relative prices of farm products have declined, despite the increasing relative importance of exports. The level of production is now limited much more by export demand than by amount of cropland.

Despite these successes, fears about the sustainability of the country's agricultural path deserve to be taken seriously. A particular concern is the supply of water, a scarce resource that in many parts of the country has been priced far below its true social cost. Enthusiasm for public water projects was high after World War II, expanding the area of irrigated farmland by more than 25 million acres in the western states. But such projects have now largely halted as the reality of limits has become more fully appreciated. For example, in the High Plains of the Southwest, irrigation had by 1990 drawn down the level of the Ogallala aquifer by more than 40 percent of its original volume. In California and elsewhere, rising salinity levels and land subsidence threaten not only agriculture but supplies of water for urban uses. Critics have voiced concern about the impact of these and many other agricultural technologies on broader regional and global ecosystems.

As serious as these resource and environmental issues may be, the historical resilience of American agriculture is the best evidence for the view that

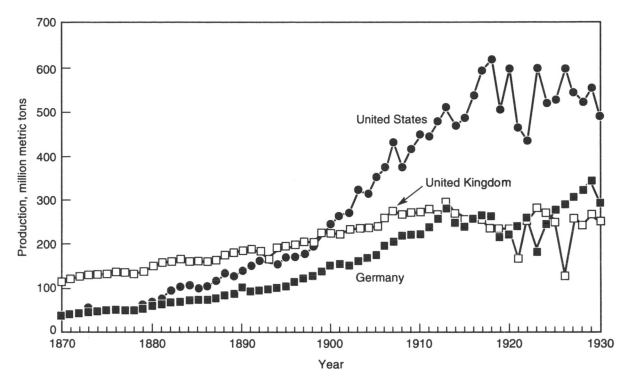

Figure 3.   Coal production in the United States, United Kingdom, and Germany, 1870–1930, in million metric tons. Source: U.S. Geological Survey, *Mineral Resources of the United States* [various issues]; *European Historical Statistics, 1750–1970* (1975), pp. 362, 364, 366, 368.

these problems need not jeopardize fundamental living standards or productivity. American agriculture has a great productive potential. The issue is not primarily the level of output but its composition and location, and the technology used to produce it. To be sure, realistic prices for water in arid regions or systems of charges or incentives to impel farmers to bear the social costs of environmental damage will raise the costs of agricultural goods. But the history of American agriculture gives us every reason to believe that technology can be developed to make these adaptations at modest cost.

THE RISE OF AMERICAN MINERAL ABUNDANCE

The rise of the United States to a position of world leadership in minerals was a post–Civil War development. As late as the 1870s, Britain was self-sufficient in iron ore, copper, lead, tin, and coal and was unquestionably the world's foremost mining nation. In 1865, however, the economist W. Stanley Jevons accurately forecast that Britain would soon be surpassed by the United States in coal production and hence (in his view) in manufacturing more generally. Although

Jevons's *The Coal Question* is commonly listed as merely one among many ill-fated pessimistic predictions about the world's resources, in fact Jevons saw the issue clearly from a national perspective. He was well aware that the world's supply of coal was "practically inexhaustible," but he argued that much of Britain's peculiar advantage was traceable to the cheapness and quality of its coal in comparison to that of other nations. It is striking that the ascendancy of the United States to leadership in industrial production and per capita gross domestic product (GDP) between 1890 and 1910 had a close parallel in the pattern of national coal production (figure 3).

Perhaps the clearest evidence that resource abundance was not merely a geological endowment lies in the breadth and variety of American minerals and the coincidence of timing in the growth of production. Between 1870 and 1910, leadership or near-leadership passed to the United States in the production of lead, copper, iron ore, antimony, magnesite, mercury, nickel, silver, and zinc. By 1913, the country was the world's leading producer of virtually every one of the major industrial minerals of that day (figure 4).

Contrary to the intuition that the importance of

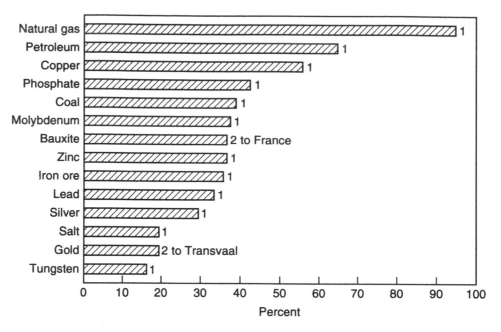

Figure 4.   United States share of world mineral production, 1913. Source: U.S. Geological Survey, *Mineral Resources of the United States* (1913).

resources should decline over time, the share of mining in the national labor force continued to rise until 1909, and its share in gross national product (GNP) did not peak until the 1920s. The indirect contribution to GNP was far greater. The relative price of material inputs declined, and American manufacturing exports became more resource-intensive between 1880 and 1920. Cain and Paterson (1986) find a significant materials-using bias in technological change in nine of twenty manufacturing industries, including many of the most prominent and successful cases. Although the production and consumption of lumber grew absolutely until 1907, the country underwent a long-term shift in the relative importance of material and energy sources, away from vegetable matter and in favor of minerals.

What were the forces propelling the national economy along this path? It is tempting to explain the rise of mineral production simply as the byproduct of territorial expansion. How could the deposits in Colorado, South Dakota, and Montana have been discovered and developed until these regions had been brought within the borders of the nation and settlement begun? Nevertheless, although the opening of the western public domain was undoubtedly an important part of the story, the process was broader. Some of the most dramatic production growth did not occur in the Far West, but in the older parts of the country; copper in Michigan, coal in Pennsylvania and Illinois, oil in Pennsylvania and later Indiana, for example. Mineral discoveries were not merely byproducts of national expansion but also the results of purposeful exploration, often in areas that were (and in many cases, still are) remote from centers of population. Many other countries in the world were large and (as we now know) well endowed with minerals. But no other country exploited its geological potential to a comparable extent.

This point is illustrated by the example of copper (figure 5). It was by no means obvious that the United States had a better natural endowment of copper ores than did Chile, and prior to 1880, Chilean copper production exceeded that of the United States. Chile had nearly recovered its supremacy by 1930, and has maintained its position since. During the 1880–1930 era of U.S. mineral ascendancy, however, the United States was far in the lead. Its performance represented much more than discovery: it also included a revolution in copper metallurgy (bessemerizing, pyritic smelting, electrolytic refining) that allowed the exploitation of low-grade coppers. By 1913, all major American copper mines were of this type.

A study by David and Wright (1992) emphasizes the following four elements in the rise of the American minerals economy.

First, an accommodating legal environment. For more than a century, mining activity in the United States has been governed by the federal Mining Law

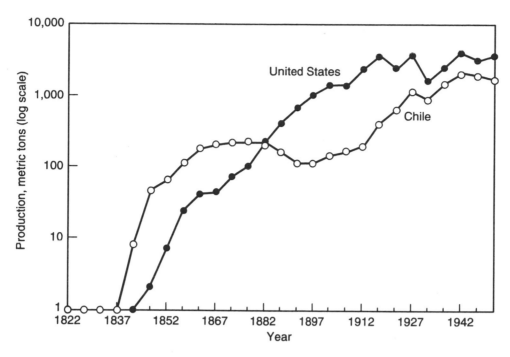

Figure 5.   Copper production in the United States and Chile, 1840–1950. Source: Christopher J. Schmitz, *World Non-ferrous Metal Production and Prices, 1700–1976* (1979).

of 1872, among the most liberal in the world. The act espoused the principle of open access to the public domain for exploration, with simple and inexpensive procedures for gaining exclusive rights (patenting a claim) upon evidence of discovery. It would be a mistake, however, to view the encouragement to mining as flowing exclusively from the effects of a simple well-specified system of rights and incentives, because much of the best mineral land was transferred into private hands outside of the procedures set down by federal law. Nearly 6 million acres of coal lands were transferred into private hands between 1873 and 1906, for example, mostly disguised as farmland. Most of the iron lands of northern Minnesota and Wisconsin were fraudulently privatized under the provisions of the Homestead Act. Nonetheless, whether through official or unofficial procedures, the posture of American legal authority toward mining was permissive and even encouraging well into the twentieth century. Behind this posture lay a broad national consensus on the desirability of resource development.

Second, investment in the infrastructure of public knowledge. Established in 1879, the United States Geological Survey (USGS) was the most ambitious and productive governmental science project of the nineteenth century. The USGS was the successor to a great many state-sponsored surveys, and to a number of more narrowly focused federal efforts. It proved to be highly responsive to the concerns of western mining interests, and the practical value to prospectors of its detailed mineral maps gave the USGS, in turn, a powerful constituency in support of its scientific research. The early-twentieth-century successes of the USGS in petroleum were instrumental in transforming the attitudes of the oil industry from hunches and folklore toward trained geologists and applied geological science.

Third, mining education. By the late nineteenth century, the United States emerged as the world's leading educator in mining engineering and metallurgy. The early leader was the Columbia School of Mines, opened in 1864, and some twenty schools granted degrees in mining from 1870 to 1890. A surge in enrollment occurred during the decade bracketing the turn of the century, at which time the University of California claimed to be the largest mining college in the world. A manpower survey for military purposes in 1917 identified 7,500 mining engineers in the country, with a remarkably broad range of professional experience and mineral specialties. American mining schools provided a steady stream of trained personnel to industry, for whose needs the curriculum was closely adapted. The most famous American mining engineer, Herbert Hoover, maintained that the increasing assignment of trained engineers to positions of combined financial and managerial, as well as technical responsibility, was largely an American development.

Fourth, the ethos of exploration. Mineral exploration, even when conducted by a decentralized army of individual prospectors, was a network activity, replete with spillovers and unexpected consequences in the acquisition of knowledge. Each new discovery provides clues regarding the location and properties of likely future discoveries. It usually turned out that the more thoroughly an area was explored, the larger its mineral potential proved to be. This regularity was noted by the compilers of an international survey of iron ore resources, conducted in 1910 by the International Geological Congress:

> One of the most striking results of the collection of the reports is that areas covered by the reports of group A [reliable calculations based on actual investigations] contain much greater quantities of known and recorded iron ores than is the case with those covered by reports of group B [figures based only on very approximate estimates]. This may be expressed in other words to the effect that the more a district becomes known and its industrial resources are developed, the greater become also its actual iron ore resources.

According to the report, the United States was not only the country most richly endowed with actual iron-ore reserves, but—even at that late date—it also had the greatest opportunity for future expansion, since it contained fully 70 percent of the world's estimated potential reserves. The very faith that important mineral discoveries were (still) possible was itself an important source of ongoing new discoveries. In the case of petroleum, the opening of major new fields continued into the 1930s and, in Alaska, into the 1970s.

NATURAL RESOURCES AND AMERICAN INDUSTRIALIZATION

Americans, including economists, tend to attribute their country's historic economic success to free enterprise, technology, and hard work, not to abundant natural resources. Perhaps "primary production" or "extractive industries" are regarded as primitive types of economic activity, which advanced countries move away from as progress unfolds. In light of these expectations, it may be unsettling to observe the extent to which American industrialization was dominated by products closely linked to natural resources. Table 1 displays a list of industries ranked by absolute growth of net exports between 1879 and 1909. Perhaps it is something of a surprise to see that raw cotton exports were by far the leader, as they had been in the decades before the Civil War. After cotton, however, nearly all the leading categories were manufactured goods clearly linked to the resource economy in one way or another: petroleum products, primary copper, meat packing and poultry, steel works and rolling mills, coal mining, vegetable oils, grainmill products, sawmill products, and so on. The only items not conspicuously resource-oriented are the various categories of machinery. Even here, however, some types of machinery serviced the resource economy directly (such as farm equipment), while virtually all were beneficiaries in that they were made of metal. These observations are not intended to debunk or diminish the American industrial achievement, only to stress that the country's industrialization was built upon its resource strength.

It may be still more surprising to look at the same table for the years 1899–1928, a time when American leadership in industry was one of the wonders of the world (table 2). The one eye-catching change is the leap of motor vehicle exports to the forefront. After that, the list is similar to that in the previous table and is highly resource-oriented: among the leaders, we still see petroleum products, cotton, primary copper, steel works and rolling mills, coal mining, tobacco, sawmill products, and farm equipment. Among the newcomers are canned foods and mining machinery, which are also tied to the resource-based economy. The pattern of international exchange implied by these tables is very different from that of the post–World War II era, characterized by a high volume of two-way trade in similar product categories. Instead, column 2 indicates that these products were mainly exports, not imports. Thus it seems fair to say that American industrialization had a strong resource-using slant well into the twentieth century, and that this was a distinctive characteristic of American industrialization.

It is more difficult to assert that American industry succeeded *because* of the advantages offered by cheap resources. In some industries breakthroughs in resource supply do seem to have been essential. American steel rails, for example, were not competitive against British and German imports without tariff protection until the 1890s, when the rich iron ore from the Mesabi Range began to arrive at the steel mills of the lower Great Lakes. Thereafter, the U.S. industry quickly moved into a position of leadership in both labor productivity and fuel efficiency. As of 1907–1909, the economist Robert Allen's estimates of total-factor productivity in iron and steel

Table 1.   HIGH ABSOLUTE NET EXPORT GROWTH INDUSTRIES, 1879–1909

Industry	Net Exports, Millions of Dollars, 1909	Exports/ (Exp + Imp), 1909[a]	Growth in Current Dollars, Millions of Dollars, 1879–1909[b]	Growth in Constant Dollars, Millions of Dollars, 1879–1909[b]
Cotton	404	.97	243	223
Petroleum products	105	1.00	67	102
Primary copper	82	1.00	79	75
Meat packing and poultry	153	.98	61	51
Steel works and rolling mills	27	.77	37	43
Coal mining	34	.91	33	32
Vegetable oils	37	.83	32	31
Farm equipment	26	.99	23	26
Special industrial machinery	22	.86	19	22
Leather tanning and finishing	25	.85	22	22
Grain mill products	51	.87	19	21
Sawmills, planing, and veneer products	26	.68	18	12
Fabricated wire products	9	1.00	9	10
Paving and roofing	10	1.00	10	10
Footwear (except rubber)	10	.98	10	9
Other commercial machinery and equipment	10	1.00	8	9
Other nonmetallic minerals	8	.98	9	8
Communication equipment	6	1.00	6	7
Logging	4	.62	10	7
Tools and general hardware	7	1.00	6	7
Other hardware	5	1.00	6	6
Motor vehicles	6	.72	6	6
Railroad equipment	5	1.00	5	6

[a] Exports are expressed as a percentage of total trade. Hence, for the items with a value of 1.00 imports are zero or close to zero.
[b] The movement from current dollars to constant dollars adjusts for changes in the relative prices of commodities in each export category.
SOURCE: Mary Locke Eysenbach, *American Manufactured Exports 1879–1914* (1976). Price deflators (1913 = 100) from Robert E. Lipsey, *Price and Quantity Trends in the Foreign Trade of the United States* (1963), pp. 142–143 and 146–147.

put the United States at a par with Germany (15 percent ahead of Britain), but the ratio of horsepower to worker in this industry was twice as large in America as in either of the other two contenders. Cheap coal and high-quality iron ore clearly played a role in the rise of the industry.

It is a mistake, however, to think that resource abundance is an alternative to technological progress as an explanation for American industrial success. As we have already seen, the process of mineral development was itself the object of extensive study and technical improvement, from the science of exploration to the machinery for extraction to the technologies of refining and use. Also, the benefits of resource abundance to industry would have been much less useful without massive investments and technological improvements in the infrastructure of transportation—most dramatically the railroad but also including canal barges and the highly efficient Great Lakes shipping system. Moreover, technological progress does not mean just finding ways to economize on scarce resources; it also means finding additional productive uses for resources that are plentiful. A good example is petroleum, originally considered a useless waste product found in drilling for coal or water. (More recently, natural gas released in the search for petroleum provides another example.) The United States pioneered both in petroleum in discoveries and production and in the development of petroleum-using technologies, including those of the sophisticated twentieth-century petrochemical industry.

Resource abundance was complementary to the distinctive mass production technologies that formed much of the basis for American industrial success. It is difficult to say, and perhaps not meaningful, whether these technologies were more advanced than those of the European rivals from a scientific or engineering perspective. They were distinctive, but American conditions were also distinctive, not just in the supply of material resources but in access to an affluent, homogeneous (and highly protected) domestic market. In an era when transportation costs and barriers to international trade were far higher than they are

Table 2.   HIGH ABSOLUTE NET EXPORT GROWTH INDUSTRIES, 1899–1928

Industry	Net Exports, Millions of Dollars, 1928	Exports/ (Exp + Imp), 1928[a]	Growth in Current Dollars, Millions of Dollars, 1899–1928[b]	Growth in Constant Dollars, Millions of Dollars, 1899–1928[b]
Motor vehicles	500	.99	497	1,037
Petroleum products	447	.92	389	539
Cotton	877	.96	672	251
Primary copper	155	1.00	121	110
Steel works and rolling mills	120	.87	102	89
Farm equipment	112	.96	99	86
Special industrial machinery and equipment	105	.87	92	80
Coal mining	87	.94	77	71
Tobacco	201	.82	185	60
Sawmills, planing, and veneer products	79	.69	57	56
Other commercial machinery and equipment	57	1.00	45	39
Canning and preserving	62	.70	59	32
Tires and inner tubes	38	1.00	38	28
Construction and mining machinery	30	1.00	30	26
Machine tools and metalworking machinery	34	.98	27	23
Miscellaneous rubber products	29	.94	28	21
Paints and allied products	22	.87	21	13
Industrial organic chemicals	11	.88	20	12

[a] Exports are expressed as a percentage of total trade. Hence, for the items with a value of 1.00 imports are zero or close to zero.
[b] The movement from current dollars to constant dollars adjusts for changes in the relative prices of commodities in each export category.
SOURCE: Mary Locke Eysenbach, *American Manufactured Exports 1879–1914* (1976). Price deflaters (1913 = 100) from Robert E. Lipsey, *Price and Quantity Trends in the Foreign Trade of the United States* (1963), pp. 142–143 and 146–147.

today, these conditions gave American firms advantages and propelled them to develop domestic-resource-using products for a domestic market.

Perhaps the epitome of these processes was the automobile, which stood at the intersection of the industries of petroleum and steel (and other metals). The United States was unquestionably the world's technological leader in automobiles during the 1920s, as the export performance clearly attests. But other nations bought the cars in spite of the fact that they were designed for the American market and were not well adapted elsewhere. (A parallel problem faced U.S. locomotive manufacturers, who found their foreign sales handicapped by their design for standard-gauge rails, heavy motive power, and heavy train loads.) These drawbacks became more evident later, when access to resources and markets became more equalized among nations.

WHAT HAPPENED TO AMERICAN RESOURCE ABUNDANCE?

Since 1940, after having led world production and exports of minerals for more than half a century, the United States has increasingly become a net importer of minerals (figure 6). Although the aggregate figures for recent years are dominated by the special case of petroleum, the trend is general among major minerals. Bauxite became a net import even before the war. Lead, zinc, and copper followed in the late 1940s. Iron ore imports became significant in the 1950s. By the 1980s, the country was a net importer of most minerals, the only major exceptions being bituminous coal and phosphate rock.

During the first decade after World War II, many national leaders viewed this trend with alarm. William L. Batt, administrator of the War Production Board, stated in 1946: "It may hurt our pride, but harden our decision, to ask ourselves if the remarkable combination of assets which enabled this country to develop its fantastic strength is not gone forever." Yale geologist Alan M. Bateman wrote in 1952: "The irony is that the more we build our industrial and military power, along with that of other countries, the faster we exhaust the very basis of this power." Concerns such as these led to the appointment of the President's Material Policy Commission (known as the Paley Commission), whose 1952 report was entitled *Resources for Freedom*.

The report called for liberalization of international trade in raw materials as well as intensification of domestic resource development. As events took their course, the ready availability of imports largely allayed both the economic and security fears of impending scarcity—with the obvious exception of petroleum. From the historical point of view, however, it is appropriate to inquire into the underlying nature of the economic process itself. The geologist Bateman and others thought that the main problem was exhaustion or depletion of domestic supplies, and it is quite true that the war seriously cut into the stock of measured reserves of many minerals. Depletion could be qualitative as well as quantitative. The best-known example was the case of iron ore, where high-grade hematite from the Mesabi Range had largely played out by about 1950, forcing the industry to invest in costly techniques for utilizing the remaining lower quality taconite ores.

The diagnosis of excessively rapid depletion of the national mineral endowment may be reinforced by evidence now available, that the United States had been utilizing its geological potential to a far greater extent than had other countries. Table 3 compares the U.S. share of 1913 world production of nine important minerals with the U.S. share of estimated world reserves as of 1989. The disproportionality is striking. The smallest differential is for coal, but even in that case the American share of output was nearly double the share of reserves. The next column presents a slightly more complex comparison, adding to 1989 reserves cumulative U.S. output of the minerals

between 1913 and 1989. This exercise gives us an estimate of the level of reserves in 1913, as seen from the vantage point of modern geological knowledge. These shares are of course larger, but it is still the case that 1913 production was far in excess of even this expanded concept of reserves in all categories with the possible exception of phosphate. The fourth column expands the concept still further to the 1989 reserve base (adding reserves now thought to be uneconomic), but the conclusion is unchanged. It is tempting to infer that the United States has moved into a position of mineral deficits largely because the country used up its natural endowment more quickly than did the rest of the world.

Yet such a conclusion is questionable. As one may infer from comparing the second and third columns of table 3, even if all U.S. mineral output between 1913 and 1989 were put back in the ground, the effect on the current American reserve position would be negligible for all cases except petroleum and phosphate. Over these years the world has not experienced a decline but an expansion of estimated reserves for virtually all minerals. The increase has come from new discoveries and from improvements in the techniques of extraction, refinement, and transportation that have given added value (hence the status of reserves) to deposits previously considered unusable.

These developments have not been geographically neutral. Figure 7 displays three sets of estimates of iron ore reserves by continent, beginning with

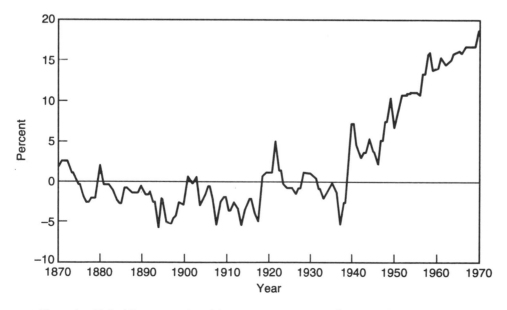

Figure 6.   United States net mineral imports as a percentage of consumption, 1870–1970.
Source: Robert S. Manthy, *Natural Resource Commodities* (1978), tables MC1 and MC2.

Table 3.   U.S. SHARE OF WORLD MINERAL PRODUCTION, PERCENT, 1913 AND 1989

	1913 Output	1989 Reserves	1989 Reserves Plus Cumulative, 1913–1989	1989 Reserve Base Plus Cumulative, 1913–1989
Petroleum	65	2.96	19.77	
Copper	56	16.40	19.94	18.50
Phosphate	43	9.80	36.30	15.43
Coal	39	23.00	23.32	
Bauxite	37	0.17	0.52	0.50
Zinc	37	13.89	13.96	15.58
Iron Ore	36	10.46	11.56	7.39
Lead	34	15.70	18.13	18.79
Gold	20	11.50	8.61	8.43

SOURCES: U.S. Geological Survey, *Mineral Resources of the United States* (1913); *Minerals Yearbook, 1989* (1990); *The Mineral Industry: Its Statistics, Technology, and Trade 1988;* American Petroleum Institute, *Basic Petroleum Data Book,* vol. 10 (September 1990); National Coal Association, *International Coal, 1989;* U.S. Department of Energy, Energy Information Administration, *Annual Prospects for World Coal Trade, 1991.*

the survey conducted by the International Geologic Congress in 1910. At that time it was thought that the world's iron ore reserves were overwhelmingly concentrated in Europe and North America. Since then, almost all major new additions have been found in other parts of the world, especially South America, Oceania, Asia, and Russia. In the United States, depletion has certainly occurred, yet estimated reserves were actually higher in 1985 than they were in 1910. Although the numerous surveys of world

iron ore resources were once motivated by fears of shortage and rising prices, it is now understood that iron ore remains abundant and widely distributed on the earth's surface. It has not even been necessary to move into the more advanced and sophisticated phases of science-based exploration.

Bauxite is another interesting case (figure 8). Bauxite is used in making aluminum. Its name comes from that of the French village where the manufacturing process was first developed, almost simultane-

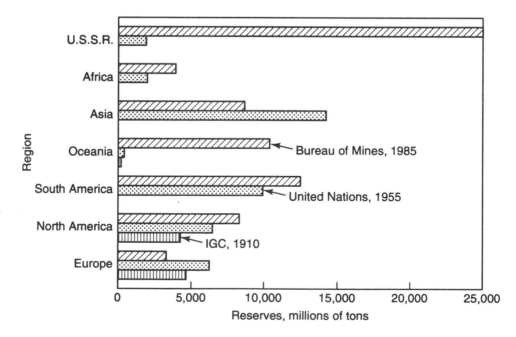

Figure 7.   World iron-ore reserves by continent (estimated), 1910, 1955, 1985. Source: International Geological Congress, 1910; United Nations, 1955; U.S. Bureau of Mines, *Bulletin 675* (1985).

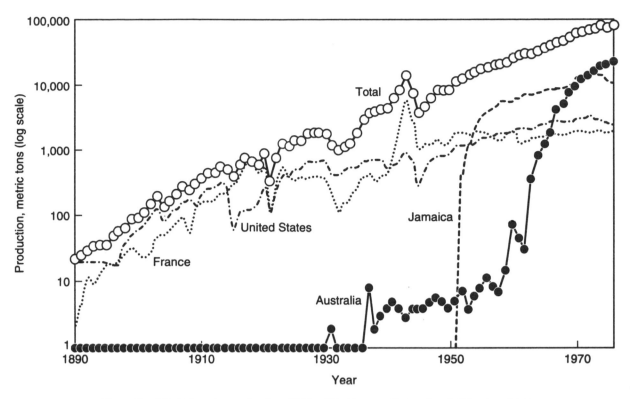

Figure 8. World bauxite production, 1890–1976. Source: Christopher J. Schmitz, *World Non-ferrous Metal Production and Prices, 1700–1976* (1979).

ously with parallel events in the United States. The United States and France alternated as first and second in world bauxite production until the 1950s. With discoveries in the West Indies in the 1950s, Jamaica quickly moved into first place, at production levels higher than those ever achieved in either France or the United States, even though production in those countries continued to grow. In the late 1960s, Australia replaced Jamaica as number one, again setting new production records without causing an absolute decline in the older countries. It is true that bauxite production in the United States did finally decline in the 1980s. But since the real price of bauxite has declined fairly steadily over time (as with other minerals), one cannot claim that the driving force was "exhaustion" of domestic reserves or that distant supplies have simply been coaxed out along a world supply curve. Rather, early discoveries and mining took place in areas near to the early centers of industry.

When we look for driving forces behind worldwide mineral exploration in the twentieth century, one of the first things we find is the active presence of American mining engineers and companies as well as Europeans. The spillover of American expertise

across national boundaries began to be important not long after the turn of the twentieth century. A 1917 preparedness survey found that more than 2,000 mining engineers (28 percent of the total surveyed) reported some experience in foreign countries, scattered over all of major continents of the earth. One of these was Herbert Hoover, who made three fortunes on three continents: in gold mining in Australia, coal mining in China, and copper mining in tsarist Russia. In more recent years, global exploration has been sponsored by giant corporations using increasingly sophisticated methods of geologic inference. Although American mining interests have often opposed subsidies for mineral development in third world countries, large American companies have been well represented in most parts of the world.

One further change completes the narrative. Even with all the new discoveries and developments around the world, the United States continues to be one of the world's largest mineral-producing nations and is certainly distinct among the advanced industrial countries in the breadth of its domestic resources. Why is it, then, that the country imports such a large share of its mineral consumption? Putting aside the special case of petroleum (discussed in the next section), the answer is that the costs of transporting minerals internationally have fallen to such an extent that industrial producers can draw upon the resources of other nations almost as cheaply as on their own. In short, natural resources are no longer part of the national factor endowment. They are internationally traded commodities, and a country's manufacturing is no longer closely tied to its own materials.

This phenomenon is illustrated by the results of a 1978 study of costs in the steel industries of Japan and the United States, sponsored by the Federal Trade Commission. As late as 1957, the study found, there was a large cost differential in favor of the United States in coking coal and iron ore. The price of iron ore to the U.S. industry was barely half that in Japan, while for coking coal the ratio was only 40 percent. Over the course of the 1960s and 1970s, however, these prices equalized. For iron ore, the two countries were essentially at par by 1966, and for coking coal equality was reached by 1975. Note the surprising feature of this comparison: the United States was losing its resource advantage not to one of the producers of coal and iron ore but to a country that had to import both. That country, however, had located its steel plants on deep ocean harbors and had invested heavily in special deepwater facilities capable of receiving a new generation of large ore carriers. With adaptations of this sort, it is possible that an importing country can obtain raw materials more cheaply than one relying on remote or inconvenient locations within its own boundaries.

The important general point is this: so long as countries import minerals at the margin, the price of inputs to producers is essentially set by the world price. Since most nations of the world now find themselves in this position, this means that the price of minerals is approximately the same to all competing firms. American industry may have lost a competitive advantage that it previously enjoyed, but there is no way to get it back. Future discoveries or intensified exploitation of mineral deposits domestic or foreign will not alter this fundamental picture.

PETROLEUM: THE ALL-AMERICAN MINERAL

Petroleum is a special case that defies conventional historical or economic formulas or intuition. The usefulness of the liquid mineral first known as "rock oil" was first recognized in America, and the country dominated world production for more than a century. New discoveries led to an ever-widening range of uses in the twentieth century. Oil-using technologies spread around the world under American leadership. It would seem to be a classic example of a nation building comparative advantage around its natural resource base and acquiring a distinctive expertise in the uses of its resources. Yet we now know that from a world perspective, the United States was never particularly well endowed with petroleum. Paradoxically, American technology launched a worldwide, century-long process of movement away from the use of a mineral for which the United States has enormous reserves (coal) in favor of a liquid mineral for which the domestic supply is drying up. It should not be surprising that the United States has increasingly relied on petroleum imports; but historical persistence is such that the country continues to be the world's largest oil consumer. To compound the paradox, the United States continues to fight against nature by persisting in its search for domestic oil, even in the face of competition from vast reservoirs elsewhere in the world.

The story of Edwin Drake's first oil strike in 1859, near Titusville, Pennsylvania, is well known, though the background conditions are less so: that the potential of rock oil as an illuminant had been widely discussed in the preceding decade as one of several strategies being explored to find an inexpensive substitute for whale oil. The first such effort to achieve some success was a liquid distilled from coal, known as coal oil. Indeed, one of the reasons petroleum was so quickly adopted was that it fit readily into an existing network of refineries, markets, and distribution channels laid out by the coal oil industry, not to mention the availability of the lamps themselves. If the forces pushing the economy along this historical path seem inexorable, however, it was only so in America. The United States was almost the world's sole source of crude and refined petroleum until the mid-1880s.

From Pennsylvania, the oil frontier moved westward and southward, in a series of sporadic jumps, in which periodic fears of exhaustion alternated with dramatic breakthroughs in new territories, followed by frenzied speculation and bursts of new production. The oil industry thus displayed the traits of the development of American minerals generally, but in much exaggerated fashion. One of the reasons for this tendency to extremes is that oil is fugacious in character—that is, it is quickly extracted—and once a field was discovered, drillers were in fact pumping from a common pool. Production took place under the legal maxim known as the "rule of capture": the owner of the land on which drilling occurred was entitled to claim all the oil extracted through that channel, regardless of its origins. This dictum had the virtue of simplicity (avoiding the disputes that would surely have arisen in an attempt to assign subterranean pools to various surface owners) and could be viewed as an extension of the "apex" rule in American mining, allowing those who undertook an investment to pursue the vein wherever it led. In the case of petroleum, however, the rule encouraged wild competitive drilling, at maximum speed and with considerable waste. The rule of capture found its chief application in judicial interpretations of the leasing agreements (since most oil production occurred under leases), in which the courts invariably decided that the landowner's interest was defined by immediate and exhaustive exploitation. Despite growing misgivings and conservationist concerns, the rule remained in force until the 1930s, when it was displaced by the compulsory production controls.

Shortly after the turn of the twentieth century, four major new producing centers came into the picture: the Gulf Coast area, triggered by the famous gusher at Spindletop, Texas, in 1901; the midcontinent region in Oklahoma and Kansas, where the major strikes occurred in 1904 and 1905; southeastern Illinois, which became the third largest producing area between 1907 and 1913; and California, where discoveries in the Los Angeles basin opened a new round of development in the southern part of the state. California became the leading oil state in 1923, after the dramatic strike at Signal Hill, near Long Beach. There were additional major discoveries in Oklahoma in 1926 (the Greater Seminole field) and in East Texas in 1930 (the Black Giant field). Although the industry by that time drew upon the best available geological knowledge of those years, the discoveries and the volume of crude-oil production persistently outran expectations and forecasts. Each new discovery was considered largely a matter of luck.

But rising consumer demand was the real force behind this kind of luck. American industry and households had become hooked on oil by the 1920s. Through most of the nineteenth century, petroleum's chief use had been as an illuminant, but it gave way to electricity in 1900. In the twentieth century, oil became the nation's primary source of energy: as fuel oil for industry, heating oil for homes, gasoline and diesel fuel for transportation. The appearance of the automobile on the American scene was the greatest of these new sources of demand. Oil was also increasingly used as a lubricant, as a source for asphalt in road making, and as a base for a sophisticated array of petrochemicals. One of the advantages of oil over coal was its cost; but the primary advantage was transportability, both from the point of origin to the point of use and in moving vehicles themselves. Industrialization in California, which had been held back by an absence of coal, flourished under the new oil regime. And California became a symbol of the oil-using high-mobility American lifestyle of the twentieth century. Although oil allowed great flexibility to firms and households, the nation as a whole became quite committed to it through massive investments in an infrastructure of pipelines and roads and through its commercial and household capital stock. This commitment proved to be a heavy burden during the oil shocks of 1973 and 1979, brought on by the steep rise in prices resulting from cutbacks in production agreed on by the Organization of Petroleum Exporting Countries (OPEC).

During much of the twentieth century, however, the dominant policy concern regarding oil was not the threat of high prices but the industry's own complaint about uncontrolled production and depressed prices. During the heyday of Standard Oil from the 1870s to the 1890s, one of the persistent goals of the company was to achieve stability in the crude oil market by controlling the rate of throughput at the refining stage. But the opening of rich new fields was too fast for Standard's reach, and the company had lost a good part of its dominant market position even before its partial dismemberment by the Supreme Court in the historic antitrust decision of 1911.

A more effective means of output control was achieved by the federal government beginning in 1909, when President William Howard Taft announced the withdrawal of some 3 million acres of public land from mineral exploration. The policy was confirmed and extended by Congress in the Land Withdrawal Act of 1910, which, however, specifically exempted exploration projects already underway at the time of the act. This legislation and the land withdrawals that continued between 1912 and 1919 were motivated by both conservation and national security considerations, the latter reflected in lands set aside as naval reserves to ensure adequate future supplies of marine fuels for the navy. But as in many other industries at this time, these motives were closely intertwined with the industry's own desire to limit the expansion of output and stabilize the market, preferably at relatively high prices. The major oil companies therefore welcomed the new federal effort to rationalize competition through the Mineral Leasing Act of 1920, which set out an intri-

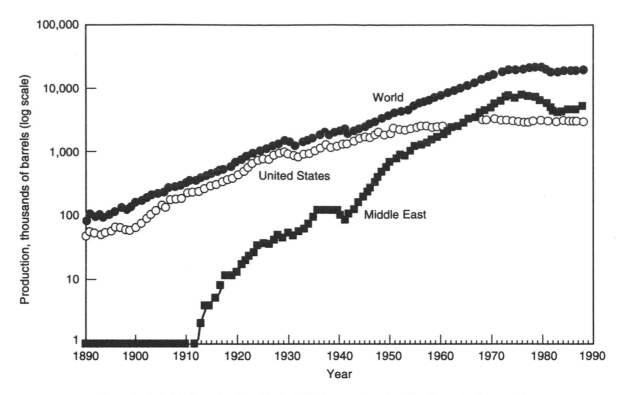

Figure 9.   World oil production, 1890–1988. Source: American Petroleum Institute, *Basic Petroleum Data Book,* vol. 8 (September 1988).

cate system of classifications and procedures for oil lands in the public domain.

The pressure for stabilization measures became overwhelming at the time of the oil market glut caused by the East Texas strikes of 1930, and aggravated by the fall in demand after the onset of the Great Depression. Again using the veneer of conservationism, the Texas Railroad Commission began to assign specific production quotas to individual wells, limits enforced by National Guardsmen and Texas Rangers. Although the commission apparently had some success in raising prices during 1932, effective control of "hot oil" (unauthorized production sent across state lines) required federal enforcement powers, which were provided under the National Industrial Recovery Act in 1933 and the Connally Hot Oil Act of 1935. When the NIRA was declared unconstitutional in 1935, its place was taken by a less compulsory but nonetheless effective system of prorationing under the Interstate Oil Compact, a "treaty" among oil-producing states. Long after the depressed conditions of the 1930s had passed, the Texas Railroad Commission (and similar bodies in other states) managed an informal cartel-like arrangement to control and allocate oil production and stabi-

lize prices. The system expired in 1972, but not before it had been carefully studied abroad as a possible model for OPEC.

The prorationing system achieved a modicum of protection against depressed oil prices, but after World War II the United States was protected against high oil prices only by a steadily rising flow of imports. Figure 9 conveys the degree to which world production was dominated by the United States until 1945 (excepting a brief period at the turn of the century when it was surpassed by Russia in a production spurt that did not last). Other producing centers did eventually emerge, most notably in the Middle East, which collectively passed the United States in 1960. The rich oil potential of the Middle East had long been suspected, but its exploitation was delayed by political turmoil and international rivalries. After agreements were successfully negotiated between Arab countries and major oil companies, however—in which American companies were well represented—important discoveries in Kuwait were announced in the 1930s. Informed people were aware even during World War II that the center of gravity of world production would shift to the Persian Gulf. The magnitude of this shift is conveyed in figure 10, which displays world reserves by continent for 1948 and 1988. In the earlier year, North America and the Middle East were closely matched, well ahead of any other regions. By 1988, however, the total of world reserves surpassed anything dreamed of in 1948, and with the Middle East holding the largest share by far, more than all the other areas put together. Although reserves in the United States have grown over the period shown, the continent of North America would appear to be no more than a minor player in the world oil drama.

The historical question persists: how did this state of affairs come about? Does the decline of the United States as a source of petroleum primarily reflect the century-long depletion of the country's initial endowment? To put this question in perspective, suppose that all the oil produced in America since 1890 were put back into the ground. Figure 11 displays the relation among estimated world reserves, U.S. reserves, and the hypothetical level of U.S. reserves if all oil produced were added to the total. Two things are clear from the graph: restoring historical oil would increase the level of U.S. reserves several times over; but the entire exercise would have no more than a marginal effect on world reserves. In other words, the fundamental fact of U.S. dependence on imported oil would hold true today, whatever the past history of American oil production had been. In light of the explosive growth in the Middle

East, the swing toward imported oil was restrained only by the protectionist response of the American industry, specifically the program of mandatory import quotas imposed in 1959 and lasting until 1973.

Even this evidence understates the matter. In a market setting, the relative shares of oil-producing regions in world totals are determined not by tabulations of reserves but by costs. Since the last discovery of a major new oil field in 1930, most additions to reserves in the United States have come not through discovery of previously unknown reservoirs, but from development drilling in known reservoirs—installing new wells and equipment in an extension of activity already underway. In neither case are the new reserves gifts of nature; they are returns on investment. According to oil economist M. A. Adelman (1990, 1992), marginal oil development cost in the United States—defined as the ratio of real annual development expenditures to reserves added during the year, showed no upward trend between 1955 and 1972, the time of the OPEC oil price increase. It is often alleged that the oil price increases of the 1970s were only incidentally due to the organization of OPEC and that the deeper cause was depletion and rising scarcity. But from a world perspective, there has been no increase in development cost over the entire century. The 1970s saw an expansion of output in high-cost areas, accompanied by a contraction in low-

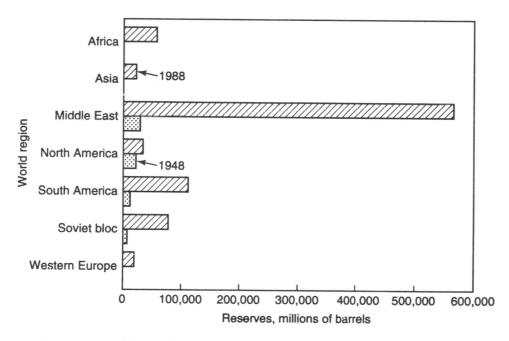

Figure 10.   World crude oil reserves, 1948 and 1988. Source: American Petroleum Institute, *Basic Petroleum Data Book,* vol. 8 (September 1988).

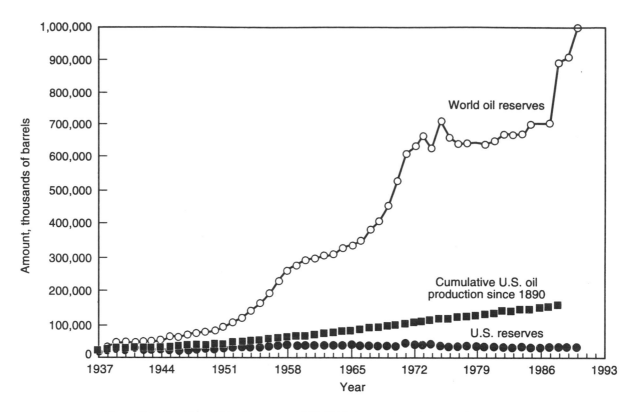

Figure 11. World and U.S. oil reserves, 1937–1990. Source: American Petroleum Institute, *Basic Petroleum Data Book,* vol. 10 (May 1990).

cost areas, a clear sign of deviation from competitive market conditions.

It is true that the actions of OPEC came at a time when the United States was in a particularly vulnerable position, in that strong demand conditions had pushed production to the point where surplus capacity was exhausted. As a result, the United States had no readily available domestic response to a cutoff of imports, a fact of which the OPEC managers were well aware. Although in retrospect the American failure was essentially a short-term mismanagement of inventories, the initial jump in prices set in motion expectations of runaway prices into the indefinite future. For a time the anticipation of shortages was self-fulfilling, as producers and suppliers slowed deliveries in hopes of profiting from higher expected prices in the future. Prices rose even further at the time of the second oil shock, during the Iranian Revolution of 1979. By the early 1980s, however, under the cumulative effects of demand-side substitutions away from oil, and supply-side expansion of production capacity in non-OPEC countries, prices began to slip until their collapse in 1986. At the time of the Persian Gulf War in 1990–1991, the familiar

cycle of rising and falling prices became even more rapid.

The events of the 1970s were only the most severe and protracted of the alternating bouts of feared shortages and glutted markets that have characterized this industry from the beginning. What has changed is that remedies for either condition can no longer be sought within the boundaries of the United States. Yet the grip of the past on behavior has been remarkably strong. Despite the country's status as the most thoroughly explored oil territory in the world, the rate of exploratory drilling in the United States reached an all-time high in 1981, though it declined precipitously after that. And despite vigorous efforts to encourage conservation and fuel efficiency, the American transportation sector continues to consume proportionally far more oil than do its counterparts in the other advanced industrial nations of the world. This persistence is facilitated by the low prevailing levels of oil prices, which are nonetheless far higher than the true costs of extracting Middle Eastern oil. The United States also stands almost alone in the low rates at which oil is taxed, a policy that dates from the days when domestic oil producers were one of the most powerful domestic lobbies in the country.

THE DECLINE AND REBIRTH OF AMERICAN FORESTS

Economic theory predicts that a nonrenewable resource will be consumed at a steady rate until exhausted, with its price rising at a pace equal to the rate of interest in the economy. Economic theory predicts, in contrast, that consumption of a renewable resource will tend toward a steady state, in which the annual harvest equals the size of the annual growth, and the stock is maintained. With this equilibrium, prices will change only in response to changes in underlying conditions of production costs or demand.

For most of American history since European settlement, this scenario was utterly irrelevant when applied to forests and wood products. From an original forestland of some 900 million acres, four-fifths of which was east of the Great Plains, only 470 million acres remained as of 1920, and the majority of these had been disrupted to the point that they were no longer self-restoring. The most rapid destruction occurred between 1800 and 1920, the very period when Americans were so ingeniously adding to the country's mineral resource base. Why the radical contrast in behavior toward these two different types of resources, minerals and timber?

Although the forests were in principle renewable, from the viewpoint of the settlers the original forestland had the character of a one-time gift of nature. To be sure, even at the time of earliest European arrival, the forests were not really in a "natural" condition, because the American Indians engaged extensively in land clearing for agricultural purposes and in regular burnings to extend grassland and encourage the growth of plants bearing nuts and berries. To the Europeans, however, the land was far more densely wooded than were the places they had come from; furthermore, the forests stood in the way of their means of livelihood, family-farm agriculture. Over the course of the seventeenth through the nineteenth centuries, most of the eastern part of the country was cleared for farming, and during this process, lumber was universally and cheaply available. Cheap timber helped give the United States world leadership in shipbuilding down to the 1830s, during the era of wooden ships, and the Americans developed expertise in woodworking technology and a wood-based lifestyle unique in the world at that time. Despite the rise of minerals, lumber continued to be one of the leading American industries in both value-added and employment until World War I. Since timber was "mined" with little thought of replacement, this renewable resource played out a sequence assigned by theory to the nonrenewables: indeed, the producer price index for wood has risen relative to the general price level (figure 12). Correspondingly, the relative utilization of wood for energy and for industrial purposes declined, at least until the middle of the twentieth century.

In contrast to minerals, there were no hidden reserves of timber to be discovered. But lumber companies could expand their reserves by moving their activities westward and southward, and by investing in transport links to carry wood from ever more distant locations to the growing urban markets. Transportation costs have been more significant for timber than for minerals, because the sources of supply are scattered across the countryside rather than concentrated at mining centers; local shortages of firfirewood and building materials presented serious problems in eastern cities very early in the nineteenth century. Much of the rising relative price of timber products is presumably attributable to increasing remoteness rather than depletion from an aggregate national standpoint. Much the way twentieth-century Americans cling to their oil-based lifestyles, nineteenth-century Americans maintained their wood-using ways by transporting lumber across previously unheard-of distances, up to one thousand miles by the 1850s.

Why the extractive behavior pattern continued in the industry as long as it did is something of a puzzle for economic historians. With the price of timber rising, one might think that some owners of forestland would have held on to their standing timber in order to capture higher prices in the future. One hypothesis argues by analogy to the common-property or common-pool problem in the case of petroleum, that property rights in timberland were not clearly enough established because much of the available acreage was found in the public domain. The forests of the Great Lakes states, however, were thoroughly logged out between 1870 and 1900, despite the fact that most of the land came into private ownership before the cutting. It is true that the forestlands were privatized under agricultural land laws intended to encourage rapid clearing and settlement. Much of the cutover land in the Lake States region was resold for farming on the traditional model, but probably more than half of it, mainly in Wisconsin and Minnesota, was too far north for commercial agriculture, and so was abandoned after cutting. An

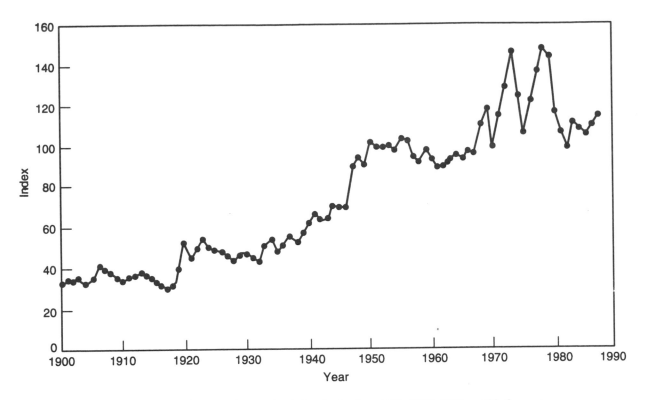

Figure 12.   Relative producer price index for lumber, 1900–1987. 1982 = 100. Source: Alice H. Ulrich, "U.S. Timber Production, Trade, Consumption, and Price Statistics, 1950–1987," U.S. Department of Agriculture–Forest Service, misc. pub. 1471 (1989), table 35.

alternative theory is that the price of standing timber in a given location was simply not rising fast enough to cover the anticipated costs of holding forestland, including taxes, interest, and the opportunity cost of resale. The risk of forest fires, which were frequent and devastating in the late nineteenth century, added to the motivation for realizing revenue quickly.

The tide began to turn early in the twentieth century. Concerns about the disappearance of the nation's forests were central to the rise of the conservationist ethic at that time. As early as 1873, the American Association for the Advancement of Science appealed to Congress to establish forest reserves for future use. In 1891 the first legislation was passed permitting the president to set aside public forest reservations. Subsequent laws led to the creation of the Forest Service in 1905, with Gifford Pinchot as its first director. In 1911 the service obtained the right to purchase land for the national forest system, and between 1916 and 1920, nine national forests were established in the eastern part of the country. Here again we encounter a mix of motivations, in which genuine farsighted concern for the public welfare blended with the newly emerging interests of

private parties. Much of the land purchased for the national forest was logged-over, burned, and unwanted by its owners. And the Forest Service's program for promoting more sustainable practices in the forests found favor with large owners as a way of stabilizing production and keeping prices up.

Eventually, attitudes and practices in the private sector also gravitated toward longer term sustainability. Even while engaged in "cut out and get out" methods in the Middle West, giants like Weyerhaeuser were planning for the future by buying thousands of forest acres in the South and in the Pacific Northwest. In fact, a 1914 report by the Bureau of Corporations accused these large companies of "hoarding" timber and acting in "restraint of trade," very likely a valid observation if not necessarily a practice deserving a hostile public response. The diffusion of enlightened sustainable private-sector practices was certainly slow, depending as it did not only on a sufficiently long organizational time horizon to make the investments worthwhile but also on improvements in the general knowledge base and level of training in forest management. Because both profit incentives and research in forestry have been

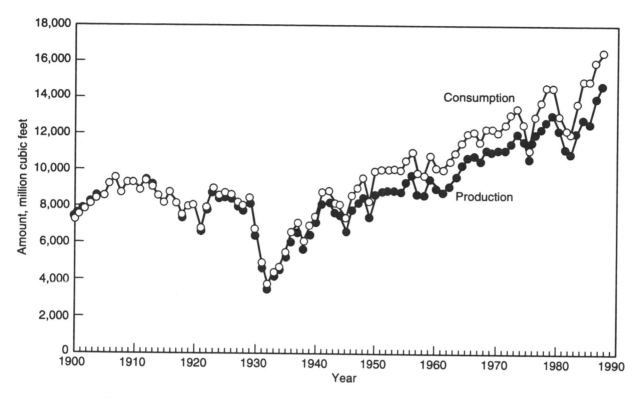

Figure 13.   U.S. production and consumption of industrial roundwood, in million cubic feet. Source: Alice H. Ulrich, "U.S. Timber Production, Trade, Consumption, and Price Statistics, 1950–1987," U.S. Department of Agriculture–Forest Service, misc. pub. 1471 (1989), table 4; *Historical Statistics of the United States* (1970), p. 539.

heavily influenced by subsidies and by federal land management programs of various types, it is probably pointless to ask whether the transition should be attributed principally to public policy or to farsighted private self-interest in response to rising timber prices. Whatever the case, through some combination of forces, American forestland has been expanding for the last fifty years or so, despite continuing growth in levels of production and consumption during that time (figure 13). Since the 1950s, the private sector has not just held its inventories for the future, but has engaged in tree planting on a large scale. Aided by genetic improvements in seedlings, this move toward intensive tree farming has been particularly pronounced in the South, where the period of regeneration is relatively fast.

Indeed, perhaps the greatest contributor to the recovery of American forests has been the rapid rate of regeneration on previously cutover land, once crop cultivation had ceased. In the 1930s, when yields for most crops began to rise for the first time in American history, crop acreage ceased to compete with the forests. Much of this abandoned land reverted passively to forest under public ownership, confounding

forecasts of impending exhaustion. Since the 1950s, managing the annual timber harvest has been a major activity of the Forest Service. In contrast to the country's relative decline as a mineral producer, the United States continues to be the world's largest producer of industrial wood by a wide margin. And despite these record outputs, forest acreage is as high as it was a century ago.

The world is never as tidy as a simple equilibrium model, but it may be that American forests are approaching a sustainable position somewhat resembling the steady-state abstraction. International trade in forest products has been much less important than in the case of minerals. Although U.S. imports from Canada are significant, by and large the national trends in production and consumption are closely linked, as shown in figure 13. The long decline in per capita levels of forest-product consumption came to an end by the 1960s (figure 14). The transition away from wood as a source of fuel is now essentially complete, despite a temporary reversal caused by the fuel price crises of the 1970s. Per capita lumber consumption has stabilized, though pulp and paper products have slowly but steadily grown in volume

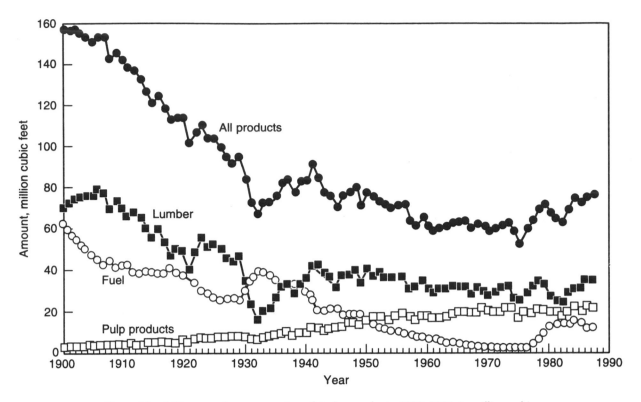

Figure 14.   U.S. per capita consumption of timber products, 1900–1987, in million cubic feet. Source: Alice H. Ulrich, "U.S. Timber Production, Trade, Consumption, and Price Statistics, 1950–1987," U.S. Department of Agriculture–Forest Service, misc. pub. 1471 (1989), table 8; *Historical Statistics of the United States* (1970), p. 540.

throughout the twentieth century. Despite these new demands, the two-century rise in relative lumber prices slowed in the 1980s and may have stopped altogether (figure 12). Perhaps it would be appropriate to say that demand and supply have come into approximate balance at the current level of relative prices.

This historical overview puts into somewhat different perspective the debate over preservation of old-growth forests in the Pacific Northwest. These areas are often portrayed as the last vestiges of a once-vast American woodland, a characterization far from accurate. But because the cycle of regeneration is much longer in this region, logging still retains much of the character of the old once-over pattern and is less amenable to change through incentives. Ironically, these tendencies may have been aggravated by the debate itself, which has accelerated cutting in many areas out of fear of an abruptly imposed termination. The issues largely turn, however, not on the need to conserve timber resources for future generations, nor on the vital importance of timber to the

national economy, but on the social value of preserving the unique ecological systems that the old-growth forests represent, particularly as habitats for diverse plant and animal life. This value is subject to great uncertainty and wide differences of opinion. But compromise is difficult because of the probable irreversibility of many of the ecological consequences, unlike the highly regenerative quality that American forests have historically displayed.

RESOURCE ISSUES

At the end of the twentieth century, natural resources are far less central to American economic prosperity than they were a hundred years before. Mineral resources were an important factor in the nation's rise to world economic leadership, but they play a much reduced role in today's production technologies. Further, the terms on which minerals are available are now determined in global rather than national markets. In modern economies, mineral endowments no longer provide the core around which a country's comparative advantage is constructed.

The products of farms and forests continue to be essential to life, and in these industries, local and regional effects have persisted to the present. The country is not in danger of running out of either farmland or forestland, but together they provide employment to no more than a tiny fraction of the nation's labor force. The price of lumber has short-term importance for the construction industry. But the longer term significance of the forests lies much more in recreation, in the protection of ecosystems, and in the country's responsibilities to global environmental regulation. These will be the resource issues of the twenty-first century.

SEE ALSO Conservation and the Environment; Infrastructure; Industrial Production; Consumption (all in this volume).

BIBLIOGRAPHY

Interest in resource and environmental economics has been growing in recent years, but good historical studies are still rare. Harold J. Barnett and Chandler Morse, *Scarcity and Growth* (1963), present detailed evidence that natural resources have not become more scarce over time. Their argument is updated in Harold J. Barnett, "Scarcity and Growth Revisited," in *Scarcity and Growth Reconsidered*, ed., V. Kerry Smith (1979). The classic theoretical analysis, to which Barnett and Morse were responding, is Harold Hotelling, "The Economics of Exhaustible Resources," *Journal of Political Economy* 39 (1931): 137–175. E. A. Wrigley, *Continuity, Chance, and Change* (1988), argues that the adoption of mineral-using technologies was crucial to the success of the industrial revolution.

For statistical reference, Robert S. Manthy, *Natural Resource Commodities: A Century of Statistics* (1978), is a useful collection of U.S. data. Christopher J. Schmitz, *World Non-Ferrous Metal Production and Prices, 1700–1976* (1979), is a valuable source for international figures. U.S. Department of Agriculture, Economic Research Service, *Economic Indicators of the Farm Sector*, Statistical Bulletin no. 679 (1980), is a good collection of agricultural statistics for the twentieth century. Alice H. Ulrich, "U.S. Timber Production, Trade, Consumption and Price Statistics, 1950–1987," USDA–Forest Service Miscellaneous Publication no. 1471 (December 1989), is the latest available compilation of statistical material from the Forest Service.

Historical studies of agricultural resource use are also rare. Pierre Crosson, "Cropland and Soils," in *America's Renewable Resources*, ed., Kenneth D. Frederick and Roger A. Sedjo (1991), is a concise summary of changing cropland use patterns and the forces behind them. Robert G. Healy, *Competition for Land in the American South* (1985), describes the interplay among competing demands for land, mainly in the South.

America's rise to world leadership in minerals is examined in Paul David and Gavin Wright, "Resource Abundance and American Economic Leadership," CEPR Publication No. 267R (1992). W. Stanley Jevons, *The Coal Question*, 2d ed. (1866), forecasts British economic decline because of exhaustion of coal. Herbert Hoover, *Principles of Mining* (1909), is a textbook by one of America's foremost mining engineers. Carl J. Mayer and George A. Riley, *Public Domain, Private Dominion* (1985), is a survey of the history of profit-driven abuse of the public domain.

Alfred Chandler, Jr., "Anthracite Coal and the Beginnings of the Industrial Revolution in the United States," *Business History Review* 46 (Summer 1972): 141–181, describes early links between energy sources and American industry. Robert Allen presents a detailed quantitative history of the American iron and steel industry in comparison with those of other countries in a series of articles: "The Peculiar Productivity History of American Blast Furnaces, 1840–1913," *Journal of Economic History* 39 (September 1977): 605–633; "International Competition in Iron and Steel, 1850–1913," *Journal of Economic History* 39 (December 1979): 911–937; "Accounting for Price Changes: American Steel Rails, 1879–1910," *Journal of Political Economy* 89 (June 1981): 512–528. Louis P. Cain and Donald G. Paterson, "Biased Technical Change, Scale and Factor Substitution in American Industry, 1850–1919," *Journal of Economic History* 46 (September 1986): 153–164, is an econometric study of the bases for American industrial ascendancy. Gavin Wright, "The Origins of American Industrial

Success, 1879–1940," *American Economic Review* 80 (September 1990): 651–668, stresses the importance of resources for American industry.

An early forecast of U.S. mineral depletion was by geologist Alan M. Bateman, "Our Future Dependence on Foreign Minerals," *Annals of the American Academy of Political and Social Science* 281 (May 1952). Alfred Eckes, *The United States and the Global Struggle for Minerals* (1979), reviews changing American attitudes and involvement in the search for foreign minerals. Michael Tanzer, *The Race for Resources* (1980), is a well-informed survey of all major minerals as of 1980. Eugene N. Cameron, *At the Crossroads* (1986), summarizes America's resource position as of the same year. Roderick G. Eggert, *Metallic Mineral Exploration: An Economic Analysis* (1987), analyzes recent developments in mineral exploration.

Petroleum has a rich and colorful history. Harold Williamson and Arnold R. Daum, *The American Petroleum Industry*, vol. 1: *The Age of Illumination 1859–1899* (1959), and Williamson et al., *The American Petroleum Industry*, vol. 2: *The Age of Energy 1899–1959* (1963), comprise the standard industry history.

M. A. Adelman, "Mineral Depletion, with Special Reference to Petroleum," *Review of Economics and Statistics* 72 (February 1990): 1–10, is a devastating critique of conventional thinking about exhaustible resources. More detailed quantitative research is presented in M. A. Adelman, "Finding and Developing Costs in the U.S., 1945–1986," in *Energy, Growth and the Environment: Advances in the Economics of Energy and Resources* 7 (1992). Richard H. K. Vietor, *Energy Policy in America since 1945* (1984), reviews U.S. fossil fuel policies since World War II. Daniel Yergin, *The Prize* (1991), is a sweeping best-seller history of the oil industry.

Michael Williams, *Americans and Their Forests: A Historical Geography* (1989), is a monumental survey of the history of forests in the United States. Roger A. Sedjo, "Forest Resources: Resilient and Serviceable," in *America's Renewable Resources*, ed. Kenneth D. Frederick and Roger A. Sedjo (1991), is a knowledgeable and up-to-date survey of historical trends and current issues relating to America's forest resources.

THE PROFESSIONS

Kenneth J. Lipartito and Paul J. Miranti, Jr.

Professional occupations have been among the fastest growing and best rewarded of all types of work in the twentieth century. Between 1900 and 1989, professional, managerial, and other white-collar workers rose from 13 percent to 66 percent of the labor force. Benefiting from the decline of American manufacturing and growth of service industries, these occupations have been responsible for most of the new jobs in the economy since World War II. Although varying widely in status and income, professional fields have held out to the educated middle class the promise of secure employment, interesting and varied work, and independence.

Professional life has changed significantly in its meaning and quality over the past century, even as it has remained associated in the public mind with such important values as public service, competence, scientific objectivity, and personal autonomy. Like other Americans, professionals have taken advantage of the entrepreneurial freedom available and the organizational structures that emerged at the beginning of this century. Both in the early years of professionalization, and more recently in response to changing economic circumstances, professionals have shown themselves capable of remaking their occupations, altering their values, and accommodating to the large-scale organizations that characterize America's private and public sectors.

The growth of professions in the twentieth century was linked to a new relationship between knowledge and society that began to emerge after the Civil War. Disturbed by the violence and corrupting materialism that had beset the nation, some thoughtful Americans came to believe that civilization and culture could only be restored through the spiritual leadership of an intellectual elite. They were joined by others worried about the closure of the frontier and the end of a long period of prosperity based on the exploitation of natural resources. Those troubled by such developments directed themselves toward the discovery of more efficient methods for producing economic abundance. Education, knowledge, and science, directed at industrial and social issues, seemed to provide the means of achieving these goals.

New forms of knowledge served as the basis for new technical disciplines and managerial skills needed in an industrial society. Beginning early in the nineteenth century, advances in technology and changes in the structure of the economy helped to transform America from an agricultural to an urban and industrial society. In this evolving social order, hierarchical bureaucratic organizations successfully coordinated the activities of many types of specialists. The prototypes of these new organizational forms appeared with the railroads. During the latter half of the century they were adopted by industry and government to coordinate activities of great scale and scope.

Before the mid-nineteenth century, institutions of higher education were ill-suited to train the many classes of specialists required by a society whose elements were becoming more complex and interdependent. The nation's colleges and universities were not geared to prepare graduates for careers in specific fields except the ministry. Instead, they aspired to turn out gentlemen well versed in cultural traditions and possessed of a modicum of scholarly skills. Their genteel curricula encompassed rudimentary instruction in science and mathematics and a heavy dose of moral philosophy. Training for professions like law, engineering, and medicine was usually not pursued through university studies but through apprenticeships or proprietary schools.

With the coming of the new urban-industrial order in the 1840s, educational institutions began to respond to the new types of specialized knowledge. Institutes of technology capable of providing more comprehensive engineering education were founded at West Point and Rensselaer in New York, Annapolis in Maryland, Stevens in New Jersey, and MIT in Massachusetts. After 1869, many liberal arts colleges adopted the elective system developed at Harvard

University, which allowed for specialized majors. Soon, at leading institutions such as Harvard's Lawrence Laboratories and Yale University's Sheffield Scientific School, natural philosophy devolved into the modern sciences of chemistry, biology, and physics. Influenced by European patterns, American universities also sponsored graduate study dedicated to the extension of knowledge through systematic research. The pioneering programs established at Johns Hopkins in 1876 served as a model for other American universities that sought to upgrade the quality of their graduate schools.

Changing perceptions about the nature of knowledge were also reflected in the experience of the social sciences. At mid-century the American Social Science Association (ASSA) had served as a debating society for amateurs interested in social questions. This approach was abandoned as Americans became aware of developments in European universities. By the end of the first decade of the twentieth century, ASSA's eclecticism gave way to the more sharply focused disciplines of anthropology, economics, political science, psychology, and sociology. These specialties sought knowledge through the methods that had enriched the natural sciences and engineering. By discovering the underlying "laws" of these new disciplines, scholars believed they could extend their control over the social world.

THE ORGANIZATION OF THE PROFESSIONS, 1900–1917

During the Progressive Era, specialized knowledge circulated through society along several new channels. One was the formalization in educational institutions of methods for developing competence. A second was a new set of linkages between universities and a growing business sector. A third was incorporation of expert knowledge within social reform programs through an extension of government's executive capacities. Each of these new circuits of knowledge shaped the occupations that became known as the modern professions.

Accessibility to education at all levels provided a strong base for professional expansion. America's wealth and ample endowments of basic food and fuel staples made schooling less of a sacrifice than it was in poorer countries. Although the nation had a long tradition of open education, it had been confined to primary schools. During the latter decades of the nineteenth century, however, states passed compulsory education laws that expanded primary and secondary schooling. The number of high school gradu-

ates increased by approximately 700 percent during the period between 1890 and 1920. The United States Bureau of Education (USBE) also worked with local educators to standardize curricula and improve the quality of instruction through the growth of state-sponsored normal schools specializing in teacher training. Subsidies from government assisted students in higher education as well, beginning with the Morrill Act of 1862, which created the nation's system of land-grant colleges.

As educational facilities expanded, professional training moved into universities. Formal education provided several advantages over traditional apprenticeships in supplying the expertise an industrial society required. University programs could be structured to assure pedagogical uniformity and to provide more objective evaluations of graduate capabilities. Freedom from distracting job responsibilities required in apprenticeships allowed university graduates more time to master the theory underlying their specializations. The broader scope and scale of university educational resources promised more efficient and effective instruction than was available in the old-fashioned apprenticeships sponsored by small firms or individual practitioners.

Law and medicine saw a rapid shift away from apprenticeships and proprietary schools to more rigorous and systematic instruction in university-based programs. In legal education there was widespread adoption of Dean Christopher Langdell's case-study method, introduced at Harvard in 1870. By 1929, forty-seven out of the sixty member institutions making up the Association of American Law Schools were employing Langdell's technique. It was thought superior to rote learning of legal compilations because it stressed the analysis of precedents established by the courts as they sought to make law more responsive to America's changing social setting. Langdell's approach was also favored by a new breed of law firm that specialized in serving a corporate clientele. Traditional advocacy of client rights in hot courtroom confrontations now coexisted with a new type of practice that emphasized cool research and consultation, while avoiding litigation.

In medicine, rising educational standards concentrated instructional resources into fewer but stronger teaching units. Abraham Flexner of the Carnegie Foundation for the Advancement of Teaching (CFAT) led this effort, in cooperation with the USBE and the Council on Medical Education of the American Medical Association (AMA). Flexner's 1910 report revealed great unevenness in medical school standards. His findings were instrumental in the disappearance through closure or merger of 102 institutions during the period 1904–1920. Following the recommendations of the Flexner report, leading medical schools improved quality by raising the requisite number of courses for both premedical and medical education.

Graduate studies in the sciences, humanities, and social studies came under pressure to strengthen scholarship by concentrating scarce educational resources in a few highly selective programs. The impetus originated with an alliance of the Rockefeller supported General Education Bureau (GEB), CFAT, and USBE. The drive to promote higher standards did not result in mass closures, as it did in medicine. Instead, it marginalized weak programs that were unable to attract substantial funding or highly qualified faculty and students. The winners were well-established private colleges of the Northeast and the more progressive state institutions in the Middle and Far West that could qualify for admission to the prestigious Association of American Universities (1900).

While traditional professions moved training into universities, new professions grew by forming their own schools of higher education. Business administration became more professionalized by this method. Although the first program was established at the University of Pennsylvania's Wharton School in 1881, the take-off in business education occurred between 1900 and 1920, with 183 institutions branching into this line of instruction by 1925.

Two models characterized these new business schools. Most popular was the Wharton model, which provided several parallel tracks at the baccalaureate level, training specialists for careers in such fields as finance, accounting, transportation, and insurance. A second approach, pioneered at Harvard (1908), adopted a case-study method similar to law in order to inculcate the principles of effective decision making. This graduate program sought to train generalists in the analytical skills necessary to manage virtually any type of enterprise.

Besides teaching business studies, universities also began to adopt businesslike methods, thereby professionalizing education administration. In 1909, CFAT engaged an associate of the engineer and efficiency expert Frederick W. Taylor, Morris L. Cooke, to study how university procedures might be made more efficient through standardization. Cooke's recommendations were published in *Academic and Industrial Efficiency*. From this document CFAT adopted its *Standard Forms for Financial Reports of Colleges, Universities and Business Schools*. It required all member institutions participating in its pension plan to apply these standards. GEB was also active in rationalizing financial administration. Its consultants advised college administrators on fiscal management and in 1913 it sponsored the publication of Trevor Arnott's *College and University Finance*.

While the growing dependency of American society on specialized knowledge increased the size, visibility, and power of professions, this transition affected particular fields in different ways. Three patterns were noteworthy. First, there were the independent professions, including accounting, law, and medicine, in which practitioners directly contracted their services to clients or patients. Second, there were those occupations such as engineering, social work, nursing, and teaching, where the application of professional skill usually had to be subordinated to the overriding goals of organizations. Lastly, there were a few professions, best typified by the ministry, whose status was being eroded by new perspectives that challenged their claims of authority.

Law, medicine, and accounting established strong foundations in the early twentieth century by incorporating new forms of knowledge within new organizational structures largely controlled by independent practitioners. Nineteenth-century medicine had an uneven record in successfully treating acute illnesses. This poor performance undermined doctors' claims to authority. Other groups, including hydrotherapists, herbalists, homeopaths, and practitioners of electric medicine, challenged their jurisdiction over the problems of health. In the twentieth century, however, physicians began to infuse their therapies with insights derived from the allied sciences of bacteriology, serology, and x-ray physics. New knowledge gained from scientific understanding of diseases improved the efficacy of practice. One striking example was found in surgery, where mortality rates for pelvic and abdominal operations declined from about 40 percent in 1880 to about 5 percent in 1900.

During this period, the ways in which physicians practiced and organized their calling changed radically. The heavy capital investment required for scientific medicine soon made hospitals the preferred locus for practice. Earlier, hospitals had primarily served the urban poor, providing little more than food and a warm place to rest. Medical progress changed hospitals from essentially charitable institutions to centers of technology providing services to a largely middle-class clientele. From 1873 to 1909, the number of hospitals increased more than twentyfold to 4,359, reflecting greater urbanization and improved quality of health care.

The rise of the modern hospital and of scientific medicine contributed to the emergence of a new elite practice based on specialization and innovation. Specialists often discovered ways of modifying the cognitive base of their fields, broadening the scope of professional jurisdiction, and raising the efficacy of practice. Although many specializations had been organized during the nineteenth century, their influence had generally been slight, reflecting the strong generalist bias of practice in a predominantly rural setting and the poor state of knowledge in many fields. By the dawn of the twentieth century, circumstances had changed dramatically. Specialties, particularly surgery, were leading the advance through the improved techniques developed by pioneers like Charles and William Mayo, William S. Halsted, and Harvey Cushing.

Researchers working on the cutting edge of knowledge were crucial to other professions as well. A pattern similar to that in medicine emerged in elite law practices associated with service to large business clients whose innovations in technology and management were transforming the American economy. The radical changes brought about by these clients raised many vexing questions about antitrust, taxes, industrial regulation, and finance. Large firms such as the one founded by Paul D. Cravath in New York assisted corporations in navigating safely through uncharted legal waters. To assure the highest quality of service, firms of this caliber recruited only candidates who had compiled excellent records at prestigious law schools and had demonstrated through contributions to law journals a capacity to perform sound research.

Patterns in corporate law contrasted sharply with the broader range of legal practice. Most attorneys still pursued careers in local practices that served individuals and small businesses. In these echelons educational qualifications were more varied. Many attorneys received instruction at night schools. Others were admitted to the bar after serving an apprenticeship. Concentrating on routine tasks requiring little research, they had few opportunities to participate in significant professional innovation.

Divisions among professionals also marked accountancy. Elite status was based on a capacity for business measurement useful to dynamic national corporations. Leading practices such as Haskins and Sells, Ernst and Ernst, Peat Marwick and Mitchell, and Price Waterhouse established branch office networks to serve far-flung, giant business clients. As in law, however, a large local practice served simpler businesses that required only routine services.

As professions reorganized in the twentieth century, they benefited from widening arcs of useful specialized knowledge that were helping to transform government as well as business. Confronted by recognition that many types of specialized knowledge could help resolve social problems, and faced with the limited executive capacities of government, reform leaders eagerly sought the support of professionals with expert skills. The voluntary service of these groups helped to extend the reach of the state in such matters as guaranteeing agricultural abundance, improving public health, conserving natural resources, and enhancing economic equity. The advocacy of experts created favorable public impressions about reform and lent needed credibility to government requests for fatter operating budgets. As an antidote to corrupt patronage politics, capable, high-minded professionals tried to increase public faith in government's ability to meet social needs. Often they succeeded.

Through government service, professional groups made contacts that provided them with tangible benefits. They gained a highly visible forum to demonstrate the power of their knowledge. In fact, they were willing to join with politicians of virtually every persuasion in ventures that would better assure a safe haven for their expertise. Government expansion during the Progressive Era provided a steady demand for new professional skills. Agencies such as the Interstate Commerce Commission (ICC) and the Federal Trade Commission (FTC) recruited attorneys for their staffs. The imposition of financial reporting requirements on private groups by agencies like the ICC, the Internal Revenue Service, and the Federal Reserve Board created work for accountants. So too did the expansion of internal accounting systems that facilitated the management of bureaucratic agencies. Physicians found opportunities in the national effort to assure the purity of food and drugs and to promote public health measures. Many joined the staffs of state and local hospitals and health institutions.

Perhaps even more important were professions' new links to corporations requiring advanced specialized knowledge. The desire to recruit well-trained scientists, engineers, and managers provided a strong incentive for corporations to cultivate contacts with universities and other institutions training experts. Forward-looking companies that sought competitive advantages through control of specialized knowledge provided financial support for faculty research projects. Business further nurtured these relationships by providing funds in the form of scholarships, work-study programs, endowed professorships, and grants-in-aid.

Business interest in education reflected the degree to which the giant bureaucracies that emerged in transportation and manufacturing depended on new forms of knowledge. Perceptive business leaders soon discovered that they could reduce costs and increase operating efficiencies by integrating specialists in marketing, manufacturing, and finance into the managerial hierarchy. Business knowledge also became increasingly formalized through the writings of Frederick W. Taylor and other management theorists.

Once firms established internal capacities for conducting scientific research, they forged ties to the estate of science. These efforts were directed either toward developing more efficient manufacturing processes or discovering useful new products. Some private sector research centers dated back to the 1880s. Independent laboratories such as those of Thomas A. Edison and Arthur D. Little had been organized before the formation of many large corporations. By 1910, companies such as AT&T, Eastman Kodak, General Electric, Standard Oil, and Westinghouse Electric had established their own R&D facilities, employing growing numbers of university-trained scientists and engineers.

During the Progressive Era, concerns about the public image of the corporation and its products spurred the development of expertise in advertising and public relations. To assure the full and profitable utilization of manufacturing capacity, many corporations engaged advertising specialists who could assess consumer preferences, build brand loyalty, and motivate buying. Public relations served to rebut the fierce public criticism of Big Business, a mistrust based on the belief that corporations served only private interests, and not the public weal. Pioneering publicists such as Ivy Lee were enlisted by leading corporations to project a more favorable impression that emphasized business contributions to social progress and material improvement.

Some of the richest opportunities for professionals belonged to independent practitioners working for the corporate sector. Elite attorneys were called upon by business clients to draft contracts, litigate disputes, and provide counsel on a wide array of issues. During the merger boom of 1900–1904, leading banks engaged accounting firms to certify corporate financial statements. Their goal was to increase the confidence of London investors in American securities. English law required annual audits of companies. Recognizing the appeal of this practice to English investors, the House of Morgan in 1902 engaged Price Waterhouse to conduct annual audits of United States Steel, the nation's first billion-dollar manufacturing enterprise. Gradually many other leading corporations embraced this practice. Only in medicine did the connections with the corporate sector remain weak. Although a few physicians were employed by the pharmaceutical industry or obtained positions as company doctors, the majority applied their knowledge to individual patients in private practice or through nonprofit hospitals.

Although often tied to powerful private and public sector institutions, professionals tried to retain independence. In part their goal was to restrict access to their fields and control their incomes. Representative associations played a key role in building professional monopolies by socializing members and drawing them closer together. The need for cohesiveness induced associational leaders to attempt to coordinate the members' activities and constrain their competitive impulses. Additionally, professional leaders sought both to build public confidence and to strengthen market control by raising qualifying standards and extending ethical codes.

For the more elite professions, unity, and cohesion were often difficult to achieve. Medical doctors imitated the American political system by forming national federations with weak central authority. The American Medical Association (AMA) failed to draw into its orbit many of the specialist associations, though it did incorporate state medical societies by 1903. Specialists chose to remain separate. They feared that the AMA's large and influential general practitioner constituency would enact policies inimical to their interests. Even the formation of specialist sections within the AMA did little to reconcile these differences. This lack of unity eventually contributed to serious conflicts over the control of postgraduate education.

Lawyers also failed to achieve unity through federation. Many local practitioners were apprehensive that the elite bar would dominate the American Bar Association. Some lawyers in southern and western states believed the association leadership reflected the interests of the industrial and financial Northeast. Others had misgivings about its Uniform Commercial Code, which aimed to eliminate the many inconsistencies in state business law. In doing so, it would also eradicate the protection that in-state attorneys enjoyed from competition with large out-of-state firms. By its very nature law was a profession that was primarily practiced locally. Even elite practices representing giant corporations maintained access to the federal judiciary through local district courts. Nor did large firms specializing in corporate practice feel the pressure to form branch networks as was the case in accounting. Instead they relied on the cooperation of correspondent firms for distant assignments.

As a group, accountants began this period by employing the federal structures introduced in medicine. They ended it by reverting to the fragmented associationalism exhibited in law. Seeking to eliminate intraprofessional competition, the American Association of Public Accountants (AAPA) reorganized as a federation in 1905. It promoted licensing legislation for state-certified public accounting (CPA). Nationwide coordination facilitated by a federated structure helped the AAPA win acceptance for its model CPA law in forty states by 1917.

Despite this achievement, many accountants soon became dissatisfied with the direction taken by their professional leadership. Some of the northeastern elite were unhappy with compromises struck over criteria for licensing. Although emphasizing educational attainment and performance on qualifying examinations, the criteria retained the older standard based on practical experience. Compromise had been necessary to secure legislation in certain states. After a decade of rapid growth, however, these members of the profession felt that accounting was becoming overcrowded. They wanted higher barriers to entry and stricter rules against disruptive competition. The more bigoted worried about the influx of immigrants. Others, anticipating America's entry into World War I, simply desired a more tightly organized body which could respond quickly to the federal government's expected call for assistance.

In 1916 the AAPA broke up on these rocky shoals. It was replaced by the more rigidly centralized American Institute of Accountants (AIA). The new body took an important step toward extending its influence over accreditation nationwide. In 1916 it sponsored a uniform examination for admission to its own ranks, which it made available the following year to nine state boards of accountancy. By 1921 the number of states that had adopted the AIA examination grew to thirty-six.

In both medicine and law, professional organizations began to raise entry barriers around World War I. Most dramatic was the reduction in medical schools resulting from Flexner's critical survey and the extension of training time in those that remained. The number of doctors increased from 130,000 to 146,000 between 1910 and 1920. This 12.3 percent increase was slightly less than the growth of the total labor force. A second set of barriers limited entry in lucrative specializations. Surgeons again led the way, using the accreditation process to control the size and number of residency programs in 1913. Soon both the AMA and specialist colleges began to widen the scope of this form of regulation. Hospitals, concerned about their own accreditation by medical boards, began limiting some types of practice in their facilities to properly certified specialists. These reforms were touted as a way of raising standards. But they also had the undesirable effect of reducing the number of schools that trained black candidates.

A more challenging bar examination helped to reduce access to the legal profession. The total number of law schools actually increased from 102 in 1900 to 143 by 1943, in spite of a critical CFAT survey. What had changed dramatically was the relevant core of legal knowledge. Law was no longer a static form of expertise that could be mastered solely through the standard compilations. Legal quandaries stemming from the great social and economic flux of this period led to a proliferation of precedent-setting court decisions that could best be learned through the systematic training provided by law schools. Increasingly, admission to the bar was governed by performance on state-administered examinations testing this knowledge.

During the decade ending in 1910 the number of attorneys increased by a scant 7,000, to 115,000 (+6.5 percent), while in the following decade these numbers only grew by a mere 8,000 (+7.0 percent). This growth paled in comparison to the over 30 percent increase in attorneys that had taken place each decade between 1870 and 1900. It was also low in comparison with the growth of the national labor force, which expanded by 28.5 percent between 1900 and 1910 and 13.2 percent from 1910 to 1920.

In accountancy, where a rigorous licensing examination provided the principal barrier to entry, education was becoming more important as well. Although collegiate training had grown rapidly, no state board required this credential. In a few states, it was not even necessary to have a high school diploma to gain a license. Many old hands were skeptical about the benefit of higher education. As noted, however, many states were adopting the AIA examination. Aspirants who prepared for licensing examinations through apprenticeships performed poorly in comparison with graduates of collegiate accounting programs. As tests grew more challenging, the advantages of education increased. In 1940, New York became the first state to mandate a college education as a prerequisite to the practice of accounting.

In addition to organizing and raising standards, elite professions began to establish codes of ethics. These rules had a dual purpose. They assured the public that practitioners would not apply their superior knowledge in ways that took unfair advantage of clients. They also permitted professional leaders to exercise control over the practitioner community. Generally, professional leaders used this power to suppress market competition. All the independent professions eventually promulgated rules against aggressive competitive activities like fee-splitting, advertising, and direct solicitation of clients. The burden of these rules fell most heavily on new entrants with few connections. The main beneficiaries were the well established, who had the most to lose from disruptive competition.

Although the new professional structures generally served economic functions, they also contributed to a growing cultural homogeneity of practitioner communities. The rising costs of qualifying for a career and the restrictions placed on practice development created competitive advantages for middle-class candidates. During this period, white men from Anglo-Saxon, Protestant backgrounds enjoyed these advantages. In an age that provided virtually no public financial assistance for professional education, the economic barriers to professional life were usually insurmountable for the less well-off. Only the existence of part-time programs—options available in accounting and law but not in medicine—afforded some relief to candidates of meager means.

These cultural patterns were also apparent in the growing stratification within individual professions. Although elite status was associated with innovative practice, access to the best jobs depended not only on ability and aptitude but also on social background. The partner rolls of the top accounting and law firms or the attending roster of prestigious hospitals reflected a predominance of men of WASP backgrounds. Because they shared with clients and professional leaders a similar education and outlook, they were considered to be more acceptable as colleagues and counselors than were those from minority cultures.

Practitioners who did not share this background, such as members of racial minorities or those of recent immigrant origin, had little chance to scale the professional heights. Worried about the corrosive effects of immigration, industrialization, and urbanization on traditional values, the middle-class mainstream of established professional practices kept hyphenated Americans on the margins of their fields, or out altogether. The purportedly alien qualities of minority groups served as a rationalization for exclusion. Unable to penetrate this glass wall in professional life, they were confined to small, local practices in law and accounting.

In medicine, professional stratification separated those who had been trained at domestic and foreign institutions. The reduction in the number of medical school places in America compelled many ambitious candidates of recent immigrant origin to seek instruction in Europe. A foreign degree was viewed by many American medical leaders as a stigma of mediocrity. Those trained overseas thus had diminished prospects for appointments to prestigious internships or residency programs. This bias against ethnic Americans was partially offset, however, by the admissions policies of hospitals sponsored by religious or ethnic groups and by public hospitals in larger municipalities. Jewish and Catholic doctors, for example, organized first-rate training hospitals such as Mount Sinai and Saint Vincent's in New York City. Appointments in municipal hospitals were often used as political patronage. Local politicians, seeking to maintain broad coalitions among their various constituents, were sensitive to the need to bring people of different ethnic, racial, religious, and social backgrounds to the staffs of public hospitals.

Although the independent professions were the most visible channels of new specialized knowledge, many experts found outlets for their skills in other types of organizational settings during the early twentieth century. In engineering, nursing, teaching, and social work, specialists were employees of public or private organizations, rather than independent contractors. These professionals had to apply their knowledge in ways that satisfied the imperatives of their employers. In return, they received compensations. By blending many sorts of professional skills, schools, hospitals, and corporations achieved social benefits that otherwise would have been unattainable. Many forms of specialized knowledge would have languished without the concentration of capital and human resources made possible by giant enterprises.

Typical of these mutually beneficial relationships was the one formed between engineers and business corporations. To attract well-trained engineers to their laboratories, corporate scientists provided scholarships, internships, faculty research grants, and financial assistance to leading technical institutions. Corporate sponsors also supported the activities of engineering and scientific professional societies. Strong industrial expansion in turn provided job opportunities for engineers. In 1900, for example, there were 38,000 engineers; by 1920, this number had increased to 134,000. Industrialization also led to the broadening of technical horizons. In 1900, the primary outlets for technical experts had been civil and mechanical engineering. By 1920, electrical, chemical, and industrial engineering were also thriving fields.

Because of the heavy business demand for their special knowledge, engineers assumed critical roles in shaping corporate cultures. Some were absorbed into the ranks of senior management with responsibility for defining strategic goals. Engineer-executives like Theodore N. Vail, Irénée du Pont, and Alfred P. Sloan exerted substantial influence on the companies they led—AT&T, Du Pont, and General Motors. Others such as Thomas Midgely, Jr. and Charles Kettering, both of General Motors, demonstrated how engineers could be instrumental in determining the direction of technological advance through their involvement in research and development activities.

As business-professional relations grew stronger, some engineers came to believe that corporate influence frustrated the possibility of reform. Morris L. Cooke, for example, held that the objectives of corporations were inconsistent with the type of public service he believed that engineering professionalism was capable of achieving. Cooke was not entirely wrong. After World War I, the deep conservatism of corporate engineers on social matters was exhibited in decisions taken by the Federated American Engineering Societies, a national umbrella organization. Its constituent groups included the American Society of Mechanical Engineers, the American Institute of Electrical Engineers, and the American Institute of Mining Engineers. Intimately bound to industry, these groups refused to support proposals to study waste in industry or the twelve-hour working day.

In contrast to male-dominated engineering, nursing provided professional opportunities primarily for American women. The popularity of nursing reflected a changing attitude about the social role of women that was first exemplified by the careers of such pioneers as Florence Nightingale in Britain and Clara Barton in the United States. Their diligence in tending to the sick and wounded during the Crimean War and the American Civil War helped to break down the traditional middle-class view of women as mothers and wives whose experience was defined exclusively by the ebb and flow of family life. Nightingale, Barton, and others demonstrated the ability of women to act decisively during crises.

Although these antecedents seemed to promise a strong, autonomous professional role for women, by the twentieth century nursing was being structured by requirements set down by other members of the medical profession. The result was that nurses became subordinated to both hospitals and male physicians. Seeking reliable assistants for their medical staffs, hospital administrators eagerly sponsored nurse training programs to create a tractable and inexpensive source of labor for routine duties. Perceiving nurses as a potential threat, physicians defined curricula and the scope of service in ways that assured a ancillary role for nursing practice.

Nevertheless, opportunities abounded for women in this field. Professional nursing grew dramatically, from 12,000 members in 1900 to 149,000 by 1920. By 1903, four states had passed legislation licensing registered nurses. Nursing provided women with modest salaries and secure professional status. The more ambitious and able could aspire to hospital supervisory positions. Those desiring greater autonomy could choose either visiting or private duty assignments.

Social work, like nursing, was also primarily a female profession. It had grown out of the visitations to the poor sponsored by late-nineteenth-century urban charitable and settlement organizations. Middle-class volunteers assisted the "deserving poor" by distributing alms and providing encouragement and moral counsel. Through these contacts, activists in charity movements believed that the social cohesiveness characteristic of small-town America might be restored in the burgeoning cities. Frugality, industry, and temperance, they hoped, would help the poor become more self-sufficient and able to improve their own condition.

After 1900 the intellectual grounding and organizational focus of social work began to change radically. Earlier emphasis on well-meaning and pragmatic appeals for personal improvement gave way to a new form of counsel rooted in a new concentration on the bases of social demoralization. In this view poverty was the product not so much of personal moral failure as of the dynamic interplay between personal and environmental factors that resulted in victimization and exploitation of the poor.

As the intellectual base of social work changed, its practice took on the dimensions of other professions. The need for more formal training to function effectively contributed to a shift away from volunteerism. By the 1920s, such educational leaders in this field as Mary Ellen Richmond of the Russell Sage Foundation in New York admonished their students to treat each of their cases as unique. Individual cases required their own social diagnosis. The professional social worker became the qualified diagnostician.

Social work proved a hardy saprophyte capable of grafting its knowledge onto many social and scientific institutions. One new branch was medical social work, which centered in hospitals. Medical social workers pursued the environmental origins of diseases, particularly tuberculosis. Another new specialty was the visiting teachers services in public schools. They provided specialized instruction to students disadvantaged by debilitating environmental or personal circumstances. A third new area was psychiatric social work. It found niches in psychopathic hospitals, in the mental health movement, and in institutions specializing in the problems of juvenile delinquency or "feeble-mindedness."

An uncertain economic base made careers in social work somewhat less appealing than those in other professions. Although social workers generally enjoyed greater autonomy in their practices than did nurses, their salaries were low (generally about half the salaries paid schoolteachers). Welfare agency budgets remained tight, dependent on community chest support or meager subsidies from state governments. Nevertheless, the ranks of social and recreational workers grew from about 20,000 in 1910 to about 46,000 in 1920.

The teaching profession, by contrast, grew to enormous proportions by the early twentieth century, providing careers for both men and women. In 1900 there were 436,000 teachers. By 1920, the number had increased to 752,000. Teachers constituted fully one-third of all professional workers.

Although an old occupation, teaching took on a new professional consciousness reflecting a fundamental redefinition of the teacher's mission in the early twentieth century. The rising industrial/service economy required a work force whose intellectual capabilities surpassed the basic literacy levels achieved earlier in the public schools. A high school education became more commonplace as the total number of diplomas granted annually grew from 95,000 in 1900 to 331,000 in 1920. Secondary school curricula were modified to make them more useful both to those who wished to enter the job market on graduation and those who desired to progress to higher education. Many larger urban high schools simultaneously supported curricula for industrial arts, commercial studies, and college preparation. Schools also modified their traditional emphasis on inculcating civic virtues in order to facilitate the assimilation into American society of new waves of immigrants, particularly those from eastern and southern Europe.

Civics and history courses extolled the superiority of America's unique liberal, democratic institutions. Normal schools began training educators in the tenets of "progressive" education. This new pedagogy encouraged sensitivity to the unique aptitudes and interests of individual students.

Representative associations composed of members imbued with this professional consciousness fought to increase teacher autonomy. With the aid of national and local professional associations, teachers sought to insulate education from the political spoils system. In many communities they achieved their goals through the institution of qualifying examinations, licensing, tenure arrangements, and the formation of independent boards of education.

Not all professional groups were on the rise during the early twentieth century. In the urban centers of the Northeast and Midwest, the ministry's prestige was in eclipse. New scientific theories about the origins of life and the structure of the physical universe began to replace ecclesiastical explanations. Ministerial authority over problems of the mind and the soul was challenged by the rise of psychiatry and psychoanalysis. Guided by doctrines that sought to explain the complexities of human behavior through scientific data, a new corps of mental health therapists competed with ministers' pastoral mission.

Ministers' authority remained high in rural settings, particularly in the South and West. Evangelists such as Billy Sunday and Aimee Semple McPherson continued to build great followings preaching the "old-time religion." The encroachment of the state and new specialist groups in many welfare functions that had earlier been predominantly the sphere of religious bodies, however, further eroded the influence of the ministry. Professional social work gradually displaced the charitable association movement which had been led by clerics since the 1880s. This intrusion increased when state and federal governments began to play more active roles in alleviating poverty.

In response to these challenges, religious groups gradually began to accept many of the new forms of knowledge transforming American society. There were some notable instances where religious outlooks clashed sharply with scientific perspectives. In 1925, a secondary school teacher, John T. Scopes, was brought to trial in Tennessee for using the theory of evolution to explain humankind's origin. Such spectacular battles between science and the Bible, however, were not the norm. Religious bodies implicitly accepted the new social and scientific paradigms through their sponsorship of universities, hospitals, and social welfare agencies that incorporated these forms of secular knowledge in their programs.

WORLD WAR I AND THE ASSOCIATIVE STATE, 1917–1930

The national emergency brought on by World War I created strong pressures for the formation of a more cooperative relationship between the federal government and professional groups. The National Research Council and the Naval Consulting Board both solicited the aid of the nation's scientific and engineering communities. The War Industries Board, which coordinated production, operated through specialized commodity sections whose members were mainly volunteers from industry. Its banking counterpart, the War Finance Board, relied on the voluntary services of leading accountants, financiers, and attorneys. Professional associations assisted government by providing evaluations of the credentials of individuals who sought to enter federal service. They also took up specific assignments that aided the war effort. The American Institute of Accountants, for example, developed financial systems for military bases and financial schedules for cost-plus contracts. The Engineering Council consulted with the Fuel Administration and the Bureau of Mines on projects dealing with essential resources.

The victory in 1918 bolstered the American public's confidence in the professions. Americans were impressed by the contributions of a broad array of specialists to national defense and to the prosperity that soon followed the war. Their achievements seemed to prove the superiority of a society which relied on the voluntary cooperation of free people over what was viewed as the stultifying statism of the vanquished Central Powers. These perceptions, in conjunction with a weariness with wartime regimentation, encouraged a laissez-faire attitude among political and governmental leaders toward the professions.

A similar attitude marked public perceptions of the business enterprises that were run by managers who had contributed to the war effort. By the 1920s large-scale, hierarchical companies dominated many of the most dynamic sectors of the American economy. They were directed by a self-consciously professional managerial class possessing specialized business skills—the visible hands responsible for coordinating and controlling the complex operations of these vast enterprises. By 1930, the national economy required the services of 3.6 million managers, or about one out of every thirteen workers in the labor force.

The American corporate sector also continued to employ large numbers of professional workers in other fields. Seeking more effective control over the physical and social environments, many companies were making substantial investments in R&D through the efforts of organized, university-trained scientists. Systematic research, the Du Pont Company learned, could provide the basis for a new business strategy, namely product diversification. Like the economist Joseph Schumpeter's notion of "creative destruction," a continuous process of discovery could sustain the corporation through the vicissitudes of the business cycle. New products and market opportunities helped to assure the full utilization of enterprise resources. Sensitive to the need to project a favorable impression about their social roles, companies also acquired public relations know-how. These efforts were highly successful, helping to crystallize broad public acceptance of the large corporation during this decade.

Greater prosperity during the 1920s enabled more Americans to purchase professional services. Growing incomes provided better access to justice, health, education, recreation, and financial counsel. Evidence of this change was clearly reflected in the increasing numbers of workers classified as "professional" by the Census. This category (which excluded business managers) grew from 2.3 million in 1920 to 3.3 million in 1930 (+50 percent). But these growth trends were not uniformly reflected in all professional categories.

Elite professional groups continued their strategies of securing their economic positions by severely limiting their numbers. In spite of the general growth of professional workers, the numbers of medical doctors increased by a scant 11,000 during the 1920s. Attorneys grew by only 38,000. Accountants increased from 74,000 to 192,000 between 1920 and 1929; the numbers actually passing the crucial CPA licensing examination, however, were considerably lower. Since the establishment of licensing requirements in 1897 the grand total of CPA licenses issued nationwide amounted to only 13,273 through 1929. Over 70 percent of these were issued during the period 1920 to 1929.

Strong foundations of professionalism established by the 1920s enabled practitioners of law, medicine, and accounting to exert such control over access. Each group was represented by highly visible and prestigious associations. Each was also well served by strong educational institutions that followed standard curricula. These professions had detailed their social responsibilities in comprehensive ethical codes. They had also made progress in winning acceptance for their uniform certifying examinations from many state licensing boards.

Tight supply and small, closely knit professional communities had varying effects on the availability of professional services in society, particularly among the poor. After 1917, organized medicine mounted a strong opposition against both private and public health insurance schemes. Many physicians feared that insurance intermediaries would regulate their incomes and interfere with their access to patients. In an age of patchy health insurance coverage, medical expenses were an onerous burden to many households. On the other hand, to assure broad accessibility (and a supply of live specimens for teaching), many urban hospitals opened free wards for the indigent. In law, practitioners sometimes provided services pro bono on behalf of charitable or civic organizations. The Legal Aid Society, established in 1905, assisted poor clients by donating services, usually those of fledgling attorneys. In civil cases the poor could engage lawyers on a contingent fee basis, though this practice was roundly condemned by the elite leaders of the bar whose corporate clients often were defendants in these suits. In lieu of cash payments, lawyers and accountants sometimes accepted equity positions in financially tenuous businesses that could not afford to pay their professional bills. Overall, elite professions made some efforts to provide their services to those below the middle class, but these efforts remained quite small.

Maintaining the impressive edifice of united and autonomous professionalism proved increasingly difficult through the decade of the 1920s. Professionals were divided by differences in the nature of their practices, their beliefs about professionalism, and their social backgrounds. Although associational structures generally were loose enough to vent the pressures of conflict, sometimes tensions boiled over spectacularly.

In 1921, the rigidly centralized American Institute of Accountants failed to neutralize differences among members. Problems started over rules banning advertising and other types of client solicitation. Promulgated at the behest of the leadership of the elite national firms, these rules were cursed by many of the local practitioners, who resented the control of their markets. Tensions mounted when dissidents imputed sinister motives to the unsuccessful drive by elite members to secure a congressional charter for their association. They suspected that this step was part of a broader design to substitute membership in the organization for state-granted CPA licenses as

the primary proof of competency. The dissidents soon deserted the AIA and formed the American Society of Certified Public Accountants. The new organization championed state licensing and also abjured the sort of ethical standards that their rivals sought to enhance market control. For more than a decade, the profession remained divided.

In other professions during the 1920s, growth depended much more on government policies and actions. Unlike the services of independent professionals, those of teachers and social workers were paid for by public agencies. Where this support was strong, professions thrived. Education, for example, was a traditional activity of government that had grown over time with the passage of compulsory education acts. Americans had long favored public spending on education because it was equated with material and spiritual improvement. Accordingly, the ranks of teachers swelled by 292,000, passing the million mark during this decade. This 39 percent increase more than doubled that of the labor force.

Social work, on the other hand, did not achieve the same level of public support. The growth of recreational and social workers was modest, rising from 46,000 to 71,000 during the decade. During a period of optimism and prosperity, when Americans celebrated the virtues of hard work and personal initiative, there was little support for governmental spending to alleviate the plight of the poor and the socially maladjusted.

Other vocations also maintained a tenuous hold on professional status during the 1920s. The growth of several health specializations—including chiropractic, osteopathy, and optics—was kept in check by strong opposition from powerful medical associations. Even when they gained a foothold, moreover, these practices were held back by their narrow base of knowledge. Unlike physicians, none of these rival health specialists demonstrated convincingly how their techniques could be generalized for the broad treatment of illness.

The trends evident in professions during the 1920s provided tentative answers to three fundamental questions about the relationship between organized knowledge and society. The first concerned the degree of autonomy that professionals should exercise in ordering their own affairs independent of outside interests such as government and consumers. The second was what influence the professions' control over access to careers would have on social mobility. The third was whether it was equitable for professions to raise practice standards in ways that augmented their market power.

With respect to autonomy, the insularity of professional systems for control led to serious shortcomings that in the future proved problematic. Professionalism was limited by the priority given to the entrepreneurial over the service dimensions of practice. Despite their ethical codes, representative associations were lax in protecting consumers. They refused to take strong steps to monitor practitioner performance and punish malpractice. The independent professions were also reluctant to apply their expertise to alleviate worrisome social problems because it was costly or inconvenient to practitioners or their clients. Most medical doctors, for example, strongly opposed publicly financed health insurance, claiming that it would lead to socialized medicine. Leading attorneys did little to increase the availability of justice to the poor. And corporate accountants were slow to standardize financial reporting so as to assist investors.

In the subordinate professions, by contrast, the priorities of employer institutions usually outweighed those of representative associations. Hospitals, business corporations, school systems, and welfare agencies all enjoyed substantial countervailing power in dealing with the professionals they employed. In this context experts had to be wary of circumstances that might lead to a misalignment between the precepts of their professional ethical codes and employers' imperatives.

With regard to social mobility, the professions also had difficulty living up to their own ideals. Access to America's rising professional meritocracy was not predicated on individual ability alone. It was also strongly influenced by economic status, race, and gender. Barriers to professional access, such as rigorous qualifying standards, were accepted because they presumably improved practice and thus protected the public interest. These measures, however, were generally advantageous to male candidates of white, middle-class backgrounds. Such aspirants were better able to afford the high cost of training and the long period of foregone income that was required in preparing for the challenge of professional life. Their progress up the professional ladder, moreover, was easier than that of other groups. They shared with leaders in their fields of expertise and with important clients a common social and cultural background.

Some social groups did not benefit from the organization of the professions in the early twentieth century. Many of those of southern or eastern European immigrant backgrounds, as well as most women, blacks, Asians, and Hispanics were left out of elite professional practices and relegated to the margins of these fields. Qualifying standards also worked against native whites who lived in economically depressed regions such as the South, where educational facilities were not yet well developed. Economic barriers encountered in the pursuit of competency were generally harder for these groups to surmount. At a time when personal qualities were commonly equated with particular social backgrounds, the seemingly alien character of minority men and women served as obstacles to their acceptance by both fellow practitioners and clients.

Opportunities for personal advancement through professional life were not completely closed off by socioeconomic barriers. Far more professional openings emerged in the United States during this period than could possibly be filled by any single social class. In addition, talent and perseverance—characteristics important for success—were broadly distributed across members of society. Some professional leaders and educators recognized that skills and proficiency were not class-bound traits. They provided financial aid and employment opportunities to candidates from a wide range of backgrounds. Leaders of minority groups who recognized the significance of professionalism in American society also provided financial support to worthy members of their communities. Educational institutions, eager to increase tuition cash flows, opened admissions to qualified members of minority groups, though usually enforcing a quota that kept out other qualified aspirants. In many fields economic barriers could still be overcome by the part-time schooling and night training available through urban universities. Lastly, many individuals, perhaps sensitive to the disdain in which their social backgrounds were held, may have been all the more driven by desires to prove their personal worth through achievement in the professions.

Although the portals to professional life gradually began to open to people of different social backgrounds, practice units themselves remained sharply differentiated in this period. Partners of elite law and public accounting firms and the senior staffs of the most prestigious hospitals were overwhelmingly middle-class WASPs. Over time this pattern would gradually change as clients of the elite firms themselves grew more socially diverse. Only then did practitioners from nontraditional backgrounds begin to advance in professional hierarchies.

By the end of the 1920s there was little doubt that professions had gained substantial market power. Nowhere was this power more apparent than in the independent practices, where control over access to professional careers was portrayed as the only secure way of assuring competency. Consumers had little say over how knowledge that affected their interests would be exercised by these bodies. Eventually, the rising costs of service and limitations on access to careers would force the independent professions to change. Through the 1920s, however, their autonomy and control remained intact.

The market power of professionals working for large organizations, on the other hand, was largely constrained by the countervailing bargaining power of their employers. From a cost standpoint, the public interest seemed better served when professional skills were primarily allocated through large hierarchical organizations, whether private or public. These institutions had the incentive to control labor costs. They were also capable of achieving efficiency by rationalizing the division of labor. Those that operated under the discipline of the market or the ballot box often passed these savings on to consumers. In the future, the power of organizations in all professional occupations would increase, driven by shifting competitive circumstances, political demands for greater access, and rising service costs.

THE GREAT DEPRESSION AND THE NEW DEAL, 1931–1949

As the Great Depression devastated the economy, so too did it overrun the professions. Incomes from independent practices plummeted. Unemployment among white-collar workers, though lower than that of blue-collar workers, was nonetheless substantial. For professionals such as teachers, social workers, and engineers working within public and private organizations, the experience of unemployment was little different from that of other workers. Some eventually found jobs in the growing federal bureaucracy spawned by the New Deal, while others benefited from the war effort in the 1940s. But many remained unemployed so long as private business firms faced low demand and so long as government programs reflected the prevailing fear of large budget deficits and a permanent bureaucracy.

For lawyers, doctors, and accountants not directly employed by the state or private business, the experience of the Great Depression was more complicated, though no less harmful. Overall, income in these occupational categories fell as sharply as that of all workers, if not more sharply. Discretionary spending on services such as medical care dropped precipitously with income. By one estimate, physicians' nominal incomes declined by 47 percent between 1929 and 1933. Hospitals found themselves with excess capacity, a calamity for such capital intensive enterprises.

An increase in the supply of potential practitioners added to the problems faced by professions. College and university enrollments grew during the Depression. By 1940, the number of annual college graduates had increased by 55 percent over its 1930 level. When added to the dramatic 160 percent increase that had taken place between 1920 and 1930, these numbers suggested a larger pool of talent seeking entry into professional occupations. The pincers of falling demand and increasing supply frustrated the strategy of professional associations, which sought to use educational attainment and practice standards to police access.

Many professions had also become dependent on channels of recruitment that were severely disrupted by the economic crisis. Hospitals and large law and accounting firms traditionally made use of practitioners in training, who worked for low wages in exchange for experience. Nursing schools leased out their students, providing cheap labor to hospitals and funds to cash-strapped schools. Physician interns and residents did much of the routine labor of patient care. Young associate lawyers and accountants handled tedious and prosaic tasks of legal research and auditing. Associates' labor augmented the incomes of partners, who divided the firms' net proceeds while paying associates a fixed annual wage. These mechanisms, too, were disrupted by the Depression. Wages of apprentices went down sharply and many had trouble securing places in the professional hierarchy.

In the general climate of despair and frustration, professional institutions, like many others, came under attack. Social scientists, economists in particular, suffered a sudden loss of prestige. The public recalled with bitter irony their prognostications of the 1920s about the permanence of the boom. Investment bankers were paraded in front of congressional committees, most notably the Senate Banking Committee of 1932–1934 and its crusading chief counsel Ferdinand Pecora. Many of them winced as Richard Whitney, patrician head of the New York Stock Exchange, was revealed as simultaneously a swindler and a sucker. As the later New Deal launched probes into monopoly practices by corporations, it revisited the tradition of self-policing in the professions. Assistant Attorney General Thurman Arnold lambasted the American Medical Association in 1938 for its iron-fisted control of medical practice and pricing and its opposition to group medical insurance.

Although the Depression and its political consequences presented a serious challenge, many professions also found opportunities during the slump to accomplish tasks with which they had long been struggling. The National Industrial Recovery Act of 1933, for example, was built around the concept of limiting competition. It briefly popularized the sort of entry barriers which professions had been establishing. Some professions profited from this short-lived New Deal flirtation with corporatism. Lawyers were finally able to close down nonaccredited, proprietary night law schools, which for decades had been turning out attorneys in competition with university law programs. Elite law schools tightened admission standards, and regional schools around the nation followed suit. Marginal practitioners in many fields found that the hard times of the 1930s forced them out of their jobs, or at the very least made them retreat from specialization and scramble for clients.

Although the fortunes of professions and individual practitioners waxed and waned during the Depression and New Deal eras, the profound changes in American politics taking place at this time had a salient effect on professional life. By the end of the 1940s, state-professional ties had expanded enormously. These ties not only transformed policy making in the United States, but reshaped the meaning of professionalism as well.

The New Deal picked up the threads of government-professional relations that had been established in the Progressive era and wove them into a grand new tapestry. In order to expand administrative capacity quickly during the crisis, yet keep the size of the government bureaucracy within acceptable limits, President Roosevelt relied on a number of different professional groups to carry out specific regulatory tasks. In one of the boldest new programs, accountants were given a broad new mandate to oversee the financial dealings of corporations and to monitor the behavior of financial markets. The Securities Act of 1933 and the Securities Exchange Act of 1934 exposed accountants to greater legal liability for failure to report financial misdeeds. The second of the acts, which created the Securities and Exchange Commission (SEC), also required publicly traded companies to file annual statements audited by independent accountants. Initially opposed by accountants fearing encroachment into their domain, the laws eventually provided a vast new source of business. They also resolved the longstanding conflict between accountants' roles as both assurers of financial probity to investors and employees of corporations. As a result, the public prestige and reliability of the profession increased.

Lawyers too found new opportunities through expanded government regulation. Staffing many of the agencies created by the New Deal, as well as making up a significant portion of Roosevelt's Brain Trust, lawyers in Washington contributed substantially to the shaping of policy. Some, like Securities and Exchange Commission architect James Landis, played highly creative roles in fashioning those policies. Even lower level practitioners, however, gained access to the new political economy of business-government relations.

Many of these lawyers took the expertise gained in Washington back into their private practices as they went through the revolving door that was opening between the private and public sectors. New York law firms as well as regional ones formed Washington offices, a development which would continue throughout the postwar period. Besides traditional lobbying exercises, capital city practices offered opportunities in what became major areas of law, such as antitrust and regulation. By providing new government-related work during the nadir of the Great Depression, the New Deal revived many sagging law firms. By greatly expanding the scope of federal law, it gave opportunities to lawyers around the country to move beyond state-level work and participate more fully in the emerging national political economy.

The new federal rules governing the economy also helped lawyers and accountants standardize their practices. To some extent, standardization had already been accomplished in accounting. But SEC rulings and the growing effect of federal regulation in specific industries such as railroads, telecommunications, energy, shipping, and banking widened its scope. The expanding importance of federal law provided a level of coherence in legal practice impossible in the days when state law predominated. After World War II the American Bar Association issued codifications and restatements of legal principles that educated members of the profession about the new standards. Most significant was the completion of the Uniform Commercial Code in 1950 and its adoption by the states over the next two decades. Law schools, which since the turn of the century had taught students through cases from federal appellate courts, could more truthfully argue that the case method got at the fundamentals of legal knowledge.

Management of the macroeconomy, the capstone of New Deal economic policy, elevated the status of professional economists. Denounced as "failed prophets" during the Depression, they gained substantial political influence after the passage of the Full

Employment Act of 1946. This new law did not go quite as far as earlier bills had proposed in setting fiscal policy. Nonetheless, it created a Council of Economic Advisers with considerable prestige and influence. Refinements in economic science during the 1930s and 1940s, including the publication and explication of John Maynard Keynes's *General Theory* (1936), Paul Samuelson's *Foundations of Economic Analysis* (1947), and Simon Kuznets's constructions of national income accounts greatly expanded the tools available for economic policy making. For a brief period, the economics profession appeared to have reached a consensus about its basic principles and knowledge.

While many of the new federal programs were aimed at business and the economy, others were directed at specific sectors such as health. These too drew on the assistance of professional groups. Agencies like the Public Health Service and the Veterans Administration expanded during the Roosevelt administration. Expenditures on public health increased 51 percent in the 1930s and then leapt an additional 200 percent between 1940 and 1944. Doctors also secured greater control over the institutions of private medicine. They defeated initiatives that contradicted their interests, such as the broadening of Social Security to include medical benefits. And they assured themselves of the right to make the key decisions in the Blue Cross and Blue Shield insurance programs.

For professionals desiring thoroughgoing social reform, the New Deal proved disappointing. Public welfare agencies, reeling from years of neglect followed by crisis, received only emergency help in the 1930s. Little of it was new and innovative in the model of the federal Works Progress Administration (WPA). Social work as an occupation prospered, growing from 71,000 members in 1930 to 136,000 by 1950. But even by 1940, 86 percent of federal, state, and local government social spending went to conservative social insurance schemes or to traditional social institutions such as schools.

There were few breakthroughs in education as well. Federal funding for schools was small and sporadic, little more than an offshoot of public works and jobs programs. Although federal aid to education rose by a factor of five between 1930 and 1940, it still stood at a scant 1.6 percent of total public school receipts by decade's end. For the poorest areas of the nation, even this small amount of federal assistance strengthened primary and secondary education and upgraded curricula. But schools remained overwhelmingly local institutions. In the South, the New Deal only scratched the surface of educational segregation. Teachers themselves were frustrated by the restricted flow of federal dollars, but at the same time fearful that more money would shift control of schools to federal hands.

Education professionals received some aid through the New Deal and World War II sponsored initiatives supporting the growth of knowledge. Through federal programs such as the GI bill, more Americans had access to universities at the end of World War II. Many enrolled in normal schools, which were turning out teachers to meet the growing enrollments of primary and secondary schools. Federal dollars also helped to standardize the training of teachers, and laid the basis for a boom in pedagogical knowledge in new academic departments of education.

This new federal presence in the generation of knowledge was particularly valuable to scientists. During World War II, the Manhattan Project had brought university scientists and the military together in the making of the atomic bomb. This successful endeavor led to increased funding of university and private industry research on weapons systems. More generally, war-related breakthroughs such as radar, jet aircraft, and penicillin gave scientists in a variety of fields greater prestige and a greater claim on the public purse. By 1953, federal contributions to research and development exceeded 50 percent of the total and continued to increase steadily through the mid-1960s.

While working on the Manhattan Project, scientists debated important questions of professional responsibility: Who should control the terrible weapons of destruction? Where did professional responsibilities to clients end and those to society at large begin? In the case of the bomb, scientists' social responsibility was limited to that of serving their clients, despite some objections from members of the professional community. This approach became the norm during the 1950s. Scientists applied their expertise to military projects, but were granted no right to control the fruits of their research. For the most part, other professions accepted a similar demarcation between professional responsibility and the authority of other institutions. Throughout the postwar decades, professionalism continued to hinge on a narrow definition that made service to clients—public or private—rather than exercise of independent judgment the main ethical responsibility of professionals.

By the end of the 1940s, professionals of all sorts had largely abandoned their fear of central government power. They grew more willing to work within governmental structures, accede to state regulations and mandates, and accept federal dollars. Professionals began to fill many of the key positions in America's new triocracy—that combination of legislatures, bureaucracies, and interest groups making public policy. Professional bodies also came before bureaucrats and legislators as interest groups lobbying for legislation that assisted their practices.

Eventually professionals and the state were fully joined in a new union. This alliance rested on the growing importance of scientific expertise in policy making. It was supported on the one side by the cohesiveness and maturity of professional organizations that could supply and direct such expertise. On the other it was buttressed by increasing public demand for services that could be met by "technocrats" drawn from the professions and housed in federal agencies.

Despite the growing power and prestige of professions in an expanded administrative state, neither statism nor corporatist traditions characterized American politics. A majority of practitioners in independent professions such as law, medicine, and accounting continued to work in the private rather than public sector. But they now enjoyed a wider political role. They had abandoned their drive to replace political functions with scientific expertise. Instead, science and bureaucracy became permanent features of a new politics that deemphasized the role of parties in policy making.

With government-supplied resources, professionals were able to fashion new specializations. They exerted greater control over their occupations and solved internal conflicts on matters of ethics, organization, and access. Doctors, dentists, lawyers, teachers, and accountants—plus a host of "quasi-professionals," such as real estate agents, morticians, and barbers—proved quite adept at manipulating the triocracy. They continued to strengthen barriers to competition through licensing laws and educational requirements. They gained competitive advantages through the manipulation of tax codes, regulations, and public sector patronage of their services. These developments, combined with trends in the private economy, would help make the following decades an age of professional prosperity.

AN AGE OF PROFESSIONAL PROSPERITY, 1950–1969

As the nation surged out of the Depression, changes in the structure of the economy, the management of business, and the international competitive position of American industry all had major effects on the professions. The role of the state in professional life did not abate. But in a booming postwar economy, private sector employment and private sector institutions—large corporations most notably—assured professional workers ample opportunities and growing incomes.

For all occupations based on specialized knowledge and the manipulation of information, the postwar years were the beginnings of a golden age. Information-related activity as a percentage of GNP recovered from the dip it had taken in the 1930s and grew substantially between 1949 and 1969. By some estimates the "information sector" accounted for nearly one-half of GNP. By the late 1960s, industries such as communications, finance, real estate, insurance, publishing, and education were providing employment for growing numbers of lawyers, accountants, statisticians, economists, sociologists, and kindred technical workers. In other industries, corporate bureaucracies housed large numbers of employees carrying out similar knowledge- and information-related functions, plus a host of scientists and engineers engaged in basic and applied research.

The growing significance of expertise, information, and knowledge in the economy fueled a general boom in white-collar work. America had emerged from the war with a dominant international position. In many industries it commanded the field in manufacturing, marketing, and finance. But the thrust of postwar policy gradually shifted America's competitive advantage away from manufacturing—and hence blue-collar jobs—and toward white-collar jobs. By 1970, professional, technical, managerial, and clerical workers constituted 47 percent of the labor force, nearly double the figure for 1950. Their share of national income rose to a similar percentage.

The United States' leadership after World War II in constructing an international economy built on free trade assured that the nation would eventually lose position in industries that involved a substantial manual labor component. In the free-trade economy, comparative advantage became a much more powerful force. With a highly educated work force and ample opportunities in higher education, America was better able to compete in high-wage than low-wage sectors. Many high-wage jobs involved the production of intangibles that could not be easily shifted offshore—information and personal services that moved only with the movement of people. Since people were less mobile than capital, these jobs tended to stay in the United States.

Professionals rode this wave of service expansion.

Corporate law partnerships and national accounting firms had around the turn of the century begun to transform themselves into bureaucratic organizations. They grew substantially larger and more powerful during the 1950s, 1960s, and 1970s. As the corporate economy spread from the East Coast and Middle West to the West and South, many regional firms began to take on work for national corporations.

Incomes for elite independent professionals were among the fastest growing in the economy between 1949 and 1969. Doctors were perhaps the major beneficiaries of the nation's preoccupation with services. Physicians' incomes in the 1960s pushed them into the economic elite of the nation and made them the highest paid of all professionals. By 1970, doctors in private practice earned on average almost $42,000 per year, at a time when median family income was $9,800.

In an economy that depended on a high-quality work force, access to education was vital. Seventy-five percent of the nation's seventeen-year-olds were graduating from high school by 1970. One-third of those between the ages of eighteen and twenty-four were attending institutions of higher leaning. Education remained the single largest profession, with over 3 million teachers.

Certain quasi-professional occupations also benefited from these broad economic trends. Real estate agents, psychological counselors, beauticians, interior decorators, and a host of others in service occupations garnered a good part of the disposable income of households. The service sector's share in national income rose to 13 percent by 1970, more than double what it had been in 1929. Sociologists debated whether these service occupations possessed sufficient autonomy and control over their output to be considered professions. The practitioners themselves, however, regulated access by gaining state support for licensing procedures and forming associative bodies.

Subordinate professionals—that is, those who worked for organizations—enjoyed similar prosperity during the latter half of the twentieth century. Structural changes in business opened up opportunities for workers who manipulated information, knowledge, and symbols rather than physical objects. Many corporations adopted the multidivisional form of organization as they diversified into related and eventually unrelated areas of business. This new structure generated greater demand for middle-level managers. In an era of economic growth, general macroeconomic stability, and few serious challenges from abroad, American business could afford to plan ahead and sacrifice immediate profits for longer range

goals. There was little incentive to slash payrolls and increase profits, so long as returns were sufficient to keep investors happy.

In this economy, business management itself became more professional. As entrepreneurship gave way to rational planning and administration, a degree from a respected university and graduate school of business provided entry into the world of corporate leadership. Some firms, more concerned about conserving existing assets than innovating, appointed professionals, lawyers in particular, to top positions. Strategic behavior and the manipulation of government regulations became significant sources of profits. Under these conditions, administrators skilled in the art of compromise, capable bureaucratic politicians, and possessors of knowledge about the world beyond the firm gained the levers of power within corporations. Those with hands-on experience in production and distribution saw their status drop.

Schools of business grew and improved to meet this demand for professional managers. Spurred by two key reports, the Ford Foundation–sponsored *Higher Education for Business* (1959) and the Carnegie Commission–funded *The Education of American Businessmen: A Study of University-College Programs in Business Administration* (1959), graduate business schools adopted a more rigorous and quantitative social science pedagogy. As in other disciplines, faculty research became a measure of distinction in business education. College graduates with undergraduate or graduate training in business soon came to see themselves as masters of an abstract body of knowledge like other professionals.

These changes on the supply side complemented changes taking place on the demand side. As the numbers of students in universities swelled in the postwar decades, many turned to business schools for career opportunities and protection from economic downturns such as the still-memorable Great Depression. Graduate and undergraduate degrees in business replaced the traditional professions and liberal arts as the course of study for many middle-class students. Undergraduate degrees in business after World War II jumped from 8 percent (1935–1945) to 14 percent (1945–1953) of the total. They climbed, though unsteadily, over the next three decades.

University-educated managers had little difficulty in seeing business as a profession. Some adopted a technocratic stance. They believed that business, shorn of its disreputable, robber baron tendencies, could be run solely by the numbers. Methodologically sophisticated managers familiar with the new sciences of operations research and systems analysis used complex quantitative measures to track performance. During the 1960s, a new type of business organization emerged—the conglomerate. In the most extreme cases, conglomerate management focused on measuring the performance of individual business units, making investment decisions, and more and more, acquiring other business units.

Professional managers had an easy time accepting the presence of other professionals within their firms. Nowhere was managerial deference to professional autonomy greater than in the industrial research laboratories of the 1950s and 1960s. Big corporations with ample budgets like AT&T, General Electric, and Du Pont spent lavishly on research and development. They let the numerous scientists and engineers in their employ create quasi-independent research units that possessed their own culture. This collegial culture was much closer to that of a university department or a professional association than a business office.

Infused with a faith in science that grew out of the successful crash development programs and numerous technological achievements of the World War II era, some large corporations began to expect miracles from industrial research. Science and technology could not only open up profitable new horizons, it was believed, they could also provide the common basis for overseeing diverse lines of business. The notion that different businesses could be profitably managed together because they shared certain technical or scientific features provided a powerful rationale for diversification. Yet when carried too far, faith in science and respect for professional autonomy led to a strange contradiction. Some corporate executives acted as though miracles would most likely be forthcoming if cranky and eccentric Ph.D.'s were left alone to run their own shop. What went on in the research end of these firms was in danger of becoming disassociated from development and production.

This same tendency to defer to professional judgments led to strong institutional relations between independent professional organizations and business firms. Investment banks, law partnerships, accounting practices, public relations and advertising firms tended to link themselves to a handful of large clients. Throughout most of the 1950s and 1960s, the willingness of clients to accept fees without question and the successful suppression of competition and crass commercial advertising kept these client relationships extremely stable. Some professional practices, in law in particular, generated such a substantial percentage of their yearly income through their largest, oldest clients that they showed little interest in seeking new business. Although this period was one of professional autonomy, experts rarely challenged or contradicted the wishes of powerful clients. Part of the reason that "independent" professional practices accorded so smoothly with dominant interests was that practitioners specialized in serving particular groups. They identified closely with those whom they served. Well-established corporate lawyers represented business firms far more often than they did workers or consumers. If possible, private physicians took only paying clients; public health was left to state institutions. Professional ethics stressed the obligation to serve the paying client above all else. In an age when most payments to professionals were made directly by the client, rather than by third parties, it was very easy to believe that service to individual clients was tantamount to service to society as a whole.

Not all members of professions enjoyed stable client relations. Although the most successful partnerships could afford to stay above the commercial fray, those at the lower end—criminal lawyers, accountants that catered to small businesses, or architects struggling for their first commission—had to scramble for business. Even here, however, stability was often obtained by the deference to professional judgment of poorer, less educated clients, and smaller, less well-endowed businesses. For a time the upper and lower strata of professions were able to cooperate within overarching associations, agreeing on fundamental questions about entry, access, competition, and ethics. A booming economy that provided plenty of work for all helped to smooth over any inherent conflicts.

To some extent, the values, practices, and culture of professionals employed in the public sector were similar to those in the private sector. The military, teaching, the sciences, and many of the social sciences, humanities, and arts grew through government funding much in the manner that independent professions grew through their largest clients. The National Science Foundation, National Institutes of Health, and Cold War spending on military hardware and space exploration funded numerous large-scale science projects. Federal contributions to social welfare expenditures grew from the stable 44 percent average of the 1950s to 53 percent by 1970. In 1965 Congress created the National Endowment for the Humanities and the National Endowment for the Arts.

Public sector professionals sought the same respect, autonomy, and deference that professionals in the private sector enjoyed. The manner of government spending in this period helped them to realize their goals. Federal funding of big science gave to university scientists substantial amounts of money with few strings attached, making life in the publicly funded research lab and the corporate research lab remarkably similar. New government interest in social problems raised the status of sociologists and social workers who diagnosed social maladies. Reform-minded doctors became involved in setting the terms on which public funding for medicine and health would be provided. It was apparent, however, that public-sector professionals had imbibed the liberal doctrines of the time, accepting the politics of consensus in the postwar period. Much of the government support for professional activity was induced by Cold War competition with the Soviet Union. Scientists employed by public or university research laboratories rarely questioned the morality of making weapons of mass destruction. In the early 1960s, an age of liberal consensus, social scientists usually did not politicize their solutions to public ills either. Under the welfare programs of the Great Society, experts armed with federal dollars and court and legislative mandates worked to change the lives of residents of rural Appalachia, the segregated South, and inner city ghettos. The myth of scientific objectivity and professional independence allowed them to propose what they believed to be objective solutions to problems—be those problems social or economic ones at home, or military ones in Vietnam. They did not see their prescriptions as political programs enmeshed in an ideology.

The high tide of this mode of state-professional relations came in medicine in the 1950s and 1960s. More than any other group, physicians successfully rode the crest of broad economic changes and benefited from the growth of government programs, while retaining command over their practices and clients. Federal money helped to build hospitals and programs such as Medicare and Medicaid brought new patients into hospitals and offices even as fees rose. Private insurance had also expanded in the period after World War II. With help from large employers and powerful unions, it was made available to substantial portions of the working class. Almost two-thirds of the population was covered by health insurance by the mid 1960s. By 1970, 7.3 percent of GNP went for health care, up from 4.5 percent two decades earlier.

Despite these impressive, publicly assisted medical achievements, doctors did not have to give up control of what remained a large and lucrative private health care delivery market. They continued to regulate access through state licensing and medical school and residency programs. Restrictions on advertising and competition were enforced by a large and cohesive American Medical Association. As a result, the availability of medical services up and down society reflected the general distribution of wealth and power. Citizens in the South and in rural areas, the unemployed and the retired, generally had less access to quality health care than did the urban middle and unionized working classes.

New government programs such as Medicare and Medicaid partly compensated for these deficiencies. Doctors, who had long opposed medical insurance, had to accommodate themselves to the growing influence of both government and insurance companies in their profession. But they largely succeeded in protecting their independence by preventing third parties from coming between themselves and their patients. They insisted that medical insurance reimburse patients, not doctors, so that patients remained financially liable for their physicians' bills. Doctors also fended off challenges from the state and from insurance carriers, who sought to set standards for care and payment. To a large degree, they were able to maintain their strategic position between patients and other health care institutions in this period.

THE PROFESSIONS IN A TURBULENT ERA, 1970–1990s

Professionals, like many other groups, were buffeted by the economic problems and cultural malaise that tore at American society in the period after 1970. New challenges to the authority of experts began to undermine the autonomy and power of professional groups. New Left critics attacked the military-industrial complex and the amorality of science. Consumer advocates exposed the monopoly privileges of professionals. A general dismay over the application of pure technique in questionable circumstances such as the Vietnam War tarnished the public image of experts of all stripes. In the 1980s era of deregulation, the Right launched similar assaults on elite intellectuals and privileged liberal professionals. As disenchantment built, people began to scrutinize the decisions of their doctors, accountants, and lawyers more carefully. Formerly docile clients were prepared to take professionals to court when not satisfied.

The very growth of specialized knowledge and expertise allowed individuals and groups to confront the autonomy of practitioners in a variety of fields. Activist citizens with scientific and technical backgrounds became leaders of popular movements such as environmentalism. They called into question the judgments of industry and government scientists on matters related to air and water pollution and chemical toxicity. Both liberal and conservative think tanks found plenty of intellectuals for hire, ready to turn out studies and position papers designed to shape political debate. The wide availability of expertise and the entrepreneurial nature of many American professionals brought new groups into the territory formerly commanded by others. Lawyers aggressively sought to profit from growing concern about medical malpractice. Chiropractors, midwives, and faith healers built up new clienteles in an atmosphere of suspicion toward scientific medicine.

One set of criticisms that professions met somewhat successfully in this period were charges of anti-Semitism, racism, and sexism. Minorities had earlier gained admittance to the lower levels of professional practice and to quasi-professions. In the later decades of the twentieth century, Jews, blacks, and women began entering the worlds of investment banking, corporate law, medicine, engineering, business management, and the physical sciences in increasing numbers. Coeducation and educational desegregation allowed them to obtain the sorts of intellectual qualifications that were becoming mandatory at elite professional institutions. By 1989, 45 percent of managerial and professional workers were women, 10 percent black or Hispanic.

Although minority groups had substantially improved their position in professional life by the late twentieth century, they were still underrepresented at the top of elite practices. Some professional occupations did no better than the rest of society in overcoming barriers to minorities or in making up for past exclusion. Engineering remained a largely male field. Corporate law practices admitted only tiny numbers of black, Mexican, and Asian Americans to partnerships. In less elite professions such as criminal law, insurance, and real estate, ethnic practitioners tended to serve clients of their own ethnic group. But by the 1980s, even top-level professional practices could no longer be characterized as institutions exclusively for the white, male, Protestant elite, which they had been just a generation earlier. These institutions were now granting access to more and more of those who had found their way up the ranks of the social order, regardless of background.

In a population that had greater access to higher education than any other in the industrial world, the professions proved more and more appealing to all members of the middle class. By 1989, professionals and managers alone made up 30 percent of the labor force; technical, clerical, and sales workers comprised an additional 31 percent. All told, white-collar and service sector workers held nearly 75 percent of the jobs in the nation.

Not all jobs classified as white collar were well paid or desirable. A considerable growth had taken place in lower level clerical, health, and food preparation categories. On the other hand, elite professionals and skilled technical and managerial workers experienced income growth throughout the 1970s and 1980s. In some cases, as with real estate agents, the entry of women into the field swelled the number of workers and expanded practice. For a time, professional organizations were able to accommodate growth by moving into new areas of business, developing new services, and charging higher fees. There appeared to be no limit to the amount of medical treatment, psychological counseling, legal advice, accounting assistance, advertising genius, not to mention hair styling, interior decorating, fitness training, and personal development that businesses and consumers were willing to pay for. Eventually, however, the growth of the professions ran headlong into some fundamental economic and technological changes. In an atmosphere already rife with skepticism about professional values, these structural shifts threatened the economic base of many white-collar occupations.

When America was inundated by foreign competition in the late 1970s, business firms were forced to cut back personnel, slash costs, and spin off activities. This restructuring threw out of work many white-collar and professional workers. It also upset the stable institutional arrangements between accounting, law, banking, public relations, and advertising partnerships and their clients. Corporations seeking to reduce costs began to scrutinize bills more carefully and inquire closely about charges. At the same time, the proliferation of professional workers in the economy and the continued fracturing of knowledge and expertise made many professional practices more and more specialized. Clients searched for the best practitioner in the nation, regardless of for whom he or she worked. Aggressive professional organizations raided each others' businesses. Client relations moved from stable and institutional to dynamic and transactional.

Similar pressures to contain costs also hit the public sector. Budget deficits, tax revolts, and dismay over perceived failures of social policies forced governments to rein in spending in such areas as welfare, education, and the arts and culture. Social scientists and social workers tried to regroup and defend their accomplishments against conservative criticism in the 1980s. They discovered, however, that they were no longer perceived as independent, scientific experts. Liberal and conservative specialists proposed widely different answers to problems of crime, homelessness, falling educational standards, and poverty. Budget deficits and political divisions subjected public sector professionals to the same depressing array of forces that were lowering the incomes and employment prospects of other types of workers.

The prestige professions too felt the belt tightening. Government spending on science and medicine continued to grow in the 1970s and 1980s, but at lower rates than in the first three postwar decades. Big science lost some of its luster, as scientists themselves debated the social and scientific value of blockbuster projects such as the mapping of the human genome and the search for extraterrestrial life. Expenditures on corporate R&D were often among the first to feel the axe when market share declined and profits dropped. Even in the high-tech sectors of the economy, industrial research and engineering was reined in. Firms moved away from the academic model of R&D that rewarded independent professionals and tried to link the corporate laboratory more closely to other parts of the company. Professionals in the business sector came under pressure to act and think more like other corporate employees.

Even medicine, long considered the most independent and autonomous of the professions, found by the 1980s that growth was a mixed blessing. The nation was spending a significant percentage of GNP on an elusive quest for health. Never-resolved problems of third-party payments and universal medical coverage emerged as major issues in presidential elections. Medical technology, specialization, and refinement of professional skills had all pushed scientific medicine into the forefront of professional life. Doctors had bested all their competitors in the health field. But by the 1980s, success had generated a strong backlash. Medicine would either have to find a way of containing costs, or those costs would be contained for it.

In a number of professions, efforts by clients and outside parties to lower costs led to the adoption of new technologies. These imperiled the position of certain occupational groups. Personal computers and prepackaged software, national and international databases, expert systems for diagnosing medical ills and legal problems, and computer-aided design seemed ready to replace human skills and knowledge. In business, the new field of management information brought forth gurus who preached the virtues of the information revolution to bloated corporations. Chief information officers were told how they could restructure their firms, cutting away whole layers of bureaucracy which had done by hand the record keeping, calculations, and quality control that could now be performed by a few microprocessors.

As a threat to professionalism—or rather, to the embodiment of expertise in people—technology was far less serious than it first appeared. In many cases, it merely eliminated routine functions, which elite practitioners were happy to slough off. The most highly skilled specialized by taking on only cutting-edge work that paid the highest fees. Physicians, for example, gained more than they lost by allowing technicians to handle complex diagnostic equipment. The medical profession continued to grow by embracing rather than fighting new technology.

A more significant challenge came from new forms of organization for expert services and knowledge. To some extent, professionals themselves led the way in organizational innovation, as they had done throughout the twentieth century. The real threat to traditional professional status came when outside parties began to look at reorganization as a means of controlling professional autonomy and costs. Examples of these changes included the substantial volume of legal work that after 1970 shifted from law firms to the legal staffs of corporations. Planning, design, and architecture also began to move from independent professional practices to larger-scale construction and building firms. In medicine, hospitals, health maintenance organizations (HMOs), and insurance carriers began to regulate and standardize medical treatments to keep costs down.

Following these trends, observers working in Marxian paradigms have predicted the proletarianization of professional life. Like blue-collar workers, they argue, professionals are becoming deskilled by capitalism's relentless pursuit of surplus value. Whether or not professionals will experience a reduction of income or status from these developments, however, will depend on specific individual situations. Certainly there has been a decline in the supposed ideals of autonomy and deference to expert judgment. But then, throughout the twentieth century those ideals have been readily abandoned by entrepreneurial professionals whenever necessary.

Some of the difficulties of recent decades appear to be either short-lived or of far less moment than they once seemed. Even if future generations of professionals will enjoy less autonomy and deference than did their forebears, expert advice is still eagerly sought by many consumers. Some of the sources that purvey such expertise perhaps cannot be termed "professional" by the standards of the 1950s. Yet this situation is little different from that of the turn of the century, when many professional boundaries were still in formation and command over particular functions was up for grabs. In the history of the professions, lines and boundaries have been continually redrawn.

Professionals must now admit that they are as political as other citizens and as subject to the laws of supply and demand as other workers. The more competitive and consumer-oriented atmosphere of the recent past has also opened up great opportunities for entrepreneurial practitioners. They can now restructure their organizations, seek new clients, and encroach on the territory of rivals. This situation is also reminiscent of the turn of the century. Then too professional associations and organizations aggressively sought business, expanded their reach, defended their territories and accommodated new technologies. The years between 1950 and 1970 were the exceptional ones. In those stable decades, professional practitioners could pretend to be above the competitive fray and free from the taint of commerce.

Possible future styles of professional life are already becoming manifest. Some professional organizations have responded to the new market for professional services with an interrelated strategy of consolidation, diversification, and internationalization. Legal, accounting, and group medical practices have grown larger. They have begun to offer a wider array of services. And they have sought opportunities in foreign markets. The Big Eight national accounting firms shrunk to the Big Six in the 1980s, absorbing many medium-sized firms in the process. Law practices grew to monstrous size in the 1980s, with some surging above the 1,000-lawyer mark. Many opened offices in London, Paris, Hong Kong, Singapore, and Tokyo. HMOs have been able to attract highly competent physicians by offering good if not spectacular wages, steady work, and reasonable hours, with less risk than in solo practice. Law and accounting firms do battle for control of work involving general financial advice to clients. Both have encroached on the territory of financial counselors, investment firms, and portfolio managers. A number of new types of professional agencies have also explored new service markets. Employee leasing firms now handle personnel matters for many small businesses. Other firms provide assistance to businesses in complying with complex regulatory and environ-

mental laws. These services do not fit neatly into the old professional categories of law or accounting.

Another organizational response of professions has been specialization. Small boutique firms in a variety of fields have tried to sell clients on the value of employing the most highly skilled and refined specialists for particular issues or problems. This move is the opposite of the one-stop shopping approach that large law, accounting, and medical practices have taken. In cases where practice size has remained small, however, it has been popular. Specialization allows individual professionals to ward off lower-cost technical and organizational alternatives to their functions.

THE PROFESSIONS AND THE NATIONAL EXPERIENCE

Since the beginning of the twentieth century, professional life has held out many promises to the educated middle class of the nation. These included independence, autonomy, status, respect, and above-average incomes. As part of the growth of scientific and specialized knowledge, professions have benefited from one of the major trends in modern, industrial civilization. Throughout most of the century, professionals have been able to stay atop these changes. The increasing economic value of knowledge, information, expertise, and judgment gave them a substantial advantage over other workers at the beginning of this century. Professionals not only profited materially, but were able to construct an ideological justification for their existence that related to some of the core values of Western society: the objective pursuit of truth and the perfection of human knowledge. In the United States, where professions were a pillar of civil society rather than an arm of the state, they also could be seen as holders of democratic values. Particularly in an age that was coming to be dominated by large institutions of business and government, the competent, autonomous professional was a figure of respect.

The values that professions seem to embody have, of course, always been in uneasy tension with the material underpinnings of professional work. For, at base, the professions are occupations—a particular division of labor. In the early decades of the twentieth century and in recent times, professionals have acted with keen awareness of this fundamental economic fact. They have taken the lead in promoting their functions. They have pursued technological and organizational innovations to fit their practices to the demands of clients. They have made effective use of the state both to build demand for their services and to protect their markets from competitors. Yet they have also been shaped by noneconomic values. In response to charges of elitism, professions have gradually opened their doors to those of different cultural backgrounds. They settled on educational attainment, rather than character or ethnicity, as the chief arbiter of admittance in a society uniquely dedicated to education.

Under the adversity experienced from the 1970s to the early 1990s, professionals responded by articulating some new core values. Professionalism now can include employment in a large nonprofessional organization. The longstanding problem of accountability has increasingly been resolved not internally through associations and statements of professional ethics, but externally in the legal and political system. The growth of professional expertise has given both the state and private parties far greater command of the specialized functions formerly carried out by independent professionals. These countervailing interests now also possess far greater ability to challenge the autonomy of professional judgments. Those who purvey independent expertise still enjoy a lively and remunerative source of employment. Increasingly, however, they must accommodate themselves to the reality of powerful organizations.

SEE ALSO The University; Philosophy (both in volume IV).

BIBLIOGRAPHY

An important treatment of the professions as a system of interlocked occupations competing for control of different types of work is Andrew Abbott, *The System of Professions: An Essay on the Division of Expert Labor* (1988). Magli Sarfatti Larson, *The Rise of Professionalism* (1977), on the other hand, provides a sophisticated general interpretation stressing professions' pursuit of collective mobility through the exercise of monopoly power. Burton Bledstein, *The Culture of Professionalism: The Middle Class and the Development of Higher Education in America* (1976), discusses the relationship between university training and professional careers and its effect on American middle-class culture and values. A broad overview of professions and business in the twentieth century is presented in Louis Galambos, "Technology, Political Economy and Professionalization: Central Themes of the Organizational Synthesis," *Business History Review* 57 (Winter 1983): 471–493.

For the context of knowledge and institutional learning in American society, see Alexandra Oleson and John Voss, eds., *The Organization of Knowledge in Modern America, 1860–1920* (1979). Laurence R. Veysey, *The Emergence of the American University* (1965), weighs the influence of academic philosophies and academic structures in shaping the modern American university during its formative period, 1865–1910. Lawrence A. Cremin, *The Transformation of the School: Progressivism in American Education* (1961), focuses on the interplay between progressive education and American progressivism. Clyde W. Barrow, "Corporate Liberalism, Finance Hegemony and Central State Intervention in the Reconstruction of American Higher Education," in *Studies in American Political Development* 6 (1992): 420–444, provides a different interpretation, stressing the cooperative relationships which developed between private foundations and the federal government in reforming higher education during the early decades of the twentieth century. David Tyack, *The One Best System: A History of American Urban Education* (1974), provides a comprehensive survey of the progress of public education in American cities.

On the medical profession, Paul Starr, *The Social Transformation of American Medicine* (1982), is a compelling portrait, focusing especially on the economic and social problems of twentieth-century health care delivery in a profession dominated by independent physicians. James G. Burrow, *Organized Medicine in the Progressive Era: The Move Toward Monopoly* (1977), perceptively evaluates how professional welfare considerations moderated medical practice reform before World War I. Charles E. Rosenberg, *The Care of Strangers: The Rise of America's Hospital System* (1987), analyzes the factors that transformed American hospitals in the twentieth century. Rosemary Stevens, *American Medicine and the Public Interest* (1971), explains how the rise of practice specializations influenced the organization and politics of American medicine from the late nineteenth century through the 1950s. Susan Reverby, *Ordered to Care: The Dilemma of American Nursing, 1850–1945* (1987), evaluates the institutional and professional factors that contributed to the subordinate nature of nursing professionalism. Eliot Freidson, *Professional Dominance: The Social Structure of Medical Care* (1970), examines how medicine established itself through its dominance of other, competing occupational categories.

Progressive Era engineering is well covered in Edwin Layton, *The Revolt of the Engineers: Social Responsibility and the American Engineering Profession* (1971), which discusses the conflict between engineers who served corporations and those who hoped that engineering would achieve an independent status from which it could contribute to social reform. Monte A. Calvert, *The Mechanical Engineer in America, 1830–1910: Professional Careers in Conflict* (1967), analyzes how the tensions that divided practitioners trained in traditional shop-based apprenticeships from those graduating from newer university training programs influenced the development of mechanical engineering. In a somewhat different vein, David Noble, *America by Design: Science, Technology and the Rise of Corporate Capitalism* (1977), argues that science and engineering were made to serve the interests of business in the Progressive era. Leonard Reich, *The Making of American Industrial Research: Science and Business at GE and Bell* (1985), provides an in-depth analysis of these issues through case studies of corporate R&D and the links between science and corporate strategy. Daniel Kevles, *The Physicists* (1979), recounts the story of a community of scientists.

On the legal profession, Jerold S. Auerbach, *Unequal Justice: Lawyers and Social Change in Modern America* (1976), presents a sharply critical analysis of the roles of elite attorneys in frustrating social reform. Wayne Karl Hobson's "The American Legal Profession and the Organizational Society, 1890–1930" (Ph.D. diss. Stanford University, 1977), discusses in rich detail the activities of representative associations in developing professional institutions for law. Robert Stevens, *Law School: Legal Education in America from the 1850s to the 1980s* (1983), surveys the history of legal education paying particular attention to the years before 1945. Kenneth Lipartito and Joseph Pratt, *Baker & Botts in the Development of Modern Houston* (1991), follows the history of a large corporate law firm throughout the twentieth century, emphasizing the links between firm organization and the economy.

Paul J. Miranti, *Accountancy Comes of Age: The Development of an American Profession, 1886–1940* (1990), concentrates on the role that representative associations played in building a cohesive practitioner community of accountants and in gaining acceptance for accountants' specialized skills. James Don Edward, *History of Public Accounting in the United States* (1965), is an overview of the major events shaping the rise of public accounting in America through the 1950s. Gary J. Previts and Barbara D. Merino, *A History of Accounting in America: An Historical Interpretation of the Cultural Significance of Accounting* (1979), is an overview of the influence of accounting in American society and business from the colonial period to modern times.

Roy Lubove, *The Professional Altruist: The Emergence of Social Work as a Career, 1880–1930* (1965), analyzes how private philanthropy gradually gave way to a new professional social work which placed greater emphasis on formal organization, bureaucracy and specialized training and function.

A major new reinterpretation of professions and the state is Brian Balogh's, "Reorganizing the Organizational Synthesis: Federal-Professional Relations in Modern America," *Studies in American Political Development* 5 (Spring 1991): 119–172. For the post–World War II economy, Marc U. Porat, *The Information Economy: Definition and Measurement* (1977), is an important economic and statistical analysis of the increasing role of information processing activities in employment and GNP. Alfred D. Chandler, Jr. *Strategy and Structure* (1962), tracks business diversification in the twentieth century and the creation of specialized managerial hierarchies.